BRIEF FOURTEENTH EDITION

AMERICAN GOVERNMENT
POWER & PURPOSE

Theodore J. Lowi
Cornell University

Benjamin Ginsberg
The Johns Hopkins University

Kenneth A. Shepsle
Harvard University

Stephen Ansolabehere
Harvard University

W.W. NORTON
NEW YORK • LONDON

W. W. Norton & Company has been independent since its founding in 1923, when William Warder Norton and Mary D. Herter Norton first published lectures delivered at the People's Institute, the adult education division of New York City's Cooper Union. The firm soon expanded its program beyond the Institute, publishing books by celebrated academics from America and abroad. By mid-century, the two major pillars of Norton's publishing program—trade books and college texts—were firmly established. In the 1950s, the Norton family transferred control of the company to its employees, and today—with a staff of four hundred and a comparable number of trade, college, and professional titles published each year—W. W. Norton & Company stands as the largest and oldest publishing house owned wholly by its employees.

Editor: Ann Shin
Associate Editor: Emily Stuart
Editorial Assistant: Shannon Jilek
Project Editor: David Bradley
Media Editor: Spencer Richardson-Jones
Associate Media Editor: Michael Jaoui
Media Editorial Assistant: Ariel Eaton
Marketing Manager: Erin Brown
Production Manager: Ben Reynolds
Book Designer: Kiss Me I'm Polish LLC, New York
Design Director: Rubina Yeh
Permissions Manager: Megan Schindel
Composition: GraphicWorld
Manufacturing: Quad/Graphics—Taunton MA

Permission to use copyrighted material is included in the credits section of this book, which begins on page A69.

ISBN: 978-0-393-28377-8 (pbk.)

W. W. Norton & Company, Inc., 500 Fifth Avenue, New York, NY 10110
wwnorton.com

W. W. Norton & Company Ltd., 15 Carlisle Street, London W1D 3BS

1 2 3 4 5 6 7 8 9 0

For Our Families

Angele, Anna, and Jason Lowi
Sandy, Cindy, and Alex Ginsberg
Rise, Nilsa, and Seth Shepsle
Laurie Gould and Rebecca and
Julia Ansolabehere

Contents

PART 2 INSTITUTIONS

10   Elections   314

11 Political Parties   360

12 Groups and Interests

Preface

This book was written for faculty and students who are looking for a little more than just "nuts and bolts" and who are drawn to an analytical perspective—but who also prefer a brief-format text. No fact about American government is intrinsically difficult to grasp, and in an open society such as ours, facts abound. The philosophy of a free and open media in the United States makes information about the government readily available. The advent of the Internet and new communication technologies have expanded further the opportunity to learn about our government. The ubiquity of information in our society is a great virtue. Common knowledge about the government gives our society a vocabulary that is widely shared and enables us to communicate effectively with each other about politics. But it is also important to reach beyond that common vocabulary and to develop a more sophisticated understanding of politics and government. The sheer quantity of facts in our society can be overwhelming. In a 24/7 news cycle it can be hard to pick out what stories are important and to stay focused on them. Today, moreover, Americans may choose among a variety of news sources, including broadcast, print, and various online formats all clamoring for attention. The single most important task of the teacher of political science is to confront popular ideas and information and to choose from among them the small number of really significant concepts that help us make better sense of the world. This book aims to help instructors and students accomplish this task.

This Fourteenth Edition continues our endeavor to make *American Government: Power and Purpose* the most authoritative and contemporary introductory text on the market. Those who have used the book in the past know that we have always emphasized the role of American political institutions. We have not strayed from this emphasis. In every chapter we encourage students to think critically and analytically about how well the institutions discussed in that chapter serve the goals of a democratic society.

The major changes in this Fourteenth Edition are intended to combine authoritative, concise coverage of the central topics in American politics with smart pedagogical features designed to get students thinking analytically about quantitative data and current issues. Highlights of the revision include:

- **More than 10 pages on the 2016 elections, including data figures**, walk students through what happened and why. This edition includes a section devoted to analyzing the 2016 elections in Chapter 10, as well as updated data, examples, and other information throughout the book.

- **New Policy Principle boxes** in every chapter each provide a mini case study on how individual preferences and institutional procedures led to a given policy outcome. These new sections make it easy to teach an analytical approach to policy throughout the course.

- **New Timeplot features** use quantitative date to illuminate long-term trends in American politics, such as shifts in party coalitions, the growth of the American electorate, and representation in Congress.

- **Six new Analyzing the Evidence units written by expert researchers** highlight the political science behind the information in the book, while the remaining units have been updated with new data and analysis. Each unit poses an important question from political science and presents evidence that can be used to analyze the question. The six new units are:

  "Constitutional Engineering: How Many Veto Gates?" in Chapter 2 Contributed by Steven L. Taylor, Troy University; and Matthew S. Shugart, University of California, Davis

  "Americans' Attitudes Toward Church and State" in Chapter 4 Contributed by David E. Campbell, University of Notre Dame

  "Why Congress Can't Make Ends Meet" in Chapter 5 Contributed by David M. Primo, University of Rochester

  "Where Do Americans Get News about Politics?" in Chapter 9 Contributed by Rasmus Kleis Nielsen, University of Oxford

  "Economic Influence on Presidential Elections" in Chapter 10 Contributed by Robert S. Erikson, Columbia University

  "Fixing Social Security?" in Chapter 13 Contributed by Rachael Vanessa Cobb, Suffolk University Boston

For the Fourteenth Edition we have profited greatly from the guidance of many teachers who have used earlier editions and from the suggestions of numerous thoughtful reviewers. We thank them by name in the Acknowledgments. We recognize that there is no single best way to craft an introductory text, and we are grateful for the advice we have received.

Theodore J. Lowi
Benjamin Ginsberg
Kenneth A. Shepsle
Stephen Ansolabehere

Acknowledgments

Our students at Cornell, Johns Hopkins, and Harvard have already been identified as an essential factor in the writing of this book. They have been our most immediate intellectual community, a hospitable one indeed. Another part of our community, perhaps a large suburb, is the discipline of political science itself. Our debt to the scholarship of our colleagues is scientifically measurable, probably to several decimal points, in the footnotes of each chapter. Despite many complaints that the field is too scientific or not scientific enough, political science is alive and well in the United States. Political science has never been at a loss for relevant literature, and without that literature, our job would have been impossible.

We are pleased to acknowledge our debt to the many colleagues who had a direct and active role in criticism and preparation of the manuscript. The First Edition was read and reviewed by Gary Bryner, Brigham Young University; James F. Herndon, Virginia Polytechnic Institute and State University; James W. Riddlesperger, Jr., Texas Christian University; John Schwarz, University of Arizona; Toni-Michelle Travis, George Mason University; and Lois Vietri, University of Maryland. We also want to reiterate our thanks to the four colleagues who allowed us the privilege of testing a trial edition of our book by using it as the major text in their introductory American Government courses: Gary Bryner, Brigham Young University; Allan J. Cigler, University of Kansas; Burnet V. Davis, Albion College; and Erwin A. Jaffe, California State University–Stanislaus.

For second through seventh editions, we relied heavily on the thoughtful manuscript reviews we received from J. Roger Baker, Wittenburg University; Timothy Boylan, Winthrop University; David Canon, University of Wisconsin; Victoria Farrar-Myers, University of Texas at Arlington; John Gilmour, College of William and Mary; Mark Graber, University of Maryland; Russell Hanson, Indiana University; Robert Huckfeldt, University of California–Davis; Mark Joslyn, University of Kansas; William Keech, Carnegie Mellon

University; Donald Kettl, University of Wisconsin; Anne Khademian, University of Wisconsin; Beth Leech, Rutgers University; James Lennertz, Lafayette College; Allan McBride, Grambling State University; William McLauchlan, Purdue University; Grant Neeley, Texas Tech University; Charles Noble, California State University, Long Beach; and Joseph Peek, Jr., Georgia State University.

For the Eighth Edition, we benefited from the comments of Scott Ainsworth, University of Georgia; Thomas Brunell, Northern Arizona University; Daniel Carpenter, Harvard University; Brad Gomez, University of South Carolina; Paul Gronke, Reed College; Marc Hetherington, Bowdoin College; Gregory Huber, Yale University; Robert Lowry, Iowa State University; Anthony Nownes, University of Tennessee; Scott Adler, University of Colorado–Boulder; John Coleman, University of Wisconsin–Madison; Richard Conley, University of Florida; Keith Dougherty, University of Georgia; John Ferejohn, Stanford University; Douglas Harris, Loyola College; Brian Humes, University of Nebraska–Lincoln; Jeffrey Jenkins, Northwestern University; Paul Johnson, University of Kansas; Andrew Polsky, Hunter College–CUNY; Mark Richards, Grand Valley State University; Charles Shipan, University of Iowa; Craig Volden, Ohio State University; and Garry Young, George Washington University.

For the Ninth Edition, we were guided by the comments of John Baughman; Lawrence Baum, Ohio State University; Chris Cooper, Western Carolina State University; Charles Finochiaro, State University of New York–Buffalo; Lisa Garcia-Bellorda, University of California–Irvine; Sandy Gordon, New York University; Steven Greene, North Carolina State University; Richard Herrera, Arizona State University; Ben Highton, University of California–Davis; Trey Hood, University of Georgia; Andy Karch, University of Texas at Austin; Glen Krutz, University of Oklahoma; Paul Labedz, Valencia Community College; Brad Lockerbie, University of Georgia; Wendy Martinek, State University of New York–Binghamton; Nicholas Miller, University of Maryland Baltimore County; Russell Renka, Southeast Missouri State University; Debbie Schildkraut, Tufts University; Charles Shipan, University of Iowa; Chris Shortell, California State University, Northridge; John Sides, University of Texas at Austin; Sean Theriault, University of Texas at Austin; and Lynn Vavreck, University of California, Los Angeles.

For the Tenth Edition, we were grateful for the detailed comments of Christian Grose, Vanderbilt University; Kevin Esterling, University of California–Riverside; Martin Johnson, University of California–Riverside; Scott Meinke, Bucknell University; Jason MacDonald, Kent State University; Alan Wiseman, Ohio State University; Michelle Swers, Georgetown University; William Hixon, Lawrence University; Gregory Koger, University of Miami; and Renan Levine, University of Toronto.

For their advice on the Eleventh Edition, we thank Scott Ainsworth, University of Georgia; Bethany Albertson, University of Washington; Brian Arbour, John Jay College; James Battista, University at Buffalo, State University of New York; Lawrence Becker, California State University, Northridge; Damon Cann, Utah State University; Jamie Carson, University of Georgia; Suzanne Chod, Pennsylvania State University; Michael Crespin, University of Georgia; Ryan

Emenaker, College of the Redwoods; Kevin Esterling, University of California–Riverside; Brad Gomez, Florida State University; Sanford Gordon, New York University; Christian Grose, Vanderbilt University; James Hanley, Adrian College; Ryan Hurl, University of Toronto; Josh Kaplan, University of Notre Dame; Wendy Martinek, Binghamton University; Will Miller, Southeast Missouri State University; Evan Parker-Stephen, Texas A&M University; Melody Rose, Portland State University; Eric Schickler, University of California–Berkeley; John Sides, George Washington University; and Lynn Vavreck, University of California–Los Angeles.

For the Twelfth Edition we looked to comments from John M. Aughenbaugh, Virginia Commonwealth University; Christopher Banks, Kent State University; Michael Berkman, Pennsylvania State University; Cynthia Bowling, Auburn University; Matthew Cahn, California State University, Northridge; Damon Cann, Utah State University; Tom Cioppa, Brookdale Community College; David Damore, University of Nevada, Las Vegas; Kevin Esterling, University of California–Riverside; Jessica Feezell, University of California–Santa Barbara; Charle J. Finocchiaro, University of South Carolina; Rodd Freitag, University of Wisconsin, Eau Claire; Richard Glenn, Millersville University; Kevin Jefferies, Alvin Community College; Nancy Jimeno, California State University, Fullerton; Gregory Koger, University of Miami; David E. Lewis, Vanderbilt University; Allison M. Martens, University of Louisville; Thomas M. Martin, Eastern Kentucky University; Michael Andrew McLatchy, Clarendon College; Ken Mulligan, Southern Illinois University, Carbondale; Geoffrey D. Peterson, University of Wisconsin, Eau Claire; Jesse Richman, Old Dominion University; Mark C. Rom, Georgetown University; Laura Schneider, Grand Valley State University; Scot Schraufnagel, Northern Illinois University; Ronald P. Seyb, Skidmore College; Martin S. Sheffer, Tidewater Community College; Charles R. Shipan, University of Michigan; Howard A. Smith, Florida Gulf Coast University; Michele Swers, Georgetown University; Charles Tien, Hunter College; Elizabeth Trentanelli, Gulf Coast State College; and Kenneth C. Williams, Michigan State University.

For the Thirteenth Edition we are indebted to: Michael M. Binder, University of North Florida; Stephen Borrelli, The University of Alabama; Dan Cassino, Fairleigh Dickinson University; Jangsup Choi, Texas A&M University–Commerce; Martin Cohen, James Madison University; Jeff Colbert, Elon University; Richard S. Conley, University of Florida; Mark Croatti, American University; David Dulio, Oakland University; Andrew M. Essig, DeSales University; Kathleen Ferraiolo, James Madison University; Emily R. Gill, Bradley University; Brad T. Gomez, Florida State University; Paul N. Goren, University of Minnesota; Thomas Halper, Baruch College; Audrey A. Haynes, University of Georgia; Diane J. Heith, St. John's University; Ronald J. Hrebenar, The University of Utah; Ryan Hurl, University of Toronto Scarborough; Richard Jankowski, SUNY Fredonia; Kevin Jefferies, Alvin Community College; Timothy R. Johnson, University of Minnesota; Kenneth R. Mayer, University of Wisconsin–Madison; Mark McKenzie, Texas Tech University; Fiona Miller, University of Toronto Mississauga; Richard M. Pious, Barnard College; Tim Reynolds, Alvin Community College; Martin Saiz, California State University, Northridge; Dante Scala, University of New Hampshire; Sean M. Theriault, University of Texas at Austin; J. Alejandro Tirado, Texas Tech University; Terri Towner, Oakland University; Nicholas Valentino, University of Michigan; Harold M. Waller, McGill University; and Jeffrey S. Worsham, West Virginia University.

We also thank the reviewers who advised us on this Fourteenth Edition: Michael E. Aleprete, Westminster College–Community College of Allegheny County; James Binney, Pennsylvania State University; William Blake, Indiana University–Purdue University, Indianapolis; Eric Boyer, Colby-Sawyer College; Chelsie L. M. Bright, Mills College; Thomas Cioppa, Brookdale Community College; Daniel Coffey, University of Akron; Darin DeWitt, California State University–Long Beach; Scott Englund, University of California–Santa Barbara; Amanda Friesen, Indiana University–Purdue University, Indianapolis; Frank Fuller, Lincoln University; Baogang Guo, Dalton State College; Eric Hanson, State University of New York at Fredonia; Jennifer Haydel, Montgomery College; Peter B. Heller, Manhattan College; Tseggai Isaac, Missouri University of Science and Technology; Vicki Jeffries-Bilton, Portland State University; Nicole Kalaf-Hughes, Bowing Green State University; Ervin Kallfa, Hostos Community College of CUNY; James Krueger, University of Wisconsin–Oshkosh; Aaron Ley, University of Rhode Island; Christine Lipsmeyer, Texas A&M University; David B. MacDonald, University of Guelph; Samantha Majic, John Jay College–City University of New York; William McLauchlan, Purdue University; Hong Min Park, University of Wisconsin–Milwaukee; Barbara Palmer, Baldwin Wallace University; John Patty, Washington University in Saint Louis; John W. Ray, Montana Tech of the University of Montana; Michael K. Romano, Georgia Southern University; Eric Sands, Berry College; Kathleen Tipler, Wake Forest University; and David Weaver, Boise State University.

An important contribution to recent editions was made by the authors of the Analyzing the Evidence units. We are grateful to the authors of the new Analyzing the Evidence units in the Fourteenth Edition, who are named in the preface. In addition, Jenna Bednar, David E. Campbell, Jeremiah D. Castle, Sean Gailmard, John C. Green, Geoffrey C. Layman, Beth L. Leech, David Lewis, Andrew D. Martin, Kenneth Mayer, and Kevin M. Quinn contributed to this feature in earlier editions, and much of their work is still reflected in this edition. We also thank Zachary Hodges, who provided valuable assistance in updating the data figures and tables throughout the book.

We would also like to thank our partners at W. W. Norton & Company, who have continued to apply their talents and energy to this textbook. The efforts of Ann Shin, Emily Stuart, Shannon Jilek, David Bradley, Ben Reynolds, Spencer Richardson-Jones, Michael Jaoui, and Ariel Eaton kept the production of the Fourteenth Edition and its accompanying resources coherent and in focus. We also thank Roby Harrington and Steve Dunn, whose contributions to previous editions remain invaluable.

We are more than happy, however, to absolve all these contributors from any flaws, errors, and misjudgments that this book contains. We wish it could be free of all production errors, grammatical errors, misspellings, misquotes, missed citations, etc. From that standpoint, a book ought to try to be perfect. But substantively we have not tried to write a flawless book; we have not tried to write a book to please everyone. We have again tried to write an effective book, a book that cannot be taken lightly. Our goal was not to make every reader a political scientist. Our goal was to restore politics as a subject of vigorous and enjoyable discourse, releasing it from the bondage of the thirty-second sound bite and the thirty-page technical briefing. Every person can be knowledgeable because everything about politics is accessible. One does not have to be a philosopher to argue about the requisites of democracy, a lawyer to dispute constitutional interpretations, an economist to debate public policy. We will be very proud if our book contributes in a small way to the restoration of the ancient art of political controversy.

Theodore J. Lowi
Benjamin Ginsberg
Kenneth A. Shepsle
Stephen Ansolabehere

AMERICAN GOVERNMENT
POWER & PURPOSE

Introduction: Making Sense of Government and Politics

American government and politics are extraordinarily complex. The United States has many levels of government—federal, state, county, city, and town—to say nothing of a host of special and regional authorities. Each of these governments operates under its own rules and statutory authority and is related to the others in complex ways. Each level of government, moreover, consists of an array of departments, agencies, offices, and bureaus undertaking a variety of sometimes overlapping tasks. At times this complexity gets in the way of effective governance, as in the case of governmental response to emergencies. America's federal, state, and local public safety agencies seldom share information and frequently use incompatible communications equipment, so they are often not even able to speak to one another. For example, on September 11, 2001, New York City's police and fire departments could not effectively coordinate their responses to the attack on the World Trade Center because their communications systems were not linked. While communication has improved in the last decade, many security and policy agencies, ranging from the Central Intelligence Agency (CIA) to the Department of Homeland Security (DHS), still possess separate computer operating systems and databases that inhibit cooperation through sharing.

The complexity of the United States' government is no accident. Complexity was one element of the Founders' grand constitutional design. The framers of the Constitution hoped that an elaborate division of power among institutions and between the states and the federal government would allow competing groups, forces, interests, and ideas to have a voice in public affairs, while preventing any single group or coalition from monopolizing power. One set of interests might be active in some states, other forces would be influential in the national legislature, and still others might prevail in the executive branch. This dispersion of power and opportunity allows many groups to achieve at least some of their political goals. In this way, the United States' political tradition associates complexity with liberty and political opportunity. But does American government work?

The United States' institutional structure sometimes makes it possible for small groups to prevent the enactment of policies that seem to be favored by the majority. For example, most Americans favor ending the billions of dollars in subsidies received by the oil and gas industries. However, every year, oil and gas backers in the House of Representatives are able to block efforts to curtail these subsidies. In cases like this, when the government's policies seem inconsistent with popular preferences, we may question whether American government works.

This same institutional structure, on the other hand, makes it possible for minorities to protect their rights against majorities. For example, after the enactment of a restrictive immigration law in Arizona in 2010, most Americans said they supported the idea of arresting individuals who could not prove they were in the United States legally. This effort seemed likely to lead to the harassment of Hispanics in particular,

CORE OF THE ANALYSIS

→ Government has become a powerful and complex force in the United States.

→ Government is necessary to maintain order, to protect property, and to provide public goods.

→ American government is based on democratic electoral institutions and popular representative bodies.

whether they were in the United States legally or not. Later in 2010, however, a federal judge struck down the most questionable provisions of the Arizona law, and in 2012, the Supreme Court nullified most of the law. When a branch of government blocks action in order to protect rights, we may be tempted to say the government works best when it is prevented from working.

America's complex institutional structure also complicates our politics and places a burden on citizens who wish to achieve something through political participation. They may be unable to discern where particular policies are actually made, who the decision makers are, and what forms of political participation are most effective. This is one of the paradoxes of political life: in a dictatorship, lines of political authority may be simple, but opportunities to influence the use of power are few; in the United States, political opportunities are plentiful, but how they should be used is far from obvious. Indeed, precisely because America's institutional and political arrangements are so complex, many Americans are mystified by government. As we see in Chapter 9, most Americans have difficulty making sense of even the basic features of the Constitution.

For most Americans, the focal point of U.S. politics is the electoral process. As we see in Chapter 10, tens of millions of Americans participate in national, state, and local elections in which they hear thousands of candidates debate what may seem to be a perplexing array of issues. Candidates fill the air with promises, charges, and countercharges, while pundits and journalists, which we discuss in Chapter 9, add their own clamor to the din. Politics, however, does not end on Election Day. Long after the voters have spoken, political struggles continue in Congress, the executive branch, and the courts; they embroil political parties, interest groups, and the mass media.

Citizens can hardly be blamed for becoming discouraged or for thinking that our political system is broken when their decisions at the polls seem only to lead to continuing institutional struggle and often fail to produce concrete results. But the framers of the Constitution were wary of making it too easy for shifts in the public's mood to be translated into shifts in policy. The framers believed that new ideas needed time to mature and to be subjected to scrutiny before being written into the law. In 2016, for example, many Americans, including President Obama, were angered at the Congress's refusal to consider gun control legislation proposed by the president and supported by a majority of Americans. However, the system of government designed by America's framers was not intended to give immediate expression to popular preferences. The framers were wary of government action and thought hasty action was more dangerous than none at all.

MAKING SENSE OF GOVERNMENT AND POLITICS

Can we find order in the apparent chaos of politics? Yes, and that is precisely the purpose of our text. It should be noted before we begin that "finding order in the apparent chaos of politics" is precisely what political scientists do. The discipline of political science, and especially the study of American politics, seeks to identify patterns in all the noise and maneuvering of everyday political life. This is motivated by two fundamental questions: What do we observe? And why?

The first question makes clear that political science is an *empirical* enterprise: it aims to identify facts and patterns that are true in the world around us. What strategies do candidates use to capture votes? What decisions do legislators make about how to vote on bills? What groups put pressure on the institutions of government? How do the media report politics? What tools are available to the president to get what he or she wants in dealing with Congress (legislative-executive relations)? How have courts intervened in regulating political life? And how do they come to the decisions they have made (judicial politics)? These and many other questions have prompted political scientists to ascertain what is true about the political world, and we will take them up in detail in later chapters.

The second question—Why?—is fundamental to any science. We not only would like to know *that* something is true about the world. We also want to know *why* it is true, which requires us to create in our minds a theory of how the world works. In this way we not only describe politics, we *analyze* it. One of the most important goals of this book is to provide concepts and tools to help readers critically analyze what they observe in politics and government. In this chapter, we offer a number of concepts that we hope will clarify why American government works the way it does. We conclude with a brief guide to analyzing evidence related to the ways these concepts play out in the American political system.

There is a third type of question that is normative, rather than empirical or analytical. Normative questions focus on "should" issues: What responsibilities should citizens have? How should legislators vote on the motions before them? How should presidents lead?

Political science grapples with all three types of questions. In this book, we believe that answers to the empirical and analytical questions help us formulate answers to the normative questions.

Forms of Government

Government is the term generally used to describe the formal political arrangements by which a land and its people are ruled. Government is composed of institutions and processes that rulers establish to strengthen and perpetuate their

> **government**
>
> The institutions and procedures through which a land and its people are ruled

autocracy

A form of government in which a single individual rules

oligarchy

A form of government in which a small group of landowners, military officers, or wealthy merchants control most of the governing decisions

democracy

A system of rule that permits citizens to play a significant part in the governmental process, usually through the selection of key public officials

constitutional government

A system of rule—a constitution—specifying formal and effective limits on the powers of the government

authoritarian government

A system of rule in which the government recognizes no formal limits but may nevertheless be restrained by the power of other social institutions

totalitarian government

A system of rule in which the government recognizes no formal limits on its power and seeks to absorb or eliminate other social institutions that might challenge it

power or control over a territory and its inhabitants. A government may be as simple as a tribal council that meets occasionally to advise the chief or as complex as our own vast establishment with its forms, rules, governmental bodies, and bureaucracies. Governments vary in structure, size, and the way they operate. Two questions are of special importance in determining how governments differ: Who governs? And, how much government control is permitted?

In some nations, political authority is vested in a single individual. This is called autocracy. When a small group of landowners, military officers, or wealthy merchants control most of the governing decisions, that government is an oligarchy. If many people participate, and if the populace has some influence over the leaders' actions, that government is tending toward democracy.

Governments also vary in how they govern. In the United States and a small number of other nations, governments are severely limited in what they are permitted to control (substantive limits), as well as in how they go about it (procedural limits). These are called constitutional governments. In other nations, including many in Europe, South America, Asia, and Africa, political and social institutions that the government is unable to control—such as autonomous territories or an organized church—may help keep the government in check, but the law imposes few real limits. Such governments are called authoritarian. In a third group of nations, including the Soviet Union under Joseph Stalin, governments not only are free of legal limits but seek to eliminate organized social groupings or institutions that might challenge their authority. Because these governments attempt to dominate political, economic, and social life, they are called totalitarian.

Foundations of Government

Whatever their makeup, governments historically have included two basic components: a means of coercion, such as an army or police force, and a means of collecting revenue. Some governments, including many in the less-developed nations today, have consisted of little more than an army and a tax-collecting agency. Other governments, especially those in the developed nations, such as the United States, also attempt to provide services to secure popular consent for control. For some, power is an end in itself. For most, power is necessary to maintain public order.

The Means of Coercion. Government must have the power to get people to obey its laws and to punish them if they do not. Coercion—forcing a person to do something by threats or pressure—takes many forms; each year, millions of Americans are subject to one form of government coercion or another. One aspect of coercion is conscription, whereby the government requires certain involuntary services of citizens. The best-known

Chapter 1: Introduction: Making Sense of Government and Politics

example of conscription is military conscription, or "the draft." Although there has been no draft since 1974, there were drafts during the Civil War, World War I, World War II, the postwar period, and the wars in Korea and Vietnam. With these drafts, the American government compelled millions of men to serve in the armed forces; one-half million of these soldiers made the ultimate contribution by giving their lives in their nation's service. If the need arose, military conscription would probably be reinstituted. Eighteen-year-old men are required to register today, just in case. American citizens can also, by law, be compelled to serve on juries; to appear before legal tribunals when summoned; to file a great variety of official reports, including income tax returns; and to attend school or to send their children to school. Government also has the power to punish those who do not obey its laws.

The Means of Collecting Revenue. Each year, American governments on every level collect enormous sums from their citizens to support their institutions and programs. Taxation has grown steadily over the years. In fiscal year 2015, the national government alone collected $1.6 trillion in individual income taxes, $1.1 trillion in social insurance taxes, $402 billion in corporate income taxes, $116 billion in estate and gift taxes, and $36 billion in custom duties. The grand total amounted to more than $3 trillion, or about $10,000 per person in the United States. But not everyone benefits equally from programs paid for by their tax dollars. One of the perennial issues in American politics is the distribution of tax burdens versus the distribution of program benefits. Every group would like more of the benefits while passing more of the burdens of taxation on to others.

Why Is Government Necessary?

As we have just seen, control is the basis for government. But what forms of government control are justifiable? To answer this question, we begin by examining the ways in which government enables a large group of people to live together as peacefully as possible.

To Maintain Order. For people to live together peacefully, law and order are required, the institutionalization of which is called government. From the standpoint of this definition, the primary purpose of government is to maintain order. But order can come about only by controlling a territory and its people. This may sound like a threat to freedom until you ponder the absence of government, or anarchy. According to the philosopher Thomas Hobbes (1558–1679), anarchy is even worse than the potential tyranny of government because anarchy is characterized by "continual fear, and danger of violent death . . . [where life is] solitary, poor, nasty, brutish and short."[1] Governmental power can be seen as a threat to our freedom, yet it is essential to maintain order so that we can enjoy that freedom.

To Protect Property. After safety of persons comes security of a person's property, or private property. Protection of property is almost universally recognized as a justifiable function of government. Hobbes's successor John Locke (1632–1704) was the first to assert clearly that whatever we have appropriated from nature with our own labor is considered our property. But even Locke recognized that although the right to own what we have produced by our own labor is absolute, it means nothing if someone with greater power than ours decides to take it or trespass on it.

So something we call our own is ours only as long as the laws against trespass improve the probability that we can enjoy, use, consume, trade, or sell it. Property, then, can be defined as all the laws against trespass that permit us not only to call something our own but also to make sure that our claim sticks. In other words, property—that is, private property—is virtually meaningless without a government of laws and policies that makes trespass prohibitive.

To Provide Public Goods. David Hume (1711–76), another successor to Hobbes, observed that although two neighbors may agree to cooperate in draining a swampy meadow, the more neighbors there are, the more difficult it will be to get the task done. A few neighbors might clear the swamp because they understand the benefits each of them will receive. But as you expand the number of neighbors who benefit from clearing the swamp, many neighbors will realize that all of them can get the same benefit if only a few clear the swamp and the rest do nothing. This is called free riding. A public good (or collective good) is, therefore, a benefit that members of a group cannot be kept from enjoying once it has been provided. The clearing of the swamp is one example; national defense is another. National defense is one of the most important public goods—especially when the nation is threatened by war or terrorism. Without government's coercive powers through a policy (backed by taxation) to build a bridge, produce an army, or issue "legal tender" (currency), there is no incentive—in fact, very often there is a disincentive—for even the richest, most concerned members to provide the benefit.[2]

America's Founders were influenced by the thinking of English philosopher John Locke (1632–1704). Locke asserted the right to private property and the need for a government of laws and policies to protect that right.

free riding
Enjoying the benefits of some good or action while letting others bear the costs

public good
A good that, first, may be enjoyed by anyone if it is provided and, second, may not be denied to anyone once it has been provided

politics
Conflict, struggle, cooperation, and collaboration over the leadership, structure, and policies of government

Influencing the Government: Politics

The term *politics* broadly refers to conflicts over the character, membership, and policies of any organizations to which people belong. As Harold Lasswell, a famous political scientist, once put it, politics is the struggle over "who gets what, when, how."[3] Although politics exists in any organization, in this book, politics refers to conflicts over the leadership, structure, and policies of governments—that is, over who governs and who has power. But politics also involves collaboration and cooperation. The goal of politics, as we define it, is to have a say in the composition of the government's leadership, how the government is organized, and what its policies will be. Having such a share is called power or influence. Most people are eager to have some "say" in matters affecting them; witness the willingness of so many individuals over the past two centuries to risk their lives for voting rights and representation. In recent years, of course, Americans have become more skeptical about their actual "say" in government, and many do not bother to vote. This skepticism, however, does not mean that Americans no longer want to have a share in the governmental process. Rather, many Americans doubt that the political system allows them real influence.

As we see throughout this book, not only does politics influence government but the character and actions of government also influence a nation's politics. The rules and procedures established by political institutions influence what forms political activity may take. The institutions of a constitutional government such as that of the United States are designed to gain popular consent by opening channels for political expression. Institutions may discourage conflict, encourage coordination, enable bargaining, and thus facilitate decision making, cooperation, and collective action.

institutions

The rules and procedures that provide incentives for political behavior, thereby shaping politics

FROM COERCION TO CONSENT

Americans have the good fortune to live in a constitutional democracy, with legal limits on what government can do and how it does it. Such democracies were unheard of before the modern era. Prior to the eighteenth and nineteenth centuries, governments seldom sought—and rarely received—the support of their ordinary subjects. But beginning in the seventeenth century, in a handful of Western nations, important changes began to take place in the character and conduct of government.

Limiting Government. The key force behind the imposition of limits on government power, beginning in seventeenth-century Europe, was a new social class called the "bourgeoisie." *Bourgeois* is French for "free-man of the city." The bourgeoisie later became associated with being "middle class" and with being in commerce or industry. In order to gain a share of control of government—to join the kings, monarchs, and gentry who had dominated governments for centuries—the bourgeoisie sought to change existing institutions, especially parliaments, into instruments of real political participation. Parliaments had existed for hundreds of years, controlling from the top and not allowing influence from below. The bourgeoisie embraced parliaments as the means by which they could wield their greater numbers and growing economic advantage against their aristocratic rivals.

Although motivated primarily by self-interest, the bourgeoisie advanced many of the principles that became the central underpinnings of individual freedom for *all* citizens—freedom of speech, of assembly, and of conscience, as well as freedom from arbitrary search and seizure. It is important to note here that the bourgeoisie generally did not favor democracy as such. They were advocates of electoral and representative institutions, but they favored property requirements and other restrictions so as to limit participation to the middle classes. Yet, once the right to engage in politics was established, it was difficult to limit it just to the bourgeoisie.

The Expansion of Democratic Politics. Along with limits on government came an expansion of democratic government. Three factors explain why rulers were forced to give ordinary citizens a greater voice in public affairs: internal conflict, external threat, and the promotion of national unity and development.

First, during the eighteenth and nineteenth centuries, many nations faced intense conflict among the landed gentry, the bourgeoisie, lower-middle-class shopkeepers and artisans, the urban working class, and farmers. Many governments came to the conclusion that if they did not deal with basic class conflicts in some constructive way, disorder and revolution would result. One of the best ways of dealing with such conflict was to extend the rights of political participation, especially voting, to each new group as it grew more powerful.

Another form of internal threat is social disorder. As a result of the Industrial Revolution, societies became much more interdependent and therefore much more vulnerable to disorder. One important approach to managing that disorder was to give the masses a bigger stake in the system itself. As one supporter of electoral reform put it, the alternative to voting was "the spoliation of property and the dissolution of social order."[4] In the modern world, social disorder helped to compel East European regimes and the republics of the former Soviet Union to take steps toward democratic reform.

The second factor that helped expand democratic government was external threat—that is, the existence of other nation-states. During the past three centuries, more and more tribes and nations—people tied together by a common culture and language—have formed into separate principalities, or nation-states, in order to defend their populations more effectively. But as more nation-states formed, the more likely it was that external conflicts would arise. War and preparation for war became constant rather than intermittent facts of national life, and the size and expense of military forces increased dramatically with the size of the nation-state and the size and number of its adversaries.

The cost of defense forced rulers to seek popular support to maintain military power. It was easier to raise huge permanent armies of citizen-soldiers and induce them to fight harder and to make greater sacrifices if they were imbued with enthusiasm for cause and country. To raise that enthusiasm and support, European regimes increased participation and representation in government.

The third factor often associated with the expansion of democratic politics was the promotion of national unity and development. In some instances, governments seek to subvert local or regional loyalties by linking citizens directly to the central government via the ballot box. America's Founders saw direct popular election of members of the House of Representatives as a means through which the new federal government could compete with the states for popular allegiance.

The expansion of democratic politics had two historic consequences. First, democracies opened up the possibility that citizens might use government for their own benefit rather than simply watch it being used for the benefit of others. This consequence is widely understood. But the second is less obvious: once citizens perceived that governments could operate in response to their demands, they became increasingly willing to support the expansion of government. The public's belief in its capacity to control the government's action is only one of the many factors responsible for the growth of government. But at the very least, this linkage of democracy and strong government set into motion a wave of governmental growth that began in the middle of the nineteenth century and has continued to the present day.

DOES AMERICAN DEMOCRACY WORK?

The growth of democracy in the United States has led to wider participation, which in turn has fulfilled the democratic ideals of popular sovereignty and majority rule. Thus, democratization creates the possibility that citizens can use government for their own benefit. But what are the trade-offs involved in democracy? Are there unintended consequences of too much democracy?[5] The answers to these questions are complex. Despite over 200 years of development, American democracy has still not worked out the inconsistencies and contradictions woven in its very fiber by the framers of the Constitution. Similarly, despite all that political scientists and political historians know about American government and politics, puzzles and anomalies remain for which we don't have fully satisfactory answers. We conclude this chapter by examining three of them.

Delegating Authority in a Representative Democracy

For over two centuries, we have expanded popular sovereignty to the point where a citizen, from the time she is roughly the age of a college freshman to the time that final breath is taken, can engage in political activity at various levels of government. Yet it is often convenient for citizens to delegate many of these activities to others. When we don't pay attention to politics or even register to vote, we concede the field entirely to representatives—chiefly legislators and executives—rather than exercising political authority directly. Ours is a representative democracy for very pragmatic reasons. Americans have lives to live and private concerns to attend to; by delegating, they do not have to be specialists and can focus on other matters.

We think of our political representatives as our agents, whom we "hire" to act on our behalf. In this relationship, citizens are the principals—those with the authority—who delegate some of that authority to politicians. This principal-agent relationship means that citizens don't always get what they want because, inadvertently or not, they allow agents to pursue their own self-interest or to be influenced unduly by those who care more or who have more at stake. Thus, popular sovereignty is qualified (some would say undermined) by our willingness to off-load governance responsibilities on to professional agents.

principal-agent relationship
The relationship between a principal and his or her agent. This relationship may be affected by the fact that each is motivated by self-interest, yet their interests may not be well aligned

The Trade-Off between Freedom and Order

If the imperfect fit between popular sovereignty and delegation of governance to a "political class" constitutes one problem, a second involves the trade-off between liberty and coercion. While governments are necessary to maintain order, to protect property, and to provide public goods, all these activities require a degree of coercion. Laws, regulations, and rulings constrain behavior and restrict the uses of property. Taxes include claims on

Representative democracy entails citizens choosing politicians who they think will promote their interests. This delegation of power gives politicians a level of independence but also makes them accountable to constituents.

Does American government work? In recent years, public trust in the federal government has declined, a trend reflected in the 2016 presidential campaign by the popularity of nonestablishment, "outsider" candidates such as Donald Trump.

labor income, on gains in the value of capital, and on the transmission of estates from one generation to another. In short, all of these things constitute limits on liberty. But coercion itself is necessary to enable liberty. A pinch of coercion is one of the ingredients in the stew of liberty. But where to draw the line? And even if we had an answer to this question, there is another: How can we arrange our political life to ensure just the right amount of coercion and no more? As the history of experiments in democratic self-government reveals, coercion is a slippery slope. Especially after the events of September 11, 2001, it is clear that a strong desire for public goods such as security from terrorism can lead us to accept extensive limitations on citizens' liberties.

The Instability of Majority Rule

A third puzzle involves the multitude of people's individual goals. It is not always easy to add them up into a collective choice without doing damage to the interest of some. As we see in subsequent chapters, majority rule, especially as manifested in constitutional democracies, is vulnerable to the powers of those in a position to influence the political agenda or veto potential courses of action, including financial fat cats and group leaders such as political bosses, union heads, corporate CEOs, and religious leaders. All democracies struggle with the fact that outcomes, because they entail disproportionate influence by some, are not always fair. In our American democracy, we put a great deal of faith in frequent elections, checks and balances among government institutions, and multiple levels of government. But again, we may ask where to draw the line: Elections how frequent? How powerful the checks? How many governmental levels? The disproportionate influence of some would appear inescapable, despite our efforts to control it. We revisit decisions. We reform institutions. We alter political practices. But still, perfection eludes us.

In all these puzzles and anomalies, normative principles sometimes clash. Popular sovereignty, individual liberty, delegation, and multiple purposes constitute the circle that cannot quite be squared. We noted earlier that making sense of the apparent chaos, puzzles, and contradictions in politics is the goal of political science. Political scientists try to develop theories that can be tested using empirical evidence. The Analyzing the Evidence unit at the end of this chapter describes some of the ways that political scientists analyze and attempt to better understand the patterns and events that shape our political system. With these concepts and tools for analysis in hand, we turn in Chapter 2 to the Founding and the Constitution.

For Further Reading

Crenson, Matthew A., and Benjamin Ginsberg. *Downsizing Democracy.* Baltimore: Johns Hopkins University Press, 2002.

Downs, Anthony. *An Economic Theory of Democracy.* New York: Harper, 1957.

Huntington, Samuel P. *Who Are We? The Challenges to America's National Identity.* New York: Simon & Schuster, 2004.

Kiewiet, D. Roderick, and Mathew McCubbins. *The Logic of Delegation.* Chicago: University of Chicago Press, 1991.

Lupia, Arthur, and Mathew D. McCubbins. *The Democratic Dilemma: Can Citizens Learn What They Need to Know?* New York: Cambridge University Press, 1998.

Olson, Mancur, Jr. *The Logic of Collective Action: Public Goods and the Theory of Groups.* Reprinted with new preface and appendix. Cambridge, MA: Harvard University Press, 1971; orig. published 1965.

Tilly, Charles. *Democracy.* New York: Cambridge University Press, 2007.

Tocqueville, Alexis de. *Democracy in America.* Isaac Kramnick, ed. New York: Norton, 2007; orig. published 1835.

Wolfe, Alan. *Does American Democracy Still Work?* New Haven, CT: Yale University Press, 2006.

How Do Political Scientists Know What They Know?

The five principles introduced in this chapter provide a foundation for understanding and explaining political life. However, to make and test arguments about politics, we need more than just an analytical framework; we also need empirical evidence. Political scientists study facts about politics and analyze and interpret these facts to assess different arguments and claims. Typically, we study data, systematically collecting facts and information, and examining the structure of data to see whether they are consistent, or not, with a given line of thinking.

Consider one of the most basic questions about voting: Why do people vote the way they do? In elections, Americans face two main alternatives in the form of the Democratic Party and the Republican Party. These parties have distinctive policy priorities, notably in the important area of economic policy. Since at least the 1930s, the Democratic Party has favored economic policies that redistribute income to poorer segments of society; Republicans, on the other hand, favor lower taxes and little or no redistribution. It is often argued that people vote according to their economic self-interest: people choose the candidate from the party that maximizes their income. On reflection, however, we can see that other factors may also affect voting decisions, including the candidates' personal qualities, important noneconomic issues, and even candidates' appearance or habits. Which factor best explains vote choice?

Table A Votes Cast for President, 2016

VOTE CAST	NUMBER*
HILLARY CLINTON (Democrat)	65.2 million
DONALD TRUMP (Republican)	62.7 million
Other candidates	8.0 million
Did not vote	101.1 million

*As of December 2, 2016.

What Are Data? Data are systematic measurements or observations that are collected as a source of information about a theoretically defined concept or idea. In our example there is a political behavior that we want to explain, *vote choice*. Vote choice is a general concept, and we can define it before we ever observe an election. The first step in collecting data is to represent the concept that we are interested in as a variable. A variable defines all possible outcomes of a concept that could occur and assigns them a unique label or value. Vote choice, for instance, may take four possible values or outcomes: vote for the Democratic Party candidate, vote for the Republican Party candidate, vote for another party or candidate, or don't vote.

The second step in collecting data is to measure the behavior of interest. This requires the collection of information. Observation of a small set of events can be quite enlightening.

We might, for instance, conduct in-depth interviews with a dozen or so people about how they decided to vote. However, we often require more evidence to support a given claim; a small number of people might not be sufficiently representative.

Censuses and random sample surveys allow social scientists to collect information systematically on a large number of cases. These means of collecting data are staples of social sciences. With a census we observe all individuals in the population at a given moment. Every 10 years, the United States conducts a comprehensive enumeration of all people living in the country, including information on families, education levels, income, race and ethnicity, commuting, housing, and employment. An election is a census, as it is a comprehensive count of all votes cast in a given election. So we can measure a variable such as vote choice by taking count of all electoral votes and nonvotes in the voting-eligible population (Table A).

A survey, on the other hand, consists of a study of a relatively small subset of individuals. We call this subset a sample. We can measure a variable for those individuals in the sample, and extrapolate patterns from the sample to the entire population. One of the most important social science research projects of the second half of the twentieth century is the American National Election Study, or ANES. The ANES is a national survey that has been conducted during every presidential election and most midterm congressional elections since 1948 to gauge how people voted and to understand why. In recent years, the ANES has used a sample of 2,000 Americans to make inferences about the entire voting population of over 100 million. Today, most of the information used by public policy makers, businesses, and academic researchers, including estimates of variables like unemployment and inflation, television and radio ratings, and most demographics of the population, are measured using surveys.

Summarizing Data. Communicating the information in a census or survey requires tools for summarizing data. First, we compute the frequency with which each value of a variable occurs. Frequency may be either the *number of times* that a specific behavior or value of a variable occurs or the percent of the observations in which it occurs.

Second, we construct a graph or statistic that summarizes the frequencies of all values of the variable. The distribution of a variable expresses how often each of the values of the variable occurs. A bar chart displays all possible values of a variable on one axis, usually the horizontal axis; the heights of the bars equal the frequency or *percent* of cases observed for each value (Figure A).

Votes Cast for President, 2016

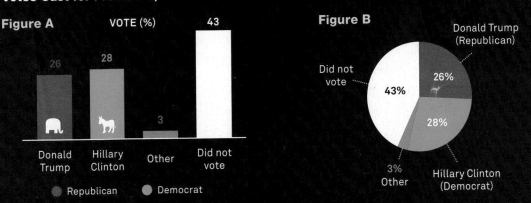

Figure C Party Identification, 1952-2016

PERCENTAGE

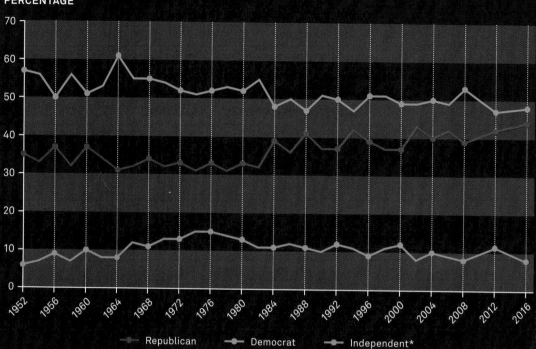

Republican ●—— Democrat ●—— Independent*

*Independents who said thay leaned toward one party are counted with that party.

In a pie chart, the frequency for each value is depicted as a share of the whole (Figure B). A line graph is often used to show frequency over time (Figure C).

The distribution of income in the United States offers a somewhat different example. This variable takes a range of values, from the smallest household income to the largest household income. For ease of presentation, we can organize this variable into categories. In Figure D, the first category is "less than $10,000," the second category is "$10,000 to $19,999," and so forth up to the top category, "$200,000 or more." All possible income levels are covered in this classification.

Variables such as income can also be characterized with statistics, such as the median or mean. In this example, the median is the value of household income such that half of all households have incomes below the value and half have income above it. Fifty percent of all cases have income above the median value, and 50 percent have income below it; thus the median is also called the 50th percentile. The median household income in the United States in 2015 was $56,516, meaning that half of all households have income below that value and half have income above that amount. The mean is the average value for the variable. In the case of household income, the mean equals the sum of all households' incomes divided by the number of households. Personal income received by households totaled approximately $10 trillion in 2015, and there were 126 million households. So the average household income was $79,263.

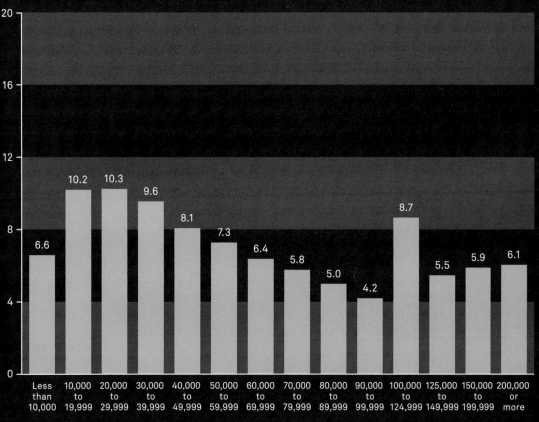

PERCENTAGE OF ALL HOUSEHOLDS

HOUSEHOLD INCOME (U.S. DOLLARS)

Why do the median and mean differ? In calculating the median, every household is equal. We merely count the percent above and below a certain income level. The mean value weights households according to their incomes; consequently, a household with $200,000 income contributes 10 times as much to the calculation of the mean as a household with $20,000. If there were only a small difference in income among households, the mean would be very close to the median. The difference between the median income and the mean income thus provides a way to measure inequality. Only about one-third of households had income above the mean value of $79,263.

Testing Arguments Using Data. Let's return to the idea discussed at the beginning of the section: that people vote their economic self-interest. Is this claim correct?

To test this idea, we need to formulate a hypothesis. In the social sciences, hypotheses often take the form of stating a relationship between two variables, such as income and vote choice.

o test the hypothesis that people vote their economic self-interest, we want to know to what extent voting decisions match up with individuals' income levels. As stated earlier, in the United States today, the Republican Party generally favors lower income taxes and less income redistribution, and the Democratic Party favors higher income taxes and more income redistribution. We therefore want to know if people in high-income households vote Republican more often than people in low-income households. The difference we observe in vote choice between high- and low-income groups is considered to be the effect of income on vote choice.

To see whether the effect of income on the vote is indeed large, we can use the data in Table B to examine the actual voting behavior of different sorts of individuals. The national exit polls in 2016 reveal that 41 percent of voters with income less than $30,000 chose the Republican candidate, Donald Trump. By comparison, 48 percent of those with income over $100,000 chose Donald Trump. This difference (7 percentage points) reveals that income is associated with vote choice, but it is not absolutely determinative: not every person of high income voted Republican in this election, and not everyone in low-income groups voted Democrat.

Table B Vote by Level of Income

INCOME	🐴 CLINTON	🐘 TRUMP
Under $30,000	53%	41%
$30,000–$49,999	51%	42%
$50,000–$99,999	46%	50%
$100,000 or more	47%	48%

As we explore alternative arguments about what determines vote choice, we can make many different comparisons—men versus women, college graduates versus high school graduates, and so forth. Our goal is to find which, if any, of these potential explanations best accounts for the variation in vote choice. Throughout this book, we will consider other political outcomes besides voter behavior, such as the support by members of Congress for different types of legislation and how often the executive succeeds in passing legislation.

Many times we will look for a relationship or association between two variables to see if the predictions from an argument hold true, and if they do, we take that as evidence supporting the argument. A relationship or association between two variables, sometimes called a correlation, should not be taken to mean that one of the variables caused the other to occur. Causation is more difficult to establish. A correlation between two variables X (say X is a measure of education) and Y (say Y is a measure of income) is consistent with a theory that education increases one's earning power. From a simple correlation, however, one cannot tell whether many years of education caused high income or high income led to many years of education. It is also possible that some other variable, say high intelligence, caused both many years of education and high income.

Social scientists design experiments and carefully controlled comparisons in order to measure causal relationships. Observing simple associations and correlations, though, is not the final step in verifying our arguments, ideas, or theories about how politics works.

Be a Savvy Consumer of Quantitative Data. Beyond the figures and tables in this book, which reflect data from sources that we consider reliable and accurate, you will undoubtedly encounter other data about politics in the news and elsewhere. Before you take such data—and whatever argument they seem to support—at face value, it is worth asking a few questions about how the data were gathered and presented.

 What is the source of the data? Is it a respected source like a government office or a major mainstream news organization, which may be relied upon to gather and report data accurately? Or are they from a source that is likely to have a goal other than accurate presentation of the data, like an interest group, a campaign, or an entertainment website?

 When were the data collected and how? What is the date (or date range) for the data? Are the data from a census or sample, and how large is the sample?

 What is being measured? For example, in a poll showing support for a candidate, is it the percent of all Americans? The percentage of likely voters? The percentage of Democrats or Republicans?

 Why are the data presented a certain way? Is this the best way to present these data? Does it distort the data in any way? What relationships and patterns do we observe in the data?

Thinking through the questions above can help you better understand the information in the data figures and tables found throughout this book as well as in other academic writing and in the news. In each of the chapters to follow, you will find an Analyzing the Evidence unit, highlighting arguments and evidence on some of the subjects of that chapter. Many of these sections discuss how political scientists use the basic methodology discussed above to test arguments about American politics.

SOURCES:

Table A "2016 Presidential General Election Results," U.S. Election Atlas, www.uselectionatlas.org/RESULTS/national.php (accessed 11/28/16).

Table B "Election 2016: Exit Polls," *The New York Times*, www.nytimes.com/interactive/2016/11/08/us/politics/election-exit-polls.html (accessed 11/12/16).

Figure C Gallup, "Party Affiliation," www.gallup.com/poll/15370/party-affiliation.aspx (accessed 11/7/16).

Figure D U.S. Census Bureau, Household Income in 2015, www.census.gov/data/tables/time-series/demo/income-poverty/cps-hinc.html (accessed 11/3/16).

2

The Founding and the Constitution

The story of America's Founding and the Constitution is generally presented as something both inevitable and glorious: it was inevitable that the American colonies would break away from England to establish their own country successfully; and it was glorious that they established the best of all possible forms of government under a new Constitution, which was easily adopted and quickly embraced, even by its critics. In reality, though, America's successful breakaway from England in 1776 was by no means assured, and the Constitution that we revere today as one of the most brilliant creations of any nation was in fact highly controversial. Moreover, its ratification and durability were often in doubt. George Washington, the man venerated as the father of the country and chosen to preside over the Constitutional Convention of 1787, thought the document produced that hot summer in Philadelphia would probably last no more than 20 years, at which time leaders would have to convene again to come up with something new.

That Washington's prediction proved wrong is, indeed, a testament to the enduring strength of the Constitution. Nonetheless, the Constitution was not carved in stone. It was a product of political bargaining and compromise, formed very much in the same way political decisions are made today. As this chapter shows, the Constitution reflects political self-interest and high principle, too. It also defines the relationship between American citizens and their government. To understand the character of the American Founding and the meaning of the American Constitution, it is essential to look beyond the myths and rhetoric and explore the conflicting interests and forces at work during the revolutionary and constitutional periods. Thus, we first assess the political backdrop of the American Revolution, and then we examine the Constitution that ultimately emerged as the basis for America's government.

Does the Constitution work? Not every feature of the Constitution has been a success. One of the Constitution's most famous failures was the Eighteenth Amendment (ratified in 1919), which, until its repeal by the Twenty-First Amendment (ratified in 1933), launched America's brief and disastrous experiment with the prohibition of alcoholic beverages. Most scholars agree that the framers did not intend for the amendment process to be used to address substantive social problems normally handled through legislation, but in this case it was. In an example from recent years, the constitutional features intended to leash what James Madison called the "dogs of war" by assigning the power to declare war to Congress rather than the president have been undermined by the expansion of presidential war powers (see Chapter 6).

On the whole, however, we would have to judge the Constitution a success and attribute to it at least some of the credit for America's success as a

CORE OF THE ANALYSIS

➡ The framers of the Constitution, although guided by underlying values, also had conflicting goals and interests.

➡ The first attempt at a new arrangement for self-government relied on institutions that were too weak to achieve collective action on behalf of the nation.

➡ The conflicting interests of the Founders were eventually accommodated through a complex set of rules and procedures set forth in the Constitution, which divided power among three branches of the federal government and between states and the federal government.

➡ The Constitution not only provides a framework for government but also often guides the policy process, even to this day.

nation. Not only is America a great economic, military, and political power but Americans are relatively free and prosperous. One important way in which the Constitution has contributed to America's success as a nation is by firmly establishing the rule of law.

The rule of law means that a government's actions cannot be arbitrary but must, instead, be based upon a fairly stable body of published, clearly stated statutes that are binding upon government officials as well as citizens. The rule of law is a safeguard for citizens, protecting them from arbitrary action by government officials. At the same time, it enhances the quality of governance and generally promotes the development of a nation's economy. Who would invest in creating a new technology if their property was not protected by the law? Who would purchase a government's bonds if they could not be sure of repayment? Indeed, who would bother to obey any law if the law itself was arbitrarily enforced and constantly changing? The rule of law is the foundation of a successful government.

The framers of the Constitution understood this concept. James Madison's views, expressed in *Federalist 62*, are instructive. Madison writes

> It will be of little avail to the people that the laws are made by men of their own choice if the laws be so voluminous that they cannot be read, or so incoherent that they cannot be understood; if they be repealed or revised before they are promulgated, or undergo such incessant changes that no man, who knows what the law is today, can guess what it will be tomorrow.

Such a state of affairs, according to Madison, reduces popular respect for government and undermines economic development. "What prudent merchant will hazard his fortunes in any new branch of commerce when he knows not but that his plans may be rendered unlawful before they can be executed?"[1] Similar concerns have inspired a number of regimes, including such authoritarian states as Russia and China, to endeavor to strengthen the rule of law in their domains in recent years. The Chinese leadership has viewed the rule of law as essential to economic development and, in Russia, former president Dmitri Medvedev said, "Shortcomings in implementing laws . . . are basically macro-economic factors which restrain the growth of national prosperity."[2] In many instances, the strength of a regime and well-being of a nation could be increased if the arbitrary power of rulers and officials were reduced. James Madison understood this principle, but it is one that many rulers, protective of their personal powers and prerogatives, fail to grasp. In China, for example, the central government's efforts to promote legalism as a spur to economic development are often thwarted by local officials accustomed to exercising discretionary power.[3]

The U.S. Constitution, enforced by an independent judiciary, has helped to impose limits upon the arbitrary exercise of governmental power. Under the Constitution, the powers of government officials are defined by law and may only be exercised according to law. The same laws apply to officials and citizens alike. Those accused of offenses must be treated according to law. These principles safeguard the citizenry and promote the well-being and prosperity of the nation as well. In this chapter, we will explore the institutions and procedures established in the Constitution, and how the framers settled on these features of government.

THE FIRST FOUNDING: INTERESTS AND CONFLICTS

Competing ideals often reflect competing interests, and so it was in Revolutionary America. The American Revolution and the American Constitution were outgrowths of a struggle among economic and political forces within the colonies. Five economic sectors of society were important in colonial politics: (1) the New England merchants; (2) the southern planters; (3) the "royalists"—holders of royal lands, offices, and patents (licenses to engage in a profession or business activity); (4) shopkeepers, artisans, and laborers; and (5) small farmers. Throughout the eighteenth century, these groups differed over issues of taxation, trade, and commerce. For the most part, the merchants, the planters, and the royalists—in other words, the colonial elite—maintained a political alliance that held in check the more radical forces representing shopkeepers, laborers, and small farmers. After 1750, however, British tax and trade policies split the elite, permitting radical forces to expand their political influence and setting off a chain of events that culminated in the American Revolution.[4]

Political Strife and the Radicalizing of the Colonists

The political strife within the colonies was the background for the events of 1773–74. With the Tea Act of 1773, the British government granted the politically powerful East India Company a monopoly on the export of tea from Britain, eliminating a lucrative trade for colonial merchants. Together with their southern allies, the merchants called upon their radical adversaries—shopkeepers, artisans, laborers, and small farmers, all of whom had their own grievances against the established colonial government—for support. The most dramatic result was the Boston Tea Party of 1773, led by Samuel Adams.

The Boston Tea Party played a decisive role in American history. The merchants hoped to force the British government to rescind the Tea Act, but they certainly did not seek independence from Britain. Samuel Adams and the other radicals, however, hoped to provoke the British to take actions that would alienate their colonial supporters and pave the way for a rebellion. By dumping the East India Company's tea into Boston Harbor, they goaded the British Parliament into enacting harsh reprisals. A series of acts closed the port of Boston to commerce, changed the provincial government of Massachusetts, provided for the removal of accused persons to Britain for trial, and added new restrictions on movement to the West—further alienating the southern planters who depended on access to new western lands. These acts of retaliation helped radicalize the American colonists.

Thus, the Boston Tea Party sparked a cycle of provocation and retaliation that in 1774 resulted in the convening of the First Continental Congress with delegates attending from all parts of the country. The Congress called for a total boycott of British goods and, under the radicals' prodding, began to consider independence from British rule. The result was the Declaration of Independence.

The Declaration of Independence

In 1776, the Second Continental Congress appointed a committee consisting of Thomas Jefferson of Virginia, Benjamin Franklin of Pennsylvania, Roger Sherman of Connecticut, John Adams of Massachusetts, and Robert Livingston of New York to draft a statement of American independence from British rule. The Declaration of Independence was written by Jefferson, drawing on ideas from the British philosopher John Locke, whose work was widely read in the colonies. Adopted by the Second Continental Congress, the Declaration was an extraordinary document in both philosophical and political terms. Philosophically, the Declaration was remarkable for its assertion (derived from Locke) that certain "unalienable rights"—including life, liberty, and the pursuit of happiness—could not be abridged by governments. In the world of 1776, in which some kings still claimed to rule by divine right, this was a dramatic statement. Politically, the Declaration was remarkable because it focused on grievances, aspirations, and principles that might unify the various colonial groups. The Declaration was an attempt to articulate a history and set of principles that might help to forge national unity.[5]

The Revolutionary War

In 1775, even before formally declaring their independence, the colonies had begun to fight the British, most notably at Lexington and Concord, Massachusetts, where colonial militias acquitted themselves well against trained

British soldiers. Nevertheless, the task of defeating Britain, then the world's premier military power, seemed impossible. To maintain their hold on the colonies, the British sent a huge expeditionary force composed of British regulars and German mercenaries along with artillery and equipment. To face this force, the colonists relied on inexperienced and lightly armed militias. To make matters worse, the colonists were hardly united in their opposition to British rule. Many colonists saw themselves as loyal British subjects and refused to take up arms against the king. Thousands, indeed, took up arms *for* the king and joined pro-British militia forces.

The war was brutal and bloody with tens of thousands of casualties among the colonists, among British troops, and among the Native Americans who fought on both sides. Eventually, the revolutionary armies prevailed, mainly because the cost to England of fighting a war thousands of miles from home became too great. As colonial militias prevented British forces from acquiring enough food and supplies locally, these had to be brought from Europe at enormous expense. With the eventual help of Britain's enemy, France, the colonists fought until Britain decided it had had enough of a seemingly endless colonial war. The war ended with the signing of the Treaty of Paris, which officially granted the 13 American colonies their independence.

The Articles of Confederation

Having declared independence, the colonies needed to establish a government. In November 1777, the Continental Congress adopted the Articles of Confederation and Perpetual Union—the first written constitution of the United States. Although it was not ratified by all the states until 1781, it served as the country's constitution for almost 12 years, until March 1789.

The Articles of Confederation were concerned primarily with limiting the powers of the central government. They created no executive branch. Congress constituted the central government, but it had little power. Execution of its laws was left to the individual states. Its members were not much more than messengers from the states: they were chosen by the state legislatures, paid out of the state treasuries, and subject to immediate recall by state authorities. Each state, regardless of size, had only a single vote. Furthermore, amendments to the articles required the unanimous agreement of the 13 states.

Congress was given the power to declare war and make peace, to make treaties and alliances, to coin or borrow money, and to regulate trade with Native Americans. It could also appoint the senior officers of the United States Army. But it could not levy taxes or regulate commerce among the states. Moreover, the army officers it appointed had no army to serve in

Articles of Confederation and Perpetual Union

America's first written constitution. Adopted by the Continental Congress in 1777, the Articles of Confederation and Perpetual Union were the formal basis for America's national government until 1789, when they were superseded by the Constitution

because the nation's armed forces were composed of the state militias. An especially dysfunctional aspect of the Articles of Confederation was that the central government could not prevent one state from discriminating against other states in the quest for foreign commerce.

In brief, the relationship between Congress and the states under the Articles of Confederation was much like the contemporary relationship between the United Nations and its member states—a relationship in which the states retain virtually all governmental powers. It was called a confederation because, as provided under Article II, "each state retains its sovereignty, freedom and independence, and every power, jurisdiction, and right, which is not by this confederation expressly delegated to the United States, in Congress assembled." Not only was there no executive, there was also no judicial authority and no means of enforcing Congress's will. If there was to be any enforcement, the states would have to do it.[6] In essence, each state was an independent nation-state.

THE SECOND FOUNDING: FROM COMPROMISE TO CONSTITUTION

The Declaration of Independence and the Articles of Confederation were not sufficient to hold the nation together as an independent and effective nation-state. From almost the moment of armistice with the British in 1783, moves were afoot to reform and strengthen the Articles.

International Standing, Economic Difficulties, and Domestic Turmoil

Many Americans were concerned about the country's international position. Competition for foreign commerce allowed the European powers to play the states against one another, which created confusion on both sides of the Atlantic. At one point, John Adams, a leader in the independence struggle, was sent to negotiate a new treaty with the British, one that would cover disputes left over from the war. The British government responded that, since the United States under the Articles of Confederation was unable to enforce existing treaties, it would negotiate with each of the 13 states separately.

At the same time, well-to-do Americans—in particular the New England merchants and southern planters—were troubled by the influence of "populist" forces in the Continental Congress and several state governments.

The colonists' victory in the Revolutionary War had not only meant the end of British rule but also significantly changed the balance of political power within the new states. As a result, one key segment of the colonial elite—the holders of royal land, offices, and patents—was stripped of its economic and political privileges. In fact, many of these individuals, along with tens of thousands of other colonists who considered themselves loyal British subjects, left for Canada after the British surrender. And as the elite was weakened, the radicals gained control in such states as Pennsylvania and Rhode Island, where they pursued economic and political policies that struck terror in the prerevolutionary political establishment. The central government under the Articles of Confederation was powerless to intervene. Commerce within the states stagnated, and several states borrowed money just to finance their Revolutionary War debts.

The new nation's weak international position and domestic turmoil led many Americans to consider whether a new version of the Articles might be necessary. In the fall of 1786, delegates from five states met in Annapolis, Maryland, and called on Congress to send commissioners to Philadelphia at a later time to devise adjustments to the Articles. Their resolution took on force as a result of an event that occurred the following winter in Massachusetts: Shays's Rebellion. Daniel Shays led a mob of farmers, who were protesting foreclosures on their land, in a rebellion against the state government. In January 1787, Shays and the rebels attempted to seize a federal armory in Springfield, Massachusetts. The state militia dispersed the mob within a few days, but the threat posed by the rebels scared Congress into action. The states were asked to send delegates to Philadelphia to discuss constitutional revision, and eventually delegates were sent from every state but Rhode Island.

The Constitutional Convention

In May 1787, 29 of a total of 73 delegates selected by the state governments convened in Philadelphia. Recognizing that political strife, international embarrassment, national weakness, and local rebellion were symptoms of fundamental flaws in the Articles of Confederation, the delegates soon abandoned plans for revision and undertook a second Founding instead—an ultimately successful attempt to create a legitimate and effective national system.

The Great Compromise. The proponents of a new government fired their opening shot on May 29, 1787, when Edmund Randolph of Virginia offered a resolution that proposed corrections and enlargements in the Articles of Confederation. Not a simple motion, it provided for virtually every

Representation in Congress: States' Ranks

Rank of Top Five States

At the nation's founding, Virginia and Massachusetts were the most populous states and thus had the greatest representation in Congress.

Rank	1789	1790	1800	1810	1820	1830	1840	1850	1860	1870	1880	1890
1	VA	VA	VA	NY	NY	NY	NY	NY	NY	NY	NY	NY
2	MA / PA	MA	PA	PA / VA	PA	PA	PA	PA	PA	PA	PA	PA
3		PA / MA	NY / MA	NY	VA	VA	OH	OH	OH	OH	OH	IL
4	NY / MD	NY / NC			MA	OH	OH	VA	VA	IL	IL	OH
5			NC	NC	MA / NC	TN / NC / KY	TN	MA / IN	VA / IN	MO / IN	MO	MO

aspect of a new government, and it was in fact the framework for what ultimately became the Constitution.[7]

The portion of Randolph's motion that became most controversial was known as the Virginia Plan. This plan provided for a system of representation in the national legislature based upon the population of each state or the proportion of each state's revenue contribution, or both. (Randolph also proposed a second branch of the legislature, but it was to be elected by the members of the first branch.) Because the states varied enormously in size and wealth, the Virginia Plan appeared heavily biased in favor of the large states, which would have greater representation.

While the convention was debating the Virginia Plan, additional delegates arriving in Philadelphia were beginning to mount opposition to it. In particular, delegates from the less populous states, which included Delaware, New Jersey, Connecticut, and New York, asserted that the more populous states, such as Virginia, Pennsylvania, North Carolina, and Massachusetts, would dominate the new government if representation were to be determined by population. The smaller states argued that each state should be equally represented regardless of its population. The proposal, called the

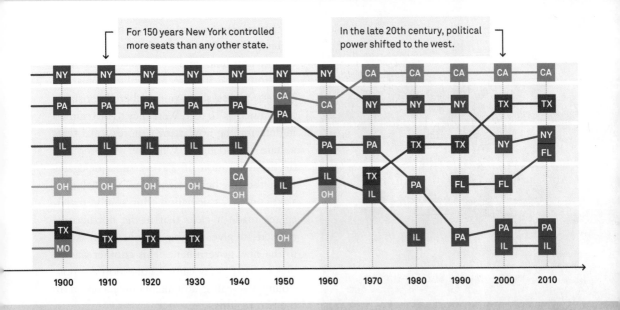

For 150 years New York controlled more seats than any other state.

In the late 20th century, political power shifted to the west.

New Jersey Plan (it was introduced by William Paterson of New Jersey), focused on revising the Articles rather than replacing them. Their opposition to the Virginia Plan's system of representation was sufficient to send the proposals back to committee for reworking into a common document.

The outcome was the Great Compromise, also known as the Connecticut Compromise. Under its terms, in the first branch of Congress—the House of Representatives—the members would be apportioned according to the number of inhabitants in each state. This was what delegates from the large states had sought. But in the second branch—the Senate—each state would have an equal vote regardless of its size; this addressed the small states' concerns. This compromise was not immediately satisfactory to all the delegates. In the end, however, both sides preferred compromise to the breakup of the Union, and the plan was accepted. The timeplot above shows the top five most represented states in Congress from 1789 to today.

◀ **Great Compromise**

An agreement reached at the Constitutional Convention of 1787 that gave each state an equal number of senators regardless of its population but linked representation in the House of Representatives to population

The Question of Slavery: The Three-Fifths Compromise.

Many of the conflicts facing the Constitutional Convention reflected the

The issue of how to count slaves in determining state populations and apportioning congressional seats nearly prevented the passage of the new constitution. Here, slaves are auctioned in Charleston, South Carolina, around the time of the Founding.

fundamental differences between the slave and the nonslave states—differences that pitted the southern planters and New England merchants against one another. This was the first premonition of a conflict that would almost destroy the Republic in later years.

Over 90 percent of all slaves resided in five states—Georgia, Maryland, North Carolina, South Carolina, and Virginia—where they accounted for 30 percent of the population. In some places, slaves outnumbered nonslaves by as much as 10 to 1. Were they to be counted in determining how many congressional seats a state should have? Whatever they thought of the institution of slavery, most delegates from the northern states opposed including slaves in this calculation. But southern delegates made it clear that if the northerners refused to give in, they would never agree to the new government. This conflict was so divisive that many came to question the possibility of creating and maintaining a union of the two regions.

Northerners and southerners eventually reached agreement through the Three-Fifths Compromise. The seats in the House of Representatives would be apportioned according to a "population" in which only three-fifths of slaves would be counted. This arrangement was supported by the slave states, which included some of the biggest and some of the smallest states at that time. It was also acceptable to many delegates from nonslave states who supported the principle of property representation, whether that property was expressed in slaves or in land, money, or stocks.

The issue of slavery was the most difficult one the framers faced, and it nearly destroyed the Union. Although some delegates considered slavery morally wrong, morality was not the issue that caused the framers to support or oppose the Three-Fifths Compromise. A compromise that acknowledged the legitimacy of slavery was probably necessary to keep the South from rejecting the Constitution.

THE CONSTITUTION

The political significance of the Great Compromise and the Three-Fifths Compromise was to restore the alliance of the southern planters and northern merchants. The Great Compromise reassured those of both groups who feared that a new governmental framework would reduce their own local or regional influence, and the Three-Fifths Compromise temporarily defused the rivalry between the groups (see the Policy Principle section on p. 34). Their unity secured, members of the alliance supporting the establishment of a new government moved to fashion a constitutional framework consistent with their economic and political interests.

First, the framers sought a new government strong enough to promote commerce and protect property from radical state legislatures. This goal led them to establish national control over commerce and finance, as well as national judicial supremacy and a strong presidency. Second, the framers sought to prevent the threat posed by the "excessive democracy" of the state and national governments under the Articles of Confederation. This goal led to such constitutional principles as bicameralism (the division of Congress into two chambers), checks and balances, staggered terms in office, and indirect election of the president and senators (by an electoral college and state legislatures rather than by voters directly).

Third, to prevent the new government from abusing its power by interfering with the interests of the merchants and planters, the framers incorporated principles such as the separation of powers and federalism into the Constitution. Finally, despite some misgivings, the framers provided for direct popular election of representatives and promised to add a Bill of Rights to the Constitution. Many of the framers were dubious about these provisions but were concerned that without them, the Constitution would not be ratified and the provisions they favored would come to naught. Let us now assess the major provisions of the Constitution to see how each relates to these objectives.

The Legislative Branch

The first seven sections of Article I of the Constitution provided for a Congress consisting of two chambers—a House of Representatives and a Senate. Members of the House of Representatives were given two-year terms in office and directly elected—though generally only white males had the right to vote. State legislatures were to appoint members of the Senate (this was changed in 1913 by the Seventeenth Amendment, providing for direct election of senators) for six-year terms. These terms were staggered

Three-Fifths Compromise
An agreement reached at the Constitutional Convention of 1787 stipulating that for purposes of the apportionment of congressional seats, only three-fifths of slaves would be counted

bicameralism
The division of a legislative body into two chambers, or houses

The Constitution and Policy Outcomes

Large states and small states debated representation at the Constitutional Convention.

Individuals involved in politics try to create institutions that will help them achieve policy outcomes they favor and prevent ones they oppose. In conflicts over policy, the right institutional arrangements can put them at an advantage, and their opponents at a disadvantage, for many years.

This idea is illustrated by the struggles at the Constitutional Convention. Delegates from the smaller states thought their states had much to gain by creating legislative institutions that gave each state an equal vote regardless of population. The larger states, however, especially Virginia, Massachusetts, New York, and Pennsylvania, were centers of commerce, and their delegates believed that over time the new government's commercial policies would be more likely to serve those states' interests if its legislative institutions reflected their advantage in population. Nevertheless, representatives of both groups of states agreed that a new government was likely to produce better policies than those developed under the Articles of Confederation and so were willing to compromise: they eventually settled, in what is

known as the Great Compromise, on an institutional arrangement that gave the larger states more weight in the House of Representatives and the smaller states equality of representation in the Senate.

In a similar vein, the Southern delegates knew that a system of apportioning House seats that counted slaves as part of their states' populations would increase Southern states' legislative representation and thereby strengthen their hands in political struggles for years to come. The Northern delegates, for their part, were determined not to provide this institutional advantage to the South in future policy making. Again, though, both groups of delegates calculated that the benefits of new national institutions were substantial and thus agreed to the Three-Fifths Compromise, in which, for the purposes of apportionment of House seats, only three-fifths of slaves would be counted.

The Three-Fifths Compromise became moot with the abolition of slavery, but the impact of the Great Compromise continues to be felt today. For example, the Constitution assigns each state a number of electors in the Electoral College equal to its number of senators plus representatives. Because the Great Compromise assigned each state an equal number of senators, small states have more electoral votes *per capita* in presidential elections than large states. One Wyoming voter, for example, has as much influence as three New York voters. Equal representation in the Senate plus a disproportionate share of electoral votes may help to explain why some of America's smallest states, such as South Carolina and North Dakota, are leading beneficiaries of federal tax and spending policies, receiving far more in federal spending than their citizens pay in taxes.

so that the appointments of one-third of the senators expired every two years. The Constitution assigned somewhat different tasks to the House and Senate. Though the approval of each body was required for the enactment of a law, the Senate alone can ratify treaties and approve presidential appointments. The House has the sole power to originate revenue bills.

The character of the legislative branch reflects the framers' major goals. The House of Representatives was designed to be directly responsible to the people in order to encourage popular consent for the new Constitution and, as we saw in Chapter 1, to help enhance the power of the new government. At the same time, to guard against "excessive democracy," the power of the House was checked by the Senate, whose members were to be appointed for long terms rather than elected for short terms.

Staggered terms in the Senate would make that body even more resistant to popular pressure. Because only one-third of the senators would be selected at any given time, the Senate's composition would be somewhat protected even from changes in public opinion transmitted by the state legislatures. Thus, the structure of the legislative branch was designed to contribute to governmental power, promote popular consent for the new government, and at the same time place limits on the popular political currents that many framers saw as a radical threat to the economic and social order.

The Powers of Congress and the States. The issues of power and consent were important throughout the Constitution. Section 8 of Article I specifically listed the powers of Congress, which include the authority to collect taxes, to borrow money, to regulate commerce, to declare war, and to maintain an army and navy. By granting it these powers, the framers indicated clearly that the new government would be far more influential than its predecessor. At the same time, by giving these important powers to Congress rather than to the executive branch, the framers sought to reassure citizens that their views would be fully represented whenever the government exercised its new powers.

As a further guarantee to the people that the new government would pose no threat, the Constitution implied that any powers *not* listed were not granted to the government at all. This is the doctrine of expressed powers: the Constitution grants only those powers specifically *expressed* in its text. But the framers wanted an active and powerful government, and so they included the necessary and proper clause, sometimes known as the elastic clause, which signified that the expressed powers were meant to be a source of strength to the national government, not a limitation on it. Each power could be used with the utmost vigor, although no additional powers could be assumed by the national government without a constitutional amendment. Any power not enumerated was stated to be "reserved" to the states (or the people).

> **expressed powers**
> The powers that the Constitution explicitly grants to the federal government

> **necessary and proper clause**
> Article I, Section 8 of the Constitution, which enumerates the powers of Congress and provides Congress with the authority to make all laws "necessary and proper" to carry them out; also referred to as the elastic clause

The Executive Branch

The Constitution provided for the establishment of the presidency in Article II. As Alexander Hamilton put it, the presidential article aimed at "energy in the Executive." It did so in an effort to overcome the natural stalemate that was built into both the bicameral legislature and the separation of powers among the legislative, executive, and judicial branches. The Constitution afforded the president a measure of independence from the people and from the other branches of government—particularly Congress.

Some of the framers had wanted a plural executive or executive council to avoid the evils that many associated with a monarch. However, Hamilton argued that "energy" required a single rather than a plural executive. While abuse of power should be guarded against by checks and balances and other devices, energy also required that the executive hold "competent powers" to direct the nation's business.[8] These would include the unconditional power to accept ambassadors from—to "recognize"—other countries; the power to negotiate treaties, although their acceptance requires Senate approval; the unconditional right to grant reprieves and pardons, except in cases of impeachment; and the power to appoint major departmental personnel, to convene Congress in special session, and to veto congressional enactments. (The veto power is not absolute, because Congress can override it by a two-thirds vote. The Analyzing the Evidence unit on pp. 38–9 explores the various points at which legislation can be halted in the United States as compared to other countries.)

The framers debated whether a plural executive would better protect against tyranny but ultimately decided that the energy required to overcome government stalemates required a single executive. In 1789, George Washington was unanimously elected as America's first president.

Chapter 2: The Founding and the Constitution

At the same time, the framers sought to help the president withstand (excessively) democratic pressures by making him subject to indirect rather than direct election (through a separate electoral college). The extent to which the framers' hopes were actually realized is the topic of Chapter 6.

The Judicial Branch

Article III established the judicial branch. This provision reflects the framers' concern with giving more power to the national government and checking radical democratic impulses, while guarding against potential interference with liberty and property by the new national government itself.

The framers created a court that was to be literally a supreme court of the United States and not merely the highest court of the national government. The Supreme Court was given the power to resolve any conflicts that might emerge between federal and state laws and to determine to which level of government—national, state, or both—a power belonged. In addition, the Supreme Court was assigned jurisdiction over controversies between citizens of different states. The long-term significance of this provision was that as the country developed a national economy, it came to rely increasingly on the federal judiciary, rather than on the state courts, for resolution of disputes.

Judges were given lifetime appointments to protect them from popular politics and interference by the other branches. To further safeguard judicial independence, the Constitution also prohibited Congress from reducing the salary of any sitting judge. But they would not be totally immune to politics or to the other branches, for the president was to appoint the judges and the Senate was to approve the appointments. Congress would also have the power to create inferior (lower) courts, change the federal courts' jurisdiction, add or subtract federal judges, and even change the size of the Supreme Court.

The Constitution does not specifically mention judicial review—the power of the courts to render the final decision when there is a conflict of interpretation of the Constitution or of laws. This conflict could be between the courts and Congress, the courts and the executive branch, or the federal government and the states. Scholars generally feel that judicial review is implicit in the existence of a written Constitution and in the power given to the federal courts over "all Cases . . . arising under this Constitution, the Laws of the United States, and Treaties made, or which shall be made, under their Authority" (Article III, Section 2). The Supreme Court eventually assumed the power of judicial review. Its assumption of this power, as we will see in Chapter 8, was based not on the Constitution itself but on the politics of later decades and the membership of the Court.

judicial review
The power of the courts to determine whether the actions of the president, the Congress, and the state legislatures are or are not consistent with the Constitution. The Supreme Court asserted the power to review federal statutes in *Marbury v. Madison* (1803).

Constitutional Engineering: How Many Veto Gates?

Contributed by

Steven L. Taylor
Troy University

Matthew S. Shugart
University of California, Davis

Any given constitution contains a number of individual elements that interact to produce a specific policy-making environment. These parameters determine how policy decisions are made as well as which political actors can stop them from proceeding through the process. One area of comparative constitutional structures is how many *veto gates* a system contains. A veto gate is an institution that serves as a point in the legislative process where the progress of a proposal can be halted. This notion conceives of the legislative process as being made up of one or more such gates that have to be opened to allow an idea to "flow" past on its way to becoming law. Each gate, however, is locked and can be opened only by institutional actors who hold the keys.

The simplest possible model of such a system would be an absolute dictator who has to consult only his own preferences before acting. Democratic governance, on the other hand, is a system that builds complex (and often multiple) gates and then creates and empowers players to open (or not) those gates.

The exact mix of institutional elements in a given constitution has a profound impact not only on how policy is made but also on what kinds of policies are made. More veto gates and players in a given system will generate more need for negotiation and compromise versus systems with fewer such actors. In counting veto gates, we can ask three questions:

1. **Presidential veto:** Is there an elected president who can veto legislation? In parliamentary systems, like the United Kingdom and India, there is no elected presidency at all. Other systems have elected presidents who may be important in some respects but who are not empowered with a veto (for instance, France). The strongest presidents are both elected and have a veto, such as the U.S. president.

2. **Number of legislative chambers:** How many legislative chambers are there? Does the government have one chamber (unicameral) or two (bicameral)? If there is only one legislative chamber, as in Costa Rica and Denmark, then obviously there can be only one veto gate among legislative actors—but we need a final question to differentiate different forms of bicameralism.

3. **Symmetry of chambers:** If there is a second chamber, are they symmetrical in their powers? Many second chambers are less powerful in their systems than the U.S. Senate, which is fully symmetrical. Some other bicameral legislatures are asymmetrical, meaning the second chamber has minimal powers beyond delaying power, as in Austria, or it has substantial powers in some areas but not others, as with the Canadian Senate and the United Kingdom's House of Lords.

We can see from the table of 40 established democracies that there are multiple ways in which national constitutions can configure the lawmaking process in terms of the type and number of veto gates. Moreover, the United States is not typical. It is only 1 of 9 of these 40 democracies to have three veto gates in the lawmaking process. Most other established democracies have fewer veto gates, although several have multiple veto players—such as frequent coalition governments where political parties have to compromise with one another. This combination of veto gates and veto players directly impacts the policies and may help us understand why policies are different across different democracies.

	ELECTED PRESIDENT WITH VETO?	NO. OF LEGISLATIVE CHAMBERS	LEVEL OF CHAMBER SYMMETRY	NUMBER OF VETO GATES
ARGENTINA, BRAZIL, CHILE, COLOMBIA, DOMINICAN REPUBLIC, *MEXICO*,* PHILIPPINES, *UNITED STATES*, URUGUAY	Yes	● ●	High	✖ ✖ ✖
COSTA RICA,** PANAMA, SOUTH KOREA	Yes	●	Unicameral	✖ ✖
POLAND	Yes	● ●	Low *1 strong chamber 1 weak chamber*	✖ ✖
AUSTRALIA, ITALY, **SWITZERLAND**	No	● ●	High *2 strong chambers*	✖ ✖
CANADA, GERMANY, INDIA, JAPAN, **NETHERLANDS,** *SOUTH AFRICA*, **UNITED KINGDOM**	No	● ●	Medium *1 strong chamber 1 chamber with limitations*	✖ ✖
AUSTRIA, BELGIUM, CZECH REPUBLIC, FRANCE, *SPAIN*	No	● ●	Low	✖
BULGARIA, DENMAR K, **FINLAND**, GREECE, HUNGARY, IRELAND, ISRAEL, **NEW ZEALAND**, NORWAY, PORTUGAL, SLOVAKIA, **SWEDEN**	No	●	Unicameral	✖

Beyond the legislative process, there are other constitutional factors that can create veto gates for policy implementation: a federal system may empower states to block the implementation of policy passed at the national level; Supreme Courts or constitutional tribunals may have the ability to declare laws unconstitutional, and therefore null and void. All of these factors derive from constitutional design.

SOURCES: Steven L. Taylor, Matthew S. Shugart, Arend Lijphart, and Bernard Grofman, *A Different Democracy: American Government in a Thirty-One-Country Perspective* (New Haven, CT: Yale University Press, 2014); and authors' classifications.

Although the power of judicial review is not mentioned in the Constitution, the courts have assumed this power. When President Obama issued an executive order that would shield millions of immigrants from deportation, opponents of his order challenged the legality of his actions. In 2016 the Supreme Court issued a 4–4 tie, calling into question Obama's plan.

National Unity and Power

Various provisions in the Constitution addressed the framers' concern with national unity and power. Article IV provided for comity (reciprocity) among states, which we discuss in more detail in Chapter 3. Each state was also prohibited from discriminating against the citizens of other states in favor of its own citizens, with the Supreme Court being the arbiter in each case.

The framers' concern with national supremacy was also expressed in Article VI, in the supremacy clause, which provided that national laws and treaties "shall be the supreme law of the land." This meant that all laws made under the "authority of the United States" would be superior to laws adopted by any state or other subdivision, and that the states must respect all treaties made under that authority—a clear effort to keep the states from dealing separately with foreign nations or businesses. The supremacy clause also bound all state and local as well as federal officials to take an oath to support the national Constitution if disputes arose between national and state laws.

supremacy clause ➡

A clause of Article VI of the Constitution that states that all laws and treaties approved by the national government are the supreme laws of the United States and superior to all laws adopted by any state or other subdivision

Amending the Constitution

The Constitution established procedures for its own revision in Article V. Its provisions are so difficult that Americans have succeeded in the amending process only 17 times since 1791, when the first 10 amendments were adopted.

IN BRIEF

The Seven Articles of the Constitution

I. The Legislative Branch

House: two-year terms, elected directly by the people

Senate: six-year terms (staggered so that only one-third of the Senate changes in any given election), appointed by state legislatures (changed in 1913 to direct election)

Expressed powers of the national government: collecting taxes, borrowing money, regulating commerce, declaring war, and maintaining an army and a navy; all other power belongs to the states, unless deemed otherwise by the elastic (necessary and proper) clause

Exclusive powers of the national government: states are expressly forbidden to issue their own paper money, tax imports and exports, regulate trade outside their own borders, and impair the obligation of contracts

II. The Executive Branch

Presidency: four-year terms (limited in 1951 to a maximum of two terms), elected indirectly by the electoral college

Powers: can "recognize" other countries, negotiate treaties, grant reprieves and pardons, convene Congress in special sessions, and veto congressional enactments

III. The Judicial Branch

Supreme Court: lifetime terms, appointed by the president with the approval of the Senate

Powers: include resolving conflicts between federal and state laws, determining whether power belongs to national government or the states, and settling controversies between citizens of different states

IV. National Unity and Power

Reciprocity among states: establishes that each state must give "full faith and credit" to official acts of other states and guarantees citizens of any state the "privileges and immunities" of every other state

V. Amending the Constitution

Procedures: requires approval by two-thirds of Congress and three-fourths of the states

VI. National Supremacy

The Constitution and national law are the supreme law of the land and cannot be overruled by state law

VII. Ratification

The Constitution became effective when approved by nine states

Many other amendments have been proposed, but fewer than 40 have even come close to fulfilling the Constitution's requirement of a two-thirds vote in Congress, and only a fraction have approached adoption by three-fourths of the states. (A breakdown of these figures and further discussion of amending the Constitution appear in Chapter 3.) The Constitution could also be amended by a constitutional convention, but no national convention has been called since the Philadelphia Convention of 1787; Congress has submitted all proposed amendments to the state legislatures for ratification.

Ratifying the Constitution

Rules for ratification of the Constitution of 1787 made up Article VII of the Constitution. This provision actually violated the procedure for constitutional change in the Articles of Confederation. For one thing, it adopted a nine-state requirement for ratification in place of the unanimity required by the Articles. For another, it provided for ratification by special state conventions rather than by state legislatures. All the states except Rhode Island eventually did set up conventions to ratify the Constitution.

Constitutional Limits on the National Government's Power

separation of powers

The division of governmental power among several institutions that must cooperate in decision making

As we have indicated, though the framers wanted a powerful national government, they also wanted to guard against possible misuse of that power. Thus they incorporated two key principles into the Constitution—the separation of powers and federalism (see also Chapter 3). A third set of limitations, the Bill of Rights, was added to the Constitution to help secure its ratification when opponents charged that it paid insufficient attention to citizens' rights.

federalism

The system of government in which a constitution divides power between a central government and regional governments

The Separation of Powers. No principle of politics was more widely shared at the time of the 1787 Founding than the principle that power must be used to balance power. The French political theorist Montesquieu (1689–1755) believed that this balance was an indispensable defense against tyranny, and his writings "were taken as political gospel" at the Philadelphia Convention.[9] This principle is not stated explicitly in the Constitution, but it is clearly built into Articles I, II, and III, which provide for

Bill of Rights

The first 10 amendments to the U.S. Constitution, adopted in 1791. The Bill of Rights ensures certain rights and liberties to the people

1. Three separate branches of government (Figure 2.1).

2. Different methods of selecting the top personnel, so that each branch is responsible to a different constituency. This arrangement is intended to

Figure 2.1
THE SEPARATION OF POWERS

LEGISLATIVE	EXECUTIVE	JUDICIAL
Passes federal laws	Enforces laws	Reviews lower-court decisions
Controls federal appropriations	Serves as commander in chief of armed forces	Decides constitutionality of laws
Approves treaties and presidential appointments	Makes foreign treaties	Decides cases involving disputes between states
Regulates interstate commerce	Nominates Supreme Court justices and federal court judges	
Establishes lower-court system	Pardons those convicted in federal court	

produce a "mixed regime," in which the personnel of each department will develop very different interests and outlooks on how to govern, and different groups in society will be assured of some access to governmental decision making.

3. Checks and balances, a system under which each of the branches is given some power over the others. Familiar examples are the presidential veto power over legislation and the requirement that the Senate approve high-level presidential appointments.

This system has also been described not as separated powers but as "separated institutions sharing power,"[10] thus diminishing the chance that power will be misused.

Federalism. Federalism was a step toward greater centralization of power. Aiming to place more power at the national governmental level without completely undermining the power of state governments, the delegates

checks and balances

The mechanisms through which each branch of government is able to participate in and influence the activities of the other branches

devised a system of two sovereigns, or supreme powers—the states and the nation—with the hope that competition between the two would limit the power of both.

The Bill of Rights. Late in the Philadelphia Convention, a motion was made to include a bill of rights in the Constitution. After a brief debate, it was almost unanimously rejected. Most delegates felt that since the federal government was already limited to its expressed powers, further protection of citizens from it was unnecessary. Many argued that it was the states that should adopt bills of rights because their greater powers needed greater limitations. But almost immediately after the Constitution was ratified, a movement arose to adopt a national bill of rights. This is why the Bill of Rights, adopted in 1791, comprises the first 10 amendments to the Constitution rather than being part of the body of it. We explore the Bill of Rights further in Chapter 4.

THE FIGHT FOR RATIFICATION

The first hurdle faced by the new Constitution was ratification by state conventions of delegates elected by white, propertied male voters. This struggle for ratification encompassed 13 separate campaigns, each influenced by local as well as national considerations. Two sides faced off in all the states, however, taking the names of Federalists and Antifederalists.[11] The Federalists supported the Constitution and preferred a strong national government. The Antifederalists opposed the Constitution and preferred a more decentralized government; they took on their name by default, in reaction to their better-organized opponents. Whereas the Federalists were united in their support of the Constitution, the Antifederalists were divided as to what the alternative should be. (See the "In Brief" box on p. 45.)

Under the name Publius, Alexander Hamilton, James Madison, and John Jay wrote 85 articles in New York newspapers supporting ratification of the Constitution. These *Federalist Papers*, as they are collectively known today, defended the principles of the Constitution and sought to dispel the fears of a national authority.[12] The Antifederalists, however, such as Richard Henry Lee and Patrick Henry of Virginia and George Clinton of New York, argued that the new Constitution betrayed the Revolution and was a step toward monarchy. The Antifederalists wanted a bill of rights to protect against government.

By the beginning of 1788, the conventions of five states had ratified the Constitution. Delaware, New Jersey, and Georgia ratified it unanimously, and

Federalists

Those who favored a strong national government and supported the constitution proposed at the American Constitutional Convention of 1787

Antifederalists

Those who favored strong state governments and a weak national government and who were opponents of the constitution proposed at the American Constitutional Convention of 1787

Chapter 2: The Founding and the Constitution

Federalists versus Antifederalists

	Federalists	Antifederalists
✔ Who were they?	Property owners, creditors, merchants	Small farmers, frontiersmen, debtors, shopkeepers
✔ What did they believe?	Believed that elites were best fit to govern; feared "excessive democracy"	Believed that government should be closer to the people; feared concentration of power in the hands of the elites
✔ What system of government did they favor?	Favored strong national government; believed in "filtration" so that only elites would obtain governmental power	Favored retention of power by state governments and protection of individual rights
✔ Who were their leaders?	Alexander Hamilton, James Madison, George Washington	Patrick Henry, George Mason, Elbridge Gerry, George Clinton

Connecticut and Pennsylvania by wide margins. Opposition was overcome in Massachusetts by the inclusion of nine amendments to protect human rights. Ratification by Maryland and South Carolina followed. In June 1788, New Hampshire became the ninth state to ratify. That put the Constitution into effect, but for the new national government to have real power, Virginia and New York needed to approve it. After impassioned debate and many recommendations for future amendments, especially for a bill of rights, the Federalists mustered enough votes for approval of the Constitution in Virginia in June and New York in July. North Carolina joined the new government in 1789, after Congress actually submitted a bill of rights to the states for approval, and Rhode Island held out until 1790 before finally voting to become part of the new union.

CHANGING THE FRAMEWORK: CONSTITUTIONAL AMENDMENT

The Constitution has endured for over two centuries as the framework of government. But it has not endured without change. Without change, the Constitution might have become merely a sacred text, stored under glass.

Amendments: Many Are Called, Few Are Chosen

The framers of the Constitution recognized the need for change, and provisions for amendment were incorporated into Article V. Since 1791, when the first 10 amendments, the Bill of Rights, were added, only 17 amendments have been adopted. And two of them—Prohibition (Eighteenth) and its repeal (Twenty-First)—cancel each other out, so that overall, only 15 amendments have been added since 1791, despite vast changes in American society and its economy.

As Figure 2.2 illustrates, Article V provides for four routes of amendment:

1. Passage in House and Senate by two-thirds vote; then ratification by majority vote of the legislatures of three-fourths (38) of the states.

2. Passage in House and Senate by two-thirds vote; then ratification by conventions called for the purpose in three-fourths of the states.

3. Passage in a national convention called by Congress in response to petitions by two-thirds of the states; ratification by majority vote of the legislatures of three-fourths of the states.

4. Passage in a national convention, as in route 3; then ratification by conventions called for the purpose in three-fourths of the states.

Because no amendment has ever been proposed by national convention, however, routes 3 and 4 have never been employed. And route 2 has been employed only once (for the Twenty-First Amendment, which repealed the Eighteenth, or Prohibition, Amendment). Thus, route 1 has been used for all the others.

The Twenty-Seven Amendments

The Constitution and its 27 amendments are reproduced at the end of this book. All but two of the amendments are concerned with the structure or

Figure 2.2

ROUTES OF AMENDMENT

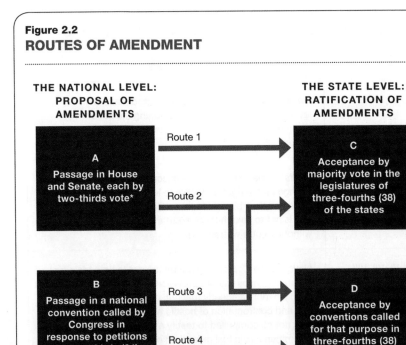

THE NATIONAL LEVEL: PROPOSAL OF AMENDMENTS

THE STATE LEVEL: RATIFICATION OF AMENDMENTS

A
Passage in House and Senate, each by two-thirds vote*

Route 1

Route 2

C
Acceptance by majority vote in the legislatures of three-fourths (38) of the states

B
Passage in a national convention called by Congress in response to petitions by two-thirds (34) of the states**

Route 3

Route 4

D
Acceptance by conventions called for that purpose in three-fourths (38) of the states

*For each amendment proposal, Congress has the power to choose the method of ratification, the time limit for consideration by the states, and other conditions of ratification.
**This method of proposal has never been employed. Thus, amendment routes 3 and 4 have never been attempted.

composition of the government. This is consistent with the concept of a constitution as "higher law," because the whole purpose of a higher law is to establish a framework within which government and the process of making ordinary law can take place. There is great wisdom in this principle. A constitution enables legislation and public policies to take place, but it should not attempt to determine what that legislation or those policies ought to be.

The purpose of the 10 amendments in the Bill of Rights was to give each of the three branches clearer and more restricted boundaries (Table 2.1). The First Amendment clarified Congress's turf. Although its powers under Article I, Section 8, do not justify laws regulating religion, speech, and the like, the First Amendment makes this limitation explicit: "Congress shall make no law. . . ." The Second, Third, and Fourth Amendments similarly spell out limits on the executive branch, a necessity given the abuses of executive power Americans had endured under British rule.

Table 2.1

THE BILL OF RIGHTS: ANALYSIS OF ITS PROVISIONS

AMENDMENT	PURPOSE
I	*Limits on Congress:* Congress is not to make any law establishing a religion or abridging the freedom of speech, press, or assembly or the right to petition the government.
II, III, IV	*Limits on the Executive:* The executive branch is not to infringe on the right of people to keep arms (II), is not to force people arbitrarily to let soldiers live in their houses (III), and is not to search for or seize evidence or to arrest people without a court warrant (IV).
V, VI, VII, VIII	*Limits on the Courts:* The courts are not to hold trials for serious offenses without provision for a grand jury (V), a petit (trial) jury (VII), a speedy trial (VI), presentation of charges (VI), and confrontation of hostile witnesses (VI). Individuals may not be compelled to testify against themselves (V) and are immune from trial more than once for the same offense (V). Neither bail nor punishment may be excessive (VIII), and no property may be taken for public use without just compensation (V).
IX, X	*Limits on National Government:* All rights not enumerated are reserved to the states or the people.

The Fifth, Sixth, Seventh, and Eighth Amendments contain some of the most important safeguards for individual citizens against the arbitrary exercise of government power. And they do so by defining the judicial branch more concretely than had been done in Article III of the Constitution. The Ninth and Tenth Amendments reinforce the idea that the Constitution creates a government of limited powers. The Ninth declares that failure to mention a right does not mean it is not possessed by the people, while the Tenth states that powers not granted to the federal government are reserved to the states and the people.

Five amendments adopted since 1791 are concerned with expansion of the electorate (Table 2.2).[13] The Founders were unable to agree on uniform national voting qualifications, although they provided in the final draft of Article I, Section 2, that eligibility to vote in a national election would be the same as "the Qualification requisite for Elector of the most numerous branch of the state Legislature." Article I, Section 4, added that Congress

Table 2.2

AMENDING THE CONSTITUTION TO EXPAND THE ELECTORATE

AMENDMENT	PURPOSE	YEAR PROPOSED	YEAR ADOPTED
XIV	Section 1 provided national definition of citizenship	1866	1868
XV	Extended voting rights to all races	1869	1870
XIX	Extended voting rights to women	1919	1920
XXIII	Extended voting rights to residents of the District of Columbia	1960	1961
XXIV	Extended voting rights to all classes by abolition of poll taxes	1962	1964
XXVI	Extended voting rights to citizens ages 18 and over	1971	1971

could alter state regulations as to the "Times, Places and Manner of holding Elections for Senators and Representatives." But any important expansion of the American electorate would almost certainly require a constitutional amendment.

Six more amendments are also electoral in nature, although not concerned directly with voting rights and the expansion of the electorate. These amendments deal with the elective offices themselves or with the relationship between elective offices and the electorate (Table 2.3).

Another five amendments have sought to expand or to limit the powers of the national and state governments (Table 2.4). The Eleventh Amendment protected the states from suits by private individuals and took away from the federal courts any power to take suits by private individuals of one state (or a foreign country) against another state. The other three amendments in Table 2.4 aim to reduce state power (Thirteenth), to reduce state power and expand national power (Fourteenth), and to expand national

Table 2.3

AMENDING THE CONSTITUTION TO CHANGE THE RELATIONSHIP BETWEEN THE ELECTED OFFICES AND THE ELECTORATE

AMENDMENT	PURPOSE	YEAR PROPOSED	YEAR ADOPTED
XII	Created separate ballot for vice president in the electoral college	1803	1804
XIV	Penalized states for depriving freed slaves of the right to vote	1866	1868
XVII	Provided direct election of senators	1912	1913
XX	Shortened the time between election of new Congress and president and their inauguration	1932	1933
XXII	Limited presidential terms	1947	1951
XXV	Provided presidential succession in case of disability	1965	1967

power (Sixteenth). The Twenty-Seventh limits Congress's ability to raise its members' salaries.

The Eighteenth, or Prohibition, Amendment underscores the meaning of the rest: this is the only amendment that the country used to *legislate*, to deal directly with a substantive social problem. And it was the only amendment ever to have been repealed. Two other amendments—the Thirteenth, which abolished slavery, and the Sixteenth, which established the power to levy an income tax—essentially had the effect of legislation. But the purpose of the Thirteenth was to restrict the power of the states by forever forbidding them to treat any human being as property. As for the Sixteenth, it is true that income tax legislation followed immediately, but the amendment itself deals only with establishing the power of Congress to enact such legislation.

Table 2.4

AMENDING THE CONSTITUTION TO EXPAND OR LIMIT THE POWER OF GOVERNMENT

AMENDMENT	PURPOSE	YEAR PROPOSED	YEAR ADOPTED
XI	Limited jurisdiction of federal courts over suits involving the states	1794	1795
XIII	Eliminated slavery and eliminated the right of states to allow property in persons	1865	1865
XIV	Established due process of law in state courts for all persons. Later used to apply the entire Bill of Rights to the states.	1866	1868
XVI	Established national power to tax incomes	1909	1913
XXVII	Limited Congress's power to raise its own salary	1789	1992

DOES THE CONSTITUTION WORK?

The final product of the Constitutional Convention would have to be considered an extraordinary victory for those who wanted a new system of government to replace the Articles of Confederation. In contrast to the relatively weak Articles of Confederation, the new Constitution laid the groundwork for a government that would be sufficiently powerful to promote trade, to protect property, and to restrain radical state legislatures. It established the rule of law to protect citizens and strengthen the government. Moreover, this new government was so constructed through internal checks and balances, indirect selection of officeholders, lifetime judicial appointments, and other similar provisions to preclude the "excessive democracy" feared by many of the Founders. Some of the framers favored going even further in limiting popular influence, but the consensus

The framers gave each branch of government a means of blocking the other branches. In 2015, President Obama announced that he would veto congressional legislation authorizing the construction of the Keystone XL Pipeline due to concerns about its impact on the environment.

at the Convention was that a thoroughly undemocratic document would never receive the popular approval needed to be ratified by the states.[14]

Although the Constitution was the product of a particular set of political forces, the principles of government it established have a significance that goes far beyond the interests of its authors. Two of these principles, federalism and civil liberties, are discussed in Chapters 3 and 4, respectively. A third important constitutional principle that has affected America's government for the past 200 years is checks and balances. As we saw earlier, the framers gave each of the three branches of government a means of intervening in and blocking the actions of the others. Often, checks and balances have seemed to prevent the government from getting much done. In recent years, liberals have been outraged as they watched Congress block presidential initiatives in such areas as environmental policy and gun control, while conservatives seethed as they watched President Obama take action to overhaul the U.S. health care system and provide a path toward permanent residence and citizenship for undocumented immigrants. At various times, all sides have vilified the judiciary for invalidating legislation enacted by Congress and signed by the president.

Checks and balances also help to explain why groups seldom have been able to bring about dramatic changes in governmental policy or institutions in a short period of time. Instead, checks and balances have slowed the pace of change and increased the need for compromise and accommodation.

Groups who take control of the White House, for example, must negotiate with their rivals who remain entrenched on Capitol Hill. New forces in Congress must reckon with the influence of other forces in the executive branch and in the courts. Checks and balances inevitably frustrate those who desire change, but they also function as a safeguard against rash action. During the 1950s, for example, Congress was caught up in a nearly hysterical effort to unmask subversive activities in the United States, which might have led to a serious erosion of civil liberties if not for the checks and balances provided by the executive branch and the courts. Thus, a governmental principle that serves as a frustrating limitation one day may become a vitally important safeguard the next.

Comparing the Articles of Confederation and the Constitution

	Articles of Confederation	Constitution
Legislative Branch	**Power to:** Declare war and make peace Make treaties and alliances Coin or borrow money Regulate trade with Native Americans Appoint senior officers of the U.S. Army **Limits on power:** Could not levy taxes, regulate commerce among the states, or create national armed forces	**Power to:** Collect taxes Borrow money Regulate commerce Declare war Maintain an army and navy **Limits on power:** All other powers belong to the states
Executive Branch	No executive branch was created	**Power to:** Recognize other countries Negotiate treaties Grant reprieves and pardons Appoint major departmental personnel Convene special sessions of Congress Veto congressional actions **Limits on power:** Senate must approve treaties Congress can override a veto by a two-thirds vote
Judicial Branch	No judicial branch was created	**Power to:** Resolve conflicts between state and federal laws Determine whether a power belongs to federal government or states or both Decide conflicts between citizens of different states **Limits on power:** Judicial appointments are made by the president and approved by the Senate Congress creates lower courts and can change the jurisdiction of the federal courts Congress can add or subtract federal judges and can change the size of the Supreme Court

Although the Constitution sought to lay the groundwork for a powerful government, the framers struggled to reconcile government power with freedom. They surrounded the powerful institutions of the new regime with a variety of safeguards—a continual array of checks and balances—designed to make certain that the power of the national government could not be used to undermine the states' power and their citizens' freedoms. Thus, the framers were the first Americans to confront head-on the dilemma of coercion and power that we discussed briefly in Chapter 1. Whether their solutions to this dilemma were successful is the topic of the remainder of our chapters.

To Whose Benefit?

Of course, the groups whose interests were served by the Constitution in 1789, mainly the merchants and planters, are not the same groups that benefit from the Constitution's provisions today. Once incorporated into the law, political principles often take on lives of their own and have consequences that were never anticipated by their original champions. Indeed, many of the groups that benefit from constitutional provisions today did not even exist in 1789. Who would have thought that the principle of free speech would influence the transmission of data on the Internet? Who would have predicted that commercial interests that once sought a powerful government might come, two centuries later, to denounce governmental activism as "socialistic"? Perhaps one secret of the Constitution's longevity is that it did not confer permanent advantage on any one set of economic or social forces.

Although they were defeated in 1789, the Antifederalists present us with an important picture of a road not taken and of an America that might have been. Would the country have been worse off if it had been governed by a confederacy of small republics linked by a national administration with severely limited powers? Were the Antifederalists correct in predicting that a government given great power in the hope that it might do good would, through "insensible progress," inevitably turn to evil purposes? Two hundred years of government under the federal Constitution are not necessarily enough to definitively answer these questions. Time must tell.

To What Ends?

The Constitution's framers placed individual liberty ahead of all other political values, leading many of them to distrust both democracy and equality. They feared that democracy could degenerate into a majority tyranny in which the populace, perhaps led by a rabble-rousing demagogue, would trample on liberty. As for equality, the framers were products of their time and place; our contemporary ideas of racial and gender equality would have been foreign to them. They were concerned primarily with another manifestation of equality: they feared that those without property or position might be driven by what some called a "leveling spirit" to infringe on liberty in the name of greater economic or social equality. Indeed, the framers believed that this leveling spirit was most likely to produce demagoguery and majority tyranny. As a result, the basic structure of the Constitution—separated powers, internal checks and balances, and federalism—was designed to safeguard liberty, and the Bill of Rights created further safeguards for liberty. Many of the Constitution's other key provisions, such as indirect election of senators and the president, as well as the appointment of judges for life, were designed to limit democracy and, hence, the threat of majority tyranny.

By championing liberty, however, the framers virtually guaranteed that democracy and even a measure of equality would sooner or later evolve in the United States, for liberty inevitably leads to the growth of political activity and the expansion of political participation. In James Madison's famous phrase, "Liberty is to faction as air is to fire."[15] Where they have liberty, more and more people, groups, and interests will almost inevitably engage in politics and gradually overcome any restrictions placed on their participation. This is precisely what happened in the early years of the American Republic. During the Jeffersonian period, political parties formed. During the Jacksonian period, many state voting restrictions were removed, and popular participation greatly expanded. Over time, liberty is conducive to democracy.

Liberty does not guarantee that everyone will be equal. It does, however, reduce the threat of inequality in one very important way. Historically, the greatest inequalities of wealth, power, and privilege have arisen where governments have used their power to allocate status and opportunity among individuals or groups. The most extreme cases of inequality are associated with the most tyrannical regimes. In the United States, however, by promoting democratic politics, over time liberty unleashed forces that militated against inequality. As a result, over the past 200 years, groups that have learned to use the political process have achieved important economic and social gains.

One limitation of liberty as a political principle, however, is that the idea of limits on government action can also inhibit effective government. Take one of the basic tasks of government: the protection of citizens' lives and property. A government limited by concerns over the rights of those accused of crimes may be limited in its ability to maintain public order. For the last decade, the U.S. government has asserted that protecting the nation against terrorists requires law enforcement measures that seem at odds with legal and constitutional formalities. The conflict between liberty and governmental effectiveness is another tension at the heart of the American constitutional system.

For Further Reading

Allison, Robert. *The American Revolution: A Concise History*. New York: Oxford University Press, 2011.

Amar, Akhil Reed. *America's Constitution: A Biography*. New York: Random House, 2005.

Bailyn, Bernard. *The Ideological Origins of the American Revolution*. Cambridge, MA: Harvard University Press, 1967.

Beard, Charles A. *An Economic Interpretation of the Constitution of the United States*. New York: Macmillan, 1913.

Chernow, Ron. *Alexander Hamilton*. New York: Penguin, 2004.

Ellis, Joseph. *His Excellency: George Washington*. New York: Knopf, 2004.

Farrand, Max, ed. *The Records of the Federal Convention of 1787*. Rev. ed., 4 vols. New Haven, CT: Yale University Press, 1966.

Ferling, John. *Whirlwind: The American Revolution and the War That Won It*. New York: Bloomsbury Press, 2015.

Hamilton, Alexander, James Madison, and John Jay. *The Federalist Papers*, no. 10 and no. 51. Clinton Rossiter, ed. New York: New American Library, 1961.

Newton, Michael. *Angry Mobs and Founding Fathers: The Fight for Control of the American Revolution*. New York: Eleftheria, 2011.

Stewart, David O. *Madison's Gift: Five Partnerships That Built America.* New York: Simon & Schuster, 2015.

Storing, Herbert J., ed. *The Complete Anti-Federalist.* 7 vols. Chicago: University of Chicago Press, 1981.

3

Federalism and the Separation of Powers

The great achievement of American politics in the eighteenth century was the fashioning of an effective constitutional structure of political institutions. Although it is an imperfect and continuously evolving work in progress, this structure of law and political practice has served well for more than two centuries. Two of its most important institutional features are federalism and the separation of powers. Federalism seeks to limit government by dividing it into two levels, national and state. Often the two levels must cooperate, as in the investigation of the mass shooting in San Bernardino, California, in 2015, when FBI and other federal officials worked with local law enforcement to investigate the terrorist attack that left 14 dead. Yet each level is also granted sufficient independence to compete with the other, thereby restraining the power of both.[1] The separation of powers seeks to limit the national government's power by dividing government against itself—by giving the legislative, executive, and judicial branches separate functions, thus forcing them to share power.

Both federalism and the separation of powers complicate policy making in the United States. If governmental power were arranged neatly and simply in a single hierarchy, decisions could certainly be made more easily and efficiently. But would they be better decisions? The framers thought that complexity, multiple checks, and institutionalized second-guessing, though messy, would allow more interests to have a voice and would eventually produce better results. And along the way, messy decision processes might preserve liberty and prevent tyranny. Yet, although the constitutional dispersion of power among federal institutions and between the federal government and the states may well protect our liberties, it often seems to make it impossible to get anything done collectively. This lack of decisiveness sometimes appears to negate the most important reason for building institutions in the first place.

Since the adoption of the Constitution, political decision makers have developed a variety of strategies for overcoming the impediments to policy change that inevitably arise in our federal system of separated powers. Most commonly, those promoting a new program find ways of dispersing its benefits so that other politicians controlling institutional veto powers find it in their interest to go along. For example, if the executive branch hopes to win congressional support for a new weapons system, it generally ensures that portions of the system are subcontracted to firms in as many congressional districts as possible. In this way, dispersion of benefits helps to overcome the separation of powers between the executive and legislative branches. Similarly, as we will see next, federal officials often secure state cooperation with national programs by offering the states funding, called grants-in-aid, in

CORE OF THE ANALYSIS

➡️ Federalism limits national power by creating two sovereigns: the national government and the state governments.

➡️ Under "dual federalism," which lasted from 1789 to 1937, the national government limited itself primarily to promoting commerce, while the states directly coerced citizens.

➡️ After 1937, the national government exerted more influence, yet the states maintained many of their traditional powers.

➡️ Checks and balances ensure the sharing of power among separate institutions of government. Within the system of separated powers, the framers of the Constitution provided for legislative supremacy.

exchange for their compliance. These programs help to overcome the limitations of federalism. Spending on public works and other "pork barrel" projects, a term used to describe federal dollars that members of Congress bring home to their states and districts, offers yet another strategy for achieving policies by dispersing their benefits.

Unfortunately, having to convert needed measures into pork-barrel programs often dilutes their effectiveness. Take the federal government's effort to enhance the nation's level of readiness for terrorist attacks following September 2001. Under the terms of the 2001 USA PATRIOT Act, Congress appropriated billions of dollars to improve communications, police and fire protection, and intelligence collection at the state and local levels to avert future disasters.

Much of the money—some $40 billion—was not allocated to states and cities on the basis of some assessment of the threat they actually faced. Instead, Congress insisted that every state receive at least 0.75 percent of the funds appropriated during any given year in case terrorists adopted what some politicians dubbed the "heartland strategy," attacking obscure targets in rural and small-town America. Terrorists, of course, had no known interest in the heartland, but members of Congress from heartland states and districts certainly did.

Thus, cities like New York, Los Angeles, and Washington, D.C., which seemed likely to be the main targets for future terrorist attacks, never had enough money for needed preparedness and warning programs. Meanwhile, other localities that faced virtually no threat of terrorism were happy to receive federal funds for new fire trucks, radio equipment, and educational programs. For example, in 2011, Middleton, Rhode Island, a small city unlikely to attract international terrorists' attention, received $188,000 for fire equipment; in 2005, the 1,600 residents of North Pole, Alaska, were awarded $500,000 in homeland security grants. Such grants have also gone disproportionately to states and districts represented by powerful politicians. Nevada, for example, represented by Harry Reid, Senate majority leader from 2007 through 2014, has been a major recipient of homeland security dollars.

The homeland security grant program is criticized every year by some fiscally prudent members of Congress who see it as a waste of taxpayer dollars. However, the program survives year after year. Billions of dollars in spending may not have made the nation much safer, but it may have helped enhance the safety of some congressional seats. In this instance, we may wonder if the institutions of federalism worked properly. Would a unitary central government have been better able to spend precious resources where they were needed most? If federalism and the separation of powers work most of the time, what explains the exceptions?

FEDERALISM

Federalism can be defined as the division of powers and functions between the national government and the state governments. As we saw in Chapter 2, the 13 original states were individual colonies before independence, and for nearly 13 years they were virtually autonomous units under the Articles of Confederation. In effect, the states had retained too much power relative to the national government, a problem that led directly to the Annapolis Convention in 1786 and the Constitutional Convention in 1787. Under the Articles, disorder within states was beyond the reach of the national government, and conflicts of interest between states were not manageable. For example, states were making their own trade agreements with foreign countries and companies, which might then play one state against another for special advantages. Some states adopted barriers to foreign commerce that were contrary to the interests of another state.[2] Tax and other barriers were also erected between states.[3] Even after ratification of the Constitution, the states remained more important than the national government. For nearly a century and a half, virtually all of the fundamental policies governing Americans' lives were made by the state legislatures, not by Congress.

> **federalism**
> The system of government in which a constitution divides power between a central government and regional governments

Federalism in the Constitution

The United States was the first nation to adopt federalism as its governing framework. With federalism, the framers sought to limit the national government by creating a second layer of sovereignty, or independent political authority, in the state governments. American federalism recognized two sovereigns in the original Constitution and reinforced the principle in the Bill of Rights by granting a few expressed powers to the national government and reserving all the rest to the states. A federal system also allows geographically concentrated groups to wield more power than they could weild in a central system (see the Policy Principle on page 62).

> **sovereignty**
> Independent political authority. A sovereign possesses such authority

The Powers of the National Government. As we saw in Chapter 2, the expressed powers granted to the national government are found in Article I, Section 8, of the Constitution. These 17 powers include the power to collect taxes, to coin money, to declare war, and to regulate commerce (which became a very important power for the national government). Article I, Section 8, also contains another important source of power for the national government: the implied powers that enable Congress "to make all Laws which shall be necessary and proper for carrying into Execution the foregoing Powers." Not until several decades after the Founding did

> **implied powers**
> Powers derived from the necessary and proper clause (Article I, Section 8) of the Constitution. Such powers are not specifically expressed but are implied through the expansive interpretation of delegated powers

Federalism and Support for Corn Farmers

An ethanol plant in Missouri.

One of the United States' key institutional arrangements is federalism. Because members of Congress are elected from districts and states rather than chosen on a national basis, and because states also elect governments of their own that possess considerable powers, well-organized local groups often find it possible to work through Congress to develop national government policies that serve their interests.

Take the case of ethanol. Because ethanol (ethyl alcohol) can be made from a renewable resource—agricultural crops such as corn—grown in the United States, ethanol producers have argued that its increased use in motor fuel would help to preserve nonrenewable resources such as oil and thus reduce American dependence on energy suppliers in the volatile Middle East. The U.S. government has been heavily subsidizing the production and use of ethanol since the 1970s by mandating its addition to motor fuel. In 2015, the Environmental Protection Agency proposed again increasing the required use of ethanol in motor fuel, but supporters of the product charged that the agency's proposal did not go far enough.

If ethanol could indeed become a renewable, domestically produced substitute for foreign oil,

these billions in federal subsidies would have been well spent. However, the claims by pro-ethanol forces may be based more on political considerations than on economic and technological reality. The energy needed to produce a gallon of ethanol from corn is greater than the energy that can be produced by that gallon; thus, on balance, ethanol production actually consumes rather than creates energy.

If ethanol is not the answer to dependence on foreign oil, why does the government require its use? The answer has to do with the structure of government institutions and how these institutions shape policies. As a federal republic, the United States elects its legislature—Congress—in local contests, rather than in national ones (as in some other countries, in which citizens vote for a political party rather than individual candidates and national party officials select the individuals to fill the number of seats proportional to the party's share of the vote). In addition, in the United States each state has a separate and powerful level of government, whose governor is elected at the state level rather than appointed by the national government. This decentralized system allows geographically concentrated interest groups to wield more power through their local members of Congress and state governments than they could possibly wield in a centralized system where decision making was concentrated at the national level. Ethanol producers are highly organized and concentrated in several Midwestern agricultural states such as Iowa, and the campaign for ethanol subsidies and tax breaks is strongly backed by virtually all the members of Congress and governors representing these states. Thus, federalism magnifies the political influence of the pro-ethanol forces, that would otherwise be minor players, by giving them a chance to wield power within several states.

the Supreme Court allow Congress to exercise the power granted in this necessary and proper clause, but ultimately the doctrine allowed the national government to expand the scope of its authority. In addition to expressed and implied powers, the Constitution affirmed the national government's power in the supremacy clause (Article VI), which made all national laws and treaties "the supreme Law of the Land."

The Powers of State Governments. One way in which the framers preserved a strong role for the states was through the Tenth Amendment, which states that the powers that the Constitution does not delegate to the national government or prohibit to the states are "reserved to the States respectively, or to the people." The Antifederalists, who feared that a strong central government would encroach on individual liberty, pressed for such an amendment as a way of limiting national power. Federalists agreed to it because they did not think it would do much harm, given the powers that the Constitution already granted to the national government. The Tenth Amendment is also called the reserved powers amendment.

The most fundamental power that is retained by the states is that of coercion—the power to develop and enforce criminal codes, to administer health and safety rules, and to regulate the family via marriage and divorce laws. The states have the power to regulate individuals' livelihoods; if you're a doctor, lawyer, plumber, or a barber, you must be licensed by the state. Even more fundamental, the states have the power to define private property—private property exists because state laws against trespassing define who is and is not entitled to use a piece of property. If you own a car, your ownership isn't worth much unless the state is willing to enforce your right to possession by making it a crime for anyone else to take your car. Similarly, your "ownership" of a house or piece of land means that the state will enforce your possession by prohibiting others from occupying the property against your will. At the same time, however, under its power of eminent domain, the state may seize your property (and compensate you) for anything it deems to be a public purpose.

A state's authority to regulate these fundamental matters, commonly referred to as the police power of the state, encompasses its power to regulate the health, safety, welfare, and morals of its citizens. Policing is what states do—they coerce you in the name of the community in order to maintain public order. And this was exactly the type of power that the Founders intended the states to exercise.

In some areas, the states share concurrent powers with the national government. The two levels both have some power to regulate commerce and to affect the currency—for example, by being able to charter banks, grant or deny corporate charters, and regulate the quality of products or the conditions of labor. This issue of concurrent versus exclusive power has

reserved powers
Powers that are not specifically delegated to the national government or denied to the states by the Constitution; under the Tenth Amendment, these powers are reserved to the states

eminent domain
The right of the government to take private property for public use, with reasonable compensation awarded

concurrent powers
Authority possessed by both state and national governments, such as the power to levy taxes

come up at times in our history, but wherever there is a direct conflict of laws between the national and the state levels, the issue has generally been resolved in favor of national supremacy.

States' Obligations to One Another. The Constitution also creates obligations among the states. These obligations, spelled out in Article IV, were intended to promote national unity. By requiring the states to recognize actions and decisions taken in other states as legal and proper, the framers aimed to make the states less like independent countries and more like parts of a single nation. Article IV, Section 1, calls for "Full Faith and Credit" among states, meaning that each state is expected to honor the "public Acts, Records, and judicial Proceedings" that take place in any other state. So, for example, if a couple is married in Texas—marriage being regulated by state law—Missouri must also recognize that marriage, even though they were not married under Missouri state law.

In recent years, the full faith and credit clause became entangled in the controversy over same-sex marriage. As some states began to allow individuals of the same gender to marry, a number of other states passed "defense of marriage acts" that defined marriage as a union only between a man and a woman. In 1996, eager to show its own disapproval of same-sex marriage, Congress passed the federal Defense of Marriage Act (DOMA), declaring that states did *not* have to recognize a same-sex marriage legally contracted in another state. In 2015, however, the Supreme Court ruled that states were required to issue marriage licenses to same-sex couples and to recognize such marriages performed in other jurisdictions.[4]

Article IV, Section 2, known as the comity clause, also promotes national unity. It provides that citizens enjoying the "privileges and immunities" of one state should be entitled to similar treatment in other states; that is, a state cannot discriminate against someone from another state or give special privileges to its own residents. For example, when Alaska passed a law in the 1970s that gave residents preference over nonresidents in obtaining work on the state's oil and gas pipelines, the Supreme Court ruled the law illegal because it discriminated against citizens of other states.[5] This clause also regulates criminal justice among the states by requiring states to return fugitives to the states from which they have fled. Thus in 1952, when an inmate escaped from an Alabama prison and sought to avoid being returned on

Previously a state-level policy, same-sex marriage was declared a fundamental right nationwide by the Supreme Court in 2015, and is now no longer an issue of federalism.

full faith and credit clause

The provision in Article IV, Section 1, of the Constitution, requiring that each state normally honor the government actions and judicial decisions that take place in another state

Chapter 3: Federalism and the Separation of Powers

the grounds that he was subject to "cruel and unusual punishment" there, the Supreme Court ruled that he must be returned according to Article IV, Section 2.[6] This example highlights the difference between the obligations among states and those among different countries. In 1997, France refused to return an American fugitive because he might be subject to the death penalty, which does not exist in France.[7] The Constitution clearly forbids states to do something similar.

States' relationships to one another are also governed by the interstate compact clause (Article I, Section 10), which states that "No State shall, without the Consent of Congress . . . enter into any Agreement or Compact with another State." The Supreme Court has interpreted this clause to mean that two or more states may enter into legally binding agreements with one another, subject to congressional approval, to solve a problem that crosses state lines. In the early years of the Republic, states turned to compacts primarily to settle border disputes. Today they are used for a wide range of issues but are especially important in regulating the distribution of river water, addressing environmental concerns, and operating transportation systems that cross state lines.[8]

Local Government and the Constitution. Local government, including counties, cities, and towns, occupies a peculiar but very important place in the American system. In fact, local government has no status in the American Constitution. *State* legislatures created local governments, and *state* constitutions and laws permit local governments to take on some of the responsibilities of the state governments. Most states amended their own constitutions to give their larger cities home rule—a guarantee of noninterference in various areas of local affairs. But local governments enjoy no such recognition in the national Constitution. They have always been mere conveniences of the states.[9]

Local governments became important in the early Republic because the states possessed little administrative capability or bureaucracy and so relied on cities and counties to implement state laws. Today, like the national and state governments, the state and local governments within each state both cooperate and compete with each other as shown, for example, in the mix of collegiality and rivalry beween their police forces.

The Slow Growth of the National Government's Power

Before the 1930s, America's federal system was one of dual federalism, a two-layered system—national and state—in which the states and their local governments did most of the governing. We call it the traditional system

comity clause
Article IV, Section 2, of the Constitution, which prohibits states from enacting laws that treat the citizens of other states in a discriminatory manner

home rule
The power delegated by a state to a local unit of government to manage its own affairs

dual federalism
The system of government that prevailed in the United States from 1789 to 1937, in which most fundamental governmental powers were shared between the federal and state governments, with the states exercising the most important powers

because almost nothing about it changed during two-thirds of American history. The only exception was the four years of the Civil War, after which the traditional system resumed.

But there was more to dual federalism than merely the existence of two tiers. They were functionally quite different from each other, and every generation since the founding has debated how to divide responsibilities between them. As we have seen, the Constitution delegated specific powers to the national government and reserved all the rest to the states. That arrangement left a lot of room for interpretation, however, because of the final "elastic" clause of Article I, Section 8. The three words *necessary and proper* amounted to an invitation to struggle over the distribution of powers between national and state governments. We confront this struggle throughout the book. However, it is noteworthy that federalism remained dual for nearly two-thirds of American history, with the national government remaining steadfastly within a "strict construction" of Article I, Section 8.

The Supreme Court has at times weighed in on the debate over the distribution of powers between national and state governments, starting in 1819 with a decision favoring national power, *McCulloch v. Maryland.*[10] The issue was whether Congress had the power to charter a bank, in particular the Bank of the United States (created by Congress in 1791 over Thomas Jefferson's constitutional opposition), because no power to create banks is mentioned in Article I, Section 8. Chief Justice John Marshall stated that such a power could be "implied" from other powers authorized in Article I, Section 8. Specifically, he cited the commerce clause, which gives Congress the power "to regulate Commerce with foreign nations, and among the several States and with Indian tribes," plus the final necessary and proper clause. Thus the Court created the potential for significant increases in national governmental power.

A second question of national power arose in the same case: whether Maryland's attempt to tax the bank was constitutional. Once again, Marshall and the Supreme Court sided with the national government, arguing that a bank created by a legislature representing all the American people (Congress) could not be taxed out of business by a state legislature (Maryland) representing only a small portion of the people. Here also the Supreme Court reinforced the supremacy clause: whenever a state law conflicts with a federal law, the state law is invalid because "the Laws of the United States . . . shall be the supreme Law of the Land." (For more on federal supremacy, see Chapters 2 and 8.)

This nationalistic interpretation of the Constitution was reinforced by *Gibbons v. Ogden* in 1824. At issue was whether the state of New York could grant a monopoly to a steamboat company to operate an exclusive service between New York and New Jersey. Aaron Ogden had secured his license from the company, whereas Thomas Gibbons, a former partner of Ogden's, had secured a competing license from the U.S. government. Chief Justice

commerce clause

The clause found in Article I, Section 8, of the Constitution, which delegates to Congress the power "to regulate Commerce with foreign Nations, and among the several States and with the Indian Tribes." This clause was interpreted by the Supreme Court to favor national power over the economy

Marshall ruled that Gibbons could not be kept from competing because with the commerce clause giving Congress the power "to regulate Commerce . . . among the several States," the state of New York did not have the power to grant this particular monopoly. In his decision, Marshall insisted that the definition of commerce was "comprehensive" but added that the comprehensiveness was limited "to that commerce which concerns more states than one." This opinion gave rise to the legal concept that later came to be called interstate commerce.[11]

Despite the Court's expansive reading of national power in the Republic's early years, between the 1820s and the 1930s, federal power grew only slowly. During the Jacksonian period, a states' rights coalition developed in Congress. Among its most important members were state party leaders who often had themselves appointed to the Senate, where they jealously guarded the powers of the states they ruled. Of course, members of Congress from the southern states had a particular reason to support states' rights: so long as the states were powerful and the federal government weak, the South's institution of slavery could not be threatened.

Aside from the interruption of the Civil War, the states' rights coalition dominated Congress and influenced presidential nominations (which were also controlled by the state party leaders) and judicial appointments (which required senatorial confirmation) as well. Indeed, the Supreme Court turned away from John Marshall's nationalistic jurisprudence in favor of a states' rights interpretation of the Constitution—particularly in cases concerning the commerce clause. For many years, any federal effort to regulate commerce so as to discourage such things as fraud, the production of impure goods, the use of child labor, and dangerous working conditions or long hours was declared unconstitutional by the Supreme Court. Such regulation, the Court held, would mean the federal government was entering the factory and the workplace, areas inherently local because the goods produced there had not yet passed into commerce and crossed state lines. Rather, the Court held that regulation of these areas constituted police power, a power reserved to the states. No one questioned the power of the national government to regulate certain kinds of businesses, such as railroads, gas pipelines, and waterway transportation, because they intrinsically involved interstate commerce.[12] But well into the twentieth century, most other efforts by Congress to regulate commerce were blocked by the Supreme Court's interpretation of federalism, with the concept of interstate commerce as the primary barrier.

For example, in the 1918 case of *Hammer v. Dagenhart*, the Court struck down a statute prohibiting the interstate shipment of goods manufactured with the use of child labor. Congress had been careful to avoid outlawing the production of such goods within states and only prohibited their interstate shipment. The Court, however, declared that the intent had been to outlaw their manufacture and that the statutory language was merely a ruse.[13]

The past 80 years—since Franklin Delano Roosevelt's New Deal—have seen an increase in national government power. Today, some Americans question whether the balance has shifted too far toward federal power.

After his election in 1932, President Franklin Delano Roosevelt was eager to expand the power of the national government. His "New Deal" depended on governmental power to regulate the economy and to intervene in every facet of American society. Roosevelt's efforts provoked sharp conflicts between the president and the federal judiciary. After making a host of new judicial appointments and threatening to expand the size of the Supreme Court, Roosevelt managed to bend the judiciary to his will. Beginning in 1937, the Court issued a series of decisions converting the commerce clause from a barrier to a source of national power.

One key case was *National Labor Relations Board v. Jones & Loughlin Steel Company*.[14] At issue was the National Labor Relations Act, which prohibited corporations from interfering with the efforts of employees to organize into unions, to bargain collectively over wages and working conditions, and to go on strike and engage in picketing. The newly formed National Labor Relations Board (NLRB) had ordered Jones & Loughlin to reinstate workers fired because of their union activities. The appeal reached the Supreme Court because the steel company had made a constitutional issue over the argument that its manufacturing activities, being local, were beyond the government's reach. But the Court ruled that a large corporation with subsidiaries and suppliers in many states was inherently involved in interstate commerce and hence subject to congressional regulation. In other decisions, the Court upheld minimum wage laws, the Social Security Act, and federal rules controlling how much of any given commodity local farmers might grow.[15]

Cooperative Federalism and Grants-in-Aid

cooperative federalism

A type of federalism existing since the New Deal era in which grants-in-aid have been used strategically to encourage states and localities to pursue nationally defined goals. Also known as intergovernmental cooperation

Roosevelt was able to overcome judicial resistance to expansive New Deal programs. Congress, however, forced him to recognize the continuing importance of the states by crafting some programs in such a way as to encourage states to pursue nationally set goals while leaving them some leeway to administer programs according to local values and needs. If the traditional system of two sovereigns performing highly different functions could be called dual federalism, the system that prevailed after the 1930s could be called cooperative federalism, which generally refers to supportive relations, sometimes partnerships, between national government and the state and local governments. It takes the form of federal subsidies for specific state and local activities; these are called grants-in-aid. Because many of these state and local programs would not exist without the federal grants-in-aid, the grant-in-aid is also an important form of federal influence on states and localities. (Another form of federal influence, the mandate, will be covered in the next section.)

A grant-in-aid is really a kind of bribe or "carrot" whereby Congress gives money to state and local governments with the condition that it be spent for a particular purpose. Congress uses grants-in-aid because it does not usually have the direct political or constitutional power to command these governments to do its bidding. Beginning in the late 1930s, for example, Congress set national goals in specific policy categories such as public housing and assistance to the unemployed and provided grants-in-aid to meet these goals. The range of categories has expanded greatly over the decades, and the value of categorical grants-in-aid increased from $2.3 billion in 1950 to over $550 billion in 2015 (Figure 3.1). Sometimes Congress requires the state or local government to match the national contribution dollar for dollar, but for some programs, such as the interstate highway system, the grant-in-aid provides 90 percent of the cost of the program.

For the most part, the categorical grants created before the 1960s simply helped the states perform their traditional functions.[16] In the 1960s,

grants-in-aid

A general term for funds given by Congress to state and local governments

categorical grants-in-aid

Funds given to states and localities by Congress that are earmarked by law for specific policy categories, such as education or crime prevention

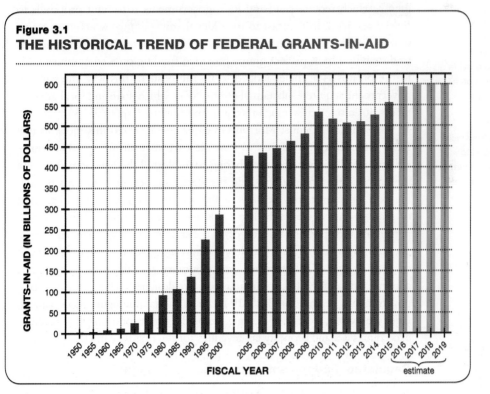

Figure 3.1
THE HISTORICAL TREND OF FEDERAL GRANTS-IN-AID

y-axis: GRANTS-IN-AID (IN BILLIONS OF DOLLARS) — 0, 50, 100, 150, 200, 250, 300, 350, 400, 450, 500, 550, 600

x-axis: FISCAL YEAR — 1950, 1955, 1960, 1965, 1970, 1975, 1980, 1985, 1990, 1995, 2000, 2005, 2006, 2007, 2008, 2009, 2010, 2011, 2012, 2013, 2014, 2015, 2016, 2017, 2018, 2019

estimate (2016–2019)

NOTE: Excludes outlays for national defense, international affairs, and net interest.

SOURCE: Office of Management and Budget, www.whitehouse.gov/omb/budget/historicals (accessed 2/10/16).

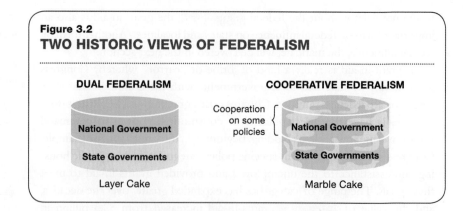

Figure 3.2
TWO HISTORIC VIEWS OF FEDERALISM

DUAL FEDERALISM

National Government

State Governments

Layer Cake

Cooperation on some policies

COOPERATIVE FEDERALISM

National Government

State Governments

Marble Cake

however, the national role expanded dramatically. For example, during the 89th Congress (1965–66) alone, the number of categorical grant-in-aid programs grew from 221 to 379.[17] The grants authorized during the 1960s announced national purposes much more strongly than did earlier grants, and central among them was to provide opportunities to the poor.

Many of the categorical grants enacted during the 1960s were project grants, which require state and local governments to submit proposals to federal agencies. In contrast to the older formula grants, which used a formula (composed of such elements as need and state and local capacities) to distribute funds, project grants provided funding on a competitive basis to the proposals agencies judged to be the best. In this way, the national government acquired substantial control over which state and local governments got money, how much they got, and how they spent it.

The political scientist Morton Grodzins characterized this move as one from "layer cake federalism" to "marble cake federalism," in which intergovernmental cooperation and sharing have blurred the line between where the national government ends and the state and local governments begin.[18] Figure 3.2 demonstrates the basis of the marble-cake idea. At the high point of grant-in-aid policies in the late 1970s, federal aid contributed about 25–30 percent of the operating budgets of all the state and local governments in the country (Figure 3.3). In 2010, federal aid accounted for more than 35 percent of these budgets. This increase was temporary, resulting from the Obama administration's $787 billion stimulus package designed to help state and local governments weather the 2008–10 recession; today the figure is 33 percent. Briefly, however, federal aid became the single largest source of state revenue, exceeding sales and property tax revenues for the first time in U.S. history.

Regulated Federalism and National Standards. Developments from the 1960s to the present have moved well beyond marble-cake federalism to what might be called regulated federalism.[19] In some areas—especially civil rights, poverty programs, and environmental protection—the national

project grants

Grants-in-aid for which state and local governments submit proposals to federal agencies, who provide funding for them on a competitive basis

formula grants

Grants-in-aid for which a formula is used to determine the amount of federal funds a state or local government will receive

regulated federalism

A form of federalism in which Congress imposes legislation on state and local governments that requires them to meet national standards

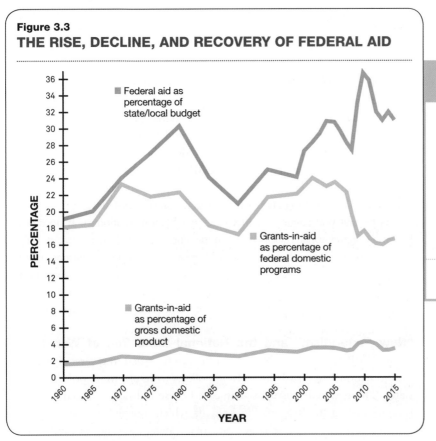

Figure 3.3

THE RISE, DECLINE, AND RECOVERY OF FEDERAL AID

Legend:
- Federal aid as percentage of state/local budget
- Grants-in-aid as percentage of federal domestic programs
- Grants-in-aid as percentage of gross domestic product

Y-axis: PERCENTAGE (0–36)
X-axis: YEAR (1960–2015)

SOURCES: Robert J. Dilger, Federal Grants to State and Local Governments, CRS, 2015.

government offers grant-in-aid financing to state and local governments for particular policies but threatens to withhold or withdraw it unless their versions of the policies conform to national standards. Such efforts to "set national standards" are also often made in interstate highway use, social services, and education. The net effect of enforcing standards in this way is that state and local policies are more uniform from coast to coast. In addition, in other programs, the national government imposes obligations on the states *without providing any funding at all.* These obligations have come to be called unfunded mandates.[20]

These burdens became a major part of the rallying cry that produced the Republican Congress elected in 1994 and its Contract with America. One of the first measures adopted by the new Congress was the Unfunded Mandates Reform Act (UMRA). A triumph of lobbying by state and local governments, UMRA was "hailed as both symbol and substance of a renewed congressional commitment to federalism."[21] Under this law, a point of order raised on the House or Senate floor can stop any mandate with an

unfunded mandates

National standards or programs imposed on state and local governments by the federal government without accompanying funding or reimbursement

uncompensated state and local cost that the Congressional Budget Office estimates will exceed $50 million a year. This so-called "stop, look, and listen" requirement forced Congress to own up to any mandate and its potential costs. During 1996, its first full year of operation, only 11 bills included mandates that exceeded the $50 million threshold—out of a total of 69 in which mandates were included. (Among the 11 were an increase in the minimum wage and extension of Federal Occupational Safety and Health Administration standards to state and local employees.) Most of these bills were modified in the House to reduce their costs. However, as one expert put it, "The primary impact of UMRA came not from the affirmative blockage of [mandate] legislation, but rather from its effect as a deterrent to mandates in the drafting and early consideration of legislation."[22]

As its first year suggests, UMRA has not been revolutionary. It does not prevent congressional members from passing unfunded mandates; it only makes them think twice before they do. Moreover, it exempts several areas from coverage, and states must still enforce antidiscrimination laws and meet other requirements to receive federal assistance. Still, UMRA is a serious effort to shift power in the national–state relationship a bit further toward the state side.

"New Federalism" and the National–State Tug of War. Even before UMRA, Presidents Nixon and Reagan had tried to reverse the trend toward national standards by crafting policies to return more power to the states. The new federalism, as they called these policies, included Nixon's revenue sharing and Reagan's block grants, which consolidated a number of categorical grants into one larger category, leaving the state (or local) government more discretion to decide how to use the money.

President Barack Obama, on the other hand, seemed to believe firmly in regulated federalism, viewing the states more as administrative arms than as independent laboratories. For example, under his new health care reform law every state was encouraged to establish a health insurance exchange where individuals in need of insurance could shop for the best rate. Citizens purchasing insurance through these exchanges would receive federal tax subsidies. Some states did not establish exchanges, but the Supreme Court ruled that their citizens could receive tax benefits for the policies they purchased through the federal government's exchange.[23] The law also required states to expand their Medicaid programs, adding as many as 15 million Americans to the Medicaid rolls. Some states were concerned that the costs of the new program would fall on their strained budgets, and 12 state attorneys general brought suit, charging that the program's mandates violate the Tenth Amendment. Ultimately, the Supreme Court upheld major provisions of the legislation, although it ruled that the federal government cannot require that Medicaid rolls be expanded. As of September 2016, 31 states and Washington, D.C. had decided to expand

block grants

Federal funds given to state governments for goods, services, or programs, with relatively few restrictions on how the funds may be spent

their rolls. The Analyzing the Evidence unit on pp. 74–5 explores the states' approaches to setting Medicaid eligibility.

The Supreme Court as Referee. For much of the nineteenth century, federal power remained limited. The Tenth Amendment was used to bolster arguments about states' rights, which in their extreme version claimed that the states did not have to submit to national laws when they believed the national government had exceeded its authority. These arguments in favor of states' rights were voiced less often after the Civil War. But the Supreme Court continued to use the Tenth Amendment to strike down laws that it thought exceeded constitutional limits on national power, including the Civil Rights Act passed in 1875.

In the early twentieth century, however, the Tenth Amendment appeared to lose its force. Reformers began to press for national regulations to limit the power of large corporations and to preserve the health and welfare of citizens, and the Supreme Court began to uphold many of these laws. By the late 1930s, the Court had approved such an expansion of federal power that the Tenth Amendment appeared irrelevant.

Recent decades have seen a revival of interest in the Tenth Amendment and important Supreme Court decisions limiting federal power. Much of the interest in the Tenth Amendment stems from conservatives who believe that a strong federal government encroaches on individual liberties and so power should be returned or "devolved" to the states. Meanwhile, the Supreme Court revived the Eleventh Amendment concept of state sovereign immunity. This legal doctrine holds that states are immune from lawsuits by private persons or groups claiming that a state has violated a statute enacted by Congress.

The Supreme Court's ruling in *United States v. Lopez* in 1995 fueled interest in the Tenth Amendment. Stating that Congress had exceeded its authority under the commerce clause, the Court struck down a federal law that barred handguns near schools.[24] This was the first time since the New Deal that the Court had limited congressional powers in this way. (The New Deal is discussed in Chapter 6.) The Court further limited federal power over the states in a 1996 ruling, based on the Eleventh Amendment, that prevented Native Americans of the Seminole tribe from suing the state of Florida in federal court. A 1988 law had given tribes the right to sue a state in federal court if the state did not negotiate in good faith over issues related to gambling casinos on tribal land. By calling into question whether individuals or groups can sue a state if it fails to uphold federal law, the Supreme Court's ruling appeared to signal a much broader limitation on national power.[25]

Another significant decision came in the 1997 case *Printz v. United States* (joined with *Mack v. United States*),[26] in which the Court struck down a key provision of the Brady Bill, enacted in 1993 to regulate gun sales. Under

states' rights

The principle that states should oppose the increasing authority of the national government. This view was most popular before the Civil War

state sovereign immunity

A legal doctrine, based on the Eleventh Amendment to the Constitution, holding that states cannot be sued for violating an act of Congress

Health Care Policy and the States

Contributed by
Jenna Bednar
University of Michigan

The 2010 Patient Protection and Affordable Care Act (ACA) was an attempt by Congress to standardize access to health care nationally as well as to contain costs. The act raised questions about responsibility for health care policy and poverty relief. The primary federalism question in the ACA was what level of government, state or federal, should set Medicaid eligibility criteria. Medicaid is a program to provide health care coverage to the poor and is jointly financed by the federal and state governments. As enacted, the ACA expanded Medicaid eligibility to adults with incomes at or below 138 percent of the federal poverty level (FPL). In 2015 the FPL was $20,090 for a family of three, making that family eligible for Medicaid if it earned up to $27,724. This provision, however, was effectively made a state option by the Supreme Court's 2012 ruling on the constitutionality of the ACA. States could choose not to accept the Medicaid expansion and instead set their own thresholds for eligibility.

As of November 2015, 31 states and Washington, D.C. had adopted the Medicaid expansion. The first map below shows the 2015 Medicaid eligibility thresholds by state for adults with dependent children. A family of three in Connecticut, a state that extended Medicaid eligibility above the ACA minimum to 155 percent of FPL for parents, could earn up to $31,139 and the family would still qualify for Medicaid benefits. The same family living in Texas, a state that did not adopt the Medicaid expansion, would be ineligible if they earned more than $3,616 (18 percent of FPL). The second map shows the percentage of nonelderly adults who lacked health insurance in each state in 2014.

Medicaid Eligibility Thresholds and Percentage Uninsured*

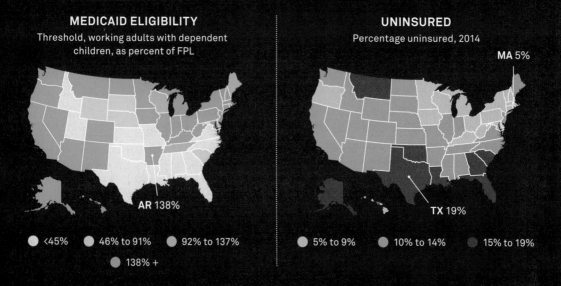

MEDICAID ELIGIBILITY
Threshold, working adults with dependent children, as percent of FPL

AR 138%

● <45%   ● 46% to 91%   ● 92% to 137%
● 138% +

UNINSURED
Percentage uninsured, 2014

MA 5%

TX 19%

● 5% to 9%   ● 10% to 14%   ● 15% to 19%

When public policy is decentralized in a federal system, not only can states set policy according to their own preferences and capacity, as demonstrated by the variation in Medicaid eligibility, but states may innovate to improve policy. For example, in 2006 Massachusetts enacted a law that required residents to obtain insurance but subsidized or offered free coverage for the poor. In the graph below, we see the proportion of the Massachusetts nonelderly adult population without health insurance compared with the proportion of nonelderly adults without health insurance nationwide. Although Massachusetts already had a far lower rate of uninsured than the national average, the introduction of health policy reform further reduced the percentage of uninsured at a time when the national average was increasing.

The ACA was modeled on the Massachusetts plan. Two aspects were politically controversial: the requirement that all individuals obtain insurance and the standardization of Medicaid eligibility. If states complied with the ACA prescription, access to Medicaid benefits expanded considerably, including extending coverage to all limited-income adults regardless of whether they had dependent children, a population that currently lacks access to Medicaid. However, the ACA did so by centralizing authority, reducing the states' control over health care policy and poverty relief.

Although the federal government would pay the lion's share of the costs of the expanded Medicare coverage through at least 2020, many states were unhappy with the dictum from the central government, and 26 states joined lawsuits to challenge Congress's authority, leading to the 2012 Supreme Court ruling that states need not accept the Medicaid expansion. In 2012 the Supreme Court ruled that states cannot be required to conform their Medicaid eligibility thresholds to the national minimum. As of November 2015, 19 states had indicated that they would not raise their Medicaid eligibility thresholds to meet the ACA minimum. Ultimately, the fate of health care responsibility will rest with the American public, as they grow to accept or reject the arguments made on both sides.

Percentage of Population without Health Insurance**

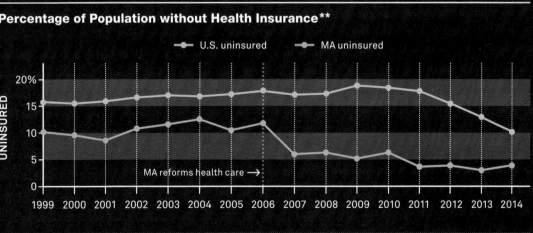

* SOURCE: Kaiser Family Foundation, "Eligibility Limits for Adults as a Percent of the Federal Poverty Level," www.kff.org/health-reform/state-indicator/medicaid-income-eligibility-limits-for-adults-as-a-percent-of-the-federal-poverty-level/#map (accessed 2/11/16); and www.kff.org/other/state-indicator/nonelderly-0-64 (accessed 2/11/16).

** SOURCE: Compiled from U.S. Census Bureau, Current Population Survey, 2012 Annual Social and Economic Supplement, Health Insurance, Table HI05 (2011, 2010), Table HI A-6, Table HI06 (2012); and Kaiser Family Foundation, (2013, 2014) and www.kff.org/other/state-indicator/total-population/#table (accessed 2/11/2016).

Evolution of the Federal System

1789–1834	Nationalization: the Marshall Court interprets the Constitution broadly so as to expand and consolidate national power.
1835–1930s	Dual federalism: the functions of the national government are very specifically enumerated. States do much of the fundamental governing that affects citizens' day-to-day life. There is tension between the two levels of government, and the power of the national government begins to increase.
1930s–1970s	Cooperative federalism: the national government uses grants-in-aid to encourage states and localities to pursue nationally defined goals.
1970s–	Regulated federalism: the national government sets conditions that states and localities must meet in order to receive certain grants. The national government also sets national standards in policy areas without providing states and localities with funding to meet them.
1980s–1990s	New federalism: the national government attempts to return more power to the states through block grants to them.

the act, state and local law enforcement officers were required to conduct background checks on prospective gun purchasers. The Court held that the federal government cannot require states to administer or enforce federal regulatory programs. This trend continued with the 2006 *Gonzales v. Oregon* case, in which the Court ruled that the federal government could not use federal drug laws to interfere with Oregon's assisted-suicide law.[27] These rulings signaled a move toward greater latitude for the states.

By 2012, however, the Court once again seemed to favor national power in the nation-state tug-of-war. In addition to a decision upholding the constitutionality of President Obama's health care initiative (the Affordable Care Act), the Court struck down portions of an Arizona immigration law, declaring that immigration was a federal, not a state, matter.[28] And in a 2013 decision, it struck down an Arizona law requiring individuals to show documentation of citizenship when registering to vote. The Court ruled that this requirement was preempted by the federal National Voter Registration Act, which requires states to use the official federal registration form.[29] In two other cases, the Court ruled against state legislatures on questions involving congressional district boundaries.[30]

THE SEPARATION OF POWERS

As we have noted, the separation of powers enables several different federal institutions to influence the nation's agenda, to affect decisions, and to prevent the other institutions from taking action—dividing agenda, decision, and veto power. The Constitution's framers saw this arrangement, although cumbersome, as an essential means of protecting liberty.

In his discussion of the separation of powers, James Madison quoted the originator of the idea, the French political thinker Baron de Montesquieu: "There can be no liberty where the legislative and executive powers are united in the same person . . . [or] if the power of judging be not separated from the legislative and executive powers."[31] Using the same reasoning, many of Madison's contemporaries argued that there was not *enough* separation among the three branches, and Madison had to backtrack to insist that complete separation was not required:

> Unless these departments [branches] be so far connected and blended as to give to each a constitutional control over the others, the degree of separation which the maxim requires, as essential to a free government, can never in practice be duly maintained.[32]

This is the secret of how Americans have made the separation of powers effective: they have made it self-enforcing by giving each branch of government the means to participate in, and partially or temporarily obstruct, the workings of the other branches.

Checks and Balances

The means by which each branch of government interacts with every other branch is known informally as checks and balances. The best-known examples are shown in Figure 3.4. The framers sought to guarantee that the three branches would in fact use these checks and balances as weapons against one another by giving each branch a different political constituency and therefore a different perspective on what the government ought to do: direct, popular election for the members of the House; indirect election of senators (until the Seventeenth Amendment, adopted in 1913); indirect election

Figure 3.4
CHECKS AND BALANCES

LEGISLATIVE

EXECUTIVE OVER LEGISLATIVE

President can veto acts of Congress

President can call a special session of Congress

President carries out, and thereby interprets, laws passed by Congress

Vice president casts tiebreaking vote in the Senate

JUDICIAL OVER LEGISLATIVE

Court can declare laws unconstitutional

Chief justice presides over Senate during hearing to impeach the president

LEGISLATIVE OVER EXECUTIVE

Congress can override presidential veto

Congress can impeach and remove president

Senate can reject president's appointments and refuse to ratify treaties

Congress can conduct investigations into president's actions

Congress can refuse to pass laws or provide funding that president requests

LEGISLATIVE OVER JUDICIAL

Congress can change size of federal court system and number of Supreme Court justices

Congress can propose constitutional amendments

Congress can reject Supreme Court nominees

Congress can impeach and remove federal judges

Congress can amend court jurisdictions

Congress controls appropriations

JUDICIAL OVER EXECUTIVE

Court can declare executive actions unconstitutional

Court has the power to issue warrants

Chief justice presides over impeachment of president

EXECUTIVE

JUDICIAL

EXECUTIVE OVER JUDICIAL

President nominates Supreme Court justices

President nominates federal judges

President can pardon those convicted in federal court

President can refuse to enforce the courts' decisions

of the president through the electoral college; and appointment of federal judges for life. All things considered, the best characterization of the separation of powers principle in action is "separated institutions sharing power."[33]

Legislative Supremacy

Although each branch was given adequate means to compete with the other branches, the framers provided for legislative supremacy by making Congress the preeminent branch. Legislative supremacy made the provision of checks and balances in the other two branches all the more important.

The system of checks and balances ensures that political power is shared by the separate institutions. Here, President Obama greets House Speaker Paul Ryan.

The most important indication of the intentions of the framers was the provisions in Article I to treat the powers of the national government as powers of Congress. The Founders also provided for legislative supremacy in their decision to give Congress the sole power over appropriations.

Although "presidential government" gradually supplanted legislative supremacy after 1937, the relative power of the executive and legislative branches since that time has varied. The power play between the president and Congress is especially intense during periods of divided government, when one party controls the White House and another controls all or part of Capitol Hill.

The Role of the Supreme Court

The role of the judicial branch in the separation of powers has depended on the power of judicial review, a power not provided for in the Constitution but asserted by Chief Justice Marshall in 1803:

> If a law be in opposition to the Constitution; if both the law and the Constitution apply to a particular case, so that the Court must either decide that case conformable to the law, disregarding the Constitution, or conformable to the Constitution, disregarding the law; the Court must determine which of these conflicting rules governs the case: This is of the very essence of judicial duty.[34]

Review of the constitutionality of acts of the president or Congress is relatively rare. For example, there were no Supreme Court reviews of congressional acts in the 50-plus years between *Marbury v. Madison* (1803)

legislative supremacy

The preeminent position within the national government that the Constitution assigns to Congress

divided government

The condition in American government in which the presidency is controlled by one party, while the opposing party controls one or both houses of Congress

and *Dred Scott v. Sandford* (1857). In the century or so between the Civil War and 1970, 84 acts of Congress were held unconstitutional (in whole or in part), but there were long periods of complete Court deference to Congress, punctuated by flurries of judicial review during periods of social upheaval. The most significant of these was 1935–36, when 12 acts of Congress were invalidated, blocking virtually the entire New Deal program.[35] Then, after 1937, when the Court made its great reversals in upholding New Deal legislation, no significant acts were voided until 1983, when the Court declared unconstitutional the legislative veto, a practice in which Congress authorized the president to take certain actions but reserved the right to veto those with which it disagreed.[36] The Supreme Court became much more activist (that is, less deferential to Congress) after the elevation of Justice William H. Rehnquist to chief justice (1986–2005), and "a new program of judicial activism"[37] seemed to be in place. Between 1995 and 2002, at least 26 acts or parts of acts of Congress were struck down on constitutional grounds.[38]

The Court has been far more deferential toward the president since the New Deal period, with only five significant confrontations. One was the so-called steel seizure case of 1952, in which the Court refused to permit President Truman to use "emergency powers" to force workers back into the steel mills during the Korean War.[39] In 1974, the Court declared unconstitutional President Nixon's refusal to respond to a subpoena to make available the infamous White House tapes as evidence in a criminal prosecution. The Court argued that although executive privilege protected confidentiality of communications to and from the president, this did not extend to data in presidential files or tapes bearing on criminal prosecutions.[40] During the Clinton administration, the Supreme Court struck down the Line-Item Veto Act of 1996, which would have allowed the president to veto certain portions of bills while accepting others, on the grounds that any such change in the procedures of adopting laws would have to be made by amendment to the Constitution, not by legislation.[41] More recently, and of far greater importance, the Supreme Court repudiated the Bush administration's claims about the president's authority to detain enemy combatants without giving detainees an opportunity to defend themselves in an open court.[42]

executive privilege

The claim that confidential communications between a president and the president's close advisors should not be revealed without the consent of the president

DO FEDERALISM AND THE SEPARATION OF POWERS WORK?

Federalism and the separation of powers are two of the most important constitutional principles upon which the United States' system of limited government is based. As we have seen, federalism limits the power of the national government in numerous ways. By its very existence, federalism recognizes the principle of two sovereigns: the national government and the state governments (hence the term *dual federalism*). In addition, the Constitution specifically restrained the power of the national government to regulate the economy. As a result, the states were free to do most of the fundamental governing for the first century and a half of American government. This began to change during and following the New Deal, as the national government began to exert more influence over the states through grants-in-aid and mandates. But even as the powers of the national government grew, so did the powers of the states. In recent decades, a countertrend to the growth of national power has developed as Congress has opted to devolve some of its powers to the states.

From 1974–87, the federal government set a national maximum speed limit at 55 miles per hour to help conserve fuel following the oil shortage of the 1970s. Since 1995, the states have been free to set their own limits, and in some areas of Texas the speed limit is as high as 85 miles per hour.

But the problem that arises with devolution is that programs that were once uniform across the country (because they were the national government's responsibility) can become highly variable, with some states providing benefits not available in other states. To a point, variation can be considered one of the virtues of federalism. But dangers are inherent in large variations and inequalities in the provision of services and benefits in a democracy. For example, the Food and Drug Administration has been under attack in recent years. Could the government address the agency's perceived problems by devolving its regulatory tasks to the states? Would people care if drugs require "caution" labels in some states but not in others? Devolution, as attractive as it may seem, is not an approach that can be applied across the board without analyzing carefully the nature of the program and of the problems it is designed to solve.

A key puzzle of federalism is deciding when differences across states reflect proper democratic decisions by the states and when such differences reflect inequalities that should not be tolerated. Sometimes a decision to eliminate differences is made on the grounds of equality and individual rights, as in the Civil Rights Act of 1964, which outlawed segregation. At other times, a stronger federal role is justified on the grounds of national interest, as in the institution of a national 55-mile-per-hour speed limit to improve fuel efficiency during the oil shortage in the 1970s. Advocates of a more limited federal role often point to the value of democracy. Public actions can more easily be tailored to fit distinctive state or local desires if states and localities have more power to make policy. Viewed this way, variation across states can be an expression of democratic will.

Another feature of limited government, separation of powers, is manifested in our system of checks and balances, whereby separate institutions of government share power with each other. Even though the Constitution clearly provided for legislative supremacy, checks and balances have functioned well. Some would say this system has worked too well. The last 50 years have witnessed long periods of divided government, when one party controls the White House while the other controls one or both houses of Congress. During these periods, the level of conflict between the executive and legislative branches has been particularly divisive, resulting in what some analysts derisively call gridlock.[43]

During President George W. Bush's first six years in office, the separation of powers did not seem to work effectively, as a Congress controlled by the president's fellow Republicans gave Bush a free rein in such important matters as the war in Iraq and the war against terrorism. In 2006, Democrats won control of both houses and began to scrutinize the president's actions carefully. With the election of Democrat Barack Obama to the presidency in 2008, Congress and the presidency were once again controlled by the same party. But in 2010, Republicans took control of the House of Representatives and in 2014, both the House and the Senate, challenging the president's domestic and foreign policies. At times, the stalemate between Congress and the president became so severe that the government was virtually paralyzed. In 2016, the Republicans won control of the White House and retained control of both houses of Congress. Though a number of Republican congressional leaders, including House Speaker Paul Ryan, had been lukewarm to Donald Trump's presidential candidacy, all pledged to work with the new president on behalf of a Republican agenda. It seemed that the GOP now had an opportunity to enact legislation based upon its vision of American foreign and domestic policy.

For Further Reading

Bednar, Jenna. *The Robust Federation*. New York: Cambridge University Press, 2008.

Ferejohn, John A., and Barry R. Weingast, eds. *The New Federalism: Can the States Be Trusted?* Stanford, CA: Hoover Institution Press, 1997.

Fisher, Louis. *Constitutional Conflicts between Congress and the President*. 5th ed., revised. Lawrence: University Press of Kansas, 2007.

LaCroix, Alison L. *The Ideological Origins of American Federalism.* Cambridge, MA: Harvard University Press, 2010.

Moellers, Christoph. *The Three Branches: A Comparative Model of Separation of Powers.* New York: Oxford University Press, 2015.

Nolette, Paul. *Federalism on Trial: State Attorneys General and National Policymaking in Contemporary America.* Lawrence, KS: University Press of Kansas, 2015.

Noonan, John T. *Narrowing the Nation's Power: The Supreme Court Sides with the States.* Berkeley: University of California Press, 2002.

Riker, William H. *Federalism: Origin, Operation, Significance.* Boston: Little, Brown, 1964.

Robertson, David. *Federalism and the Making of America.* New York: Routledge, 2011.

Samuels, David, and Matthew Shugart. *Presidents, Parties and Prime Ministers: How the Separation of Powers Affects Party Organization and Behavior.* New York: Cambridge University Press, 2010.

Van Horn, Carol E. *The State of the States.* 4th ed. Washington, DC: CQ Press, 2004.

4

Civil Liberties and Civil Rights

The first 10 amendments of the U.S. Constitution, together called the Bill of Rights, are the basis for the freedoms we enjoy as American citizens. The Bill of Rights might well have been entitled the "Bill of Liberties," because the provisions that were incorporated in the Bill of Rights were seen as defining a private sphere of personal liberty, free of governmental restrictions. These freedoms include the right to free speech, the right to the free exercise of religion, prohibitions against unreasonable searches and seizures, and guarantees of due process of law.

As Jefferson put it, a bill of rights "is what people are entitled to against every government on earth...." Civil liberties are protections from improper government action. Thus, as we will see in the first sections of this chapter, the Bill of Rights is a series of restraints imposed on government.

Whereas civil liberties are phrased as negatives (what government cannot do), civil rights are obligations (what government must do) to guarantee equal citizenship and protect citizens from discrimination. Civil rights regulate *who* can participate in the political process and civil society and *how* they can participate: for example, who can vote, who can hold office, who can have a trial or serve on juries, and when and how citizens can petition the

civil liberties

The protections of citizens from improper governmental action

civil rights

The legal or moral claims that citizens are entitled to make on the government

government to take action. Civil rights also define how people are treated in employment, education, and other aspects of American society.

In some nations, citizens have few, if any, civil rights. They have no right to vote, no right to stand for office, and no right to be judged by their peers if accused of a crime. The United States, however, began life as a nation with numerous civil rights guaranteed in both federal and state constitutions. The federal Constitution provided such rights as representation in Congress (Article I, Section 2), established who can serve in Congress and become president, and guaranteed the privilege of *habeas corpus* for all people (Article I, Section 9). The Bill of Rights, in addition to defining the major civil liberties, also provides for important civil rights, such as the right of all persons to due process of law, guaranteed in the Fifth Amendment.

Yet Americans' early conception of civil rights was much narrower than it is today. Originally, the Constitution did not guarantee a general right to vote; it left voting and many other civil rights to the states. The Founders' initial rules permitted widely disparate treatment of different categories of individuals, including women, members of minority racial and ethnic groups, owners of property, and others. The greatest restriction on civil rights at the time of the Constitution was on black people. Eight of the 13 original states permitted slavery, and slaves possessed virtually no civil rights.

The Constitution banned the importation of slaves after 1808, but permitted slavery itself to continue. Just before the Civil War, roughly 4 million African Americans were slaves in the southern states, where their labor was crucial to the region's agricultural economy. By then, slavery was prohibited in most of the northern states, and the issue of whether it should be

CORE OF THE ANALYSIS

➡ Civil liberties are rules that limit the government's authority to interfere in certain spheres of activity, such as free speech and religion.

➡ Civil rights are rules that limit the power of majorities to exclude or harm individuals based on factors such as race, gender, or ethnicity.

➡ Today's conceptions of civil liberties and civil rights have been shaped by their historical development and their interpretation by key political actors, especially the Supreme Court.

allowed in western territories bitterly divided the nation. In the 1857 *Dred Scott v. Sandford* case, the Supreme Court ruled that a slave was not a citizen, could not bring suit in federal court, and was merely his master's personal property. Moreover, said the Court, slavery could not be excluded from the territories.[1] This decision inflamed sectional divisions, infuriated antislavery groups in the North, and helped to provoke the Civil War.

Following the Civil War, Congress adopted the Thirteenth, Fourteenth, and Fifteenth amendments to the Constitution to protect civil rights that had been violated by slavery. The Thirteenth Amendment prohibited slavery and involuntary servitude in the United States. The Fifteenth extended the right to vote to blacks: "The right of citizens of the United States to vote shall not be denied or abridged by the United States or by any State on account of race, color, or previous condition of servitude." The Fourteenth Amendment asserted the idea of civil rights much more broadly for all citizens:

> All persons born or naturalized in the United States, and subject to the jurisdiction thereof, are citizens of the United States and of the State wherein they reside. No State shall make or enforce any law which shall abridge the privileges or immunities of citizens of the United States; nor shall any State deprive any person of life, liberty, or property, without due process of law; nor deny to any person within its jurisdiction the equal protection of the laws.

The last clause of this section, the equal protection clause, has transformed civil rights in the United States, as it creates the foundation for asserting equal civil rights for all persons.

The words of the equal protection clause launched more than a century of political movements and legal efforts to press for equality. African Americans' quest for civil rights in turn inspired many other groups—including other racial and ethnic groups, women, people with disabilities, gay men and lesbians, and transgender people—to seek new laws and constitutional guarantees of their civil rights. Their struggles were aided by the simplicity of the clause, which offers its guarantee to *any person*.

The enforcement of this guarantee was hard-won, and debates over the extent of the government's responsibility in ensuring equal protection persist. The reason is that the definition of civil rights depends not only on what laws are passed or how the words of the Constitution are interpreted but on the behavior of people in society. How can we understand historical patterns of discrimination? Do political divisions between whites and racial and ethnic minorities cause a majority of the white population to oppose the preferred candidates of a majority of the black or Hispanic populations? Is there evidence of intentional discrimination in election administration, employment, housing, and other activities? Before we consider these questions, we turn first to civil liberties and the long effort to make personal liberty a reality for every citizen in America.

CIVIL LIBERTIES: NATIONALIZING THE BILL OF RIGHTS

The First Amendment provides that "Congress shall make no law respecting an establishment of religion . . . or abridging freedom of speech, or of the press; or the right of [assembly and petition]." But this is the only part of the Bill of Rights that exclusively addresses the national government. For example, the Second Amendment provides that "the right of the people to keep and bear Arms shall not be infringed." The Fifth Amendment says, among other things, that "no person shall . . . be twice put in jeopardy of life or limb" for the same crime; that no person "shall be compelled in any Criminal Case to be a witness against himself"; that no person shall "be deprived of life, liberty, or property, without due process of law"; and that private property cannot be taken "without just compensation."[2] Because the First Amendment is the only part of the Bill of Rights that explicitly limits the national government, a fundamental question arises: Do the remaining parts put limits on state governments or only on the national government?

Dual Citizenship

The question of whether the Bill of Rights also limits state governments was settled in 1833 in the case *Barron v. Baltimore*, and the facts were simple. In paving its streets, the city of Baltimore had disposed of so much sand and gravel in the water near John Barron's wharf that the wharf's value for commercial purposes was virtually destroyed. Barron brought the city into court on the grounds that it had, under the Fifth Amendment, unconstitutionally deprived him of his property without just compensation. Chief Justice Marshall, in one of the most significant Supreme Court decisions ever handed down, said:

> The Constitution was ordained and established by the people of the United States for themselves, for their own government, and not for the government of the individual States. Each State established a constitution for itself, and in that constitution provided such limitations and restrictions

on the powers of its particular government as its judgment dictated. . . . If these propositions be correct, *the fifth amendment must be understood as restraining the power of the general government, not as applicable to the States.*[3] [Emphasis added]

In other words, if an agency of the national government had deprived Barron of his property, there would have been little doubt about his winning his case. But if the constitution of Maryland contained no such provision protecting citizens of Maryland from such action, then Barron had no legal leg to stand on against Baltimore, an agency of the state of Maryland.

Barron v. Baltimore confirmed "dual citizenship"—that each American was a citizen of the national government and separately a citizen of one of the states. This meant that the Bill of Rights did not apply to decisions or procedures of state (or local) governments. Even slavery could continue, because the Bill of Rights could not protect anyone from state laws treating people as property. In fact, the Bill of Rights did not become a vital instrument for the extension of civil liberties for anyone until after a bloody Civil War and a revolutionary Fourteenth Amendment intervened. And even then, nearly a second century would pass before the Bill of Rights would truly come into its own.

The Fourteenth Amendment

From a constitutional standpoint, the defeat of the South in the Civil War settled one question and raised another. It probably settled forever the question of whether secession was an option for any state. After 1865, there was more "united" than "states" to the United States. But this left unanswered just how much the states were obliged to obey the Constitution and, in particular, the Bill of Rights. The wording of the Fourteenth Amendment suggests that it was almost perfectly designed to impose the Bill of Rights on the states and thereby to reverse *Barron v. Baltimore*. Consider the amendment's very first words:

> All persons born or naturalized in the United States, and subject to the jurisdiction thereof, are citizens of the United States and of the State wherein they reside.

This statement provides for a single national citizenship, and at a minimum that means that civil liberties should not vary drastically from state to state. This interpretation of the Fourteenth Amendment is reinforced by the next clause:

> No state shall make or enforce any law which shall abridge the privileges or immunities of citizens of the United States; nor shall any state deprive any person of life, liberty, or property, without due process of law.

All of this sounds like an effort to extend the entire Bill of Rights to citizens wherever they might reside.[4] But this was not to be the Supreme Court's interpretation for nearly 100 years. Within five years of ratification of the Fourteenth Amendment, the Court was making decisions as though it had never been adopted.[5] Table 4.1 outlines the major developments in the history of the Fourteenth Amendment against the backdrop of *Barron*, citing particular provisions of the Bill of Rights as they were incorporated by Supreme Court decisions into the Fourteenth Amendment as limitations on all the states. This is a measure of the degree of "nationalization" of civil liberties.

Table 4.1

INCORPORATION OF THE BILL OF RIGHTS INTO THE FOURTEENTH AMENDMENT

SELECTED PROVISIONS AND AMENDMENTS	DATE "INCORPORATED"	KEY CASES
Eminent domain (V)	1897	Chicago, Burlington and Quincy Railroad v. Chicago
Freedom of speech (I)	1925	Gitlow v. New York
Freedom of the press (I)	1931	Near v. Minnesota ex rel. Olson
Free exercise of religion (I)	1934	Hamilton v. Regents of the University of California
Freedom of assembly (I)	1937	De Jonge v. Oregon
Freedom from unnecessary search and seizure (IV)	1949	Wolf v. Colorado
Freedom from warrantless search and seizure ("exclusionary rule") (IV)	1961	Mapp v. Ohio
Freedom from cruel and unusual punishment (VIII)	1962	Robinson v. California
Right to counsel in any criminal trial (VI)	1963	Gideon v. Wainwright
Right against self-incrimination and forced confessions (V)	1964	Malloy v. Hogan Escobedo v. Illinois
Right to privacy (III, IV, and V)	1965	Griswold v. Connecticut
Right to remain silent (V)	1966	Miranda v. Arizona
Right against double jeopardy (V)	1969	Benton v. Maryland
Right to bear arms (II)	2010	McDonald v. Chicago

The only change in civil liberties during the first 60 years after the Fourteenth Amendment came in 1897, when the Supreme Court held that the amendment's due process clause did in fact prohibit states from taking property for a public use—a power called eminent domain—without just compensation, as required by the Fifth Amendment.[6] This decision effectively overruled the specific holding in *Barron*; henceforth, a citizen of Maryland or any other state was protected from a "public taking" of property even if the state constitution did not provide such protection. But the Court had "incorporated" into the Fourteenth Amendment *only* the property protection provision of the Fifth Amendment, even though the due process clause applied to the taking of life and liberty as well as property.

No further expansion of civil liberties through incorporation occurred until 1925, when the Supreme Court held that freedom of speech is "among the fundamental personal rights and 'liberties' protected by the due process clause of the Fourteenth Amendment from impairment by the states."[7] In 1931, the Supreme Court added freedom of the press to that list; in 1934, it added freedom of religion; in 1937, it added freedom of assembly.[8] But that was as far as the Court would go.

The shadow of *Barron* extended into its second century, despite adoption of the Fourteenth Amendment. At the time of World War II, the Constitution, as interpreted by the Supreme Court, left standing the framework in which the states had the power to determine their own law on numerous fundamental issues. It left states with the power to pass laws segregating the races. It also left them with the power to engage in searches and seizures without a warrant, to indict accused persons without benefit of a grand jury, to deprive persons of trial by jury, to force persons to testify against themselves, to deprive accused persons of their right to confront adverse witnesses, and to prosecute accused persons more than once for the same crime, a practice known as double jeopardy.[9] Although few states exercised these powers, they were there for any state whose legislative majority chose to use them.

Before we leave the topic, it is worth mentioning that aside from its implications for the Bill of Rights, one specific part of the Fourteenth Amendment itself has come under political challenge today: the provision that all persons "born or naturalized" in the United States are citizens. Some politicians, most notably Donald Trump, have argued that even if born in this country, children of illegal immigrants should not be considered U.S. citizens and might be subject to deportation. Other politicians say that foreigners come to the United States specifically to have their children born here as citizens and perhaps also thereby provide the parents an advantage in securing their own American citizenship. Though we are a nation of immigrants, the grandchildren of yesterday's immigrants are not always eager to welcome the next group.

The Constitutional Revolution in Civil Liberties

strict scrutiny

The most stringent standard of judicial review of a government's actions in which the government must show that the law serves a "compelling state interest"

Signs of change in the constitutional framework came after 1954 in *Brown v. Board of Education*, when the Court found state segregation laws for schools unconstitutional.[10] Even though *Brown* was not a civil liberties case, it indicated rather clearly that the Supreme Court was going to be expansive about civil liberties, because with *Brown* the Court had effectively promised that it would actively subject the states and all actions affecting civil rights and civil liberties to strict scrutiny. In retrospect, this constitutional revolution was given a jump-start in 1954 by *Brown v. Board of Education*, even though the results were not apparent until after 1961, when the number of incorporated civil liberties increased (see Table 4.1).

As in the case of the enormous expansion in "interstate commerce" regulation discussed in Chapter 3, the constitutional revolution in civil liberties after World War II was a movement toward nationalization. But the two revolutions required opposite motions on the part of the Supreme Court. In interstate commerce (the first revolution), the Court had to assume a *passive* role by not interfering as Congress expanded the meaning of the commerce clause of Article I, Section 8. This expansion has been so extensive that the national government can now constitutionally reach a single farmer growing 20 acres of wheat or a small restaurant selling barbecue to local "whites only" without either being anywhere near interstate commerce routes. In the second revolution—involving the Bill of Rights and the Fourteenth Amendment—the Court had to assume an active role. It required close review of the actions of state legislatures and decisions of state courts in order to apply a single national Fourteenth Amendment standard to the rights and liberties of all citizens.

exclusionary rule

The requirement that courts exclude evidence obtained in violation of the Fourth Amendment

Miranda rule

The requirement derived from the Supreme Court's 1966 ruling in *Miranda v. Arizona* that persons under arrest must be informed of their legal rights, including the right to counsel, before undergoing police interrogation

Table 4.1 shows that until 1961, only the First Amendment and one clause of the Fifth Amendment had been clearly incorporated into the Fourteenth Amendment.[11] After 1961, several other important provisions of the Bill of Rights were incorporated. *Gideon v. Wainwright* expanded the Fourteenth Amendment's reach by establishing the right to counsel in a criminal trial.[12] In *Mapp v. Ohio*, the Court held that evidence obtained in violation of the Fourth Amendment ban on unreasonable searches and seizures would be excluded from trial.[13] This exclusionary rule was particularly irksome to the police and prosecutors because it meant that patently guilty defendants sometimes go free because evidence that clearly incriminated them could not be used. In *Miranda v. Arizona*, the Court's ruling required that arrested persons be informed of their right to remain silent and to have counsel present during interrogation[14]—the requirement now called the Miranda rule. By 1969, in *Benton v. Maryland*, the Supreme Court had come full circle regarding the rights of the criminally accused, explicitly reversing a 1937 ruling by incorporating a ban on double jeopardy.[15]

Beginning in the mid-1950s, the Court also expanded another important area of civil liberties: rights to privacy. In 1958, the Court recognized "privacy in one's association" in its decision to prevent the state of Alabama from using the membership list of the National Association for the Advancement of Colored People in the state's investigations.[16] As we see later in this chapter, legal questions about the right to privacy have come to the fore in more recent cases concerning birth control, abortion, homosexuality, and assisted suicide.

THE BILL OF RIGHTS TODAY

Because liberty requires restraining the power of government, the general status of civil liberties can never be considered fixed and permanent.[17] Every provision in the Bill of Rights is subject to interpretation, and interpretations always reflect the interpreter's interest in the outcome. As we have seen, the Supreme Court continuously reminds everyone that if it has the power to expand the Bill of Rights, it also has the power to contract it.[18]

The First Amendment and Freedom of Religion

The Bill of Rights begins by guaranteeing freedom of religion, and the First Amendment provides for that freedom in two distinct clauses: "Congress shall make no law [1] respecting an establishment of religion, or [2] prohibiting the free exercise thereof." The first clause is called the establishment clause, and the second is called the free exercise clause.

Separation between Church and State. The establishment clause and the idea of "no law" regarding the establishment of religion could be interpreted in several ways. One interpretation, which probably reflects the views of many of the First Amendment's authors, is that the government is prohibited only from establishing an official church. Official state churches, such as the Church of England, were common in the eighteenth century and seemed to many Americans inconsistent with a republican form of government. Indeed, many colonists had fled Europe to escape persecution for having rejected official churches. A second possible interpretation, the "nonpreferentialist" or "accommodationist" view, holds that the government may provide assistance to religious institutions or ideas so long as it shows no favoritism among them. The United States accommodates religious beliefs in a variety of ways, from the reference to God on U.S. currency to the prayer that begins every session of Congress. These forms of establishment have never been struck down by the courts.

establishment clause

The First Amendment clause that says, "Congress shall make no law respecting an establishment of religion." This law means that a wall of separation exists between church and state.

The third view regarding religious establishment, the most commonly held today, is that of a "wall of separation" between church and state that the government cannot breach. (The Analyzing the Evidence unit on pp. 96–7 explores Americans' attitudes on the separation of church and state.) Despite the absolute sound of the phrase *wall of separation*, there is ample room to disagree on its meaning. For example, the Court has been consistently strict in cases of prayer in public schools, striking down such practices as Bible reading,[19] nondenominational prayer,[20] a moment of silence for meditation or voluntary prayer, and pregame prayer at public sporting events.[21] Yet it has been quite permissive (some would say inconsistent) about the public display of religious symbols, such as city-sponsored Nativity scenes, in commercial or municipal areas.[22] In 1971, after 30 years of cases involving government assistance to religious schools, the Court specified some criteria to guide its decisions and those of lower courts about circumstances in which such aid might be constitutionally acceptable. In *Lemon v. Kurtzman,* a decision invalidating state payments for the teaching of secular subjects in parochial schools, the Court established three criteria, which collectively came to be called the *Lemon* test. Government aid to religious schools would be allowed if (1) it had a secular purpose, (2) its effect was neither to advance nor to inhibit religion, and (3) it did not entangle government and religious institutions in each other's affairs.[23]

In 2004, the question of whether the phrase "under God" in the Pledge of Allegiance violates the establishment clause came before the Court, which ruled that the plaintiff lacked a sufficient personal stake in the case to bring the complaint.[24] This inconclusive decision kept the issue alive for possible resolution in a future case.

In two cases in 2005, the Court also ruled inconclusively on government-sponsored displays of religious symbols, specifically the Ten Commandments. In *Van Orden v. Perry*, the Court ruled that a display of the Ten Commandments in the Texas state capitol did not violate the Constitution.[25] However, in *McCreary v. ACLU*, it found unconstitutional a display of the Ten Commandments inside two Kentucky courthouses.[26] Justice Stephen Breyer, the swing vote in both cases, intimated that the difference had been the purpose of the displays. Most legal observers, though, could see little difference between the two and assume that the Court will provide further clarification in future cases.

Free Exercise of Religion. The free exercise clause protects the right to believe and practice whatever religion one chooses; it also protects the right to be a nonbeliever. Although the Supreme Court has been fairly consistent in protecting the free exercise of religious belief, it has distinguished between beliefs and actions based on those beliefs. The 1940 case of *Cantwell v. Connecticut,* which arose from the efforts of two Jehovah's Witnesses to engage in door-to-door fund-raising, established the "time, place and manner" rule: Americans

Lemon test

Rule articulated in *Lemon v. Kurtzman* according to which governmental action in respect to religion is permissible if it is secular in purpose, does not lead to "excessive entanglement" of government with religion, and neither promotes nor inhibits the practice of religion. The Lemon test is generally used in relation to government aid to religious schools.

free exercise clause

The First Amendment clause that protects a citizen's right to believe and practice whatever religion he or she chooses

Different interpretations of the establishment clause have led to debates about the extent to which church and state must be separated. This monument of the Ten Commandments displayed in an Alabama courthouse was declared unconstitutional.

are free to adhere to any religious beliefs, but the time, place, and manner of exercising those beliefs are subject to regulation in the public interest.

In recent years, the principle of free exercise has been bolstered by legislation prohibiting religious discrimination by public and private entities in a variety of realms including hiring, land use, and the treatment of prison inmates. Two recent cases illustrating this point are *Holt v. Hobbs* and *E.E.O.C. v. Abercrombie and Fitch Stores*.[27] The Holt case involved a Muslim prisoner in an Arkansas jail, who asserted that his religious beliefs required him to grow a beard despite an Arkansas prison policy prohibiting beards. The Court held that the policy violated both the free exercise clause and a federal statute designed to protect the ability of prisoners to worship as they pleased. In the second case, the Equal Employment Opportunity Commission brought suit against Abercrombie for refusing to hire a Muslim woman who wore a head scarf in violation of the company's dress code. The Court held that the company's actions amounted to religious discrimination in hiring—a violation of something not allowed by federal law.

The First Amendment and Freedom of Speech and the Press

Because democracy depends on an open political process, freedom of speech and freedom of the press are considered critical. In 1938, freedom of speech (which in all important respects includes freedom of the press)

Americans' Attitudes Toward Church and State

Contributed by
David E. Campbell
University of Notre Dame

Almost all Americans agree that their nation has a separation of church and state, but translating the abstract principle of church–state separation into practice is often contentious. The phrase *separation of church and state* does not actually appear in the Constitution, but religion is mentioned twice in the document.

The first mention of religion is in the First Amendment, which states that "Congress shall make no law respecting an establishment of religion, or prohibiting the free exercise thereof." These two phrases have come to be known as the establishment and free exercise clauses.

A national survey asked Americans about their attitudes toward two applications of the First Amendment: whether the Ten Commandments can be displayed on government property such as courthouses or legislatures (the establishment clause) and whether public schools should be able to ban religious dress such as Muslim head scarves (the free exercise clause). The two graphs below compare the views of Republicans, Independents, and Democrats.

Should the Ten Commandments Be Displayed on Government Property?

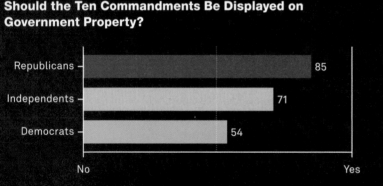

Should Public Schools Be Able to Ban Religious Dress, Such as Muslim Headscarves?

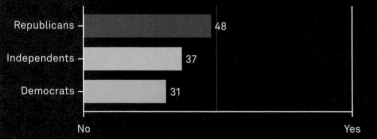

In this study, respondents placed their opinion on a 0–100 scale between "should be allowed" and "should not be allowed." The findings show that most Americans do not have a problem with the display of the Ten Commandments, although Democrats are more likely to object than Republicans. Democrats are also more likely to think that public schools should not be able to prevent students from wearing religious dress at school, but the partisan differences are more muted.

SOURCE: David E. Campbell, Geoffrey C. Layman, and John C. Green, "Secularism in America Study."

The second place that the Constitution mentions religion is Article VI, which says that "no religious test shall ever be required as a qualification to any office or public trust under the United States." Yet while formal religious tests are expressly forbidden, historically some voters have been unwilling to vote for candidates with particular religious backgrounds.

The graph below displays historical trends in the percentage of Americans who say that they would vote for a presidential candidate (from their preferred party) who is Catholic, Jewish, Mormon, Muslim, or Atheist.

Would You Vote for a _____ Candidate?

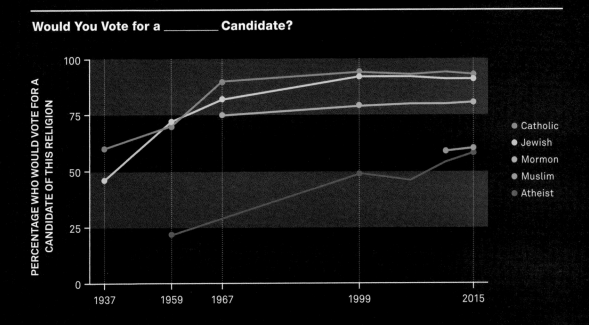

Over the decades, the percentage of Americans who say that they would vote for a Catholic or Jewish presidential candidate has risen steeply (and, of course, in 1960 Americans elected John F. Kennedy, a Catholic). The percentage saying that they would vote for a Mormon has risen only a little since the 1960s. Thus when Mitt Romney, a Mormon, ran for the presidency in 2012, he faced opposition to his religion that was comparable to the anti-Catholicism faced by Kennedy in 1960. While Americans are significantly more willing to vote for an atheist today than in the 1950s, in 2015 only 58 percent of Americans said they would be willing to vote for an atheist. This is comparable to the percentage willing to vote for a Muslim (60 percent). Antagonism toward atheist and Muslim candidates today is about the same as the opposition faced by Catholics and Jews in the 1930s.

SOURCES: Results through 2007: Jeffrey M. Jones, February 20, 2007, www.gallup.com/poll/26611/Some-Americans-Reluctant-Vote-Mormon-72Year%20Old-Presidential-Candidates.aspx (accessed 2/26/2016); 2012 results: Jeffrey M. Jones, June 21, 2012, www.gallup.com/poll/155285/atheists-muslims-bias-presidential-candidates.aspx (accessed 2/26/2016); 2015 results: Frank Newport, September 22, 2015, www.gallup.com/opinion/polling-matters/185813/six-americans-say-yes-muslim-president.aspx (accessed 2/26/2016).
NOTE: Not all religions were included in every year.

was given extraordinary constitutional status when the Supreme Court established that any legislation attempting to restrict these fundamental freedoms "is to be subjected to a more exacting judicial scrutiny . . . than are most other types of legislation."[28]

The Court was saying that the democratic political process must be protected at almost any cost. This higher standard of judicial review came to be called strict scrutiny. Strict scrutiny implies that speech—at least some kinds of speech—occupies a "preferred" position and will be protected almost absolutely. In 2011, for example, the Court ruled 8–1 that members of Westboro Baptist Church, a tiny Kansas institution, had a First Amendment right to picket the funerals of American soldiers killed in action while displaying signs reading "Thank God for Dead Soldiers." The church teaches that these deaths represent divine punishment for America's tolerance of homosexuality and other matters. In his opinion, Chief Justice John Roberts wrote, "As a nation we have chosen to protect even hurtful speech on public issues to ensure that we do not stifle public debate."[29] But even though we do protect many types of speech with which most Americans strongly disagree, only some are fully protected. Many are less so—even though they are entitled to strict scrutiny.

Political Speech. Since the 1920s, political speech has been consistently protected by the courts even when it has been deemed "insulting" or "outrageous." In the 1969 case *Brandenburg v. Ohio,* the Supreme Court ruled that as long as speech falls short of actually "inciting or producing imminently lawless action," it cannot be prohibited, even if it is hostile to or subversive of the government and its policies.

This case involved a Ku Klux Klan leader, Charles Brandenburg, who had been convicted of advocating "revengent" action against the president, Congress, and the Supreme Court, among others, if they continued "to suppress the white, Caucasian race." Although Brandenburg was not carrying a weapon, some members of his audience were. Nevertheless, the Court reversed the state courts and freed Brandenburg while declaring Ohio's Criminal Syndicalism Act unconstitutional because it punished persons who "advocate, or teach the duty, necessity, or propriety [of violence] as a means of accomplishing industrial or political reform" or who publish materials or "voluntarily assemble…to teach or advocate the doctrines of criminal syndicalism." The Court argued that the statute did not distinguish "mere advocacy" from "incitement to imminent lawless action." It would be difficult to go much further in protecting freedom of speech. Typically, courts strike down restrictions on speech if they are deemed to be "overbroad," "vague," or lacking "neutrality"—for example, if a statute prohibited the views of the political left but not the political right, or vice versa.

Another area of expansion of political speech—the loosening of limits on spending and donations in political campaigns—was opened up in 1976 with the Supreme Court's decision in *Buckley v. Valeo*.[30] Campaign finance reform laws of the early 1970s, arising out of the Watergate scandal, had put severe limits on campaign spending. But the Court declared a number of important provisions unconstitutional on the basis of a new principle that spending money by or on behalf of candidates is a form of speech protected by the First Amendment (as contrasted with contributions to campaigns, which Congress has more authority to regulate). The issue arose again in 2003, after passage of a still stricter campaign finance law, the Bipartisan Campaign Reform Act of 2002 (BCRA). This time, the Court's majority seriously reduced the area of speech protected by *Buckley v. Valeo,* holding that Congress was within its power to limit the amounts individuals could spend, the amounts of "soft money" corporations and their PACs could spend, and the amounts spent on issue advertising prior to Election Day.[31] This decision was the anomaly, however. In 2007, the Court struck down a key portion of BCRA, finding that the act's limitations on political advertising violated the First Amendment's guarantee of free speech.[32] In *Citizens United v. Federal Election Commission*, in 2010, the Court ruled that corporate funding of independent election ads could not be limited under the First Amendment.[33] And in 2014, the Court struck down aggregate limits on an individual's contributions to candidates for federal office, political parties, and political action committees. As a result of this decision, several wealthy donors have contributed more than $10 million to presidential candidates in 2016.

Symbolic Speech, Speech Plus Action, and the Rights of Assembly and Petition. The First Amendment treats the freedoms of assembly and petition as equal to the freedoms of religion and political speech. Assembly and petition are closely associated with speech but go beyond it to speech associated with action. Since at least 1931, the Supreme Court has sought to protect actions that are designed to send a political message. Thus although the Court upheld a federal statute making it a crime to burn draft cards to protest the Vietnam War on the grounds that the government had a compelling interest in preserving draft cards as part of the conduct of the war itself, it considered the wearing of black armbands to school a protected form of assembly. In such cases, a court will often use the standard articulated in the draft card case, *United States v. O'Brien*, and now known as the *O'Brien* test.[34] Under this test, a statute restricting expressive or symbolic speech must be justified by a compelling government interest and be narrowly tailored toward achieving that interest.

Another example of symbolic speech is the burning of the American flag as a symbol of protest. In 1984, at a rally during the Republican National

Convention in Dallas, a political protester burned an American flag in violation of a Texas statute that prohibited desecration of a venerated object. In a 5–4 decision, the Supreme Court declared the Texas law unconstitutional on the grounds that flag burning is expressive conduct protected by the First Amendment.[35] Subsequent efforts in Congress to make flag burning a federal crime were probably killed by the Supreme Court's 2003 decision striking down a Virginia cross-burning statute.[36] In that case, the Court ruled that states could make cross burning a crime only if the statute required prosecutors to prove that the act was intended to intimidate rather than simply express opinion.

Closer to the original intent of the assembly and petition clause is the category of speech plus—following speech with physical activities such as picketing, distributing leaflets, and other forms of peaceful demonstration or assembly. Such activities are consistently protected by courts under the First Amendment; state and local laws regulating them are closely scrutinized and frequently overturned.

Freedom of the Press. Freedom of speech includes freedom of the press. With the exception of broadcast media, which are subject to federal regulation, the press is protected under the doctrine prohibiting prior restraint. Beginning in 1931,[37] the Supreme Court has held that except under extraordinary circumstances, the First Amendment prohibits government agencies from seeking to prevent newspapers or magazines from publishing whatever they wish.

Libel, Slander, Obscenity, and Pornography. Some speech is not protected at all. If a written statement is made in "reckless disregard of the truth" and is considered damaging to the victim because it is "malicious, scandalous, and defamatory," it can be punished as libel. An oral statement of such nature can be punished as slander.

Today most libel suits involve freedom of the press. Historically, newspapers were subject to the law of libel, whereby newspapers that printed false and malicious stories could be compelled to pay damages to those they defamed. Recently, however, American courts have narrowed the meaning of libel and made it extremely difficult, particularly for public figures, to win a libel case against a newspaper.

If libel and slander cases involve difficult problems of determining whether statements are true and malicious and damaging, cases involving pornography and obscenity can be even stickier. It is easy to say that these fall outside the realm of protected speech, but it is impossible to define clearly where protection ends and unprotected speech begins. All attempts by the courts to define pornography and obscenity have proved impractical because each instance required courts to screen thousands of pages of print material or feet of film alleged to be pornographic.

speech plus
Speech accompanied by activities such as sit-ins, picketing, and demonstrations. Protection of this form of speech under the First Amendment is conditional, and restrictions imposed by state or local authorities are acceptable if properly balanced by considerations of public order.

prior restraint
An effort by a government agency to block the publication of material it deems libelous or harmful in some other way; censorship. In the United States, the courts forbid prior restraint except under extraordinary circumstances.

libel
A written statement made in "reckless disregard of the truth" and considered damaging to a victim because it is "malicious, scandalous, and defamatory"

slander
An oral statement made in "reckless disregard of the truth" and considered damaging to a victim because it is "malicious, scandalous, and defamatory"

In recent years, the battle against obscene speech has focused on Internet pornography, which opponents argue should be banned because of the easy access children have to the Internet. The first significant effort to regulate such content occurred in 1996, when Congress attached to a major telecommunications bill an amendment, the Communications Decency Act (CDA), designed to regulate the online transmission of obscene material. In the 1997 case *Reno v. ACLU*, the Supreme Court struck down the CDA, ruling that it suppressed speech that "adults have a constitutional right to receive."[38] Congress tried again with the 2001 Children's Internet Protection Act, which required public libraries to install antipornography filters on all library computers with Internet access. In 2003, the Court upheld this law, asserting that it did not violate library patrons' First Amendment rights.[39] Other conflicts have focused on the use of children in pornography rather than their access to it. In 2003, Congress enacted the Prosecutorial Remedies and Other Tools to end the Exploitation of Children Today (PROTECT) Act, which outlawed efforts to sell child pornography via the Internet. The Supreme Court upheld this act in the 2008 case of *United States v. Williams*.[40]

Fighting Words and Hate Speech. Speech can also lose its protected position when it moves from the symbolic realm toward the sphere of action. "Expressive speech," for example, is protected until it becomes direct incitement of damaging conduct with the use of fighting words. In 1942, the Supreme Court upheld the arrest and conviction of a man who had violated a state law forbidding the use of offensive language in public. He had called the arresting officer a "goddamned racketeer" and "a damn Fascist." The Court held that the First Amendment provides no protection for such offensive words because they "are no essential part of any exposition of ideas."[41] Since that time, however, the Court has reversed almost every conviction based on arguments that the speaker had used "fighting words." But this is not an absolutely settled area.

> **fighting words**
> Speech that directly incites damaging conduct

Many jurisdictions have drafted ordinances banning forms of expression that assert hatred toward a specific group, be it African Americans, Jews, Muslims, or others. Such ordinances seldom pass constitutional muster. The leading Supreme Court case in this realm is the 1992 decision in *R.A.V. v. City of St. Paul*.[42] Here, a white teenager was arrested for burning a cross on the lawn of a black family in violation of a municipal ordinance that banned cross burning. The Court ruled that the ordinance was not content neutral, because it prohibited only cross burning—typically an expression of hatred of African Americans. Since a statute banning all forms of hateful expression would be deemed overly broad, the *R.A.V.* standard suggests that virtually all hate speech is constitutionally protected.

Commercial Speech. Commercial speech, such as newspaper or television advertising, does not have full First Amendment protection because it cannot be considered political speech. Some commercial speech is still unprotected and therefore regulated. For example, regulation of false and misleading advertising by the Federal Trade Commission is a well-established power of the federal government. The Supreme Court long ago upheld the constitutionality of laws prohibiting the electronic media from carrying cigarette advertising.[43] However, gains far outweigh losses in the effort to expand the protection commercial speech enjoys. As the scholar Louis Fisher explains, "In part, this reflects the growing appreciation that commercial speech is part of the free flow of information necessary for informed choice and democratic participation."[44] For example, in a 2001 case, the Court ruled that a Massachusetts ban on all cigarette advertising violated the tobacco industry's First Amendment right to advertise its products to adult consumers.[45]

The Second Amendment and the Right to Bear Arms

The purpose of the Second Amendment is to provide for militias; they were to be the government's backup for the maintenance of local public order. The framers understood *militia* to be a military or police resource for state governments; militias were distinguished from armies and troops, which came within the sole constitutional jurisdiction of Congress. Some groups, though, have always argued that the Second Amendment also establishes an individual right to bear arms.

The mass shooting of twenty first graders in Newtown, Connecticut in 2012 fueled renewed calls for gun control legislation. In the years following, President Obama issued several executive orders on gun control, but staunch opposition on second amendment grounds has prevented any significant national legislation.

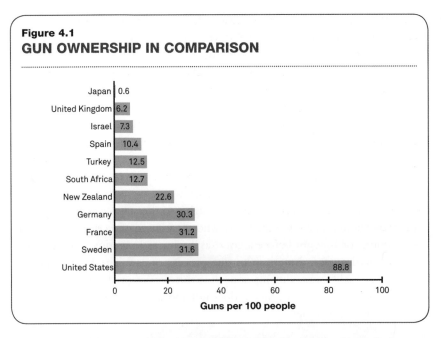

Figure 4.1
GUN OWNERSHIP IN COMPARISON

Japan 0.6
United Kingdom 6.2
Israel 7.3
Spain 10.4
Turkey 12.5
South Africa 12.7
New Zealand 22.6
Germany 30.3
France 31.2
Sweden 31.6
United States 88.8

Guns per 100 people

SOURCE: Sydney Lupkin, "U.S. Has More Guns—And Gun Deaths—Than Any Other Country, Study Finds," ABC News, September 19, 2013, http://abcnews.go.com/blogs/health/2013/09/19/u-s-hasmore-guns-and-gun-deaths-than-any-other-country-study-finds/ (accessed 5/23/16).

The judicial record of Second Amendment cases is far sparser than for First Amendment cases, and for almost 60 years, the Court made no Second Amendment decisions. The United States has a higher gun ownership rate than any other developed country (see Figure 4.1 for a comparison with selected countries). Within the United States, there is no single national policy, and different states and localities have very different gun ownership standards. For instance, in Wyoming, there is no ban on owning any type of gun, no waiting period to purchase a firearm, and no permit required to carry a concealed weapon. In California, in contrast, the possession of assault weapons is banned, there is a 10-day waiting period to purchase a firearm, and a permit is required to carry a concealed weapon. In Virginia, individuals may practice "open carry" of handguns without a permit but require a license to carry a concealed weapon. In a 2008 decision, the Supreme Court ruled that the federal government could not prohibit individuals from owning guns for self-defense in their homes.[46] The case involved a District of Columbia ordinance that made it virtually impossible for residents to possess firearms legally. In the majority opinion, Justice Antonin Scalia stated that the decision was not intended to cast doubt on all laws limiting firearm possession, such as the prohibition on gun ownership by felons or the mentally ill. In his dissenting opinion, Justice John Paul Stephens asserted that the Second

Amendment protects the right to bear arms only as part of a militia force, not in an individual capacity. The District of Columbia is an entity of the federal government, and the Court did not indicate that its ruling applied to state firearms laws. However, in a 2010 case, the Court struck down a Chicago firearms ordinance and applied the Second Amendment to the states as well.[47] Despite these rulings, the debate over gun control continues to loom large in American politics today, fueled by a recent series of mass shootings.

Rights of the Criminally Accused

Most of the battle to apply the Bill of Rights to the states was fought over the protections granted to individuals who are accused of a crime, suspected of a crime, or brought before a court as a witness to a crime. The Bill of Rights entitles every American to due process of law. The Fourth, Fifth, Sixth, and Eighth amendments constitute the essence of due process, even though this fundamental concept does not appear until the very last words of the Fifth Amendment.

due process

Proceeding according to law and with adequate protection for individual rights

The Fourth Amendment and Searches and Seizures. The purpose of the Fourth Amendment is to guarantee the security of citizens against unreasonable (that is, improper) searches and seizures. In 1990, the Supreme Court summarized its understanding of this amendment: "A search compromises the individual interest in privacy; a seizure deprives the individual of dominion over his or her person or property."[48]

The exclusionary rule, which prohibits evidence obtained during an illegal search from being introduced in a trial, is the most severe restraint ever imposed by the Constitution and the courts on the behavior of the police. It is a dramatic restriction because it often rules out precisely the evidence that produces a conviction; it frees people who are *known* to have committed the crime of which they were accused. For this reason, in recent years the federal courts have shifted to a discretionary application of the exclusionary rule, whereby they make a judgment as to the "nature and quality of the intrusion." It is thus difficult to know ahead of time whether a defendant will or will not be protected from an illegal search under the Fourth Amendment.[49]

The Fourth Amendment also applies to electronic searches and government surveillance. For example, the Apple Corporation cited its Fourth Amendment rights when it refused to provide the FBI with the information that would have been needed to access an iPhone belonging to Syed Farook, the alleged terrorist who killed 14 of his coworkers in San Bernardino, California, in 2015. The agency did not wait for a court to rule on the claim but, instead, hired a hacker to break into the phone. In the matter of surveillance, one of the most pressing issues facing the federal courts today is the extent to which the government may eavesdrop on Americans' e-mail and phone calls as it seeks to prevent terrorist attacks.

The Fifth Amendment. The right of a suspect to have a grand jury determine whether a prosecutor has sufficient evidence to bring criminal charges is "the oldest institution known to the Constitution."[50] Grand juries play an important role in federal criminal cases. However, the provision for a grand jury is the one important civil liberties provision of the Bill of Rights that the Supreme Court has not incorporated into the Fourteenth Amendment and applied to state criminal prosecutions. Thus some states operate without grand juries: the prosecuting attorney simply files a "bill of information" affirming that sufficient evidence is available to justify a trial.

The Fifth Amendment also provides the constitutional protection from double jeopardy, or being tried more than once for the same crime, and the guarantee that no citizen "shall be compelled in any criminal case to be a witness against himself." This protection against self-incrimination led to the *Miranda* case and the *Miranda* rules that police must follow when questioning an arrested criminal suspect.

Another fundamental part of the Fifth Amendment is the "takings clause," which extends to each citizen a protection against the taking of private property "without just compensation." Although this clause does not concern protecting persons accused of crimes, it does deal with an important instance where the government and the citizen are adversaries. As discussed earlier, the power of government to take private property for a public use is called eminent domain.

The Sixth Amendment and the Right to Counsel. Some provisions of the Sixth Amendment, such as the right to a speedy trial and the right to confront witnesses before an impartial jury, are not very controversial in nature. The "right to counsel" provision, however, like the exclusionary rule of the Fourth Amendment and the self-incrimination clause of the Fifth Amendment, is notable for freeing defendants who seem patently guilty as charged.

Gideon v. Wainwright is the perfect case study because it involved a disreputable person who seemed patently guilty of the crime for which he was convicted. In and out of jails for most of his 51 years, Clarence Earl Gideon received a five-year sentence for breaking into and entering a poolroom in Panama City, Florida. While serving time, Gideon became a fairly well-qualified "jailhouse lawyer," made his own appeal on a handwritten petition, and eventually won the landmark ruling on the right to counsel in all felony cases.[51] In 1964, the year after the *Gideon* decision, the Supreme Court ruled that suspects had a right to counsel during police interrogations, not just when their cases reached trial.[52] The right to counsel has since been

grand jury
A jury that determines whether sufficient evidence is available to justify a trial. Grand juries do not rule on the accused's guilt or innocence.

expanded further to encompass the quality of the counsel provided. For example, in 2003 the Court overturned a death sentence on the grounds that the defense lawyer had failed to fully inform the jury of the defendant's history of "horrendous childhood abuse."[53]

The Eighth Amendment and Cruel and Unusual Punishment.
The Eighth Amendment prohibits "excessive bail," "excessive fines," and "cruel and unusual punishment," but virtually all debate over Eighth Amendment issues focuses on the last of these provisions. One of the greatest challenges in interpreting it consistently is that what is considered "cruel and unusual" varies from culture to culture and from generation to generation. Unfortunately, it also varies by class and race.

The most important questions concerning cruel and unusual punishment are raised by the use of the death penalty. Some Americans believe that execution is inherently cruel, but in its consideration of the death penalty the Supreme Court has generally avoided this question. In 1972, the Supreme Court overturned several state death-penalty laws not because they were cruel and unusual but because they were being applied in a capricious manner.[54] Since 1976, the Court has consistently upheld state laws providing for capital punishment, although it continues to review numerous death-penalty appeals each year.

Constitutional objections to the death penalty often invoke the Eighth Amendment's protection against punishments that are "cruel and unusual." Yet supporters of the death penalty say it can hardly be considered a violation of this protection since it was commonly used in the eighteenth century and was supported by most early American leaders.

The Right to Privacy

right to privacy

The right to be left alone, which has been interpreted by the Supreme Court to entail individual access to birth control and abortions

When the Supreme Court began to take a more activist role in the mid-1950s and 1960s, the idea of a right to privacy gained traction. The Constitution does not specifically mention such a right, but the Ninth Amendment declares that the rights enumerated in the Constitution are not an exhaustive list. In 1958, the Court recognized "privacy in one's association" in its decision to prevent the state of Alabama from using the NAACP membership list in the state's investigations. The sphere of privacy was drawn in earnest in 1965, when the Court ruled that a Connecticut statute forbidding the use of contraceptives violated the right of marital privacy. Justice William O. Douglas, writing for the majority in *Griswold v. Connecticut*, argued that this right of privacy is also grounded in the Constitution because it fits into a "zone of privacy" created by a combination of the Third, Fourth, and Fifth amendments. The right to privacy was extended in 1973 in one of the most important Supreme Court decisions in American history: *Roe v. Wade*. This decision established a woman's right to seek an abortion and prohibited states from making abortion a criminal act prior to the point at which the fetus becomes viable, which in 1973 was the twenty-seventh week of pregnancy.[55]

In recent decades, the right to be left alone began to include the privacy rights of gay men and lesbians. In Atlanta in 1982, Michael Hardwick was arrested by a police officer who discovered him in bed with another man and was charged under Georgia's law against sodomy. Hardwick filed a suit challenging the constitutionality of the law and won his case in the federal court of appeals. The state of Georgia appealed the court's decision to the Supreme Court, whose majority reversed the lower-court decision, holding against Hardwick on the grounds that "the federal Constitution confers [no] fundamental right upon homosexuals to engage in sodomy" and that there was therefore no basis to invalidate "the laws of the many states that still make such conduct illegal and have done so for a very long time."[56] With *Lawrence v. Texas* in 2003, however, the Court overturned its 1986 decision in *Bowers v. Hardwick*, and state legislatures no longer had the authority to make private sexual behavior a crime.[57] The majority opinion maintained, "In our tradition the State is not omnipresent in the home. And there are other spheres of our lives and existence outside the home, where the State should not be a dominant presence." Explicitly encompassing lesbians and gay men within the umbrella of privacy, the Court concluded that the "petitioners are entitled to respect for their private lives. The State cannot demean their existence or control their destiny by making their private sexual conduct a crime." This decision added substance to the idea that the Ninth Amendment allows for the "right to privacy."

Another area ripe for litigation and public discourse is the so-called right to die. A number of highly publicized physician-assisted suicides have focused attention on whether people have a right to choose their own death and receive assistance in carrying it out. Will this become part of the privacy right, or perhaps be accepted as a new kind of right? In the 2006 case of *Gonzales v. Oregon*, the Supreme Court upheld an Oregon law that allowed doctors to use drugs to facilitate the deaths of terminally ill patients who requested such assistance.[58] This decision is not a definitive ruling on the right-to-die question, but it does suggest that the Court is not hostile to the idea.

CIVIL RIGHTS

Civil rights are the rules that government must follow in the treatment of individuals when collective decisions are made. Some civil rights concern who can be involved in collective decisions and how. Others concern how people are treated in civil society, including who has access to public facilities, such as schools and public hospitals. Increasingly, civil rights have extended to private spheres, including the right to work, the right to marry, and the question of whether clubs and organizations can exclude people on the basis of gender or race. Even when no legal right to something currently exists, such a right may be asserted as a matter of justice or morality. When there is a demand for new civil rights, society must decide whether and how rights should be extended.

Civil rights encompass three features: who, what, and how much. *Who* has a right and who does not? A right to *what*? And *how much* is any individual allowed to exercise that right? Consider the right to vote. The "what," of course, is the vote. The "who" concerns which persons are allowed to vote. Today all U.S. citizens 18 years of age and older are eligible to vote. Some states impose additional criteria, such as requirements that voters show photo IDs or prohibitions on voting by ex-felons. The "how much" concerns whether that right can be exercised equally—whether some people's votes count more than others' or whether election laws create greater obstacles for some people than for others. For instance, until the mid-1960s, the California State Senate had one senator from Los Angeles County, with 6 million people, and one senator from Inyo County, with 14,000 people. The votes of the 14,000 people translated into the same amount of representation in the state senate as the votes of the 6 million people. The U.S. Supreme Court ruled that such arrangements violated the equal protection clause and hence the civil rights of those in the more populous counties.

In the course of American history, two principles have emerged that answer "who" enjoys civil rights and "how much." First, civil rights ought to be universal—all persons should enjoy them. Second, they ought to be equal—all persons who enjoy a civil right ought to be allowed an equal ability or opportunity to practice that right. However, in practice, these principles have not always been applied.

What civil rights we enjoy and who has them are political decisions. The Constitution sets forth a small number of civil rights. The Bill of Rights asserted a larger number of legal rights. But many of the civil rights we enjoy now were left to Congress and the states to determine. Thus most of our civil rights are the result of legislation, litigation, and administration that occurred after the country was founded.

The Struggle for Voting Rights

Some of the most profound debates and divisions in American society have concerned *who* has civil rights, because those who already have those rights, such as the right to vote, are asked to extend them to those who do not.

At the time of the Founding, most states granted voting rights exclusively to white male property owners. Many states also imposed religious criteria, forbidding Catholics or Jews from voting, running for office, and engaging in other public activities. White, male property owners had disproportionate political power in 1787 because they alone had voting rights while no one else did. In order to expand voting rights to other groups, those who had power had to decide to remove property and religious qualifications, extend voting rights to women and blacks, and loosen other restrictions, such as age.

Property qualifications for voters were the first restrictions to be lifted by the various states. Throughout the first half of the nineteenth century, states began to shed the requirement that people hold property in order to vote or run for office, especially as the economy became more industrial and less agricultural, with many people moving to cities for work and thus becoming less likely to own property. By 1850, property qualifications were eliminated. Even still, many states had poll taxes well into the twentieth century: voters had to pay a nominal amount, such as $2, every time they voted. Poll taxes abridged the civil rights of poor people and often also served to discriminate against blacks. The Twenty-Fourth Amendment to the Constitution eliminated poll taxes in 1964.

The restrictions on the right to vote based on religion and property were removed with relatively little protest. The struggle to extend voting rights to women and to racial and ethnic minorities proved much more contentious, however, fueling two of the greatest struggles in American political history. The conflict over race runs so deep in U.S. politics that we will discuss that matter more broadly in the next section.

Women's Suffrage. In the early 1800s, few state or local governments granted women voting rights. It took an entire century of agitation and activism, of protest and political maneuvering, to guarantee those rights. In the decades prior to the Civil War, attitudes about women's civil rights began to change, in part because of practical problems related to property, inheritance, and settlement in new states and territories. The United States adopted laws of inheritance and property from Britain, which granted men control over all property, but those laws proved problematic in a country of settlers rather than established families and classes. It is no coincidence that many of the newer states, such as Indiana and Kentucky, were the first to give women economic rights. Around the same time, American women began to organize to advance their political and social rights, including the right to vote. In 1848, women and men attending the Seneca Falls Convention issued the "Declaration of Sentiments and Resolutions," asserting that women were entitled to rights in every way equal to those of men.

In 1869, the National Woman Suffrage Association (NWSA) was formed and began an effort to amend the U.S. Constitution to allow women to vote.

It took over a century of activism and protests for women to win the right to vote in national elections. Before the passage of the Nineteenth Amendment in 1920, activists picketed and organized marches, attracting thousands of participants.

By the 1880s, the issue of voting rights for women was the subject of mass meetings, parades, and protests, and by 1917, NWSA had 2 million members. By 1918, all of the western states and territories plus Michigan and New York had granted women full suffrage. Once a critical mass of states had acted, it was only a matter of time before federal law followed. In 1919, Congress ratified the Nineteenth Amendment, granting women the right to vote in federal elections.[59] Two months later, the amendment was ratified by the states, and women across the United States voted in the presidential election of 1920.

The Right to Vote for Black Americans. The struggle to extend full voting rights to racial minorities, especially blacks, reflects even deeper divisions in American society. It took a full century after the Civil War for Congress to guarantee minorities' voting rights with the Voting Rights Act of 1965, and the battle to protect those rights continues today.

The Fifteenth Amendment to the Constitution gives blacks voting rights, and during Reconstruction, the federal government enforced those rights. Following withdrawal of federal troops from the South, however, state legislatures and local governments there (and elsewhere) enacted practices that excluded blacks from elections or weakened their political power. In many states, blacks were excluded from primary elections, a practice called the "white primary." Poll taxes, literacy tests, registration list purges, and other tactics were used to keep blacks from voting.[60] District and municipal boundaries were drawn to place blacks in jurisdictions in which they had little or no impact on the election of representatives or the approval of public expenditures.[61]

Blacks had little hope of changing state law because state legislators had benefited electorally from them. Congress was also reluctant to pass federal legislation to enforce the Fifteenth Amendment. At last, the Supreme Court intervened. It struck down the white primary in *Smith v. Allwright* in 1944, and asserted the federal government's power to intervene in states' conduct of elections in order to protect blacks' voting rights.[62] The Court acted again in 1960, ruling that state and local governments could not draw election district boundaries so as to discriminate against blacks.[63] In 1965, Congress finally took action with the Voting Rights Act, sweeping aside many state laws and practices that had served to discriminate against blacks. That act has been amended several times to expand who is covered, including Hispanics (1975) and language groups (1982), and what sorts of activities are prohibited, most notably racial gerrymandering (see Chapter 5). In 2013, the Supreme Court declared unconstitutional an important section of the Voting Rights Act in *Shelby County v. Holder.* This section—Section 4(b)—obligated jurisdictions in Alabama, Alaska, Arizona, Georgia, Louisiana, Mississippi, South Carolina, and Texas, as well as municipalities and counties in some other states, to obtain approval of any change in election administration procedures from the Department of Justice or the Federal District Court in the District of Columbia—a procedure called *preclearance.* Other parts of the act still hold, however, and the *Shelby County* decision shifts the legal battles to those sections.[64] It also puts the question of preclearance back on Congress's agenda.

Thus the fight over minority voting rights continues. New administrative procedures, such as laws requiring that voters show a government-issued photo ID, and the redrawing of legislative district maps every 10 years, are subject to intense debate. There are frequent allegations that these practices or the way they are applied affect minorities' voting rights adversely and even embody intentional discrimination. Disputes over these laws often end up in federal courts. Since the 1960s, the courts—and not legislatures—have become the arena in which minorities, poor people, city dwellers, and many others can argue for the protection of their voting rights.

Racial Discrimination after the Fourteenth Amendment

As we saw at the start of the chapter, the Fourteenth Amendment's equal protection clause guaranteed equal protection of the laws to all Americans. However, the Supreme Court was initially no more ready to enforce the civil rights aspects of the Fourteenth Amendment than it was to enforce the civil liberties provisions discussed earlier.

equal protection clause

The provision of the Fourteenth Amendment guaranteeing citizens "the equal protection of the laws." This clause has served as the basis for the civil rights of African Americans, women, and other groups.

***Plessy v. Ferguson:* "Separate but Equal."** The Court declared the Civil Rights Act of 1875 unconstitutional on the ground that it sought to protect blacks against discrimination by private businesses, whereas the Fourteenth Amendment, according to the Court's interpretation, was intended to protect only against discrimination by *public* officials of state and local governments. In 1896, the Court went further, in the infamous *Plessy v. Ferguson* case, by upholding a Louisiana statute that required racial segregation on trolleys and other public carriers (and by implication in all public facilities, including schools). The Court held that the Fourteenth Amendment's "equal protection of the laws" was not violated by racial distinction as long as the law applied to both races equally.[65] Many people generally pretended that blacks were treated equally as long as some accommodation existed. In effect, the Court was saying that it was not unreasonable to use race as a basis of exclusion in public matters. This was the origin of the "separate but equal" rule that was not reversed until 1954.

"separate but equal" rule

The doctrine that public accommodations could be segregated by race but still be equal

Challenging "Separate but Equal." The Supreme Court had begun to change its position regarding racial discrimination before World War II by defining more strictly the criterion of equal facilities under the "separate but equal" rule. Notably, in 1938, the Court rejected Missouri's policy of paying the tuition of qualified blacks to out-of-state law schools rather than admitting them to the University of Missouri Law School.[66] After the war, modest progress resumed. In 1950, the Court rejected Texas's claim that its new "law school for Negroes" afforded education equal to that of the all-white University of Texas Law School. The Court's decision anticipated *Brown v. Board of Education* by opening the question of whether *any* segregated facility could be truly equal.[67]

As the Supreme Court was ordering the admission of blacks to all-white state law schools, it was also striking down the southern practice of white primaries, which legally excluded blacks from participation in the nominating process.[68] The most important pre-1954 decision was probably *Shelley v. Kraemer*, in which the Court ruled against the practice of "restrictive convenants," whereby the seller of a home added a clause to the sales contract requiring the buyer to agree not to resell the home to a non-Caucasian, non-Christian, and so on.[69]

Although none of those cases confronted "separate but equal" and the principle of racial discrimination as such, they gave black leaders encouragement enough to believe that at last they had an opportunity and enough legal precedent to change the constitutional framework itself. By the fall of 1952, plaintiffs had brought cases to the Supreme Court from Kansas, South Carolina, Virginia, Delaware, and the District of Columbia challenging the constitutionality of school segregation. Of these, the Kansas case became the focal point. It had the special advantage of being located in a state outside the South, which would lessen local resistance to a decision outlawing segregation.[70]

Student Nonviolent Coordinating Committee (SNCC) formed to organize protests, sit-ins, freedom rides

Interstate Commerce Commission **orders desegregation** on all buses, on all trains, and in terminals; President John F. Kennedy favors executive action over civil rights legislation

First substantive Civil Rights Act, primarily guaranteeing voting rights

President Kennedy shifts gears, **supporting strong civil rights law**; President Lyndon B. Johnson asserts strong support for civil rights

Nonviolent demonstrations in Birmingham, Alabama, lead to King's arrest and "Letter from Birmingham Jail"; march on Washington

Congress passes historic **Civil Rights Act** covering voting, employment, public accommodations, education

King announces drive to register 3 million black voters in the South

Voting Rights Act

War on Poverty in full swing

Movement dissipates but remains focusing on litigation, community action programs, antiwar protest, and more militant Black Power actions

| 1960 | 1961 | 1962 | 1963 | 1964 | 1965 | 1966 |

to white Americans now be recognized and protected for black Americans, too. By the 1960s, the many organizations making up the civil rights movement had accumulated experience and built networks capable of launching massive direct-action campaigns against southern segregationists. The Southern Christian Leadership Conference, the Student Nonviolent Coordinating Committee, and many other organizations had built a movement across the South that used the media to attract nationwide attention and support. In the massive March on Washington in 1963, the Reverend Martin Luther King, Jr., staked out the movement's moral claims in his "I Have a Dream" speech. Also in the 1960s, images of protesters being beaten, attacked by police dogs, and set on with fire hoses did much to win broad sympathy for the black civil rights cause and discredit state and local governments in the South. In this way, the movement created intense pressure for a reluctant federal government to take more assertive steps to defend black civil rights.

Protests against discriminatory practices toward African Americans did not end in the 1960s. In recent years, a variety of protests have coalesced under the banner "Black Lives Matter" to focus attention on allegations of police misconduct directed at African Americans. The movement took off in Ferguson,

Missouri, in 2014 after the shooting of an unarmed black teenager by a white police officer. It spread across the nation as the media carried reports, photos, and videos of police violence against blacks in Chicago, South Carolina, Baltimore, New York, and other cities. African Americans had long asserted that they were often victims of racial profiling and more likely than whites to be harassed, physically harmed, or arrested by the police. Police departments had always replied that blacks were more likely than whites to be engaged in criminal activity. However, reports and video recordings of killings proved difficult for the police to justify and seemed likely to lead to new rules governing police behavior.

Opportunity in Education

Education has been the focus of some of the most important battles over civil rights, largely because Americans believe that everyone should have an equal chance to succeed. Inequities in educational opportunities were painfully obvious in the 1950s. Poverty rates of blacks far exceeded those of whites. Equal access to quality education, it was thought, would reduce and perhaps eliminate those inequities.

School Desegregation. Although the District of Columbia and some school districts in border states responded almost immediately to court-ordered desegregation, states in the Deep South responded with delaying tactics. Southern legislatures passed laws ordering school districts to maintain segregated schools and state superintendents to withhold state funding from racially mixed classrooms.

Most of these plans were tested in the federal courts and were struck down as unconstitutional.[72] But southern resistance went beyond legislation. Perhaps the most serious incident occurred in Arkansas in 1957. On the first day of school, a mob assembled at Little Rock Central High School to protest integration and block black students from attending. Governor Orval Faubus ordered the Arkansas National Guard to prevent enforcement of a federal court order to integrate the school. When President Eisenhower deployed U.S. troops and placed the city under martial law, Faubus responded by closing all the city's public high schools. In 1959, the Supreme Court ordered the schools reopened.

As the southern states invented new devices to avoid desegregation, it became clear that the federal courts could not do the job alone. At last, in 1964, Congress passed a Civil Rights Act that outlawed discrimination against racial, ethnic, and religious minorities and against women. The law allowed federal agencies to withhold grants, contracts, and loans to states and municipalities found to discriminate or obstruct the law's implementation.

Further progress in the desegregation of schools came in the form of busing children across school districts, sometimes for relatively long distances,[73] and reorganizing school attendance zones. Figure 4.2 shows the increase in racial integration in southern schools as a result of such measures. However, continued progress will likely be slow unless the Supreme Court permits federal action against de facto segregation and the varieties of private schools that have sprung up for the purpose of avoiding integration.[74] A 1995 decision in which the Court signaled to the lower courts to "disengage from desegregation efforts," dimmed the prospects for further school integration. In 2007, the Court went further, declaring unconstitutional programs in the Louisville and Seattle school districts that tried to achieve racial diversity by using race as a determining factor in admissions. Provocatively, Chief Justice John Roberts quoted the counsel for Oliver Brown in

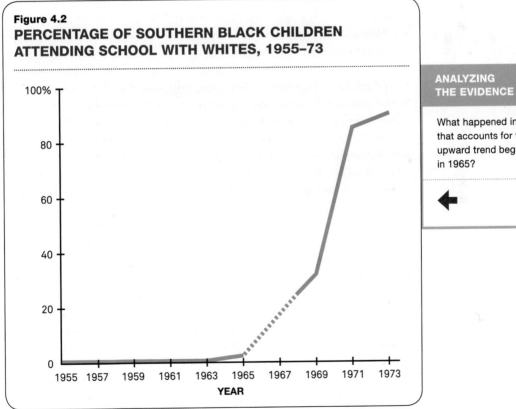

Figure 4.2

PERCENTAGE OF SOUTHERN BLACK CHILDREN ATTENDING SCHOOL WITH WHITES, 1955–73

ANALYZING THE EVIDENCE

What happened in 1964 that accounts for the upward trend beginning in 1965?

NOTE: Dashed line indicates missing data.
SOURCE: Gerald N. Rosenberg, *The Hollow Hope: Can Courts Bring About Social Change?* (Chicago: University of Chicago Press, 1991), pp. 50–1.

his decision for the majority, writing, "We have one fundamental contention which we will seek to develop in the course of this argument, and that contention is that no state has any authority under the equal-protection clause of the Fourteenth Amendment to use race as a factor in affording educational opportunities among its citizens."[75]

Women and Education. Women have also suffered from unequal access to education. Throughout the nineteenth century, relatively few colleges and professional schools admitted them. Even as late as the 1960s, elite universities such as Princeton and Yale did not admit women undergraduates, and even colleges that did offered them fewer opportunities than men to participate in programs, clubs, and athletics. Congress began to remedy these inequities with the Civil Rights Act of 1964, but the most significant federal legislation to guarantee women equal access to education is the 1972 Education Act. Title IX of this act forbids gender discrimination in education. By the mid-1970s, most universities had become fully coed. But enforcing equality was more difficult.

Although the Education Act's enforcement provisions are fairly weak, it has proven effective for litigation. A significant step came in 1992, when the Court ruled that violations of Title IX could be remedied with monetary damages.[76] This ruling both opened the door for further legal action in the area of education and led to stronger enforcement against sexual harassment, gender inequities in resources (such as lab space, research support for faculty, and athletics), and gender inequities in compensation. Over the next two years, complaints to the Education Department's Office for Civil Rights about unequal treatment of women's athletic programs nearly tripled. Subsequently, some prominent universities were ordered to create more women's sports programs; many other colleges and universities have added more women's programs to avoid potential litigation.[77]

In 1996, the Supreme Court put an end to all-male schools supported by public funds when it ruled that the Virginia Military Institute's policy of not admitting women was unconstitutional.[78] Like the Citadel, an all-male state military college in South Carolina, Virginia Military Institute (VMI) argued that its unique educational experience, including intense physical training and harsh treatment of freshmen, would be destroyed if women were admitted. The Court, however, ruled that the male-only policy denied "substantial equality" to women. Two days after the Court's ruling, the Citadel announced that it would accept women. VMI considered becoming a private institution in order to remain all male, but ultimately its board voted to admit women.

The Nineteenth Amendment, *Brown v. Board of Education*, the Civil Rights Act, and the Voting Rights Act were the signal achievements of the civil rights movements of women and blacks. They helped redefine civil rights in America not just for those groups but for all people. These movements became models for other groups to press civil rights claims, and their strategies have been widely mimicked. The principles behind equality in voting and in education have since been applied to many other areas, including employment, housing, immigration, access to public facilities, and athletics. With the push for rights in these spheres, however, there has also been a push back. Just how far do civil rights extend?

Outlawing Discrimination in Employment. Despite the agonizingly slow progress of school desegregation, there was some progress in other areas of civil rights during the 1960s and 1970s. Voting rights were established and fairly quickly began to revolutionize southern politics. Service on juries was no longer denied to minorities. But progress in the right to participate in politics and government dramatized the relative lack of economic progress, and it was in this area that battles over civil rights were increasingly fought.

The federal courts and the Justice Department entered the arena of discrimination in employment through Title VII of the Civil Rights Act of 1964, which outlaws job discrimination by all private and public employers, including governmental agencies (such as fire and police departments), that employ more than 15 workers. We have already seen that the Supreme Court gave "interstate commerce" such a broad definition that Congress had the constitutional authority to outlaw discrimination by virtually any local employer.[79] Title VII made it unlawful to discriminate in employment on the basis of color, religion, sex, or national origin, as well as race.

A potential difficulty with Title VII is that the complaining party must show that deliberate discrimination caused the failure to get a job or a training opportunity. Employers rarely admit discrimination on the basis of race, sex, or any other illegal factor. For a time, courts allowed plaintiffs to make their case if they could show that hiring practices had the *effect* of exclusion.[80] More recently, though, the Supreme Court has placed a number of limits on employment discrimination suits. In 2007, for example, it said that a complaint of gender discrimination must be brought within 180 days of the time the discrimination was alleged to have occurred.[81] In 2009, Congress effectively overturned this decision by enacting legislation greatly extending the time available to workers filing such suits.

Women and Gender Discrimination. Although women gained voting and property rights long ago, they continue to suffer discrimination in various forms, particularly in employment. Here, women benefited from the civil rights movement and especially from Title VII, which in many ways fostered the growth of the women's movement in the 1960s and 1970s.[82] The first major campaign of the National Organization for Women (NOW) involved picketing the Equal Employment Opportunity Commission (EEOC) for its refusal to ban sex-segregated employment advertisements.

Building on the growth of the women's movement, women's rights activists sought an equal rights amendment (ERA) to the Constitution. The proposed amendment's substantive passage stated that "equality of rights under the law shall not be denied or abridged by the United States or by any State on account of sex." Supporters believed that such a sweeping guarantee of equal rights was necessary to end all discrimination against women and make gender roles more equal. Opponents charged that it would be socially disruptive and would introduce changes—such as unisex restrooms—that most Americans did not want. The amendment easily passed Congress in 1972 and won quick approval in many state legislatures but fell three states short of the 38 needed for ratification by the 1982 deadline.[83]

Despite the ERA's failure, gender discrimination expanded dramatically as an area of civil rights law. In the 1970s, the conservative Burger Court helped to establish gender discrimination as a major visible civil rights issue. Although the Court refused to treat gender discrimination as equivalent to racial discrimination,[84] it did make it easier for plaintiffs to file and win gender discrimination suits by applying an "intermediate" level of review to these cases.[85] This intermediate scrutiny is midway between traditional rules of evidence, which put the burden of proof on the plaintiff, and strict scrutiny, which requires the defendant to show not only that a particular classification is reasonable but also that there is a need or compelling interest for it. Intermediate scrutiny shifts the burden of proof partially but not entirely onto the defendant.

Courts' identification of sexual harassment as a form of gender discrimination has also advanced the cause of women's civil rights. In 1986, the Supreme Court recognized two forms of sexual harassment—the quid pro quo type, which involves sexual extortion, and the hostile-environment type, which involves sexual intimidation[86]—in its decision that harassment may be legally actionable even if the employee did not suffer tangible economic or job-related losses from it. In 1993, the Court said harassment may be actionable even if the employee did not suffer tangible psychological costs as a result of it.[87] In two 1998 cases, the Court further strengthened the law when it said that whether or not harassment results in economic harm to the employee, an employer is liable for it if it was committed by someone with authority over the employee. But the Court also said that an employer may defend itself by showing that it had a sexual harassment prevention and grievance policy in effect.[88]

Many of the victories won against gender discrimination have, in recent years, been applied to discrimination against transgender individuals. In 2015,

intermediate scrutiny

The test used by the Supreme Court in gender discrimination cases. Intermediate scrutiny places the burden of proof partially on the government to show that the law in question is constitutional and partially on the challengers to show it is unconstitutional.

Chapter 4: Civil Liberties and Civil Rights

President Obama issued an executive order prohibiting federal contractors from discriminating against workers based on their sexual orientation or gender identity. Later that year, the Equal Employment Opportunity Commission filed its first-ever lawsuits to protect transgender workers under Title VII of the Civil Rights Act, and Attorney General Eric Holder announced that, going forward, the Justice Department would consider discrimination against transgender people as covered by the Civil Rights Act's prohibition of sex discrimination.[89] In 2016, the Justice Department declared that a North Carolina law restricting transgender people to the use of public restrooms consistent with the gender given by their birth certificates constituted a violation of federal civil rights laws. The state government vowed to resist this federal stance. As the legal standoff continued, many companies pulled conventions and other events out of the state, costing North Carolina's economy millions of dollars. In the midst of this battle, in June 2016, the U.S. military dropped its ban against openly transgender people serving in the uniformed services. The Policy Principle section on p. 122 looks at changing policy around the transgender movement.

Latinos. The labels "Latino" and "Hispanic" encompass a wide range of groups with diverse national origins and experiences and distinctive cultural identities. For example, the early political experiences of Mexican Americans were shaped by race and region. In 1898, Mexican Americans gained formal political rights, including the right to vote. In many places, however—especially in Texas—they were prevented from voting by such means as the white primary and the poll tax.[90] In addition, prior to World War II, segregated schools for Mexican Americans were common in Texas and California, along with housing and employment restrictions. In 1947, the League of United Latin American Citizens (LULAC) won a key victory in *Mendez v. Westminster*, which overturned an Orange County, California, policy of school segregation.[91] *Mendez* became an important precedent for *Brown v. Board of Education*.

As LULAC and other Mexican American political organizations worked to stem discrimination after World War II, the first Mexican American was elected to Congress in the late 1950s, and four others followed in the 1960s. In the late 1960s, a new kind of Mexican American political movement was born. Inspired by the black civil rights movement, Mexican American students boycotted high school classes in Los Angeles, Denver, and San Antonio; students in colleges and universities across California joined in as well. Among their demands were bilingual education, an end to discrimination, and greater cultural recognition. In Crystal City, Texas, which Anglo politicians had dominated despite an overwhelmingly Mexican American population, the newly formed La Raza Unida Party took over the city government.[92]

In recent years, Latino political strategy has developed along two tracks. One is a traditional ethnic-group path of voter registration and voting along ethnic lines, because Hispanic voter registration rates typically lag far behind

Transgender Rights and Policy

An inclusive restroom that people of any gender identity may use.

The campaign for transgender equality seeks to end discrimination against transgender persons in employment, housing, health care, and public accommodations. Roughly 700,000 Americans openly identify as transgender or gender nonconforming, meaning that they do not necessarily identify with the sex they were assigned at birth.

The United States' history of rights advocacy on the part of African Americans, women, and other groups blazed a trail for transgender people to follow, demonstrating tactics and offering potential allies for their cause. Earlier victories by these groups established legal principles, laws, and political institutions that transgender advocates could use to develop and implement policies for their own purposes.

For example, in recent years transgender advocates lobbied effectively to achieve court decisions and executive orders that applied to their own cause laws originally crafted to protect African Americans and women from workplace discrimination. The federal courts, the Justice Department, and the Equal Employment Opportunity Commission have all agreed that Title VII of the 1964 Civil Rights Act, which prohibits sex discrimination in employment, prohibits discrimination against transgender and gender-nonconforming individuals as well. Two executive orders, the first by President Bill Clinton in 1998 and the second by President Obama in 2014, prohibit discrimination in federal employment and in hiring by federal contractors, respectively, based on sexual orientation or gender identity. Thus favorable federal policies emerged because transgender individuals could channel their policy preferences through an already-existing set of institutions.

The effort to end gender identity–based discrimination in public accommodations has taken a somewhat different path. Discrimination by hotels, restaurants, theaters, and so forth was not a focus for the women's movement by the late twentieth century, and thus federal anti-discrimination laws for public accommodations cover race, religion, national origin, and disability, but not gender. As a result, the transgender movement did not inherit an existing legal framework or set of institutions through which to pursue its policy goals. While continuing to work for federal legislation in this area, advocates have made strides at other levels of government: as of 2016, seventeen states and a number of localities have expressly prohibited discrimination based on gender identity in public accommodations. In this case, preferences channeled through sympathetic state and local institutions rather than federal ones have produced the movement's desired policy outcomes.

These successes have sometimes proved only temporary, however. In 2015, an antidiscrimination ordinance in Houston was repealed in a referendum. And in 2016, a similar measure in Charlotte, North Carolina, was reversed by the state's legislature, which enacted a bill prohibiting transgender individuals from using bathrooms that correspond to their gender identity in schools and other government buildings. The bill also bans any future legislation by local governments to prevent discrimination on the basis of gender identity. After the federal Department of Justice then warned the state that the law violated the Civil Rights Act, the state and the department filed opposing lawsuits over the issue.

those for whites and blacks. Helping this strategy is the enormous growth of the Latino population, resulting in part from immigration. The second track is a legal strategy using civil rights laws designed to ensure fair access to the political system. The Mexican American Legal Defense and Education Fund (MALDEF) has played a key role in designing and pursuing this strategy.

Asian Americans. The early Asian experience in the United States was shaped by naturalization laws dating back to 1790, the first of which declared that only white immigrants were eligible for citizenship. Chinese immigrants drawn to California by the gold rush beginning in the 1850s were met with virulent antagonism, which led Congress in 1870 to declare them ineligible for citizenship. In 1882, the first Chinese Exclusion Act suspended the entry of Chinese laborers.

At the time of the Exclusion Act, the Chinese community predominantly comprised single male laborers, with few women and children. The few Chinese children in San Francisco were denied entry to public schools until parents of American-born Chinese children pressed legal action; even then, they had to attend a separate Chinese school. In 1897, the Supreme Court ruled that American-born Chinese children could not be denied citizenship.[93] Still, new Chinese immigrants were barred from the United States until 1943; China by then had become a wartime ally, and Congress repealed the Chinese Exclusion Act and permitted Chinese immigrants to become citizens.

Immigration climbed rapidly after the 1965 Immigration and Nationality Services Act, which lifted discriminatory quotas. Nevertheless, limited English proficiency barred many Asian Americans and Latinos from full participation in American life. Two developments in the 1970s, however, established rights for language minorities. In 1974, the Supreme Court ruled in a suit filed on behalf of Chinese students in San Francisco that school districts must provide education for students whose English is limited.[94] It did not mandate bilingual education, but it established a duty to provide instruction that students could understand. The 1970 amendments to the Voting Rights Act of 1965 permanently outlawed literacy tests as a prerequisite to register to vote and mandated bilingual ballots or oral assistance for those who speak Spanish, Chinese, Japanese, Korean, Native American languages, or Inuit languages.

Immigration and Rights. The United States has always struggled to define the rights of immigrants and the notion of citizenship. Waves of immigration have led to contentious questions as to whether immigrants should enjoy the same civil rights as citizens, such as the right to vote and equal access to education, or only a narrower set of rights.

Asian Americans, Latinos, and other groups have long been concerned about the impact of immigration laws on their civil rights. Many Asian American and Latino organizations opposed the Immigration Reform and Control Act of 1986 because it imposes sanctions on employers who hire

In recent years, immigration laws have become a source of debate in American politics. Some people feel that not enough is being done to prevent illegal immigration, while others worry that harsher laws violate immigrants' rights and fundamental American values.

undocumented workers—sanctions they feared would lead employers to discriminate against Latinos and Asian Americans. Indeed, a 1990 report by the General Accounting Office found that sanctions had created a "widespread pattern of discrimination" against Latinos and others who appear foreign.[95] Organizations such as MALDEF and the Asian Law Caucus monitor and challenge such discrimination, focusing as well on the rights of legal and illegal immigrants as anti-immigrant sentiment has grown in recent years.

The Supreme Court has ruled that undocumented immigrants are eligible for education and medical care but can be denied other social benefits; legal immigrants, however, are to be treated much the same as citizens. But with growing numbers of immigrants and economic insecurity mounting, many voters nationwide now strongly support drawing a sharper line between immigrants and citizens. The movement to deny benefits to noncitizens began in California, which experienced sharp economic distress in the early 1990s and has the highest levels of immigration of any state. In 1994, Californians voted to deny illegal immigrants all services except emergency medical care. Supporters of the measure hoped to discourage illegal immigration and pressure illegal immigrants already in the country to leave. Opponents contended that denying basic services to illegal immigrants risked creating a subclass whose lack of education and poor health would threaten all Americans. In 1994 and 1997, a federal court affirmed previous rulings that illegal immigrants should be granted public education.

The Constitution begins with the phrase "We the People of the United States"; likewise, the Bill of Rights refers to the rights of *people*, not the rights of citizens. Undocumented immigrants are certainly people, though not citizens. Americans continue to be divided on the question of the rights to which these particular people are entitled.

Americans with Disabilities. The concept of rights for people with disabilities emerged in the 1970s as the civil rights model spread to other groups. The seed was planted in a little-noticed provision of the 1973 Rehabilitation Act that outlawed discrimination against individuals on the basis of disabilities. As in many other cases, the law itself helped spark the movement for rights.[96] Mimicking the NAACP's Legal Defense Fund, the disability movement founded a Disability Rights Education and Defense Fund to press its legal claims. The movement's greatest success has been the passage of the Americans with Disabilities Act (ADA) of 1990, which guarantees people with disabilities equal employment rights and access to public businesses. The law's impact has been far-reaching, as businesses and public facilities have installed ramps, elevators, and other devices to meet its requirements.[97]

Gay Men and Lesbians. Beginning with street protests in the 1960s, the gay rights movement has grown into a well-financed and sophisticated lobby. The Human Rights Campaign is the primary national political action committee that raises and distributes campaign money to further gay rights; it provides campaign financing and volunteers to work for candidates endorsed by the group. The movement has also formed legal rights organizations, including the Lambda Legal Defense and Education Fund.

The 1990s witnessed both the first national anti-gay laws and the first Supreme Court declaration protecting the civil rights of gay men and lesbians. In 1993, in the first months of his presidency, Bill Clinton confronted the question of whether gays should be allowed to serve in the military. As a candidate, he had said he favored lifting the ban on gays in the military. But after much controversy and nearly a year of deliberation, his administration compromised on a "Don't Ask, Don't Tell" policy, which allowed gay men and lesbians to serve in the military as long as they did not openly proclaim their sexual orientation or engage in homosexual activity. Two years later, gay rights experienced a further setback when Clinton signed the Defense of Marriage Act (DOMA), which for the purposes of federal laws, such as those concerning taxes and spousal benefits, recognized a marriage as only the union of one man and one woman.

As with other civil rights movements, it was the Supreme Court that took a major step in protecting gay men and lesbians from discrimination, one marking an important departure from its earlier jurisprudence. The first gay rights case that the Court decided, *Bowers v. Hardwick* (1986), had ruled against a right to privacy that would protect consensual homosexual activity. Subsequently, the gay rights movement sought suitable legal cases to test the constitutionality of discrimination against gay men and lesbians, much as the civil rights movement had done in the late 1940s and 1950s. Among the possibilities were cases stemming from local ordinances restricting gay rights (including the right to marry), from job discrimination, and from family law issues such as adoption and parental rights. In 1996, the Supreme

Court explicitly extended fundamental civil rights protections to gay men and lesbians by declaring unconstitutional a 1992 amendment to the Colorado state constitution that prohibited local governments from passing ordinances to protect gay rights.[98] The decision's forceful language highlighted the connection between gay rights and civil rights as it declared discrimination against gay people unconstitutional.

Finally, in 2003, the Court overturned *Bowers* and struck down a Texas statute criminalizing certain intimate sexual conduct between consenting partners of the same sex. The decision extends at least one aspect of civil liberties to sexual minorities: the right to privacy. However, it does not undo various other exclusions that deprive lesbians and gay men of full civil rights. Another important victory occurred in 2010, when Congress repealed Don't Ask, Don't Tell. Because in 2008 then-candidate Barack Obama had promised to repeal the act, gay rights activists criticized him for not seeking to do so early in his administration. After a lengthy study by the Defense Department of the possible consequences of allowing openly gay men and women to serve, Congress voted for the repeal.

The focal point for the assertion of gay rights soon turned to the right to marry. In 2004, the Supreme Judicial Court of Massachusetts ruled that under the state's constitution, gay men and lesbians were entitled to marry. The state senate then requested the court to rule on whether a civil union statute (avoiding the word *marriage*) would satisfy the ruling, as it had a comparable ruling in Vermont. In response, the court said no, that this approach was too much like the "separate but equal" doctrine that maintained legalized racial segregation from 1896 to 1954. In the decade between 2004 and 2014, same-sex marriage became legal in 35 states through court order, voter initiative, or legislative enactment. However, these changes faced pushback; in many states, voters and legislatures approved constitutional amendments banning same-sex marriage. Some of these bans were struck down by courts, but in November 2014, same-sex marriage remained illegal in 15 states.

The discrepancy between some state laws, which recognized same-sex marriage, and the federal law under DOMA, which did not, ultimately proved the act's undoing. The nation's laws extend to everyone equally; that is the meaning of equal protection under the Fifth and Fourteenth amendments. In 2013, the Supreme Court ruled DOMA unconstitutional "as a deprivation of liberty of the person protected by the Fifth Amendment."[99] Finally, in 2015, the Court ruled definitively in *Obergefell v. Hodges* that the right to marry is guaranteed to same-sex couples by the due process clause and the equal protection clause. The decision required all states to issue marriage licenses to same-sex couples and to recognize same-sex marriages performed in other jurisdictions. Despite scattered local resistance, this decision seemed to put an end to the marriage question, though LGBTQ activists continue to fight for equal rights in other arenas.

Affirmative Action

In the past 50 years, the relatively narrow goal of equalizing opportunity by eliminating discriminatory barriers developed into the broader goal of affirmative action—compensatory action to overcome the consequences of past discrimination and encourage greater diversity. In 1965, President Lyndon Johnson issued executive orders promoting minority employment in the federal civil service and in companies doing business with the national government. But affirmative action did not become a prominent goal until the 1970s.

The Supreme Court and the Burden of Proof. As affirmative action spread, the issue of giving preference to minority-group members began to divide civil rights supporters. In 1974, Allan Bakke, a white man, brought suit against the University of California at Davis School of Medicine on the grounds that in denying him admission, the school had discriminated against him on the basis of his race. That year, the school had reserved 16 of 100 available slots for minority applicants. Bakke argued that his grades and test scores had ranked him well above many students who were accepted and that he had been rejected only because they were black or Hispanic and he was white. In 1978, Bakke won his case before the Supreme Court and was admitted to the medical school, but affirmative action was not declared unconstitutional. The Court rejected the medical school's admissions procedures because they included both a quota and a separate admissions system for minorities. The Court agreed with Bakke that racial categorizations are suspect categories that place a severe burden of proof on those using them to show a "compelling public purpose." It went on to say that achieving "a diverse student body" was such a public purpose but that the method of a rigid quota of slots assigned on the basis of race was incompatible with the equal protection clause. Thus the Court permitted universities (and other schools, training programs, and hiring authorities) to continue to take minority status into consideration but limited severely the use of quotas.[100]

For nearly a decade after *Bakke*, the Supreme Court was tentative and permissive about efforts by corporations and governments to experiment with affirmative action programs in employment.[101] But in 1989, it returned to the *Bakke* position, ruling that any "rigid numerical quota" is suspect and that any affirmative action program already approved by federal courts could be challenged by individuals (usually white men) alleging that the program had discriminated against them.[102] In 1995, another Supreme Court's ruling further weakened affirmative action. This decision stated that race-based policies, such as preferences given by the government to minority contractors, must survive strict scrutiny, placing the burden on the government to show that such affirmative action programs serve a compelling government interest and are narrowly tailored to address identifiable past

> **affirmative action**
> A policy or program designed to redress historical injustices committed against specific groups by making special efforts to provide members of these groups with access to educational and employment opportunities

discrimination.[103] In 1996, the U.S. Court of Appeals for the Fifth Circuit ruled that race could never be considered in granting admissions and scholarships at state colleges and universities, even as a factor in diversity.[104] The Supreme Court refused to hear a challenge to this decision, which in the three southern states covered by the Fifth Circuit effectively rolled back the use of affirmative action permitted by the 1978 *Bakke* case.

In 2003, affirmative action was challenged in two Supreme Court cases arising from the University of Michigan. The first suit alleged that by automatically awarding 20 points (out of 150) on a ranking system to African American, Latino, and Native American applicants, the university's undergraduate admissions policy discriminated unconstitutionally against white students with otherwise equal or superior academic qualifications. The Supreme Court agreed, arguing that something tantamount to a quota was involved.[105]

The second case broke new ground. Barbara Grutter sued the University of Michigan Law School on the grounds that it had discriminated in a race-conscious way against white applicants with grades and law boards equal or superior to those of minority applicants. A 5–4 vote aligned the majority of the Supreme Court with Justice Lewis Powell's opinion in *Bakke* for the first time. Powell had argued that diversity in education is a compelling state interest and that constitutionally race could be considered as a positive factor in admissions decisions. In *Grutter v. Bollinger*, the Court reiterated Powell's holding and, applying strict scrutiny to the law school's policy, found that its admissions process was narrowly tailored to the school's compelling state interest in diversity because it gave a "highly individualized, holistic review of each applicant's file," in which race counted but was not used in a "mechanical way."[106] This ruling put affirmative action on stronger ground.

Today, the subject of affirmative action has not yet been fully settled. In 2013, the Court upheld the principles stated in *Grutter* and *Bakke*, ruling that universities, municipalities, and other agencies can engage in affirmative action but that those programs are subject to strict scrutiny by the courts; the Court sent the case back to the lower courts for further consideration.[107] In 2016, the Court ruled on the plan and declared that some intrusion on equal protection was warranted by the importance of creating a diverse student body.[108]

CAN RIGHTS AND LIBERTIES BE BALANCED?

As we observed at the beginning of this chapter, the Constitution's Bill of Rights includes both rights and liberties. A liberty is a limit on the government's intrusion into an area such as speech or religious belief. A right, on the other hand, is an obligation imposed upon the government. When citizens have a right, such as the right to vote or to a jury trial, the government must not only respect that right but act vigorously to protect it.

In the real world, of course, nothing is ever neat. Without any regulation, speech can lead to riots and violence. As a result, we tolerate a variety of restrictions on speech designed to keep the peace. Liberties and rights may clash. Today, for example, some assert that governmental recognition of gay rights violates their own deeply held religious beliefs. The courts are constantly asked to adjudicate and balance these and a host of other conflicts among rights and liberties.

Civil rights and civil liberties are among America's most important promises and aspirations. Perfection is impossible, but we must always strive to be better.

For Further Reading

Ackerman, Bruce. *Before the Next Attack: Preserving Civil Liberties in an Age of Terrorism*. New Haven, CT: Yale University Press, 2006.

Baer, Judith, and Leslie Goldstein. *The Constitutional and Legal Rights of Women*. Los Angeles: Roxbury, 2006.

Dawson, Michael. *Not in Our Lifetimes: The Future of Black Politics*. Chicago: University of Chicago Press, 2011.

Klarman, Michael. *From Jim Crow to Civil Rights: The Supreme Court and the Struggle for Racial Equality*. New York: Oxford University Press, 2004.

Koppelman, Andrew M. *Same Sex, Different States: When Same-Sex Marriages Cross State Lines*. New Haven, CT: Yale University Press, 2006.

Lewis, Anthony. *Gideon's Trumpet*. New York: Random House, 1964.

Lewis, Anthony. *Freedom for the Thought That We Hate: A Biography of the First Amendment*. New York: Basic Books, 2010.

Tushnet, Mark, and Michael Olivas. *"Colored Men" and "Hombres Aquí:" Hernandez v. Texas and the Emergence of Mexican American Lawyering*. Houston, TX: Arte Público Press, 2006.

Yoshino, Kenji. *Covering: The Hidden Assault on Our Civil Rights*. New York: Random House, 2007.

5

Congress: The First Branch

The U.S. Congress is the "first branch" of government under Article I of the Constitution and is also among the world's most important representative bodies. Most of the world's representative bodies only represent—that is, their governmental functions consist mainly of affirming and legitimating the national leadership's decisions. The U.S. Congress is one of the few national representative bodies that actually possesses powers of governance. It has vast authority over the two most important powers given to any government: the power of force (control over the nation's military forces) and the power over money. Specifically, according to Article I, Section 8, Congress can "lay and collect Taxes," deal with indebtedness and bankruptcy, impose duties, borrow and coin money, and generally control the nation's purse strings. It also may "provide for the common Defence and general Welfare," regulate interstate commerce, undertake public works, acquire and control federal lands, promote science and "useful Arts" (pertaining mostly to patents and copyrights), and regulate the militia.

In the realm of foreign policy, Congress has the power to declare war, deal with piracy, regulate foreign commerce, and raise and regulate the armed forces and military installations. Further, the Senate has the power to ratify treaties (by a two-thirds vote) and to approve the appointment of ambassadors. Capping these powers, Congress is charged to make laws "which shall be necessary and proper for carrying into Execution the foregoing Powers, and all other Powers vested by this Constitution in the Government of the United States, or in any Department or Officer thereof."

It is extraordinarily difficult for a large representative assembly to formulate, enact, and implement laws. The internal complexities of conducting business within Congress—the legislative process—are daunting. These difficulties are exacerbated by partisanship. For example, the framers of the Constitution viewed bicameralism, or the division of the legislature into two distinct bodies, as a "salutary check on government."[1] James Madison averred that requiring two houses to agree on legislation would lessen the risk that ambitious politicians could carry out schemes inconsistent with the public good. Bicameralism, however, can sometimes thwart needed legislative action, particularly if the two houses are controlled by different political parties.

Recent struggles over the federal debt limit have been difficult to resolve in part because of divided control of Congress. On May 16, 2011, the U.S. government reached its legal debt limit of $14.3 trillion, which is the statutory limit on the amount the government can borrow to meet its obligations. Congress created the original debt limit in 1917 but has raised it many times since then. Reaching the debt limit means that the government is no longer able to borrow money to pay its bills. In order to meet the federal government's expected expenses for the fiscal year ending in September 2011, the government would need an additional $738 billion more than its anticipated revenues.

CORE OF THE ANALYSIS

➡ Congress is the most important representative institution in American government.

➡ Constituents hold their representatives to account through elections.

➡ The legislative process is driven by numerous political forces: political parties, committees, staffs, caucuses, rules of lawmaking, and the president.

➡ Congress also makes the law. Before a bill can become law, it must pass through the legislative process—a complex set of procedures.

When the debt limit was reached, the U.S. Treasury announced that it would adopt a number of fiscal measures that would avert a crisis until approximately August 4, 2011. After that date, the government would no longer be able to meet all of its obligations and would need to institute significant spending cuts that could include outlays for federal social and military programs as well as interest payments on U.S. government securities. Each of these types of cuts could have serious consequences. If, for example, the government failed to meet its debt obligations, bond holders, who include foreign governments, might dump U.S. securities, causing interest rates to rise dramatically throughout the economy. The result might then be an extremely severe economic downturn.

As the potential crisis approached, Congress began discussing its options. Usually the debt ceiling is raised as needed without much fanfare, but in 2011, differences between the House and Senate complicated the picture. The Senate was controlled by Democrats and the House by Republicans, many of whom had been elected in 2010 with Tea Party support on an anti-tax and anti-spending platform. House Republicans declared that they would agree to an increase in the debt ceiling only if Senate Democrats accepted substantial cuts in domestic spending that would bring about long-term reductions in the federal debt. Indeed, Republicans sought $1.7 trillion in cuts by severely reducing spending on such domestic programs as education, food safety, health research, and criminal justice. Senate Democrats, replied that they, too, saw the need to reduce the federal deficit, but that this could only be accomplished through a mix of spending cuts and what they characterized as tax increases for the wealthy. They vowed to defend certain domestic programs against the GOP's budget axe. House Republicans retorted that they would not allow any new taxes.

Though the potential consequences of a default seemed dire, neither side was anxious to compromise. In June 2011, House Republican Majority Leader Eric Cantor (R-Va.) denounced the Democrats and walked out of budget talks organized by Vice President Joseph Biden. In the end, with just one day remaining before a default, the two sides reached an agreement that was widely seen as a victory for the Republicans. The president accepted their formula of spending cuts with no tax increases. Republicans also secured a promise of a vote on a balanced-budget amendment to the Constitution. Again in the spring of 2013, U.S. borrowing approached the debt ceiling. This time, spending cuts combined with higher government revenue (a result of improved economic conditions as the country emerged from recession) pushed the date by which a new debt ceiling must be negotiated into the future.

Many individuals and institutions have the capacity to influence the legislative process. To exercise its power to make the law, Congress must first bring about something close to an organizational miracle. In this chapter, after a brief consideration of representation, we examine the organization of Congress and the legislative process. Throughout, we point out the connections between these two aspects—the ways in which representation affects congressional operations and the ways in which congressional institutions enhance or diminish representation.

REPRESENTATION

Congress is the most important representative institution in American government. Each member's primary responsibility is to the district, to his constituency, not to the congressional leadership, a party, or even Congress itself. Yet the task of representation is not simple. Views about what constitutes fair and effective representation differ, and constituents can make very different demands on their representatives. Members of Congress must consider these diverse views and demands as they represent their districts (Figure 5.1).

Some legislators see themselves as having been elected to do the bidding of those who elected them, and they act as delegates. Others see themselves as having been selected to do what they think is "right," and they act as trustees. Most legislators are a mix of these two types. And all need to survive the next election in order to pursue their chosen role.

Legislators not only represent others; they may be representative *of* others as well. The latter point is especially salient in terms of gender and race, where such representation is symbolically significant at the very least. Legislators who are women or members of minority groups can serve and draw support from those with whom they share an identity, both inside their formal constituency and in the nation at large. (See Table 5.1 for a summary of demographic characteristics of members of Congress.) In the process of drawing new district boundaries within states every 10 years following the decennial census of the population, descriptive representation (also called sociological representation) for African American and Hispanic minorities has been facilitated by creating some districts where racial or ethnic minorities are a majority—so-called majority-minority districts.

As discussed in Chapter 1, we think of our political representatives as our agents. Agency representation means that constituents have the power to hire and fire their representatives. Frequent competitive elections constitute an important means by which constituents hold their representatives to account and keep them responsive to constituency views and preferences. The relationship of representative and constituent is similar in some respects to the relationship of lawyer and client. True, the relationship between a

constituency
The district making up the area from which an official is elected

delegate
A legislator who votes according to the preferences of his or her constituency

trustee
A legislator who votes based on what he or she thinks is best for his or her constituency

agency representation
The type of representation in which representatives are held accountable to their constituents if they fail to represent them properly. That is, constituents have the power to hire and fire their representatives.

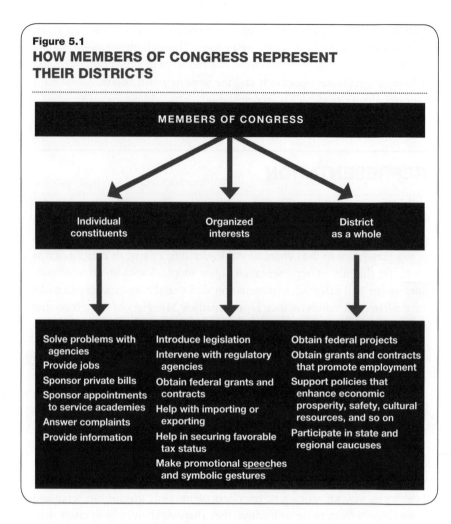

Figure 5.1

HOW MEMBERS OF CONGRESS REPRESENT THEIR DISTRICTS

MEMBERS OF CONGRESS

Individual constituents	Organized interests	District as a whole
Solve problems with agencies	Introduce legislation	Obtain federal projects
Provide jobs	Intervene with regulatory agencies	Obtain grants and contracts that promote employment
Sponsor private bills	Obtain federal grants and contracts	Support policies that enhance economic prosperity, safety, cultural resources, and so on
Sponsor appointments to service academies	Help with importing or exporting	
Answer complaints	Help in securing favorable tax status	Participate in state and regional caucuses
Provide information	Make promotional speeches and symbolic gestures	

member of the House and 700,000 "clients" in the district or that between a senator and millions of clients in the state is very different in scale from that of a lawyer and an individual client. But the criteria of performance are comparable.

We would expect at the very least that representatives will constantly seek to discover the interests of their constituencies and will speak for those interests in Congress and other centers of government.[2] We expect this because we believe that members of Congress, like politicians everywhere, are ambitious. For many, this ambition is satisfied by maintaining a hold on their present office and advancing up the rungs of power in that legislative body. Some may be looking ahead to the next level—a Senate seat, their state's governorship, or even the presidency.[3] (This means that members of Congress may not be concerned only with their present *geographic* constituency. They may

Table 5.1

DEMOGRAPHICS OF MEMBERS OF THE 114TH CONGRESS

	HOUSE	SENATE
AGE*		
Average	57 years	61 years
Range	30–85 years	37–81 years
OCCUPATION**		
Business	231 representatives	42 senators
Education	80	25
Law	151	51
Public service/politics	271	60
EDUCATION†		
High school is highest degree	20	0
College degree	400	100
Law degree	159	54
PhD	23	1
MD	22	3
RELIGION††		
Protestant	251	55
Catholic	138	26
Jewish	19	9
Mormon	9	7
GENDER		
Women	88	20
Men	347	80
RACE/ETHNICITY		
White	340	93
African American	46	2
Hispanic/Latino	34	4
Asian/Pacific Islander	13	1
American Indian	2	0
CONGRESSIONAL SERVICE		
Number serving in first term	61	13
Average length of service	8.8 years (4.4 terms)	9.7 years (1.6 terms)

*Age at time of election (November 4, 2014).

**Most members list more than one occupation.

†Education categories are not exclusive (for example, a representative with a law degree might also be counted as having a college degree).

††Ninety-eight percent of members cite a specific religious affiliation. Other affiliations not listed here include Buddhist, Muslim, Hindu, Orthodox Christian, Unitarian, and Christian Science.

SOURCE: Jennifer E. Manning, "Membership of the 114th Congress: A Profile," Congressional Research Service, March 31, 2015.

want to appeal to a different geographic constituency, for instance, or seek support from a broader gender, ethnic, or racial community.) In each of these cases, the legislator is eager to serve the interests of constituents, either to enhance the prospects of contract renewal at the next election or to improve the chances of moving to another level.[4]

House and Senate: Differences in Representation

bicameral legislature

A legislative assembly composed of two chambers, or houses

money bill

A bill concerned solely with taxation or government spending

The framers of the Constitution provided for a bicameral legislature—a legislative body consisting of two chambers. As we saw in Chapter 2, the framers intended each chamber to serve a different constituency. Members of the House of Representatives were to be "close to the people," elected by popular vote every two years. Because they saw the House as the institution closest to the people, the framers gave it a special power. All money bills—that is, bills authorizing new taxes or authorizing the government to spend money for any purpose—were required to originate in the House. Members of the Senate were to be appointed by state legislatures for six-year terms, were to represent the elite members of society, and were to be attuned more to the interests of property owners than to those of the general population. Today, since the Seventeenth Amendment (1913) provided for direct popular election of senators, members of both chambers are elected directly by the people. The 435 members of the House are elected from districts apportioned among the states according to population: the 100 members of the Senate are elected by state, with two senators from each.

The House and Senate play different roles in the legislative process. In essence, the Senate is the more deliberative body—the forum in which all ideas can receive a thorough public airing. The House is the more centralized and organized body—better equipped to play a role in the routine governmental process. In part, this difference stems from the different rules governing the two bodies. These rules give House leaders more control over the legislative process and encourage House members to specialize in certain legislative areas. The rules of the much smaller, more freewheeling Senate give its leadership relatively little power and discourage specialization.

Other formal and informal factors contribute to differences between the two chambers. Differences in the length of terms and requirements for holding office generate differences in how members of each body develop their constituencies and exercise their powers of office. The small size and relative homogeneity of their constituencies and the frequency with which they must seek re-election make House members more attuned than senators to local interest groups with specific legislative agendas—used-car dealers seeking relief from regulation, labor unions seeking easier organizing rules, or farmers looking for higher subsidies. This was the intent of the

Constitution's drafters—that the House of Representatives be the "people's house" and that its members reflect public opinion in a timely manner.

Senators, in contrast, serve larger and more heterogeneous constituencies. As a result, they are better able than members of the House to be the agents for groups and interests organized on a statewide or national basis. Moreover, with longer terms in office, senators have the luxury of considering new ideas or seeking to bring together new coalitions of interests, rather than simply serving existing ones. This, too, is what the framers intended when they drafted the Constitution.

For much of the late twentieth century, the House exhibited more intense partisanship and ideological division than the Senate. Because of their diverse constituencies, senators were more inclined to seek compromises than members of the House, who with their more homogeneous districts were more willing to stick to their partisan and ideological guns.

Citizens often feel that officials who share their race, gender, or other demographic characteristics will better represent their interests in government. Linda Sanchez and Loretta Sanchez, who are sisters, were elected to the House of Representatives with support from women's and Hispanic groups.

However, beginning with the presidency of George W. Bush, even the Senate grew more partisan and polarized—especially on social issues and the war in Iraq. During Barack Obama's presidency, many of the president's initiatives dealing with the economic crisis, health care, gay rights, and most other areas received virtually no Republican support. Initially, Democrats sought compromise but were rebuffed by Republicans, whose objective was to "make Obama a one-term president." Ultimately, neither party was inclined to compromise.

The Electoral System

In light of their role as agents for various constituencies in their states and districts, and the importance of elections as a mechanism by which principals (constituents) reward and punish their agents, representatives are very much influenced by electoral considerations. Three factors related to the U.S. electoral system affect who gets elected and what that person does once in office. The first factor concerns who decides to run for office and which candidates have an edge over others. The second factor is the advantage incumbents have in winning re-election. Finally, the way congressional district lines are drawn can greatly affect the outcome of an election. Let us examine the impact these considerations have on who serves in Congress.

Running for Office. Voters' choices are restricted from the start by who decides to run for office. In the past, local party officials decided who would run for a particular office; they might nominate someone who had a record of service to the party, or who was owed a favor, or whose "turn" had come up. Today, few party organizations have the power to slate candidates in that way. Instead, the decision to run for Congress is a more personal choice. One of the most important factors determining who runs for office is a person's ambition.[5] A potential candidate may also assess whether he or she can raise enough money to mount a credible campaign, using connections to other politicians, interest groups, and the national party organization.

Features distinctive to each congressional district also affect the field of candidates. For any candidate, decisions about running must be made early because once money has been committed to already declared candidates, it is harder for new candidates to break into a race. Thus the outcome of a November election is partially determined many months earlier, when decisions to run are finalized.[6]

incumbency

Holding the political office for which one is running

Incumbency. Incumbency plays a key role in the American electoral system and in the kind of representation citizens get in Washington. Once in office, members of Congress are typically eager to remain in office and make politics a career. And incumbent legislators have created an array of tools that stack the deck in favor of their re-election. Through effective use of these tools, an incumbent establishes a reputation for competence, imagination, and responsiveness—the attributes most principals look for in an agent.

Perhaps the most important advantage of incumbency is the opportunity to serve on legislative committees. Doing so enables legislators to burnish their policy credentials, develop expertise, and help constituents, either by affecting the legislative agenda or by interceding with the bureaucracy. By serving on committees, incumbents establish a track record of accomplishments that compares favorably with the mere promises of electoral challengers.

The opportunity to help constituents—and thus gain support in the district—goes beyond the particular committees in which a member serves. A considerable share of a representative's time and even more of that of staff members is devoted to constituency service, or casework, which includes talking to constituents, providing them with minor services, introducing special bills for them, and attempting to influence decisions by agencies and regulatory commissions on their behalf.

One significant way in which members of Congress serve as agents of their constituencies on a larger scale is through patronage, direct services and benefits that members provide for their districts. One of the most important forms of patronage is pork-barrel legislation, through which representatives seek to capture federal projects and funds for their districts (or states in the case of senators) and thus "bring home the bacon" for their constituents. A common form of pork barreling is the "earmark," the practice by which members of Congress insert language into otherwise pork-free bills that provides special benefits for their own constituents.[7] Congressional rules now require that earmarks be explicitly associated with their sponsoring legislators, who must list them on their official web sites and certify that neither they nor family members benefit financially from them.

Finally, all of these incumbent benefits are publicized through another incumbency advantage—the franking privilege. Under a law enacted by the first U.S. Congress in 1789, members of Congress may send mail to their constituents free of charge to keep them informed of government business and public affairs. The franking privilege provides incumbents with a valuable resource for making themselves and their activities visible to voters.

The incumbency advantage is evident in the high rates of re-election: over 90 percent for House members and nearly 90 percent for senators

casework

An effort by members of Congress to gain the trust and support of constituents by providing personal services. One important type of casework is helping constituents obtain favorable treatment from the federal bureaucracy.

patronage

The opportunities available to legislators to provide direct services and benefits to their constituents, especially making partisan appointments to offices and conferring grants, licenses, or special favors to supporters

pork-barrel legislation

Legislative appropriations that legislators use to provide government funds for projects benefiting their home district or state

Alaska's "bridge to nowhere" (shown here in a computer rendering) became an infamous example of pork-barrel legislation after Alaskan members of Congress inserted earmarks for $320 million into a highway bill. The bridge, which would have connected the town of Ketchikan to an almost uninhabited island, was never built.

in recent years (Figure 5.2).[8] The advantage is also evident in what is called sophomore surge—the tendency for candidates to win a higher percentage of the vote when seeking their second term than in their initial victory. Incumbents with their "brand name" are in a position to raise campaign funds throughout their term, often in such quantities as to scare off prospective challengers. And even when they draw challengers, incumbents are almost always able to outspend them.[9] Over the past quarter-century, despite campaign-finance regulations seeking to level the playing field, the gap between incumbent and challenger spending has grown (House) or held steady (Senate). Members of the majority party in the House and Senate are particularly attractive to donors who want access to those in power.[10] Potential challengers are often discouraged not only by an incumbent's war-chest advantages but also by the fear that the incumbent simply has brought too many benefits to the district or is too well liked or too well known to be defeated.[11]

The role of incumbency also has implications for the social composition of Congress. For example, the incumbency advantage makes it harder for women to increase their numbers in Congress because most incumbents are men. Women who run for open seats (for which there are no incumbents) are just as likely to win as male candidates.[12] Supporters of term limits argue that the incumbency advantage and the tendency of legislators to view politics as a career mean that very little turnover will occur in Congress unless limits are imposed on the number of terms a legislator can serve.

Chapter 5: Congress: The First Branch

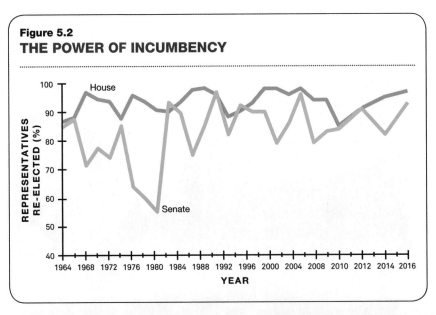

Figure 5.2

THE POWER OF INCUMBENCY

SOURCES: Center for Responsive Politics, www.opensecrets.org/bigpicture/reelect.php (accessed 10/15/13), and author updates.

Congressional Districts. The final factor that affects who wins a seat in Congress is the way congressional districts are drawn. Every 10 years, state legislatures must redraw congressional districts to reflect population changes. In 1929, Congress enacted a law fixing the total number of congressional seats at 435. As a result, when states with fast-growing populations gain districts, they do so at the expense of states with slower growth. In recent decades, this has meant that the South and West have gained congressional seats at the expense of the Northeast and the Midwest (Figure 5.3). Redrawing congressional districts is a highly political process: in most states, districts are shaped to create an advantage for the majority party in the state legislature, which controls the redistricting process (subject to a possible veto by the governor, who may be of a different party). As we see in Chapter 10, this practice, called gerrymandering, can have a major effect on the outcome of congressional elections.

Since the passage of the 1982 amendments to the 1965 Voting Rights Act, race has become a major—and controversial—consideration in drawing voting districts. These amendments, which encouraged creation of districts in which members of racial minorities have decisive majorities, have greatly increased the number of minority representatives in Congress. At the same time, the growing number of majority-minority districts has meant that minority voter proportions in other districts have been diluted, opening up the possibility that representatives from these districts will be less

gerrymandering
The apportionment of voters in districts in such a way as to give an advantage to one political party

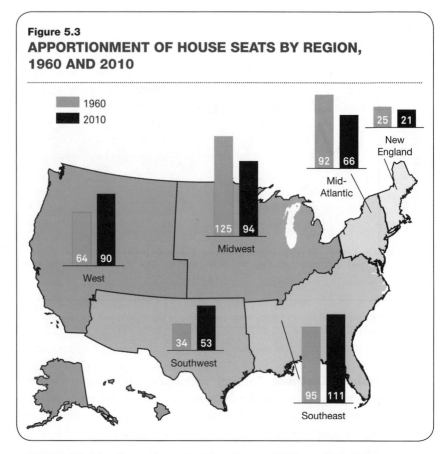

Figure 5.3

APPORTIONMENT OF HOUSE SEATS BY REGION, 1960 AND 2010

■ 1960
■ 2010

New England: 25 | 21

Mid-Atlantic: 92 | 66

Midwest: 125 | 94

West: 64 | 90

Southwest: 34 | 53

Southeast: 95 | 111

SOURCE: U.S. Census Bureau, Congressional Apportionment, 2010 Census Briefs, Table 1, www.census.gov/prod/cen2010/briefs/c2010br-08.pdf (accessed 2/16/13).

responsive to minority policy concerns. Nonetheless, there is no doubt that descriptive representation has grown. After the 2014 and 2016 elections, the House has more minority-group members than ever before.

THE ORGANIZATION OF CONGRESS

We now examine the basic building blocks of congressional organization: political parties, the committee system, congressional staff, the caucuses, and the parliamentary rules of the House and Senate. Each of these factors plays a key role in the process through which Congress formulates and enacts laws. We also look at powers Congress has in addition to lawmaking and explore the role of Congress in relation to the executive.

Party Leadership and Organization in the House and the Senate

One significant aspect of legislative life is not even part of the *official* organization: political parties. The legislative parties—primarily Democratic and Republican in modern times, but also numerous others over the course of American history—foster cooperation, coalitions, and compromise. They are the vehicles of collective action by legislators, both for pursuing common policy objectives inside the legislature and for competing in election contests back home.[13] In short, political parties in Congress are the fundamental building blocks from which policy coalitions are fashioned to pass legislation and monitor its implementation, thereby providing a track record on which members build electoral support.

Every two years, at the beginning of a new Congress, the parties in each chamber choose leaders. In the House, members gather into partisan groups—called the party caucus by the Democrats and the party conference by the Republicans—to elect leaders and decide other matters of party policy. The elected leader of the majority party is later proposed to the whole House and is automatically elected to the position of Speaker of the House, with voting along straight party lines. The House majority caucus or conference then also elects a majority leader. The minority party goes through the same process and selects the minority leader. Both parties also elect "whips," who line up party members on important votes and relay voting intentions to the leaders.

At one time, party leaders strictly controlled committee assignments, using them to enforce party discipline. Today, representatives expect to receive the assignments they want and resent leadership efforts to control assignments. The leadership's best opportunities to use committee assignments as rewards and punishments come when more than one member seeks a seat on a committee.

Generally, representatives seek assignments that will allow them to influence decisions of special importance to their districts. Representatives from farm districts, for example, may request seats on the Agriculture Committee.[14] Seats on powerful committees such as Ways and Means, which is responsible for tax legislation, and Energy and Commerce, responsible for health, energy, and regulatory policy, are especially popular.

Within the Senate, the president pro tempore exercises mainly ceremonial leadership. Usually, the majority party designates the member with the greatest seniority to serve in this capacity. Real power is in the hands of the majority leader and minority leader, each elected by party caucus or conference. The majority and minority leaders, together, control the Senate's calendar or agenda for legislation. In addition, the senators from each party elect a whip.

party caucus, or party conference

A nominally closed meeting of a political or legislative group to select candidates or leaders, plan strategy, or make decisions regarding legislative matters

Speaker of the House

The chief presiding officer of the House of Representatives. The Speaker is elected at the beginning of every Congress on a straight party vote. He or she is the most important party and House leader.

majority leader

The elected leader of the party holding a majority of the seats in the House of Representatives or in the Senate. In the House, the majority leader is subordinate in the party hierarchy to the Speaker.

minority leader

The elected leader of the party holding less than a majority of the seats in the House or Senate

Party leaders reach outside their respective chambers in an effort to augment their power and enhance prospects for their party programs. One important external strategy involves fund-raising. In recent years, congressional leaders have frequently established their own political action committees. Interest groups are usually eager to contribute to these "leadership PACs" to curry favor with powerful members of Congress. The leaders, in turn, use these funds to support the various campaigns of their party's candidates and thereby create a sense of obligation.

In addition to the tasks of organizing Congress, congressional party leaders may also seek to set the legislative agenda. Since the New Deal, presidents have taken the lead in creating legislative agendas. (This trend will be discussed in the next chapter.) But in recent years, congressional leaders, especially when facing a White House controlled by the opposing party, have attempted to devise their own agendas.

The Committee System

The committee system provides Congress with its second organizational structure, but it is more a division and specialization of labor than the hierarchy of power that determines leadership arrangements.

Six fundamental characteristics define the congressional committee system:

standing committee

A permanent legislative committee that considers legislation within its designated subject area; the basic unit of deliberation in the House and the Senate

1. *The official rules give each standing committee a permanent status*, with a fixed membership, officers, rules, staff, offices, and, above all, a jurisdiction that is recognized by all other committees and usually the leadership as well (Table 5.2).

2. *The jurisdiction of each standing committee is defined by the subject matter of the legislation it deals with.* Except for the Rules Committee in the House and the Rules and Administration Committee in the Senate, all the important committees are organized to receive proposals for legislation and to process them into official bills. The House Rules Committee decides the order in which bills come up for a vote and determines the specific rules that govern the length of debate and the opportunity for amendments. Rules can be used to help or hinder particular proposals.

3. *Standing committees' jurisdictions usually parallel those of the major departments or agencies in the executive branch.* There are important exceptions, but by and large the division of labor is designed to parallel executive-branch organization.

4. *Bills are assigned to standing committees on the basis of subject matter*, but the Speaker of the House and the Senate's presiding officer have some discretion in the assignment. Most bills "die in committee"—that is, they

Table 5.2

STANDING COMMITTEES OF CONGRESS, 2016*

HOUSE COMMITTEES	
Agriculture	Intelligence
Appropriations	Judiciary
Armed Services	Natural Resources
Budget	Oversight and Government Reform
Education and the Workforce	Rules
Energy and Commerce	Science and Technology
Ethics	Small Business
Financial Services	Transportation and Infrastructure
Foreign Affairs	Veterans' Affairs
Homeland Security	Ways and Means
House Administration	

SENATE COMMITTEES	
Agriculture, Nutrition, and Forestry	Finance
Appropriations	Foreign Relations
Armed Services	Health, Education, Labor, and Pensions
Banking, Housing, and Urban Affairs	Homeland Security and Governmental Affairs
Budget	Judiciary
Commerce, Science, and Transportation	Rules and Administration
Energy and Natural Resources	Small Business and Entrepreneurship
Environment and Public Works	Veterans' Affairs

*These are the committees in the 114th Congress (2015–17). Committee names and jurisdictions change over time, as does the number of committees.

are not sent to the full House or Senate for consideration. Ordinarily, this ends a bill's life. There is only one way for a legislative proposal to escape committee processing: a bill passed in one chamber may be permitted to move directly to the calendar of the other chamber. Even here, however, the bill must receive the full committee treatment before passage in the first chamber.

5. *Each standing committee is unique.* No effort is made to compose the membership of any committee to be representative of the total House or

Senate membership. Members with a special interest in the subject matter of a committee are expected to seek membership on it. In both the House and the Senate, each party has established a Committee on Committees, which determines the committee assignments of new members and of established members who wish to change committees. Ordinarily, members can keep their committee assignments as long as they like.

6. *Traditionally, each standing committee's hierarchy is based on seniority.* Seniority is determined by years of continuous service on a particular committee, not by years of service in the House or Senate. In general, each committee is chaired by the most senior member of the majority party. Since the 1970s, committee chairs have been elected by the majority-party members of the full legislature, though there remains a presumption (which may be rebutted) that the most senior committee member will normally assume the chair.

The Staff System: Staffers and Agencies

A congressional institution second in importance only to the committee system is the staff system. Every member of Congress employs a large number of staff members, whose tasks include handling constituency requests and, to a growing extent, dealing with legislative details and overseeing the activities of administrative agencies. Increasingly, staffers bear the primary responsibility for drafting proposals, organizing hearings, dealing with administrative agencies, and negotiating with lobbyists. Indeed, legislators typically deal with one another through staff rather than through direct, personal contact. Representatives and senators together employ nearly 11,000 staffers in their Washington and home offices.

In addition, Congress employs roughly 2,000 permanent committee staffers. These individuals, attached to every House and Senate committee, stay regardless of turnover in Congress and are responsible for administering the committee's work, including research, scheduling, organizing hearings, and drafting legislation.

Congress has also established three *staff agencies* to provide the legislative branch with resources and expertise and to enhance its capacity to oversee administrative agencies as well as evaluate presidential programs and proposals. They are the Congressional Research Service, which performs research for legislators who wish to know the facts and competing arguments relevant to policy proposals or other legislative business; the Government Accountability Office, through which Congress can investigate the financial and administrative affairs of any government agency or program; and the Congressional Budget Office, which assesses the economic implications and likely costs of proposed federal programs.

Informal Organization: The Caucuses

In addition to the official organization of Congress, an unofficial organizational structure also exists—the caucuses, or *legislative service organizations* (LSOs). Caucuses are groups of senators or representatives who share certain opinions, interests, or social characteristics. They include ideological caucuses such as the liberal Democratic Study Group and the conservative Democratic Forum. There are also a large number of caucuses representing particular economic or policy interests, such as the Travel and Tourism Caucus, the Steel Caucus, and the Concerned Senators for the Arts. Legislators who share common backgrounds or social characteristics have organized caucuses such as the Congressional Black Caucus, the Congressional Caucus for Women's Issues, and the Hispanic Caucus. All these caucuses advance the interests of specific groups by promoting legislation, encouraging Congress to hold hearings, and pressing administrative agencies for favorable treatment.

RULES OF LAWMAKING: HOW A BILL BECOMES A LAW

The institutional structure of Congress is one key factor that helps to shape the legislative process. An equally important factor is the rules of congressional procedures. These rules govern everything from the introduction of a bill through its submission to the president for signing. Not only do they influence the fate of every bill, they also help to determine the distribution of power in Congress (Figure 5.4).

Committee Deliberation

Even if a member of Congress, the White House, or a federal agency has spent months developing a piece of legislation, it does not become a bill until it is submitted officially by a senator or representative to the clerk of the House or Senate and referred to the appropriate committee for deliberation. No floor action on any bill can occur until the committee with jurisdiction over it has taken all the time it needs to deliberate. During its deliberations, the committee typically refers the bill to a subcommittee, which may hold hearings, listen to expert testimony, and amend the proposed legislation before referring it to the full committee for consideration. The full committee may accept the recommendation of the subcommittee or hold its own

Figure 5.4
HOW A BILL BECOMES A LAW

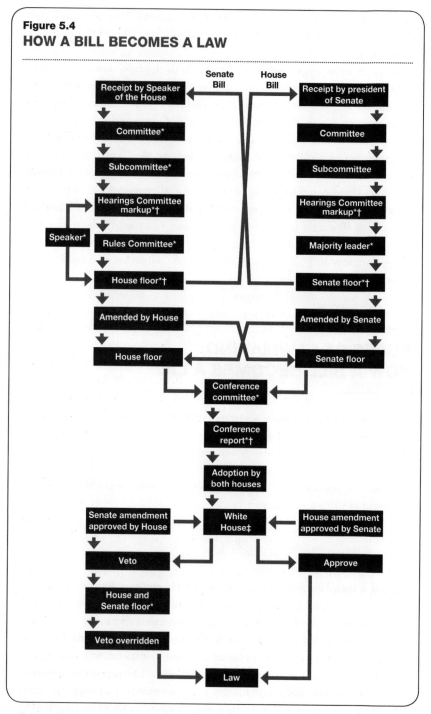

*Points at which the bill can be amended.
†Points at which the bill can die.
‡If the president neither signs nor vetoes the bill within 10 days, it automatically becomes law.

Chapter 5: Congress: The First Branch

hearings and prepare its own amendments. Or, even more frequently, the committee and subcommittee may do little or nothing with a bill and simply allow it to die in committee.

Once a bill's assigned committee or committees in the House have reported it, the bill must pass one additional hurdle: the Rules Committee. This powerful committee determines the rules that will govern action on the bill on the House floor. In particular, the Rules Committee allots the time for debate and decides to what extent amendments to the bill can be proposed from the floor. A bill's supporters generally prefer a closed rule, which severely limits floor debate and amendments. Opponents usually prefer an open rule, which permits potentially damaging floor debate and makes it easier to add amendments that may cripple the bill or weaken its chances for passage.

Debate

Before members vote on a bill that has been reported out of committee, supporters and opponents of the bill speak for or against it on the chamber floor. Party control of the agenda is reinforced by the rule giving the Speaker of the House and the majority leader of the Senate the power to recognize members—or not—during debate. Usually the chair knows the purpose for which a member intends to speak well in advance, and spontaneous efforts to gain recognition are often foiled. For example, the Speaker may ask, "For what purpose does the member rise?" before deciding whether to grant recognition.

In the House, a bill's sponsor and its leading opponent control virtually all of the time allotted by the Rules Committee for debate on the bill. These are almost always the chair and the ranking minority member of the committee that processed the bill—or those they designate. These two participants have the power to allocate most of the debate time in small amounts to members seeking to speak for or against the measure.

In the Senate, other than the power of recognition, the leadership has much less control over the floor debate. Indeed, the Senate is unique among the world's legislative bodies for its commitment to unlimited debate. Once given the floor, a senator may speak as long as he wishes unless a three-fifths majority (now sixty senators) votes to end debate, a procedure called cloture. On a number of memorable occasions, senators have used this right to prevent action on legislation that they opposed. Through this tactic, called the filibuster, a small minority or even one individual in the Senate can thwart the majority. During the 1950s and 1960s, for example, opponents of civil rights legislation often sought to block it by filibustering. The filibuster remains potent today, though Senate rule

closed rule

The provision by the House Rules Committee that restricts the introduction of amendments during debate

open rule

The provision by the House Rules Committee that permits floor debate and the addition of amendments to a bill

cloture

A procedure by which a super-majority of the members of a legislative body can set a time limit on debate over a given bill.

filibuster

A tactic in which members of the Senate prevent action on legislation they oppose by continuously holding the floor and speaking until the majority abandons the legislation. Once given the floor, senators have unlimited time to speak, and it requires a cloture vote of three-fifths of the Senate to end a filibuster.

From the Patriot Act to the Freedom Act

Rand Paul spoke for over 10 hours to prevent the renewal of the Patriot Act in 2015.

Shortly after the 9/11 terror attacks in 2001, Congress passed and President George W. Bush signed the USA Patriot Act, which authorized extensive data collection and domestic surveillance by the National Security Agency. This legislation, giving officials tools to forestall acts of terrorism, was reauthorized in 2006 and again in 2011 despite criticisms by both Democrats and Republicans for its disregard of individual liberties and privacy. However, by 2015, when the Patriot Act was again set to expire, significant opposition arose to another reauthorization. This time, opponents worked through the specific institutions of the House and the Senate to produce a different outcome: a new law to replace the Patriot Act.

As we've seen in this chapter, the House and the Senate are organized quite differently, which influences how members' policy preferences are translated into outcomes in each chamber. The House is tightly controlled by its leadership and thus can act expeditiously. There, the Patriot Act was discarded completely, and in its place the USA Freedom Act—an entirely new document intended to place a much higher premium on individual liberties and privacy—passed comfortably with 338 supporters.

The Senate is a much less centralized institution. Senate Majority Leader Mitch McConnell favored a "clean" reauthorization of the Patriot Act, with no amendments. However, his Kentucky colleague, Senator Rand Paul, wanted to allow amendments, which could include protections for privacy and civil liberties. Under Senate rules allowing any senator unlimited time when speaking on the floor, Paul spoke against McConnell's position for 10 hours and 30 minutes, and it appeared his filibuster would cause the Patriot Act to expire before it could be renewed. Paul didn't talk right up to the deadline, but he ensured that those with reservations about the Patriot Act had time to go public about them. Because the rules of the Senate require unanimous consent to bypass committee hearings and bring a bill to the floor, Paul had the power to prevent slight variations of the Patriot Act—McConnell's preferred option—from being considered by forcing the bill to go through committee. Senate rules mattered decisively here, and Paul exploited them smartly.

The Senate then turned to the USA Freedom Act already passed by the House. The act faced stiff opposition from key senators, but eventually agreement was reached to vote on several amendments that satisfied the concerns of opponents. These amendments were ultimately rejected, however, and the Senate passed the unchanged USA Freedom Act by a margin of 67-32 on June 2, 2015, two days after the Patriot Act had expired. Institutional rules and practices, combined with individual preferences and persistence, revised a policy from one that had been permissive of domestic surveillance to one that, at least in the opinion of its proponents, restrained government a bit more.

changes have reduced its value for blocking the confirmation of executive and judicial appointments (it still may be used against Supreme Court nominations). The Policy Principle section on p. 150 gives an example of how Rand Paul used the filibuster and other maneuvers in 2015 to prevent the renewal of the Patriot Act.

Conference Committee: Reconciling House and Senate Versions of a Bill

Getting a bill out of committee and through both of the houses of Congress is no guarantee that a bill will be enacted into law. Frequently, bills that began with similar provisions in both chambers emerge from them at variance to one another. For example, a bill may be passed unchanged by one chamber but undergo substantial revision in the other. If the first chamber will not simply accept the other's changes, a conference committee composed of the senior members of the committees or subcommittees that initiated the bills may be required to iron out differences. Sometimes members or leaders will let objectionable provisions pass on the floor with the idea that they will be eliminated in conference. Usually, conference committees meet behind closed doors. Agreement requires majority support from each of the two delegations. Legislation that emerges from a conference committee is more often a compromise than a clear victory of one set of political forces over another.

When a bill comes out of conference, it faces one more hurdle. Before a bill can be sent to the president for signing, the House–Senate conference report must be approved on the floor of each chamber. Usually, such approval is given quickly. Occasionally, however, opponents use this one last opportunity to defeat a piece of legislation.

conference committee

A joint committee created to work out a compromise between House and Senate versions of a bill

Presidential Action

Once adopted by the House and Senate, a bill goes to the president, who may choose to sign the bill into law or veto it. The veto is the president's constitutional power to reject a piece of legislation. To veto a bill, the president returns it within 10 days to the house of Congress in which it originated, along with his objections to it. If Congress adjourns during the 10-day period, and the president has taken no action, the bill is also rejected; this outcome is called a pocket veto. The possibility of a presidential veto affects how willing members of Congress are to push for different pieces of legislation at different times. If they think the president is likely to veto a

veto

The president's constitutional power to reject acts of Congress within 10 days of their passage while Congress is in session. A presidential veto may be overridden by a two-thirds vote of each house of Congress.

pocket veto

A veto that occurs when Congress adjourns during the 10 days a president has to approve a bill and the president has taken no action on it

Acts Passed by Congress, 1789–2014

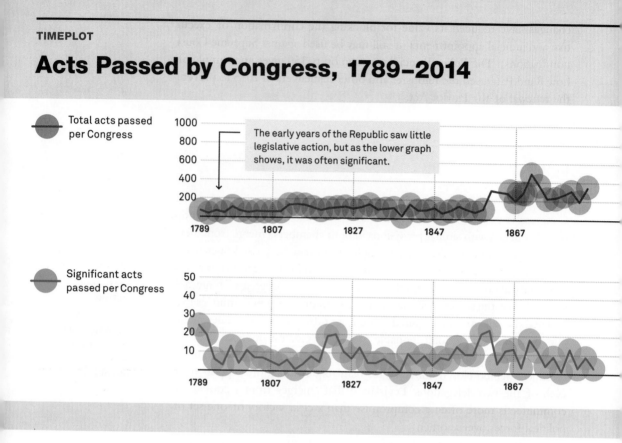

Total acts passed per Congress

The early years of the Republic saw little legislative action, but as the lower graph shows, it was often significant.

1000 800 600 400 200

1789   1807   1827   1847   1867

Significant acts passed per Congress

50 40 30 20 10

1789   1807   1827   1847   1867

proposal, they might shelve it for a later time. Alternatively, the sponsors of a popular bill opposed by the president might push for passage to force the president to pay the political costs of vetoing it.[15]

A presidential veto may be overridden by a two-thirds vote in both the House and the Senate. A veto override delivers a stinging blow to the president, and presidents will often back down from a veto threat if they believe that Congress will override the veto.

HOW CONGRESS DECIDES

What determines the kinds of legislation that Congress ultimately produces? The process of creating a legislative agenda, drawing up a list of possible measures, and deciding among them is very complex, and a variety of

1887   1907   1927   1947   1967   1987   2007

Franklin D. Roosevelt's New Deal saw extraordinary legislative activity to cope with the Great Depression.

Lyndon B. Johnson's Great Society program included numerous acts supported by the Democratic Congress.

1887   1907   1927   1947   1967   1987   2007

influences from inside and outside government play important roles. External influences include a legislator's constituency and various interest groups. Influences from inside government include party leadership, congressional colleagues, and the president. Let us examine each of these influences individually and then consider how they interact to produce congressional policy decisions.

Constituency

Because members of Congress want to be re-elected, their constituents' views have a key influence on their decisions. Yet constituency influence is not straightforward. In fact, most constituents do not even know what policies their representatives support. The number of citizens who *do* pay attention to such matters—the attentive public—is usually very small.

Nonetheless, members of Congress worry about what their constituents think because they realize that the choices they make may be used as ammunition by an opposing candidate in a future election. In this way, constituents may affect congressional policy choices even when there is little direct evidence of their influence.[16] For example, because a large number of voters will not support a candidate who opposes cuts to mandatory spending programs such as Medicare, legislators are unwilling to support such cuts even as those programs approach unsustainable levels (see the Analyzing the Evidence unit on pp. 156–7). Similarly, even moderate Republicans in Congress support very conservative positions on issues like gay marriage, abortion, and gun control because they fear that angry voters will support a more conservative Republican in the next primary election.

Interest Groups

Interest groups are another important external influence on the policies that Congress produces. When members are making voting decisions, interest groups that have some connection to constituents in particular members' districts are most likely to be influential. For this reason, interest groups with the ability to mobilize followers in many districts may be especially influential in Congress. The small business lobby, for example, played an important role in defeating President Bill Clinton's proposal for comprehensive health care reform in 1993–94. Because of the mobilization of networks of small businesses across the country, virtually every member of Congress had to take their views into account. In 2009, the Obama administration brought small business groups and the insurance industry into their planning for health care reform very early in the process precisely for this reason.

The AARP is an interest group representing senior citizens and has been successful in lobbying Congress to support programs affecting the elderly, such as Social Security and Medicare.

In addition to mobilizing voters, interest groups contribute money. In the 2016 electoral cycle, interest groups and political action committees (PACs) donated many millions of dollars in campaign contributions to incumbent legislators and challengers. What does this money buy? A popular conception is that it buys votes: that legislators vote for whatever benefits the bulk of their contributors. Although the vote-buying hypothesis makes for good campaign rhetoric, it has little factual

Chapter 5: Congress: The First Branch

support. Studies by political scientists show little evidence that contributions from large PACs influence legislative voting patterns.[17]

If contributions don't buy votes, what do they buy? Our claim is that they influence legislative behavior in ways difficult for the public to observe and for political scientists to measure. The institutional structure of Congress provides opportunities for interest groups to influence legislation outside the public eye.

Committee proposal power enables legislators, if they are on the relevant committee, to introduce legislation that favors contributing groups. Gate-keeping power enables committee members to block legislation that harms such groups. (The *exclusion* of certain provisions from a bill is just as much an indicator of PAC influence as the *inclusion* of others. The difference is that it is hard to measure what you don't see.) Committee oversight powers enable members to intervene in bureaucratic decision making on behalf of contributing groups.

The point here is that voting on the floor, the alleged object of campaign contributions according to the vote-buying hypothesis, is a highly visible public act, one that could get a legislator in trouble with her broader electoral constituency. The committee system, in contrast, provides numerous opportunities for legislators to deliver to PAC contributors and other donors "services" that are more subtle and hidden from public view. Thus, we suggest that the most appropriate places to look for traces of campaign contribution influence are in the manner in which committees deliberate, mark up proposals, and block legislation from the floor.

Interest groups mobilize voters and contribute campaign finance, but they also convey information. Although legislators become specialists, acquire expertise, and hire expert staff to assist them, for much specialized knowledge, especially about how aspects of policy will affect local constituencies, they depend on lobbyists. Informational lobbying is a very important inside-the-beltway activity. Interest-group expenditures on lobbying dwarf money given in campaign contributions.[18]

Party Discipline

In both the House and the Senate, party leaders have substantial influence over their party members' behavior. This influence, sometimes called party discipline, was once so powerful that it dominated the lawmaking process. Because of their control of patronage and the nominating process, party leaders could often command the allegiance of more than 90 percent of their members. A vote on which 50 percent or more of the members of one party take a particular position while at least 50 percent of the members

Why Congress Can't Make Ends Meet

Contributed by
David M. Primo
University of Rochester

For most of the past half century, Congress has chosen to exercise its constitutionally granted "power of the purse" by authorizing spending in excess of revenues. The result of this deficit spending is a federal debt that stood at nearly $19 trillion at the end of 2015.

How did we get here? The answer begins with congressional rules. In the 1970s, Congress constructed a budget process under which entitlement programs, such as Social Security and Medicare, were left to operate on "autopilot," meaning that spending on these programs is mandatory and continues to increase unless Congress intervenes.

Reforming the process is easier said than done. Some scholars point to the success of the U.S. states in balancing their budgets as a model for Congress. Every state except for Vermont requires a balanced budget, and research shows that deficits and spending are lower in states with constitutional, effectively enforced budget rules.[1]

The federal government has no such constitutional rule and is unlikely to implement one anytime soon, meaning that Congress has to rely on internal enforcement of its budget rules. Because it is much easier to break the rules than to reach bipartisan agreement on difficult spending and tax policy questions, Congress has not managed to meet its own budget deadlines in nearly 20 years.

As the population ages and health care costs increase, programs on autopilot are soaking up an increasing share of government spending. In every year since 1990, mandatory spending has exceeded discretionary spending, and the gap is projected to widen significantly in the coming decades.

Federal Government Spending by Category as a Percentage of GDP

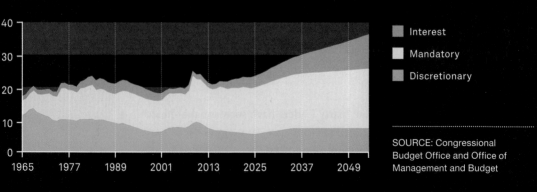

Interest
Mandatory
Discretionary

SOURCE: Congressional Budget Office and Office of Management and Budget

---

1 David M. Primo, *Rules and Restraint: Government Spending and the Design of Institutions* (Chicago: University of Chicago Press, 2007); and Henning Bohn and Robert P. Inman, "Balanced Budget Rules and Public Deficits: Evidence from the U.S. States," *Carnegie Rochester Conference Series on Public Policy* 45 (1996): 13–76.

If Congress is not able to design effective budget rules to overcome institutional inertia, the federal government's debt will continue to grow, with future generations being left with a big bill to pay. Legislators, however, are reluctant to insist on reforms in these areas for fear of upsetting their constituents and losing their seats in Congress. In a 2013 survey, very few voters said they would be more likely to support a candidate who wanted to cut Medicare to reduce the deficit; in fact, a majority of voters in all age groups but one said they would be less likely to support that candidate. The exception? Young people aged 18 to 29, who cast ballots at much lower rates than older voters.

Opposition to Medicare Cuts

This survey asked, "If a candidate for Congress supports making major cuts in Medicare spending to reduce the federal budget deficit, would that make you more likely or less likely to vote for that candidate specifically because of this issue, or would it not make much difference in your vote?"

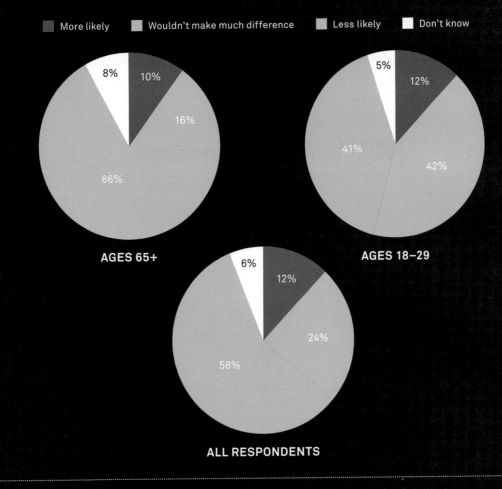

SOURCE: Robert J. Blendon and John M. Benson, "The Public and Conflict over Future Medicare Spending," *New England Journal of Medicine* 369 (2013): 1072.

party vote

A roll-call vote in the House or Senate in which at least 50 percent of the members of one party take a particular position and are opposed by at least 50 percent of the members of the other party. Party votes are less common today than they were in the nineteenth century.

roll-call vote

Voting in which each legislator's yes or no vote is recorded

of the other party take the opposing position is called a party vote. At the beginning of the twentieth century, most roll-call votes in the House of Representatives were party votes. Today, primary elections have deprived party leaders of the power to decide who receives the party's official nomination. The patronage resources available to the leadership, moreover, have become quite limited. As a result, party-line voting happens less often. It is, however, fairly common to find at least a majority of Democrats opposing a majority of Republicans on any given issue.

Typically, party unity is greater in the House than in the Senate. House rules grant greater procedural control of business to the majority and minority party leaders, which gives them more influence over their members. In the Senate, however, the leadership has few controls over its members. Party unity has increased as a consequence of the intense partisan struggles in recent decades (Figure 5.5). In the first six years of the Obama administration, party voting in both chambers was strong. Republican votes supporting Obama initiatives were quite rare. After the Republicans won complete control of Congress in the 2014 midterm elections, however, they had to assume some responsibility for governing; a degree of bargaining between them and the minority Democrats emerged as a consequence.

To some extent, party divisions are based on ideology and background. Republican members of Congress are more likely than Democrats to be

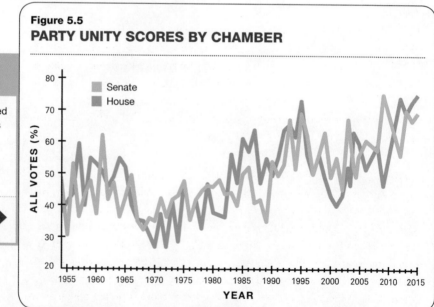

Figure 5.5
PARTY UNITY SCORES BY CHAMBER

ANALYZING THE EVIDENCE

Party voting increased in the 1970s and has remained fairly high since then. What contributes to party voting?

NOTE: The scores represent the percentage of recorded votes on which the majority of one party voted against the majority of the other party.

SOURCES: Voteview, http://voteview.com/Party_Unity.htm (accessed 9/16/13) and "2015 Vote Studies: Party Unity Remained Strong," *CQ Weekly*, February 8, 2016.

drawn from rural or suburban areas. Democrats are likely to be more liberal on economic and social questions than their Republican colleagues. Beginning in the 1970s, legislative parties grew more homogeneous and more polarized. Conservative southern districts began electing Republicans, and liberal northeastern districts began sending Democrats to Congress. This meant that there were fewer conservatives in the ranks of Democratic legislators, and fewer moderates and liberals among Republican legislators. Party members were becoming more alike, but the parties themselves were becoming more different—the very essence of polarization.

This ideological gap has been especially pronounced since 1980 (Figure 5.6). By the end of President Obama's second term in 2016, party polarization had produced "gridlock," a state of affairs in which virtually no legislation could be enacted. These differences certainly help to explain roll-call divisions between the two parties. Ideology and background, however, are only part of the explanation of party unity. The other part has to do with organization and leadership.

Although party organization has weakened over the last century, today's party leaders still have some resources at their disposal: (1) committee assignments, (2) access to the floor, (3) the whip system, (4) logrolling, and (5) the presidency. These resources are often very effective in securing the support of party members.

Committee Assignments. Leaders can create debts among members by helping them get favored committee assignments. These assignments are made early in the congressional careers of most members and cannot be taken from them if they later balk at party discipline. Nevertheless, if the leadership goes out of its way to get the assignment a member prefers, this effort is likely to create a bond of obligation that can be called on without any other payments or favors.

Access to the Floor. The most important everyday resource available to the parties is control over access to the floor. With thousands of bills awaiting passage and most members clamoring for access in order to influence a bill or to publicize themselves, floor time is precious. In the House, the Speaker, as head of the majority party (in consultation with the minority leader), allocates large blocks of floor time. More important, the Speaker of the House and the majority leader in the Senate possess the power of recognition. This formidable authority can be used to block a piece of legislation completely or to frustrate a member's attempts to speak on a particular issue. Because the power is significant, members of Congress usually attempt to stay on good terms with the Speaker and the majority leader to ensure that they will continue to be recognized.[19]

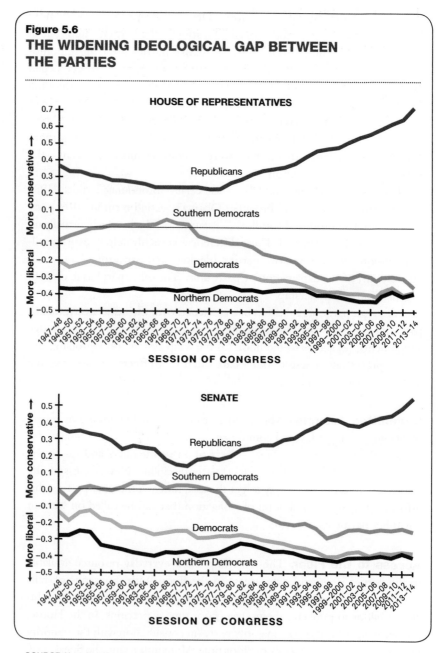

Figure 5.6

THE WIDENING IDEOLOGICAL GAP BETWEEN THE PARTIES

HOUSE OF REPRESENTATIVES

More conservative ↑ / More liberal ↓

Republicans

Southern Democrats

Democrats

Northern Democrats

SESSION OF CONGRESS

SENATE

More conservative ↑ / More liberal ↓

Republicans

Southern Democrats

Democrats

Northern Democrats

SESSION OF CONGRESS

SOURCE: Voteview, Voteview.com/party-unity.htm. (accessed 8/15/16).

The Whip System. Some influence accrues to party leaders through the whip system, which is primarily a communications network. Between 12 and 20 assistant and regional whips are selected by zones to operate at the direction of the majority or minority leader and the whip. They take polls of their party's members to learn their intentions on specific bills. This information tells the leaders whether they have enough support to allow a vote and whether the vote is so close that they need to put pressure on a few swing votes. Leaders also use the whip system to convey their wishes and plans to the members.

whip system

A party communications network in each house of Congress. Whips poll their party's members to learn their intentions on specific bills and also convey to members the leadership's views and plans to members.

Logrolling. An agreement between two or more members of Congress who have nothing in common except the need for reciprocal support is

IN BRIEF

Party Discipline

The influence that party leaders have over the behavior of their party members is maintained in a number of ways:

✔ **Committee assignments:** By giving favorable committee assignments to members, party leaders create a sense of debt.

✔ **Access to the floor:** Ranking committee members in the Senate and the Speaker of the House control the allocation of time for floor debate on bills; legislators want to stay on good terms with these party leaders so that their bills get floor time.

✔ **Whip system:** The system allows party leaders to keep track of how many votes they can count on for a bill; if the vote is close, they can try to influence members to switch sides.

✔ **Logrolling:** Party leaders help arrange deals between members who have nothing in common to support one another's legislation because each needs the vote.

✔ **Presidency:** The president's legislative proposals are often the most important part of Congress's agenda. Party leaders use partisan support for or opposition to the president's program to rally members.

logrolling

Reciprocal agreements between legislators, usually in voting for or against a bill. In contrast to bargaining, logrolling unites legislators who have nothing in common but their desire to exchange support.

called logrolling. The agreement states, in effect, "You support me on bill X, and I'll support you on another bill of your choice." Since party leaders are the center of the communications networks in the two chambers, they can help members create large logrolling coalitions. Hundreds of logrolling deals are made each year. Although there are no official record-keeping books, it would be a poor party leader whose whips did not know who owed what to whom.

The Presidency. Of all the influences that maintain the clarity of party lines in Congress, that of the presidency is probably the most important. Indeed, it is a touchstone of party discipline in Congress. Since the late 1940s, under President Truman, presidents each year have identified a number of bills to be considered part of the administration's program. By the mid-1950s, both parties in Congress began to look to the president for these proposals, which became the most significant part of Congress's agenda. Support for or opposition to the president's program has become a criterion for party loyalty, and party leaders in Congress are able to use it to rally some members.

Weighing Diverse Influences

Clearly, many factors affect congressional decisions. But at various points in the decision-making process, some factors are more influential than others. For example, interest groups may be more effective at the committee stage, when their expertise is especially valued and their visibility is less obvious. Because committees play a key role in deciding what legislation reaches the floor of the House or Senate, interest groups can often put a halt to bills they dislike, or they can ensure that options that do reach the floor are ones they support. Once legislation reaches the floor and members of Congress are deciding among alternatives in visible roll-call votes, constituent opinion becomes more important.

The influence of the external and internal forces described in the preceding section also varies according to the kind of issue under consideration. On policies of great importance to powerful interest groups—farm subsidies, for example—those groups are likely to have considerable influence. On other issues, members of Congress may be less attentive to narrow interest groups and more willing to consider what they see as the general interest.

Finally, the mix of influences varies according to the historical moment. The 1994 electoral victory of Republicans allowed their party to control both houses of Congress for the first time in 40 years. That fact, combined with an unusually assertive Republican leadership, meant that party leaders became especially important in decision making. The willingness of moderate Republicans to support measures they had once opposed indicated the unusual importance of party leadership in this period.[20] Likewise, the historical significance in 2008 of the election of the first African American president gave Democratic party leaders that extra weight and credibility to rally their fellow partisans in support of the new president's agenda.

BEYOND LEGISLATION: ADDITIONAL CONGRESSIONAL POWERS

In addition to the power to make the law, Congress has at its disposal an array of other instruments through which it may influence the process of government. As we saw in Chapter 2, the Constitution gives the Senate the power to approve treaties and appointments. And Congress has drawn to itself a number of other powers through which it can share with the other branches the capacity to administer the laws.

Oversight

Oversight, as applied to Congress, refers not to something neglected but to the effort to oversee or supervise how the executive branch carries out legislation. Individual senators and members of the House can engage in a form of oversight simply by calling or visiting administrators, sending out questionnaires, or talking to constituents about programs. But in a more formal sense, oversight is carried out by committees or subcommittees of the Senate or House, which conduct hearings and investigations in order to analyze and evaluate bureaucratic agencies and the effectiveness of their programs. The purpose may be to locate inefficiencies or abuses of power, to explore the relationship between what an agency does and what a law intended, or to change or abolish a program. Most programs and agencies are subject to some oversight every year during the course of hearings on appropriations; that is, the funding of agencies and government programs. Committees or subcommittees have the power to subpoena witnesses, administer oaths, cross-examine, compel testimony, and bring criminal charges for contempt (refusing to cooperate) and perjury (lying).

Hearings and investigations resemble each other in many ways, but they differ on one fundamental point. A hearing is usually held on a specific bill, and the questions asked there are usually intended to build a record with regard to that bill. In an investigation, the committee or subcommittee examines a broad area or problem and then concludes its investigation with one or

oversight
The effort by Congress, through hearings, investigations, and other techniques, to exercise control over the activities of executive agencies

The House Select Committee on Benghazi was formed to investigate the 2012 attack on the U.S. embassy in Benghazi, Libya. The committee reconvened in 2015 after revelations that Hillary Clinton had used a private e-mail server at the time for official State Department business.

more proposed bills. One example of an investigation is the Senate hearings on the abuse of prisoners in Iraq's Abu Ghraib prison. Many Democrats and some Republicans complained that congressional oversight of the entire Iraq war had been too lax. Reflecting on the prison abuse scandal, Representative Christopher Shays (R-Conn.) stated, "I believe our failure to do proper oversight has hurt our country and the administration. Maybe they wouldn't have gotten into some of this trouble if our oversight had been better."[21]

Advice and Consent: Special Senate Powers

The Constitution has given the Senate a special power, one that is not based on lawmaking. The president has the power to make treaties and to appoint top executive officers, ambassadors, and federal judges—but only "with the Advice and Consent of the Senate" (Article II, Section 2). For treaties, two-thirds of senators present must concur; for appointments, a majority is required.

The Senate only occasionally exercises its power to reject treaties and appointments. More common than rejection of appointees is a senatorial "hold" on an appointment. Any senator may place an indefinite hold on the confirmation of a mid- or lower-level presidential appointment. The hold typically aims to wring concessions from the White House on matters unrelated to the appointment. During George W. Bush's administration, Senate Democrats prevented final confirmation votes on a dozen especially conservative judicial nominees. Of course, Republicans had done the same thing to many judicial nominations in the preceding Clinton administration and continued the practice in the Obama administration.

Most presidents make every effort to take potential Senate opposition into account in treaty negotiations and frequently resort to executive agreements with foreign powers instead of treaties when they find the prospects of Senate consent unlikely. The Supreme Court has held that such agreements are equivalent to treaties, but they do not need Senate approval.[22] Congress can also limit the president's ability to conduct foreign policy through executive agreement by refusing to appropriate the funds needed to implement an agreement. In this way, for example, Congress can modify or even cancel executive agreements to provide economic or military assistance to foreign governments. In the past, presidents sometimes concluded secret agreements without informing Congress. In 1972, Congress passed the Case Act, which requires that the president inform Congress of any executive agreement within 60 days of its having been reached.

executive agreement

An agreement between the president and another country that has the force of a treaty but does not require the Senate's "advice and consent"

Impeachment

The Constitution also grants Congress the power of impeachment over the president, vice president, and other executive officials. To impeach means to charge a government official with "Treason, Bribery, or other high Crimes and Misdemeanors" and bring him or her before Congress to determine guilt. The procedure is similar to a criminal indictment in that the House of Representatives acts like a grand jury, voting (by simple majority) on whether the accused ought to be impeached. If a majority of the House votes to impeach, the impeachment trial is held in the Senate, which acts like a trial jury by voting whether to convict and remove the person from office. (This vote requires a two-thirds majority.)

impeachment

The charging of a governmental official (president or other) with "Treason, Bribery, or other high Crimes and Misdemeanors" and bringing him or her before Congress to determine guilt

Controversy over Congress's impeachment power has arisen over the meaning of "high Crimes and Misdemeanors." A strict reading of the Constitution suggests that the only impeachable offense is an actual crime. But a more commonly agreed-on definition is that an impeachable offense is whatever the majority of the House of Representatives considers it to be at a given time. In other words, impeachment, especially of a president, is a political decision.

During the course of American history, only two presidents have been impeached. In 1867, President Andrew Johnson, a Southern Democrat who had battled a congressional Republican majority over Reconstruction,

Critics of Congress want it to be both more representative and more effective. On the one hand, Congress is frequently criticized for falling victim to gridlock and failing to reach decisions on important issues such as Social Security reform. (Or, as we saw earlier with the debt ceiling crisis, allowing partisanship to dominate legislative decision making.) This was one reason why, in 1995, the Republican House leadership reduced the number of committees and subcommittees in the lower chamber. Having fewer committees and subcommittees generally means greater centralization of power and more expeditious decision making. On the other hand, critics demand that Congress become more representative of the changing makeup and values of the American populace. In recent years, for example, some reformers have demanded limits on the number of terms that any member of Congress can serve. Term limits are seen as a device for producing a more rapid turnover of members and, hence, a better chance for new political and social forces to be represented in Congress. The problem, however, is that although reforms such as term limits and greater internal diffusion of power may make Congress more representative, they may also make it less efficient and effective. By the same token, policies that may make Congress better able to act—such as strong central leadership, reduction of the number of committees and subcommittees, and retention of members with seniority and experience—may make Congress less representative. This is the dilemma of congressional reform. Efficiency and representation are often competing principles in our system of government; we must be wary of gaining one at the expense of the other.

For Further Reading

Arnold, R. Douglas. *The Logic of Congressional Action.* New Haven, CT: Yale University Press, 1990.

Binder, Sarah. *Stalemate: Causes and Consequences of Legislative Gridlock.* Washington, DC: Brookings Institution, 2003.

Brady, David W., and Mathew D. McCubbins, eds. *Party, Process, and Political Change in Congress: New Perspectives on the History of Congress.* Palo Alto, CA: Stanford University Press, 2002.

Cox, Gary W., and Mathew D. McCubbins. *Legislative Leviathan: Party Government in the House.* 2nd ed. Berkeley: University of California Press, 2006.

Cox, Gary W., and Mathew D. McCubbins. *Setting the Agenda: Responsible Party Government in the U.S. House of Representatives.* New York: Cambridge University Press, 2005.

Frisch, Scott A., and Sean Q. Kelly. *Committee Assignment Politics in the U.S. House of Representatives.* Norman: University of Oklahoma Press, 2006.

Harbridge, Laurel, and Neil Malhotra. "Electoral Incentives and Partisan Conflict in Congress: Evidence from Survey Experiments." *American Journal of Political Science* 55 (2011): 494–510.

Krehbiel, Keith. *Pivotal Politics: A Theory of U.S. Lawmaking.* Chicago: University of Chicago Press, 1998.

Mayhew, David. *Congress: The Electoral Connection.* New Haven, CT: Yale University Press, 1974.

Sinclair, Barbara. *Unorthodox Lawmaking: New Legislative Processes in the U.S. Congress.* 3rd ed. Washington, DC: CQ Press, 2007.

Stewart, Charles H. *Analyzing Congress.* 2nd ed. New York: W. W. Norton, 2012.

6

The Presidency

Presidential power generally seems to increase during times of war. For example, President Abraham Lincoln's 1862 declaration of martial law and Congress's 1863 legislation giving the president the power to make arrests and imprisonments through military tribunals amounted to a "constitutional dictatorship" that lasted through the war and Lincoln's re-election in 1864. But these measures were viewed as emergency powers that could be revoked once the crisis of union was resolved. In less than a year after Lincoln's death, Congress had reasserted its power, leaving the presidency in many respects the same as, if not weaker than, it had been before the war.

During World War II, Franklin Delano Roosevelt, like Lincoln, did not bother to wait for Congress but took executive action first and expected Congress to follow. Roosevelt brought the United States into an undeclared naval war against Germany a year before Pearl Harbor, and he ordered the unauthorized use of wiretaps and other surveillance as well as the investigation of suspicious persons for reasons not clearly specified. The most egregious (and revealing) of these was his segregation and eventual confinement of 120,000 individuals of Japanese descent, many of whom were American citizens. The Supreme Court validated Roosevelt's treatment of the Japanese on the grounds of military necessity. One dissenter on the Court called the president's assumption of emergency powers "a loaded weapon ready for the hand of any authority that can bring forward a plausible claim of an urgent need."[1]

The "loaded weapon" was seized again on September 14, 2001, when Congress defined the World Trade Center and Pentagon attacks as an act of war and proceeded to adopt a joint resolution authorizing the president to use "all necessary and appropriate force against those nations, organizations or persons he determines planned, authorized, committed or aided the terrorist attacks that occurred on September 11, 2001, or harbored such organizations or persons. . . ."[2] On the basis of this authorization, President George W. Bush ordered the invasion of Afghanistan and began the reorganization of the nation's "homeland security."

The question then arises of whether presidents have too much power. The framers of the Constitution were concerned with what they saw as the tendency of "executive magistrates" to engage in "ambitious intrigues" to enhance their powers and prerogatives.[3] The framers hoped that this threat to citizens' liberties would be mitigated by the system of checks and balances they devised to prevent any branch of government from improperly expanding its power. In recent decades, as we see in this chapter, successive presidents have greatly enhanced the power of the executive branch, expanding presidential war power and devising a host of administrative instruments the framers would hardly recognize.

Even before World War II, President Franklin Delano Roosevelt enhanced the president's control over the federal budget, made executive orders and executive agreements routine instruments of presidential power, and built the Executive Office of the President. Ronald Reagan introduced the use of regulatory review and bolstered presidential war powers. George W. Bush made

CORE OF THE ANALYSIS

➡ The Constitution endows the president with a limited number of expressed powers. Other presidential powers are delegated by Congress or claimed by presidents without specific statutory authority.

➡ Since the 1930s, the presidency has been the dominant branch of American government.

➡ Contemporary presidents have also increased the power of the executive branch through "administrative strategies" that often allow them to achieve policy goals without congressional approval.

signing statements an instrument through which presidents seek to rewrite the law. (We will discuss each of these sources of power in this chapter.)

The framers might not have been familiar with the precise mechanisms of presidential power used today, but they were familiar with the ambition that seems to drive executives, be they kings or presidents. For example, as a senator, Barack Obama was a frequent critic of George W. Bush's expansion of executive authority, claiming that Bush had exceeded his constitutional war powers. In 2007, then-Senator Obama said, "The president does not have power under the Constitution to unilaterally authorize a military attack in a situation that does not involve stopping an actual or imminent threat to the nation."[4] As president, however, Obama ordered U.S. forces into combat against Libyan leader Mu'ammar Qaddafi, asserting that congressional authorization was not needed for his action, which was undertaken in the context of a NATO effort to oust Qaddafi. In this case, Obama did not hesitate to assert the powers of the executive office.

In this chapter, we examine the foundations of the American presidency and assess the origins and character of presidential power today. National emergencies are one source of presidential power, but presidents are also empowered by democratic political processes and, increasingly, by their ability to control and expand the institutional resources of the office. The Supreme Court, to be sure, can sometimes check presidential power. For example, in the 2006 *Hamdan v. Rumsfeld* decision, the Court invalidated the military tribunals established by President Bush to try terror suspects. And, of course, through legislative investigations and its budgetary powers, Congress can oppose the president. With Democratic majorities in both houses of Congress after the 2006 elections, congressional opposition to President Bush's policies in Iraq and the war on terrorism increased. And President Obama encountered congressional opposition to his economic and foreign policies, among other matters, after the GOP won control of the House in 2010 and the Senate in 2014.

This chapter explains why the American system of government could be described as presidential government and how it got to be that way. We also explore how and why the president, however powerful, is nevertheless vulnerable to the popular will. But first, we begin with a look at the presidential powers provided for in the Constitution.

THE CONSTITUTIONAL ORIGINS AND POWERS OF THE PRESIDENCY

The presidency was established by Article II of the Constitution, which asserts, "The executive power shall be vested in a President of the United States of America." It goes on to describe the manner in which the president is to be chosen and to define the basic powers of the presidency. By vesting the executive power in a single president, the framers were emphatically rejecting proposals for collective leadership, most of which aimed to avoid undue concentration of power in the hands of one individual. Most of the framers were anxious to provide for "energy" in the executive and to have a president capable of taking quick and aggressive action. They believed that a powerful executive would help to protect the nation's interests vis-à-vis other nations and promote the federal government's interests relative to those of the states.

Immediately following its first sentence, Article II, Section 1, defines the manner in which the president is to be chosen. This odd sequence says something about the difficulty the delegates to the Constitutional Convention were having over how to give power to the executive and at the same time balance that power with limitations. This conflict reflected the twin struggles etched in the memories of the Founding generation—against the powerful executive authority of King George III and the dismal low energy of the government under the Articles of Confederation. Some delegates wanted the president to be selected by, and thus responsible to, Congress; others preferred that the president be elected directly by the people. Direct popular elections would create a more independent and more powerful presidency. But by adopting a scheme of indirect election through an electoral college, in which the electors would be selected by the state legislatures (and close elections would be resolved in the House of Representatives), the framers hoped to achieve a "republican" solution: a strong president responsible to state and national legislators rather than directly to the electorate.

Sections 2 and 3 of Article I outline the powers and duties of the president. These sections identify two sources of presidential power. One source is the specific language of the Constitution. For example, the president is authorized to make treaties, grant pardons, and nominate judges and other public officials. These specifically defined powers, called the expressed powers of the office, cannot be revoked by Congress or any other agency without an amendment to the Constitution. Other expressed powers include the power to receive ambassadors and to command the nation's military forces.

In addition to establishing the president's expressed powers, Article II declares that the president "shall take Care that the Laws be faithfully executed." Since the laws are enacted by Congress, this language implies that Congress is to delegate to the president the power to implement or execute its will. Powers given to the president by Congress are called delegated powers. In principle, Congress delegates to the president only the power to identify or develop the means to carry out congressional decisions. So, for example, if Congress determines that air quality should be improved, it might delegate to the executive branch the power to determine the best

expressed powers
The powers that the Constitution explicitly grants to the federal government

delegated powers
Constitutional powers assigned to one branch of the government but exercised by another branch with the express permission of the first

means of improvement as well as the power to implement the process. In practice, of course, decisions about how to clean the air are likely to have an enormous impact on businesses, organizations, and individuals throughout the nation. As it delegates power to the executive branch, Congress substantially enhances the importance of the presidency. In most cases, Congress delegates power to executive agencies rather than directly to the president. As we shall see, however, contemporary presidents have found ways to capture a good deal of this delegated power for themselves.

Presidents have claimed a third source of institutional power beyond expressed and delegated powers. These inherent powers are not specified in the Constitution or the law but are said to stem from "the rights, duties and obligations of the presidency."[5] They are most often asserted by presidents in times of war or national emergency. For example, after the fall of Fort Sumter and the outbreak of the Civil War, President Abraham Lincoln issued a series of executive orders for which he had no clear legal basis. Without even calling Congress into session, Lincoln combined the state militias into a national volunteer force, called for 40,000 new volunteers, enlarged the regular army and navy, diverted $2 million in unspent appropriations to military needs, instituted censorship of the U.S. mail, ordered a blockade of southern ports, suspended the writ of *habeas corpus* in the border states, and ordered the arrest by military police of individuals whom Lincoln deemed guilty of engaging in or even contemplating treasonous actions.[6] Lincoln asserted that these extraordinary measures were justified by the president's inherent power to protect the nation.[7]

Expressed Powers

The president's expressed powers, as defined by Sections 2 and 3 of Article II, fall into several categories, including military, judicial, diplomatic, executive, and legislative powers.

Military and Domestic Defense Power. The president's military powers are among the most important that the chief executive exercises. The position of commander in chief makes the president the highest military officer in the United States, with control of the entire military establishment. The president is also the head of the nation's intelligence hierarchy, which includes not only the Central Intelligence Agency (CIA) but also the National Security Council (NSC), the National Security Agency (NSA), the Federal Bureau of Investigation (FBI), and a host of lesser-known but very powerful international and domestic security agencies.

The president's military powers extend into the domestic sphere. Although Article IV, Section 4, provides that the "United States shall [protect] . . . every State . . . against Invasion . . . and . . . domestic Violence," Congress has made

---

inherent powers

Powers claimed by a president that are not expressed in the Constitution but are said to stem from "the rights, duties and obligations of the presidency," claimed mostly during war and national emergencies

---

commander in chief

The power of the president as commander of the national military and the state national guard units (when called into service)

Chapter 6: The Presidency

Though the constitutional power to declare war is given to Congress, the past 60 years have seen the president become the most dominant figure in military affairs. Thus, the public's dissatisfaction with the handling of the war in Afghanistan has been charged mostly against the presidents who oversaw it, George W. Bush and Barack Obama.

this an explicit presidential power through statutes directing the president as commander in chief to discharge these obligations.[8] The Constitution restrains the president's use of domestic force by providing that a state legislature (or governor when the legislature is not in session) must request federal troops before the president can send them into the state to provide public order. Yet this proviso is not absolute. First, presidents are not obligated to deploy national troops merely because the state legislature or governor makes such a request. And more important, presidents may deploy troops without a specific request if they consider it necessary to maintain an essential national service, to enforce a federal judicial order, or to protect federally guaranteed civil rights.

One historic example was the decision by President Dwight Eisenhower in 1957 to send troops into Little Rock, Arkansas, to enforce court orders to integrate Little Rock's Central High School; he did so only after failed negotiations with the state's governor, who had posted the Arkansas National Guard at the school entrance to prevent the admission of nine black students. However, in most instances of domestic disorder—whether from human or natural causes—presidents tend to exercise unilateral power by declaring a "state of emergency," thereby making available federal grants, insurance, and direct assistance as well as troops. President George W. Bush sent various military units to the Gulf Coast in response to Hurricanes Katrina and Rita in 2005, and President Obama sent the Coast Guard and teams from other agencies following the BP *Deepwater Horizon* explosion and oil spill in the Gulf of Mexico in 2010.

Military emergencies have also led to expansion of the domestic powers of the executive branch. This was true during World Wars I and II and during the ongoing "war on terrorism" as well. Within a month of the September 11 attacks, the White House drafted and Congress enacted the USA PATRIOT Act, expanding the power of government agencies to engage in domestic surveillance activities, including electronic surveillance, and restricting judicial review of such efforts. The following year, Congress created the Department of Homeland Security, combining offices from 22 federal agencies into one huge new cabinet department responsible for protecting the nation from attack. The White House drafted the reorganization plan, but Congress weighed in to make certain that the new agency's workers had civil service and union protections. President Obama signed a four-year extension of the Patriot Act in 2011. In 2015, Congress passed and Obama signed the USA Freedom Act, renewing expiring sections of the Patriot Act but scaling back the domestic surveillance authority of the National Security Agency.

reprieve

Cancellation or postponement of a punishment

pardon

Forgiveness of a crime and cancellation of relevant penalty

amnesty

A pardon extended to a group of persons

Judicial Power. The presidential power to grant reprieves, pardons, and amnesties as well as to "commute" or reduce the severity of sentences, literally gives the president the power of life and death over individuals. Presidents may use this power on behalf of a particular individual, as did Gerald Ford when he pardoned Richard Nixon in 1974 "for all offenses against the United States which he . . . has committed or may have committed." Or they may use it on a large scale, as Jimmy Carter did in 1977 when he declared an amnesty for all Vietnam War draft evaders.

Diplomatic Power. The president is America's chief representative in dealings with other nations. As "head of state," the president has the power to make treaties for the United States (with the advice and consent of the Senate). When President George Washington received Edmond Genêt ("Citizen Genêt") as the formal emissary of the revolutionary government of France in 1793, he transformed the power to "receive Ambassadors and other public Ministers" into the power to "recognize" other countries. That power gives the president the almost unconditional authority to review the claims of any new ruling groups to determine whether they indeed control the territory and population of their country, so that they can commit it to treaties and other agreements.

The president is the United States' chief representative in dealings with other nations. Here, Obama meets with Cuban President Raúl Castro in 2015.

In recent years, presidents have expanded the practice of using executive agreements to conduct foreign policy.[9] An executive agreement is like a treaty because it is a contract between two countries, but it is different because it does not require a two-thirds vote of approval by the Senate. Ordinarily, executive agreements are used to carry out commitments already made in treaties or to arrange for matters well below the level of policy. But when presidents have found it expedient to use an executive agreement in place of a treaty, Congress has typically acquiesced.

executive agreement

An agreement between the president and another country that has the force of a treaty but does not require the Senate's "advice and consent"

Executive Power. The most important basis of the president's power as chief executive is found in the sections of Article II that stipulate that the president must see that all the laws are faithfully executed and that the president will appoint all executive officers and all federal judges. In this manner, the Constitution focuses executive power and legal responsibility upon the president. The famous sign on President Truman's desk, "The buck stops here," was not merely an assertion of Truman's personal sense of responsibility. It acknowledged his acceptance of the constitutional imposition of that responsibility upon the president.

The president's executive power is not absolute, as many presidential appointments, including ambassadors, cabinet officers and other high-level administrators, and federal judges, are subject to a majority approval by the Senate. But these appointments are at the discretion of the president.

Another component of the president's power as chief executive is executive privilege—the claim that confidential communications between a president and close advisers should not be revealed without the president's consent. Presidents have made this claim ever since George Washington refused a request from the House of Representatives to deliver documents concerning negotiations of an important treaty. Washington refused (successfully) on the grounds that, first, the House was not constitutionally part of the treaty-making process and, second, that diplomatic negotiations required secrecy.

Executive privilege became a part of the "checks and balances" between the president and Congress, and presidents have usually had the upper hand when invoking it. Although many presidents have claimed executive privilege, the concept was not tested in the courts until the Watergate affair of the early 1970s, when President Nixon refused congressional demands that he turn over secret White House tapes that congressional investigators thought would establish Nixon's complicity in illegal activities. In *United States v. Nixon*, the Supreme Court ordered Nixon to turn over the tapes.[10] The president complied with the order and resigned from office to avoid impeachment and conviction. *United States v. Nixon* is often seen as a blow to presidential power, but actually the Court's ruling recognized for the first time the validity of executive privilege, although it held that the claim did not apply in this instance. Subsequent presidents have cited *United States v. Nixon* in support of their claims of executive privilege. Thus in 2012, the Obama administration cited executive privilege in refusing to comply with a subpoena from the House of Representatives for documents related to "Operation Fast and Furious," a Justice Department program to combat drug trafficking.

Legislative Power. Two constitutional provisions are the primary sources of the president's power in the legislative arena. Article II, Section 3, provides that the president "shall from time to time give to the Congress Information of the State of the Union, and recommend to their Consideration such Measures as he shall judge necessary and expedient." This first legislative power has been important, especially since Franklin Delano Roosevelt began to use it to propose specific action in Congress. Roosevelt established the presidency as the primary initiator of legislation.

The second of the president's legislative powers is the "veto power" assigned by Article I, Section 7—the president's constitutional power to turn down acts of Congress. This power alone makes the president the most important single legislative leader. No bill vetoed by the president can become law unless both the House and the Senate override the veto by a two-thirds vote. In the case of a pocket veto, Congress does not even have the option of overriding the veto, but must reintroduce the bill in the next session. The president may exercise a pocket veto when presented with a bill during the last 10 days of a congressional session. Usually, if a president does not sign a bill within 10 days, it automatically becomes law. But this is true only while Congress is in session. If a president chooses not to sign a bill presented within the last 10 days that Congress is in session, then the 10-day limit expires while Congress is out of session, and instead of becoming law the bill is vetoed. Figure 6.1 illustrates the president's veto options. In 1996, Congress added the line-item veto, giving the president

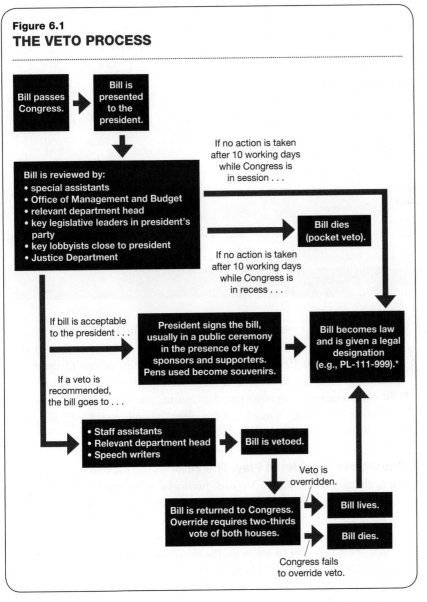

line-item veto
The power of the executive to veto specific provisions (lines) of a bill passed by the legislature

Figure 6.1
THE VETO PROCESS

Bill passes Congress. → Bill is presented to the president.

Bill is reviewed by:
• special assistants
• Office of Management and Budget
• relevant department head
• key legislative leaders in president's party
• key lobbyists close to president
• Justice Department

If no action is taken after 10 working days while Congress is in session . . .

Bill dies (pocket veto).

If no action is taken after 10 working days while Congress is in recess . . .

If bill is acceptable to the president . . .

President signs the bill, usually in a public ceremony in the presence of key sponsors and supporters. Pens used become souvenirs.

Bill becomes law and is given a legal designation (e.g., PL-111-999).*

If a veto is recommended, the bill goes to . . .

• Staff assistants
• Relevant department head
• Speech writers

Bill is vetoed.

Veto is overridden.

Bill is returned to Congress. Override requires two-thirds vote of both houses.

Bill lives.

Bill dies.

Congress fails to override veto.

*PL stands for "public law"; 111 is the Congress (e.g., the 111th Congress was in session in 2009–11); 999 is the number of the law.

Presidential Vetoes, 1789–2016

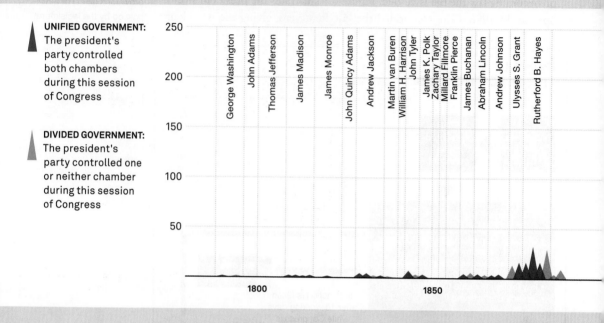

UNIFIED GOVERNMENT:
The president's party controlled both chambers during this session of Congress

DIVIDED GOVERNMENT:
The president's party controlled one or neither chamber during this session of Congress

the power to strike specific spending items from appropriations bills passed by Congress, unless a two-thirds vote of both the House and the Senate reenacted them. In 1997, President Clinton used this power 11 times to strike 82 items from the federal budget. But, as we saw in Chapter 5, in 1998 the Supreme Court ruled that the Constitution does not authorize the line-item veto power.[11] Only a constitutional amendment would give this power to the president.

The Games Presidents Play: The Veto. Use of the veto varies according to the political situation that each president confronts. George W. Bush vetoed only one bill during his first six years in office, a period during which his party controlled both houses of Congress. After the Democrats won control of Congress in 2006, Bush's use of the veto increased markedly.[12] In President Obama's first term, with Democratic control of both the House and the Senate, he vetoed only two bills. In his second term, during which his party did not control the House and controlled the Senate for only one Congress, Republicans pursued the strategy of obstruction, and very little legislation was produced. Obama's vetoes nevertheless increased to the low

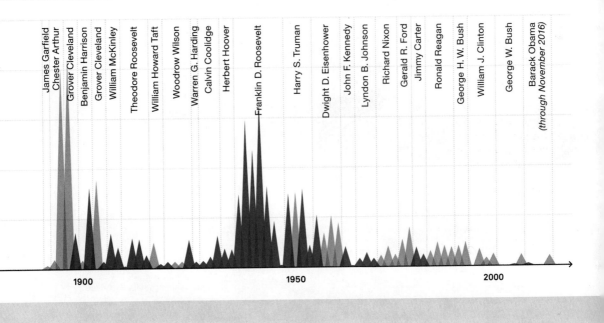

double digits. In general, presidents have used the veto to equalize or upset the balance of power with Congress. The politics surrounding the veto is complicated, and it is usually part of an intricate bargaining process between the president and Congress, involving threats of vetoes, repassage of legislation, and second vetoes.[13] As the timeplot above shows, divided government does not necessarily result in more vetoes.

Although presidents rarely veto legislation, in many cases the *threat* of a veto is sufficient to make members of Congress alter the content of a bill to make it more to a president's liking. Thus the veto power can be influential even when the veto pen rests in its inkwell.

What about the relationship between mass public support for the president and the use of the veto? At least for the modern presidency, a crucial resource for the president in negotiating with Congress has been public approval as measured by opinion polls.[14] In some situations, members of Congress pass a bill not because they want to change policy but because they want to force the president to veto a popular bill that he disagrees with in order to hurt his approval ratings.[15] As a result, vetoes may come at a price to the president. The Policy Principle case study on page 182 looks at Obama's veto of a bill

The Veto and the Keystone XL Pipeline

Demonstrators protest the Keystone XL Pipeline.

President Obama, despite presiding over congresses with at least one house controlled by Republicans through most of his two terms, did not use his veto pen very often. However, his veto of a 2015 bill concerning the Keystone XL pipeline provides a clear example of how institutions shape policy outcomes.

The Keystone XL pipeline would have taken crude oil from Alberta, Canada, through Montana, South Dakota, and Nebraska, and on to refineries in Illinois and on the Gulf Coast. Proponents of the pipeline—including most Republicans as well as business groups—pointed to its economic benefits, such as construction jobs and ongoing employment at U.S. refineries. Opponents of the pipeline—environmental groups and many Democrats—argued that the construction jobs would not last and that the project posed serious environmental risks. The pipeline was planned to travel through fragile wetlands, threatened large aquifers, and was said to be vulnerable to ruptures.

In 2012, Obama announced his opposition to the pipeline plans because of the environmental dangers. The pipeline corporation adjusted the route in response, and the governor of Nebraska (where the risks were especially alarming) signed off on the new proposal. Obama then announced that any further consideration would be suspended until various lawsuits against the pipeline were resolved. In 2015, the Nebraska Supreme Court allowed the project to go forward. The table was now set for federal action.

In February 2015, a bill approving the Keystone XL pipeline passed the House, was amended by the Senate, and then passed the House again. The institutional rules of Congress mattered: Republican majorities controlled the agenda in both chambers, had the Democrats held a majority in either chamber, they could have blocked consideration of the bill. The vote splits on the bill were important, too: 62–36 in the Senate and 270–152 in the House. Neither total indicated that the votes were there to override a presidential veto with the two-thirds required under the Constitution.

On February 24, 2015, the bill was sent to President Obama for his signature. Although opinion polls indicated that a majority of the public supported the pipeline, it was not a top issue for most people. It was very important to environmental organizations, however, and thus to their Democratic allies in Congress and in the White House. This was enough to persuade the president to wield his veto pen. On that very same day, he communicated to the Senate his decision to veto the bill. A week later, the Senate held a vote to override the veto, which failed to reach the necessary two-thirds (62-37).

The very exacting standard for the legislature to override a president's veto means that presidents require only a sufficiently large minority in at least one chamber to block legislative action. A president facing a hostile Congress may be handicapped in accomplishing his or her own policy goals, but the president nevertheless may succeed in blocking policies he or she opposes.

authorizing the Keystone XL pipeline, a project that was supported by a majority of Americans but strongly opposed by Democrats in Congress. In this case, the president risked a dip in public approval in order to promote his own policy preferences and those of the politicians who supported him.

Delegated Powers

Many of the powers exercised by the president and the executive branch are not set forth in the Constitution but are the products of congressional statutes and resolutions. Over the past three-quarters of a century, Congress has voluntarily delegated a great deal of its own legislative authority to the executive branch. To some extent, this delegation has been an almost inescapable consequence of the expansion of governmental activity since the New Deal. Given the vast range of the federal government's responsibilities, Congress cannot execute and administer all the programs it creates and the laws it enacts. Inevitably it must turn to the hundreds of departments and agencies in the executive branch or, when necessary, create new agencies to implement its goals. Thus, for example, in 1970, when Congress enacted legislation designed to improve the nation's air and water quality, it assigned the task of implementing its goals to the new Environmental Protection Agency (EPA) created by Nixon's executive order. Congress gave the EPA substantial power to set and enforce air- and water-quality standards.

As they implement congressional legislation, federal agencies interpret Congress's intent, promulgate thousands of rules aimed at implementing that intent, and issue thousands of orders to individuals, firms, and organizations designed to impel them to conform to the law.

In the nineteenth and early twentieth centuries, Congress typically wrote laws that provided fairly clear principles and standards to guide executive implementation. At least since the New Deal, however, Congress has tended to give executive agencies broad mandates through legislation that offers few clear standards or guidelines for implementation. The 1972 Consumer Product Safety Act, for example, authorizes the Consumer Product Safety Commission to reduce unreasonable risk of injury from household products but offers no suggestions of what constitutes reasonable and unreasonable risks or how these are to be reduced.

Inherent Powers

A number of presidential powers are neither expressed explicitly in the Constitution nor delegated by congressional statute or resolution. They are said to be "inherent" powers of a sovereign nation exercised by its chief executive. One inherent power of sovereign nations is self-protection. Today, this power is mainly exercised by the White House.

War and Inherent Presidential Power. The Constitution gives Congress the power to declare war. Presidents, however, have gone a long way toward capturing this power for themselves. Congress has not declared war since December 1941, yet since then American military forces have engaged in numerous campaigns throughout the world under the orders of the president. When North Korean forces invaded South Korea in June 1950, Congress was prepared to declare war, but President Harry S. Truman decided not to ask for congressional action. Instead, Truman asserted the principle that the president and not Congress could decide when and where to deploy America's military might. He dispatched American forces to Korea without a congressional declaration, and in the face of the emergency, Congress felt it had to acquiesce. It passed a resolution approving the president's actions, and this became the pattern for future congressional-presidential relations in the military realm. The wars in Vietnam, Bosnia, Afghanistan, and Iraq, as well as a host of smaller-scale conflicts, were all fought without declarations of war.

In 1973, Congress responded to presidential unilateralism by passing the War Powers Resolution over President Nixon's veto. This resolution reasserted the principle of Congress's power to declare war, required the president to inform Congress of any planned military campaign, and stipulated that forces must be withdrawn within 60 days in the absence of a specific congressional authorization for their continued deployment. Presidents, however, have generally ignored the War Powers Resolution, claiming inherent executive power to defend the nation. Thus, for example, President George W. Bush responded to the 2001 attacks by Islamic terrorists by organizing a major military campaign to overthrow the Taliban regime in Afghanistan, which had sheltered the terrorists. In 2003, Bush ordered a major American campaign against Iraq, which he accused of posing a threat to the United States. In both instances, Congress passed resolutions approving the president's actions; the War Powers Resolution was barely mentioned on Capitol Hill and was ignored by the White House. However, tensions stemming from the separation of powers between the president and Congress have not ceased. The powers of the purse and investigation give Congress levers with which to constrain the executive. For these reasons, presidents often restrain themselves to minimize adverse political consequences. Thus in 2013, with public opinion running against

War Powers Resolution

A 1973 resolution of Congress declaring that the president can send troops into action abroad only by authorization of Congress or if U.S. troops are already under attack or seriously threatened. For the most part, presidents have ignored the resolution.

On September 20, 2001, President George W. Bush addressed Congress and the public with a speech declaring a "war on terror." Congress passed a resolution approving the military campaign in Afghanistan (and, in 2002, the invasion of Iraq), but Bush insisted he did not need congressional authorization to go to war.

Chapter 6: The Presidency

him, President Obama sought authorization from Congress for an airstrike on Syria as punishment for its use of chemical weapons, in part to implicate Congress in the action and thereby share accountability. Throughout 2015 and 2016, the president and Congress negotiated over a congressional "authorization for the use of military force" against the Islamic State of Iraq and Syria (ISIS) and debated the legal rationale for a continuing American military effort without such authorization.

Legislative Initiative. Although it is not explicitly stated, the Constitution provides the president with the power of legislative initiative, which the framers clearly saw as one of the keys to executive power. Initiative obviously implies the ability to formulate proposals for important policies, and the president, as an individual with a great deal of staff assistance, is able to initiate decisive action more frequently than Congress, with its large assemblies that have to deliberate before taking action. It should be emphasized that Congress is under no constitutional obligation to take up proposals from the president. With some important exceptions, however, Congress banks on the president to set the policy agenda. And there is power in being able to set the terms of discourse in the making of public policy.

For example, in 2009, soon after taking office, President Obama presented Congress with a record-breaking $3 trillion budget proposal that included a host of new programs in such areas as health and human services, transportation, housing, and education. Obama told Congress that he would soon be requesting several hundred billion more for the financial bailout to rescue the United States' banks and revive the nation's credit markets. Not only was Congress responsive to the president's initiatives, but lawmakers also expected the president to take the lead in responding to the United States' financial emergency and other problems.

The president's initiative does not end with policy making involving Congress and the making of laws in the ordinary sense of the phrase. The president has still another legislative role (in all but name) within the executive branch: the power to issue executive orders. The executive order is foremost simply a management tool, the power virtually any CEO has to make "company policy"—rules-setting procedures, etiquette, chains of command, functional responsibilities, and so on. But evolving out of this practice is a presidential power to promulgate rules that have the effect of legislation. Most executive orders of the president provide for the reorganization of structures and procedures or otherwise direct the affairs of the executive branch. The power to issue executive orders illustrates that although reputation and persuasion are typically required in presidential policy making, the practice of issuing executive orders, within limits, allows a president to govern without the necessity to persuade.[16]

legislative initiative
The president's inherent power to bring a legislative agenda before Congress

executive order
A rule or regulation issued by the president that has the effect of legislation

THE RISE OF PRESIDENTIAL GOVERNMENT

Most of the real influence of the modern presidency derives from the powers granted by the Constitution and the laws made by Congress. Presidential power is institutional. Thus, any person properly sworn in as president will possess all of the power held by the strongest presidents in American history. But what variables account for a president's success in exercising these powers? Why are some presidents considered great successes, others colossal failures, and most somewhere in between? The answer relates broadly to the very concept of presidential power. Is that power a reflection more of the president's personal attributes or of the political situations that a president encounters?

The personal view of presidential power dominated political scientists' view for several decades,[17] but recently scholars have argued that presidential power should be analyzed in terms of the strategic interactions that a president has with other political actors. With the occasional exception, it took more than a century before presidents came to be seen as consequential players in these strategic encounters. A bit of historical review will be helpful in understanding how the presidency has risen to its current level of influence.

The Legislative Epoch, 1800–1933

In 1885, a then-obscure political science professor named Woodrow Wilson titled his general textbook *Congressional Government* because American government was just that—government by Congress. There is ample evidence that Wilson's description of the national government was consistent not only with nineteenth-century reality but also with the intentions of the framers. Within the system of three separate and competing powers, the clear intent of the Constitution was legislative supremacy. In the early nineteenth century, some observers saw the president as little more than America's chief clerk. Indeed, most historians agree that between Thomas Jefferson and the beginning of the twentieth century, Andrew Jackson and Abraham Lincoln were the only exceptions to a succession of weak presidents. Both Jackson and Lincoln are considered great presidents because they used their power in momentous ways. But it is important in the history of the presidency that neither of them left his powers as an institutional legacy to his successors. That is to say, once Jackson and Lincoln left office, the presidency reverted to the subordinate role that it played throughout the nineteenth century.

One reason that so few great men became presidents in the nineteenth century is that there was rarely room for greatness in such a weak office.[18] As Chapter 3 indicated, the national government of that period was not particularly powerful. Another reason is that during this period, the presidency was not closely linked to major national political and social forces. Federalism had fragmented political interests and diverted the energies of interest groups toward state and local governments, where most key decisions were made.

The presidency was strengthened somewhat in the 1830s with the introduction of the national convention system of nominating presidential candidates. Until then, presidential candidates had been nominated by their party's members of Congress. The national nominating convention arose in order to provide some representation for a party's voters who lived in districts where they weren't numerous enough to elect a member of Congress. It was seen as a victory for democracy against the congressional elite, and it gave the presidency a base of power independent of Congress. This independence did not transform the presidency into the office we recognize today, though, because Congress was long able to keep tight reins on the president's power. The real turning point came during the administration of Franklin Delano Roosevelt.

The New Deal and the Presidency

The "first hundred days" of the Roosevelt administration in 1933 have no parallel in U.S. history. The policies proposed by Roosevelt and adopted by Congress during this period so changed the size and character of the national government that they constitute a moment in American history equivalent to the Founding or to the Civil War. But this period was only the beginning. The president's constitutional obligation to see "that the laws be faithfully executed" became, during Roosevelt's presidency, virtually a responsibility to shape the laws before executing them.

An Expanded Role for the National Government. Many of the New Deal programs were extensions of the traditional national government approach, which was described in Chapter 3. But the New Deal also included policies never before tried on a large scale by the national government; it began intervening into economic life in ways that had hitherto been reserved to the states. For example, in the throes of the Great Depression, the Roosevelt administration created the Works Progress Administration, seeking to put the able-bodied back to work; the federal government became the nation's largest employer at this time. The Social Security Act, to give another example, sought to improve the economic condition of the most impoverished segment of the population—the elderly. In other words, the national government discovered that it could directly regulate individuals as well as provide roads and other services.

The new programs were such dramatic departures from the traditional policies of the national government that their constitutionality was in doubt, and the Supreme Court did in fact declare several of them unconstitutional. The turning point came in 1937 with *National Labor Relations Board v. Jones & Laughlin Steel Corporation*, a case challenging the federal government's authority to regulate relations between businesses and labor unions. The Court's decision affirmed a federal role in the regulation of the national economy. After the end of the New Deal, the Court has never again seriously questioned the legitimacy of interventions of the national government in the economy or society.

Delegation of Power. The most important constitutional effect of Congress's actions and the Supreme Court's approval of those actions during the New Deal was the enhancement of presidential power. Most major acts of Congress in this period involved significant exercises of control over the economy, but few of them specified the actual controls to be used. Instead, Congress authorized the president or in some cases a new agency to determine what the controls would be. Although some of the new agencies were independent commissions responsible to Congress, most of the new agencies and programs were placed in the executive branch directly under presidential authority.

The growth of the national government through acts delegating legislative power tilted the American national structure away from a Congress-centered government toward a president-centered government, which has become an established fact of American life. Nevertheless, Congress continues to be the constitutional source of policy, and it can rescind these delegations of power or restrict them with later amendments, committee oversight, or budget controls.

PRESIDENTIAL GOVERNMENT

Presidents have at their disposal a variety of formal and informal resources that enable them to govern. Indeed, without these resources, presidents would lack the tools needed to make much use of the power and responsibility given to them by the Constitution and by Congress. Let us first consider the president's formal or official resources (Figure 6.2) and then turn to the more informal ones that affect a president's capacity to govern, in particular a base of popular support.

Figure 6.2
THE INSTITUTIONAL PRESIDENCY, 2016

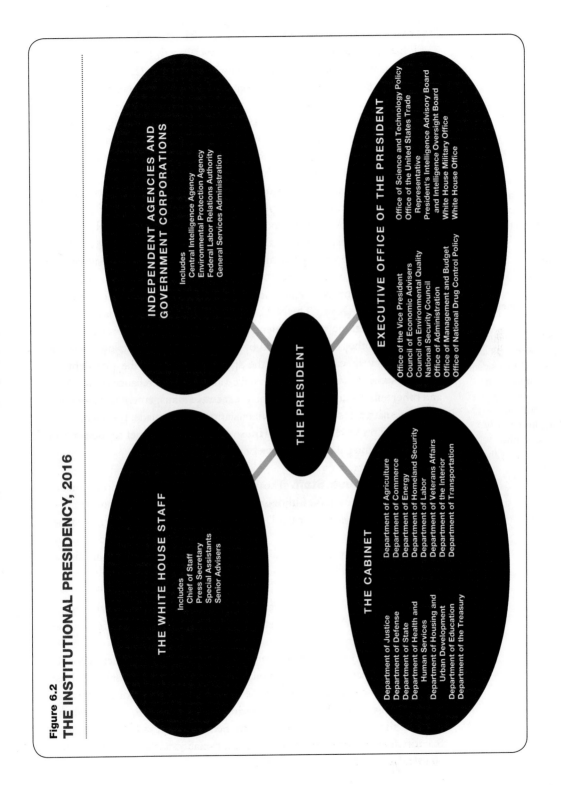

INDEPENDENT AGENCIES AND GOVERNMENT CORPORATIONS

Includes
Central Intelligence Agency
Environmental Protection Agency
Federal Labor Relations Authority
General Services Administration

THE WHITE HOUSE STAFF

Includes
Chief of Staff
Press Secretary
Special Assistants
Senior Advisers

THE PRESIDENT

EXECUTIVE OFFICE OF THE PRESIDENT

Office of the Vice President
Council of Economic Advisers
Council on Environmental Quality
National Security Council
Office of Administration
Office of Management and Budget
Office of National Drug Control Policy
Office of Science and Technology Policy
Office of the United States Trade
  Representative
President's Intelligence Advisory Board
  and Intelligence Oversight Board
White House Military Office
White House Office

THE CABINET

Department of Justice
Department of Defense
Department of State
Department of Health and
  Human Services
Department of Housing and
  Urban Development
Department of Education
Department of the Treasury
Department of Agriculture
Department of Commerce
Department of Energy
Department of Homeland Security
Department of Labor
Department of Veterans Affairs
Department of the Interior
Department of Transportation

Formal Resources of Presidential Power

The formal resources of presidential power include the Cabinet, the White House staff, the Executive Office of the President, and the vice presidency.

The Cabinet. In the American system of government, the Cabinet is the traditional but informal designation for the heads of all the major federal government departments. The Cabinet has only a limited constitutional status. Unlike that of Great Britain and many other parliamentary countries, where the cabinet *is* the government, the American Cabinet makes no decisions as a group; it is made up of directors but is not a board of directors. Each appointment to it must be approved by the Senate, but the person appointed is not responsible to the Senate or to Congress at large. Cabinet appointments help build party and popular support for the president, but the Cabinet is not a party organ.

Some presidents have relied heavily on an "inner cabinet," the National Security Council (NSC). The NSC, established by law in 1947, is composed of the president, the vice president, the secretary of state, the secretary of defense, and other officials invited by the president. It has its own staff of foreign-policy specialists run by the special assistant to the president for national security affairs. Presidents have varied in their reliance on the NSC and other sub-Cabinet bodies, because executive management is inherently a personal matter. However, one generalization can be made: presidents have increasingly preferred the White House staff to the Cabinet as their means of managing the gigantic executive branch.

The White House Staff. The White House staff is composed mainly of analysts and advisers. Although many of the top White House staffers carry the title "special assistant" for a particular task or sector, the types of judgments they are expected to make and the kinds of advice they are supposed to give are a good deal broader and more generally political than those that come from the Cabinet departments or the Executive Office of the President.

The White House staff is a crucial information source and management tool for the president. But it may also insulate the president from other sources of information. Managing this trade-off between in-house expertise and access to independent outside opinion is a major challenge for the president. Sometimes it is botched, as when President George W. Bush depended too heavily on his staff for information about WMDs in Iraq, leading him to erroneous conclusions. In 2009, President Obama merged the White House Homeland Security staff with the National Security Council staff to create a new National Security staff to deal with all security problems.[19]

Cabinet

The secretaries, or chief administrators, of the major departments of the federal government. Cabinet secretaries are appointed by the president with the consent of the Senate.

National Security Council (NSC)

A presidential foreign-policy advisory council comprising the president; the vice president; the secretaries of state, defense, and the treasury; the attorney general; and other officials invited by the president

The Executive Office of the President. The development of the White House staff can be appreciated only in relation to the still larger Executive Office of the President (EOP). Created in 1939, the EOP is what is often called the "institutional presidency"—the permanent agencies that perform defined management tasks for the president. The most important and the largest EOP agency is the Office of Management and Budget (OMB). Its roles in preparing the national budget, designing the president's program, reporting on agency activities, and overseeing regulatory proposals make OMB personnel part of virtually every presidential responsibility. The status and power of the OMB within the EOP has grown in importance from president to president.

The process of budgeting was at one time a bottom-up procedure, with expenditure and program requests passing from the lowest bureaus through the departments to "clearance" in OMB and hence to Congress, where each agency could be called in to reveal what its original request had been before OMB got hold of it. Now the process is top-down, with OMB setting the budget guidelines for agencies as well as for Congress.

The Vice Presidency. The Constitution created the vice presidency for two purposes: its occupant succeeds the president in the case of a vacancy and presides over the Senate, casting the tie-breaking vote when necessary.[20] The main value of the vice presidency as a political resource for the president is electoral. Traditionally, a presidential candidate's most important rules for choosing a running mate are that the vice-presidential nominee should bring the support of at least one state (preferably a large one) not otherwise likely to support the ticket and should come from a region and, if possible, an ideological or ethnic subsection of the party differing from the presidential nominee's. It is very doubtful that John Kennedy would have won in 1960 without the contribution his vice-presidential candidate, Lyndon Johnson, made in carrying Texas.

In 2016, Donald Trump chose Governor Mike Pence of Indiana as his running mate. A devout Christian, Pence increased Trump's electoral appeal among social conservatives. Before serving as governor, Pence had served in Congress for twelve years. He worked to reassure skeptical party leaders that Trump was a qualified candidate.

Presidential candidates often choose their vice presidential running mate to gain a specific electoral advantage. Mike Pence helped improve Donald Trump's electoral appeal among social conservatives and establishment Republicans.

As the institutional presidency has grown in size and complexity, most recent presidents have sought to use their vice presidents as a management resource after the election. The presidency of George W. Bush resulted in unprecedented power and responsibility for his vice president, Dick Cheney. For the Obama administration, Vice President Biden has played important roles as a liaison to Congress and a sounding board on foreign affairs.

The Contemporary Bases of Presidential Power

Generally, presidents can expand their power in three ways: party, popular mobilization, and administration. In the first instance, presidents may construct or strengthen national partisan institutions with which to influence the legislative process and through which to implement their programs. Alternatively, or in addition, presidents may use popular appeals to create a mass base of support that enables them to subordinate their political foes. This tactic has sometimes been called the strategy of "going public" or the "rhetorical" presidency.[21] Third, presidents may seek to bolster their control of executive agencies or to create new administrative institutions and procedures that will reduce their dependence on Congress and give them a more independent governing and policy-making capability. Use of executive orders to achieve policy goals in lieu of seeking to persuade Congress to enact legislation is, perhaps, the most obvious example.

Party as a Source of Power. All presidents have relied on the members and leaders of their own party to implement their legislative agendas—as, for example, President George W. Bush did on such matters as energy policy and Medicare reform. But the president does not control the party, whose members have considerable autonomy. Moreover, in the United States' system of separated powers, the president's party may be in the minority in Congress and unable to do much for the chief executive's programs (Figure 6.3). Consequently, although their party is valuable to chief executives, it has not been a fully reliable presidential tool. The more unified the president's party is behind his legislative requests, the more unified the opposition party is also likely to be. The president often poses as being above partisanship to win "bipartisan" support in Congress. But to the extent that he pursues a bipartisan strategy, he cannot throw himself fully into building the party loyalty and discipline that would maximize the value of his own party's support in Congress. This is a dilemma for every president, particularly one with an opposition-controlled Congress.

Going Public. Popular mobilization as a technique of presidential power has its historical roots in the presidencies of Theodore Roosevelt and Woodrow

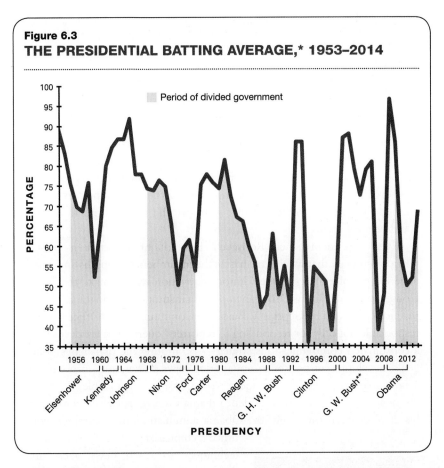

Figure 6.3

THE PRESIDENTIAL BATTING AVERAGE,* 1953–2014

*Percentage of congressional votes in which the president took the position supported by Congress.
**In 2001, the government was divided for only part of the year.
NOTE: Percentages are based on votes on which presidents took a position.
SOURCES: *Congressional Quarterly Weekly Report*, January 3, 2011, pp. 18–24, and authors' update.

Wilson and has become a weapon in the political arsenals of most presidents since the mid-twentieth century. During the nineteenth century, it was considered inappropriate for presidents to engage in personal campaigning on their own behalf or in support of programs and policies. When Andrew Johnson broke this unwritten rule and made a series of speeches vehemently seeking public support for his Reconstruction program, even some of Johnson's most ardent supporters were shocked at what they saw as his lack of decorum.

The president who used public appeals most effectively was Franklin Delano Roosevelt. The political scientist Sidney Milkis observes that Roosevelt was "firmly persuaded of the need to form a direct link between the executive office and the public.[22] He developed a number of tactics aimed at forging such a link. Like Theodore Roosevelt and Wilson, he often embarked on speaking trips around the nation to promote his programs. In addition, Roosevelt made limited but important use of the new electronic medium, the radio, to reach millions of Americans. In his famous "fireside chats," the president, or at least his voice, came into living rooms across the country to discuss programs and policies and generally to assure Americans that Roosevelt was aware of their difficulties and working diligently toward solutions.

Roosevelt also made himself available for biweekly press conferences, offering candid answers to reporters' questions and making important policy announcements that would provide the reporters with significant stories to file.[23] Roosevelt was especially effective in designating a press secretary, who organized press conferences and made certain that reporters distinguished presidential comments that were off the record from those that could be attributed.

Every president since Roosevelt has sought to craft a public-relations strategy that would emphasize the incumbent's strengths and maximize his popular appeal. One Clinton innovation was to make the White House Communications Office an important institution within the EOP. In a practice continued by George W. Bush, the Communications Office became responsible not only for responding to reporters' queries but for developing a coordinated communications strategy—promoting the president's policy goals, developing responses to unflattering news stories, and ensuring that a favorable image of the president would, insofar as possible, dominate the news. Consistent with President Obama's use of social networking in his 2008 election campaign, the Obama administration's communications office emphasized social networking techniques to reach newsmakers and the American people directly. The White House posted several tweets a day on topics as varied as immigration reform, climate change, and the Chicago Blackhawks' Stanley Cup win. In addition to using the media, recent presidents have reached out directly to the American public to gain its approval (Figure 6.4).

However, popular support has not been a firm foundation for presidential power. To begin with, it is notoriously fickle. President George W. Bush maintained an approval rating of over 70 percent for more than a year after the September 11 terrorist attacks. By 2003, however, his rating had fallen nearly 20 points as

Today, presidents use an array of strategies, including appearances on popular television shows, to reach constituents, shape their image, and attempt to win support for their policies.

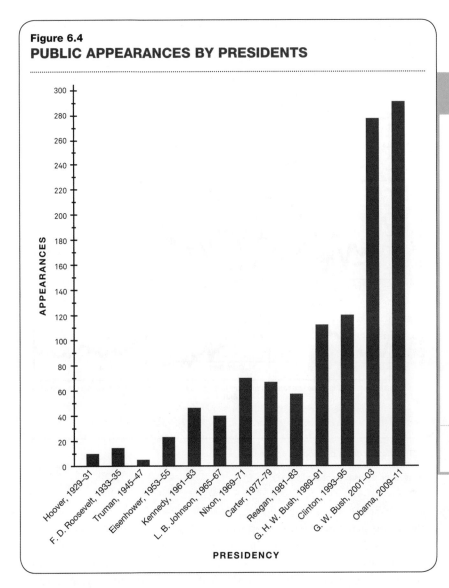

Figure 6.4

PUBLIC APPEARANCES BY PRESIDENTS

Y-axis: APPEARANCES (0 to 300)

X-axis (PRESIDENCY): Hoover, 1929–31; F. D. Roosevelt, 1933–35; Truman, 1945–47; Eisenhower, 1953–55; Kennedy, 1961–63; L. B. Johnson, 1965–67; Nixon, 1969–71; Carter, 1977–79; Reagan, 1981–83; G. H. W. Bush, 1989–91; Clinton, 1993–95; G. W. Bush, 2001–03; Obama, 2009–11

NOTE: Only the first two years of each term are included, because the last two years include many purely political appearances for the president's re-election campaign.
SOURCES: Kernell, *Going Public*, p.118; Lyn Ragsdale, *Vital Statistics on the Presidency*, 3rd ed. (Washington, DC: CQ Press, 2009), Table 4-9, pp. 202–3; POTUS Tracker, *Washington Post*, http://projects.washingtonpost.com/potus-tracker/ (accessed 8/8/11); and authors' updates.

American casualties in Iraq mounted, and it steadily declined through the remainder of his presidency. Obama began his presidency with a very high approval rating, but since 2010 it has hovered in the 40s and 50s. Such declines in popular approval during a president's term in office are nearly inevitable and follow a predictable pattern (Figure 6.5).[24]

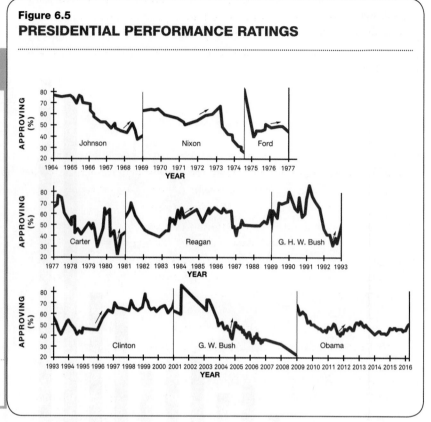

Figure 6.5

PRESIDENTIAL PERFORMANCE RATINGS

In the presidential performance-rating poll, respondents are asked, "Do you approve of the way the president is handling his job?" The graphs show the percentage of positive responses. What factors help explain changes in presidential approval ratings? Does popular approval really affect presidential power? How can popular feelings about the president affect the president's conduct and influence?

NOTE: Arrows indicate pre-election upswings.
SOURCES: Gallup, Presidential Job Approval Center, www.gallup.com/poll/124922/presidential-approval-center.aspx (accessed 5/9/16).

Presidents generate popular support by promising to undertake important programs that will contribute directly to the well-being of large numbers of Americans, but presidential performance almost inevitably falls short of those promises, leading to a sharp decline in support. Reagan and Clinton are the exceptions among modern presidents—leaving office at least as popular as when they arrived.

Technological change has affected the tactics of going public. The growing heterogeneity of media outlets—cable stations, streamed radio, the blogosphere, social media such as Twitter—and the declining viewership and readership of formerly "mainstream" outlets have fragmented the public. This has necessitated newly crafted approaches—"narrowcasting" to reach targeted demographic categories rather than broadcasting to reach "the public." Instead of going "capital P" public, new approaches seek to appeal to myriad "small p" publics (plural). Shrinking and fragmented audiences have raised the costs and cast doubt on the effectiveness of presidential efforts to educate and mobilize public opinion. The limitations of going public as a route to presidential power have also led contemporary presidents to make use of a third technique: expanding their administrative capabilities.

The Administrative State

Contemporary presidents have increased the administrative capabilities of their office in two important ways. First, they have sought to increase White House control over the federal bureaucracy. Second, they have expanded the role of executive orders and other instruments of direct presidential governance. Taken together, these components of administrative strategy have given presidents the potential to achieve their programmatic and policy goals even when they are unable to secure congressional approval. Indeed, some recent presidents have been able to accomplish quite a bit without much congressional, partisan, or even public support.

Appointments and Regulatory Review. Presidents have sought to increase their influence through bureaucratic appointments and regulatory review. By appointing loyal supporters to top jobs in the bureaucracy, presidents make it more likely that agencies will follow the president's wishes. As the Analyzing the Evidence unit on pp. 198–9 shows in more detail, recent presidents have increased the number of political appointees in the bureaucracy. Through regulatory review, presidents have tried to control rule making by the agencies of the executive branch. Whenever Congress enacts a statute, its implementation requires the promulgation of hundreds of rules by the agency charged with administering the law. Some congressional statutes are quite detailed and leave agencies with relatively little discretion. Typically, however, Congress enacts a relatively broad statement of legislative intent and delegates to the appropriate agency the power to fill in many important details.[25] In other words, Congress often says to an administrative agency, "Here is the problem. Deal with it."[26]

The discretion Congress delegates to administrative agencies has provided recent presidents with an important avenue for expanding their power. For example, after President Clinton ordered the Food and Drug Administration (FDA) to develop rules to restrict the marketing of tobacco products to children, White House and FDA staffers prepared nearly 1,000 pages of new regulations affecting tobacco manufacturers and vendors.[27] Although Republicans denounced Clinton's actions as a usurpation of power,[28] President George W. Bush continued the practice of ordering agencies to issue new regulations, and Obama also continued the practice.

> **regulatory review**
> The Office of Management and Budget function of reviewing all agency regulations and other rule making before they become official policy

Presidential Appointees in the Executive Branch

Contributed by
David Lewis
Vanderbilt University

Article II of the Constitution states that "The executive power shall be vested in a President of the United States of America" and details one of the president's most important constitutional roles: leading the executive branch. Today, this means the president must manage 15 cabinet departments and 55 to 60 independent agencies—and the over 2 million civilian employees who work in the federal government. Given the system of separation of powers, the president often competes with Congress for control of the executive branch. Congress also has a legitimate interest in the actions of executive branch officials since Congress creates programs and agencies and determines their budgets. The stakes of this competition between the branches are increasing. As the scope and complexity of government work have grown, Congress has delegated important policy-making responsibility to government officials working in the executive branch. These officials determine important public policies such as allowable levels of pollutants in the environment, eligibility rules for government benefits like medical care and Social Security, and safety rules in workplaces. Modern presidents have sought to exert more control over these agencies by a number of means, including increasing the number of presidential appointments.

Civil Service Systems

Government agencies are generally staffed by a mix of two types of employees: civil servants and political appointees. Civil servants staff the lower strata of government agencies and are to be hired, fired, promoted, and demoted on the basis of merit, and they cannot be removed without good cause. Political appointees, however, are generally selected from outside the civil service by the president, and most can be removed at the president's discretion.

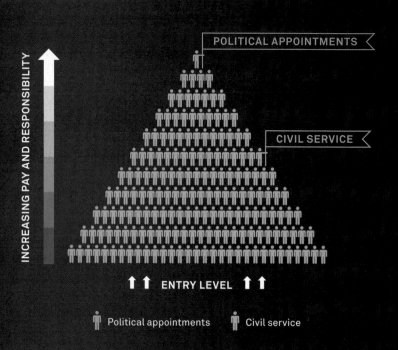

INCREASING PAY AND RESPONSIBILITY

POLITICAL APPOINTMENTS

CIVIL SERVICE

↑ ↑ ENTRY LEVEL ↑ ↑

Political appointments   Civil service

SOURCE: David E. Lewis,
The Politics of Presidential Appointments (Princeton, NJ: Princeton University Press, 2008).

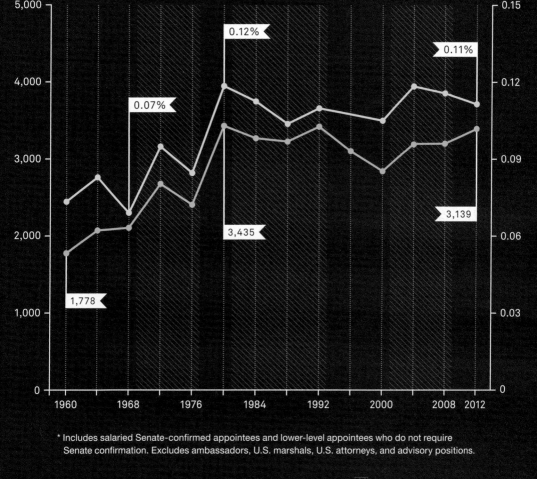

* Includes salaried Senate-confirmed appointees and lower-level appointees who do not require
  Senate confirmation. Excludes ambassadors, U.S. marshals, U.S. attorneys, and advisory positions.

●—● Percent appointed   ●—● Number of appointees   ▨ Republican president

Presidents since the middle of the twentieth century have sought to push down the dividing line between appointees and civil servants in government agencies. The figure above presents the total number of presidential appointees as well as the percentage of appointees in the federal government workforce over the last five decades. First, it should be noted that appointees make up a very small percentage of the federal workforce. However, and interestingly, the proportion of federal employees who are appointees has grown during this time period, as presidents have tried to exert greater influence over the executive branch.

Executive Orders. Another mechanism through which contemporary presidents have enhanced their power to govern unilaterally is the use of executive orders and other forms of presidential decrees, including executive agreements, national security findings and directives, proclamations, reorganization plans, signing statements, and others.[29] Presidents may not use executive orders to issue whatever commands they please. If a president issues an executive order, proclamation, directive, or the like, in principle he does so under powers granted to him by the Constitution or delegated to him by Congress, usually through a statute. When presidents issue such orders, they generally state the constitutional or statutory basis for their actions. For example, when President Truman ordered the desegregation of the armed services, he cited his constitutional powers as commander in chief. In a similar vein, when President Johnson issued Executive Order No. 11246, he asserted that the order was designed to implement the 1964 Civil Rights Act, which prohibited employment discrimination. Where an executive order has no statutory or constitutional basis, the courts have held it to be void. The most important case illustrating this point is *Youngstown Sheet & Tube Co. v. Sawyer*, the so-called steel seizure case of 1952.[30] Here the Supreme Court ruled that President Truman's seizure of the nation's steel mills during the Korean War had no statutory or constitutional basis and was thus invalid.

A number of court decisions, though, have held that Congress might approve a presidential action after the fact or through "acquiescence"—for example, by not objecting for long periods or by continuing to fund programs established by executive orders. In addition, the courts have indicated that some areas, most notably military policy, are inherently presidential in character and have allowed presidents wide latitude to make policy by executive decree. Thus, within the very broad limits established by the courts, presidential orders can be important policy tools (Figure 6.6).

President George W. Bush issued more than 40 executive orders during his first year in office alone, and continued to employ them regularly during his presidency. During his first months in office, Bush issued orders prohibiting the use of federal funds to support international family-planning groups that provided abortion-counseling services and placing limits on the use of embryonic stem cells in federally funded research projects. Bush also made very aggressive use of executive orders in response to the threat of terrorism; for example, he issued a directive authorizing the creation of military tribunals to try noncitizens accused of involvement in terrorism against the United States.

On his second full day in office, President Obama signed executive orders that reversed Bush's orders on stem cell research and on federal funding for international family-planning groups that performed or advocated abortion. By the end of his second term, Obama had issued over 250

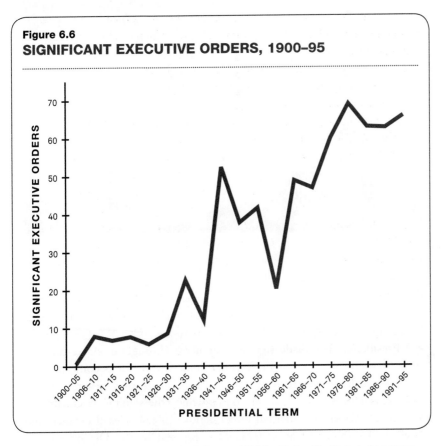

Figure 6.6

SIGNIFICANT EXECUTIVE ORDERS, 1900–95

SIGNIFICANT EXECUTIVE ORDERS (y-axis)

PRESIDENTIAL TERM (x-axis: 1900–05, 1906–10, 1911–15, 1916–20, 1921–25, 1926–30, 1931–35, 1936–40, 1941–45, 1946–50, 1951–55, 1956–60, 1961–65, 1966–70, 1971–75, 1976–80, 1981–85, 1986–90, 1991–95)

SOURCE: William G. Howell, "The President's Powers of Unilateral Action: The Strategic Advantages of Acting Alone" (Ph.D. diss., Stanford University, 1999).

executive orders including a controversial one that would protect some 4 million undocumented immigrants from the threat of deportation. This order provoked an outcry from congressional Republicans, who declared that the president had exceeded his constitutional authority. The order also spurred a variety of legal challenges and one federal court ruling blocking its implementation. In June of 2016, the Supreme Court sustained the lower-court decision, a major blow to Obama's immigration policy.

Signing Statements. The signing statement has become another instrument of presidential power, used frequently by recent presidents to negate congressional actions to which they objected.[31] A signing statement is an announcement by the president at the time of signing a bill into law, sometimes presenting the president's interpretation of the law as well as remarks

signing statement
An announcement made by the president when signing a bill into law

President Reagan, shown here signing the Deficit Reduction Act of 1984, often issued signing statements to point to elements of the law he deemed unconstitutional.

predicting the benefits it will bring to the nation. Occasionally, presidents have used signing statements to point to sections of the law they deemed improper or unconstitutional or to instruct executive branch agencies how to execute the law.[32]

Presidents have made signing statements throughout American history, though many were not recorded and so did not become part of the official legislative record. Ronald Reagan's attorney general, Edwin Meese, is generally credited with transforming the signing statement into a routine tool of presidential direct action.[33] Reagan used detailed and artfully designed signing statements—prepared by the Department of Justice—to attempt to reinterpret certain congressional enactments. Despite subsequent court rulings that the president lacked the power to declare acts of Congress unconstitutional[34] or to "excise or sever provisions of a bill with which he disagrees,"[35] the same tactic of reinterpreting and nullifying congressional enactments was continued by George H. W. Bush and Bill Clinton, and even more so by George W. Bush. The latter Bush challenged more than 800 legislative provisions with his signing statements, including a number of important domestic and security matters, such as a congressional effort to ban the use of torture by American interrogators. Though he had denounced George W. Bush's use of signing statements when running for president, soon after taking office Barack Obama began to make use of the same tactic. As he neared the end of his presidency, by November 2016, Obama had issued 36 signing statements in which he offered his own interpretation of portions of the bills he signed into law. In recent years, as presidents had hoped, courts have begun giving weight to presidential signing statements when interpreting the meaning of statutes.[36] Still, the legal status of signing statements has not been fully resolved.

Presidents are powerful political actors and have become increasingly so during the past century. This is the take-home point of this chapter. But there are limits to presidential power. Indeed, presidents have had to resort to institutional and behavioral invention—signing statements, executive orders, public appeals—precisely because their official powers are limited. As the framers intended, the separation of powers is a mighty constraint— "the president proposes; the Congress disposes." The president cannot always bend the Congress to his will, though it is an easier task when his party controls the two chambers. And yet the agendas of powerful congressional players must obtain the president's consent, as the presentment clause of the Constitution requires. Through the veto power, the president can defeat—but more important, can influence in advance—congressional aspirations. Presidential power is real, but it is tempered by the necessity of bargaining with the legislature and managing the bureaucracy along with the constraints imposed by rulings of the federal judiciary. The growth in presidential power of the last hundred years has required the acquiescence if not the outright support of all the other players in the game.

IS THE PRESIDENCY TOO STRONG?

The framers of the Constitution, as we saw, created a unitary executive branch because they thought this would make the presidency a more energetic institution. At the same time, they checked the powers of the executive branch by creating a system of separated powers. Did the framers' work make the presidency a strong or weak institution?

At one time, historians and journalists liked to debate the question of strong versus weak presidents. Some presidents, such as Lincoln and Franklin Delano Roosevelt, were called "strong" for their leadership and ability to guide the nation's political agenda. Others, such as James Buchanan and Calvin Coolidge, were seen as "weak" for failing to develop significant legislative programs and seeming to observe rather than shape political events. Today, the strong versus weak categorization has become moot. Despite the limits mentioned in the preceding section, *every president is strong*. This strength is a reflection not so much of personal charisma as of the increasing powers of the institution of the presidency. Of course, as we noted earlier, political savvy in interacting with other politicians and mobilizing public opinion can account for a president's success in exercising these powers. But contemporary presidents all possess a vast array of resources and powers.

Indeed, presidents seek to dominate the policy-making process and claim the inherent power to lead the nation in time of war. The expansion of presidential power over the past century has come about not by accident but as the result of ongoing efforts by successive presidents to expand the power of the office. Some of these efforts have succeeded and others have failed. One recent president, Richard Nixon, was forced to resign, and others have left office under clouds. Most presidents, nevertheless, have sought to increase the office's power. As the framers of the Constitution predicted, presidential ambition has been a powerful and unrelenting force in American politics. Why has it gone virtually unchecked? What are the consequences of such a development?

As is often noted by the media and in the academic literature, popular participation in American political life has declined precipitously since its nineteenth-century apogee. Voter turnout in presidential elections barely reaches the 60 percent mark; hardly a third of those eligible participate in off-year congressional races. Turnout in state and local contests is typically even lower. These facts are well known, and their implications for the representative character of American government frequently deplored.

The decay of popular political participation, however, also has institutional implications that are not often fully appreciated. To put the matter succinctly, the decline of voting and other forms of popular involvement in American political life reduce congressional influence while enhancing the power of the presidency. For all its faults, Congress is the nation's most representative political institution and remains the only entity capable of placing limits on unwise or illegitimate presidential conduct. Certainly, the courts have seldom been capable of thwarting a determined president, especially in the foreign-policy realm. Unfortunately, however, in recent decades our nation's undemocratic politics has undermined Congress while paving the way for aggrandizement of power by the executive and the presidential unilateralism that inevitably follows.

The framers of the Constitution created a system of government in which the Congress and the executive branch were to share power. In recent years, however, the powers of Congress have waned while those of the presidency have expanded dramatically. To take one instance of congressional retreat in the face of presidential assertiveness, in October 2002, pressed by President George W. Bush, both houses of Congress voted overwhelmingly to authorize him to use military force against Iraq. The resolution adopted by Congress allowed the president complete discretion to determine whether, when, and how to attack Iraq. Indeed, Bush's legal advisers had pointedly declared that the president did not actually need specific congressional authorization to attack Iraq if he deemed such action to be in America's interest. Few members of Congress even bothered to object to this apparent rewriting of the U.S. Constitution.

There is no doubt that Congress continues to be able to harass presidents and even, on occasion, to hand the White House a sharp rebuff. In the larger view, however, presidents' occasional defeats—however dramatic—have to be seen as temporary setbacks in a gradual and decisive shift toward increased presidential power in the twenty-first century.

For Further Reading

Canes-Wrone, Brandice. *Who Leads Whom? Presidents, Policy, and the Public.* Chicago: University of Chicago Press, 2006.

Crenson, Matthew, and Benjamin Ginsberg. *Presidential Power: Unchecked and Unbalanced.* New York: Norton, 2007.

Deering, Christopher, and Forrest Maltzman. "The Politics of Executive Orders: Legislative Constraints on Presidential Power." *Political Research Quarterly* 52 (1999): 767–83.

Howell, William, G. *Power without Persuasion: The Politics of Direct Presidential Action.* Princeton, NJ: Princeton University Press, 2003.

Krutz, Glen, and Jeffrey Peake. *Presidential-Congressional Governance and the Rise of Executive Agreements.* Ann Arbor: University of Michigan Press, 2009.

Milkis, Sidney M. *The President and the Parties: The Transformation of the American Party System Since the New Deal.* New York: Oxford University Press, 1993.

Nelson, Michael, ed. *The Presidency and the Political System.* 9th ed. Washington, DC: CQ Press, 2009.

Neustadt, Richard E. *Presidential Power and the Modern Presidents: The Politics of Leadership from Roosevelt to Reagan.* 1960. Rev. ed. New York: Free Press, 1990.

Skowronek, Stephen. *The Politics Presidents Make: Leadership from John Adams to Bill Clinton.* Cambridge, MA: Harvard University Press, 1997.

7

The Executive Branch

The bureaucracies of the executive branch are the administrative heart and soul of government. They are where the policies formulated and passed into law by elected officials are interpreted, implemented, and ultimately delivered to a nation's citizens. Government touches the lives of ordinary citizens most directly in their interactions with bureaucratic agents—at the Department of Motor Vehicles when obtaining a driver's license; in filing an income-tax return with the Internal Revenue Service; at the recruiting center when enlisting in one of the armed services; at the Board of Elections when registering to vote.

Public bureaucracies are powerful because legislatures and chief executives—and, indeed, the people—delegate to them vast power to make sure a particular job is done, leaving the rest of us freer to pursue our private ends. The public sentiments that emerged after September 11 revealed this underlying appreciation of public bureaucracies. Faced with the challenge of making air travel safe again, the public strongly supported giving the federal government responsibility for airport security even though this meant expanding the federal bureaucracy. In 2008 and 2009, Americans again looked to the federal bureaucracy to help solve the financial crisis. However, Americans have often been more suspicious of bureaucracy.

One reason for this suspicion is concern about organizational bias. Bureaucracies are created to give effect to the will of the nation's elected representatives. However, the practices of bureaucratic agencies often reflect their own external or internal interests more than Congress's plans or some broader conception of the public purpose. Two types of organizational interests or biases are especially likely to drive the behavior of bureaucratic agencies. First, agency executives are often concerned with their budget, power, and autonomy vis-à-vis other institutions and political forces.[1] For example, since the creation of the Department of Defense (DOD) and the Central Intelligence Agency (CIA) in 1947, the secretary of Defense and the director of Central Intelligence have engaged in continual bureaucratic struggle over control of the nation's intelligence assets and budgets.

A second type of organizational bias often results from an organization's internal politics. Just as organizations vie with one another, factions within an agency compete with rival groups for money, power, and prestige. A particularly important factor in such internal struggles is the agency's definition of its central mission and core responsibilities. Usually, one or another faction within the organization bases its claim to power and

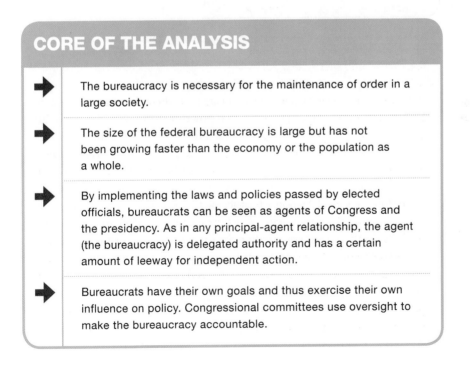

CORE OF THE ANALYSIS

➡ The bureaucracy is necessary for the maintenance of order in a large society.

➡ The size of the federal bureaucracy is large but has not been growing faster than the economy or the population as a whole.

➡ By implementing the laws and policies passed by elected officials, bureaucrats can be seen as agents of Congress and the presidency. As in any principal-agent relationship, the agent (the bureaucracy) is delegated authority and has a certain amount of leeway for independent action.

➡ Bureaucrats have their own goals and thus exercise their own influence on policy. Congressional committees use oversight to make the bureaucracy accountable.

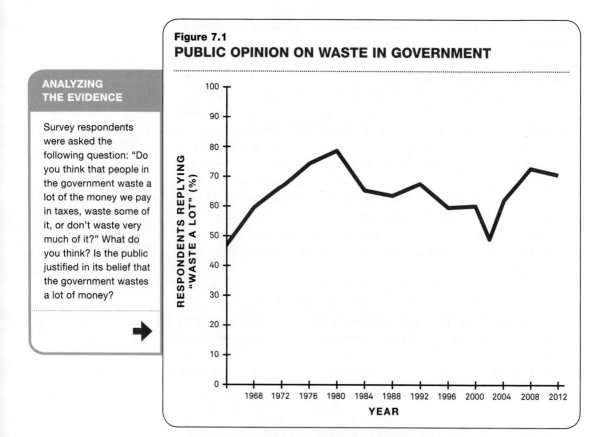

Figure 7.1
PUBLIC OPINION ON WASTE IN GOVERNMENT

SOURCES: American National Election Studies, Cumulative Data File, 1958–2008, www.electionstudies. org/nesguide/toptable/tab5a_3.htm (accessed 12/7/11), and www.electionstudies.org/studypages/ anes_timeseries_2012/anes2012TS_codebook.pdf (accessed 6/11/13).

preferment on its particular ability to carry out the agency's core mission. A change in mission might threaten that power. For example, when aircraft carriers were developed, the top commanders of many countries' navies resisted their introduction. These officers had generally built their careers on the command of battleships and other surface combatants and feared that a shift in naval missions and tactics would diminish their influence and empower a rival faction of officers—effects that, indeed, eventually took place.[2] The commitment of a bureaucracy's leaders to the mission that bolsters their own power within the organization is a major reason that bureaucracies often seem reluctant to change their practices and priorities in response to shifts in the external environment. Over time, this mission and associated practices can become so deeply ingrained in the minds of agency executives and staffers that adherence to them becomes a matter of habit and reflex. Students of bureaucracy refer to this set of established practices and beliefs about the organization's role and purpose as the agency's institutional "culture."[3]

The political scientist James Q. Wilson observed, "Every organization has a culture . . . a persistent, patterned way of thinking about the central tasks of and human relationships within an organization. Culture is to an organization what personality is to an individual . . . it is passed from one generation to the next. It changes slowly, if at all."[4] All agencies, civilian as well as military, are almost certain to resist efforts to compel them to undertake activities that are foreign to their institutional cultures and, thus, seem to pose a threat to their institutional autonomy or internal balance of power.

We can shed light on public attitudes toward government bureaucracy by examining one of the standard questions posed in election years by the American National Election Studies (ANES). In surveying the American public, the ANES asks a range of questions, including "Do you think that people in the government waste a lot of money we pay in taxes, waste some of it, or don't waste very much of it?" Although it doesn't elicit a nuanced assessment of bureaucratic performance, the question allows respondents to register a blunt evaluation. Results from the past several decades appear in Figure 7.1.

We examine the federal bureaucracy in this chapter both as an organizational setting within which policies are interpreted and implemented and as a venue in which politicians (called bureaucrats or bureaucratic agents) pursue their own and public interests. We first seek to define and describe bureaucracy as a social and political phenomenon. Second, we look in detail at American bureaucracy in action by examining the government's major administrative agencies, their role in the governmental process, and their political behavior.

HOW DOES BUREAUCRACY WORK?

Despite their tendency to criticize bureaucracy, most Americans recognize that maintaining order in a large society is impossible without a large governmental apparatus staffed by professionals with expertise in public administration. When we approve of what a government agency is doing, we give the phenomenon a positive name, administration; when we disapprove, we call the phenomenon bureaucracy.

Although *administration* and *bureaucracy* are often used interchangeably, it is useful to distinguish between the two terms. Administration is the more general term; it refers to all the ways human beings might rationally coordinate their efforts to achieve a common goal, in private as well as public

bureaucracy

The complex structure of offices, tasks, rules, and principles of organization that all large institutions use to coordinate the work of their personnel

organizations. Bureaucracy refers to the actual offices, tasks, rules, and principles of organization that large institutions use to coordinate their work.

Bureaucratic Organization Enhances Efficiency

The core of bureaucracy is the division of labor. The key to bureaucratic effectiveness is the coordination of experts performing complex tasks. If each job is specialized to increase efficiency, then each worker must depend on other workers' output, and that requires careful allocation of jobs and resources. Inevitably, bureaucracies become hierarchical, often pyramidal. At the base of the organization are workers with the fewest skills and specializations; one supervisor can oversee a large number of them. At the next level of the organization, involving more highly specialized workers, the coordination of work involves fewer workers per supervisor. Toward the top, a handful of high-level executives engage in the "management" of the organization, meaning the coordination and oversight of all its tasks, plus the allocation of supplies and the distribution of the organization's outputs to the market (if it is a private-sector organization) or to the public.

Bureaucracies Allow Governments to Operate

By dividing up tasks, matching them to a labor force that develops appropriately specialized skills, routinizing procedures, and providing the incentive structure and oversight arrangements to get large numbers of people to operate in a coordinated fashion, bureaucracies accomplish tasks and missions in a manner that would otherwise be unimaginable. The provision of "government goods" as broad as the defense of people, property, and national borders or as narrow as a subsidy to a wheat farmer requires organization, routines, standards, and, ultimately, the authority for someone to cut a check and put it in the mail. Bureaucracies are created to do these things.

Bureaucracy also consolidates complementary programs and insulates them from opposing political forces. By creating clienteles—in the legislature, interest groups, and public opinion—a bureaucracy establishes a coalition of supporters, some of whom will fight to keep it in place. Clienteles, after all, value consistency, predictability, and durability. It is well known that everyone in the political world cares deeply and intensely about certain policies and related agencies and opposes other policies and agencies, but not with nearly the same passion. Opponents, to succeed, must clear many hurdles, whereas proponents, to maintain the status quo, must only marshal their forces at a few veto points. Typically, opponents eventually give up and concentrate on protecting that about which they care most deeply.

Politicians acknowledge this fact of life. Consequently, both opponents and proponents of particular government activities wage the fiercest battles at the time programs are enacted and a bureaucracy is created. Once created, this bureaucracy assumes a position of relative permanence.

So, in terms of how bureaucracy makes government possible, efficiency and credibility both play a part. The creation of a bureau is both a way to deliver government goods efficiently and a device by which to "tie one's hands," thereby providing a credible commitment to the long-term existence of a policy.

Bureaucrats Fulfill Important Roles

Bureaucracy conveys to most people a picture of hundreds of office workers shuffling millions of pieces of paper. There is truth in that image, but we have to look more closely at what papers are being shuffled and why.

Implementing Laws. Bureaucrats, whether in public or private organizations, communicate with one another to coordinate all the specializations within their organization. This coordination is necessary to carry out the primary task of bureaucracy, which is implementation—that is, carrying out the organization's objectives as laid down by its board of directors (if a private company) or by law (if a public agency). In government, the "bosses" are ultimately the legislature and the chief executive.

> **implementation**
> The efforts of departments and agencies to the development of rules, regulations, and bureaucratic procedures to translate laws into action

Making and Enforcing Rules. When the bosses—Congress, in particular, when it is making the law—are clear in their instructions to bureaucrats, implementation is fairly straightforward. Bureaucrats translate the law into specific routines for each of the employees of an agency. But what happens to routine implementation when several bosses disagree as to what the instructions ought to be? This requires a fourth job for bureaucrats: interpretation. Interpretation is a form of implementation, in that the bureaucrats still have to carry out what they see as the intentions of their superiors. But when bureaucrats have to interpret a law before implementing it, they are in effect engaging in lawmaking.[5] Congress often deliberately delegates to an administrative agency the responsibility of lawmaking; for example, members conclude that some area of industry needs regulation or some area of the environment needs protection, but they are unwilling or unable to specify just how to do it. In such situations, Congress delegates to the appropriate agency a broad authority within which to make law, through the procedures of rule making and administrative adjudication.

Rule making is essentially the same as legislation; in fact, it is often called quasi-legislation. The rules issued by government agencies provide

The rules made by bureaucracies have the force of law. Bureaucracies may charge a person or business with violating the law, such as when peanut processing companies were found to have engaged in practices that caused a salmonella outbreak in 2007.

more detailed indications of what a policy actually will mean. For example, the Forest Service is charged with making policies that govern the use of national forests. Just before President Bill Clinton left office in 2001, the agency issued rules that banned new road building and development in the forests. This was a goal long sought by environmentalists and conservationists. In 2005, the Forest Service relaxed the rules, allowing states to make proposals for building new roads within the national forests. Just as the timber industry had opposed the Clinton rule banning road building, environmentalists challenged the new ruling and sued the Forest Service in federal court for violating clean-water and endangered-species legislation.

New rules proposed by an agency take effect only after a period of public comment, and reaction from the people or businesses that will be affected may cause the agency to modify its draft rules. Public participation takes the form of filing statements and giving testimony in public forums. The rule-making process is thus highly political. Once rules are approved, they are published in the *Federal Register* and have the force of law.

Settling Disputes. Administrative adjudication is very similar to what the judiciary ordinarily does: applying rules and precedents to specific cases in order to settle disputes. The agency charges the person or business suspected of violating the law, and the ruling applies only to the specific case being considered. Many regulatory agencies use administrative adjudication to make decisions about specific products or practices. For example, the National Labor Relations Board (NLRB) uses administrative adjudication to decide union certification. Groups of workers seek the right to vote on forming a union or the right to affiliate with an existing union as their bargaining agent and are opposed by their employers, who assert that relevant provisions of labor law do not apply. The NLRB takes testimony case by case and makes determinations for one side or the other, acting essentially like a court.

In sum, government bureaucrats do essentially the same things that bureaucrats in large private organizations do. But because of the coercive nature of government, far more constraints are imposed on public bureaucrats than on private bureaucrats. Public bureaucrats are required to maintain a more thorough paper trail and are subject to more access from the public, such as newspaper reporters. Public access has been vastly facilitated by the Freedom of Information Act (FOIA), adopted in 1966. This act gives ordinary citizens the right of access to agency files and data to determine whether those materials contain derogatory information about them and to learn about what the agency is doing in general.

Bureaucracies Serve Politicians

In principle, the legislature could make all bureaucratic decisions itself, writing very detailed legislation each year. In some areas—tax policy, for example—this is in fact done. Tax policy is promulgated in significant detail by the House Ways and Means Committee, the Senate Finance Committee, and the Joint Committee on Taxation. The Internal Revenue Service, the agency charged with implementation, engages in relatively less discretionary activity than many other regulatory and administrative agencies. But it is the exception.

The norm is for statutory authority to be delegated to the bureaucracy, often in vague terms, with the bureaucracy being expected to fill in the gaps. This, however, is not a blank check for unconstrained discretion. The bureaucracy will be held to account by the legislature's oversight of bureaucratic performance. The latter is monitored by the staffs of relevant legislative committees, which also serve as repositories for complaints from affected parties.[6] Poor performance or the exercise of discretion inconsistent with important legislators' preferences invites sanctions ranging from the browbeating of senior bureaucrats to the trimming of budgets and the clipping of authority.

HOW IS THE EXECUTIVE BRANCH ORGANIZED?

Cabinet departments, agencies, and bureaus are the operating parts of the bureaucratic whole. These parts can be separated into four general types: (1) cabinet departments, (2) independent agencies, (3) government corporations, and (4) independent regulatory commissions.

Although Figure 7.2 is an organizational chart of the Department of Agriculture, any other department could serve as an illustration. At the top is the department head, called the secretary of the department. Below the secretary and a deputy secretary are several top administrators, such as the general counsel and the chief economist, whose responsibilities span the various departmental functions and enable the secretary to manage the

Figure 7.2

ORGANIZATIONAL CHART OF THE DEPARTMENT OF AGRICULTURE

Secretary

Deputy Secretary

Director of Communications

Inspector General

General Counsel

Assistant Secretary for Congressional Relations

Assistant Secretary for Administration

Assistant Secretary for Civil Rights

Chief Economist

Director, National Appeals Division

Chief Information Officer

Chief Financial Officer

Executive Operations

Under Secretary for Natural Resources and Environment
- Forest Service
- Natural Resources Conservation Service

Under Secretary for Farm and Foreign Agricultural Services
- Farm Service Agency
- Foreign Agricultural Service
- Risk Management Agency

Under Secretary for Rural Development
- Rural Utilities Service
- Rural Housing Service
- Rural Business Cooperative Service

Under Secretary for Food, Nutrition, and Consumer Services
- Food and Nutrition Service
- Center for Nutrition Policy and Promotion

Under Secretary for Food Safety
- Food Safety and Inspection Service

Under Secretary for Research, Education, and Economics
- Agricultural Research Service
- National Institute of Food and Agriculture
- Economic Research Service
- National Agricultural Library
- National Agricultural Statistics Service

Under Secretary for Marketing and Regulatory Programs
- Agricultural Marketing Service
- Animal and Plant Health Inspection Service
- Grain Inspection Packers and Stockyards Administration

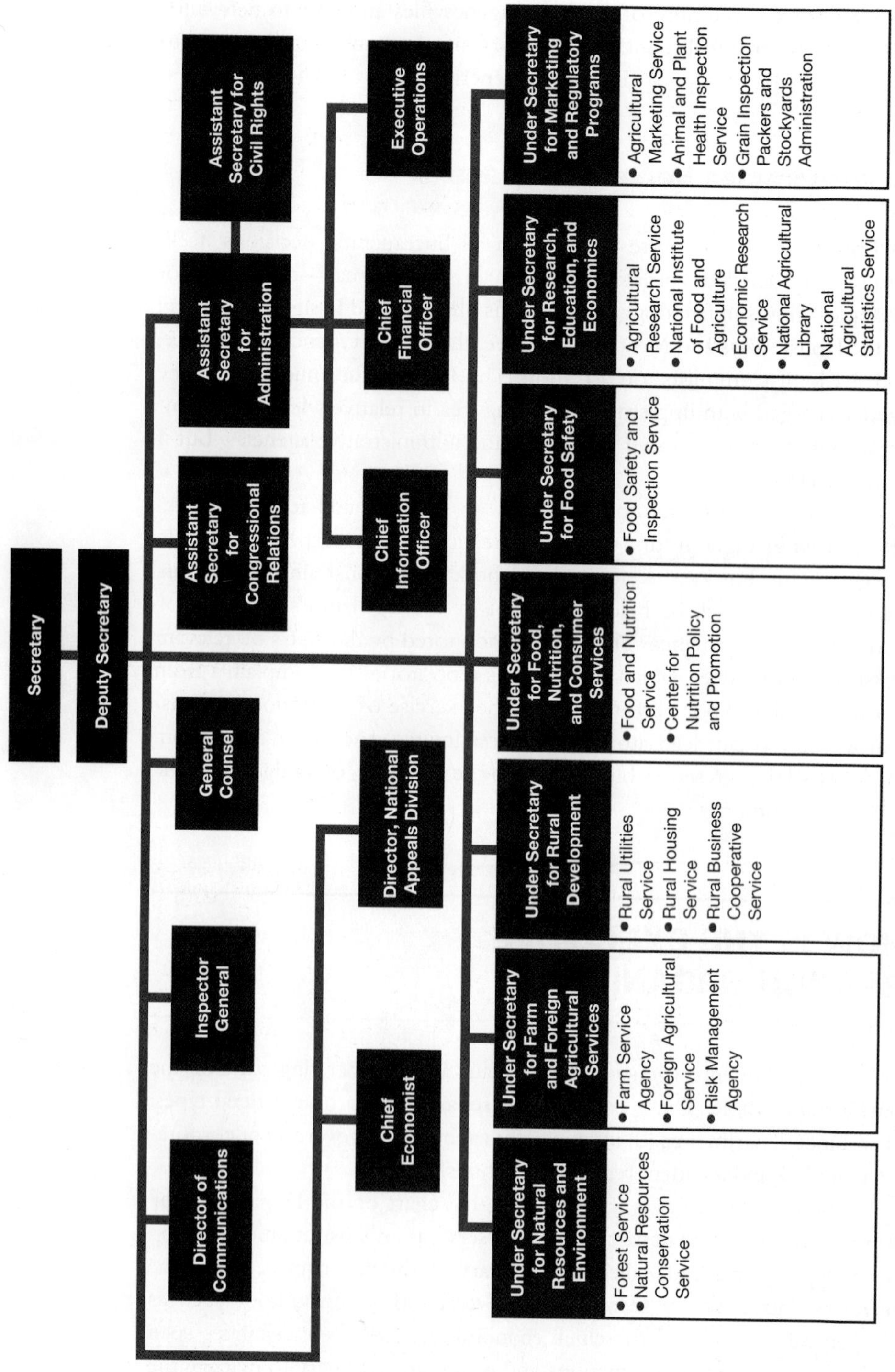

SOURCE: U.S. Department of Agriculture, www.usda.gov/documents/AgencyWorkflow.pdf.

entire organization. Working alongside these officials are the assistant and undersecretaries, each with management responsibilities for a group of operating agencies, which are arranged vertically below the undersecretaries.

The next tier, generally called the bureau level, is the highest level of responsibility for specialized programs. These bureau-level agencies are often very well known to the public: the Forest Service and the Food Safety and Inspection Service are examples. Sometimes they are officially called bureaus, such as the Federal Bureau of Investigation (FBI) in the Department of Justice. Within the bureaus are divisions, offices, services, and units.

Not all government agencies are part of cabinet departments. Some, called independent agencies, are set up by Congress outside the departmental structure, even though the president appoints and directs their heads. Independent agencies usually have broad powers to provide public services that are either too expensive or too important to be left to private initiatives. Some examples are the National Aeronautics and Space Administration (NASA), the Central Intelligence Agency (CIA), and the Environmental Protection Agency (EPA). A third type of government agency, government corporations, are more like private businesses performing and charging for a market service, such as transporting railroad passengers (Amtrak).

A fourth type of agency is the independent regulatory commission, given broad discretion to make rules. The first regulatory agencies established by Congress, beginning with the Interstate Commerce Commission in 1887, were set up as independent regulatory commissions because Congress recognized that regulatory agencies are "mini-legislatures," whose rules are the same as legislation but require the kind of expertise and full-time attention

As an independent agency, the National Aeronautics and Space Administration (NASA) is not part of a cabinet department but provides public services that are too important to be left to private initiatives. Here, NASA public affairs officer Dwayne Brown announces the presence of water on Mars.

Types of Government Agencies

There are four main types of bureaucratic agencies within the U.S. federal government.

✓ **Cabinet departments:** The largest subunits of the executive branch. Each of the 15 departments is headed by a cabinet secretary, and departments encompass related agencies and bureaus.

Example: Department of Justice (encompasses more than 50 agencies, including the Federal Bureau of Investigation, the Office of Tribal Justice, and the U.S. Parole Commission)

✓ **Independent agencies:** Agencies set up by Congress outside the cabinet departments to provide specific public goods and services, such as protection of the environment or information from space exploration.

Examples: Environmental Protection Agency (EPA), National Aeronautics and Space Administration (NASA)

✓ **Government corporations:** Government agencies that perform and charge for a market service, such as transporting rail passengers.

Example: Amtrak

✓ **Independent regulatory commissions:** Agencies given broad discretion to make rules regulating a specific type of activity.

Examples: Federal Communications Commission (FCC), Financial Stability Oversight Council

that is beyond the capacity of Congress. Until the 1960s, most of the regulatory agencies set up by Congress, such as the Federal Communications Commission (1934), were independent regulatory commissions. But beginning in the late 1960s, all new regulatory programs, with only a few exceptions (such as the Federal Election Commission), were placed within existing departments and made directly responsible to the president. After the 1970s, no major new regulatory programs were established until the financial crisis of 2008–09. The Dodd-Frank Wall Street Reform and Consumer Protection Act of 2010 brought major changes to the regulation of banks and other financial institutions. The act created several new regulatory bodies, including the Financial Stability Oversight Council, the Office of Financial Research, and the Bureau of Consumer Financial Protection.

There are too many agencies in the executive branch to identify them all here, so a simple classification will be helpful. The classification that follows organizes each agency by its mission, as defined by its jurisdiction: clientele agencies, agencies for maintenance of the Union, regulatory agencies, and redistributive agencies.

Clientele Agencies

The entire Department of Agriculture is an example of a clientele agency. So are the departments of the Interior, Labor, and Commerce. Although all administrative agencies have clienteles, certain agencies are specifically directed by law to promote the interests of their clientele. For example, the Department of Commerce and Labor was founded in 1903 as a single department "to foster, promote, and develop the foreign and domestic commerce, the mining, the manufacturing, the shipping, and fishing industries, and the transportation facilities of the United States."[7] It remained a single department until 1913, when legislation created the two separate departments of Commerce and Labor, with each statute providing for the same obligation: to support and foster their respective clienteles.[8] The Department of Agriculture serves the many farming interests that, taken together, are one of the United States' largest economic sectors.

Most clientele agencies have many of their personnel in field offices dealing directly with the clientele. A familiar example is the Extension Service of the Department of Agriculture, with its local "extension agents" who consult with farmers on farm productivity. These same agencies also provide "functional representation"; that is, they learn what their clients' interests and needs are and then operate almost as a lobby in Washington on their behalf. In addition to the departments of Agriculture, Commerce, and Labor, clientele agencies include the Department of Interior and five of the newest cabinet departments: Housing and Urban Development (HUD), created in 1966; Transportation (DOT), 1966; Energy (DOE), 1977; Education (ED), 1979; and Health and Human Services (HHS), 1979.[9]

clientele agency
A department or bureau of government whose mission is to promote, serve, or represent a particular interest

Agencies for Maintenance of the Union

The Constitution entrusts many vital functions of public order, such as the police, to state and local governments. But some agencies vital to maintaining national bonds do exist in the national government, and they can be grouped into three categories: (1) agencies for control of the sources of government revenue, (2) agencies for control of conduct defined as a threat to internal national security, and (3) agencies for defending American security from external threats. The most powerful departments in these three areas are Treasury, Justice, Defense, State, and Homeland Security.

Revenue Agencies. The Treasury Department's Internal Revenue Service (IRS) is the most important revenue agency and one of the federal government's largest bureaucracies. Over 100,000 employees are spread through 4 regions, 63 districts, 10 service centers, and hundreds of local offices.

Agencies for Internal Security. The United States is fortunate to enjoy national unity maintained by civil law rather than imposed by military force. As long as the country is not in a state of insurrection, most of the task of maintaining the Union involves legal work, and the main responsibility for that lies with the Department of Justice (DOJ). The most important agency in the DOJ is the Criminal Division, which enforces all federal criminal laws except a few assigned to other divisions. Criminal litigation is actually done by the U.S. attorneys. A presidentially appointed U.S. attorney is assigned to each federal judicial district, and he supervises the work of assistant U.S. attorneys. The work or jurisdiction of the Antitrust and Civil Rights Divisions is described by their official names. The FBI, another bureau of the DOJ, is the information-gathering agency for all the other divisions.

In 2002, Congress created the Department of Homeland Security (DHS) to coordinate the nation's defense against the threat of terrorism. This department's responsibilities include protecting commercial airlines from would-be hijackers. Most visible to the traveling public are the employees of the Transportation Security Administration (TSA). Consisting of 50,000 security officers and employees protecting airports and rail and bus depots, and staffing security screening operations, the TSA is the largest unit of the DHS.

Agencies for External National Security. Two departments occupy center stage here: State and Defense. A few key agencies outside State and Defense also have external national-security functions.

Although diplomacy is generally considered the State Department's primary task, that is only one of its organizational dimensions. The State Department also comprises geographic, or regional, bureaus concerned with all problems within specific regions of the world; "functional" bureaus, which handle such things as economic and business affairs, intelligence, and research; and relationships with international organizations and bureaus of internal affairs, which handle such areas as security, finance and management, and legal issues.

Despite the State Department's importance in foreign affairs, fewer than 20 percent of all U.S. government employees working abroad are directly under its authority. By far, the largest number of career government professionals working abroad are under the authority of the Department of Defense (DOD).

The creation of the DOD between 1947 and 1949 was an effort to unify the two historic military departments, the War Department and the Navy Department, and integrate them with a new department, the Air Force Department. Real unification did not occur, however. Instead, the DOD added more pluralism to national security.

The United States' primary political problem with its military has been relatively mundane compared to the experience of many other countries, which have struggled to keep their militaries out of the politics of governing. Rather, the problem is that of pork-barrel politics: defense contracts are often highly lucrative for local districts, so military spending becomes a matter of parochial interests as well as military need. For instance, President Bill Clinton's proposed military-base closings, a major part of his budget-cutting drive for 1993, caused a firestorm of opposition even in his own party and even from some members of Congress who otherwise favored slashing the Pentagon budget. Emphasis on jobs rather than strategy and policy means pork-barrel use of the military for political purposes. This is a classic way for a bureaucracy to defend itself politically in a democracy. It is an example of the distributive tendency, in which the bureaucracy ensures political support among elected officials by distributing things—military bases, contracts, facilities, and jobs—to the states and districts that elected the legislators.

Regulatory Agencies

The United States has many regulatory agencies. Some are bureaus within departments, such as the Food and Drug Administration (FDA) in the Department of Health and Human Services, the Occupational Safety and Health Administration (OSHA) in the Department of Labor, and the Animal and Plant Health and Inspection Service (APHIS) in the Department of Agriculture. Others are independent regulatory commissions—for example, the Federal Trade Commission (FTC). But whether departmental or independent, an agency or commission is regulatory if Congress delegates to it broad powers over a sector of the economy or a type of commercial activity and authorizes it to make rules governing the conduct of people and businesses within that jurisdiction. Rules made by regulatory agencies have the force of legislation; indeed, such rules are referred to as administrative legislation. And when these agencies make decisions or orders settling disputes between parties or between the government and a party, they are acting like courts.

regulatory agencies

A department, bureau, or independent agency whose primary mission is to ensure that individuals and organizations comply with the statutes under its jurisdiction

administrative legislation

Rules made by regulatory agencies which have the force of legislation

Agencies of Redistribution

Welfare, fiscal, and monetary agencies transfer hundreds of billions of dollars annually between the public and the private spheres, and through such transfers these agencies influence how people and corporations spend and invest trillions of dollars annually. We call them agencies of redistribution because they influence the amount of money in the economy and who has it, who has credit, and whether people will invest or save their money rather than spend it.

Fiscal and Monetary Policy Agencies. Government activity relating to money comprises *fiscal* and *monetary* policy. Fiscal policy includes taxing and spending activities. Monetary policies have to do with banks, credit, and currency. (We will discuss these policies in Chapter 13.)

Administration of fiscal policy is primarily a Treasury Department role. It is no contradiction to include the Treasury both here and among the agencies for maintenance of the Union. This dual classification indicates that (1) the Treasury performs more than one function of government and (2) traditional controls have been adapted to modern economic conditions and new technologies.

Today, in addition to administering and policing income tax and other tax collections, the Treasury manages the enormous federal debt. The Treasury also prints currency, but currency represents only a tiny portion of the entire money economy. Most of the trillions of dollars exchanged in the private and public sectors of the U.S. economy exist on printed accounts and computers, not in currency.

Federal Reserve System

A system of 12 Federal Reserve banks that facilitates exchanges of cash, checks, and credit; regulates member banks; and uses monetary policy to fight inflation and deflation

Another important fiscal and monetary policy agency is the Federal Reserve System, headed by the Federal Reserve Board. The Federal Reserve System (the Fed) has authority over the credit rates and lending activities of the nation's most important banks. Established by Congress in 1913, it is responsible for adjusting the supply of money to the needs of banks in the different regions and of the commerce and industry in each. It also ensures that the banks do not overextend themselves by overly liberal lending policies. The basis for this responsibility is the fear of a sudden economic scare that makes dubious loans uncollectible and thus destabilizes the banking system. At its worst, such a shock to the economy could cause another financial crash like the one in 1929 that ushered in the Great Depression. The Federal Reserve Board sits at the top of a pyramid of 12 district Federal Reserve banks, which are "bankers' banks," serving the hundreds of member banks in the national bank system (see also Chapter 13).

Welfare Agencies. No single agency is responsible for all the programs that make up the "welfare state." The largest agency in this field is the

Social Security Administration (SSA), which manages the social insurance aspects of Social Security and Supplementary Security Income (SSI). Other agencies in the Department of Health and Human Services administer Temporary Assistance to Needy Families (TANF) and Medicaid, and the Department of Agriculture is responsible for the food stamp program. With the exception of Social Security, these are means-tested programs, requiring applicants to demonstrate that their annual cash earnings fall below an officially defined poverty line. These public-assistance programs impose a large administrative burden.

THE PROBLEM OF BUREAUCRATIC CONTROL

Two centuries, millions of employees, and trillions of dollars after the Founding, we must return to James Madison's observation that "you must first enable the government to control the governed; and in the next place oblige it to control itself."[10] Today the problem is the same, but the form has changed. Our problem now is the challenge of keeping the bureaucracy accountable to elected political authorities.

Motivational Considerations of Bureaucrats

The economist William Niskanen proposed that a bureau or department of government is analogous to a division of a private firm and that a bureaucrat is like the manager who runs that division.[11] In particular, Niskanen stipulated that a bureau chief or department head can be thought of as trying to maximize her budget (just as the private-sector counterpart tries to maximize his division's profits).

There are many motivational bases on which bureaucratic budget maximizing might be justified. A cynical (though some would say realistic) explanation is that the bureaucrat's own compensation and fringe benefits are often tied to the size of her budget. A second, related motivation is nonmaterial personal gratification. An individual understandably enjoys the prestige that comes from running a major enterprise, and her self-esteem and status are surely buoyed by the conspicuous fact that her bureau has a large budget.

But salary and status are not the only forces driving a bureaucrat to gain as large a budget as possible. Some bureaucrats, perhaps most, actually *care* about their mission[12] and believe in the importance of helping people in their community. As they rise through the ranks and assume management

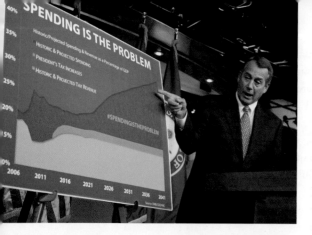

Government agencies depend on Congress to approve their budgets, and bureaucrats work to convince Congress that they are using the funds effectively. When Congress makes cuts to limit spending, some agencies suffer more than others.

responsibilities, this orientation still drives them. Thus they try to secure as large a budget as possible to succeed in the mission to which they have devoted their professional lives.

This does not mean that the legislature has to fork over whatever the bureau requests. In making budget allocations, Congress often evaluates a bureau's performance. Legislative committees hold hearings, request documentation, assign investigatory staff to research tasks, and query bureau personnel. After the fact, the committees engage in oversight; making sure that what the legislature was told at the time when authorization and appropriations were voted on actually holds in practice.

Before leaving motivational considerations, we should remark that budget maximizing is not the only objective that bureaucrats pursue. We must emphasize and reemphasize that career civil servants and high-level political appointees are politicians. They spend their professional lives pursuing political goals, bargaining, forming alliances and coalitions, solving cooperation and collective action problems, making policy decisions, operating within and interfacing with political institutions—in short, doing what other politicians do. Being subject to the oversight and authority of others, bureaucrats must be strategic and forward thinking. Whichever party wins control of the House or the Senate, and the presidency, whoever becomes chair of the legislative committee with authorization or appropriation responsibility over their agency, bureau chiefs have to adjust to the prevailing political winds. To protect and expand their authority and resources, bureaucratic politicians seek, in the form of autonomy and discretion, insurance against political change. They don't always succeed, but they do try to insulate themselves from changes in the broader political world.[13] So their motivations include budget-maximizing behavior, to be sure, but they also seek the autonomy to weather changes in the political atmosphere and the discretion and flexibility to achieve their goals.

The Bureaucracy and the Principal-Agent Problem

How does the principal-agent problem introduced in Chapter 1 apply to the president's and Congress's control of the bureaucracy? Let's suppose that legislation creating the EPA required that after 10 years new legislation be passed in order to renew the agency's existence and mandate. The issue facing the House, the Senate, and the president in considering renewal involves how much authority to give this agency and how much money to permit it to spend. Eventually majorities in the House and the Senate and the president agree on a policy reflecting a compromise among their various points of view.

The EPA bureaucrats are not pleased with this compromise because it gives them considerably less authority and funding than they had hoped for. If they flout their principals' wishes and implement a policy exactly to their liking, they risk the unified wrath of the House, the Senate, and the president. Undoubtedly the politicians would react with new legislation (and might also replace the current EPA leadership). If, however, the EPA implements a policy in between its own preferences and those of its principals, it might get away with it. That is, at the margins, the bureau tilts policy toward its own preferences, but not so far as to stimulate a legislative response.

Thus we have a principal-agent relationship in which a political principal—a collective principal consisting of the president and coalitions in the House and Senate—formulates policy and creates an implementation agent to execute its details. The agent, however, has policy preferences of its own and, unless subjected to further controls, will inevitably implement a policy that drifts toward its ideal. (The Policy Principle section on p. 224 looks at a real case in which the EPA and President Obama worked together against a Republican-controlled Congress to expand the agency's authority. In this case, the shift toward the policy preferences of the bureaucratic agents and the president *did* provoke an outcry from legislators in Congress.)

Various controls might conceivably restrict this bureaucratic drift. Indeed, legislative scholars often point to congressional hearings in which bureaucrats may be publicly rebuked, annual appropriations decisions that may serve to punish out-of-control bureaus, and watchdog agents, such as the Government Accountability Office, that may be used to scrutinize the bureau's performance. But these all come after the fact and may be only partially credible threats to the agency. The most powerful before-the-fact political weapon is the appointment process. The adroit control of a bureau's political stance by the president and Congress, through their joint powers of nomination and confirmation (especially if they can arrange for appointees who share the political consensus on policy) is a mechanism for ensuring reliable agent performance. A second powerful before-the-fact weapon is procedural controls. The general rules and regulations that direct the manner in which federal agencies operate are specified in the Administrative Procedure Act. This act is almost always the boilerplate of legislation for creating and renewing federal agencies. Sometimes, however, an agency's procedures are tailored to suit particular circumstances.

bureaucratic drift
The oft-observed phenomenon of bureaucratic implementation that produces policy more to the liking of the bureaucracy than faithful to the original intention of the legislation that created it, but without triggering a political reaction from elected officials

The EPA: Regulating Clean Air

A coal-burning power plant in Ohio.

In 1970, Congress passed the Clean Air Act to provide a platform for policy initiatives focused on reducing air pollution across the United States. It was closely aligned with the National Environmental Policy Act, passed earlier that year, which created the Environmental Protection Agency. Congress delegated authority to the EPA to regulate substances deemed harmful to air quality. Originally the list of such substances was limited, including only carbon monoxide, nitrogen oxide, sulfur dioxide, and lead. Over time, as preferences about environmental regulation changed from one presidential administration to another, the federal bureaucracy helped to shape new policies (and reshape old ones) related to air pollution.

On September 20, 2013, more than 40 years after the passage of the Clean Air Act, President Obama announced his intention to extend the EPA's authority to require polluters to cut their emissions of harmful substances, and in particular to begin regulating emissions of carbon dioxide (CO_2). Obama's objective was to reduce CO_2 emissions by 30 percent by 2030. In 2014, the EPA published its proposed plan to achieve this goal and invited commentary from the general public. By December 1, 2014, the end of a 165-day comment period during which the agency received over 2 million responses, the EPA began writing its regulations. In addition, President Obama announced plans for his administration to issue other rules governing CO_2 emissions, such as restricting coal-burning power plants directly or engaging states to devise their own plans for carbon dioxide reduction. This is an example of how the powers delegated the president and a regulatory agency by the environmental statutes change in response to a change in an administration's goals (reducing carbon emissions).

Continued pressure to combat greenhouse gases associated with climate change pitted bureaucratic agents in the Obama White House and the EPA against legislators in Congress. Obama sought to leave a legacy of environmental protection, and the EPA wished to interpret its regulatory mandate broadly, but many in Congress were anxious to protect industries in their states and districts that depend on carbon-based fuels. The majority leader in the Senate, Mitch McConnell, from coal-rich Kentucky, was eager to prevent the EPA's expanded interpretation of its authority to regulate CO_2. For example, in 2015 he introduced a bill that would block new EPA regulations on carbon emissions from going into effect unless a review by the Labor Department found they would not reduce jobs or the reliability of the electricity supply. Thus, as in many struggles involving the federal bureaucracy, executive, regulatory, and legislative agents all have pressed forward with their respective preferences, producing policy that is never truly settled.

The President as Manager-in-Chief

In 1937, President Franklin Delano Roosevelt's Committee on Administrative Management gave official sanction to an idea that had been growing increasingly urgent: "The president needs help." The national government had grown rapidly during the preceding 25 years, but the structures and procedures necessary to manage the burgeoning executive branch had not yet been established. The response to the call for help for the president initially took the form of three management policies: (1) all communications and decisions related to executive policy decisions must pass through the White House; (2) to cope with such a flow, the White House must have an adequate staff of specialists in research, analysis, legislative and legal writing, and public affairs; and (3) the White House must have additional staff to follow through on presidential decisions—to ensure that those decisions are made, communicated to Congress, and carried out by the appropriate agency.

The story of the modern presidency can be told largely as a series of responses to the plea for managerial help. Indeed, each expansion of the national government into new policies and programs in the twentieth century was accompanied by a parallel expansion of the president's management authority. This pattern began even before Roosevelt's presidency, with the policy innovations of President Woodrow Wilson between 1913 and 1920. Congress responded to Wilson's policies with the 1921 Budget and Accounting Act, which conferred on the White House agenda-setting power over budgeting. The president, in his annual budget message, transmits comprehensive budgetary recommendations to Congress. Because Congress retains ultimate legislative authority, a president's proposals are sometimes said to be dead on arrival on Capitol Hill. Nevertheless, the power to frame deliberations constitutes an important management tool. Each successive president has continued this pattern of setting the congressional agenda, creating what we now know as the managerial presidency.

For example, President Bill Clinton inaugurated one of the most systematic efforts to change the way government does business in his National Performance Review. Heavily influenced by the theories of management consultants who prize decentralization, customer responsiveness, and employee initiative, Clinton sought to infuse these new practices into government.[14] Ironically, Clinton's own management style in the White House was informal, and often compared to college bull sessions. George W. Bush, the first president with a graduate degree in business, followed a standard business-school dictum: select skilled subordinates and delegate responsibility to them. Although Bush followed this model closely in appointing highly experienced officials to cabinet positions, this was no guarantee of policy success, as doubts emerged about his administration's conduct of the Iraq War and mishandling of relief after Hurricane Katrina. Barack Obama's administrative style fell somewhere in between the styles of his two predecessors. He received high marks for the quality of his appointees but was heavily dependent on a personal staff inexperienced in dealing with Congress and the bureaucracy.

Congressional Oversight and Incentives

Congress is constitutionally essential to responsible bureaucracy because, in a "government of laws," legislation is the key to government responsibility. When a law is passed and its intent is clear, the president knows what to "faithfully execute," and the agency assigned responsibility understands its guidelines. But when Congress enacts vague legislation, everybody, from president to agency to courts to interest groups, gets involved in its interpretation. In that event, to whom is the agency responsible?

oversight

The effort by Congress, through hearings, investigations, and other techniques, to exercise control over the activities of executive agencies

The answer lies in oversight. The more legislative power Congress delegates to agencies, the more power it seeks to regain through committee and subcommittee oversight of those agencies. (See the Analyzing the Evidence unit on pp. 228–9 for a discussion of control of the bureaucracy.) The standing committee system of Congress is well suited for oversight, as most congressional committees and subcommittees have jurisdictions roughly parallel to one or more executive departments or agencies. Appropriations committees and authorization committees have oversight powers, as do their subcommittees. In addition, there is a committee on government operations in both the House and the Senate, with oversight powers not limited by departmental jurisdiction. Committees and subcommittees oversee agencies through public hearings. Representatives from agencies, the White House, and major interest groups, as well as other concerned citizens, are called as witnesses to present testimony at these hearings.

However, often the most effective control over bureaucratic behavior is the power of the purse—the ability of the congressional committees and subcommittees on appropriations to look at agency performance through the microscope of the annual appropriations process. This process makes bureaucrats attentive to Congress because they know that it has a chance each year to reduce their funding.[15] This may be another explanation for why there may be some downsizing but almost no terminations of federal agencies.

Congressional Oversight: Abdication or Strategic Delegation?

Congress often grants the executive branch bureaucracies discretion in determining certain features of a policy during the implementation phase. Although the complexities of governing a modern industrialized democracy make the granting of discretion necessary, some argue that Congress delegates too much policy-making authority to unelected bureaucrats. By enacting vague statutes that give bureaucrats broad discretion, in this view, members of Congress abdicate their constitutionally designated roles and render themselves ineffectual.

Others claim that Congress fails to use its tools for effective oversight, as we do not see Congress carrying out much oversight activity.[16] However, Mathew McCubbins and Thomas Schwartz argue that these critics have missed a type of oversight that benefits members of Congress in their bids for re-election.[17] McCubbins and Schwartz distinguish between two types of oversight: police patrol and fire alarm. Under police-patrol oversight, Congress systematically initiates investigation into the agencies' activity. Under fire-alarm oversight, Congress waits for adversely affected citizens or interest groups to bring bureaucratic perversions of legislative intent to the attention of the relevant congressional committee. To ensure that such parties bring these violations to members' attention—set off the fire alarm, so to speak—Congress passes laws that help individuals and groups make claims against the bureaucracy, granting them legal standing before administrative agencies and federal courts and giving them access to government-held information through the Freedom of Information Act.

Some citizens worry that Congress does not engage in sufficient oversight of bureaucratic agencies until after a problem has emerged. Here, citizens of Flint, Michigan, testify before the House Committee on Oversight and Government Reform after it was discovered that drinking water in the city was contaminated.

McCubbins and Schwartz argue that fire-alarm oversight is more efficient than the police-patrol variety, given the costs and the incentives of elected officials. Why should members spend their scarce resources (mainly time) to initiate investigations without having any evidence that they will reap electoral rewards? Police-patrol oversight can waste taxpayers' dollars, too, because many investigations will not turn up evidence of violations of legislative intent. It is much more cost effective for members to conserve their resources and then claim credit for fixing the problem after the fire alarms have been sounded.

On the other hand, bureaucratic drift might be contained if Congress spent more time on clarifying its legislative intent and less time on oversight activity. If its original intent in the law were clearer, Congress could afford to defer to presidential management to maintain bureaucratic responsibility. Bureaucrats are more responsive to clear legislative guidance than to anything else. But when Congress and the president (or coalitions within Congress) are at odds, bureaucrats can evade responsibility by playing one side against the other.

Congressional Design and Control of the Bureaucracy

Contributed by
Sean Gailmard
University of California, Berkeley

Who controls the bureaucracy? Scholars usually argue that political principals try to make bureaucratic agents responsive to their own direction. For example, Congress tries to make agencies choose policies that Congress prefers through oversight and threat of budget reductions. Paradoxically, however, in some cases the best agent for Congress is not one that is controlled by Congress itself but by some other political principal.

When might this be true? On some issues, the president exercises substantially more authority over the direction of public policy than other issues. This is true of foreign policy and defense. The president sets the agenda for U.S. diplomacy, can commit U.S. troops to battle without the prior approval of Congress, and plays an important role in the use of U.S. armed forces as commander in chief.

In order to use this authority effectively, the president needs advice that he trusts. Congress could try to control the bureaucratic agents that advise the president on foreign and defense policy. But if congressional interests conflict with those of the president, such agents might not be effective or trusted advisers to the president. A better alternative for Congress is to let the president control these agents himself. This will build trust and make the agencies' advice more helpful to the president as he exercises his formidable policy authority in foreign affairs and defense. Ultimately, informed use of this policy authority by the president is good for Congress too.[1]

Congress can influence how much control different political principals exert over agencies in its decision about where the agencies are "located" within the executive branch. The location of an agency within the executive branch is determined in the legislation creating that agency.

Organization of the Executive Branch

- President
- Executive office of the president
- Cabinet departments
- Independent agencies

The president's closest advisers (e.g., national security adviser, budget director) are in the executive office of the president (EOP). Senior members serve at the pleasure of the president and help him formulate policy. In cabinet departments (e.g., Department of State, Department of Agriculture), senior staff also serve at the pleasure of the president, and major policy decisions are reviewed by the EOP. Independent agencies (e.g., Securities and Exchange Commission, Federal Communications Commission) are the furthest removed from presidential control. Senior officers cannot be dismissed by the president simply for disagreements over policy, and major policy decisions are not reviewed by the EOP.

If Congress wishes the president to have relatively more control over agencies involved in foreign policy and defense than over agencies involved primarily in domestic affairs, then it should locate those agencies closer to the president within the executive branch. This expectation is borne out.[2]

Percentage of Agencies in Each Sphere of the Executive Branch

For all agencies created in legislation between 1946 and 2000, Congress was twice as likely to locate foreign and defense policy agencies in the EOP than domestic policy agencies. The reverse is true for independent agencies and commissions. Overall, when Congress designs agencies, it appears to consider the effect of bureaucratic structure on the ease of control by the relevant political principals.

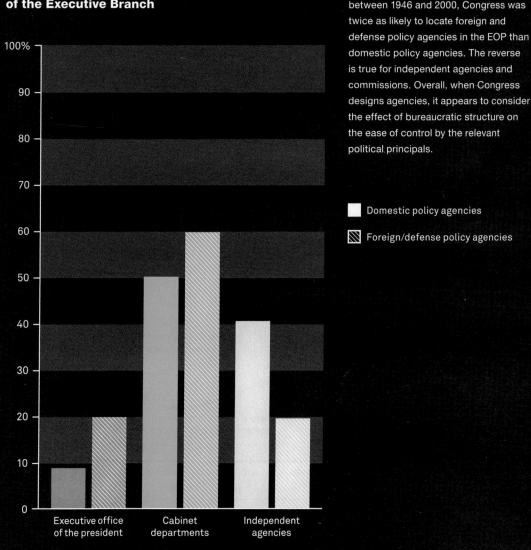

Domestic policy agencies

Foreign/defense policy agencies

1   Sean Gailmard and John W. Patty, *Learning While Governing: Institutions and Accountability in the Executive Branch* (Chicago: University of Chicago Press, 2012).

2   Data are from David E. Lewis, *Presidents and the Politics of Agency Design: Political Insulation in the United States Government Bureaucracy, 1946–1997* (Palo Alto, CA: Stanford University Press, 2003).

REFORMING THE BUREAUCRACY

Americans don't like big government because it means big bureaucracy, and bureaucracy means the federal service—about 2.7 million civilian and 1.5 million military employees.[18] Promises to cut the bureaucracy are popular campaign appeals; "cutting out the fat" by reducing the number of federal employees is touted as a surefire way of cutting the deficit.

Yet the federal service has hardly grown at all during the past 35 years; it reached its peak post–World War II level in 1968 with 2.9 million civilian employees and 3.6 million military personnel (a figure swollen by the Vietnam War). The number of civilian federal executive branch employees has since remained close to that figure. The size of the federal service is even less imposing when placed in the context of the total workforce and of state and local government employment, which was 15 million full- and 3.7 million part-time employees in 2014.[19] Figure 7.3 indicates

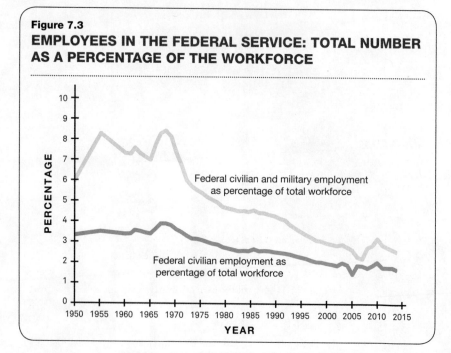

Figure 7.3

EMPLOYEES IN THE FEDERAL SERVICE: TOTAL NUMBER AS A PERCENTAGE OF THE WORKFORCE

Federal civilian and military employment as percentage of total workforce

Federal civilian employment as percentage of total workforce

NOTE: Workforce includes unemployed persons.
SOURCES: Tax Foundation, *Facts and Figures on Government Finance* (Baltimore: Johns Hopkins University Press, 1990), pp. 22, 44; Office of Management and Budget, *Budget of the U.S. Government, Fiscal Year 2009*, table 17.5, https://www.whitehouse.gov/sites/default/files/omb/budget/fy2009/pdf/hist.pdf (accessed 5/9/16); U.S. Bureau of Labor Statistics, http://stats.bls.gov/webapps/legacy/cpsatab1.htm, table A1 (accessed 5/9/16); U.S. Office of Personnel Management, Historical Federal Workforce Tables, www.opm.gov/policy-data-oversight/data-analysis-documentation/federal-employment-reports/historical-tables/total-government-employment-since-1962/ (accessed 5/9/16); and authors' update.

Figure 7.4
ANNUAL FEDERAL OUTLAYS

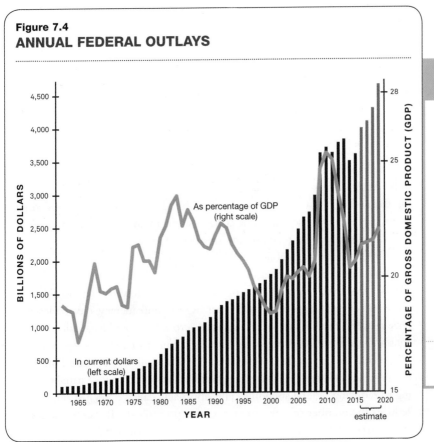

NOTE: Data for 2016–19 are estimated.
SOURCE: Office of Management and Budget, Historical Tables, Table 1.1 and 1.2 www.whitehouse. gov/omb/budget/Historicals (accessed 5/9/16).

ANALYZING THE EVIDENCE

Annual federal outlays have increased steadily over time. So has the size of the U.S. economy (not shown in figure). But the ratio of federal expenditures to annual GDP has varied over time. What might explain these fluctuations, and what might be the consequences when the federal government contributes more or less to the economy?

that, since 1950, the ratio of federal service employment to the total workforce has been steady and in fact has declined slightly in the past 25 years. Figure 7.4 offers another useful comparison: although the dollar increase in federal spending shown by the bars looks impressive, the horizontal line indicates that even here the national government has simply kept pace with the growth of the economy.

To sum up, the federal service has not been growing any faster than the U.S. economy or population. The same is roughly true of state and local public employment. Bureaucracy keeps pace with our society, despite our seeming dislike for it, because we can't operate the control towers, the prisons, the Social Security system, and other essential elements without bureaucracy. And we could not conduct wars in Iraq and Afghanistan without a gigantic military bureaucracy.

Termination

The only certain way to reduce the size of the bureaucracy is to eliminate programs. But most agencies have a supportive constituency—people and groups that benefit from the programs and will fight to reinstate any cuts. Termination is the only way to ensure an agency's reduction, and it is a rare occurrence.

The overall lack of success in terminating bureaucracy is a reflection of Americans' love/hate relationship with the national government. As antagonistic as Americans may be toward bureaucracy in general, they grow attached to the services and protections offered by particular agencies. A good example was the agonizing problem of closing military bases following the end of the Cold War, when the United States no longer needed so many. Since every base is in some congressional member's district, Congress was unable to decide to close any of them. Consequently, between 1988 and 1990, Congress established a Defense Base Closure and Realignment Commission to decide on base closings, taking the matter out of Congress's hands altogether.[20] Even so, the process has been slow and agonizing. In a more incremental approach to downsizing the bureaucracy, elected leaders have reduced the budgets of all agencies across the board by small percentages and cut some less-supported ones by larger amounts.

deregulation

The policy of reducing the number of rules promulgated by federal regulatory agencies

Another approach targets highly unpopular regulatory agencies, but they are so small (relatively) that cutting their budgets contributes virtually nothing to reducing federal spending. This approach, called deregulation, simply reduces the number of rules these agencies promulgate. But deregulation is still incremental and, like budget reduction, has not yielded a genuine reduction of bureaucracy.

Devolution

devolution

The policy of delegating a program or passing it down from one level of government to a lower level, such as from the national government to state and local governments

An alternative to genuine reduction is devolution—downsizing the federal bureaucracy by delegating program implementation to state and local governments. Indirect evidence of devolution appears in Figure 7.5, which shows the increase in state and local government employment against a backdrop of flat or declining federal employment. This evidence suggests a growing share of governmental actions taking place on the state and local levels. Devolution often alters patterns of who benefits most from government programs. In the early 1990s, a major devolution of transportation policy sought to open up decisions to a new set of interests. Since the 1920s, transportation policy in the federal and state governments had been dominated by road-building interests. Many advocates for cities and many environmentalists believed that the emphasis on road building hurt both cities and the environment. The 1992 reform, initiated

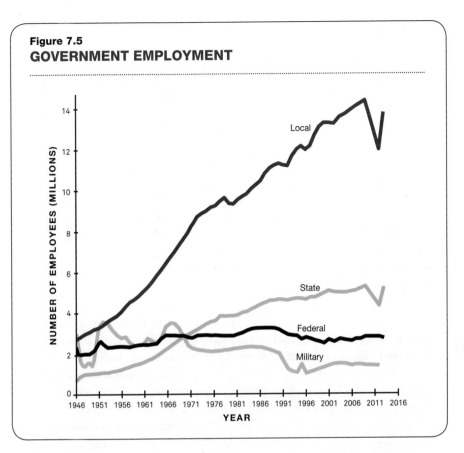

Figure 7.5
GOVERNMENT EMPLOYMENT

by environmentalists, gave more power to metropolitan planning organizations and lifted many federal restrictions on how the money should be spent. Reformers hoped that through these changes those advocating alternatives to road building, such as mass transit, bike paths, and walking, would gain more influence over federal transportation spending. Although change has been slow, devolution has indeed brought new voices into decisions about transportation spending, and alternatives to highways have received increasing attention.

Often devolution is intended to provide more efficient and flexible government services. Yet, by its very nature, it entails variation across the states. In some states, government services may improve as a consequence; in others, services may deteriorate as devolution leads to spending cuts. This pattern has characterized implementation of the welfare reform passed in 1996, the most significant devolution of federal government social programs in many decades. Some states, such as Wisconsin, have designed innovative programs that respond to clients' needs; others, such as Idaho, have virtually dismantled their welfare programs. Because the legislation placed a five-year lifetime limit on receiving welfare, the states will take on an even greater role in the future as existing clients lose their eligibility for federal benefits. Many have praised welfare reform for reducing welfare rolls and responding to the public desire that welfare be a temporary program. At the same time, however, it has placed more low-income women and their children at risk of being left with no assistance at all.

Privatization

Privatization, another downsizing option, may seem like a synonym for termination, but that is true only at the extreme. Most privatization involves the provision of government goods and services by private contractors under direct government supervision. Except for top-secret strategic materials, virtually all military hardware, from boats to bullets, is produced by private contractors. And billions of dollars of research services are bought under contract by government; these private contractors are universities, industrial corporations, and private think tanks. Privatization simply means that a formerly public activity is picked up under contract by a private company or companies. But such programs are still paid for and supervised by government. Privatization downsizes the government only in that the workers performing the activity are no longer counted as part of the bureaucracy.

privatization

The act of moving all or part of a program from the public sector to the private sector

The aim of privatization is to reduce the cost of government. When private contractors can perform a task as well as government but for less money, taxpayers win. Often the losers in such situations are the workers. Government workers are generally unionized and, therefore, receive good pay and benefits. Private-sector workers are less likely to be unionized, and private firms often provide lower pay and fewer benefits. For this reason, public-sector unions have been one of the strongest voices against privatization. Other critics observe that private firms may not be more efficient or less costly than government, especially when there is little competition among private firms

Privatization can reduce the costs of certain government activities, but it can also create issues of accountability and transparency. In recent years, the practice has become particularly controversial with regard to security contracting in Iraq and Afghanistan.

and when public bureaucracies cannot bid in the contracting competition. When private firms have a monopoly on service provision, they may be more expensive than government. Moreover, there are important questions about how private contractors can be held accountable. For example, as security has become the nation's paramount concern, some Pentagon officials fear that too many tasks vital to national security have been contracted out and that security might best be served by limiting privatization.

Indeed, the new demands of domestic security have altered the thrust of bureaucratic reform. Despite strong agreement on the goal of fighting terrorism, the effort to streamline the bureaucracy around a single purpose is likely to face considerable obstacles. Strong constituencies may attempt to block changes that they believe will harm them, and initiatives for improved coordination among agencies may provoke political disputes if the proposed changes threaten to alter groups' access to the bureaucracy. And groups that oppose bureaucratic changes can appeal to Congress to intervene on their behalf.

DOES BUREAUCRACY WORK?

Bureaucracy is one of humanity's most significant inventions. It is an institutional arrangement that allows for division and specialization of labor, harnesses expertise, and coordinates collective action for social, political, and economic purposes. It enables governments to exist and perform.

At a theoretical level, public bureaucracy is the concrete expression of rational, purposeful, political action. Elected politicians have goals—as broad as defending the realm, maintaining public health and safety, or promoting economic growth; as narrow as securing a post office for Possum Hollow, Pennsylvania, or an exit off the interstate highway for Springfield, Massachusetts. Bureaucracy is the instrument by which political objectives, established by elected legislators and executives, are transformed from ideas and intentions into the actual "bricks and mortar" of implemented policies.

At a practical level, this transformation depends upon the motivations of bureaucratic agents and the institutional machinery that develops around every bureaucratic entity. Elected politicians engage in institutional design in creating agencies. They have their greatest impact at this point. Once an agency is operating, elected officials only imperfectly control their bureaucratic agents. Institutional arrangements, and simple human nature, provide some insulation to agencies, enabling bureaucrats to march to their own drummers—at least some of the time. Of course, bureaucrats are not entirely free agents. But control is a constant and recurring problem for elected officials.

Americans' feelings toward bureaucracy are complicated, and Americans often disagree about the appropriate role of government agencies. While many people support the Environmental Protection Agency's regulation of practices that could harm the environment, others feel that these kinds of regulations go too far when they endanger jobs.

We cannot live without bureaucracy—it is the most efficient way to organize people to get a large job done. But we can't live comfortably with it either. Bureaucracy requires hierarchy, appointed authority, and professional expertise. Those requirements make it the natural enemy of representation, which requires discussion and reciprocity among equals. Yet the task is not to retreat from bureaucracy but to take advantage of its strengths while trying to make it more accountable to the demands that democratic policies and representative government make upon it.

Indeed, as the president and Congress seek to translate the ideal of democratic accountability into practice, they struggle to find the proper balance between administrative discretion and the public's right to know. An administration whose every move is subject to intense public scrutiny may be hamstrung in its efforts to carry out the public interest. On the other hand, a bureaucracy that is shielded from the public eye may wind up pursuing its own interests rather than those of the public. The last century has seen a double movement toward strengthening the managerial capacity of the presidency and making bureaucratic decision making more transparent. The purpose of these reforms has been to create an effective, responsive bureaucracy. But reforms alone cannot guarantee democratic accountability. Presidential and congressional vigilance in defense of the public interest is essential.

Another approach to bureaucratic accountability is for Congress to spend more time clarifying its legislative intent and less time on committee or individual oversight. If the intent of the law were clear, Congress

How the Three Branches Regulate Bureaucracy

The president may	• Appoint and remove agency heads • Reorganize the bureaucracy (with congressional approval) • Make changes in agencies' budget proposals • Initiate or adjust policies that would alter the bureaucracy's activities
Congress may	• Pass legislation that alters the bureaucracy's activities • Abolish existing programs • Investigate bureaucratic activities and force bureaucrats to testify about them • Influence presidential appointments of agency heads and other officials
The judiciary may	• Rule on whether bureaucrats have acted within the law and require policy changes to comply with the law • Force the bureaucracy to respect the rights of individuals through hearings and other proceedings • Rule on the constitutionality of all rules and regulations

could then count on the president to maintain a higher level of bureaucratic responsibility, because bureaucrats are more responsive to clear legislative guidance than to anything else. Nevertheless, this is not a sure solution, because Congress and the president can still be at odds, giving bureaucrats an opportunity to evade responsibility by playing one branch off against the other.

As for the vast apparatus, bureaucracy is here to stay. The administration of myriad government functions and responsibilities in a large, complex society will always require "rule by desks and offices" (the literal meaning of *bureaucracy*). No "reinvention" of government, however well conceived or executed, can alter that basic fact, nor can it resolve the problem of reconciling bureaucracy with democracy. President Bill Clinton's National Performance Review accomplished some impressive things: the national bureaucracy has become somewhat smaller, and in the next few years, it will become smaller still; government procedures are being streamlined and are under tremendous pressure to become even more efficient. But these efforts are no guarantee that the bureaucracy itself will become more malleable. Congress will not suddenly change its practice of loose and vague legislative draftsmanship. Presidents will not suddenly discover new reserves of power or vision to draw more tightly the reins of responsible management. No deep solution can be found in quick fixes. As with all complex social and political problems, the solution lies mainly in a sober awareness of the nature of the problem. This awareness enables people to avoid fantasies and myths about the abilities of a democratized presidency—or the potential of a reform effort, or the powers of technology, or the populist rhetoric of a new Congress—to change the nature of governance by bureaucracy.

For Further Reading

Aberbach, Joel, and Bert A. Rockman. *In the Web of Politics: Three Decades of the U.S. Federal Executive.* Washington, DC: Brookings Institution, 2000.

Downs, Anthony. *Inside Bureaucracy.* Boston: Little, Brown, 1966.

Gailmard, Sean, and John W. Patty. *Learning While Governing: Expertise and Accountability in the Executive Branch.* Chicago: University of Chicago Press, 2013.

Goodsell, Charles. *The Case for Bureaucracy.* 4th ed. Washington, DC: CQ Press, 2003.

Heclo, Hugh. *On Thinking Institutionally.* Boulder, CO: Paradigm, 2007.

Kerwin, Cornelius M., and Scott R. Furlong. *Rulemaking.* 4th ed. Washington, DC: CQ Press, 2010.

Kettl, Donald F. *The Politics of the Administrative Process.* 5th ed. Washington, DC: Brookings Institution, 2011.

Light, Paul C. *The True Size of Government.* Washington, DC: Brookings Institution, 1999.

McCubbins, Mathew, and Thomas Schwartz. "Congressional Oversight Overlooked: Police Patrols versus Fire Alarms." *American Journal of Political Science* 28 (1984): 165–79.

Meier, Kenneth J., and John Bohte. *Politics and the Bureaucracy.* 5th ed. Belmont, CA: Wadsworth, 2007.

Seidman, Harold. *Politics, Position, and Power: The Dynamics of Federal Organization.* 5th ed. New York: Oxford University Press, 1997.

Wilson, James Q. *Bureaucracy: What Government Agencies Do and Why They Do It.* New York: Basic Books, 1989.

8

The Federal Courts

Courts serve an essential function. When disputes arise, an impartial arbiter is needed to help settle the matter. When laws must be enforced, justice requires an impartial judge to determine guilt and innocence and—if the accused is found guilty—the appropriate punishment. And when questions arise about the meaning of the laws, we rely on the wisdom of judges to determine what Congress means and how that meaning applies in a given circumstance. It is not wise, or even possible, to pass a law to cover every contingency. Thus nearly every nation has established a judiciary system to satisfy the need for an arbiter and interpreter.

Perhaps the most distinctive feature of the American judiciary is its independence. The Constitution, as it was written and as it has evolved, set up the courts as an entity separate from the legislature, the executive, and the states, and insulated them from electoral politics. As we will see, four institutional features of the American judiciary ensure a powerful, independent legal system. First, the federal courts are a separate branch of government from Congress and the president. Second, authority among American courts is hierarchical, with federal courts able to overturn decisions of state courts, and the U.S. Supreme Court as the ultimate authority. Third, the

Supreme Court and other federal courts of appeals can strike down actions of Congress, the president, or states that judges deem to be violations of the Constitution. This authority is the power of judicial review. Fourth, federal judges are appointed for life. They are not subject to the pressures of running for re-election and need not be highly responsive to changes in public opinion.[1]

The framers of the Constitution looked to the judiciary not only to resolve legal disputes but also to play an important role in the national system of checks and balances, guarding against the improper expansion of both presidential and congressional power. Yet some question whether the judiciary has restrained these two branches equally. Over the years, the federal courts have certainly acted against congressional power, striking down more than 180 acts of Congress (see Figure 8.3 on p. 255). When it comes to presidential power, however, they have not been as vigilant. For example, only 14 of the thousands of executive orders issued by presidents have been rejected by the Supreme Court, and most of these only in part.

Indeed, the growth of presidential power has largely been reinforced, not restrained, by the federal courts. At least since the New Deal and World War II, assertions of presidential power in such realms as foreign policy, war and emergency powers, legislative power, and administrative authority have, more often than not, been upheld by the federal bench. Rather than curb presidential power, the federal judiciary has sometimes taken extraordinary presidential claims made for limited and temporary purposes and rationalized them—that is, converted them into routine and permanent instruments of presidential government. One example is Richard

CORE OF THE ANALYSIS

➡ The power of judicial review makes the Supreme Court not just a judicial agency but also a major lawmaking body.

➡ Judicial decisions are highly constrained by the past, in the form of common law and precedents, but every decision also contributes to the evolution of the law.

➡ The courts maintain their independence from the legislature and executive because federal judges are appointed for life and are not elected. Independence allows the courts to act as a check on the democratically chosen branches of government.

Nixon's sweeping claims of executive privilege. In *United States v. Nixon*, the Supreme Court rejected the president's refusal to turn over secret White House audiotapes to congressional investigators. For the first time, though, the justices also recognized the validity of the principle of executive privilege and discussed the situations in which such claims might be appropriate.[2] This judicial recognition encouraged presidents Bill Clinton and George W. Bush to make broad claims of executive privilege during their terms in office.

The support given the executive branch by the federal courts has often been noted by legal scholars, who have offered a number of explanations for it. For example, constitutional historian Edward Corwin thought that the courts tended to defer to the president because presidential exercises of power often produced some change in the world that the judiciary felt powerless to negate.[3] Political scientists Terry Moe and William Howell, on the other hand, point to the courts' dependence on the goodwill of the executive branch for enforcement of their decisions.[4] Other scholars emphasize the reluctance of the courts to risk their prestige in disputes with popular presidents.[5]

Another factor that has played an important role in linking the courts to the White House is the process of judicial appointment. Although presidents naturally do like to appoint judges who will support them, the actual significance of the appointment process as it pertains to presidential power is more subtle. During the nineteenth century, federal judges were typically drawn from—and often had continuing ties to—electoral politics. Not only were most judicial nominees active in party politics, but many, including a number of Supreme Court justices, had previously held elective office. Chief Justice John Marshall, for example, had served in both the Virginia House of Delegates and the U.S. House of Representatives.

Today, hardly any federal judges (fewer than 5 percent) have a legislative background. Most are recruited from the legal profession, the state courts, and the executive branch. Members of these bodies tend to look to the executive branch, rather than to Congress and the state legislatures, for guidance on matters of law and policy. These judges may be more inclined to check Congress but less likely to restrain the executive.

In this chapter, we first examine the judicial process, including the types of cases that the federal courts consider. We then assess the structure of the federal court system and consider how judicial review makes the Supreme Court a "lawmaking body." Last, we examine various influences on the Supreme Court and analyze the role and power of the federal courts in the American political process, looking in particular at the growth of judicial power in the United States.

THE COURT SYSTEM

Court cases in the United States proceed under three broad categories of law: criminal law, civil law, and public law.

In cases of criminal law, the government charges an individual with violating a statute enacted to protect the public health, safety, morals, or welfare. In criminal cases, the government is always the plaintiff (the party that brings charges) and alleges that a named defendant has committed a criminal violation. Most criminal cases arise in state and municipal courts and involve matters ranging from traffic offenses to robbery and murder. Although the bulk of criminal law is still a state matter, a growing body of federal criminal law deals with such matters as tax evasion, mail fraud, and the sale of narcotics. Defendants found guilty of criminal violations may be fined or sent to prison.

Cases of civil law involve disputes among individuals or between individuals and the government where no criminal violation is charged. Unlike in criminal cases, the losers in civil cases cannot be fined or sent to prison, although they may be required to pay monetary damages. In a civil case, the one who brings a complaint is the plaintiff and the one against whom the complaint is brought is the defendant. The two most common types of civil cases involve contracts and torts. In a typical contract case, an individual or corporation charges that it has suffered because of another's violation of an agreement between the two. For example, Smith Manufacturing Corporation may charge that Jones Distributors failed to honor an agreement to deliver raw materials at a specified time, causing Smith to lose business. Smith asks the court to order Jones to compensate it for the damage allegedly suffered. In a typical tort case, one individual charges that he or she has been injured by another's negligence or malfeasance. Medical malpractice suits are one example of tort cases.

In deciding civil cases, courts apply statutes (laws) and legal precedents (prior decisions). State and federal statutes, for example, often govern the conditions under which contracts are and are not legally binding. Jones Distributors might argue that it was not obliged to fulfill its contract with Smith because actions by Smith, such as the failure to make promised payments, constituted fraud under state law. Attorneys for a physician being sued for malpractice, on the other hand, may search for prior cases in which courts ruled that actions similar to their client's did not constitute negligence. Such precedents are applied under the doctrine of *stare decisis*, a Latin phrase meaning "let the decision stand."

A civil or criminal case becomes a matter of public law when plaintiffs or defendants seek to show that their case involves the powers of government or rights of citizens as defined under the Constitution or by statute.

criminal law
The branch of law that regulates the conduct of individuals, defines crimes, and specifies punishment for criminal acts

civil law
The branch of law that deals with disputes that do not involve criminal penalties

precedents
Prior cases whose principles are used by judges as the bases for their decisions in present cases

public law
Cases involving the powers of government or rights of citizens

IN BRIEF

Types of Laws and Disputes

Type of Law	Type of Case or Dispute	Form of Case
Criminal law	Cases arising out of actions that violate laws protecting the health, safety, and morals of the community. The government is always the plaintiff.	*U.S. (or state) v. Jones* *Jones v. U.S. (or state)*, if Jones lost and is appealing
Civil law	"Private law," involving disputes between citizens or between government and citizen where no crime is alleged. Two general types are contract and tort. *Contract cases* are disputes that arise over voluntary actions. *Tort cases* are disputes that arise out of obligations inherent in social life. Negligence and slander are examples of torts.	*Smith v. Jones* *New York v. Jones* *U.S. v. Jones* *Jones v. New York*
Public law	All cases where the powers of government or the rights of citizens are involved. The government is the defendant. *Constitutional law* involves judicial review of the basis of a government's action in relation to specific clauses of the Constitution as interpreted in Supreme Court cases. *Administrative law* involves disputes of the statutory authority, jurisdiction, or procedures of administrative agencies.	*Jones v. U.S. (or state)* *In re Jones* *Smith v. Jones*, if a license or statute is at issue in their private dispute

One major form of public law is constitutional law, under which a court determines whether the government's actions conform to the Constitution as it has been interpreted by the judiciary. Thus, what begins as an ordinary criminal case may enter the realm of public law if a defendant claims that the police violated her constitutional rights. Another arena of public law is administrative law, which involves disputes over the jurisdiction, procedures, or authority of administrative agencies. Under this type of law, civil litigation between an individual and the government may become a matter of public law if the individual asserts that the government is violating a statute or abusing its constitutional power. For example, landowners have asserted that federal and state administrative regulations on land use constitute violations of the Fifth Amendment's restrictions on the government's ability to confiscate private property. Recently, the Supreme Court has been very sympathetic to such claims, which effectively transform an ordinary civil dispute into a major issue of public law.

Most of the Supreme Court cases we examine in this chapter involve judgments concerning the constitutional or statutory basis of the actions of government agencies. In this arena of public law, the Supreme Court's decisions can have significant consequences for American politics and society.

Types of Courts

In the United States, court systems have been established both by the federal government and by individual state governments. Both systems have several levels (see Figure 8.1), though the one federal system and the fifty

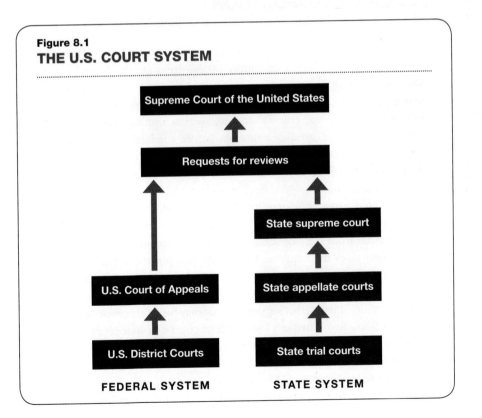

Figure 8.1
THE U.S. COURT SYSTEM

Supreme Court of the United States

Requests for reviews

State supreme court

U.S. Court of Appeals

State appellate courts

U.S. District Courts

State trial courts

FEDERAL SYSTEM **STATE SYSTEM**

state systems are all distinctive in a number of ways. More than 99 percent of all court cases in the United States are heard in state courts. Most criminal cases, for example, involve violations of state laws prohibiting such actions as murder, robbery, fraud, theft, and assault. If such a case is brought to trial, it will be heard in a state trial court, in front of a judge and sometimes a jury, who will determine whether the defendant violated state law. If the defendant is convicted, he may appeal the conviction to a higher court, such as a state court of appeals, and from there to a state's supreme court. Similarly, in civil cases, most litigation is brought in the courts of the state where the activity in question occurred. For example, a patient bringing suit against a physician for malpractice would file the suit in the appropriate court in the state where the alleged malpractice occurred. The judge hearing the case would apply state law and state precedent to the matter. (In both criminal and civil matters, however, most cases are settled before trial through negotiated agreements between the parties. In criminal cases, these agreements are called plea bargains.)

trial court

The first court to hear a criminal or civil case

court of appeals (or appellate court)

A court that hears the appeals of trial-court decisions

supreme court

The highest court in a particular state or in the United States. This court primarily serves an appellate function.

FEDERAL JURISDICTION

Cases are heard in the federal courts if they involve federal laws, treaties with other nations, or the U.S. Constitution; these areas are the federal courts' official jurisdiction. In addition, any case in which the U.S. government is a party is heard in the federal courts. If, for example, an individual is charged with violating a federal criminal statute, such as evading the payment of income taxes, charges would be brought before a federal judge by a federal prosecutor. Civil cases involving the citizens of more than one state and in which more than $75,000 is at stake may be heard in either the federal or the state courts.

jurisdiction

The types of cases over which a court has authority

But even if a matter belongs in federal court, which federal court should exercise jurisdiction? The answer is complex. Each federal court's jurisdiction is derived from the Constitution and federal statutes. Article III of the Constitution gives the Supreme Court appellate jurisdiction (the authority to hear appeals) in all federal cases and original jurisdiction (the authority to hear new cases) in cases involving foreign ambassadors and issues in which a state is a party. That is, the Supreme Court may hear cases appealed to it by a party to a case first heard in a lower federal court or a state court (appellate jurisdiction), or it may be the initial destination of cases involving a state or an ambassador (original jurisdiction). Article III assigns original jurisdiction in all other federal cases to the lower courts that Congress was authorized to establish. Over the years, as Congress enacted statutes creating the federal judicial system, it specified the jurisdiction of each type of court it established. It has generally assigned jurisdictions on the basis of geography. The nation is currently, by statute, divided into 94 judicial districts, including one court for each of three U.S. territories: Guam, the U.S. Virgin Islands, and the Northern Marianas. Each of the 94 U.S. district courts exercises jurisdiction over federal cases arising within its territorial domain. The judicial districts are, in turn, organized into 12 regional circuits plus the District of Columbia circuit. Each circuit court exercises appellate jurisdiction over cases heard by the district courts within its region. The circuit court of appeals for the District of Columbia has nationwide jurisdiction to hear appeals in specialized cases, including those arising from actions by federal agencies, and is generally considered to be the nation's second most important federal court after the Supreme Court.

Cases are heard in federal court if they involve federal law or if the U.S. government is a party in the case. After the Boston Marathon bombing suspect Dzhokhar Tsarnaev was arrested in 2013, he was tried in federal court on federal criminal charges, including using a weapon of mass destruction.

Congress has also established specialized courts with nationwide original jurisdiction in certain types of cases. These include the U.S. Court of International Trade, which deals with trade and customs issues, and the U.S. Court of Federal Claims, which handles damage suits against the United States. Congress has also established a court with nationwide appellate jurisdiction: the U.S. Court of Appeals for the Federal Circuit, which hears appeals involving patent law and those arising from the decisions of the trade and claims courts.

The federal courts' appellate jurisdiction also extends to cases originating in the state courts. In both civil and criminal cases, a decision of the highest state court can be appealed to the U.S. Supreme Court by raising a federal issue. Appellants might assert that they were denied the right to counsel or otherwise deprived of the due process guaranteed by the federal Constitution, for example, or that important issues of federal law were at stake in the case. The Supreme Court accepts such appeals only if it believes that the matter has considerable national significance. (We return to this topic later in this chapter.) In addition, in criminal cases defendants who have been convicted in a state court may request a writ of *habeas corpus* from a federal district court. *Habeas corpus* is a court order to authorities to show cause for the incarceration of a prisoner. Generally speaking, state defendants seeking a federal writ of *habeas corpus* must have exhausted all available state remedies and raise issues not previously raised in their state appeals. Federal courts of

due process

Proceeding according to law and with adequate protection for individual rights

writ of *habeas corpus*

A court order demanding that an individual in custody be brought into court and shown the cause for detention. *Habeas corpus* is guaranteed by the Constitution and can be suspended only in cases of rebellion or invasion.

appeals and, ultimately, the U.S. Supreme Court have appellate jurisdiction over federal district court *habeas* decisions.

Although the federal courts hear only a fraction of the civil and criminal cases decided each year, their decisions are extremely important. It is in the federal courts that the Constitution and federal laws governing all Americans are interpreted and their meaning and significance established. Moreover, it is in the federal courts that the powers and limitations of the increasingly powerful national government are tested. Finally, through their power to review the state courts' decisions, it is ultimately the federal courts that dominate the American judicial system.

Federal Trial Courts

Federal district courts are trial courts of general jurisdiction, and their cases are, in form, indistinguishable from cases in state trial courts.

There are 89 district courts in the 50 states, one each in the District of Columbia and Puerto Rico, and three territorial courts. These courts are staffed by 678 federal district judges. District judges are assigned to district courts according to the workload; the busiest of these courts may have as many as 28 judges. The procedures of the federal district courts are essentially the same as those of the lower state courts, except that federal procedural requirements tend to be stricter. States, for example, do not have to provide a grand jury, a 12-member trial jury, or a unanimous jury verdict. Federal courts must provide all of these.

Federal Appellate Courts

Roughly 20 percent of all federal lower-court cases, along with appeals from some federal agency decisions, are subsequently reviewed by a federal appeals court. The country is divided into 12 judicial circuits, each of which has a U.S. Court of Appeals. A thirteenth appellate court, the U.S. Court of Appeals for the Federal Circuit, is defined by subject matter rather than geographic jurisdiction. This court accepts appeals regarding patents, copyrights, and international trade.

Except for cases selected for Supreme Court review by the Supreme Court, decisions by the appeals courts are final. Because of this finality, certain safeguards have been built into the system. The most important is the provision of more than one judge for every appeals case. Each court of appeals has 3 to 28 permanent judgeships. Although normally three judges hear appealed cases, in some instances a larger number sit *en banc*.

Another safeguard is the assignment of a Supreme Court justice as the circuit justice for each of the 12 circuits. The circuit justice deals with requests for special action by the Supreme Court, most frequently that of reviewing requests for stays of execution when the full Court cannot— mainly during its summer recess.

The Supreme Court

Article III of the Constitution vests "the judicial power of the United States" in the Supreme Court, which comprises a chief justice and eight associate justices. The chief justice presides over the Court's public sessions and conferences. In the Court's actual deliberations and decisions, however, the chief justice has no more authority than his colleagues. Each justice casts one vote. The chief justice, though, always speaks first when the justices deliberate. In addition, if the chief justice has voted with the majority, he decides which justice will write the formal Court opinion. To some extent, the chief justice's influence is a function of his leadership ability. Some chief justices, such as Earl Warren, have led the Court in a new direction; in other instances, a forceful associate justice, such as Felix Frankfurter, is the dominant figure.

chief justice
The justice on the Supreme Court who presides over the Court's public sessions

The Constitution does not specify how many justices should sit on the Supreme Court; Congress has the authority to change the Court's size. In the early nineteenth century, there were six justices; later, seven. Congress set the number at nine in 1869, and the Court has remained that size ever since. In 1937, President Franklin Delano Roosevelt, infuriated by several Court decisions that struck down New Deal programs, asked Congress to enlarge the Court so that he could add sympathetic justices to it. Although Congress balked, the Court gave in to Roosevelt's pressure and began to view his policy initiatives more favorably. The president, in turn, dropped his efforts to enlarge the Court. The Court's surrender to Roosevelt came to be known as "the switch in time that saved nine."

How Judges Are Appointed

The president appoints federal judges. Nominees are typically prominent or politically active members of the legal profession: former state court judges or state or local prosecutors, prominent attorneys or elected officials, or highly regarded law professors. Prior experience as a judge is not necessary. In general, presidents try to appoint judges with legal experience, good character, and partisan and ideological views similar to their own. During the presidencies of Richard Nixon, Ronald Reagan, George H. W. Bush, and George W. Bush, most federal judicial appointees were conservative Republicans. Bill Clinton's and Barack Obama's appointees, in contrast, tended to be liberal Democrats. George W. Bush made a strong effort to appoint

Though Franklin Delano Roosevelt attempted to increase the number of justices in 1937, the size of the Supreme Court has remained at nine since 1869. This political cartoon from 1937 reflects the concern that Roosevelt's strategy threatened the independence of the judiciary.

senatorial courtesy ➡

The practice whereby the president, before formally nominating a person for a federal district judgeship, finds out whether the senators from the candidate's state support the nomination

Hispanics. Bill Clinton and Barack Obama also appointed many women and African Americans to the federal courts. (See Figure 8.2 for more information on diversity of court appointees.)

The Constitution requires the Senate to "advise and consent" to federal judicial nominations, thus imposing an important check on the president's influence over the judiciary. Before the president formally nominates someone for a federal district judgeship, senators from the candidate's state must indicate that they support him or her. This practice is called senatorial courtesy. If one or both senators from a prospective nominee's home state belong to the president's political party, the nomination will almost invariably receive their blessing. Because the president's party in the Senate will rarely support a nominee opposed by a home-state senator from their ranks, these senators hold virtual veto power over appointments to the federal bench in their own states. Senators often see this power as a way to reward important allies and contributors. If the state has no senator from the president's party, the governor or members of the state's House delegation may make suggestions. Senatorial courtesy is less consequential for appellate court appointments and plays no role in Supreme Court nominations.

Once the president has formally nominated an individual, the appointment must be approved by the Senate Judiciary Committee and confirmed by a majority vote in the full Senate. The politics and rules of the Senate determine the fate of a president's judicial nominees and influence the types of people who are nominated. There is always the risk of a filibuster, and ending it requires the approval of three-fifths of the senators. (See Chapter 5 for discussion of these procedures.) The composition of the Senate Judiciary Committee, as well as the Senate as a whole, is critical in determining whether a particular nominee will succeed. Moreover, in recent years the most important judicial nominations have been given intense scrutiny by the media, thus engaging the broader public in the process.

Before the mid-1950s, the Senate Judiciary Committee rarely questioned nominees on their judicial views, focusing instead on qualifications. Since then, however, judicial appointments have become increasingly partisan and, ultimately, ideological. Today, the Senate Judiciary Committee subjects nominees to lengthy questioning about issues ranging from gun rights to

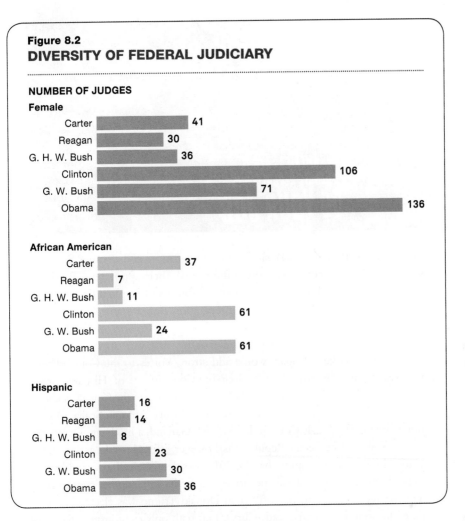

Figure 8.2

DIVERSITY OF FEDERAL JUDICIARY

NUMBER OF JUDGES

Female

President	Number
Carter	41
Reagan	30
G. H. W. Bush	36
Clinton	106
G. W. Bush	71
Obama	136

African American

President	Number
Carter	37
Reagan	7
G. H. W. Bush	11
Clinton	61
G. W. Bush	24
Obama	61

Hispanic

President	Number
Carter	16
Reagan	14
G. H. W. Bush	8
Clinton	23
G. W. Bush	30
Obama	36

NOTE: Carter appointed 261 federal judges; Reagan appointed 364; G. H. W. Bush appointed 188; Clinton appointed 372; G. W. Bush appointed 321; and Obama appointed 324 (as of March 2016). SOURCE: The Federal Judicial Center, History of the Federal Judiciary, www.fjc.gov/history/home.nsf/page/research_categories.html (accessed 8/17/16).

abortion to federal power under the commerce clause. Senators' support or opposition turns on the nominee's ideological and judicial views as much as on his or her qualifications. And, for their part, presidents nominate individuals who share their own political philosophy. Reagan and George H.W. Bush, for example, sought appointees who believed in reducing government intervention in the economy and who supported the moral positions taken by the Republican Party in recent years, particularly opposition to abortion. Not all the Reagan and Bush appointees fulfilled their sponsors' expectations. Bush appointee David Souter, for example, was attacked by conservatives as a turncoat for his decisions on school prayer and abortion rights.

Partisan politics tends to play a large role in judicial appointments. Following the death of Supreme Court Justice Antonin Scalia in 2016, Senate Republicans urged Obama to let the next president appoint Scalia's replacement. At the same time, Democrats called on Republicans to do their duty and allow a vote on Obama's nominee.

Nevertheless, Reagan and Bush did create a far more conservative Supreme Court. Hoping to counteract the influence of their appointees, President Bill Clinton named liberals Ruth Bader Ginsburg and Stephen Breyer to the Court. But George W. Bush's appointees, John Roberts and Samuel Alito, helped bolster the conservative bloc.

Similarly, President Obama hoped that his first two appointees, Sonia Sotomayor and Elena Kagan, would add strong voices to the Court's liberal wing. Sotomayor became the first Supreme Court justice of Hispanic origin and thus made judicial history even before participating in the Court's deliberations. In 2016, after the death of conservative justice Antonin Scalia, Obama nominated U.S. Appeals Court judge Merrick Garland, a moderate Democrat, to take Scalia's place. Senate Republicans, however, refused to take action on the Garland nomination, hoping that the 2016 presidential election would bring a Republican president and a chance to replace Scalia with another conservative. This strategy seemed to pay off when Donald Trump was elected and prepared to nominate a conservative jurist. Left with only eight justices for most of 2016, the Supreme Court tied 4–4 in several important cases. A tie lets stand the lower court decision. (Table 8.1 shows more information about the current Supreme Court justices.) These fierce struggles over judicial appointments reflect the growing intensity of partisanship today and the critical importance that competing political forces attach to Supreme Court appointments.

Presidents also try to shape the judiciary through their appointments to the lower federal courts. For example, with a combined total of 12 years in office, Reagan and Bush were able to exercise a good deal of influence on the composition of the federal district and appellate courts. By the end of Bush's term, he and Reagan together had appointed nearly half of all the federal judges. President Clinton promised to appoint more liberal jurists to the district and appellate courts and to increase the number of women and minorities serving on the federal bench. During his years in office, Clinton held to this promise (Figure 8.2).

Table 8.1

SUPREME COURT JUSTICES, 2016

NAME	YEAR OF BIRTH	PRIOR EXPERIENCE	APPOINTED BY	YEAR OF APPOINTMENT
John G. Roberts, Jr. *Chief Justice*	1955	Federal judge	G. W. Bush	2005
Anthony M. Kennedy	1936	Federal judge	Reagan	1988
Clarence Thomas	1948	Federal judge	G. H. W. Bush	1991
Ruth Bader Ginsburg	1933	Federal judge	Clinton	1993
Stephen G. Breyer	1938	Federal judge	Clinton	1994
Samuel A. Alito, Jr.	1950	Federal judge	G. W. Bush	2006
Sonia Sotomayor	1954	Federal judge	Obama	2009
Elena Kagan	1960	Solicitor general	Obama	2010
(vacant seat)*				

*As of November 2016.

The increasing role of partisanship or ideology in the nomination process creates a potential danger for the court system. Because courts derive much of their authority from their position of political independence, as nonpartisan arbiters in our society, the politics of appointments risks tainting judges and the judicial process as little more than extensions of the political views of those who nominate them. Fortunately, the individuals appointed to the federal judiciary tend to have a strong independent sense of themselves and their mission. Throughout the history of the federal courts are instances of judges who have frustrated the presidents who appointed them.

JUDICIAL REVIEW

The phrase judicial review refers to the power of the judiciary to examine and, if necessary, invalidate actions by the legislative and executive branches. Sometimes the phrase is also used to describe the scrutiny that appeals courts give to the actions of trial courts but, strictly speaking, this is an improper usage.

judicial review
The power of the courts to determine whether the actions of the president, the Congress, and the legislatures are or are not consistent with the Constitution. The Supreme Court asserted the power to review federal statutes in *Marbury v. Madison* (1803).

Because the Constitution does not give the Supreme Court the power of judicial review of congressional enactments, the Court's exercise of it may be seen as a usurpation. Among the proposals debated at the Constitutional Convention was one to create a council composed of the president and the judiciary that would share veto power over legislation. Another proposal was to route all legislation through both the Supreme Court and the president; overruling a veto by either would have required a two-thirds vote of the House and the Senate. Those and other proposals were rejected, and no further effort was made to give the Supreme Court review power over the other branches. This does not prove that the framers opposed judicial review, but it does indicate that "if they intended to provide for it in the Constitution, they did so in a most obscure fashion."[6]

Disputes over the framers' intentions were settled in 1803 in *Marbury v. Madison*.[7] In that case, William Marbury sued Secretary of State James Madison for Madison's failure to complete Marbury's appointment to a lower judgeship, an appointment initiated by the outgoing administration of President John Adams. Apart from the details of the case, Chief Justice John Marshall used it to declare a portion of a law unconstitutional. In effect, he stated that although Marbury's request was not unreasonable, the Court's jurisdiction in the matter was based on a section of the Judiciary Act of 1789 that the Court declared unconstitutional.

Although Congress and the president have often been at odds with the Court, its legal power to review acts of Congress has not been seriously questioned since 1803. One reason is that judicial power has come to be accepted as natural, if not intended. Another reason is that during the early years of the Republic, the Supreme Court used its power sparingly, striking down only two pieces of legislation during the first 75 years of its history. In recent years, with the power of judicial review securely accepted, the Court has been more willing to use it. Between 1985 and 2014, the Supreme Court struck down 58 acts of Congress, in part or in their entirety.[8] (See Figure 8.3.) In 2013, for example, the Court struck down a portion of the 1965 voting rights act that had required certain state and local governments to obtain federal preclearance before making any changes to their voting rules.[9] Also in 2013, the Supreme Court invalidated the 1996 Defense of Marriage Act, which had denied federal spousal benefits to gay couples.

Judicial Review of State Actions

The power of the Supreme Court to review state legislation or other state action and to determine its constitutionality is neither granted by the Constitution nor inherent in the federal system. But the logic of the

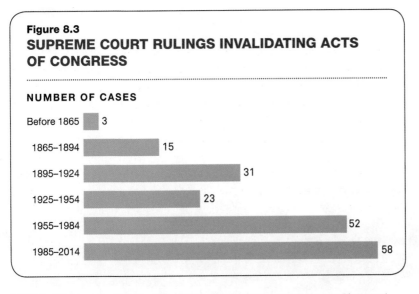

Figure 8.3

SUPREME COURT RULINGS INVALIDATING ACTS OF CONGRESS

NUMBER OF CASES

Before 1865	3
1865–1894	15
1895–1924	31
1925–1954	23
1955–1984	52
1985–2014	58

SOURCE: U.S. Government Printing Office, www.congress.gov/constitution-annotated (accessed 8/17/16).

supremacy clause of Article VI, which declares that it and laws made under its authority to be the supreme law of the land, is very strong. Furthermore, the Judiciary Act of 1789 conferred on the Supreme Court the power to reverse state constitutions and laws whenever they are clearly in conflict with the U.S. Constitution, federal laws, or treaties.[10] This power gives the Court jurisdiction over all of the millions of cases handled by American courts each year.

The history of civil rights protections abounds with examples of state laws that were overturned because the statutes violated the Fourteenth Amendment's guarantees of due process and equal protection. For example, in the 1954 case of *Brown v. Board of Education*, the Court overturned statutes in Kansas, South Carolina, Virginia, and Delaware that either required or permitted segregated public schools, on the basis that such statutes denied black schoolchildren equal protection of the law.[11] In 1967 in *Loving v. Virginia*, the Court invalidated a Virginia statute prohibiting interracial marriages.[12] Almost fifty years later, the Court cited the *Loving* case numerous times in its 2015 decision in *Obergefell v. Hodges* declaring state bans on same-sex marriage unconstitutional (see the Policy Principle section on p. 256).[13]

supremacy clause

A clause of Article VI of the Constitution that states that all laws and treaties approved by the national government are the supreme laws of the United States and superior to all laws adopted by any state or other subdivision

Judicial Review of Federal Agency Actions

Although Congress makes the law, to administer the thousands of programs it has enacted it must delegate power to the president and to a huge bureaucracy. For example, if Congress wishes to improve air quality, it

Changing Judicial Direction: Gay Marriage

Gay rights advocates celebrate the Court's 2015 decision.

In 1970, Richard Baker and James McConnell applied for a marriage license in Hennepin County, Minnesota. The county clerk, Gerald Nelson, refused to give them a license because they were both men. The couple sued Nelson, claiming that the Minnesota statute barring them from receiving a marriage license was unconstitutional. They appealed the case all the way to the Minnesota Supreme Court, which held in *Baker v. Nelson* (1971) that "The institution of marriage as a union of man and woman, uniquely involving the procreation and rearing of children within a family, is as old as the book of Genesis." In 1972, the U.S. Supreme Court issued a brief affirmation of the Minnesota ruling.

In the years and decades following this setback, the gay rights movement proceeded down other litigation avenues, bringing a series of lawsuits aimed at changing policies that discriminated against gay men and lesbians. Their collective effort to use the institution of the courts to change policy gradually saw results. A quarter of a century after *Baker v. Nelson*,

the U.S. Supreme Court struck down a provision of Colorado state law that denied gay and lesbian residents a variety of privileges that the law labeled "special rights." Justice Anthony Kennedy, writing in the 6–3 majority in *Romer v. Evans* (1996) reversing this view, states "We find nothing special in the protections [being withheld]. These protections . . . constitute ordinary civil life in a free society."

The *Romer* opinion, written in the same year Congress passed the Defense of Marriage Act (DOMA), limiting marriage to one man and one woman, shows how the Court can turn away from both its own precedents and congressional policy to actively chart a new direction.

Justice Kennedy went on to author opinions on decriminalizing sodomy in *Lawrence v. Texas* (2003), declaring DOMA unconstitutional in *United States v. Windsor* (2013), and eventually establishing a right for gays to marry across the United States in *Obergefell v. Hodges* (2015). Though by the time of *Obergefell*, many states had already legalized gay marriage, the Court was consistently on the front edge of the debate in one of its most consistent shows of judicial activism in recent times. Kennedy's *Obergefell* opinion was aimed at history, not merely at setting a legal precedent. It showed clearly his intention to shape a policy and enshrine a right, rather than argue over semantics or precedent.

Though public opinion on same-sex marriage has been changing rapidly in its favor, the *Obergefell* decision did not silence dissent. In August 2015, post-*Obergefell*, another county clerk (this time in Kentucky) refused to issue a marriage license to a gay couple. Yet, rather than affirming her action, as had happened in Minnesota four decades earlier, a court held her in contempt and jailed her.

cannot possibly anticipate all the circumstances that may arise with respect to that general goal. Inevitably, Congress must delegate to the executive substantial discretionary power to determine the best ways to improve air quality in the face of changing circumstances. Thus, over the years, almost any congressional program will result in thousands of pages of administrative regulations developed by executive agencies.

The issue of delegation of power has led to a number of court decisions over the past two centuries, generally involving the question of the scope of the delegation. Courts have also been called on to decide whether the rules and regulations adopted by federal agencies are consistent with Congress's express or implied intent.

As presidential power expanded during the New Deal era, one measure of increased congressional subordination to the executive was the enactment of laws, often at the president's behest, that gave the executive virtually unfettered authority to address a particular concern. For example, the Emergency Price Control Act of 1942 authorized the executive to set "fair and equitable" prices without indicating what those terms might mean.[14] Although the Court initially challenged these delegations of power, a confrontation with President Franklin Delano Roosevelt caused it to retreat from its position. Perhaps as a result, no congressional delegation of power to the president has been struck down as impermissibly broad in more than six decades. In the last two decades in particular, the Supreme Court has found that as long as federal agencies developed rules and regulations "based upon a permissible construction" or "reasonable interpretation" of Congress's statute, the judiciary would accept the views of the executive branch.[15] Generally, the courts defer to administrative agencies as long as those agencies have engaged in a formal rule-making process and have carried out the conditions prescribed by statutes governing agency rule making. These include the 1946 Administrative Procedure Act, which requires agencies to notify parties affected by proposed rules as well as allow them time to comment before the rules go into effect.

Judicial Review and Presidential Power

The federal courts may also review the actions of the president. As we saw in Chapter 6, presidents increasingly make use of unilateral executive powers rather than relying on congressional legislation to achieve their objectives. Often, presidential orders and actions have been challenged in the federal courts by members of Congress and by other individuals and groups. In recent decades, however, assertions of presidential power have generally been upheld and made standard executive practice. We saw one example of this earlier in the chapter, with the 1974 case *United States v. Nixon*, in which the Court first acknowledged the legitimacy of the executive privilege principle.

Executive privilege has also been invoked to protect even the deliberations of the vice president from congressional scrutiny. This pattern of judicial deference to presidential authority is also manifest in the Supreme Court's decisions regarding President George W. Bush's war on terrorism.

Perhaps the most important of these cases was *Hamdi v. Rumsfeld*.[16] In 2004, the Court ruled that Yaser Esam Hamdi, a U.S. citizen captured in Afghanistan and incarcerated in the United States as an "enemy combatant," was entitled to a lawyer and "a fair opportunity to rebut the government's factual assertions." However, the Court affirmed that the president possessed the authority to declare a U.S. citizen an enemy combatant and to order such an individual held in federal detention. Several justices intimated that once designated an enemy combatant, a U.S. citizen might be tried before a military tribunal and the normal presumption of innocence suspended. In 2006, however, in *Hamdan v. Rumsfeld*, the Court ruled that the military commissions established to try enemy combatants and other detainees violated both the Uniform Code of Military Justice and the Geneva Conventions.[17] Thus, the Supreme Court did assert that presidential actions were subject to judicial scrutiny and placed some constraints on the president's power. But at the same time it affirmed the president's unilateral power to declare individuals, including U.S. citizens, "enemy combatants" whom federal authorities could detain under adverse legal circumstances. In June, 2016, the Supreme Court sustained an appeals court decision blocking President Obama's ambitious program to prevent millions of undocumented immigrants from being deported. At issue was whether President Obama had abused his office in formulating immigration policy by using an executive order instead of the legislative and administrative processes. The eight-member Court (in the wake of the death of Justice Antonin Scalia) split 4–4, thereby letting stand the lower-court decision.[18] The Court thus thwarted an attempt to create new policy through executive action alone.

The Supreme Court has the power to review the actions of the president. When President Obama issued an executive order that would shield millions of immigrants from deportation, opponents charged that he did not have the authority to do so. The Supreme Court tied 4–4, calling the legality of his actions into question.

Much of the work of the courts involves applying statutes to particular cases. Over the centuries, however, judges have developed a body of rules and principles of interpretation that are not grounded in specific statutes. This body of judge-made law is called common law.

The appellate courts are a different realm. Their rulings can be considered laws, but ones governing only the behavior of the judiciary. When a court of appeals hands down its decision, it accomplishes two things. First, of course, it decides who wins—the person who won in the lower court or one who lost there. At the same time, it expresses its decision in a manner that provides guidance to the lower courts for handling future cases in the same area. Appellate judges try to give their reasons and rulings in writing so that the "administration of justice" can take place most of the time at the lowest judicial level. They try to make their ruling or reasoning clear so as to avoid confusion, which can produce a surge of litigation at the lower levels.

THE SUPREME COURT IN ACTION

The Supreme Court plays a vital role in government, as it is part of the structure of checks and balances that prevents the legislative and executive branches from abusing their power. The Court also operates as an institution unto itself with its own internal rules for decision making.

How Cases Reach the Supreme Court

Given the millions of disputes that arise every year, the job of the Supreme Court would be impossible if it were not able to control the flow of cases and its own caseload. The Court has original jurisdiction in a limited variety of cases defined by the Constitution, including (1) cases between the United States and one of the states, (2) cases involving two or more states, (3) cases involving foreign ambassadors or other ministers, and (4) cases brought by one state against citizens of another state or against a foreign country. The most important of these are disputes between states over land, water, or old debts. Generally, the Court deals with such cases by appointing a "special master," usually a retired judge, who actually hears the case and presents a report. The Court then allows the disputing states to present arguments for or against the master's opinion.[19]

Rules of Access. Over the years, the federal courts have developed rules governing which cases within their jurisdiction they will and will not hear. To be heard, cases must meet certain criteria that are initially applied by the trial court but may be reconsidered by appellate courts. These rules of access fall into three major categories: case or controversy, standing, and mootness.

Article III of the Constitution and past Supreme Court decisions define judicial power as extending only to "cases and controversies." That is, a case before a court must involve an actual controversy, not a hypothetical one, with two truly adversarial parties. These criteria are called ripeness. The courts have interpreted this language to mean that they do not have power to render advisory opinions to legislatures or agencies about the constitutionality of proposed laws or regulations. Furthermore, even after a law is enacted, the courts generally refuse to consider its constitutionality until it is actually applied.

Those seeking to bring a case must also have standing—they must have a substantial stake in the outcome. The traditional requirement for standing has been to show injury to oneself; that injury can be personal, economic, or even aesthetic, for example. For a group or class of people to have standing (as in a class-action suit, in which a large number of persons with common interests join together to bring or defend a lawsuit), each member must show specific injury. A general interest in the environment, for instance, does not provide a group with sufficient basis for standing.

The Supreme Court also uses a third criterion in determining whether it will hear a case: mootness. In theory, this requirement disqualifies cases that are brought too late—after the relevant facts have changed or the problem has been resolved by other means. Mootness, however, is subject to the discretion of the courts, which have begun to relax the rules about it, particularly in cases where a situation that has been resolved is likely to recur. In the abortion case *Roe v. Wade*, for example, the Supreme Court rejected the lower court's argument that because the pregnancy had already come to term, the case was moot. The Court agreed to hear the case because no pregnancy was likely to outlast the lengthy appeals process.

Putting aside the formal criteria, the Supreme Court is most likely to accept cases that involve conflicting decisions by federal circuit courts, cases that present important questions of civil rights or civil liberties, and cases that the federal government is appealing.[20] Ultimately, however, the question of which cases to accept can come down to the justices' preferences and priorities of the justices. If several justices believe that the Court should intervene in a particular area of policy or politics, they are likely to look for a case or cases that can be vehicles for doing so. For several decades, for example, the Court was not interested in considering challenges to affirmative action or other programs designed to provide particular benefits to minorities. Eventually, however, several conservative

ripeness

A criterion used by courts to avoid hearing cases that depend on hypothetical future events

standing

The right to initiate a court case, requiring that one show a substantial stake in the outcome

class-action suit

A lawsuit in which a large number of persons with common interests join together under a representative party to bring or defend a lawsuit, as when hundreds of workers join together to sue a company

mootness

A criterion used by courts to avoid hearing cases that no longer require resolution

justices eager to push back the limits of affirmative action and racial preference accepted cases that allow them to do so. In 1995, the Court's decision in three cases placed new restrictions on federal affirmative action programs, school desegregation efforts, and attempts to increase minority representation in Congress through the creation of "minority districts" (see Chapter 10).[21]

Writs. Most cases reach the Supreme Court through a write of *certiorari*, a formal request to have the Court review a lower-court decision. *Certiorari* is an order to a lower court to deliver the records of a particular case to be reviewed for legal errors (Figure 8.4). The term *certiorari* is sometimes shortened to *cert*; cases deemed to merit *certiorari* are referred to as "certworthy." A litigant who loses in a lower federal court or state court and wants the Supreme Court to review the decision has 90 days to file a petition for a writ of *certiorari* with the clerk of the Court. There are two types of petitions: paid petitions and petitions *in forma pauperis* (in the form of a pauper). The former requires payment of filing fees, submission of a certain number of copies, and compliance with numerous other rules. For *in forma pauperis* petitions, usually filed by prison inmates, the Court waives the fees and most other requirements.

writ of *certiorari*

A formal request to have the Supreme Court review a decision of a lower court. *Certiorari* is from a Latin word meaning "to make more certain."

Since 1972, most of the justices have participated in a "*certiorari* pool" in which throughout the term their law clerks evaluate the petitions. Each petition is reviewed by one clerk, who writes a memo for all the justices participating in the pool. The memo summarizes the facts and issues and makes a recommendation about whether to grant *certiorari*. Clerks for the other justices add their comments. After the justices review the memos, any justice may place any case on the "discuss list." If a case is not placed on the list, it is automatically denied *certiorari*. Cases placed on the list are considered and voted on during the justices' closed-door conference.

For *certiorari* to be granted, four justices must be convinced that the case satisfies Rule 10 of the Rules of the U.S. Supreme Court: that *certiorari* is to be granted only where there are special and compelling reasons. These include conflicting decisions by two or more circuit courts or two or more state courts of last resort; conflicts between circuit courts and state courts of last resort; decisions by circuit courts on matters of federal law that the Supreme Court should settle; and a circuit court decision on an important question that conflicts with Supreme Court decisions. The Court usually takes action only when there are conflicts among the lower courts about what the law should be; when an important legal question raised in the lower courts has not been definitively answered; or when a lower court deviates from the principles and precedents established by the high court. The support of four justices is needed for *certiorari,* and few cases satisfy this requirement. In recent sessions, though thousands

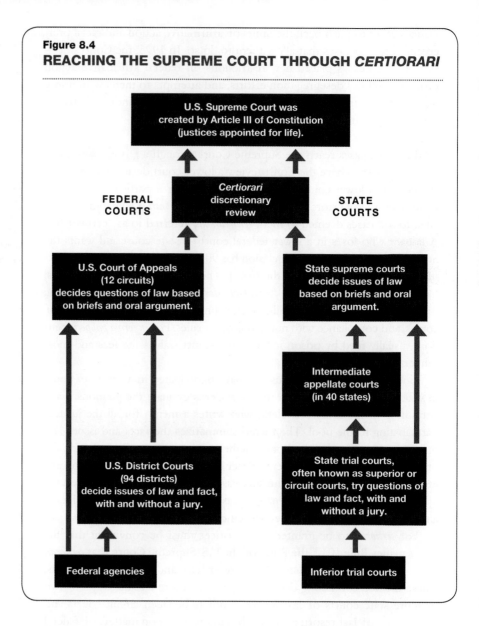

Figure 8.4

REACHING THE SUPREME COURT THROUGH *CERTIORARI*

U.S. Supreme Court was created by Article III of Constitution (justices appointed for life).

Certiorari discretionary review

FEDERAL COURTS

STATE COURTS

U.S. Court of Appeals (12 circuits) decides questions of law based on briefs and oral argument.

State supreme courts decide issues of law based on briefs and oral argument.

Intermediate appellate courts (in 40 states)

U.S. District Courts (94 districts) decide issues of law and fact, with and without a jury.

State trial courts, often known as superior or circuit courts, try questions of law and fact, with and without a jury.

Federal agencies

Inferior trial courts

of petitions have been filed (Figure 8.5), the Court has granted *certiorari* to fewer than 90 petitioners each year—about 1 percent of those seeking a Supreme Court review.

A handful of cases reach the Supreme Court through avenues other than *certiorari*. One is the "writ of certification," which can be used when a U.S. Court of Appeals asks the Supreme Court for instructions on a point of law that has never been decided. Another avenue is the "writ of appeal," used to appeal the decision of a three-judge district court.

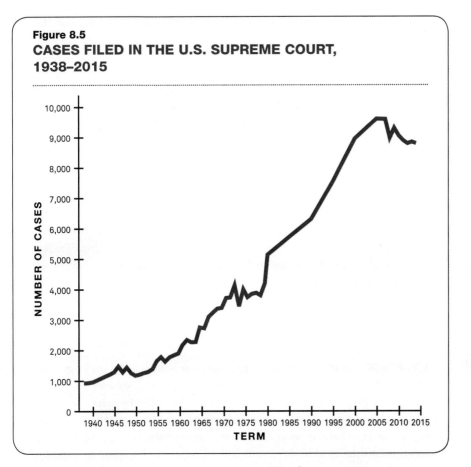

Figure 8.5

CASES FILED IN THE U.S. SUPREME COURT, 1938–2015

SOURCES: Years 1938–69: successive volumes of U.S. Bureau of the Census, *Statistical Abstract of the United States* (Washington, DC: Government Printing Office); 1970–79: Office of the Clerk of the Supreme Court; 1980–2010: The 2012 Statistical Abstract, Table 331, www.census.gov/prod/2011pubs/12statab/law.pdf (accessed 6/11/13); and Supreme Court of the United States, Cases on Docket, www.uscourts.gov/statistics-reports/caseload-statistics-data-tables (accessed 7/11/16).

Controlling the Flow of Cases: The Role of the Solicitor General

If any person has greater influence than individual justices over the work of the Supreme Court, it is the solicitor general of the United States. The solicitor general is third in status in the Justice Department (below the attorney general and the deputy attorney general) but is the top government lawyer in almost all cases before the appellate courts to which the government is a party. Although others can regulate the flow of cases, the solicitor general has the greatest control, with no review of his or her actions by any higher authority in the executive branch. More than half the

Supreme Court's total workload consists of cases under the charge of the solicitor general.

The solicitor general exercises especially strong influence by screening cases involving the federal government long before they approach the Supreme Court; the justices rely on the solicitor general to do so. Agency heads may lobby the president or otherwise try to circumvent the solicitor general, and a few of the independent agencies have a statutory right to make direct appeals, but without the solicitor general's support, these are seldom reviewed by the Court.

The solicitor general can enter a case even when the federal government is not a direct litigant by writing an *amicus curiae* ("friend of the court") brief. A "friend of the court" is not a direct party to a case but has a vital interest in its outcome. Thus, when the government has such an interest, the solicitor general can file an *amicus curiae*, or the Court can invite such a brief because it wants an opinion in writing. Other interested parties may file briefs as well.

amicus curiae ⇒

"Friend of the court," an individual or group that is not a party to a lawsuit but has an interest in influencing the outcome

brief ⇒

A written document in which an attorney explains—using case precedents—why a court should rule in favor of his or her client

The Supreme Court's Procedures

The Preparation. The Court's decision to accept a case is the beginning of a lengthy and complex process (Figure 8.6). First, attorneys on both sides must prepare briefs—written documents explaining why the Court should rule in favor of their client. The document filed by the side bringing the case, called the petitioner's brief, summarizes the facts of the case and presents the legal basis on which the Court is being asked to overturn the lower court's decision. The document filed by the side that prevailed in the lower court, called the respondent's brief, explains why the Court

Figure 8.6
THE SUPREME COURT'S DECISION-MAKING PROCESS

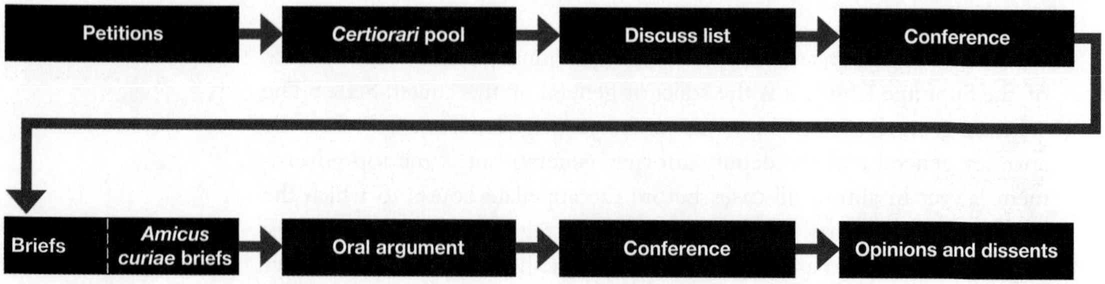

Petitions → *Certiorari* pool → Discuss list → Conference →

Briefs | *Amicus curiae* briefs → Oral argument → Conference → Opinions and dissents

should affirm the lower court's verdict. The petitioner then files another brief, the petitioner's reply brief, that attempts to refute the points made in the respondent's brief. Briefs contain many references to precedents showing that other courts have frequently ruled in the same way that the Supreme Court is being asked to rule.

As the attorneys prepare their briefs, they often ask sympathetic interest groups for help by means of *amicus curiae* briefs. In a case involving separation of church and state, for example, liberal groups such as the American Civil Liberties Union and People for the American Way are likely to file *amicus* briefs in support of strict separation, whereas conservative religious groups are likely to file ones advocating government support for religious causes. Often, dozens of briefs are filed on each side of a major case.

Oral Argument. In the next stage, oral argument, attorneys for both sides appear to present their positions before the Court and answer the justices' questions. Each attorney has only a half hour to present his or her case, including interruptions for questions. Oral argument can be very important to the outcome, for it allows justices to better understand the heart of the case and to raise questions that the opposing sides' briefs do not address. Sometimes justices go beyond the strictly legal issues and ask opposing counsel to discuss the case's implications for the Court and the nation at large. In oral arguments on the constitutionality of President Obama's executive order on immigration (discussed above), Justice Kennedy expressed his concern regarding the administration's understanding of the constitutional separation of powers. Kennedy said, "The briefs go on for pages to the effect that the president has admitted a certain number of people and then

oral argument
The stage in Supreme Court proceedings in which attorneys for both sides appear before the Court to present their positions and answer questions posed by the justices

The oral argument stage of a Supreme Court case is the last opportunity both sides have to present their positions to the Court. In addition to the immediate legal issues at stake, the attorneys may also discuss thte larger political and social ramifications of the case.

Congress approves it. That seems to me to have it backwards. It's as if . . . the president is setting the policy and the Congress is executing it. That's just upside down."[22]

The Conference. Following oral argument, the Court discusses the case in its Wednesday or Friday conference, attended only by the justices themselves. The chief justice presides and speaks first; the others follow in order of seniority. A decision is reached by a majority vote. In discussing the case, justices may try to influence one another's opinions. At times, this may result in compromise decisions.

Opinion Writing. After a decision has been reached, one of the members of the majority is assigned to write the opinion. This assignment is made by the chief justice or by the most senior justice in the majority if the chief justice is on the losing side. The assignment of the opinion can make a significant difference to the interpretation of a decision, as its wording and emphasis can have important implications for future litigation. Thus, the justice assigning an opinion must consider the impression the case will make on lawyers and on the public, as well as the probability that one justice's opinion will be more widely accepted than another's.

One of the more dramatic instances of this tactical consideration occurred in 1944, when Chief Justice Harlan F. Stone chose Justice Felix Frankfurter to write the opinion in the "white primary" case *Smith v. Allwright*, which overturned the Southern practice of excluding black voters from nominating primaries. The next day, Justice Robert H. Jackson wrote a letter to Stone arguing that Frankfurter, a foreign-born Jew from New England, would not win over the South with his opinion, regardless of its brilliance. Stone accepted the advice and substituted Justice Stanley Reed, an American-born Protestant from Kentucky and a Southern Democrat in good standing.[23]

Once the majority opinion is drafted, it is circulated to the other justices. Some members of the majority may agree with both the outcome and the rationale presented in the majority opinion but wish to highlight a particular point, and so they draft a concurring opinion for that purpose. In other cases, one or more justices agree with the majority's decision but disagree with the rationale. These justices may draft a special concurrence, explaining their disagreements with the majority.

Dissent. Justices who disagree with the majority decision may publicize the character of their disagreement in the form of a dissenting opinion, which is generally assigned by the senior justice among the dissenters. Dissenting opinions can signal to political forces on the losing side in the case that some members of the Court support their position. Ironically, the most dependable way an individual justice can exercise a direct

opinion ➡
The written explanation of the Supreme Court's decision in a particular case

concurrence ➡
An opinion agreeing with the decision of the majority in a Supreme Court case but not with the rationale provided in the majority opinion

dissenting opinion ➡
A decision written by a justice who voted with the minority opinion in a particular case, in which the justice fully explains the reasoning behind his or her opinion

influence on the Court is to write a dissent. Because there is no need to please a majority, dissenting opinions are often more eloquent and less guarded than majority opinions.

The size of the division on the Court, as well as the reasons for dissent, are often taken as an indication of the strength of the position and principles espoused by the majority. A large majority of, say, seven or more indicates that it will be hard to overturn a ruling in the future, but the one-vote margin of a 5–4 decision might be hard to sustain in future cases involving a given question. In recent years, the Supreme Court has often split 5–4, with dissenters writing long and detailed opinions that they hope will convince a swing justice to join their side on the next round of cases dealing with a similar topic.

Dissent plays a special role in the work and impact of the Court because it amounts to an appeal to lawyers nationwide to keep bringing cases of the sort at issue. Therefore, an effective dissent influences the flow of cases through the Court as well as the arguments that will be used by lawyers in later cases.

Judicial Decision Making

The judiciary is conservative in its procedures, but its impact on society can be radical. That impact depends on numerous factors, two of which stand out above the rest. The first is the individual members of the Supreme Court, their attitudes, and their relationships with each other. The second is the other branches of government, particularly Congress.

The Supreme Court Justices. The Supreme Court explains its decisions in terms of law and precedent. But ultimately the Court itself decides what laws mean and what importance precedent will have. Throughout its history, the Court has shaped and reshaped the law.

From the 1950s to the 1980s, the Court took an active role in such areas as civil rights, civil liberties, abortion, voting rights, and police procedures. It was more responsible than any other governmental institution for breaking down America's system of racial segregation. It virtually prohibited states from interfering with a woman's right to seek an abortion, sharply curtailed state restrictions on voting rights, and restricted the behavior of local police and prosecutors in criminal cases.

But since the early 1980s, resignations, deaths, and new appointments have led to many shifts in the mix of ideologies represented on the Court. In a series of decisions between 1989 and 2001, conservative justices appointed by Ronald Reagan and George H. W. Bush were able to swing the Court to a more conservative position on civil rights, affirmative action, abortion rights, property rights, criminal procedure, voting rights, desegregation, and the power of the national government.

However, because the Court was so evenly split during this period, the conservative bloc did not always prevail. Among the justices serving at the beginning of 2005, William Rehnquist, Antonin Scalia, and Clarence Thomas took conservative positions on most issues and were usually joined by Sandra Day O'Connor and Anthony Kennedy. Stephen Breyer, Ruth Bader Ginsburg, David Souter, and John Paul Stevens were reliably liberal. This produced many 5–4 conservative victories. On some issues, though, O'Connor or Kennedy tended to side with the liberal camp, producing a 5–4 and sometimes a 6–3 victory for the liberals.

George W. Bush's appointment of Samuel Alito to replace O'Connor was touted in the media as heralding a shift in a much more conservative direction, but it moved the pivotal vote on the Court only from O'Connor to the ideologically similar Kennedy. During the 2007 term, Kennedy found himself the swing voter on numerous 5–4 decisions. One-third of all cases in 2007 were decided by just one vote. President Obama's appointments of Sonia Sotomayor and Elena Kagan to replace Souter and Stevens did not promise to alter this arithmetic. The death of Justice Antonin Scalia left the Court with a 4–4 liberal-conservative division, but Republican Donald Trump promised to nominate a conservative jurist in 2017, tipping the balance back in favor of the conservatives. The Analyzing the Evidence unit on pp. 270–1 looks at ideology in the Court.

We should note that the conservative-liberal bloc structure on the Court is not always predictive, even in important cases. In *National Federation of Independent Business v. Sebelius*, the 2012 case on the constitutionality of Obama's health care law, Chief Justice John Roberts, a firm member of the conservative bloc, joined the four liberals to uphold the law.[24] Similarly, in the 2015 case of *King v. Burwell,* Roberts again sided with the liberal bloc to uphold provisions of the Affordable Care Act.[25]

Of course, the meaning of any decision rests not just on which justices vote with the majority but also on the majority's written opinion, which presents the constitutional or statutory rationale for future policy. These options establish the guidelines that govern how federal courts must decide similar cases in the future.

Activism and Restraint. One element of judicial philosophy is the issue of activism versus restraint. Over the years, some justices have believed that courts should interpret the Constitution according to the framers' stated intentions and defer to the views of Congress when interpreting federal statutes. Felix Frankfurter, for example, advocated judicial deference to legislative bodies and avoidance of the "political thicket" the Court entangled itself in by deciding questions that were essentially political rather than legal. Advocates of judicial restraint are sometimes called "strict constructionists," because they look strictly to the words of the Constitution in interpreting its meaning.

The alternative to restraint is judicial activism, which involves going beyond the words of the Constitution or a statute to consider the broader societal implications of court decisions. Activist judges sometimes strike out in new directions, promulgating new interpretations or inventing new legal and constitutional concepts when they deem them socially desirable. For example, Justice Harry Blackmun's opinion in *Roe v. Wade* was based on a constitutional right to privacy that is not found in the words of the Constitution. Blackmun and the other members of the majority in *Roe* argued that other constitutional provisions implied the right to privacy. In this instance of judicial activism, the majority knew the result it wanted to achieve and was not afraid to make the law conform to the desired outcome.

Political Ideology. The second component of judicial philosophy is political ideology. The liberal or conservative attitudes of justices play an important role in their decisions.[26] Indeed, the philosophy of activism versus restraint is, in part, a smoke screen for political ideology. In the past, liberal judges have often been activists, willing to use the law to achieve social and political change, whereas conservatives have been associated with judicial restraint. In recent years, however, some conservative justices have become activists in seeking to undo some of the work of liberal jurists over the past three decades.

Congress. At both the national and state levels in the United States, courts and judges are "players" in the policy game because of the separation of powers. Essentially, the legislative branch formulates policy (defined constitutionally and institutionally by a legislative process); the executive branch implements policy (according to well-defined administrative procedures, and subject to initial approval by the president or the legislative override of his veto); and the courts, when asked, rule on the faithfulness of the legislated and executed policy either to the substance of the statute or to the Constitution itself. The courts, that is, may strike down an administrative action either because it exceeds the authority granted in the relevant statute (statutory rationale) or because the statute itself exceeds the authority granted the legislature or executive by the Constitution (constitutional rationale).

If a court declares an administrative action outside the permissible bounds, the majority opinion can impose whatever alternative policy the majority wishes. If the legislature is unhappy with this judicial action, it may either recraft the legislation (if the rationale for striking it down was statutory)[27] or initiate a constitutional amendment that would enable it to pass constitutional muster (if the rationale for striking it down was constitutional).

judicial restraint
The judicial philosophy whose adherents refuse to go beyond the text of the Constitution in interpreting its meaning

judicial activism
The judicial philosophy that the Court should see beyond the text of the Constitution or a statute to consider the broader societal implications of its decisions

Ideological Voting on the Supreme Court

Contributed by
Andrew D. Martin
University of Michigan
Kevin M. Quinn
UC Berkeley School of Law

Do the political preferences of Supreme Court justices influence their behavior? The starting point for the analysis of the behavior of Supreme Court justices is to look at their votes.[1] For non-unanimous cases, we can compute agreement scores—the fraction of cases in which a pair of justices vote the same way. We display these agreement scores for the Court's 2014–15 term in the first figure below. If you examine this figure, you will see that two groups of justices emerge. Within each group, the justices agree with one another a lot; almost 90 percent of the time for justices on the left, and between 60 and 70 percent of the time for justices on the right. Voting is more structured than we would expect by chance.

One way to represent that structure is by arranging the justices on a line as in the diagram below to the right.[2] Justices who agree a lot should be close to one another; justices who disagree a lot should be far apart.

Does the fact that there are patterns of agreement mean that the justices are deciding based on political ideology? Not necessarily. These patterns are consistent with ideological decision making, but other things might explain the patterns as well. However, when we read the cases and see who wins or loses, there is a great deal of support for the idea that political ideology influences how justices vote.[3]

Agreement Scores for the 2014–15 Term

	Sotomayor	Ginsburg	Kagan	Breyer	Kennedy	Roberts	Scalia	Alito	Thomas
Sotomayor	1	.85	.85	.89	.72	.49	.31	.36	.13
Ginsburg	.85	1	.9	.89	.62	.49	.31	.31	.23
Kagan	.85	.9	1	.89	.72	.44	.41	.31	.23
Breyer	.89	.89	.89	1	.66	.55	.37	.39	.16
Kennedy	.72	.62	.72	.66	1	.46	.49	.49	.36
Roberts	.49	.49	.44	.55	.46	1	.72	.67	.44
Scalia	.31	.31	.41	.37	.49	.72	1	.64	.62
Alito	.36	.31	.31	.39	.49	.67	.64	1	.67
Thomas	.13	.23	.23	.16	.36	.44	.62	.67	1

POSITION

Sotomayor
Ginsburg
Kagan
Breyer

Kennedy

Roberts

Scalia
Alito

The figure to the left contains the agreement scores for the 2014–15 term of the U.S. Supreme Court for all non-unanimous cases. These scores are the proportion of cases when each justice agreed with every other justice. Two justices that always disagreed with each other would get a zero; two justices who always agreed would get a one. Red indicates low agreement scores; green indicates high agreement scores. The policy dimension to the right of the figure is one that best represents the patterns in the agreement scores.

This type of analysis can be done for any court, but it becomes more difficult if we are interested in comparing justices across time instead of during just one term. What if we are interested in whether the Supreme Court is becoming more ideologically polarized over time? Or whether individual justices have become more liberal or conservative? Martin-Quinn scores based on a statistical model of voting on the Court help solve this problem.[4]

A number of interesting patterns emerge. Consider the case of Justice Harry Blackmun, who often claimed, "I haven't changed; it's the Court that changed under me."[5] The figure below shows that Justice Blackmun's position did in fact change ideologically over the course of his career. This evidence is consistent with some clear changes in Justice Blackmun's behavior, especially in the area of the death penalty.

We can also look at patterns in the positions of chief justices. While the chief's vote counts just the same as the other justices, he or she plays an important role in organizing the court. Justice Rehnquist was the most conservative justice on the Court when he arrived in 1971, but as the figure below shows, after he was elevated in 1986 he too drifted more toward the middle. This is what we would expect to see of a justice who was working strategically to build coalitions, as any good chief would.

Ideological Trajectories of Selected Justices

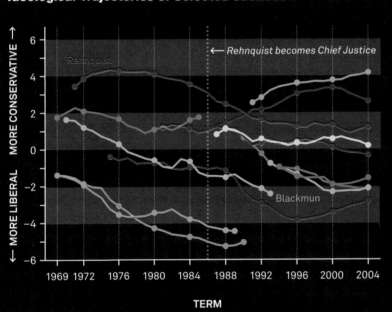

JUSTICES

- Blackmun
- Brennan
- Breyer
- Burger
- Ginsburg
- Kennedy
- Marshall
- O'Connor
- Rehnquist
- Scalia
- Souter
- Stevens
- Thomas

This figure shows the Martin-Quinn score for selected justices serving in the Burger (1969–86) and Rehnquist Courts (1986–2004). Each line represents the trajectory of each justice on the ideological dimension.

1 C. Herman Pritchett, *The Roosevelt Court: A Study in Judicial Politics and Values, 1937–1947* (New York: Macmillan, 1948).

2 Glendon A. Schubert, *The Judicial Mind: The Attitudes and Ideologies of Supreme Court Justices, 1946–1963* (Evanston, IL: Northwestern University Press, 1965).

3 Jeffry A. Segal and Harold J. Spaeth, *The Supreme Court and the Attitudinal Model* (New York: Cambridge University Press, 1993).

4 Andrew D. Martin and Kevin M. Quinn, "Dynamic Ideal Point Estimation via Markov Chain Monte Carlo for the U.S. Supreme Court, 1953–1999," *Political Analysis* 10, no. 2, (2002): 134–53, http://mqscores.wustl.edu (accessed 10/18/11).

5 Linda Greenhouse, *Becoming Justice Blackmun* (New York: Times Books, 2005).

In reaching their decisions, Supreme Court justices must anticipate Congress's response. As a result, they do not always vote according to their true preferences, because doing so may provoke Congress to overturn their decision by enacting legislation that moves the policy at issue even further away from what the justices prefer. In short, the interactions between the Court and Congress are part of a complex strategic game.[28]

The President. The president's most direct influence on the Court is the power to nominate justices. Presidents typically nominate those who seem close to their policy preferences and close enough to the preferences of a majority of senators, who must confirm the nomination.

Yet the efforts by presidents to reshape the federal judiciary are not always successful. Often in American history, judges have surprised and disappointed the presidents who named them to the bench. The president must also confront Congress in shaping the judiciary. By using the filibuster (see Chapter 5), both parties have blocked judicial nominees. In 2013, frustration over Republican blocking of President Obama's judicial nominees led Senate Democrats to eliminate the possibility of a filibuster for most presidential nominees (although it remains for Supreme Court nominations). Of course, opponents of a nomination may block it in other ways. The judiciary committee may refuse to consider the nominee, as in the case of Judge Merrick Garland, Obama's Supreme Court nominee to replace the late Justice Antonin Scalia. As we saw, the appointment process has subtly tied the judiciary to the executive and, perhaps, helped to upset the constitutional balance of power.

HOW POWERFUL IS THE JUDICIARY?

Over the past 50 years, the place of the judiciary in American politics and society has changed dramatically. Demand for legal solutions has increased, and the judiciary's reach has expanded. Some now call for reining in the power of the courts and the discretion of judges in areas ranging from criminal law and sentencing to property rights to liability and torts. How our society deals with these issues will shape the judiciary's future independence and effectiveness. Even the most conservative justices now seem reluctant to relinquish their newfound power—authority that has become accepted and thus established.

Federal judges enjoy great latitude because they are not subject to electoral pressures. More than any other politicians in the United States, they can pursue their own ideas about what is right—their own ideologies.

They are, however, constrained by rules governing access to the courts, by other courts, by Congress and the president, by their lack of enforcement powers, and most important, by the past in the form of precedent and common law. For much of its history, the federal judiciary acted very cautiously. The Supreme Court rarely challenged laws passed by Congress or actions of the president, and the scope of its decisions was limited to those individuals granted access to the courts.

Two judicial revolutions have expanded the power and reach of the federal judiciary since World War II. The first revolution brought about the liberalization of a wide range of public policies in the United States. As we saw in Chapter 4, in certain policy areas—including school desegregation, legislative apportionment, criminal procedure, obscenity, abortion, and voting rights—the Supreme Court was at the forefront of sweeping changes in the role of the U.S. government and, ultimately, the character of American society. The Court put many of these issues before the public long before Congress or the president was prepared to act.

At the same time that the courts were introducing important policy innovations, they were also bringing about a second, less visible revolution. During the 1960s and 1970s, the Supreme Court and other federal courts liberalized the concept of standing to permit almost any group seeking to challenge an administrative agency's actions to bring its case before the federal bench. It thus encouraged groups to come to the judiciary to resolve disputes, rather than to Congress or the executive branch.

Complementing this change, the federal courts broadened the scope of relief to permit themselves to act on behalf of broad categories of persons in "class-action" cases, rather than just on behalf of individuals.[29]

Finally, the federal courts began to employ so-called structural remedies, in effect retaining jurisdiction of cases until the court's mandate had actually been implemented to its satisfaction.[30]

Through these judicial mechanisms, the federal courts paved the way for an unprecedented expansion of national judicial power. Thus, during the 1960s and 1970s, the power of the federal courts expanded through links with constituencies—such as civil rights, consumer, environmental, and feminist groups—that staunchly defended the Supreme Court in its battles with Congress, the executive, or other interest groups.

During the 1980s and 1990s, the Reagan and George H. W. Bush administrations sought to end the relationship between the Court and liberal political forces. Conservative judges appointed by these Republican presidents modified the Court's position in areas such as abortion, affirmative action, and judicial procedure, though not as completely as some conservative writers and politicians had hoped. Within one week in 2003, for example, the Supreme Court affirmed the validity of affirmative action, reaffirmed abortion rights, strengthened gay rights, offered new protection to individuals facing the death penalty, and ruled in favor of a congressional apportionment plan that dispersed minority voters across several districts—a practice that appeared to favor the Democrats.[31] The Court had made these decisions based on the justices' interpretations of precedent and law, not simply their personal beliefs.

Despite its more conservative ideology in recent decades, moreover, the Court has not become conservative in another sense. It has not been eager to surrender the expanded powers carved out by earlier Courts, especially in areas that assert the power of the national government over the states. Indeed, the early opponents to the U.S. Constitution (the Antifederalists discussed in Chapter 2) feared the assertion of the national interest over the states through the independent judiciary. Over more than two centuries of U.S. history, the reach and authority of the federal judiciary have expanded greatly, and it has emerged as a powerful arm of our national politics. Whatever their policy beliefs or partisan orientations, judges and justices understand the new importance of the courts among the three branches of American government and act not just to interpret and apply the law but also to maintain the power of the courts.

For Further Reading

Abraham, Henry J. *The Judicial Process: An Introductory Analysis of the Courts of the United States, England, and France.* 7th ed. New York: Oxford University Press, 1998.

Baum, Lawrence. *Judges and Their Audiences: A Perspective on Judicial Behavior.* Princeton, NJ: Princeton University Press, 2006.

Bickel, Alexander M. *The Least Dangerous Branch: The Supreme Court at the Bar of Politics.* Indianapolis, IN: Bobbs-Merrill, 1962.

Epstein, Lee, and Jack Knight. *The Choices Justices Make.* Washington, DC: CQ Press, 1998.

Kahn, Ronald. *The Supreme Court and Constitutional Theory, 1953–1993.* Lawrence: University Press of Kansas, 1994.

Marbury v. Madison, 5 U.S. (1 Cranch) 137, 1803.

O'Brien, David M. *Storm Center: The Supreme Court in American Politics.* 10th ed. New York: Norton, 2014.

Perry, H. W., Jr. *Deciding to Decide: Agenda Setting in the United States Supreme Court.* Cambridge, MA: Harvard University Press, 1991.

Rosenberg, Gerald. *The Hollow Hope: Can Courts Bring About Social Change?* 2nd ed. Chicago: University of Chicago Press, 2008.

Segal, Jeffrey A., and Harold J. Spaeth. *The Supreme Court and the Attitudinal Model Revisited.* New York: Cambridge University Press, 2002.

Silverstein, Mark. *Judicious Choices: The New Politics of Supreme Court Confirmations.* 2nd ed. New York: Norton, 2007.

Toobin, Jeffrey. *The Nine: Inside the Secret World of the Supreme Court.* New York: Knopf, 2008.

Whittington, Keith. *Political Foundations of Judicial Supremacy: The President, the Supreme Court, and Constitutional Leadership in U.S. History.* Princeton, NJ: Princeton University Press, 2008.

9

Public Opinion
and the Media

In the United States, as in other democracies, citizens expect their government to pay close attention to popular preferences. Most Americans believe that the government does listen to popular opinion most or at least some of the time. This view is bolstered by a number of scholarly studies that have identified a reasonable correlation between national policy and public opinion over time. The political scientist Alan D. Monroe, for example, found that in a majority of cases, changes in public policy followed shifts in popular preferences. Conversely, in most cases, if opinion did not change, neither did policy.[1] These findings are certainly affirmed by hosts of politicians who not only claim to be guided by the will of the people in all their undertakings, but seem to poll constituents assiduously to find out what that will is.

But does public opinion influence public policy as much as we think? Though there is some congruence or consistency between the two, this does not mean that the public's preferences always control the government's conduct. Most citizens do not have strong preferences about most public issues, and many lack basic information that might help them to understand and evaluate policy choices. For example, 40 percent of Americans responding to a recent survey did not know that each state has two senators; 43 percent did not know what an economic recession is; 68 percent did not know that a two-thirds majority in each house is required for a congressional override of a presidential veto; and 70 percent did not know that the term of a U.S. House member is two years.[2] These findings should give us pause when we examine poll data concerning topics as complicated as the federal debt limit, immigration reform, or economic inequality. Many Americans did not have a good understanding of the economic and political implications of the various plans put forward to address these issues and probably took their cues from politicians they admired. Hence, most Democrats supported President Obama while most Republicans found merit in the GOP's position.

Indeed, many Americans' knowledge of contemporary political issues is limited to a fact or claim they saw in an ad or heard on a newscast. And, once they acquire a piece of information, many people will retain it long after it ceases to be relevant. In a 2005 Harris poll, for example, more than a third of the respondents believed that Iraq possessed weapons of mass destruction at the time of the 2003 American invasion—even though President George W. Bush, who launched the invasion, had long since acknowledged that no such weapons had existed.

Lack of basic political knowledge and accurate, up-to-date information makes many Americans quite vulnerable to manipulation by politicians and advocates wielding the instruments of advertising, publicity, and measurement. Their goal, as researchers Lawrence Jacobs and Robert Shapiro note, is to "simulate responsiveness," by developing arguments and ideas that will

CORE OF THE ANALYSIS

➡ Public opinion is the aggregation of individuals' views. It expresses the range of attitudes and beliefs and on which side of any question a majority of people fall.

➡ There are a wide range of interests at stake in any question that the government must decide, as well as differing preferences, beliefs, and opinions about what ought to be done.

➡ Politicians follow public opinion as part of the representative process. They take signals from polls and other indicators of public sentiment to gauge whether a particular decision might affect their prospects at the next election.

➡ The media are an important influence in shaping public opinion.

persuade citizens to agree with their own policy goals.[3] This effort begins with polling. As Bill Clinton's pollster Dick Morris affirmed, "You don't use a poll to reshape a program, but to reshape your argumentation for the program so the public supports it."[4] The effort continues with advertising, publicity, and propaganda, making use of the information gleaned from the polls.

Thus, for example, a coalition that succeeded in eliminating the federal estate tax in 2001 first used extensive polling and publicity over several years to persuade the public that what they labeled the "death tax" was unfair and un-American. As Michael Graetz and Ian Shapiro show in their research, while the tax actually affected only the wealthiest 2 percent of the population, the intensive campaign for its repeal seemed to persuade many Americans that it actually affected them. One poll taken in the wake of the repeal campaign showed that 77 percent of respondents believed the tax affected all Americans, and several polls indicated that more than one-third of the public believed they themselves would have to pay it.[5] When the tax was finally annulled by Congress, its elimination was supported by public opinion. But, does this mean that a change in public opinion brought about this change in policy? Hardly. Instead, a particular set of political forces engineered a shift in opinion that helped them to persuade Congress to change national policy. A similar pattern was observed by political scientists Jacob Hacker and Paul Pierson when they studied recent changes in tax policy. Citizens, they say, "proved vulnerable to extensive manipulation," as political elites framed a discussion that generated popular support for policy changes serving the interests of a small minority of wealthy Americans.[6]

In this chapter, we examine further the role of public opinion in American politics, including these questions: Do Americans know enough to form meaningful opinions about important policy issues? What factors account for differences in opinion? To what extent can the government manipulate popular sentiment? How do the media influence public opinion? Then we take a closer look at one of the most important influences on public opinion, the media.

WHAT IS PUBLIC OPINION?

public opinion
Citizens' attitudes about political issues, personalities, institutions, and events

Public opinion is the aggregation of many citizens' views and interests. It encompasses assessments of those in office, attitudes toward political organizations and social groups, and preferences about how government ought to address important problems. The term sometimes gives the impression that the public has a single opinion on a given matter; however, that is rarely the case.

In some cases, Americans do hold common views on questions vital to governance and society. There is consensus on the legitimacy of the U.S. Constitution and trust in the rule of law—that is, the principle that no one is above the law. There is consensus that we are a democratic society and that the outcomes of elections, whether or not a person likes the winners, determine who governs. These commonly held opinions and values are essential to maintaining a well-functioning democracy in the United States. They ensure peaceful transitions of government after each election and respect for laws produced by a legitimately chosen government.

There is also wide agreement on fundamental political values, such as equality of opportunity, liberty, and democracy.[7] Nearly all Americans agree that all people should have equal rights, regardless of race, gender, or social standing. Americans hold a common commitment to freedom. People who live in the United States are free to live where they want, travel where they want, work where they want, say what they want, and practice whatever religion they wish, or no religion at all. And Americans have an undying belief in democracy, that whenever possible public officials should be chosen by majority vote.[8] It makes sense to think of the American public as having a single opinion on these elemental questions.

On most matters that come before the government, however, the public does not hold a single view. Usually, opinions are divided between those who support the government or a proposed action and those who do not. Politicians are still attuned to public opinion when it is divided, but what matter most are the balance and direction of opinion. What do the majority of constituents want? Which way is opinion trending? Is it possible to find a popular middle ground?

People express their views to those in power in a variety of ways. Constituents contact their members of Congress directly through letters, phone calls, e-mails, and even personal visits to members' offices. Most questions before Congress elicit little reaction from the public, but some questions start a maelstrom of objections. In 2008, when Congress was considering a $700 billion bailout of financial institutions, the volume of e-mail on the bill was so great that at one point the House of Representatives had to limit incoming e-mail to keep its computers from crashing.[9]

People also express their opinions more publicly, by writing blogs, tweets, letters to newspapers, and op-ed pieces; by talking with others; by displaying lawn signs and bumper stickers; by working on campaigns; by giving money to candidates, groups, and party organizations; and, most simply, by voting.

Expressions of opinions and preferences are not always easy to interpret. If a constituent votes against a member of Congress, did she do so because of something the legislator did in Congress, or because she decided to vote against all politicians from the legislator's party? Or for some other reason?

Political scientists and political consultants try to provide more refined and structured descriptions of public opinion using surveys. On any important issue, the government may pursue different policy options. Public opinion on a given issue can often be thought of as the distribution of opinion across the different options. Likewise, public opinion may represent the division of support for a leader or party. Surveys try to gauge where majority support lies and how intensely or firmly citizens across the spectrum hold their views. More and more, politicians rely on opinion polls to anticipate the effects of their decisions, to develop ways to blunt objections to those decisions, and to identify opportunities to change opinions. Answering a survey, then, can also be a form of political action, because it may influence political decisions.

ORIGINS AND NATURE OF PUBLIC OPINION

To understand the meaning and origins of the public's opinions, we must have some sense of the basis for individuals' preferences and beliefs. One's opinions are the products of one's personality, social characteristics, and interests. They mirror who a person is, what she wants, and how she is related to her family and community and to the broader economy and society. But opinions are also shaped by institutional, political, and governmental forces that make it more likely that an individual will hold some beliefs and less likely that he will hold others.

Foundations of Preferences

At a foundational level, individual opinion is shaped by several factors, including self-interest, values about what is right and wrong, and the process of socialization.

Self-Interest. Individuals' preferences about politics and public policy are usually rooted in self-interest. Laws and other governmental actions directly affect people's interests—their disposable income, their safety, and the quality of public services and goods, to give just a few examples. It is not surprising, then, that when people express their political opinions, they react to the effects that government actions have on them personally.

Economic interests are perhaps the most salient preferences when it comes to people's opinions. Virtually every American has an interest in the government's role in the nation's economy and strong preferences about tax rates and spending priorities. Given the enormous influence of the federal government in the economy, assessments of the president and the party in power often correspond to how well the economy performs.

Individuals' attitudes toward government reflect other forms of self-interest as well. Laws affect families, the status of civic and religious organizations, and communities. Zoning laws and urban redevelopment programs shape the nature of neighborhoods, including the mix of commercial and residential housing and the density of low-income housing in an area. Family law affects how easy it is for families to stay together, what happens when they break down, and what rights and responsibilities parents have. Proposed changes in such laws bring immediate reaction from those affected.

Values. Much of what individuals want from their government is rooted in values about what is right or wrong—our philosophies about morality, justice, and ethics. Our values systems originate in many places—families, religion, education, groups, and so forth—and often determine our preferences in particular circumstances. For example, values of economic justice may shape preferences about whether and how government redistributes income. Americans generally believe in equal opportunity, an idea that has driven our society to try to root out discrimination in employment, housing, and education and to create a universal public education system. In some states, courts have invoked this principle of equality to insist that the states try to equalize public school expenditures per pupil across districts.

Values also shape our notions of what is a crime and what is a suitable punishment. One of the most morally laden debates in American history focuses on capital punishment. Does the government have the right to take someone's life if that person has taken the life of someone else? An ancient sense of justice seems to call for exactly that: an eye for an eye. Other ideas of morality speak against capital punishment. In addition, our values about government and its appropriate powers say that people must be protected against arbitrary and capricious governmental acts. The possibility of an error has led some to claim that the government should never have the power to take the life of an individual.

Our values also reflect established social norms of our community, analogous to common law. What, for example, is marriage? One might consider it an economic convenience, as defined by laws that tie taxes and inheritance to marital status. Most people, however, express more complex ideas of marriage, and those principles dictate whether they think that same-sex marriages ought to be allowed. Such norms change over time.

At a societal level, conflicting values are particularly difficult to resolve. Unlike economic interests, it is hard to bargain over differences based on fundamental principles of right and wrong. By the same token, there are many values that unite us. If Americans had few common values or perspectives, it would be very difficult for them to reach agreement on particular issues. Over the past half-century, political philosophers and political scientists have reflected on what those values are and have settled on three important precepts. Americans almost universally agree with (1) the democracy principle (that majority rule is a good decision rule), (2) the equal opportunity principle, and (3) the principle that the government is best that governs least.

Social Groups. Another source of political preferences is social groups. People use race, religion, place, language, and many other characteristics to describe and define themselves. These descriptors tap fundamental psychological attachments that go beyond self-interest and values, though they are often reinforced by our interests and values.

Membership in a social group may affect individual opinion. For example, Catholics and other religious groups are more likely than the religiously unaffiliated to oppose abortion.

The process through which our social interactions and social groups affect our perspectives and preferences is called socialization. Most 18-year-olds already have definite political attitudes that they have learned from parents and grandparents, friends, teachers and religious leaders, and others in their social groups and networks. Of course, socialization does not end upon leaving home. We continue to learn about politics and what we should think about political questions from our family members, coworkers, and others we see and speak with daily.

Socialization works in many ways. First, it is a means of providing information about what is going on in the community and even in national politics. Socialization also takes the form of education or instruction. Parents teach their children how to think about a problem, how to decide what is a right or wrong choice or action, and even how to participate in politics. This is how we as humans have learned to survive and adapt. But it means that we have, by the time we are adults, already learned much about what we want government to do, what sorts of people we want in government, and even whether it is worth our while to participate.

socialization

A process through which individuals assimilate community preferences and norms through social interactions

Political Ideology

An ideology is a comprehensive way of understanding political or cultural situations. It is a set of assumptions about the way the world and society works that helps us to organize our beliefs, information, and reactions to new situations. It ascribes values to different alternatives and helps us balance competing values. In the United Satates today, people often describe themselves as liberals or conservatives. Liberalism and conservatism are political ideologies that include beliefs about the proper role of government, about appropriate public policies, and about the proper groups to exercise power in society. In earlier times, these terms were defined somewhat differently. As recently as the nineteenth century, a liberal was an individual who favored freedom from state control, whereas a conservative was someone who supported the use of governmental power and favored continuation of the rule of elites.

Today, in the United States, the term liberal has come to imply support for political and social reform; government intervention in the economy; the expansion of federal social services; more vigorous efforts on behalf of the poor, immigrants, minorities, and women; and greater concern for consumers and the environment. In social and cultural areas, liberals generally support abortion rights, the rights of gay and transgender citizens, and oppose state involvement with religious institutions and religious expression. In international affairs, liberal positions usually include support for arms control, support for aid to poor nations, opposition to the use of American troops to influence the domestic affairs of developing nations, and support for international organizations such as the United Nations. Of course, liberalism is not monolithic. For example, among individuals who view themselves as liberal, many call for humanitarian intervention in the civil war in Syria though this would require the use of American military force.

By contrast, the term conservative today is used to describe those who generally support the social and economic status quo and favor markets as solutions to social and economic problems. Conservatives believe that a large and powerful government poses a threat to citizens' freedom, and in the domestic arena they generally oppose the expansion of governmental activity. In particular, they oppose government regulation of business, arguing that it is frequently economically inefficient and can ultimately lower the nation's standard of living. As for social and cultural positions, many conservatives oppose abortion and favor traditional definitions of marriage In international affairs, conservatism has come to mean support for the maintenance of the United States' superpower military status. Like liberalism, however, conservatism is far from a monolithic ideology. Some conservatives support many government social programs, and some oppose efforts to outlaw abortion, arguing that government intrusion in this area is as misguided as it is in the economy. Some conservatives are isolationists and oppose American military intervention around the globe. The real political world is far too complex to be seen in terms of a simple struggle between liberals and conservatives.

There are many other ideologies besides liberalism and conservatism. Libertarians, for example, seek to expand liberty above all other principles and to minimize government intervention in all aspects of the economy and

liberal

A person who generally supports political and social reform; governmental intervention in the economy; the expansion of federal social services; more vigorous efforts on behalf of the poor, minorities, and women; and greater concern for consumers and the environment

conservative

A person who generally supports the social and economic status quo and believes that a large and powerful government poses a threat to citizens' freedom

society. Other ideologies seek a particular outcome, such as environmental protection, or emphasize certain issues, such as economic growth, and de-emphasize others, such as abortion. Communism and fascism are ideologies that support government control of all aspects of the economy and society. These ideologies dominated politics in many European countries from the 1920s through the 1940s. Political discourse in the United States, however, has revolved around the division between liberals and conservatives for most of the last century.

Political scientists often think of liberal and conservative ideologies as anchors on a spectrum of possible belief systems. An individual's values and interests might make him or her adhere to many elements of one of these ideologies but not all. The Pew Center on People and the Press offers just such a classification in its American Values Survey, conducted annually since 1987.[10] The survey asks respondents about a wide range of political, social, and cultural preferences, behaviors, and beliefs. Classifying people this way, the Pew Center finds that most Americans are in fact fairly moderate—having as many conservative views as liberal views, and favoring more centrist, less extreme versions of both kinds.

Identity Politics

Ideology offers one lens through which people can discern where their political interests and values lie. Identity provides an alternative simplification of the political world. Political identities are distinctive characteristics or group associations that individuals carry, reflecting their social connections or common values and interests with others in that group. A harm or benefit to any individual with a given identity is viewed as a harm or benefit to all people with that identity. Common identities in politics include race and ethnicity, language, religion, and gender.

Identity politics are often zero-sum: if one group wins, another loses. The term *identity politics* is sometimes used today to refer to groups that have been oppressed and that seek to assert their rights. But the concept is much broader. The term *political identity* describes not just the situation of groups that have suffered harm; it applies to any collective identity. In fact, political identity often has a very positive side, as the glue that holds society together and as another way to overcome problems of collective action.[11]

Identity politics are quite obvious in the United States today. All citizens and even many noncitizens identify themselves as Americans. During international sporting competitions, therefore, we root for athletes representing the United States, and when those athletes win, as Americans we feel happy and proud. We may feel similarly when an American wins a Nobel Prize or makes a significant scientific discovery. The same is true of people from any country, who feel pride in the accomplishments of others from that country.

One of the most salient political identities in the United States is political party. The authors of *The American Voter* (1960), a now classic work of political science research on the social and psychological foundations of electoral behavior in the United States, characterize party identification as a stable psychological attachment usually developed in childhood and carried throughout one's adult life. Party identifications are, of course, shaped by interests and values as well as by current events, but partisanship also has deep roots in family, local culture, and other factors. People commonly rely on their partisan identities in filtering information—as in, for example, deciding who won a presidential debate. Party also has a unique hold on voting behavior. Even after taking into account self-interest, moral values, and other identities, partisanship remains one of the best predictors of how someone will vote.[12] (See the discussion of party voting in Chapters 10 and 11.) This is not to say that party does not reflect ideological choices or self-interest. It does. But it is certainly also the case that party functions as a social identity.

People who hold a specific identity often express strong affinity for others of the same identity—for example, voting for someone of the same national background or ethnicity quite apart from, or in spite of, the sorts of laws that the particular politician promises to enact. Political scientists call this preference for people of the same identity "descriptive representation," and it is an important subject in the area of race and elections. The Voting Rights Act tries to protect African Americans, Hispanics, and other racial and ethnic groups against discriminatory electoral practices that prevent those voters from electing their preferred candidates. Since the act was passed in 1965, the percentage of members of Congress who are African American or Hispanic has increased from 1 percent (6 in 1965) to 21 percent (90 in 2015). Race, gender, social class, and place all create strong identities that shape voting behavior.

People have a wide range of social, cultural, and political identities. Gender, race, and age or generation are especially obvious because of physical characteristics, but religions, regions of the country, sexual orientations, occupations, and many other distinctive characteristics of people also function as identities. Americans have identities based on who they are, where they live, and how they live, and these identities can have a large impact on individuals' preferences and political behavior.

Blacks. The practice of slavery in the colonies and early American states created a deep, lasting divide in our society between whites and blacks. That division is reflected in a staggering number of statistics, from wages and education levels to poverty levels to neighborhood integration to political ideals. There are, for example, stark differences between blacks and whites in their beliefs about government's responsibilities for providing shelter, food, and other basic necessities to those in need.[13] Blacks and whites also differ in their views of equality of opportunity in the United States, which can impact their preferences for policies that address perceived disadvantages (Figure 9.1).

More striking still, race seems to affect how other factors, like income and education, shape preferences. Among whites, there is a definite correlation between conservatism and income. Higher-income whites tend to support more conservative economic policies and are more likely to identify with the Republican Party, while lower-income whites tend to favor more liberal economic policies and align with the Democratic Party. Nearly all African Americans, on the other hand, side with the Democrats and support liberal economic policies, regardless of income. Why are high-income African Americans not as supportive of Republicans as their white counterparts? There are many other such instances, including differences across religious groups, between men and women, and between young and old. Some of these differences may be traced to self-interest, but most cannot. The explanations for differences in opinions and voting behaviors among social groups surely have something to do with the position of such groups in American society.

Latinos. Latinos are another major American subgroup with distinctive opinions on some public issues. For instance, in a 2014 poll, 60 percent of Hispanic voters approved of the Affordable Care Act, while 61 percent of non-Hispanic whites disapproved.[14] In addition, Hispanic voters routinely identify immigration as one of their top concerns, while the issue ranks lower in priority among non-Hispanic white voters.

In one respect, Hispanic and Latino political identities have a different character than those of blacks. Hispanic and Latino group identities are often rooted in particular immigrant communities such as Mexican Americans, Cubans, and Puerto Ricans[15] and are strongly tied to particular issues of immigration.[16] These differences have led to heterogeneity in opinion among Latinos on certain issues. Cuban Americans were

Racial and ethnic identity can influence political attitudes. Many Latinos oppose restrictive immigration laws, even if they are not personally affected by these laws.

Although America's
system of legally
mandated racial
segregation ended
nearly half a century
ago, its effects
continue to linger. In
contemporary America,
blacks and whites have
different perspectives
on race relations. Do
you think that black–
white differences
have increased or
decreased in the past
few decades? Are these
differences of opinion
important?

Figure 9.1
DISAGREEMENT AMONG BLACKS AND WHITES

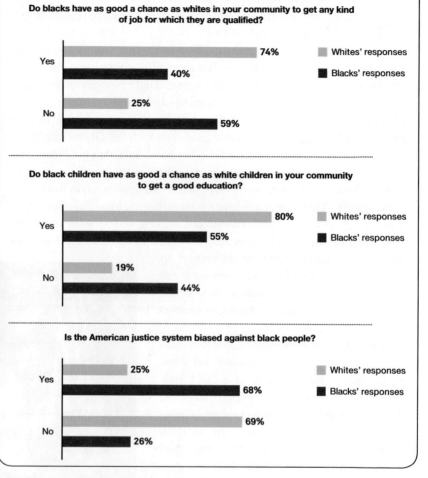

Do blacks have as good a chance as whites in your community to get any kind of job for which they are qualified?

Yes — Whites: 74%, Blacks: 40%
No — Whites: 25%, Blacks: 59%

Whites' responses
Blacks' responses

Do black children have as good a chance as white children in your community to get a good education?

Yes — Whites: 80%, Blacks: 55%
No — Whites: 19%, Blacks: 44%

Whites' responses
Blacks' responses

Is the American justice system biased against black people?

Yes — Whites: 25%, Blacks: 68%
No — Whites: 69%, Blacks: 26%

Whites' responses
Blacks' responses

SOURCE: Gallup Editors, "Gallup Review: Black and White Differences in Views on Race," December 12, 2014, www.gallup.com/poll/180107/gallup-review-black-white-differences-views-race.aspx, (Accessed 6/12/15).

long disproportionately Republican, while those of Mexican, Puerto Rican, and Central American descent identify more often as Democrats (Table 9.1). That difference reflected Cuban Americans' relationship with their homeland and the long-standing policy differences between the Republicans and Democrats over U.S. relations with Cuba. Interestingly, the difference had largely vanished by 2008; surveys during the presidential campaign found that Cuban Americans were nearly as Democratic as other Hispanic groups.

Table 9.1

CHANGING PARTY AFFILIATION IN THE LATINO COMMUNITY

BACKGROUND	2004		2008		2012		2015	
	DEM. (%)	REP. (%)	DEM. (%)	REP. (%)	DEM. (%)	REP. (%)	DEM. (%)	REP. (%)
Cuban	17	52	53	20	51	37	38	32
Mexican	47	18	50	18	64	18	48	22
Puerto Rican	50	17	61	11	74	10	56	19

SOURCES: 2004–12: Pew Hispanic Center, www.pewhispanic.org (accessed 11/13/14); 2015: Stephen Ansolabehere and Brian Schaffner, "2015 Cooperative Congressional Election Survey, Common Content," projects.iq.harvard.edu/cces/data (accessed 10/31/16).

As with blacks, Latino identity tempers the way other demographic characteristics translate into political identities and values. Although higher-income Latinos identify as Republican more than lower-income Latinos do, the differences are not as stark as among whites, and low-income Latinos are much more likely to identify as Democratic than low-income whites. Latinos' identity mutes the political effects of other characteristics.

Gender. Men and women express differing political opinions as well. Women tend to be less militaristic than men on issues of war and peace, more likely to favor measures to protect the environment, and more supportive of government social and health care programs (Table 9.2). Perhaps because of these differences on issues, women are more likely than men to vote for Democratic candidates, whereas men have become increasingly supportive of Republicans.[17] This tendency for men's and women's opinions to differ is called the gender gap. The gender gap in voting first became evident in the 1980 election and has persisted, averaging about 8 percentage points. In the 2016 presidential election, Hillary Clinton became the first female major-party candidate. The gender gap was the widest in history: she won 54 percent of the votes of women, but only 41 percent of the votes of men.

Why the gender gap emerged almost 40 years ago and persists today is something of a puzzle. Many speculate that reproductive rights and abortion politics lie at the root of this division, yet a Pew Research Center poll from 2006 indicates little or no opinion gap between men and women on the abortion issue.[18] Rather, the gender gap appears more attributable to differences in wages, life experience, the efforts of Democrats to reach out to women, and other factors reflecting the ways that men and women are

gender gap
A distinctive pattern of voting behavior reflecting the differences in views between women and men

Table 9.2

DISAGREEMENTS AMONG MEN AND WOMEN ON ISSUES OF WAR AND PEACE

GOVERNMENT ACTION	APPROVE OF ACTION (%)	
	MEN	WOMEN
Sending U.S. ground troops to fight Islamic militants in Iraq and Syria (2015)	52	41
Support U.S. missile strikes against Syria (2013)	43	30
Use U.S. troops to attack a terrorist camp (2012)	71	55
Support withdrawal of troops from Iraq (2008)	70	52
Use U.S. troops to intervene in a genocide or civil war (2008)	53	42
Go to war against Iraq (2003)	66	50
Broker a cease-fire in Yugoslavia instead of using NATO air strikes (1999)	44	51
Go to war against Iraq (1991)	72	53

SOURCES: Gallup polls, 1991, 1993, and 1999; *Washington Post*, 2003; Cooperative Congressional Election Study, 2008 and 2012; Langer Research, 2013; Pew Research Center (2015).

treated in the economy and society, and to women's sense of a shared objective of ensuring equal treatment for all women.[19]

Religion. Religion shapes peoples' values and beliefs and, thus, political ideologies, but it also serves as a strong source of political identity quite apart from what values are at play. One of the clearest examples was the decades-long attachment of Catholics to the Democratic Party, which began in 1928 with the Democrats' nomination of Al Smith, a Catholic, for president. When Democrat John Kennedy became the country's first Catholic president in 1961, that bond was strengthened.[20] The lesson of the Kennedy election is clear: people are much more likely to vote for candidates of the same religion, even after controlling for ideology, party, and other factors.

This pattern held true for born-again Christians and Jimmy Carter in 1976 and for Mormons and Mitt Romney in 2012.

Geography. Where we live also molds our sense of identity, affecting characteristics such as accent or mode of dress. People from different regions of the country, or even specific states, often strongly identify with others from the same region or state and are thus more likely to trust and to vote for someone from that background. Also, some people hold negative stereotypes of those from other regions. An unfortunate consequence of the Civil War is a lasting discomfort that many people from the North and South still feel around one another—and that conflict was 150 years ago. Yet to this day Americans contest the symbols of that conflict, such as whether a southern state should have a Confederate battle flag as part of its state's symbol or flying in the statehouse.

Other geographic identities are tied to the type of community one lives in (or prefers to live in). The division between those in urban and rural areas often reflects self-interest—for instance, people from states with predominantly agricultural economies express stronger support for government farm subsidies. But geography also reflects different ways of living, and we tend to identify with people who live like us. Such differences are cultural. Where we shop, what restaurants we frequent, what we like to do in our spare time, and so forth—all are aspects of local culture that shape our identification with others of similar backgrounds and ways of living.

Residential segregation can also strengthen other aspects of identity politics. People segregate according to income, which might strengthen social class identities, and to race and ethnicity, which reinforces racial and ethnic identities. Those who live in highly segregated neighborhoods have much stronger identities with their own racial groups, and they also express much stronger prejudices against other groups.[21]

Outgroups. Some groups are defined not by who they are but by who they are not; they are the outgroups in society. Discrimination is one manifestation of the treatment of an outgroup. Often an outgroup is clearly identifiable and ostracized, leading to systematic discrimination or persecution. When the discrimination is intense, systematic, and long-lasting, the outgroup can develop a distinctive psychology. Social psychologist James Sidanius argues that more numerous groups in all societies systematically discriminate against less numerous groups, whose members therefore develop a common identity and come to see their own situation in the treatment of others of their group.[22] Writing about the psychology of African Americans in the United States, Professor Michael Dawson calls this perception the "linked fate" of African Americans.[23]

Political, social, and economic discrimination is not limited to race and ethnicity. As we discussed in Chapter 4, the United States has witnessed struggles for equity for many different groups, including women, Catholics, Jews, gays, divorced fathers, and even urban residents. In all of these cases, members of the group had to assert themselves politically to establish or protect their rights to property, to vote, or to equal protection under the laws. Because it is difficult for those with diminished political rights to work inside the legislative process, these people often had to pursue outsider strategies, including protests, propaganda, and litigation. Their rights had been abrogated because they were treated as a class or group, and their identity was the target of discrimination. That same identity, however, served as a source of power, leading these groups to organize and to defend their political rights and identities.

KNOWLEDGE AND INSTABILITY IN PUBLIC OPINION

People are constantly confronted with new political events, issues, and personalities as they watch television, browse the Web, talk to friends and family, or read newspapers and magazines. In our democracy we expect every citizen to have views about how current issues should be addressed and who should be entrusted with political leadership, and we expect people to cast informed votes about what government ought to do. Issues, however, come and go, and people are continually learning about new ones.

Political Knowledge and Democracy

Some Americans know quite a bit about politics, and many hold opinions on several issues. Few Americans, though, devote sufficient time, energy, or attention to politics to really understand or evaluate the myriad issues that face us. Since the advent of polling in the 1930s, studies have repeatedly found that the average American appears to know little about current events or even basic facts of American government.[24]

Why do people seem to know so little, and what might be the consequence for the long-run health of democracy of low levels of information about current events and political institutions? Attending to the daily goings-on in Washington or the state capital or city council means spending time, and often money as well, to collect, organize, and digest political information.[25] Because individuals also anticipate that even political actions they take based on being well-informed will rarely make much difference, they may feel that it makes more sense to remain ignorant. That is, they find it more profitable to devote their personal resources—particularly their time—to more narrowly personal matters. Of course, because some kinds of information take little time or money to acquire, such as sound bites from television news shows or tweets from politicians, many people become partially informed, but rarely in detail.

Precisely because becoming truly knowledgeable about politics requires a substantial investment of time and energy, many Americans seek to acquire political information and to make political decisions by using shortcuts, labels, and stereotypes, rather than by following current events closely. One "inexpensive" way to become informed is to take cues from trusted others—the local minister, the television commentator or newspaper editorialist, an interest-group leader, friends, and relatives.[26] A common shortcut for political evaluation and decision making is to assess new issues and events through the lenses of one's general beliefs and orientation. Thus if a conservative learns of a plan to expand federal social programs, she might express opposition without needing to pore over the proposal's details.

These shortcuts are handy, but not perfect. Taking cues from others may lead individuals to accept positions that they would reject if they had more information. And general ideological orientations can be coarse guides to decision making on concrete issues. For example, what position should a liberal take on immigration? Should he favor keeping the United States' borders open to poor people from all over the world, or should he be concerned that open borders create a pool of surplus labor that permits giant corporations to drive down the wages of American workers? Many other issues defy easy ideological characterization.

Although understandable and perhaps inevitable, widespread inattentiveness to politics weakens American democracy in two ways. First, those who lack political information often do not understand where their political interests lie, and thus do not effectively defend them. Second, the large number of politically inattentive or ignorant individuals means that public opinion and the political process can be more easily manipulated by institutions and forces that seek to do so.

One example of the first of these problems is U.S. tax policy. Over the past several decades, the United States has substantially reduced the rate of taxation for its wealthiest citizens.[27] Tax cuts signed into law by President George W. Bush in 2001 and mostly maintained over the next decade benefited mainly the top 1 percent of the nation's wage earners, and further cuts proposed by Bush offered additional breaks to this privileged stratum. Polling data show that millions of less well-off Americans who did not stand to benefit from these tax cuts seemed to favor them nonetheless. Their support might have been based on principle, but it might also have arisen out of ignorance or from following the wrong cue-givers,[28] who led these individuals to believe that they *would* derive advantage from President Bush's tax policy.[29] Knowledge may not always translate into political power, but lack of knowledge is almost certain to translate into political weakness.

Campaigns and other forums for public discourse can change public attitudes on issues by altering the nature of the policy choices or by informing the public about their effects. Continued debate over the tax issue in the 2008 and 2012 presidential election campaigns brought about changes in public attitudes toward taxes, especially on the wealthiest segment of the population. During the 2008 campaign, Barack Obama seized on the tax issue at a time when the economy was worsening and most voters' economic prospects looked bleak. He returned to that theme during the 2012 campaign, promising to raise taxes on the top 2 percent of income earners—those who make at least $250,000 a year. That promise was instrumental in Obama's success in both campaigns. In January 2013, facing potential automatic tax increases on all Americans, Obama was able to outmaneuver the Republican leadership in Congress and increase taxes on those with incomes over $400,000 per year—an increase that affected only 1 percent of the population but nearly failed to make it through Congress.

Instability in Opinion

On most issues and political attitudes, there is great stability to public opinion in the United States. What people want government to do on specific issues and whom they want to have in charge usually changes little from election to election. For example, party identification for a large portion of the American public remains stable for life, as do notions of what is right and wrong, racial and ethnic identities, gender identities, and other cultural identities that are formed early in life. Our occupations and educational achievement also shape our economic interests, which tend to be constant throughout our adult lives. Interests, identities, and values, in turn, influence attitudes about when and how government should act.

But at times in history, the majority of Americans' opinions have changed dramatically and rapidly. Between 1945 and 1965, public opinion about federal action to promote racial equality swung from majority opposition to majority support for the Civil Rights Act and Voting Rights Act, as well as for integration of schools and public conveyances. And since the mid-1990s, there has been a near about-face in public attitudes toward same-sex marriage. In 1996, Congress passed the Defense of Marriage Act, which defined marriage as a union between one man and one woman for the purpose of federal benefits. A CNN/USA Today/Gallup poll in 1996 showed that 68 percent of Americans opposed same-sex marriage and only 27 percent supported it. By 2015, though, the year same-sex marriage was legalized nationwide, a Pew poll found that 55 percent of Americans supported same-sex marriage and 39 percent opposed it.[30]

In both cases, public attitudes changed greatly within the span of one or two decades. How and why does public opinion change? In part, the answer lies in the evolving positions of the political parties and the overall discourse of political elites. As party leaders, celebrities, and other elites debate an issue, the public often follows their cues and shifts sides. The answer also surely lies with public learning. As the public learns about an issue, the implications of government action or inaction become clearer, as does the right thing to do. In the 2016 presidential campaign, for example, Donald Trump raised several issues including sharp restrictions on immigration, such as a temporary ban on Muslim immigration, and curtailing free trade policies. Trump put these issues on the agenda and caused people to develop opinions about them.

SHAPING OPINION: POLITICAL LEADERS, PRIVATE GROUPS, AND THE MEDIA

The fact that many Americans are inattentive to politics and lack even basic political information creates opportunities to influence how the public thinks. Although direct efforts to manipulate opinion often don't succeed, three forces play especially important roles in shaping opinion. These are the government, private groups, including groups backed by politically active billionaires like the Koch brothers, Tom Styer and several others, and the news media.

Government and Political Leaders

All governments attempt, to a greater or lesser extent, to influence their citizens' beliefs. But the extent to which public opinion is affected by

IN BRIEF

Influences on Public Opinion

Government

Political leaders try to present their initiatives and accomplishments in a positive light and to generate positive media coverage. However, their claims are often disputed by the media, interest groups, and opposing forces within the government.

Private Groups

Interest groups work to draw attention to issues and ideas that will further their cause.

The Media

The mass media are Americans' main source of information about government and politics. They influence opinion by bringing attention to particular issues (the agenda-setting effect), priming the public to take a certain view of a political actor, and framing issues and events in a certain way.

governmental public relations efforts is probably limited. Despite its size and power, the government is only one source of information in the United States, and very often, governmental claims are disputed by the media, by interest groups, and at times by opposing forces within the government itself.

Often, too, governmental efforts to manipulate public opinion backfire when the public is made aware of them. Thus, in 1971, the government's efforts to build popular support for the Vietnam War were hurt when CBS News aired its documentary *The Selling of the Pentagon*, which purported to reveal the techniques, including planted news stories and faked film footage, that had been used to misrepresent the government's activities in Vietnam. These revelations undermined popular trust in all government claims.

After he assumed office in 2001, President George W. Bush asserted that political leaders should base their programs on the public interest rather than the polls. This did not mean, however, that Bush ignored public opinion. He relied on a low-key polling operation, sufficiently removed from the limelight to allow the president to renounce polling while continuing to make use of survey data.[31] At the same time, the Bush White House developed an extensive public-relations program to bolster popular support for the president's policies. These efforts included presidential speeches, media appearances by administration officials, numerous press conferences, and thousands of press releases presenting the administration's views. The White House also sought to sway opinion in foreign countries, even sending officials to present the administration's views on television networks serving the Arab world.

President Obama, seeking to maintain the political momentum from his 2008 election campaign, attempted to use social media to keep up the same enthusiasm about his legislative agenda. He brought the expert who had developed the campaign's social media strategy into the White House team to organize the effort. The Obama White House maintained a newsy website, a blog, a YouTube channel, a Facebook page, and a Twitter account, but the low level of actual engagement with the public drew criticism. Each of these new media was used like the old media—to talk at people rather than with them, to disseminate information to reporters rather than answer their questions. Indeed, many White House reporters felt that the Obama press office was less accessible than its predecessors.[32]

Social media, however, has continued to be an effective and popular means of communicating ideas to the public. Other political leaders, such as candidates for office, have increasingly used social media to communicate with supporters and attempt to influence opinion. In the 2016 presidential

Political leaders have increasingly sought to make the most of new technologies in communicating with the public and promoting their political agendas. Today, most politicians have Facebook and Twitter pages.

primary elections, every serious candidate had a Facebook page and Twitter account. Social media proved to be one of Donald Trump's most distinctive campaign advantages over his Republican opponents. By the end of the primary season, Trump had 10.7 million Twitter followers, while Senators Marco Rubio and Ted Cruz each had 1.5 million followers, and Governor John Kasich had only 400,000.

Private Groups

The ideas that become prominent in political life are also developed and spread by important economic and political groups seeking to advance their causes. In some instances, private groups espouse values in which they truly believe in the hope of bringing others over to their side—as in the campaign against so-called partial birth abortion that resulted in the Partial Birth Abortion Ban Act of 2003. Proponents believed that prohibiting particular sorts of abortions would be a first step toward eliminating all abortions—something they view as a moral imperative.[33] In other cases, groups promote principles designed mainly to further hidden agendas. One famous example is the campaign to outlaw cheap, imported handguns—the so-called Saturday night specials—that was covertly financed by domestic manufacturers of more expensive firearms. The campaign's organizers claimed that cheap handguns posed a grave risk to the public, but the real goal was protecting the economic well-being of the domestic gun industry. A more recent example is the campaign against the alleged "sweatshop" practices of some American companies manufacturing products in less developed countries. This campaign is mainly financed by U.S. labor unions seeking to protect their members' jobs by discouraging American firms from manufacturing products abroad.

Typically, ideas are best marketed by groups with access to financial resources and to institutional support. Thus, the development and promotion of conservative ideas in recent years have been greatly facilitated by the millions of dollars that conservative corporations and business organizations, such as the Chamber of Commerce and the Public Affairs Council, spend each year on public information and "issues management." In addition, conservative businesses have contributed heavily to such conservative research institutions as the Heritage Foundation, the Hoover Institution, and the American Enterprise Institute.[34]

Although they usually lack access to financial assets that match those available to their conservative opponents, liberal intellectuals and professionals have ample organizational skills, access to the media, and practice in communicating and using ideas. During the past three decades, the chief vehicle through which they have advanced their ideas has been public interest groups, organizations that rely heavily on voluntary contributions of time and effort, and interest from their members. Such groups include Common Cause, the National Organization for Women, the Sierra Club, Friends of the Earth, and Physicians for Social Responsibility.[35]

The Media

The communications media are among the most powerful forces operating in the marketplace of ideas. Most Americans say that their primary source of information about public affairs is news media—newspapers, broadcast and cable news, radio, and Internet news providers. Alternative sources are direct contact with politicians, communications from groups and organizations, and conversations with other individuals, such as family members or coworkers. Certainly, few people actually go to Washington to find out what's going on in American politics, and the broad public access to media outlets dwarfs the number of households that receive direct mail from organizations and elected officials. Personal conversation is also an important source for information, but people tend to avoid controversial political topics in casual conversation.

The mass media, as the term suggests, can be thought of as mediators. They are the conduits through which information flows. Through newspapers, radio, television, magazines, and the Internet, we can learn about what's going on in the world and in our government. As we see in the following section, providing this opportunity to learn about the world and about politics is the most important way in which the media contribute to public opinion.

THE MEDIA AS AN INSTITUTION

People rely on the media, rather than other sources of information, to find out what's going on in politics and public affairs because it is easy to do so. Media outlets are ubiquitous. Almost every community has a newspaper, an increasing number of which appear online in addition to or instead of in print. More households in the United States have television than have indoor plumbing, and the availability of television news has expanded tremendously in recent decades. In the 1960s, there were only three television news outlets—CBS, NBC, and ABC. They aired evening and nightly national news programs and allowed a half-hour slot for news from local affiliates. The rise of cable television in the 1980s brought a 24-hour news station, Cable News Network (CNN); expanded news programming through the Public Broadcasting System (PBS); and a network devoted exclusively to broadcasting proceedings of Congress and government agencies, C-SPAN. Important competitors to the big three networks emerged, including Fox and the Spanish-language networks Univision and Telemundo. Today there is no shortage of televised news programming available at all hours.[36]

Technological innovations continue to push change in political communication in the United States. As of 2015, almost 84 percent of Americans use the Internet.[37] Traditional media—from the United States and around the world—have moved much of their content online, often provided for free. The Internet has also spawned new forms of communication, most notably blogs and Twitter, which provide a platform for anyone to have a say. Several websites, such as Google News and realclearpolitics.com, are clearinghouses for traditional media, newswire stories, and blogs. The new, highly competitive media environment has radically changed the flow and nature of communication in the United States and the availability of information to the public.

Types of Media

Americans obtain their news from three main sources: broadcast media (radio and television), print media (newspapers and magazines), and, increasingly, the Internet. Each of these sources has distinctive institutional characteristics that help to shape the character of its coverage of political events.

Broadcast Media. Television news reaches more Americans than any other kind of news source. Tens of millions of individuals watch national and local news programs every day. Even in the era of digital news, the most frequented sources of news online are the websites of ABC, CBS, NBC, CNN, and Fox News. Television news, however, covers relatively few topics and provides little depth of coverage. More like a series of newspaper headlines connected to pictures, it alerts viewers to issues and events but provides little else.

The 24-hour news stations such as CNN offer more detail and commentary than the networks' evening news shows. In 2003, for example, CNN, Fox, and MSNBC provided 24-hour coverage of the start of the war in Iraq, including on-the-scene reports, expert commentary, and interviews with government officials. In this instance, these networks' depth of coverage rivaled that of the print media. Normally, they offer more headlines than analysis; nevertheless, cable continues to grow in importance as a news source (Figure 9.2).

Radio news is essentially a headline service without pictures. Usually devoting five minutes per hour to news, radio stations announce the

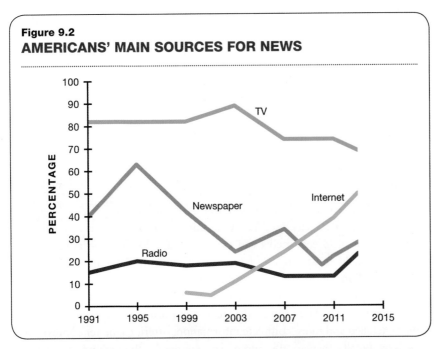

Figure 9.2
AMERICANS' MAIN SOURCES FOR NEWS

SOURCE: Pew Research Center, "Amid Criticism, Support for Media's 'Watchdog' Role Stands Out," August 8, 2013, www.people-press.org/2013/08/08/amid-criticism-support-for-medias-watchdog-role-stands-out/ (accessed 9/8/16).

day's major events with little detail. News stations such as WTOP (Washington, D.C.) and WCBS (New York City) generally repeat the same stories each hour to present them to new listeners. Radio talk shows have also become important sources of commentary and opinion. Numerous conservative radio hosts, such as Rush Limbaugh, have huge audiences and have helped mobilize support for conservative political causes and candidates. Liberals have had less success in talk radio and complain that biased radio coverage has hurt them in elections.

In recent years, much news content, especially of local news, has shifted away from politics toward "soft news"—focusing on celebrities, health tips, consumer advice, and other topics more likely to entertain than enlighten. Even much political coverage is soft. For example, in the 2016 presidential campaign, when Donald Trump held a press conference in which he touted one of his golf courses, his winery, "Trump steaks," and "Trump water," he drew significant media attention at the expense of other candidates.

Print Media. Newspapers remain an important source of news even though they are not most Americans' primary news source. Also important are magazines of opinion such as the *Economist*, the *New Republic,* and the *National Review.* These magazines have relatively small circulations but are read by politically influential Americans who count on them for news and analysis. Two Washington periodicals, the *Hill* and *Roll Call,* are important sources of political news for Washington insiders including members of Congress, congressional staffers, and lobbyists.

The general print media are important for three reasons. First, as we see later in this chapter, the broadcast media rely on leading newspapers such as the *New York Times* and the *Washington Post* to set their news agenda. The broadcast media do very little actual reporting; they primarily cover stories that have been initially reported by the print media. One might almost say that if an event is not covered in the *New York Times*, it is not likely to appear on the *CBS Evening News.* One important exception is "breaking" news, which broadcast media can carry as it unfolds or soon after, while the print media must catch up later. For example, on September 11, 2001, tens of millions of Americans saw dramatic real-time videos of the collapsing World Trade Center towers before the print media could publish the news the next day. The print media are also important because they provide more detailed and more complete information, offering a better context for analysis. Finally, they are the prime news source for the nation's economic, social, and political elites, who rely on print media's detailed coverage to inform their views about important public issues. The print media have a smaller audience than their cousins in broadcasting, but it is an audience that matters.

Today, however, the newspaper industry is in serious economic trouble. Online competition has dramatically reduced newspapers' revenues from traditional advertising, such as retail, "help wanted," and personal ads. Newspaper advertising revenue has dropped by over 50 percent over the past decade—from $50 billion in 2006 to $20 billion in 2014—as the loss of revenue from print advertising has far surpassed the rise in revenue from papers' own online advertising.[38] Facing serious financial difficulties, some papers have closed (such as the *Rocky Mountain News* in Denver) or switched to an online format only (such as the *Seattle Post-Intelligencer*). Major newspapers serving dozens of large U.S. cities and metropolitan areas have announced that they face serious financial difficulties. And in 2013, the Graham family, which had owned the *Washington Post* for three generations, surprised the industry by announcing the sale of the paper to Jeffrey Bezos, founder and CEO of Amazon.com. All these changes signal a wider transformation of print media that may leave the country with few or no print newspapers—the traditional "press"—in the future. The great unknown is whether online venues, such as social media, blogs, or news apps for mobile devices, can adequately replace print newspapers, especially in providing news about state and local politics and public affairs.[39]

The Internet. The Internet combines the depth of print media coverage with the timeliness of television and radio, but it goes much further. Internet news providers have become significant competitors to traditional media outlets, and most daily newspapers and television outlets—such as the *Wall Street Journal* and the *New York Times*, CNN and Fox News—also sponsor websites through which they attract audiences to their traditional media. Viewers see content that resembles a traditional newspaper or headline news on a television broadcast, but can choose which stories or items to click on for the full content, including video and audio material not available in a print paper.

Unlike a print newspaper, which is wholly new every day, a website can keep important stories up for many days, and most websites focusing on news also contain easily searchable archives. Besides those sponsored by traditional print or broadcast media, other news sites have emerged, some of which function as aggregators, accumulating news on a given topic from many different sources. Perhaps the most powerful aggregator is Google, whose news service compiles information from outlets as different as the *Wall Street Journal* and Al Jazeera, Reuters and the Associated Press, and the *Lebanon Daily Star* and *Shanghai Daily*. More specialized sites, like BuzzFeed, Politico, and the Huffington Post—three of the most frequently visited sites for news online—offer a wide range of content, including commentary and analysis in addition to reporting. Some sites provide more focused content. Slate.com, for instance, specializes in commentary, while Cook Political Report offers analytics.

Increasingly, social media are transforming online provision of the news by changing both how news information is distributed, through person-to-person sharing, and how it is generated. Both Facebook and Twitter have contributed to political mobilization and information sharing by creating virtual social networks where groups of like-minded individuals can quickly and easily share information. In 2016, a majority of American adults—62%—said they got news on social media.[40] (The Analyzing the Evidence unit on pp. 304–5 explores where Americans get news about politics). Social media also provides a platform for citizens to be directly engaged with political candidates and elected officials, who have been quick to adopt Facebook and Twitter as means of communicating with their supporters and providing them with a continual feed of new information. Obama was the first American president to use social media extensively for governing in his 2008 campaign for president. During the 2012 and 2016 presidential campaigns, the Internet was the medium of choice. In 2016, Hillary Clinton kicked off her presidential campaign with a YouTube video. Both she and Donald Trump made particular use of Twitter, with their campaigns often tweeting multiple times a day.

Twitter demonstrates how social media have altered not just the way news is distributed but also the way it is generated and even the form and format it takes. The immediacy of Twitter feeds, in which anyone

Where Do Americans Get News About Politics?

Contributed by
Rasmus Kleis Nielsen
University of Oxford

Most of political life is distant from our own personal experience and social circles. Thus when we know something about a recent international summit, a deal made in Congress, or a war abroad, it is usually because someone covered it as news.

How people get news, however, is changing and varies across generations. Throughout the twentieth century, news media were Americans' number one source of information about politics. Traditionally, newspapers have produced the most detailed and extensive coverage, and television has reached the widest audiences and was for several decades the most important source of news for many.

The development and spread of digital media from the 1990s onward has changed the news media landscape. Newspapers have seen declining readership, make less money, and therefore invest less in news production. Television audiences have been more stable but are increasingly made up of older people. Younger people increasingly get news online.

By 2015, 85 percent of all Americans used the Internet, and 64 percent had a smartphone.[1] Among people who are online, digital media have now overtaken television as the most important sources of news. In 2015, 43 percent of American Internet users named digital sources as their most important sources of news, compared to 40 percent who named television and 5 percent who named printed newspapers.

Main Source of News by Age

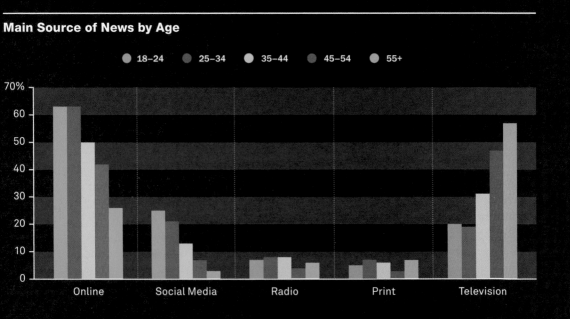

● 18–24   ● 25–34   ● 35–44   ● 45–54   ● 55+

1 Aaron Smith, "U.S. Smartphone Use in 2015," Pew Research Center, April 1, 2015, www.pewinternet.org/2015/04/01/us-smartphone-use-in-2015 (accessed 5/27/2016).

There are clear generational differences in how people get news. Older Americans rely far more on traditional media, such as television, than do younger people, who mostly get news online. For some people, getting news online is about going directly to the websites and apps of news organizations, whether newspapers like the *New York Times*, broadcasters like NBC, or digital-only news sites like the Huffington Post. But for many, online news is increasingly accessed via digital intermediaries like search engines, messaging apps, and social media. In 2015, 11 percent of American Internet users named social media their main sources of news.

Relative Importance of News: Twitter and Facebook Compared

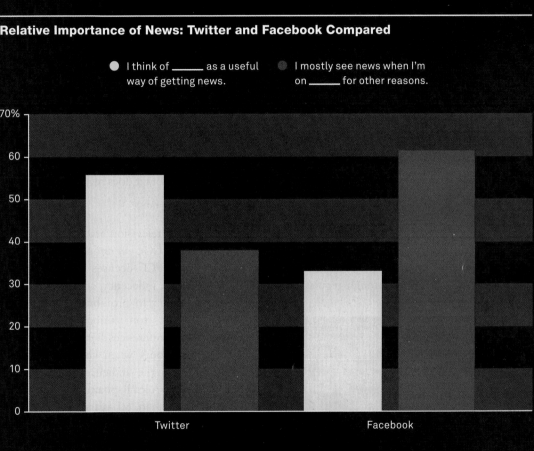

The graph above shows that some social media, such as Twitter, are often directly linked with news. In contrast, people mostly visit Facebook for other reasons but often stumble upon news when on the site. A changing media environment has sometimes been associated with the rise of "selective exposure," where people seek out information that reflects their existing views. However, the rise of widely used social media like Facebook seems to be associated with a resurgence in "incidental exposure," where people come across news unintentionally.

SOURCE: Nic Newman, Rasmus Kleis Nielsen, and David Levy, "2015 Digital News Report," University of Oxford, Reuters Institute for the Study of Journalism, 2015.

experiencing an event can provide reactions and reports in real-time without editorial filters, has made Twitter into a frequently used medium by government offices and politicians seeking to distribute information and commentary. For example, during the hunt for the bombers of the Boston Marathon in 2013, local police departments posted moment-to-moment tweets to keep the public informed about their actions and any immediate danger.

The Internet differs from traditional outlets in another important way: it enables people to get involved directly. Individual citizens can now more easily help create the news and interpret it. Most news sites provide space for people to post their own photos, video, and blogs of events, and those at the scene of a crime, natural disaster, or important political event can often provide more coverage of the story (and sometimes even better and faster coverage) than a reporter.

Regulation of the Media

In most countries, the government controls media content and owns the largest media outlets. In the United States, the government neither owns nor controls the communications networks, but it does regulate content and ownership of the broadcast media.

Broadcast Media. American radio and television are regulated by the Federal Communications Commission (FCC), an independent agency. Radio and TV stations must renew their FCC licenses every five years. Through regulations prohibiting obscenity, indecency, and profanity, the FCC has sought to prohibit radio and television stations from airing explicit sexual and excretory references between 6 A.M. and 10 P.M., the hours when children are most likely to be in the audience, though it has enforced these rules haphazardly.

For more than 60 years, the FCC also sought to regulate and promote competition in the broadcast industry, but in 1996 Congress passed the Telecommunications Act, a broad effort to eliminate most regulations in this area. The act loosened restrictions on media ownership and allowed for telephone companies, cable television providers, and broadcasters to compete for the provision of telecommunication services. Following the passage of the act, several mergers between telephone and cable

The sheer number of news outlets has ensured that different perspectives are well represented in the media. Popular political commentators such as Sean Hannity and Rachel Maddow, for example, offer clear conservative and liberal viewpoints, respectively.

Chapter 9: Public Opinion and the Media

companies and among different segments of the entertainment media produced greater concentration of media ownership.

The federal government has used its licensing power to impose several regulations that can affect the political content of radio and TV broadcasts. The first is the equal time rule, under which broadcasters must provide candidates for the same political office equal opportunities to communicate their messages to the public. The second regulation is the right of rebuttal, which requires that broadcasters give individuals the opportunity to respond to the airing of personal attacks on them. For many years, a third important federal regulation was the fairness doctrine, which required broadcasters airing programs on controversial issues to provide air time for opposing views. In 1985, the FCC stopped enforcing the fairness doctrine on the grounds that there were so many radio and television stations—to say nothing of newspapers and newsmagazines—that in all likelihood many different viewpoints were being presented even without the requirement that each station present all sides of an argument.

Freedom of the Press. Unlike broadcast media, print media are not subject to federal regulation. Indeed, the great principle underlying the federal government's relationship with the press is the doctrine against prior restraint. Beginning with the landmark 1931 case of *Near v. Minnesota*, the U.S. Supreme Court has held that, except under the most extraordinary circumstances, the First Amendment prohibits government agencies from seeking to prevent newspapers or magazines from publishing whatever they wish.[41]

Even though newspapers may not be restrained from publishing whatever they want, they may be subject to sanctions after the fact. Historically, the law of libel has provided that newspapers that print false and malicious stories can be compelled to pay damages to those they defame. Over time, however, American courts have greatly narrowed the meaning of libel and made it extremely difficult, particularly for public figures, to win a libel case against a newspaper.

Sources of Media Influence

The power of the media to affect political knowledge and public opinion stems from several sources. Learning through mass media occurs both actively and passively. Active learning occurs when people search for a particular type of program or information: by turning on the television news to find out what has happened in national and international affairs, or searching the Web for information about your member of Congress. Passive learning may be just as important. Many entertainment programs discuss current affairs and issues, such as social issues or an election. When that occurs, learning takes a passive form. You watch the program

---

equal time rule
An FCC requirement that broadcasters provide candidates for the same political office an equal opportunity to communicate their messages to the public

right of rebuttal
An FCC requirement that broadcasters give individuals the opportunity to respond to the airing of personal attacks on them

fairness doctrine
An FCC requirement that broadcasters who air programs on controversial issues provide time for opposing views

prior restraint
An effort by a government agency to block publication of material it deems libelous or harmful in some other way; censorship. In the United States, the courts forbid prior restraint except under the most extraordinary circumstances.

for entertainment but gain information about politics at the same time. One study of information gain among voters found that people learned as much from *Oprah* as from the evening news.[42] Political advertising is perhaps the most common form of passive information. During the last month of national political campaigns, three or four political advertisements often air during one commercial break in a prime-time television program.

Mass media are our primary source for information about current affairs. They influence how Americans understand politics not just through how much information is available but also through what is presented and how. Editors, reporters, and others involved in preparing the content of the news must ultimately decide what topics to cover, what facts to include, and whom to interview. Journalists usually try to present issues fairly, but it is difficult, perhaps impossible, to be perfectly objective.

What the media cover and how news is presented and interpreted can affect public opinion. Psychologists have identified two potential pathways through which media coverage shapes what people think. First, the news sets the public's agenda. Through this agenda-setting effect, the media cue people to think about some issues rather than others; they make some considerations more salient than others. Suppose, for example, that the local television news covers crime to the exclusion of all else. When someone who regularly watches the local news thinks about the mayoral election, crime is more likely to be his or her primary consideration, compared with someone who does not watch the local news. Psychologists call this effect priming.

In addition, news coverage of an issue frames the way the issue is seen in the public mind. Coverage of crime, to continue the example, may include a report on every murder that happens in a large city. Such coverage would likely make it seem that murder occurs much more often than it actually does. This misperception might in turn give viewers an exaggerated sense of their risk of violent crime, and thus increase their support for tough police practices.[43] Framing refers to the media's power to influence how events and issues are interpreted.

Priming and framing are often viewed as twin evils. One can distract us from other important problems, and the other can make us think about an issue or a politician in a biased way. Their cumulative effects on public opinion depend ultimately on the variety of issues covered and the diversity of perspectives represented. That, after all, is the idea behind the guarantee of a free press in the First Amendment. Free and open communication media yield the greatest likelihood that people will learn about important issues, gain the information to distinguish good ideas from bad ones, and learn which political leaders and parties can best represent their interests.

agenda-setting effect

The power of the media to focus public attention on particular issues and problems

priming

The use of media coverage to make the public take a particular view of an event or a public figure

framing

The influence of the media over how events and issues are interpreted

In this regard, the most significant framing effects take the form of the balance in the information available to people. Those in politics—elected officials, candidates, leaders of organized groups—work hard to influence what the news covers. A competitive political environment usually translates into a robust flow of information. However, in some political environments only one view gets expressed and is reflected in the media. Congressional elections are a case in point. Incumbent members today typically raise about three times as much money as their challengers. As a result, House elections often have a significant imbalance in the amount of advertising and news coverage between the campaign of the incumbent and that of the challenger. This imbalance will likely affect public opinion, because voters hear the incumbent's message so much more often.

Similarly, presidential press conferences and events receive much more coverage than their counterparts featuring leaders of the House or Senate. This imbalance gives the president the upper hand in setting the public agenda, because the public is more likely to hear presidential arguments for a particular policy than congressional challenges to it.

Today, it is easy to learn about public affairs and to hear different opinions—even when we don't want to. Furthermore, new forms of media have likely facilitated learning and muted some of the biases growing out of priming and framing. No one voice or perspective dominates our multifaceted media environment and competitive political system. And biases in the media often reflect not the lack of outlets or restrictive editorial control but failures of political competition.

TO WHAT EXTENT DOES GOVERNMENT POLICY FOLLOW PUBLIC OPINION?

In democratic nations, leaders should pay attention to public opinion, and most evidence suggests that they do. Although public policy and public opinion do not always coincide, in general the government's actions are consistent with citizens' preferences. The Policy Principle case study on p. 310 gives an example of how the George W. Bush administration dropped its effort to reform Social Security after not gaining sufficient public support. To take another example, one study found that between 1935 and 1979, in about two-thirds of all cases, significant changes in public opinion were followed within one year by changes in government policy consistent with the shift in the popular mood.[44] Other studies have come to similar conclusions about public opinion and government policy at the state level.[45] Do these results suggest that politicians pander to the public? The answer is

Public Opinion and Reforming Social Security

Demonstrators protest Social Security reform proposed in 2005.

Presidents consider many factors when putting together a major policy initiative, including likely support for the proposed law in Congress, reactions of organized interests, the coherence of the policy, and whether the public supports or opposes the law. Presidents need to muster public support behind a law in order to move forward, and failing to do so can lead to the end of important presidential initiatives.

Reform of Social Security has been particularly difficult because of widespread support for the benefit program. The looming surge in retirements of baby boomers (those born between 1946 and 1964) has threatened to bankrupt Social Security, as payments to retirees exceed contributions made by younger workers into the fund. President George W. Bush decided to take on the Social Security problem.

The president made Social Security reform the centerpiece of his domestic policy agenda at the start of his second term. His plan was to "privatize" Social Security. Younger workers would have the option to invest some of their Social Security tax in private accounts. Those workers would earn the interest on that investment, but would get a smaller

check from the government when they retired. Bush's State of the Union address in January 2005 emphasized the need for reform and the promise of private retirement accounts, and over the succeeding months his administration undertook a massive campaign, orchestrated by Karl Rove and Kevin Mehlman, to promote the privatization plan.

However, the campaign failed to win over the American public. A Pew Research survey conducted in 2005 noted that "Despite Bush's intensive campaign to promote the idea, the percentage of Americans who say they favor private accounts has tumbled to 46% in Pew's latest nationwide survey, down from 54% in December and 58% in September. Support has declined as the public has become increasingly aware of the president's plan. More than four-in-ten (43%) say they have heard a lot about the proposal, nearly double the number who said that in December (23%)."[1]

Eventually, the negative public reaction to the plan started to drag down the president's approval ratings. Conservative commentator Bill Kristol, editor of the *Weekly Standard*, put the matter bluntly, "The negative effect of the Social Security [campaign] is underestimated. Once you make that kind of mistake, people tend to be less deferential to your decisions."[2]

The public had spoken. By summer of 2005, it was evident that the plan, however sound it was as a policy, had failed to muster the public support needed to win approval in Congress. Fearing further damage to President Bush's reputation and to his efforts on other policies, the administration decided to drop what had been, just six months earlier, the central focus of his domestic policy agenda. Even a popular president with the advantage of a unified government usually cannot get his policy agenda enacted into law without public support for those specific policies.

[1] Pew Research Center, "Bush Failing in Social Security Push," March 2, 2005, www.people-press.org/2005/03/02/bush-failing-in-social-security-push (accessed 4/8/16)

[2] Jim VandeHei and Peter Baker, "President Struggles to Regain His Pre-Hurricane Swagger," September 24 2005, *Washington Post*, www.washingtonpost.com/wp-dyn/content/article/2005/09/23/AR2005092302182.html (accessed 5/23/16).

no. Elected leaders don't always follow the results of public-opinion polls, but instead use polling to sell their policy proposals and thereby shape the public's views.[46]

Nevertheless, there are always areas of disagreement between opinion and policy. For example, despite the support of large majorities of Americans for some form of screening of prospective gun owners in the wake of frequent mass shootings in recent years, Congress has not been responsive. Similarly, most Americans—blacks as well as whites—oppose busing children out of their local neighborhoods to achieve racial balance in public schools, yet such busing continues to be used extensively throughout the nation. Most Americans are far less concerned with the rights of the accused than the federal courts seem to be. And even though most say they oppose U.S. military intervention in other nations' affairs, interventions continue to take place and often win public approval after the fact.

Several factors can contribute to a lack of consistency between opinion and government policy. First, those in the majority on a particular issue may not be as intensely committed to their preference as supporters of the minority viewpoint, who may be more willing to commit time, energy, efforts, and resources to the affirmation of their opinions. In the case of gun control, for example, although proponents are in the majority by a wide margin, most do not regard the issue as critically important to themselves and are unwilling to commit much effort to advancing their cause. Opponents, by contrast, are intensely committed, well organized, and well financed; as a result, they usually carry the day.

A second important reason that public policy and public opinion may not coincide has to do with the nature of the American system of government. The framers of the Constitution, as we saw in Chapter 2, sought to create a system of government that was based on popular consent but that did not invariably translate shifting popular sentiments into public policies. As a result, the system includes arrangements such as an appointed judiciary that can produce policy decisions running contrary to prevailing popular sentiment—at least for a time.

Inconsistencies between opinion and policy might be reduced if the federal government of the United States used ballot initiatives and referenda as many states do. These processes allow proposals to be enacted into law (or rejected) directly by the voters, bypassing most of the normal machinery of representative government. Among other issues, ballot measures in the states have been used to restrict property tax increases; ban the use of racial or gender preferences in government employment, contracting, and university admissions; enact environmental regulations; legalize marijuana; limit campaign spending; regulate auto insurance; change the rules governing redistricting; and opt out of the Affordable Care Act. Some states even use referenda to pass budget agreements when the legislature does not want to be held responsible for casting unpopular votes.

However, government by initiative and referendum offers little opportunity for reflection and compromise. Voters are presented with a proposition, usually sponsored by a special interest group, and must take it or leave it. Perhaps public opinion on the issue lies somewhere between the positions held by various interest groups. In a representative assembly, as opposed to a referendum campaign, the outcome might be a compromise measure more satisfactory to more voters than either ballot alternative. This capacity for compromise is one reason the Founders strongly favored representative government rather than direct democracy.

When all is said and done, however, there can be little doubt that in general the actions of the American government do not remain out of line with popular sentiment for very long. A major reason for this is, of course, the electoral process, to which we turn next.

For Further Reading

Ansolabehere, Stephen, Jonathan Rodden, and James M. Snyder, Jr. "Purple America." *Journal of Economic Perspectives* 20, no. 2 (Spring 2006): 97–118.

Bartels, Larry. *Unequal Democracy: The Political Economy of the New Gilded Age.* Princeton, NJ: Princeton University Press, 2008.

Erikson, Robert S., and Kent L. Tedin. *American Public Opinion: Its Origins, Content, and Impact.* 8th ed. New York: Pearson, 2010.

Fiorina, Morris, Samuel Abrams, and Jeremy Pope. *Culture War?* 3rd ed. New York: Pearson, 2010.

Hamilton, James. *All the News That's Fit to Sell.* Princeton, NJ: Princeton University Press, 2004.

Lee, Taeku. *Mobilizing Public Opinion.* Chicago: University of Chicago Press, 2002.

Kinder, Donald, and Cindy Kam. *Us against Them: Ethnocentric Foundations of American Opinion.* Chicago: University of Chicago Press, 2010.

Lupia, Arthur, and Mathew D. McCubbins. *The Democratic Dilemma: Can Citizens Learn What They Need to Know?* New York: Cambridge University Press, 1998.

Stimson, James A. *Public Opinion in America: Moods, Cycles, and Swings.* 2nd ed. Boulder, CO: Westview Press, 1999.

Zaller, John R. *The Nature and Origins of Mass Opinion.* New York: Cambridge University Press, 1992.

10

Elections

Most Americans think that voting gives them a measure of control over the government and its policies. This belief, like the more general idea that public opinion is important, is regularly affirmed by politicians, taught in public schools, and frequently reiterated by mass media. Democratic elections, after all, permit ordinary citizens to select and depose powerful public officials. This electoral authority compels candidates to vie with one another for popular approval and forces leaders to pay heed to citizens' wishes and welfare if they wish to retain their positions. As James Madison observed in *Federalist 57*, "the restraint of frequent elections" induces public officials to "anticipate the moment when their power is to cease . . . unless a faithful discharge of their trust shall have established their title to a renewal of it."[1]

This view of elections certainly has merit. But elections may also displace other forms of political activity that could influence government to an equal, or perhaps even greater, degree. They offer a formal and institutional channel to take the place of the more impromptu tactics—including protest and violence—that might be employed by citizens seeking to force a government to listen to them, such as those used by participants in the 2011 Occupy Wall Street movement. Despite official efforts to suppress popular agitation, the citizenry is seldom politically impotent in the absence of elections. Perhaps some regimes are sufficiently powerful and ruthless to stamp out most vestiges of popular dissent. But no government is all-powerful all the time. In recent years, much-feared authoritarian regimes such as those in Libya and Algeria—seemingly protected by enormous armies and powerful security forces—disappeared almost overnight. Often, it is precisely because clandestine or spontaneous forms of popular political activity are having too great an impact that governments seek to introduce electoral mechanisms or expand existing voting rights and to persuade citizens of their value. As the late Walter Lippman observed, "New numbers were enfranchised because they had power, and giving them the vote was the 'least disturbing way' of letting them exercise their power."[2]

An example from American history appears to illustrate Lippman's proposition: the Twenty-Sixth Amendment to the Constitution, added in 1971, which lowered the U.S. voting age from 21 to 18. This amendment was adopted during a period of civil disorder during which young people—college students in particular—engaged in sometimes violent protests over the Vietnam War, military conscription, race relations, and other aspects of American politics and society. While the protesters made many demands, these did not include voting rights for young people. Even though students

CORE OF THE ANALYSIS

➡ The United States holds frequent elections as a means of keeping politicians close to the preferences of a majority of the people.

➡ The institutional features of American elections regulate who votes, what form the ballot takes, how voting districts are drawn, and what it takes to win an election.

➡ The United States uses a system of plurality rule in which the candidate with the most votes wins the electoral district. Plurality rule creates a strong pressure toward two-party politics.

➡ Voters who identify with a political party vote with that party nearly all of the time. Issues and candidate characteristics also influence voters' decisions.

➡ Campaigns try to mobilize their candidate's supporters and persuade undecided voters.

may not have been especially interested in voting, many political leaders seemed eager to give them the right to do so.

Senate Judiciary Committee hearings on the measure indicated a belief among Democrats and Republicans alike that the right to vote would channel students' political activities from the street into the polling places. For example, the late senator Jacob Javits (R-N.Y.) said, "I am convinced that self-styled student leaders who urged such acts of civil disobedience would find themselves with little or no support if students were given a more meaningful role in the political process. In short, political activism . . . is all happening outside the existing political framework. Passage of [the voting rights resolution] would give us the means, sort of the famous carrot and the stick, to channel this energy into our major political parties."[3] In a similar vein, Senator Birch Bayh (D-Ind.) said, "This force, this energy, is going to continue to build and grow. The only question is whether we should continue to ignore it, perhaps leaving this energy to dam up and burst and follow less-than-wholesome channels, or whether we should let this force be utilized by society through the pressure valve of the franchise."[4] Three years later, the resolution under discussion became a constitutional amendment.

Electoral institutions also offer benefits to the government in the form of increased popular support from lawful citizen participation. Denying citizens an opportunity to participate in political life tends to alienate those who have political interests and ambitions. Providing those who wish to participate with a lawful outlet for their political energies, on the other hand, is likely to have the opposite effect, generating support for rather than opposition to the regime. A good deal of evidence suggests that an opportunity to participate in the decision-making processes of the institutions that rule them affords many individuals enormous psychic gratification that is not dependent upon their approval of the specific decisions that ultimately result.[5]

In this chapter, we look at how citizens might benefit from voting and how the institutional features of American elections shape the way citizens' goals and preferences are reflected in their government. Then we will consider how voters decide among the candidates and questions put before them on the ballot. We should, however, not lose sight of the fact that voting serves the government as well as the citizenry.

INSTITUTIONS OF ELECTIONS

We have suggested that the relationship between citizens and elected politicians is that of a principal and an agent. There are two basic ways to view this relationship: the consent approach and the agency approach. The consent approach emphasizes the historical reality that the right of the citizen to participate in his or her own governance, mainly through the act of voting or other forms of consent, is designed by those in power to legitimate and strengthen their rule. By giving their consent, citizens provide this legitimation. The agency approach treats the typical citizen as someone who would much rather spend time and effort on his or her own private affairs than on governance. He or she therefore chooses to delegate governance to agents—politicians—who are controlled through elections. In this approach, the control of agents is emphasized.

Whether seen as a means to control delegates (the agency approach) or to legitimate governance (the consent approach), elections allow citizens to participate in political life on a routine and peaceful basis. Indeed, American voters have the opportunity to select and, if they so desire, remove some of their most important leaders. In this way, they can intervene in and influence the government's policies. Yet it is important to recall that elections are not spontaneous affairs, but formal governmental institutions. While giving citizens a chance to participate in politics, they also give the government a good deal of control over when, where, how, and which of its citizens will participate. Electoral processes are governed by rules and procedures that are a mix of state and federal laws, legal decisions, and local administrative practices. These rules provide those in power with significant power to regulate the character—and perhaps also the consequences—of mass political participation. The Policy Principle case study on p. 318 shows how the decisions by local officials can affect the outcomes.

Four features of U.S. election laws deserve particular emphasis:

- First, *who*. The United States provides for universal adult suffrage—all citizens over the age of 18 have the right to vote.[6]

- Second, *how*. Americans vote in secret and choose among candidates for office using a form of ballot called the Australian ballot.

- Third, *where*. The United States selects almost all elected officials through single-member districts with equal populations.

- Fourth, *what* it takes to win. For most offices in the United States, the candidate who wins a plurality—the most votes among all of those competing for a given seat—wins the election, whether or not he or she wins a majority of the total votes cast.

Each of these rules has substantial effects on elections and representation. Before we explore them in more detail, it is important to note that the rules governing elections are not static. The features of American electoral institutions have evolved over time—through legislation, court decisions, administrative rulings of agencies, and public agitation for electoral reform—to our present system of universal suffrage with secret voting and

Local Control of Elections and Voter ID Laws

Voters show IDs before casting a ballot.

Through elections, Americans choose their leaders and, in doing so, which policies are likely to be enacted. We saw in Chapter 1 that political behavior is purposive and that institutions "choreograph" political activity, making some outcomes more likely and others less likely. This concept applies to even the most basic aspects of the electoral process. In this chapter we discuss the major institutions of elections, including who votes, how we vote, where we vote, and what it takes to win; but the nuts and bolts of *running* elections also affect the results. Someone must register voters, certify the eligibility of the candidates, print the ballots, manage the polling places, count the votes, and, ultimately, ascertain who won and lost. Each of these functions requires many tasks, such as selecting voting technologies, programming voting machines to read voters' ballots, finding voting locations, setting up polling places, and recruiting poll workers.

The U.S. Constitution gives the authority to organize national elections to the states, as it gives the states the power to determine the "time, place, and manner" of federal elections. States, in turn, generally shift the task of running elections to the county

and municipal governments. There are 8,000 local election offices in the United States, each of which is responsible for choosing voting equipment, software, polling place locations, and staff for running elections. Though some offices have large staffs and budgets, most are led by minor officials who manage elections as only one of many other responsibilities.

The decisions that state and local officials make in organizing their electoral machinery affect voter turnout, the composition of the electorate, and thus the outcomes of elections. Officials are very much aware of these implications. For example, the location of polling places may increase turnout of voters for whom the location is convenient and decrease turnout of those who have more difficulty reaching the polls. Similarly, understaffing a polling place will produce long lines that may discourage people from voting. In every state, these seemingly routine decisions frequently become hot button issues as their potential to affect election results is assessed by competing political forces.

Currently, one of the most controversial topics in election administration is the matter of voter ID laws. Some states have adopted laws requiring voters to show some form of photo identification at the polling place. Proponents of these laws say that identification is necessary to prevent voting fraud. Opponents of voter ID laws, on the other hand, assert that such laws are designed to reduce voting on the part of poor (often minority) voters who may not have drivers' licenses or other required forms of identification.

This ongoing debate demonstrates that institutions matter. Even the most ordinary aspects of electoral machinery that we hardly notice when we go to cast our votes can be used to influence who wins, and thus the policies that will be prioritized by the government.

to the use of single-member districts with plurality rule. But this is only one era, and the future will likely bring further innovations. This fluidity raises new issues about secrecy and the form of the ballot; it also provides new opportunities for reform (such as instant runoff voting). Such changes rarely come about through carefully planned federal legislation. Instead, new election institutions typically emerge out of the experiences and experiments of local election officials and state laws. Let us take a closer look at the key institutional features of American elections.

Who Can Vote: Defining the Electorate

Over the course of American history the electorate has expanded greatly. At the beginning of the Republic, voting rights in most states were restricted to white men over 21 years of age, and many states further required that those people owned property. Today, all citizens over 18 years of age are allowed to vote, and the courts, the Department of Justice, and activist organizations work to ferret out discrimination in elections.[7] The timeplot on pp. 320–1 compares the percentage of the American population eligible to vote with the percentage of the population that did vote in national elections.

While the right to vote is universal, the exercise of this right is not. In a typical U.S. presidential election, approximately 60 percent of those eligible to vote in fact do so; in midterm elections for Congress, around 45 percent of the eligible electorate votes. And in local elections the percentage of people who vote can be quite low: some city elections attract only 10 to 20 percent of the eligible electorate. Some of the most basic questions about the functioning and health of our democracy concern the exercise of the franchise. Who votes and why? How does nonparticipation affect election outcomes, and would election outcomes be different if everyone voted? Does low voter turnout threaten the legitimacy of government?

Voting in the United States is a right, not a requirement. If we do not feel strongly about government, we do not have to participate. If we want to express dissatisfaction, one way to do so is not to vote. While most democracies view voting as a right and a voluntary act, some also treat it as a responsibility of citizenship. In Mexico and Australia, for example, adult citizens are required to vote in national elections; those who fail to vote must either receive a medical exemption or pay a fine. That requirement guarantees turnout rates in the range of 90 percent and makes election results a better reflection of the preferences of all citizens. The idea of compulsory voting is not viewed favorably in the United States, however. Those who don't vote don't want to face a potential fine; those who do may not want the "nonvoters" diluting their power, and most Americans simply do not

The Growth of the American Electorate, 1790–2016

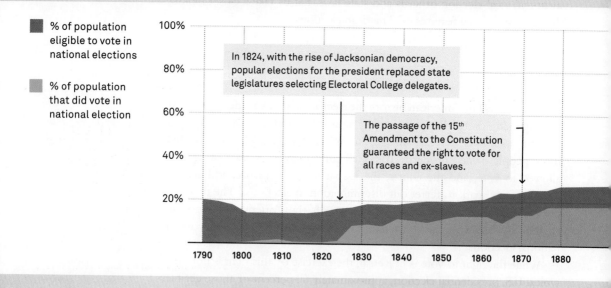

■ % of population eligible to vote in national elections

■ % of population that did vote in national election

In 1824, with the rise of Jacksonian democracy, popular elections for the president replaced state legislatures selecting Electoral College delegates.

The passage of the 15th Amendment to the Constitution guaranteed the right to vote for all races and ex-slaves.

like the notion that the government can compel us to do something. Even without compelling participation, the United States is one of the world's most participatory democracies. Besides voting, citizens can participate in electoral politics by blogging and posting on social media, speaking with others, joining organizations, giving money, and in many other ways. On nearly all of these activities, Americans participate in politics at much higher rates than people in nearly every other country.[8]

That said, levels of U.S. voter participation in the latter half of the twentieth century were quite low compared with participation in other Western democracies[9] and in earlier eras of American history, especially the late nineteenth century (see Figure 10.1).[10] The five decades after World War II saw a steady erosion of voter turnout, with participation in presidential elections falling below 50 percent in 1996. That decline stirred Congress to reform voter registration rules in the mid-1990s. Turnout rates have grown since then, in response both to legal changes and to the recognition by the political parties and candidates that they could influence elections by bringing people back to the polls. In 2016, 59 percent of adult citizens in the United States voted.

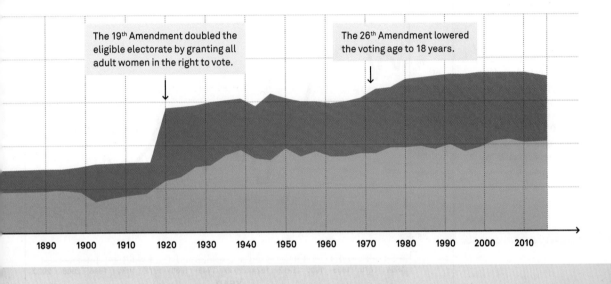

The 19th Amendment doubled the eligible electorate by granting all adult women in the right to vote.

The 26th Amendment lowered the voting age to 18 years.

1890 1900 1910 1920 1930 1940 1950 1960 1970 1980 1990 2000 2010

Who votes and why? The answers lie partly in the motivations and behavior of individuals and partly in the laws of democracy, which are the institutions of elections. Later in this chapter we will discuss the correlates of voting to understand who chooses to vote. We discuss here the institutions and how they define and constrain behavior.

Measuring Voter Turnout and the Effects of Restrictions on Voting. The turnout rate is a term that is simple to define, but some of the subtleties of the definition are important to understand, especially when making comparisons over time or across countries. It is defined as the number of people who vote in a given election divided by the number of people who are allowed to vote. The first part of this ratio is relatively uncontroversial—the number of individuals who cast ballots[11] The appropriate baseline in the turnout ratio is more difficult to define. Most commonly, the turnout rate given for the United States (and other countries) is actual voters as a percentage of the voting-age population (all adults). This baseline understates the true turnout rate, because it includes noncitizens and people who are institutionalized or (in some states) not allowed to

◀ **turnout rate**

The number of people who vote in a given election divided by the number of people who are allowed to vote

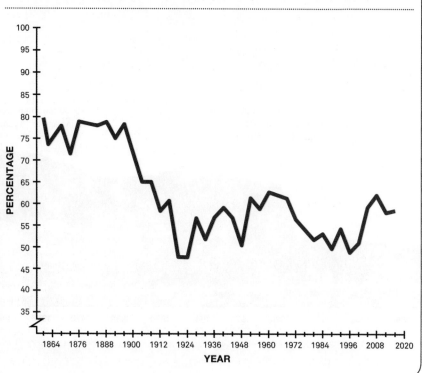

Figure 10.1

VOTER TURNOUT IN U.S. PRESIDENTIAL ELECTIONS

ANALYZING THE EVIDENCE

Voter turnout for American presidential elections was significantly higher in the nineteenth century than in the twentieth. What institutional change caused the sharp decline in turnout between 1890 and 1910? Why did this change have such a dramatic effect? Did it have any positive outcomes?

NOTE: Data reflect the population of eligible voters; the percentage of the voting-age population that voted would be smaller.
SOURCES: For 1860–1928, U.S. Bureau of the Census, *Historical Statistics of the United States, Colonial Times to 1970*, pt. 2, p. 1071, www.census.gov/prod/www/abs/statab.html (accessed 6/17/08); for 1932–92, U.S. Bureau of the Census, *Statistical Abstract of the United States*, 1993 (Washington, DC: Government Printing Office, 1993), p. 284; for 1996–2016, U.S. Census Bureau data.

vote because they are ex-felons. It is difficult to get reliable figures on the populations of these groups, so calculating the voting-*eligible* population can be controversial. Following the usual conventions, we focus here on the voting-age population.

How big is the U.S. electorate? There are approximately 320 million people in the United States today. But many of them are not allowed to vote, including children under 18, noncitizens, people in prison, and ex-felons in most states. There are approximately 74 million people under age 18 in the United States. Noncitizenship reduces the eligible electorate by another 13 million adults.[12] Finally, the total ineligible prison and felon population is approximately 3.3 million. Hence, the eligible electorate is approximately 237 million persons, or about two-thirds of the people living in the United States.

Of course, throughout the nineteenth century and much of the twentieth there were even more restrictions on the franchise, including gender, race, and property ownership. Perhaps the most significant changes in election institutions over the 200-year history of the nation have been to break down historical barriers to voting.

To put the changes in election laws in perspective, suppose that the nineteenth century's rules applied today: that only white male citizens over 21 were allowed to vote. If that had been the case in 2016, the eligible electorate would have totaled only about 76 million—about 1 in 4 people. Those restrictions would have made for a very different electorate in terms of interests, values, and preferences; they would have altered the political parties' strategies; and they would have surely resulted in very different election outcomes.

The Registration Requirement. Other restrictions on the franchise relate to how local officials run elections. As Figure 10.1 indicates, voter turnout declined markedly in the United States between 1890 and 1910, years coinciding with two important changes in the institutions of elections. Many states (1) imposed rules such as literacy tests to keep immigrants, blacks, and other groups out of the electorate and (2) began to create registration systems so that people had to be on a formal list of eligible voters in order to be allowed to vote on Election Day. Personal registration was one of several "progressive" reforms initiated early in the twentieth century, ostensibly to discourage fraud and "corruption"—a category in which reformers included machine politics in large cities, where political parties had organized immigrant and ethnic populations. Election reforms tried not only to rein in actual corruption but to weaken urban factions within parties and keep immigrants and blacks from voting.

Over the years, voter registration restrictions have been modified somewhat to facilitate the process. In 1993, for example, Congress approved and President Bill Clinton signed the National Voter Registration Act, commonly known as the "motor voter" law, which allows individuals to register when applying for driver's licenses as well as in public-assistance and military-recruitment offices.[13] In many jurisdictions, casting a vote automatically registers the voter for the next election. In Europe, in contrast, voter registration is handled automatically by

People who register to vote are highly likely to turn out and actually vote on Election Day, so getting new voters into the registration system is one way to increase voter participation.

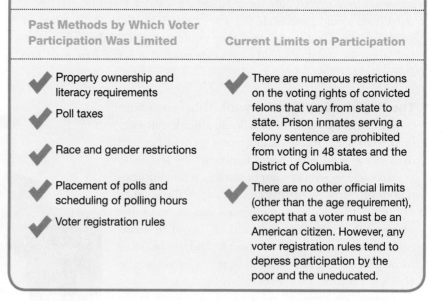

IN BRIEF

Determining Who Votes

Manipulation of the electorate's composition is a device used to regulate voting and its consequences. As we saw in Chapter 4, most restrictions on adult voters have been removed.

Past Methods by Which Voter Participation Was Limited	Current Limits on Participation
✓ Property ownership and literacy requirements	✓ There are numerous restrictions on the voting rights of convicted felons that vary from state to state. Prison inmates serving a felony sentence are prohibited from voting in 48 states and the District of Columbia.
✓ Poll taxes	
✓ Race and gender restrictions	
✓ Placement of polls and scheduling of polling hours	✓ There are no other official limits (other than the age requirement), except that a voter must be an American citizen. However, any voter registration rules tend to depress participation by the poor and the uneducated.
✓ Voter registration rules	

the government. This is one reason that voter turnout rates there are higher than in the United States.

The mere requirement that people register in order to vote significantly affects turnout rates. Studies of contemporary voter registration lists find that almost 90 percent of registered voters in fact vote, but only about 80 percent of the eligible electorate is currently registered to vote. In other words, the eligible electorate is really only about 189 million people—those who are actually registered to vote. There are approximately 47 million eligible voters who have not yet registered—disproportionately those ages 18 to 29. Getting those people into the registration system, and keeping them on the rolls, is an important way to increase the turnout rate. If you are not registered to vote, you cannot vote.[14]

Why, then, have a registration system? Such systems contain a fairly reliable list of all people who are interested in voting. Local election offices and campaigns use the lists to communicate with voters about when, where, and how to vote. Campaigns also use them to prepare grassroots organizing efforts and direct-mail campaigns.

Registration lists are also the basis for administering elections. Local election offices rely on their registration databases to format ballots, set up precincts, determine which voters should vote in which place, and communicate with people. Any given area contains many overlapping election jurisdictions, creating many different combinations of unique sets of offices. For example, one voter might reside in Congressional District 1, State Senate District 7, State Representative District 3, City Council District 1, and so forth. Variations in district boundaries may mean that a few blocks away, another voter lives in entirely different districts. Although they live in the same city, these voters must vote on different ballots. The first voter is not supposed to vote in Congressional District 2, for instance. Registration lists have become vitally important in sorting out where and on which ballots people should vote.

Efforts to eliminate or reform registration requirements must confront this very practical problem. Some states, such as Minnesota and Wisconsin, allow registration at the polls on Election Day (called same-day registration or Election Day registration). These states have noticeably higher turnout but also must recruit additional poll workers to handle the new registrants in the precincts. Five states, California, Connecticut, Oregon, Vermont, and West Virginia, have gone even further, and will automatically register voters when they renew their driver's licenses or state ID cards. In other states, electronic voting equipment now makes it possible to program many different ballots on a single machine, so that each voter just keys in his or her address to get the appropriate ballot and vote. Innovations like these may lead to an election system that does not require or rely heavily on registration before Election Day, but even these mechanisms still require the voter to register.

The past decade has seen a push to create new ways of authenticating voters at the polls. Two-thirds of all states require that voters provide some form of identification when voting, such as a driver's license, and some specifically require that voters provide government-issued photo identification. Such rules have been adopted out of fear of voter fraud. The other states either have no such requirement or prohibit election officials from asking for photographic identification. Legislators and voters there either view the risk of voter fraud as low or view the potential barrier to voting or potential discriminatory effects of such laws as outweighing any possible fraud. Social scientists have tended to find minimal levels of fraud, minimal effects of such laws on voter turnout, and minimal effects on people's confidence in the electoral system.[15]

Laws alone, however, cannot explain the variations in turnout. Perhaps the biggest systematic differences in turnout occur between election years. When the president is on the ticket, turnout exceeds 60 percent of the eligible electorate. But in midterm elections, when the president is not on the ticket, turnout plummets. This pattern of surge and decline in turnout is a function partly of the election calendar, but also of campaign activities and of voter interest in the election outcomes. These are behavioral matters, which we will discuss later in this chapter.

How Americans Vote: The Ballot

The way Americans cast their votes reflects some of our most cherished precepts about voting rights. Most people view voting as a private matter, choosing whether or not to tell others how they voted. Polling places provide privacy and keep an individual's vote secret. In some respects, the secret ballot seems incongruous with voting, because elections are a very public matter. Indeed, for the first century of the Republic, voting was conducted in the open. Public voting led to vote buying and voter intimidation, however, and at the end of the nineteenth century the secret ballot became widespread in response to such corrupt practices.

Australian ballot

An electoral format that presents the names of all the candidates for any given office on the same ballot. Introduced at the end of the nineteenth century, the Australian ballot replaced the partisan ballot and facilitated split-ticket voting.

With the secret ballot came another innovation, the Australian ballot, which lists the names of all candidates running for a given office and allows the voter to select any candidate for each office. This procedure was introduced in Australia in 1851, and in the United States today it is universal. Before the 1880s, some Americans voted in public meetings; others voted on paper ballots printed by the political parties or by slates of candidates. Voters chose which ballot they wished to submit—a Republican ballot, a Democratic ballot, a Populist ballot, a Greenback ballot, and so forth. The ballots were often printed on different-colored paper so that voters could easily distinguish them—and so that local party workers could observe who cast which ballots. With these party ballots, voters could not choose candidates from different parties for different offices; they had to vote the party line. Under the Australian form, all ballots are identical, making it difficult to observe who votes for which party. More important, voters could choose any candidate for each office, breaking the hold of parties over the vote. The introduction of the Australian ballot gave rise to split-ticket voting, whereby voters became able to select candidates from different parties for different offices.[16]

The secret and Australian ballot enabled voters to choose candidates as well as parties, and facilitated the rise of the personal vote and the incumbency advantage in American politics. (See the discussion of the incumbency advantage in Congress in Chapter 5.) The possibility of split-ticket voting also created greater fragmentation in the control of government in the United States. With the party ballot, an insurgent party could more readily be swept to power at all levels of government in a given election. A strong national tide toward one of the parties in the presidential election would change not just the presidency but also political control of every state and

One change under way in American electoral rules involves the rise of "convenience voting"—such as voting early or voting by mail.

locality that gave a majority of its votes to that party's presidential candidate. In contrast, because the Australian ballot permitted voters to choose for each office separately, it made the electorate less likely to sweep one party into power and another out at all levels.

Where Americans Vote: Electoral Districts

Elected officials in the United States represent places as well as people. Today, the president, representatives, senators, governors, and many other state and local officials are elected on the basis of geographic areas called electoral districts. Generally speaking, the United States employs single-member districts with equal populations. This means that the U.S. House of Representatives, almost all state legislatures, and almost all local governments have their own districts and elect one representative per district, and all of the districts for a given legislative body must have equal populations.

Elections for the U.S. Senate and the presidency are the odd cases. In the Senate, the states are the districts. Senate districts, then, have multiple members and unequal populations. In presidential elections, every state is allocated votes in the Electoral College equal to its number of U.S. senators (two) plus its number of House members. The District of Columbia is assigned three electors. The states are the districts, and with two exceptions (Maine and Nebraska, which employ proportional representation) each state chooses all of its electors in a statewide vote. The electors commit to casting their votes in the Electoral College for the winner of the popular vote

single-member district

An electoral district that elects only one representative—the typical method of representation in the United States

Electoral College

An institution established by the Constitution for the election of the president and vice president of the United States. Every four years, voters elect electors who, in turn, cast votes for the president and vice president. The candidate receiving a majority of the electoral vote for president or vice president is elected.

in that state. Within the political parties, the nomination process in most states allocates delegates to the parties' national conventions on the basis of House districts and their populations. However, some states choose delegates on a statewide basis, with all districts selecting multiple delegates to the party conventions. When the framers of the Constitution established the Electoral College, they mandated that each state's legislature assign the state's electoral votes, but since the 1860s, all the states have chosen electors by popular vote.

The U.S. Senate and the Electoral College remain the two great exceptions to the requirements of single-member districts with equal populations. The apportionment of Senate seats to states makes that chamber inherently unequal. California's 39 million people have the same number of senators as Wyoming's 586,000 people. The allocation of Electoral College votes creates a population inequity in presidential elections, with larger states selecting fewer electors per capita than smaller states. In the 1960s, the Supreme Court let stand the unequal district populations in the Senate and the Electoral College, because the representation of states in the Senate is specified in the Constitution. The reason lies in the politics of the Constitutional Convention (see Chapter 2), which consisted of delegations of states, each of which held equal numbers of votes under the Articles of Confederation. To create a House of Representatives that reflected the preferences of the general population, the large states had to strike a deal with the smaller states, which stood to lose representation under the initial plan of a single chamber based on population. That deal, the Connecticut Compromise, created the U.S. Senate to balance representation of people with representation of states and led to a clause in Article V of the Constitution that guarantees equal representation of the states in the Senate.

Nevertheless, the Senate and the Electoral College share the salient feature of elections for the House and for state and local offices: the use of districts to select representatives. All elections in the United States and all elected officials are tied to geographically based constituencies rather than to the national electorate as a whole. This is certainly true for the House and Senate. It applies also to presidential elections, in which candidates focus on winning enough states in the Electoral College rather than a majority of the popular vote.

Drawing Electoral Districts. House and state legislative districts are not static. To ensure equal population representation, they must be remade every decade after the U.S. Census updates the states' official population data to a fine level of geographic detail. Responsibility for drawing new boundaries for U.S. House and state legislative districts rests, in most states, with the state legislature and the governor, with the supervision of the courts, and sometimes the consultation of a commission (Figure 10.2). The politicians and others with a stake in the outcome use the census data to craft a new

Figure 10.2

CONGRESSIONAL REDISTRICTING

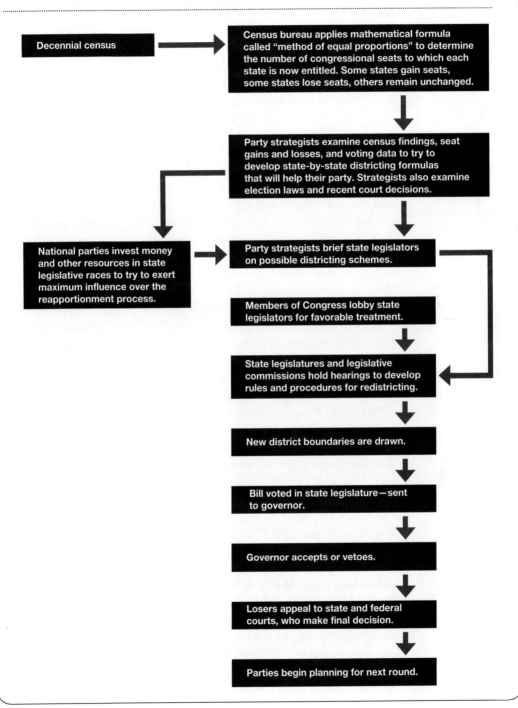

Decennial census

Census bureau applies mathematical formula called "method of equal proportions" to determine the number of congressional seats to which each state is now entitled. Some states gain seats, some states lose seats, others remain unchanged.

Party strategists examine census findings, seat gains and losses, and voting data to try to develop state-by-state districting formulas that will help their party. Strategists also examine election laws and recent court decisions.

National parties invest money and other resources in state legislative races to try to exert maximum influence over the reapportionment process.

Party strategists brief state legislators on possible districting schemes.

Members of Congress lobby state legislators for favorable treatment.

State legislatures and legislative commissions hold hearings to develop rules and procedures for redistricting.

New district boundaries are drawn.

Bill voted in state legislature—sent to governor.

Governor accepts or vetoes.

Losers appeal to state and federal courts, who make final decision.

Parties begin planning for next round.

district map; ultimately, the legislature must pass and the governor must sign a law defining the new districts. This job is forced on the legislatures by their state constitutions and by the courts. However, periodic redistricting, although it corrects one problem, invites another. Those in charge may manipulate the new map to increase the likelihood of a particular outcome, such as an electoral majority for one party or interest group. This problem arose with some of the earliest congressional district maps. In a particularly egregious example, a map of the 1812 Massachusetts House districts, drawn with the imprimatur of Governor Elbridge Gerry, prompted a *Boston Gazette* editorial writer to dub a very strangely shaped district the "Gerry-Mander" because he thought it resembled a salamander. The term stuck, and gerrymandering refers broadly to any attempt at creating electoral districts for political advantage.

gerrymandering
The apportionment of voters in districts in such a way as to give advantage to one political party

It is easy to draw an intentionally unfair electoral map, especially with the sophisticated software and data on local voting patterns and demographics that are available today. To facilitate districting, the Census Bureau divides the nation into very small geographic areas, called census blocs, which typically contain a few dozen people. U.S. House districts contain over 700,000 people. Political mapmakers combine various local areas, down to census blocs, to construct legislative districts. Those seeking political advantage try to make as many districts as possible that contain a majority of their own voters, maximizing the number of seats won for a given division of the vote. There are constraints on political cartography: the district populations must be equal, and all parts of a district must touch (be contiguous). Even so, the number of possible maps that could be drawn for any state's legislative districts is extremely large.[17]

Politicians can use gerrymandering to dilute the strength not only of a party but also of a group. Consider racial minorities. One common strategy has involved redrawing congressional district boundaries so as to divide a black population that would otherwise constitute a majority within the original district. This form of gerrymandering was used in Mississippi during the 1960s and 1970s to prevent the election of black candidates to Congress. Historically, the state's black population was clustered along the Mississippi River, a region called the Delta. From 1882 until 1966, the Delta constituted one congressional district where blacks were a clear majority, but discrimination in voter registration and at the polls guaranteed the continual election of white congressmen. With passage of the Voting Rights Act in 1965, this district would almost surely have been won by a black candidate or one favored by the black majority. To prevent that, the state legislature drew new House districts that split the Delta's black population across three districts so that it constituted a majority in none. This gerrymandering helped prevent the election of any black representative until 1987, when Mike Espy became the first African American since Reconstruction to represent Mississippi in Congress.

Continuing controversies about legislators' involvement in drawing their own districts have raised deep concerns about the fairness of the process. Many states have created commissions or appointed "special masters" to draw the maps. Other states have opened the redistricting process up to input from the public, as new developments in GIS software and provision of census data enable anyone to draw credible district maps. Opening up the process, it is hoped, will lessen the extent and effect of gerrymandering.

What It Takes to Win: Plurality Rule

The fourth prominent feature of U.S. electoral law is the criterion for winning. Although Americans often embrace majority rule as a defining characteristic of democracy, the real standard is plurality rule. The candidate who receives the most votes in the relevant district or constituency wins the election, even if that candidate doesn't receive a majority of votes. Suppose three parties nominate candidates for a seat and divide the vote such that one wins 34 percent and the other two each receive 33 percent of the vote. Under plurality rule, the candidate with 34 percent wins the seat. There are different types of plurality systems. The system most widely used in the United States combines plurality rule with single-member districts and is called *first past the post*. In choosing delegates for the Electoral College, most states use a plurality system in which the candidate who receives the most votes wins all of the delegates. This is called *winner take all*.[18]

plurality rule
A type of electoral system in which victory in an election goes to the individual who gets the most votes, but not necessarily a majority of the votes cast

In state-wide elections, two states, Louisiana and Georgia, require a candidate to receive at least 50 percent of all votes in order to win. This is majority rule. If no candidate in an election receives a majority, a runoff election is held about one month later between the two candidates who received the most votes in the first round. Other ways of voting also use plurality- and majority-rule criteria. For instance, some city councils still have multimember districts. The top vote getters win the seats. If there are, say, seven seats to fill, the seven candidates who win the most votes each win a seat.

majority rule
A type of electoral system in which, to win an office, a candidate must receive a majority (50 percent plus one) of all the votes cast in the relevant district

Plurality rule is often criticized for yielding electoral results that do not reflect the public's preferences. Votes for the losing candidates seem wasted, because they do not translate into representation. Indeed, as the example of the three-candidate race above suggests, it is possible that a majority of voters wanted someone other than the winner. In the aggregate, plurality rule with single-member districts tends to inflate the share of seats won by the largest party and deflate the other parties' shares. A striking example of this effect comes from Britain, where in 2015 the British Conservative Party won 37 percent of the vote and 51 percent of seats, while the Labour party placed second with 30 percent of the vote and 36 percent of seats. The remainder of the votes and seats were distributed very unevenly among

Who Wins? Translating Voters' Choices into Electoral Outcomes

Majority System

Winner must receive a simple majority (50 percent plus one).

Plurality System

Winner is the candidate who receives the most votes, regardless of the percentage.

Proportional Representation

Winners are selected to a representative body in proportion to the votes their party received.

three other parties. For example, the UK Independence Party came in third with 13 percent of the vote, but only won one seat. Nevertheless, plurality rule offers certain advantages. It enables voters to choose individuals to represent them personally, not just political parties, and it picks a definite winner without the need for runoff elections.

Among the world's democracies, the main alternative to plurality rule is proportional representation, or PR. Under proportional representation, competing parties win legislative seats in proportion to their overall share of the popular vote. For example, if three parties are running and one wins 34 percent of the vote and the other two each 33 percent, the first party receives 34 percent of the seats and the other two 33 percent.

PR is used rarely in the United States, with the most substantial instances being the Democratic presidential primary elections. During the 1988 primary season, Jesse Jackson routinely won 20 percent of the vote in primaries but ended up with only about 5 percent of the delegates to the Democratic National Convention, because the Democratic Party awarded all delegates from each congressional district to the candidate who won a plurality of the vote there. To make the convention and the party more representative of its disparate voting groups, Jackson negotiated with other party leaders to change the rules so that delegates within congressional districts would be allocated on a proportional basis. If a district elects five delegates, a candidate wins one delegate if he or she receives at least 20 percent of the vote in the district, two delegates for winning at least 40 percent, and so forth.

Plurality rule in single-member districts has a very important consequence: the dominance of two-party politics in the United States. Worldwide,

proportional representation

A multiple-member district system that awards seats to political parties in proportion to the percentage of the vote each party won

countries with plurality rule in single-member districts have far fewer political parties than other nations. Typically, elections under plurality rule boil down to just two major parties that routinely compete for power, with one of them winning an outright majority of legislative seats. Proportional representation systems, on the other hand, tend to have many more than two parties. Rarely does a single party win a majority of seats, and governments form as coalitions of many parties.

How votes are cast and counted, and what it takes to win a seat, then, have substantial consequences for American politics. Plurality rule with single-member districts creates strong pressures toward two-party politics and majority rule in the legislature.

Direct Democracy: The Referendum and Recall

In addition to choosing between candidates, voters in some states also vote directly on proposed laws or other governmental actions through the referendum process. Referendums may come about in two ways. First, some state constitutions and laws require that certain types of legislation (such as bonds or property tax increases) be approved by popular vote. Second, advocates may get a measure put on the ballot by obtaining enough signatures of registered voters to a petition. In recent years, voters in several states have voted to set limits on tax rates, to define marriage, and to prohibit social services for illegal immigrants. Although it involves voting, a referendum is not an election. The election is an institution of representative government; through it, voters choose officials to act for them. The referendum, by contrast, is an institution of direct democracy; it allows voters to act directly. Like legislative action, however, a referendum result is subject to judicial review. If a court finds that the outcome violates the state or national constitution, it can overturn it. For example, in 2008, California voters passed Proposition 8, which stated, "Only marriage between a man and a woman is valid or recognized in California." A federal district court ruled Proposition 8 unconstitutional in 2010. The Supreme Court let stand the district court's ruling in 2013 and in 2015, the Supreme Court ruled in *Obergefell v. Hodges* that marriage is a fundamental right guaranteed to all people.[19]

Besides referendums, there are other ways to place issues on the ballot. Twenty-four states permit various forms of the initiative. Whereas the referendum process allows citizens to affirm or reject a policy already produced by legislative action, the initiative provides citizens with a way forward in the face of legislative *in*action. They can place a policy proposal (legislation or state constitutional amendment) on the ballot to be approved or disapproved by the electorate. To gain a place on the ballot, a petition must be accompanied by a minimum number of voter signatures—a requirement that varies from state to state—that are certified by the state's secretary of state.

referendum

A measure that is decided by the vote of the electorate for approval or rejection

initiative

A process by which citizens may petition to place a policy proposal on the ballot for public vote

The initiative process allows voters to make policy directly. In 2010, voters in California successfully petitioned to put legalization of marijuana on the ballot. Though the measure did not pass in 2010, California successfully passed legalization of marijuana in 2016.

Ballot propositions often involve policies the state legislature cannot (or does not want to) resolve. Like referendum issues, these are often highly emotional and, consequently, not well suited to resolution via popular voting. On the other hand, one of the "virtues" of the initiative is that it may force action: legislative leaders may induce recalcitrant colleagues to move ahead on controversial issues by raising the possibility that a worse outcome will result from inaction.[20]

recall

The removal of a public official by popular vote

Eighteen states also have legal provisions for recall elections. The recall is an electoral device that allows voters to remove governors and other state officials from office prior to the expiration of their terms. Federal officials such as the president and members of Congress are not subject to recall. Generally, a recall effort begins with a petition campaign. For example, in California, the site of a tumultuous recall battle in 2003, if 12 percent of those who voted in the last general election sign petitions demanding a special recall election, the state board of elections must schedule one. Such petition campaigns are relatively common, but most fail to garner enough signatures to bring the matter to a statewide vote. In the California case, however, a conservative Republican member of Congress led a successful effort to recall the Democratic governor, Gray Davis. Voters were unhappy about the state's economy and dissatisfied with Davis's performance, blaming him for a $38 billion budget deficit. Davis became the second governor in American history to be recalled by his state's electorate (the first was North Dakota's governor Lynn Frazier, who was recalled in 1921). Under California law, voters in a special recall election also choose a replacement for the official whom they dismiss. Californians in 2003 elected the movie star Arnold Schwarzenegger to be their governor.

Chapter 10: Elections

HOW VOTERS DECIDE

An election expresses the preferences of millions of individuals about whom they want as their representatives and leaders. Electoral rules and laws—the institutional side of elections—impose order on that process, but ultimately, elections reflect many millions of people's personal preferences about politics.

The voter's decision can be understood as two linked decisions: whether to vote and for whom. Social scientists have examined both facets by studying election returns, survey data, and laboratory experiments as well as field experiments conducted during elections. Generations of research into these questions yield a broad picture of how voters decide. First, the decision to vote or not correlates strongly with individuals' social characteristics, especially age and education, but it also depends on the electoral choices and context. An individual who knows nothing about the candidates or dislikes all of the choices is unlikely to vote. Second, which candidates or party a voter chooses depends primarily on three factors: partisan loyalties, issues, and candidate characteristics. Partisan loyalties are the strongest single predictor of the vote, though party attachments also reflect issues and individuals' experience with candidates.

Voters and Nonvoters

As we saw earlier, turnout in modern American presidential elections is less than two-thirds of the voting-age population. In 2012, 62 percent of citizens of voting age turned out; thus, almost 40 percent of those who could have voted did not. Why do so many people not vote?

A general explanation is elusive, but social scientists find that a few demographic characteristics are strong predictors of who votes. Most important are age, education, and residential mobility. Other factors, such as gender, income, and race, also matter, but to a much smaller degree. According to the 2012 Current Population Survey, only 41 percent of those under age 25 voted that year; by comparison, 71 percent of those over age 65 voted. The difference in participation between these groups surely translates into the interests of retirees being much more likely to receive attention by the government than the interests of people in college or just entering the labor force.

Education shows similarly large differences. More than 75 percent of people with a college education voted, and the rate was 81 percent among those with a professional degree. In contrast, slightly fewer than 40 percent of those without a high school diploma voted, as did 52 percent of those with only a high school diploma. Finally, consider residency and mobility. Only 51 percent of people who had lived in their current residence less than a year reported voting, compared with 76 percent of people who had lived there at least five years. Those who owned their home or apartment voted at a 67 percent rate, but only 49 percent of those who rented voted.[21] Turnout patterns were similar in the 2016 election. Politicians listen to those who vote, and they are disproportionately older, better educated, and more rooted in their communities.

As discussed earlier, election laws have historically had a large effect on the size and character of the electorate. The decision to vote itself consists of two steps—registration and turnout. Minimizing registration requirements may increase participation, as the option of Election Day registration has shown. As of 2015, 14 states plus the District of Columbia allow people to register on Election Day at the polls or at a government office.[22] The three states with the longest experience with same-day registration—Minnesota, Wisconsin, and Maine—do have higher turnout than most other states, and most studies suggest that in a typical state, adopting such a law would increase turnout by about 3 to 5 percent.[23]

Demographics and laws are only part of what accounts for voting and nonvoting. The choices presented to voters are also important. People who do not like the candidates or dislike politics altogether tend not to vote. The top four reasons people say they do not vote are that they are "too busy," "sick or disabled," "not interested," or "did not like the choices."

Partisan Loyalty

The strongest predictor of how a person will vote is that individual's attachment to a political party. The American National Election Studies (ANES), exit polls, and media polls have found that even in times of great political change, the overwhelming majority of Americans identify with one of the two major political parties and vote almost entirely in accordance with that identity. Researchers ascertain party identification with simple questions along the following lines: "Generally speaking, do you consider yourself to be a Democrat, a Republican, an independent, or what?"[24] Those who choose a party are further classified by asking whether they identify strongly or weakly with it, and independents are asked whether they lean toward one party or another.

Party identifications capture voters' predisposition toward their party's candidates. Many of these predispositions are rooted in public policies, such as those on taxes or civil rights. Those long-standing policy positions lead to divisions in party identifications and voting patterns among different demographic groups. Large majorities of African Americans and Hispanics, for example, identify and vote with the Democratic Party. Women also tend to

party identification

An individual's attachment to a particular political party, which may be based on issues, ideology, past experience, upbringing, or a mixture of these elements

identify more and vote more with the Democrats than men do. That gap has persisted, averaging 7 percentage points over the past three decades. The 2016 election saw the widest gender gap in history, with the first female candidate running for a major party—Democrat Hillary Clinton: Clinton received 54 percent of women's votes, but only 41 percent of men's votes, a difference of 13 points. That difference is significant because women now comprise a majority of voters (53 percent).

Although specific features of the choices and context matter as well, party identifications express how voters would likely vote in a "neutral" election. Party identifications are extremely good predictors of voting behavior in less prominent elections, such as for state legislature or lower-level statewide offices, about which voters may know relatively little. Even in presidential elections, with their extensive advertising and news coverage, party predispositions predict individual voting behavior. Figure 10.3 displays the percentages of Democratic identifiers, Republican identifiers, and self-described independents who voted for Donald Trump, Hillary Clinton, or someone else in 2016. Approximately 90 percent of party identifiers voted for their own party's standard bearer. Independents broke 48 to 42 for Trump. Sometimes the independent vote decides the election. However, in this case, Hillary Clinton's popular vote victory was due to Democrats making up the single largest group in the electorate (even though Donald Trump still won the Electoral College).

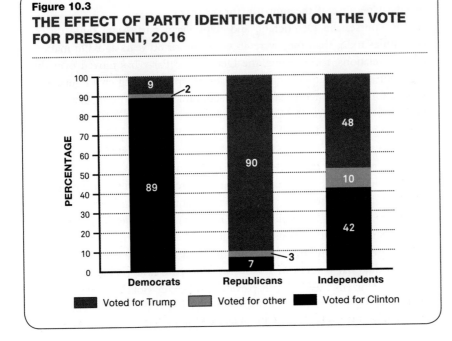

Figure 10.3

THE EFFECT OF PARTY IDENTIFICATION ON THE VOTE FOR PRESIDENT, 2016

Research into party identification has produced three distinct views about what it is, and they point to very different understandings of its effect on elections.[25] In fact, debate over the meaning of party identification cuts to the heart of the meaning of elections.

First, party identification is viewed as a psychological attachment that individuals hold, often throughout adulthood, to one of the parties. Individuals learn about politics as children and adolescents from parents, other adults, and peers, and as part of that socialization they develop attachments to a party that continue to form into early adulthood. The first few presidential elections that an individual experiences as an adult are thought to have particularly profound influence in shaping understanding of the parties and politics. And as different cohorts come into politics, their experiences carry forward throughout their lives. Those who were 18 to 24 years old in 1984, for example, identify overwhelmingly with the Republican Party, because those elections marked the triumph of Ronald Reagan's presidency and political philosophy, the rise of a revitalized Republican Party, and the beginning of the end of the Cold War. Those 18 to 24 years old in 2008, on the other hand, identify disproportionately with the Democratic Party, because the Obama campaign galvanized young voters around a new vision for the future. However it is developed, an individual's psychological affinity for a party makes that person want that party to win and want to support it, even when he or she disagrees with the party on important policies or disapproves of its nominees for office. In some instances, party identification is also a function of "negative partisanship." That is, voters may identify with one party because of the antipathy for the other.

Of course, the Democratic and Republican parties are quite different entities today than they were 40 years ago or 80 years ago. On matters of race relations, for example, the Democratic Party has moved over the past century from supporting segregation to spearheading civil rights. The Republican Party, once a bastion of economic protectionism, has championed free trade for the past several decades. In the 2016 presidential campaign, however, Donald Trump questioned the basic principles of free trade and sought to lead the GOP back to its protectionist roots. However strong generational transmission of party identifications may be, the dissonance between identities and issues must surely weaken the pull of party, which suggests a second theory: that party identifications reflect underlying ideologies of voters and policy positions of parties. Parties in government are meaningful organizations for producing public policies. The relatively high degree of party loyalty in Congress and other branches of government means that voters can reasonably anticipate how politicians will act in office. Citizens identify with parties that pursue policies more to their liking. For example, a union worker will feel a stronger attachment to the Democratic Party because the Democrats have historically protected union interests. A high-income earner may feel a strong pull toward the Republican Party because that party pushes lower taxes overall, whereas the Democrats promote higher tax rates for higher-income households. The party labels act as brand names and help voters choose the candidates that will best match their preferences. As such, party labels provide an informational shortcut. In part, party identifiers feel that one party represents their interests better than others; hence, an identifier is highly likely to vote for that party without even knowing a candidate's voting record or campaign promises.[26]

A third explanation of party identification is that it reflects experiences with political leaders and representatives, especially presidents. Americans hold their presidents, and to a lesser extent Congress, accountable for the country's economic performance and success in foreign affairs. A bad economy or a disastrous military intervention will lead voters to lower their assessment of the president's party's ability to govern. Parties are, by this account, teams seeking to run the government: they consist of experts who conduct foreign policy, economic policy, and domestic policies (such as environmental protection and health care). When things go well, voters infer that the incumbent party has a good approach to running national affairs; when things go badly, they infer that the party lacks the people needed to run the government competently or the approach needed to produce prosperity, peace, and other desirable outcomes. With each successive presidency and their experience of it, individuals update their beliefs about which party is better able to govern.

Psychological attachments, ideological affinities, and past experiences combine to form an individual's current party identifications. But party is not the only factor in voting. We consider next how issues and candidates shape voting behavior.

Issues

Voting on issues and policies cuts to the core of our understanding of democratic accountability and electoral control over government. A simple, idealized account of issue voting goes as follows. Governments make policies and laws on a variety of issues that affect the public. Voters who disagree with those policies and laws on principle, or who think those policies have failed, will vote against those who made the decisions. Voters who support the policies or like the outcomes will support the incumbent legislators or party. It is important to note that politicians' choices of what laws to enact and what administrative actions to take are made with the express aim of attracting electoral support. Voters choose the candidates and parties that stand for the policies and laws most in line with voters' preferences. Even long-term factors like party identification are related to voters' policy preferences.

issue voting
An individual's propensity to select candidates or parties based on the extent to which the individual agrees with one candidate more than others on specific issues

prospective voting

Voting based on the imagined future performance of a candidate

retrospective voting

Voting based on the past performance of a candidate or party

Voters' issue choices usually involve a mix of their judgments about the past behavior of competing parties and candidates and their hopes and fears about candidates' future behavior. Political scientists call choices that focus on future behavior prospective voting, while those based on past performance are called retrospective voting. To some extent, whether prospective or retrospective evaluation is more important in a particular election depends on the strategies of competing candidates. Candidates always endeavor to define election issues in terms that will serve their interests. Incumbents running during a period of prosperity will seek to take credit for the strong economy and define the election as revolving around their record of success. This strategy encourages voters to make retrospective judgments. In contrast, an insurgent running during a period of economic uncertainty will tell voters it is time for a change and ask them to make prospective judgments. Thus, Barack Obama focused on the need for change in 2008, but the White House repeatedly stressed the need to stay the course in 2010 and 2012. In 2016, Hillary Clinton campaigned on staying the course with Obama's policies, a stance buoyed by President Obama's rising popularity in the final two years of his second term.

Economic voting is one way that voters solve a problem inherent in representative democracy: they cannot stay informed about every government policy. They do, however, have a rudimentary way to hold the government accountable—staying the course when times are good and voting for change when the economy sours. Richard Nixon, Ronald Reagan, Bill Clinton, and George W. Bush won re-election easily in the midst of favorable economies. Jimmy Carter in 1980 and George H. W. Bush in 1992 ran for re-election in the midst of economic downturns, and both lost. The Analyzing the Evidence unit on pp. 342–3 explores voters' perceptions of the economy in relation to their support for the incumbent party.

The Consumer Confidence Index is calculated on the basis of a public opinion survey designed to measure citizens' confidence in America's economic future, has been a fairly accurate predictor of presidential outcomes. A generally rosy public view of the economy's current state and future prospects, indicated by an index score greater than 100, augurs well for the party holding the White House. A score of less than 100 suggests that voters are pessimistic about the economy and that incumbents should worry about their job prospects. In October of 2016, the index stood at 87.2, and the Democrats lost control of the White House and failed to retake either the Senate or the House.

Candidate Characteristics

Candidates' personal attributes always influence voters' decisions. Some analysts claim that voters prefer tall candidates to short candidates, candidates with shorter names to candidates with longer names, and candidates with lighter hair to candidates with darker hair. Perhaps these rather frivolous criteria do play some role. But the more important candidate characteristics that affect voters' choices are race, ethnicity, religion, gender, geography, and social background. Voters presume that candidates with similar backgrounds to their own are likely to share their views. Moreover, they may be proud to see someone of their background in a position of leadership. This is why politicians have often sought to "balance the ticket" by including members of as many important groups as possible.

Of course, personal characteristics that attract some voters may repel others. Many voters are prejudiced against candidates of certain ethnic, racial, or religious groups. For most of American history, an African American or woman president seemed unthinkable, but those barriers fell in 2008 and 2016 respectively. Voters also consider candidates' personality characteristics, such as their competence, honesty, and vigor

Economic Influence on Presidential Elections

Contributed by
Robert S. Erikson
Columbia University

The state of the economy is a key factor in presidential elections. When the United States prospers, the presidential party performs much better than when economic conditions are poor. The economic influence on presidential elections can be seen by predicting the vote based on objective indicators such as GDP growth leading up to the election. The simplest measure, however, is a subjective one—voters' responses when asked in polls whether the economy has been performing well or badly. When survey respondents are asked early in the election year how they plan to vote, candidate and party preferences show little relationship to economic perceptions at that time. By election day, however, the national vote falls surprisingly in line with the voters' perceptions of economic performance. In short, the election campaign increases the importance of the economy to voters.

The precise indicator of economic perceptions used here is the average response to the following question, asked regularly by the Survey of Consumers at the University of Michigan in April and November of the election year: "Would you say that at the current time business conditions are better or worse than they were a year ago?"

April Poll Results

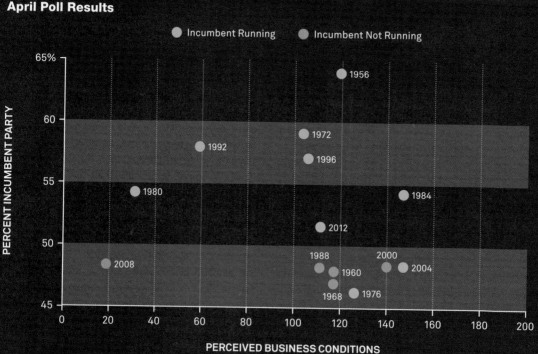

The lack of any consistent pattern in the first graph (at left) shows that what voters think about the economy in April of an election year has little bearing on their vote intentions at that time—as if voters had not yet thought about the November election sufficiently to factor in the economy. Especially noteworthy examples are 1980 and 1992 when incumbents Jimmy Carter and George H. W. Bush, respectively, were favored in the early polls, despite being seen as presiding over poor economies. Both lost the general election. John McCain (representing the incumbent Republican Party) was only slightly behind Barack Obama in early 2008, despite an economy that already was almost universally seen as worsening.

The clear pattern in the second graph (below) shows that by November, the vote fell into rough alignment with economic perceptions: The better the average perception of business conditions, the greater the support for the incumbent party. The three weakest economies in terms of perceptions (1980, 1992, 2008) all saw the incumbent party lose.

November Poll Results

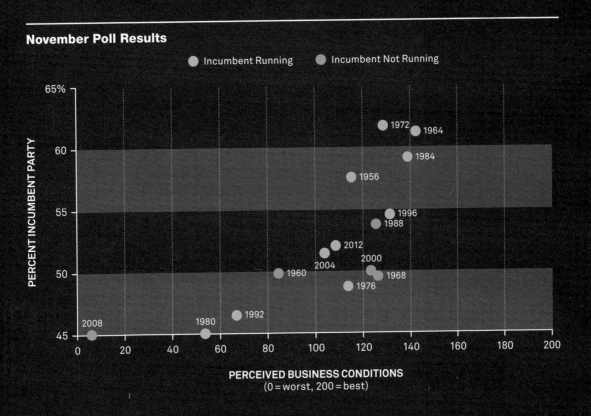

SOURCE: Surveys of Consumers, www.sca.isr.umich.edu/tables.html (accessed 12/16/2015); and author's compilation.

(or lack thereof), because they figure that politicians with these attributes are likely to produce good outcomes, such as laws that work, fair and honest administration of government, and the ability to address crises. Candidates, for their part, emphasize qualities that they think all voters will value. In the 2008 primary election between Hillary Clinton and Barack Obama, for example, Clinton ran an ad intended to show her experience and ability to deal with crises: "It's 3 A.M. and your children are safely asleep. But there's a phone in the White House and it's ringing. Something's happening in the world. Your vote will decide who answers that call. . . . Whether it's someone tested and ready to lead in a dangerous world. . . ."

One of the most distinctive features of American politics is the incumbency advantage, as we saw in Chapter 5. Why this advantage has emerged and grown remains something of a puzzle. Redistricting is almost certainly not the explanation: incumbency effects are as large in gubernatorial elections, where there are no districts, as in House elections. Researchers believe about half of the incumbency advantage reflects the activities of the legislator in office; it is voters rewarding incumbents for their performance. The other half evidently reflects the incumbents' opponents.[27] The typical challenger may not have the personal appeal of the typical incumbent, who after all has already won office once. Moreover, challengers usually lack incumbents' experience in and resources for running a campaign. This critical ability to communicate with voters can give an incumbent the edge in close elections.

While party, issues, and candidate characteristics are perhaps the three most important factors shaping voting decisions, political scientists disagree as to the relative importance of each. Recent scholarship suggests that they have roughly equal weight in explaining the division of the vote in national elections.[28] Part of the difficulty in parsing their importance is that the extent to which they matter depends on the electorate's information levels. In the absence of much information, most voters rely almost exclusively on party cues. A highly informed electorate relies more heavily on issues and candidate characteristics.[29]

CAMPAIGNS: MONEY, MEDIA, AND GRASS ROOTS

American political campaigns are freewheeling events with few restrictions on what candidates may say or do. Candidates in hotly contested House and Senate races spend millions of dollars to advertise on television, radio, and the Internet, as well as direct mail and door-to-door canvassing. Those seeking office are in a race to become as well known and as well liked as possible and to get more of their supporters to vote. Federal laws limit how much an individual or organization may give to a candidate but, with the exception of presidential campaigns, place no restrictions on how much a candidate or party committee may spend.

Adding to the freewheeling nature of campaigns is their organizational structure. Most political campaigns are temporary organizations, formed for the sole purpose of winning the coming elections and disbanding shortly afterward. To be sure, political parties in the United States have permanent, professional campaign organizations that raise money, strategize, recruit candidates, and distribute resources. On the Republican side of the aisle are the Republican National Committee, the National Republican Senatorial Committee, and the National Republican Congressional Committee; on the Democratic side are the Democratic National Committee, the Democratic Senatorial Campaign Committee, and the Democratic Congressional Campaign Committee. These account for roughly one-third of the money in politics and have considerable expertise. But most campaigns are formed by and around individual candidates, who often put up the initial cash to get the campaign rolling and rely heavily on family and friends as volunteers. Thousands of such organizations are at work during a presidential election year, with relatively little partisan coordination. The two major-party presidential campaigns operate 50 separate state-level operations, with other campaigns competing for 33 or 34 Senate seats, 435 House seats, dozens of gubernatorial and other statewide offices, and thousands of state legislative seats. All simultaneously work to persuade as many people as possible to vote for their candidate on Election Day.

What It Takes to Win. All campaigns face similar challenges—how to mobilize volunteers, how to raise money, how to coordinate activities, what messages to run, and how to communicate with the public. There is no one best way to run a campaign. There are many tried-and-true approaches, especially building up a campaign from local connections, from the grass roots. Candidates have to meet as many people as possible and get their friends and their friends' friends to support them. In-person campaigning becomes increasingly difficult in larger constituencies. Candidates continually experiment with new ways of reaching larger segments of the electorate. In the 1920s, radio advertising eclipsed handbills and door-to-door canvassing; in the 1960s, television began to eclipse radio; in the 1980s and 1990s, cable television, phone polling, and focus groups allowed targeting of specific demographic groups. The great innovation of the 2008 Obama campaign was to meld Internet networking tools with old-style organizing methods to develop a massive communications and fund-raising network that came to be called a "netroots" campaign. The Clinton campaign in 2016 capitalized on the infrastructure built by Obama and sought the advice of many of the same consultants. The Trump campaign, by contrast, relied heavily on Twitter and media coverage, and ignored the typical organization and mobilization activities considered essential for modern campaigns.

It has become an assumption of American elections and election law that candidates and parties will mount campaigns that spend millions, even billions of dollars, to persuade people to vote and how to vote. And because of those efforts, voters will understand better what choices they face. In short, campaigns inform voters through competition. In addition to being costly, American political campaigns are long. Presidential campaigns officially launch a year and a half to two years in advance of Election Day. Serious campaigns for the U.S. House of Representatives begin at least a year ahead and often span the better part of two years. To use the term of the Federal Election Commission, an election is a two-year *cycle*, not a single day or even the period between Labor Day and Election Day loosely referred to as "the general election."

Long campaigns are due largely to the effort required to mount them. There are roughly 320 million people in the United States, and the voting-age population exceeds 245 million people. Communicating with all of them is expensive and time-consuming. Suppose you ran for president of the United States. Sending one piece of mail to each household in the United States—probably the minimum imaginable campaign effort—would cost approximately $150 million dollars. How long would it take to raise that amount and mobilize such a mailing? In the 2016 election cycle, the Clinton campaign and allied committees spent $1.3 billion; the Trump campaign and allied committees spent $800 million—a combined total of just over $2 billion. Approximately half of that sum purchased airtime for television advertising. The money was raised through personal and political networks that the campaigns and candidates built up over months, even years, of effort.

The campaign season is further extended by the election calendar. American national, state, and local elections proceed in two steps: the party primary elections and the general election. General elections for federal offices are set by the U.S. Constitution to take place on the first Tuesday after the first Monday in November. The first presidential caucuses and primaries come early in January and last through the beginning of June. Primaries for congressional seats and state offices do not follow the same calendar, but most occur in the spring and early summer, with a few states waiting until September. The result of this calendar of elections is to stretch the campaigns over the entire election year.

Campaign Finance. The expense, duration, and chaos of American campaigns have prompted many efforts at reform, including attempts to limit campaign spending, shorten the campaign season, and restrict what candidates and organizations may say in advertisements. The most sweeping campaign reforms came in 1971, when Congress passed the Federal

Elections Campaign Act (or FECA). It limited the amounts that a single individual could contribute to a candidate or party to $1,000 per election for individuals and $5,000 for organizations (these limits have since been increased, as Table 10.1 indicates). It further regulated how business firms, unions, and other organizations could give money, prohibiting donations directly from the organization's treasury and requiring the establishment of a separate fund—a political action committee (PAC). It established public funding for presidential campaigns and tied those funds to expenditure limits. And it set up the Federal Election Commission (FEC) to oversee public disclosure of information and to enforce the laws.[30] Congress has amended FECA several times, most importantly in the Bipartisan Campaign Reform Act of 2002 (BCRA, also called the McCain-Feingold Act, after senators John McCain and Russell Feingold, its primary sponsors in the Senate). This amendment prohibited unlimited party spending (called *soft money*) and banned certain sorts of political attack advertisements from interest groups in the last weeks of a campaign. Table 10.1 summarizes some of the rules governing campaign finance in federal elections.

> **political action committee (PAC)**
> A private group that raises and distributes funds for use in election campaigns

The FECA also established public funding for presidential campaigns. If a candidate agrees to abide by spending limits, that candidate's campaign is eligible for matching funds in primary elections and full public funding in the general election. Until 2000, nearly all candidates bought into the system. George W. Bush chose to fund his 2000 primary election campaign outside this system and spent $500 million to win the Republican nomination. Barack Obama and Hillary Clinton ignored the public-financing system in their 2008 primary contest, and Obama opted out of the public system in the general election as well, allowing him to spend several hundred million more dollars than the Republican nominee, John McCain. In 2016, only Martin O'Malley (Democrat) and Jill Stein (Green Party) received public funding for their presidential campaigns.

FECA originally went much further than the law that survives today. Congress originally passed mandatory caps on spending by House and Senate candidates and prohibited organizations from running independent campaigns on behalf of or in opposition to a candidate (and not coordinated with any candidate). James Buckley, a candidate for U.S. Senate in New York, challenged the law, arguing that the restrictions on spending and contributions limited his rights to free speech and that the FEC had excessive administrative power. In the 1976 landmark case *Buckley v. Valeo*, the U.S. Supreme Court agreed in part.[31] The Court ruled that "money is speech," but the government also has a compelling interest in protecting elections from corrupt practices, such as bribery through large campaign donations. The justices declared the limits on candidate spending unconstitutional because they violated free speech rights of candidates and groups. However, the need to protect the integrity of the electoral process led the justices to leave contribution limits in place. The presidential public-funding system was also

Table 10.1

FEDERAL CAMPAIGN FINANCE CONTRIBUTION LIMITS

	To each candidate or candidate committee per election	To national party committee per calendar year	To state, district, and local party committee per calendar year	To each PAC* (ssf and nonconnected) per calendar year
Individual may give	$2,700**	$33,400**	$10,000 (combined limit)	$5,000
National party committee may give	$5,000	No limit	No limit	$5,000
State, district, and local party committee may give	$5,000	No limit	No limit	$5,000
PAC (multicandidate)*** may give	$5,000	$15,000	$5,000 (combined limit)	$5,000
PAC (not multicandidate) may give	$2,700	$32,400**	$10,000 (combined limit)	$5,000
Authorized campaign committee may give	$2,000	No limit	No limit	$5,000

*PAC refers to a committee that makes contributions to other federal political committees. Super PACs may accept unlimited contributions.

**Indexed for inflation in odd-numbered years

***A multicandidate committee is a political committee with more than 50 contributors that has been registered for at least six months and, with the exception of state party committees, has made contributions to five or more candidates for federal office.

SOURCE: Federal Election Commission, www.fec.gov/pages/brochures/contrib.shtml#Chart (accessed 7/2/15).

validated because it is voluntary: candidates are not required to opt into it. What survived *Buckley* is a system in which candidates, groups, and parties may spend as much as they like to win office, but donations must come in small amounts. This is a more democratic process of campaign finance, but it increases the effort and time needed to construct a campaign.

In 2010, the Court reinforced its reasoning in *Buckley* in the case *Citizens' United v. Federal Election Commission*.[32] Here the justices ruled that the BCRA of 2002 had erred in imposing restrictions on independent spending by corporations. It overturned key components of the law and reversed its ruling in a case that had upheld it.[33] The majority opinion struck down limits on independent expenditures from corporate treasuries but kept in place limits on direct contributions from corporations and other organizations to candidates. However, it also solidified corporations' right to free political speech, on par with the right to free speech of individuals. In the wake of this decision, two sorts of organizations formed—501c(4) organizations, which derive their name from the section of the tax code that allows such entities, and Super PACs. Each can raise and spend unlimited amounts on campaigns, though Super PACs are subject to more disclosure laws. Super PACs spent approximately $1.2 billion in 2016, mostly on the presidential election. In 2014, Super PACs spent $339.4 million, substantially more than all independent spending in 2010, the prior midterm election.

Congressional Campaigns. Congressional campaigns share a number of important features with presidential campaigns, but they are also distinctive. The two-term limit on the president means that incumbency is a more important advantage for congressional representatives, who have no term limits. In recent decades, the incumbency advantage has grown in both magnitude and importance in U.S. elections. Today, almost every elective office at the state and federal level exhibits this advantage, ranging from about 5 percent in state legislative elections to 10 percent for U.S. House, U.S. Senate, and governor. A 10 percent incumbency advantage is a massive electoral edge. It turns a competitive race into a blowout for the incumbent.[34]

Congressional incumbents' advantages arise in spending as well as votes. Like presidential campaigns, congressional campaigns have witnessed increased spending over time. The average U.S. House incumbent in 2014 spent $1.5 million; the typical challenger spent $260,000.[35]

Incumbent members of Congress have particular advantages in campaign fund-raising. They have already been tested; they have their campaign organizations in place; and they have connections in their constituencies, as well as in Washington, D.C.

THE 2016 ELECTIONS

In the fall of 2016, 136 million Americans went to the polls to elect a new president. Republican Donald Trump defied the expectations of most pundits and observers to defeat Democrat Hillary Clinton. The outcome reflected a unique feature of American presidential elections: Because of the Electoral College system, the winner is not necessarily the candidate who receives the most votes. In 2016, one candidate, Hillary Clinton, won the popular vote and another candidate, Donald Trump, won the Electoral College vote (see Figure 10.4). The result of the 2016 presidential election highlighted the distortions that can occur with electoral systems in which the winner is determined by who wins a majority of many districts or states, rather than by who wins a majority of votes, as discussed earlier in this chapter. But, as we will see in this section, the election outcomes more broadly were not solely a result of the Electoral College.

Political Parties in 2016

Over time, the Democratic Party has become increasingly liberal, and the Republican Party increasingly conservative. The growing ideological split between the two parties has not meant that each party is ideologically uniform, however. In 2016, factional splits in both parties deepened. For the

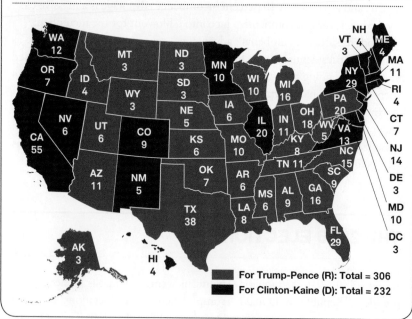

Figure 10.4

DISTRIBUTION OF ELECTORAL VOTES IN THE 2016 PRESIDENTIAL ELECTION

For Trump-Pence (R): Total = 306
For Clinton-Kaine (D): Total = 232

NOTE: Maine and Nebraska allocate Electoral College votes by congressional district. Donald Trump won one of Maine's four electoral votes.
SOURCE: "Presidential Election Results: Donald J. Trump Wins," *New York Times*, www.nytimes.com/elections/results/president (accessed 11/18/16).

first time in recent history, both parties had primary election fights that were not settled until the last primary election votes were cast in June.

Initially, it appeared that Hillary Clinton would coast to the Democratic nomination. Clinton was one of the most prominent Democratic leaders, having served as first lady, then as a U.S. Senator from New York, and later as secretary of state under President Obama. On the issues, she represented a more moderate approach to public policy, as a Democrat who embraces free trade rather than protectionism, and is known for being hawkish on national defense. Clinton, however, was challenged from the far left wing of the party when Bernie Sanders, a senator from Vermont and self-described Democratic Socialist, emerged as her biggest rival. Sanders seized on economic issues that energized key segments of the Democratic electorate. In particular, he championed free college tuition, a message that won 80 percent of the votes of people under 30 in the Democratic primaries.[36] Clinton, meanwhile, emphasized health care, racial and gender equality, and her experience. She won strong support among minority voters and older voters.

Throughout the spring, the race for the Democratic nomination remained close. By the time the last votes were cast in California's primary in June 2016, Sanders had won 23 caucuses or primaries compared to Clinton's 34, and 1,865 delegates compared to her 2,842.

It was a highly unusual primary contest for the Democrats. Sanders, a relatively unknown "outsider" candidate, presented a serious challenge to one of the most prominent political leaders, tapping into many Democratic voters' sense of unrest and unease with their party. Although Sanders eventually endorsed Clinton, many people who voted for Sanders in the primary stated that they would not support Clinton in the general election.

The Republican nomination contest was more unusual still. The Republican field attracted 17 candidates for president, including several prominent Republican governors and senators. Florida Governor Jeb Bush, son of President George H. W. Bush and brother of President George W. Bush, was the early pick of many experts. The Bush campaign, however, failed to gain much traction. Through the last six months of 2015 and into 2016 the consistent leader in the polls was not Bush, nor any of the establishment candidates, but real estate mogul and TV personality Donald Trump.

Trump announced his candidacy in June 2015, and from the outset his campaign was widely dismissed by the media and most party leaders as a gimmick. The heart of his appeal, however, was not to the media elite or the party establishment, but to working-class conservative white voters in the United States.

Trump campaigned strenuously against free trade, promising to bring jobs back to America. He also promised to cut taxes on individuals and corporations. He took a staunch stand against immigration, proposing to build a wall at the U.S.-Mexican border as well as to place a temporary ban on

Muslim immigration. These kinds of provocative statements soon came to characterize Trump's campaign. While many called Trump's style offensive, and labeled him as xenophobic and racist, to many Americans he seemed an authentic candidate unafraid to assert his views and defy a politically correct culture. As Trump's many controversial and inflammatory comments continued to dominate headlines, the field of 17 Republican candidates was winnowed to 4: Donald Trump, Senator Ted Cruz (Texas), Senator Marco Rubio (Florida), and Governor John Kasich (Ohio). Ultimately Trump won only 45 percent of all votes cast in the primaries, but that was sufficient to earn him 1,441 delegates, 204 more than were needed to secure the nomination.

The primary campaign was a divisive one. Trump's strategy was to challenge the Republican establishment directly. His attacks on John McCain (the 2008 Republican nominee), Mitt Romney (the 2012 nominee), House Speaker Paul Ryan, and other prominent party leaders left many in the GOP reluctant to embrace their party's nominee. Heading into the general elections, both parties' nominees needed to heal rifts among their rank-and-file voters.

The General Election

The general election season began at the parties' nominating conventions. In 2016, each night of the national conventions drew 30 million prime-time viewers.[37] Both parties' conventions put on a show aimed to inspire their supporters and to demonize their opponents. The main message of the Trump campaign was to "make America great again" by reversing eight years of Obama's policies, and to bridge the divisions within the party by focusing on their common enemy. The Democrats followed suit with a convention filled with attacks on Trump. When not attacking Trump, the Democratic convention focused on appealing to nonwhite voters as to well as women, emphasizing the potential to elect the first woman president of the United States and to make sweeping changes in public policies, from health care to employment to education.

As the summer rolled into August, the campaigns shifted from a broad national message to a direct appeal to voters in swing states that are neither strongly Democratic nor strongly Republican. Fourteen swing states—Arizona, Colorado, Florida, Iowa, Maine, Michigan, Minnesota, Nevada, New Hampshire, North Carolina, Ohio, Pennsylvania, Virginia, and Wisconsin—loomed large in the campaigns' strategies, but the two campaigns went about appealing to swing state voters in very different ways.

Trump's general election campaign focused on motivating his core supporters. During the primaries, Trump had proved masterful in the use of social media, especially Twitter, in stirring controversy and attracting news coverage. As effective as his mastery of the "short media" was, Trump was perhaps even more at home giving hour-long stump speeches. He held energetic rallies, each typically lasting several hours, throughout the swing states. Ultimately, it was Trump's use of social media and campaign rallies to motivate his core supporters that proved to be the staple of his campaign.

The Clinton campaign focused on a strategy of mobilization, rather than motivation, following more closely the playbook written by the Obama campaigns of 2008 and 2012. The Clinton campaign invested heavily in get-out-the-vote activities, which target specific people to make sure they are registered to vote and to remind them to vote. This strategy was a stark contrast to the motivational approach that Trump employed, which was designed to inspire enthusiasm among potential supporters more broadly.

Clinton and Trump squared off in three presidential debates. By most pundits' accounts, Clinton won the debates handily.[38] Additionally, scandals

During the 2016 general election campaign, Donald Trump and Hillary Clinton faced each other in three televised debates. The candidates addressed important issues, such as the economy, but also attacked each other's character and fitness to be president.

that emerged in the fall, including the release of a 2005 video in which Trump was heard boasting that his celebrity status allowed him to touch women inappropriately and his acknowledgment that he had avoided paying federal income tax for decades, raised questions about his electability. Clinton, however, was embroiled in controversy of her own, having been under investigation by the FBI for her use of a private e-mail server during her tenure as secretary of state, a fact that Republicans seized on as evidence that Clinton was not trustworthy. Although Clinton held a strong lead coming into the general election season, the November exit polls revealed that the debates, rallies, Tweets, ads, and other activities of the general election campaigns in fact helped push undecided voters toward Trump.[39]

Republican Victory

Based on preliminary tallies, Clinton received 65.2 million votes, or around 48 percent of the popular vote, while Trump won 62.7 million votes, or around 46 percent of the popular vote. However, Trump carried states totaling 306 votes in the Electoral College and thus won the presidency.

Five times in U.S. history, the Electoral College outcome has flipped the result of the popular vote. The reason for the reversal in 2016 was that Clinton won big in states where Democrats safely win, and Trump racked up electoral votes in key swing states by narrow margins. Among the states deemed relatively safe for one party or the other, Clinton did well. In these 36 "safely" Democratic or "safely" Republican states, Clinton won 49 percent of the popular vote and 190 electoral votes, while Trump won 45 percent of the popular vote in these states and 178 electoral votes. The 14 swing states, however, held the key to the election. Trump won 48 percent of the popular vote in these states and 125 electoral votes, while Clinton won 47 percent of the popular vote in these states for just 42 electoral votes.[40] In the end, the election was determined by four states where Trump won by 1 percentage point or less: Florida, Michigan, Wisconsin, and Pennsylvania.

In the 2016 election, Americans also elected all members of the House of Representatives, a third of the Senate, new state legislatures in 43 states, and new governors in 12 states. Prior to the election, Democrats had high hopes of taking back the U.S. Senate and making significant inroads into the state governments. But the election cemented the gains that the Republican Party had made in congressional and state elections in 2010 and 2014. Republicans suffered only minor losses in the 2016 congressional elections, retaining their majority in both the House of Representatives and the Senate. The GOP gained ground in the state governments as well. After the election, the Republicans controlled both chambers of the state legislatures in 32 states, and the governorships in 34 states.

The 2016 election signaled a shift to the right in U.S. politics and public policy making, but a shift with strong populist overtones. The 2016 elections in the United States had an eerie similarity to recent elections in Europe. In the United Kingdom, France, and Germany, right-wing and populist parties, whose messages were centrally against immigration and were nationalist and isolationist, scored stunning victories in recent elections. One of the most surprising was the referendum vote in June 2016 in the UK to leave the European Union. The pollsters got the "Brexit" vote wrong, widely predicting that Britons would not vote to leave the E.U. and isolate themselves from Europe. Forecasters and pollsters were similarly wrong in their predictions for the presidential election in the United States. In the week leading up to the election, for example, the UpShot put Hillary Clinton's chances of winning at 85 percent, FiveThirtyEight gave her a 71 percent chance of winning, and the Princeton Election Consortium put her chances at greater than 99 percent. As for the polls, survey-based estimates of the national vote for Clinton and Trump were within the margin of error. The typical poll put her lead at 3 to 4 points. She won by 2 percentage points in the popular vote nationwide. Where the polls erred was in the states, especially the upper Midwest. The most likely problem with the state polls is that they used the 2012 presidential election as their baseline estimates of the composition of the electorate. In states where there had been a significant and unexpected shift in the composition of the electorate and the voting behavior of white working-class voters, the survey estimates were biased. That differential shift in turnout made it difficult for pollsters to measure who was likely to vote. It may also have made it difficult for polls to elicit how people who were in the process of changing their minds about politics were actually going to vote. The states where many such changes occurred, it turns out, were in the upper Midwest, and the shift reflected the jump in enthusiasm among white working-class voters for Trump compared with the 2012 Republican nominee, Mitt Romney (see Figure 10.5).

The broader economic and political context in the United States may also shed light on Trump's victory. From 2008 to 2016, the U.S. economy never grew faster than 2.5 percent a year and averaged 7 percent unemployment. Growth in GDP from January to October of 2016 was less than 1.5 percent. Against this background of tepid economic growth and relatively high unemployment, many Americans wanted change. In fact, economic models of the election forecasted a very close race. Economic models of elections typically explain the election results as a function of peace and prosperity: whether we are at war and how strongly the economy is growing. A growth rate of 2.5 percent or better usually bodes well for the incumbent party's candidate.[41] The weak 1.5 percent growth rate in 2016 created a strong headwind into which the Democratic nominee—whoever it was—would have to sail.

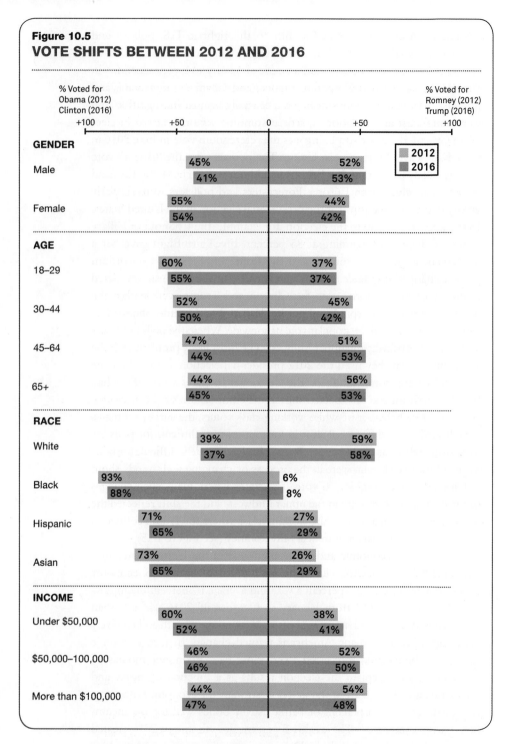

Figure 10.5

VOTE SHIFTS BETWEEN 2012 AND 2016

% Voted for
Obama (2012)
Clinton (2016)

% Voted for
Romney (2012)
Trump (2016)

+100   +50   0   +50   +100

Legend: 2012 / 2016

GENDER

Male: 45% / 41% (left); 52% / 53% (right)

Female: 55% / 54% (left); 44% / 42% (right)

AGE

18–29: 60% / 55% (left); 37% / 37% (right)

30–44: 52% / 50% (left); 45% / 42% (right)

45–64: 47% / 44% (left); 51% / 53% (right)

65+: 44% / 45% (left); 56% / 53% (right)

RACE

White: 39% / 37% (left); 59% / 58% (right)

Black: 93% / 88% (left); 6% / 8% (right)

Hispanic: 71% / 65% (left); 27% / 29% (right)

Asian: 73% / 65% (left); 26% / 29% (right)

INCOME

Under $50,000: 60% / 52% (left); 38% / 41% (right)

$50,000–100,000: 46% / 46% (left); 52% / 50% (right)

More than $100,000: 44% / 47% (left); 54% / 48% (right)

Source: "Exit Polls 2012: How the Vote Has Shifted," *Washington Post*, November 6, 2012, www.washingtonpost.com/wp-srv/special/politics/2012-exit-polls/table.html (accessed 11/28/12) and www.washingtonpost.com/graphics/politics/2016-election/exit-polls/ (accessed 11/28/16).

The months following the election saw deep soul-searching among Democrats. How did the party lose an election that seemed in its grasp? What could the party do moving forward? Such self-examination usually follows an electoral defeat. The Republican Party had conducted a similar inquiry following the 2012 election and used their loss to develop a roadmap for the future.

The Democratic Party leadership did not only look to the future but also saw immediate opportunities to work with President Trump on shared issues. For example, one of Trump's main policy promises during the campaign was a massive increase in spending on infrastructure, such as highways and airports, legislation the Democrats in Congress have long championed.

Looking further ahead, Trump's victory may put the Democratic Party in a strong position for the 2018 midterm elections, as the president's party almost always loses seats in the midterms. The 2018 midterm will elect most states' governors and most states' legislatures. A strong showing in 2018 will be essential for rebuilding the Democratic Party, not just for the 2020 presidential campaign, but beyond.

The 2018 elections will also shape which party controls the states leading into the 2021 redistricting process. Following the 2020 census, the United States will reapportion its congressional seats among the states and every congressional district and state legislative district in the country will be redrawn. In nearly every state, this responsibility follows the normal legislative process. The state legislature passes a redistricting law and the governor may sign the law or veto it. Whoever controls the state legislatures and governorships in 2021, then, will determine the contours of representation in the states and U.S. Congress for the next decade.

DO ELECTIONS ENSURE ACCOUNTABILITY?

Elections are not the only form of popular political action, but they are the most peaceful means of linking citizens and governments—providing governments with popular support and citizens with a measure of influence.

The institutions of American elections are designed to facilitate majority rule. Single-member districts and plurality rule create strong pressures toward a two-party system and majority rule. Even in elections in which one party wins a plurality but not a majority, that party typically wins a majority of legislative seats. The election itself, then, determines the government. Other systems often produce multiparty outcomes, resulting in a period of negotiation and coalition formation among the parties to determine who will govern.

The significance of elections derives less from election laws as from the voters' expression of their preferences. Voting behavior depends in no small part the tendency to vote for a given party as a matter of ingrained personal identity. If that were all there is to voting behavior, then elections might not provide a meaningful way of governing. However, voters' preferences are as strongly rooted in the issues at hand as in the choices themselves, the candidates. Voting decisions reflect individuals' assessments about whether it makes sense to keep public policies on the same track or to change direction, whether those in office have done a good job and deserve to be re-elected, or whether they have failed and it is time for new representation. The aggregation of all voters' preferences responds collectively to fluctuations in the economy, to differences in the ideological and policy orientations of the parties, and to the personal attributes of the candidates.

For Further Reading

Ansolabehere, Stephen, and James M. Snyder, Jr. *The End of Inequality: One Person, One Vote and the Transformation of American Politics.* New York: Norton, 2008.

Brady, David W. *Critical Elections and Congressional Policy Making.* Palo Alto, CA: Stanford University Press, 1988.

Carmines, Edward G., and James A. Stimson. *Issue Evolution: Race and the Transformation of American Politics.* Princeton, NJ: Princeton University Press, 1989.

Conway, M. Margaret. *Political Participation in the United States.* 3rd ed. Washington, DC: CQ Press, 2000.

Fowler, Linda L. *Candidates, Congress, and the American Democracy.* Ann Arbor: University of Michigan Press, 1994.

Gelman, Andrew. *Red State, Blue State, Rich State, Poor State: Why Americans Vote the Way They Do.* Princeton, NJ: Princeton University Press, 2008.

Ginsberg, Benjamin, and Martin Shefter. *Politics by Other Means: Politicians, Prosecutors, and the Press from Watergate to Whitewater.* 3rd ed. New York: Norton, 2002.

Green, Donald, and Alan Gerber. *Get Out the Vote!: How to Increase Voter Turnout.* 2nd ed. Washington, DC: Brookings Institution, 2008.

Jacobson, Gary C. *The Politics of Congressional Elections*. 8th ed. Boston: Pearson, 2013.

McCarty, Nolan, Keith Poole, and Howard Rosenthal. *Polarized America: The Dance of Ideology and Unequal Riches*. Cambridge, MA: MIT Press, 2006.

Morton, Rebecca B. *Analyzing Elections*. New York: Norton, 2006.

Rosenstone, Steven, and John Mark Hansen. *Mobilization, Participation, and Democracy in America*. New York: Macmillan, 1993.

11

Political Parties

Political parties are teams of politicians, activists, and voters whose goal is to win control of government. They do so by recruiting and nominating candidates to run for office; by accumulating the resources needed to run campaigns, especially manpower and money; and by pursuing a policy agenda that can appeal to large numbers of voters and secure electoral majorities. Once in office, parties organize the legislature and attempt to put their stamp on the laws passed by Congress and the president. Their potential political power is immense.

We often refer to the United States as a nation with a "two-party system," meaning that the Democratic and Republican parties compete for office and power. Most Americans believe that party competition contributes to the health of the democratic process. Certainly, we are suspicious of nations that claim to be ruled by their people but do not tolerate the existence of opposing parties.

The idea of party competition was not always accepted in the United States, however. In the early years of the Republic, parties were seen as threats to the social order. In his 1796 "Farewell Address," President George Washington warned his countrymen to shun partisan politics:

Let me warn you in the most solemn manner against the baneful effects of the spirit of party generally. This spirit exists under different shapes in all government, more or less stifled, controlled, or repressed, but in those of the popular form it is seen in its greater rankness and is truly their worst enemy.

Often, those in power viewed the formation of political parties by their opponents as acts of treason that merited severe punishment. Thus, in 1798, the Federalist party, which controlled the national government, in effect sought to outlaw its Jeffersonian Republican opponents through the infamous Alien and Sedition acts, which, among other things, made it a crime to publish or say anything that might tend to defame or bring into disrepute either the president or Congress. Under this law, 25 individuals—including several Republican newspaper editors—were arrested and convicted.

Over the past 200 years, our conception of political parties has changed considerably—from subversive organizations to bulwarks of democracy. In some instances, however, such as the 2011 struggle over increasing the nation's debt limit or the 2016 battle over appropriations, the two parties seemed ready to send the nation's economy over a precipice as they struggled for advantage. Rather than contribute to democratic governance, the parties seemed about to cause democratic collapse.

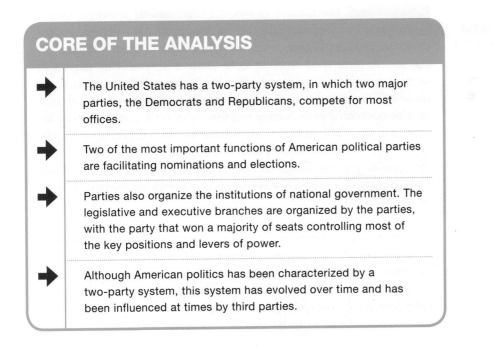

CORE OF THE ANALYSIS

➡ The United States has a two-party system, in which two major parties, the Democrats and Republicans, compete for most offices.

➡ Two of the most important functions of American political parties are facilitating nominations and elections.

➡ Parties also organize the institutions of national government. The legislative and executive branches are organized by the parties, with the party that won a majority of seats controlling most of the key positions and levers of power.

➡ Although American politics has been characterized by a two-party system, this system has evolved over time and has been influenced at times by third parties.

One concern that has become especially acute in recent years is ideological polarization. At one time, each party included liberal, moderate, and conservative factions. Today, there are few conservative Democrats and hardly any liberal Republicans. Moreover, within each party, the most ideologically motivated groups are also most likely to vote, especially in primary elections. This polarization makes it difficult for the parties to achieve compromise solutions to the nation's problems.

FUNCTIONS OF THE PARTIES

It is difficult to imagine how American politics and government would work without political parties. Our inability to conceive of democracy without parties is not a failure of our imaginations or an accident of American history. Rather, it reflects a law of democratic politics. Parties form to solve key problems in a democracy. Throughout this chapter we highlight some of the general functions of parties in any democracy, but we are especially attentive to party politics in the United States.

Why Do Political Parties Form?

political party

An organized group that attempts to influence the government by electing its members to important government offices

Political parties, like interest groups, are organizations seeking influence over government. Ordinarily, they can be distinguished from interest groups (which we consider in more detail in Chapter 12) on the basis of their orientation. A party seeks to control the entire government by electing its members to office, thereby controlling the government's personnel. Interest groups, through campaign contributions and other forms of assistance, are also concerned with electing politicians—in particular, those who are inclined in their policy direction. But interest groups ordinarily do not sponsor candidates directly, and between elections they usually accept government and its personnel as givens and try to influence government policies through them. They are *benefit seekers*, whereas parties are composed largely of *office seekers*.[1]

Parties are mainly involved in nominations and elections—recruiting candidates for office, getting out the vote, and making it easier for citizens to choose their leaders. They also influence the institutions of government—providing the leadership and organization of the various congressional committees. The political parties in the United States were ultimately formed by politicians to serve their aims. Parties make easier the basic tasks of political life—running for office, organizing one's supporters, and forming a government.

Recruiting Candidates

One of the most important party activities is the recruitment of candidates for office. Each election year, candidates must be found for thousands of state and local offices as well as congressional seats. Where an incumbent is not seeking re-election or an incumbent in the opposing party appears vulnerable, party leaders identify strong candidates and try to interest them in entering the campaign.

The recruiting season begins early, because the dates by which candidates must file for office come as early as January in some states. Candidate recruitment in the spring shapes the parties' message and fortunes in the November general election. In 2010 and 2012, Republicans capitalized on public opposition to President Obama's health care law and managed to recruit a very strong class of candidates. On the other hand, sometimes parties fail to recruit anyone to run for a seat. In 2016, candidate recruitment became particularly difficult as campaigns came to involve much mudslinging and intense media scrutiny of candidates' personal lives.[2]

An ideal candidate will be charismatic, organized, knowledgeable, and an excellent debater; have an unblemished record; and be able to raise enough money to mount a serious campaign. Party leaders usually will not provide financial backing to candidates who cannot raise substantial funds on their own. For a House seat, this can mean between $500,000 and $1 million; for a Senate seat, several million dollars; and for the presidency, upwards of $1 billion.

Nominating Candidates

Nomination is the process of selecting one party candidate to run for each elective office. The nominating process can precede the election by many months, as it does when many presidential candidates for the presidency are eliminated through a grueling series of debates and state primaries, conventions, and caucuses until there is only one survivor in each party—that party's nominee. Figure 11.1 summarizes the types of nominating processes described below.

nomination
The process by which political parties select their candidate for election to public office

Nomination by Convention. A nominating convention is a formal meeting of members of a political party that is bound by rules that govern participation and procedures. Conventions are meetings of delegates elected by party members from the relevant county (county convention) or state (state convention). Delegates to each party's national convention (which nominates the party's presidential candidate) are chosen by party members on a state-by-state basis; there is no single national delegate-selection process.

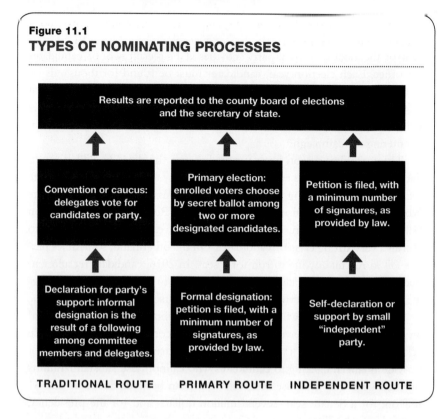

Figure 11.1
TYPES OF NOMINATING PROCESSES

Results are reported to the county board of elections and the secretary of state.

| Convention or caucus: delegates vote for candidates or party. | Primary election: enrolled voters choose by secret ballot among two or more designated candidates. | Petition is filed, with a minimum number of signatures, as provided by law. |

| Declaration for party's support: informal designation is the result of a following among committee members and delegates. | Formal designation: petition is filed, with a minimum number of signatures, as provided by law. | Self-declaration or support by small "independent" party. |

TRADITIONAL ROUTE   **PRIMARY ROUTE**   **INDEPENDENT ROUTE**

Nomination by Primary Election. In primary elections, party members select the party's nominees directly. Primaries are the dominant method of nomination in the United States.[3]

Primary elections fall mainly into two categories: closed and open. In a closed primary, participation is limited to individuals who have declared their affiliation by registering with the party prior to the primary. In an open primary, individuals declare their affiliation on the day of the primary—they simply go to the polling place and ask for the ballot of a particular party. The open primary allows each voter an opportunity to consider candidates and issues before deciding whether to participate and in which party's contest to participate. Open primaries, therefore, are less conducive to strong political parties. But in either case, primaries are more open than conventions or caucuses to new issues and new types of candidates.

Nomination by Caucus. In several states, including Iowa and Nevada, the presidential nominating process begins with meetings, called caucuses. Registered voters are eligible to participate in the caucuses, but the nomination process consists of extensive discussions among those present, and the meetings can last several hours. At the local caucuses, those present select

closed primary

A primary election in which only those voters who registered with the party a specified period before the primary election day can participate

open primary

A primary election in which voters can choose on the primary election day which party's primary to vote in

delegates to county-level conventions, and, in turn, the county conventions select delegates to go to the state party convention. It is at the state party convention where these states elect delegates to the party's national convention.

Getting Out the Vote

The election period begins immediately after the nominations. Historically, this has been a time of glory for the political parties, whose popular base of support is fully displayed. All the paraphernalia of party committees and all the committee members are activated into local party workforces.

The first step in the electoral process involves voter registration, which takes place all year round. At one time, party workers were responsible for virtually all registration, but they have been supplemented (and in many states displaced) by civic groups such as the League of Women Voters, unions, and chambers of commerce.

Those who have registered must decide on Election Day whether to go to the polling place, stand in line, and actually vote for the various candidates and referenda on the ballot. Political parties, candidates, and campaigning can make a big difference in convincing the voters to vote. Because it is costly for voters to participate in elections (they have to take time off from work to vote or spend the time to learn about the issues and candidates) and because many of the benefits that winning parties bestow are public goods (that is, parties cannot exclude any individual from enjoying them), people will often enjoy the benefits without incurring the costs of electing the party that provided the benefits. Parties help overcome this *free-rider problem* (see Chapter 1) by mobilizing the voters to support the candidates.

In recent years, the parties themselves and not-for-profit groups have mobilized large numbers of people to vote and raised millions of dollars for election organizing and advertising. Legions of workers, often volunteers, have used new technologies to build and communicate with networks of supporters, with some groups mobilizing Democrats and others Republicans. These are the "netroots" organizations of politics. To comply with federal election and tax law, the not-for-profit groups must maintain their independence from the parties[4], although they have the same objectives and essentially act as shadow appendages of the two parties. The netroots have become integral to campaign organizations, and these new forms of direct campaigning have produced a noticeable uptick in voter turnout.

Facilitating Electoral Choice

Parties make the electoral choice much easier for voters. It is often argued that we should vote for the best person regardless of party affiliation. But on

Party labels provide a "brand name" and help voters make choices even when they are less familiar with the candidates. Voters can infer from party labels what principles and policies the candidate is likely to support.

any general-election ballot, only a handful of candidates are likely to be well known to the voters: certain candidates for president, U.S. Senate, U.S. House, and governor. As one moves down the ballot, voters' familiarity with the candidates declines. Without party labels, voters would constantly confront a bewildering array of new choices and might have difficulty making informed decisions. Without a doubt, candidates' party affiliations help voters make reasonable choices.

Parties lower the information costs of participating in elections by providing a recognizable "brand name." Without knowing much about a given candidate for office, voters can infer from party labels how the candidate will likely behave once elected. In the United States, the Democratic Party is associated with a commitment to more extensive government regulation of the economy and a larger public sector; the Republican Party favors a limited government role in the economy and reduced government spending paired with tax reductions. The Democrats favor aggressive protection of civil rights for women and for sexual and racial minorities and a secular approach to religion in public life. The Republicans generally want to ban abortion and favor government participation in expanding the role of religion in society. The parties' positions on the economy were cemented in the 1930s, and their division on social issues emerged during the 1960s and 1970s. The Democratic positions are loosely labeled liberal and those of the Republicans conservative.

Party labels also benefit politicians. By having recognizable labels, candidates in most districts and states are spared the great expense of educating voters about what they stand for. The labels "Democrat" and "Republican" are usually sufficient. The labels' content is validated because like-minded people identify with the respective organizations. People who broadly share the principles espoused by a party and who wish to participate on a high level will attend party meetings, run for leadership positions in local and state party organizations, attend state and national conventions, and even run for elected office. Each party, then, draws on a distinct pool for activists and candidates. Each successive election reinforces the division between the parties.

Influencing National Government

The two major parties are often called "big tents," meaning that they try to bring together as broad a coalition of groups and ideas as possible. Positioning themselves as broad coalitions prevents effective national third parties from emerging and guarantees that the Democrats and Republicans vie for control of Congress.

The coalitions that come together in the Democratic and Republican parties shape the parties' platforms on public policy, determining which interests and social groups align with which party and also what issues emerge. The Democratic Party today embraces a philosophy of active government intervention in the economy, based on the premise that regulation is necessary to ensure orderly economic growth, prevent the emergence of monopolies, and address certain costs of economic activity, such as pollution, poverty, and unemployment. In addition, the Democratic Party espouses protection and expansion of civil rights, especially for women and racial minorities. The Republican Party espouses a philosophy of laissez-faire economics and a minimal government role in the economy. The coalition that Ronald Reagan built in the late 1970s paired this vision of limited government intervention in the economy with an expanded role for religion in society and opposition to affirmative action, and abortion, views that continue to represent the party today (see the Policy Principle section on p. 368).

The American major parties appeal to distinctly different core constituencies. The Democratic Party at the national level seeks to unite organized labor, the poor, members of racial minorities, and liberal upper-middle-class professionals. The Republicans, by contrast, appeal to business, upper-middle- and upper-class groups in the private sector, and social conservatives. Often, party leaders seek to develop issues they hope will add new groups to their constituent base. As noted above, during the 1980s, under President Reagan, the Republicans devised a series of "social issues," including support for school prayer, opposition to abortion, and opposition to affirmative action, designed to cultivate the support of white southerners. This effort was extremely successful in increasing Republican strength in the once solidly Democratic South. In the 1990s, under President Bill Clinton, the Democratic Party sought to develop new social programs designed to solidify the party's base among working-class and poor voters, and new, somewhat conservative economic programs aimed at attracting middle- and upper-middle-class voters.

As these examples suggest, party leaders can act as policy entrepreneurs, seeking ideas and programs that will expand their party's base of support while eroding that of the opposition. Both parties, for example, have aggressively sought the support of Hispanic and Latino voters, one of the fastest growing segments of the electorate. Both President George W. Bush and President Obama supported policies to ease immigration restrictions, which are popular with Hispanic and Latino voters. It can, however, be difficult to balance appeals to a party's primary electorate and the general electorate. Throughout the 2016 presidential primary season, Donald Trump proposed restrictive immigration rules, such as building a wall along the U.S.-Mexico border, which alienated many Hispanic voters but

Party Coalitions and Abortion Policy

An anti-abortion protest in Washington, D.C., in 2016.

Political action is collective. It involves merging people's individual preferences in order to pursue some collective purpose. For interest groups, collective action is relatively straightforward: people who share a common policy goal work together to achieve that goal. For political parties, however, collective action is more complicated. Parties hope not only to achieve policy goals but also to capture public offices. In some instances, party leaders find that they must subordinate policy goals in order to enhance the party's overall electoral chances.

To complicate matters, the two major American political parties, the Republican Party and the Democratic Party, are coalitions of disparate forces and individuals who agree on some things but not on others. The Republican Party, for example, includes economic conservatives who favor lower taxes, social and religious conservatives who oppose abortion and same-sex marriage, libertarians who seek a smaller government, populists who oppose free trade policies, and a number of other factions.

Every four years, the parties write platforms summarizing their core principles and policy positions. Platforms are declarations of collective policy preferences, but the road from collective policy statement to policy action can be complex. Take the case of abortion. In 1973, the Supreme Court affirmed, in the case of *Roe v. Wade*, that women have the right to seek an abortion under the Fourteenth Amendment. Until that time, neither party had mentioned abortion in its platform, but in 1976, the first presidential election following the Court decision, both parties issued broad statements on the issue. Republicans opposed abortion but called it "a moral and personal issue," on which people might disagree.

Over time, the Republican position hardened. By 1980, the Republican platform stated that the party supported a constitutional amendment protecting "the right to life for unborn children." The 2012 and 2016 Republican Party platforms called for a constitutional amendment to overturn *Roe v. Wade*, opposed the use of public funds for abortion, demanded the prohibition of "partial birth abortion," called on the president to appoint judges who opposed abortion, and demanded an end to federal funding of embryonic stem cell research.

The Republicans' increasingly staunch opposition to abortion reflected the growing importance of social conservatives in the electorate and the recognition that the party needed their support in many districts. On the other hand, despite electing three presidents since 1980 and frequently controlling the House, the Senate, or both, Republicans in government have enacted few policies to actually bring an end to abortion.

The explanation for this apparent contradiction between principles and practices is rooted in the complexities of collective action. Antiabortion rhetoric energizes one faction of the party, but antiabortion action runs counter to the views of many other Republicans and might offend moderate and independent voters whom the party also needs at the polls. This example illustrates how engaging in successful collective action in the electoral arena may preclude collective action in the policy arena.

were supported by many Republican primary voters. At the beginning of the general election, Democratic candidate Hillary Clinton led Donald Trump by 45 percentage points among Hispanic voters. To broaden his campaign's appeal among Latinos, Trump and the Republican National Committee established the National Hispanic Advisory Council to guide their message. Nonetheless, November exit polls revealed that Clinton won 65 percent of the Latino vote compared to Trump's 29 percent.

Both parties translate their general goals into concrete policies through the members they elect to office. Republicans, for example, implemented tax cuts, increased defense spending, cut social spending, and enacted restrictions on abortion during the 1980s and 1990s. Democrats defended consumer and environmental programs against Republican attacks and sought to expand domestic social programs in the late 1990s. In 2009, President Obama and a Democratic-controlled Congress created a national health insurance system that guarantees all people access to health care, a key item on the Democratic Party's platform since the 1940s. In 2016, Democratic candidates pledged to expand national health care if elected.

PARTIES IN GOVERNMENT

Parties operate in three spheres: elections, political institutions, and government. The ultimate test of a political party is its influence on the institutions of government and the policy-making process. We begin there.

Most parties originate inside the government. Political parties form as those who support the government's actions and those who do not; in the United Kingdom, these groups are called Government and Opposition.[5] In the American context, parties vie to control both Congress and the presidency.

The Parties and Congress

The two major U.S. political parties have a profound influence on the organization and day-to-day operation of Congress. The Speaker of the House, perhaps the most powerful person in Congress, holds a party office. All House members take part in electing the Speaker, but the actual selection is made by the majority party. When the majority party caucus presents a nominee to the entire House, its choice is invariably ratified in a straight party-line vote.

The parties also organize the committee system of both houses of Congress. Although the whole membership adopts the rules organizing committees and defining the jurisdiction of each one, party leadership and caucuses shape all other features of the committees. For example, each party is assigned

majority party

The party that holds the majority of legislative seats in either the House or the Senate

a quota of members for each committee, depending on the percentage of total seats held by the party. On the rare occasions when an independent or third-party candidate is elected, the leaders of the two parties must agree against whose quota this member's committee assignments will count.

The assignment of individual members to committees is a party decision, as is the choice of who advances to committee chair. Since the late nineteenth century, most advancements have been automatic—based upon the length of continual service on the committee. This seniority system has existed only because of the support of the two parties, and either party can depart from it by a simple vote. During the 1970s, both parties reinstituted the practice of reviewing each chair—voting anew every two years on whether to continue each chair. In 2001, Republicans limited House committee chairs to three terms. Existing chairs are forced to step down but are replaced generally by the next most senior Republican member of each committee.

President and Party

The president carries the mantle of his or her party, and the electoral fortunes of the parties rise and fall with the success of the president. During midterm congressional elections, when the president is not on the ballot, voters hold the president's party accountable for current problems. When the economy does poorly, Americans punish the president's party, even when the opposing party controls Congress.

The president of the United States also relies heavily on fellow party members in organizing the executive and passing legislation. Unlike parliamentary governments, such as in the United Kingdom, the heads of executive departments are not members of the legislature. With few exceptions, heads of the departments and other key presidential appointments are people loyal to the president and his or her political party: most have served as governors of states or members of Congress or are close advisers who worked with the president in previous offices or campaigns.

The president and White House staff also work closely with congressional party leaders to shepherd legislation through Congress. With few exceptions (such as nominations and treaties), the president cannot introduce legislation and must rely on members of Congress to do so. Nearly all of the president's legislative initiatives begin as bills introduced by fellow party members in the House and Senate. The leadership of the president's party also negotiates with individual members of Congress to construct majority support for a White House–sponsored bill. Sometimes even the president will try to persuade individual legislators to support a particular bill.

The president's ability to prevail in Congress depends on which party controls the House and Senate. When the president's party enjoys majorities in both chambers, his or her legislative agenda succeeds most of the time. A typical president whose party controls the House and Senate will win more than 80 percent of the time on bills. President Obama, during his first year in office, had the highest degree of support for a president since World War II, with a majority of Congress supporting his position 96 percent of the time.[6] When another party controls at least one chamber, however, the president has a much more difficult time. In the 113th Congress (2013–2015), Democrats controlled the Senate and Republicans controlled the House. Bills supported by President Obama were passed in the Senate 93 percent of the time and in the House only 15 percent of the time.[7]

PARTIES IN THE ELECTORATE

Political parties are more than just political leaders; they comprise millions of people and organizations such as labor unions, corporations, and other interest groups. This large-scale membership helps parties organize and influence elections.

Party Identification

As we saw in Chapter 10, individual voters tend to develop party identification, a personal attachment to one of the parties. Party identification partly reflects a psychological attachment developed in childhood or adolescence and carried throughout life. But it also has a rational component, rooted in evaluations of

party identification
An individual's attachment to a particular political party, which may be based on issues, ideology, past experience, upbringing, or a mixture of these elements

the performance of the parties in government, the policies they pursue, and an individual's interests and ideology.[8] Voters generally form attachments to parties that reflect their views and interests. Once an attachment is formed, it is likely to persist and even be handed down to children unless very strong factors convince the individual to reject the party. In some sense, party identification is similar to brand loyalty in the marketplace: consumers choose a brand of automobile for its appearance or mechanical characteristics and stick with it out of loyalty, habit, and unwillingness to reexamine their choices. But they may eventually switch if the old brand no longer serves their interests.

Although the strength of partisan ties in the United States seemed to decline in the 1960s and 1970s, most Americans continue to identify with either the Republican Party or the Democratic Party (Figure 11.2). Party identification gives citizens a stake in election outcomes that goes beyond the race at hand. It is why people who identify strongly with a party are more likely than other Americans to go to the polls and, of course, to support their party. Although identification with a party does not guarantee voting for that party's candidates, "strong identifiers" do so almost always, and "weak identifiers" do so most of the time. For example, according to exit polls, 90 percent of people who called themselves Republicans said

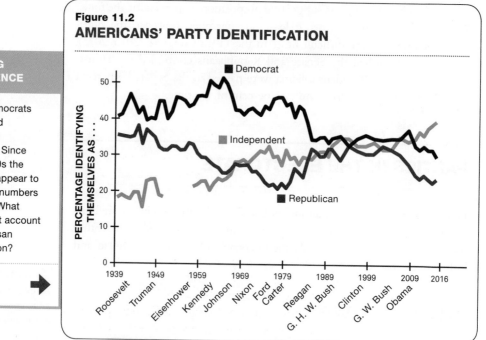

Figure 11.2
AMERICANS' PARTY IDENTIFICATION

NOTE: Independent data not available for 1951–56.
SOURCE: Pew Research Center for the People & the Press, "Trends in Party Identification," www.peoplepress.org/interactives/party-idtrend/ (accessed 6/19/15); and "Party Identification," Pew Research Center, www.pewresearch.org/data-trend/political-attitudes/party-identification/ (accessed 10/11/16).

they voted for the Republican candidate in the 2016 presidential election, and 89 percent of people who called themselves Democrats voted for the Democratic candidate.[9] Party activists are strong identifiers who not only vote but also volunteer their time and energy to party affairs. Activists ring doorbells, stuff envelopes, attend meetings, and contribute money to the party—essential work that keeps the organization going.

party activist

A partisan who contributes time and energy beyond voting to support a party and its candidates

Group Basis of Politics

One view of political parties, a pluralist view, is that they consist of coalitions of many organized groups. The leaders of organizations may choose to side with a party in an effort to influence what government does by influencing the party's policy orientation. A group can offer resources such as campaign workers, contributions, and votes; the party, in exchange, can pursue policies in line with what the group wants. Once aligned with a party, a group's leaders can then signal to members for whom they should vote. The more disciplined the group and the more resources it can offer, the more power it will have in the party. Party leaders try to build coalitions consisting of many different groups, each seeking a distinct policy or political benefit. The challenge for parties is to build coalitions that can win majorities in elections but not create too many conflicting demands.[10]

Broader social groups are also important. In the United States today, a variety of group characteristics are associated with party identification. These include race and ethnicity, gender, religion, class, region, and age.

Race and Ethnicity. Since the 1960s and Democratic support for the Civil Rights Movement, African Americans have been overwhelmingly Democratic in party identification. More than 90 percent of African Americans describe themselves as Democrats and support Democratic candidates in national, state, and local elections. Approximately 25 percent of Democratic votes in presidential races come from African American voters.

Republicans, on the other hand, depend heavily upon the support of white voters. Roughly 60 percent of the white electorate has supported the GOP in recent years. In 2016, Donald Trump appealed heavily to white working class voters on issues of trade and immigration, hoping to increase the Republican percentage of the white vote.

Latino and Hispanic voters comprise people whose ancestors came from many different countries, with disparate political orientations. Mexican Americans, the single largest group, have historically aligned with the Democratic Party, as have Puerto Ricans and Central Americans. Historically, Cuban Americans have identified and voted as Republican; recently, however, they have shifted toward the Democrats. Asian Americans have been somewhat divided as well, though more support the Democrats than the

Republicans. Japanese, Chinese, Filipino, and Korean communities have been long established in the United States and have influential business communities, and their higher-income members tend to be as Republican as higher-income whites. It is not clear whether newer Asian immigrant groups, such as the Hmong, the Vietnamese, Thais, and Indians, will follow the same trajectory as the older Asian American communities.

gender gap

A distinctive pattern of voting reflecting the differences in views between women and men

Gender. Women are somewhat more likely to support Democrats and men to support Republicans. This difference is known as the gender gap. In the 2012 election, Barack Obama won 55 percent of the women's vote and 45 percent of the men's vote, a 10-point gap. The 2016 election saw the first female presidential candidate for a major party—Democrat Hillary Clinton—which contributed to the especially large gender gap that year. Exit polls showed that Clinton won 54 percent of the women's vote and 41 percent of the men's vote, a 13-point gap.

Religion. Jews are among the Democratic Party's most loyal constituent groups and have been since the New Deal. Nearly 90 percent of all Jewish Americans describe themselves as Democrats, although the percentage is declining among younger Jews. Catholics were once a strongly pro-Democratic group as well but more conservative white Catholics have been shifting toward the Republican Party since the 1970s, when the Republicans began to focus on abortion and other social issues deemed important to Catholics. Leaders and members of more religiously conservative Protestant denominations tend to identify as Republicans, while Protestants who are religiously liberal, such as Unitarians and Episcopalians, tend to identify as Democrats. Evangelical Protestants, in particular, have been drawn to the Republicans' conservative stands on social issues, such as gay marriage and abortion. (See the Analyzing the Evidence unit on pp. 376–7 for a discussion of candidate religion and partisan voting.)

Class. Upper-income Americans are likely to affiliate with the Republicans, whereas lower-income Americans are likely to identify with the Democrats. Middle-class voters split evenly between the two parties, and this divide reflects the differences between the parties on economic issues. In general, Republicans support cutting taxes and social spending—positions that reflect the interests of the wealthy. Democrats favor increased social spending, even if this requires increasing taxes—a position consistent with the interests of less affluent Americans.

Age. Age is also associated with partisanship, mainly because individuals from the same age cohort likely experienced similar events during the period when their party loyalties were forming. Thus Americans in their sixties and seventies came of political age (that is, became aware of political issues and ideas) during the Cold War, the Vietnam War, and the civil rights movement. Apparently, voters whose initial perceptions of politics formed during these periods responded more favorably to the actions of Democrats at the time than to those of the Republicans. Among young adult Americans in their twenties and thirties who came of age during an era of political scandals that tainted both parties, most describe themselves as independents.

Figure 11.3 indicates the relationship between party identification and various social criteria. Race, religion, income, and ideology seem to have

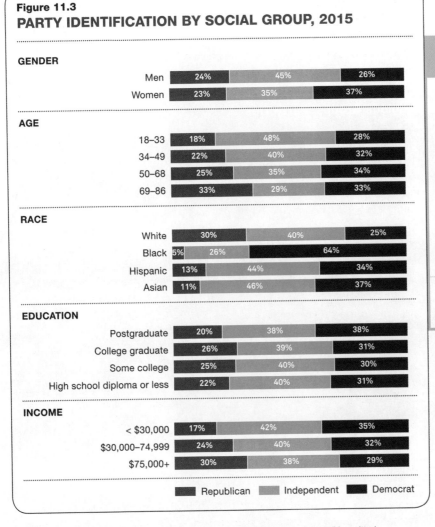

Figure 11.3

PARTY IDENTIFICATION BY SOCIAL GROUP, 2015

GENDER

	Republican	Independent	Democrat
Men	24%	45%	26%
Women	23%	35%	37%

AGE

	Republican	Independent	Democrat
18–33	18%	48%	28%
34–49	22%	40%	32%
50–68	25%	35%	34%
69–86	33%	29%	33%

RACE

	Republican	Independent	Democrat
White	30%	40%	25%
Black	5%	26%	64%
Hispanic	13%	44%	34%
Asian	11%	46%	37%

EDUCATION

	Republican	Independent	Democrat
Postgraduate	20%	38%	38%
College graduate	26%	39%	31%
Some college	25%	40%	30%
High school diploma or less	22%	40%	31%

INCOME

	Republican	Independent	Democrat
< $30,000	17%	42%	35%
$30,000–74,999	24%	40%	32%
$75,000+	30%	38%	29%

■ Republican　■ Independent　■ Democrat

NOTE: Percentages do not add to 100 because the category "Other/don't know" is omitted.
SOURCE: Pew Research Center, www.people-press.org/2015/04/07/a-deep-dive-into-party-affiliation (accessed 2/27/16).

ANALYZING THE EVIDENCE

The political parties do not draw equal support from members of each social stratum. What patterns in party identification do you see? How might these patterns influence which people are selected as political candidates by political parties and which policies the parties support?

←

Candidate Religion and Partisan Voting

Contributed by

Geoffrey C. Layman
University of Notre Dame

John C. Green
University of Akron

David E. Campbell
University of Notre Dame

Jeremiah J. Castle
University of Notre Dame

Individuals identify with a political party for many reasons, including their own social group memberships and feelings toward other social groups.[1] To what extent do the social group characteristics of political candidates affect the connection between citizens' party identifications and their support for those candidates? One important social group for many people is religion. In recent decades, the American public has come to view the Republican Party as the party of religious people and the Democratic Party as the party of nonreligious people.[2]

Public Perception of Religious Groups' Party Ties

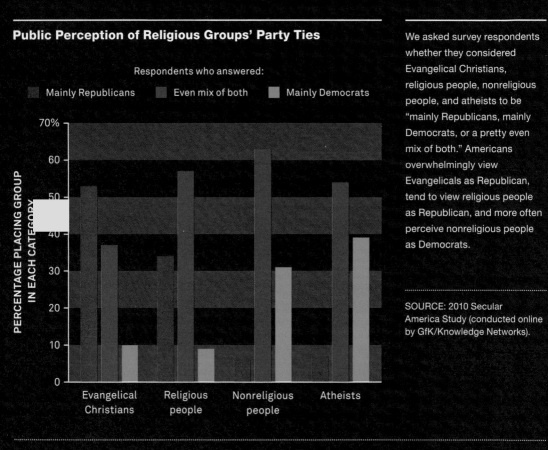

Respondents who answered:

■ Mainly Republicans   ■ Even mix of both   ■ Mainly Democrats

We asked survey respondents whether they considered Evangelical Christians, religious people, nonreligious people, and atheists to be "mainly Republicans, mainly Democrats, or a pretty even mix of both." Americans overwhelmingly view Evangelicals as Republican, tend to view religious people as Republican, and more often perceive nonreligious people as Democrats.

SOURCE: 2010 Secular America Study (conducted online by GfK/Knowledge Networks).

1 Angus Campbell, Philip E. Converse, Warren E. Miller, and Donald E. Stokes, The American Voter (Chicago: University of Chicago Press); Donald Green, Bradley Palmquist, and Eric Schickler, Partisan Hearts and Minds (New Haven, CT: Yale University Press, 2002).

2 Geoffrey Layman, The Great Divide: Religious and Cultural Conflict in American Party Politics (New York: Columbia University Press, 2001); John C. Green, The Faith Factor: How Religion Influences American Elections (Westport, CT: Praeger, 2007).

How does the public's perception of political parties' social group profiles affect the connection between individuals' party ties and their voting decisions? To find out, we presented survey respondents with descriptions of candidates that were identical except for what they said about the candidate's religion.[3] We found that the support of Republican and Democratic identifiers for the candidate changed markedly with the candidate's religious profile. Our findings suggest that because voters make assumptions about candidates' political orientations based on their social characteristics, these characteristics are quite important for electoral behavior.

The Electoral Impact of Candidate Religiosity

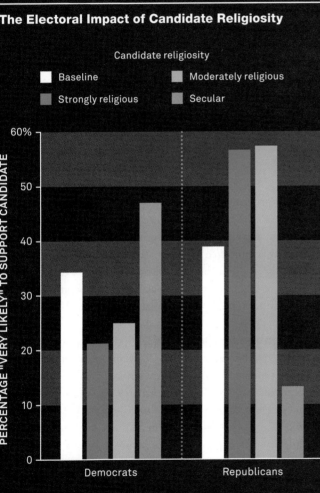

Candidate religiosity

■ Baseline ■ Moderately religious
■ Strongly religious ■ Secular

PERCENTAGE "VERY LIKELY" TO SUPPORT CANDIDATE

60%
50
40
30
20
10
0

Democrats   Republicans

RESPONDENT PARTY IDENTIFICATION

We randomly varied what we told survey respondents about the religiosity of a hypothetical state legislative candidate with a nonpartisan issue profile (focusing on goals such as good jobs, a strong economy, and efficient government) and no identified party affiliation. In the baseline (or control) condition, no mention was made of the candidate's religious orientation. When we told respondents that the candidate was moderately religious ("a man of faith") or strongly religious (a "deeply religious" person with a "personal relationship with God"), support decreased among Democrats and increased among Republicans. When we described the candidate as a secular critic of religion in public life (a "man of science" belonging to Americans United for the Separation of Church and State), support strongly increased among Democrats and strongly decreased among Republicans.

SOURCE: 2009 Cooperative Congressional Election Study (conducted online by YouGov/Polimetrix).

3 David E. Campell, John C. Green, and Geoffrey C. Layman, "The Party Faithful: Partisan Images, Candidate Religion, and the Electoral Impact of Party Identification," *American Journal of Political Science* 55, no. 1 (2011): 42–58; and Jeremiah J. Castle, Geoffrey C. Layman, David E. Campbell, and John C. Green, "Survey Experiments on Candidate Religiosity, Political Attitudes, and Vote Choice," *Journal for the Scientific Study of Religion*, forthcoming.

the greatest influence on Americans' party affiliations, although none of these characteristics is inevitably linked to partisan identification. There are, for example, union Republicans and business Democrats. The general party identifications just discussed are broad tendencies that both reflect and reinforce the issue and policy positions the two parties take in national and local political arenas. They reflect the general tendency of groups—organized and unorganized—to sort into partisan camps.

PARTIES AS INSTITUTIONS

Political parties in the United States today are not tightly disciplined, hierarchical organizations. Indeed, they never have been. Rather, they comprise extensive networks of politicians, interest groups, activists and donors, consultants, and, ultimately, voters.

Contemporary Party Organizations

The United States has party organizations at virtually every level of government (Figure 11.4). These are usually committees made up of active party members, with state law and party rules prescribing how such committees are constituted. Usually, committee members are elected at a local party meeting—a political caucus—or as part of the regular primary election. The best-known examples of these committees are the Democratic National Committee (DNC) and the Republican National Committee (RNC).

caucus (political)
A normally closed meeting of a political or legislative group to select candidates, plan strategy, or make decisions regarding legislative matters

The National Convention. At the national level, the party's most important institution is the quadrennial national convention. There delegates from all of the states nominate the party's presidential and vice-presidential candidates, draft the party's campaign platform for the presidential race, and approve changes in the rules and regulations governing party procedures. Before World War II, presidential nominations occupied most of the convention's time; the nomination process required days of negotiation and compromise among state party leaders and often many ballots before a nominee was selected. In recent years, however, presidential candidates have essentially nominated themselves by gaining enough delegate support in primary elections to win the official nomination on the first ballot. The convention itself has played little or no role in selecting the candidates.

The convention's other two tasks, establishing the party's rules and platform, remain important. Party rules can determine the relative influence

Chapter 11: Political Parties

Figure 11.4
HOW AMERICAN PARTIES ARE ORGANIZED

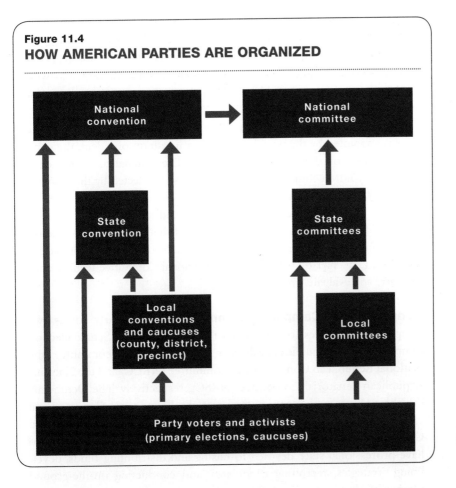

of competing factions within the party as well as the party's chances for electoral success. In the late 1970s, for example, the Democratic National Convention adopted new rules favored by the party's liberal wing, under which state delegations to the Democratic convention were required to include women and minority group members in rough proportion to those groups' representation among the party's membership in that state. The convention also approves the party platform. Platforms are often dismissed as documents filled with platitudes that voters seldom read. Furthermore, the parties' presidential candidates make little use of the platforms in their campaigns; usually they promote their own themes. Nonetheless, the platform should be understood as a "treaty" in which the various factions of the party state their terms for supporting the ticket.

The National Committee. Between conventions, each party is technically headed by its national committee: the DNC and the RNC. These committees raise campaign funds, head off factional disputes within the party, and endeavor to enhance its media image. Since 1972, the size of staff and the amount of money raised have increased substantially for both national committees. The work of each national committee is overseen by its chairperson. Other committee members are generally major party contributors or fund-raisers.

For the party that controls the White House, the national committee chair is appointed by the president. Under a first-term president, the committee focuses on the re-election campaign. The national committee chair of the party not in control of the White House is selected by the committee itself; this person usually raises money and performs other activities on behalf of the party's members in Congress and state legislatures. In the wake of Hillary Clinton's surprising defeat and the Democrats' disappointing showing in the Senate elections in 2016, the Democratic Party looked to appoint a new chair of the Democratic National Committee to help unite the party and evaluate what went wrong.

Congressional Campaign Committees. Each party forms two campaign committees to raise funds for the House and Senate election campaigns. The Republicans call their House and Senate committees the National Republican Congressional Committee (NRCC) and the National Republican Senatorial Committee (NRSC), respectively. The Democrats call their House and Senate committees the Democratic Congressional Campaign Committee (DCCC) and the Democratic Senatorial Campaign Committee (DSCC), respectively. Although these organizations also have professional staff devoted to raising and distributing funds, developing strategies, recruiting candidates, and conducting on-the-ground campaigns, they are accountable to the caucuses inside the House and Senate. The chairs of these committees come from within the respective chambers and rank high in the party leadership hierarchy. The national committees and the congressional committees are sometimes rivals. Both groups seek donations from the same pool of people but for different candidates: the national committee seeks funds primarily for the presidential race, while the congressional committees focus on House and Senate seats.

State and Local Party Organizations. Each major party has a central committee in each state. The parties traditionally also have county committees and, in some instances, state senate district committees, judicial district committees, and, in the case of larger cities, citywide party committees and local assembly district "ward" committees. Congressional districts also may have party committees.

These organizations are very active in recruiting candidates and conducting voter-registration drives. Federal law permits them to spend unlimited amounts of money on "party-building" activities such as voter-registration and get-out-the-vote drives, with the result that the national party organizations, which are restricted in how much they can spend on candidates, transfer millions of dollars to the state and local organizations. The state and local parties, in turn, spend these funds, sometimes called *soft money*, to promote national, as well as state and local, candidates. As local organizations have become linked financially to the national parties, American political

Local party organizations are important in conducting voter registration drives and getting out the vote.

parties have grown more integrated and nationalized than ever before. At the same time, the state and local party organizations came to control large financial resources and play important roles in elections despite the collapse of the old patronage machines.[11]

The Contemporary Party as Service Provider to Candidates.

Party leaders have adapted to the modern age. Parties as organizations are more professional, better financed, and more organized than ever before.[12] Political parties have evolved into "service organizations," without which it would be extremely difficult for candidates to win and hold office. For example, the national organizations of the political parties collect information, ranging from lists of likely supporters and donors in local areas to public-opinion polls in states and legislative districts, and they provide this information directly to their candidates for state and federal offices. They also have teams of experienced campaign organizers and managers who provide assistance to local candidates who are understaffed.[13]

PARTY SYSTEMS

Our understanding of political parties would be incomplete if we considered only their composition and roles. America's two major parties compete with each other for offices, policies, and power. Their struggle for control of government shapes the policies that they put forth, the coalitions of interests that they represent, and their ability, indeed the government's ability, to respond to the demands of the time. In short, the fate of each major party is inextricably linked to that of its rival.

Political scientists often call the constellation of parties that are important at any given moment a nation's party system. The most obvious feature of a party system is the number of major parties competing for power. Usually the United States has had a two-party system, meaning that only two parties have had a serious chance to win national elections. Of course, we have not always had the same two parties, and minor parties have often put forward candidates. The term *party system*, however, refers to more than just the number of parties competing for power. It also connotes the parties' organization, the balance of power between and within party coalitions, the parties' social and institutional bases, and the issues and policies around which party competition is organized.

The character of a nation's party system changes as the parties realign their electoral coalitions and alter their public philosophies. Such realignment sometimes comes subtly and sometimes suddenly. Today's American party system is very different from the system of 1950, even though the Democrats and the Republicans continue to be the major competitors (Figure 11.5). Over the course of American history, changes in political forces and alignments have produced six party systems, each with distinctive political institutions, issues, and patterns of political power and participation. Of course, some political phenomena persist across party systems—such as conflicts over the distribution of wealth, an enduring feature of American political life. But even such phenomena manifest themselves in different ways during different political eras.

The First Party System: Federalists and Democratic-Republicans

Although George Washington and many other leaders of the time deplored partisan politics, the two-party system emerged early in the history of the new Republic. Competition in Congress between northeastern mercantile and southern agrarian factions led Alexander Hamilton and the northeasterners to form a voting bloc within Congress. The southerners, led by Thomas Jefferson and James Madison, responded by cultivating a popular following to change the balance of power within Congress. The result of this regional rivalry was the birth of America's first national parties—the Democratic-Republicans, whose primary base was in the South, and the Federalists, whose strength was greatest in New England. The Federalists supported protective tariffs to encourage manufacturers, the assumption by the federal government of responsibility for the states' Revolutionary War

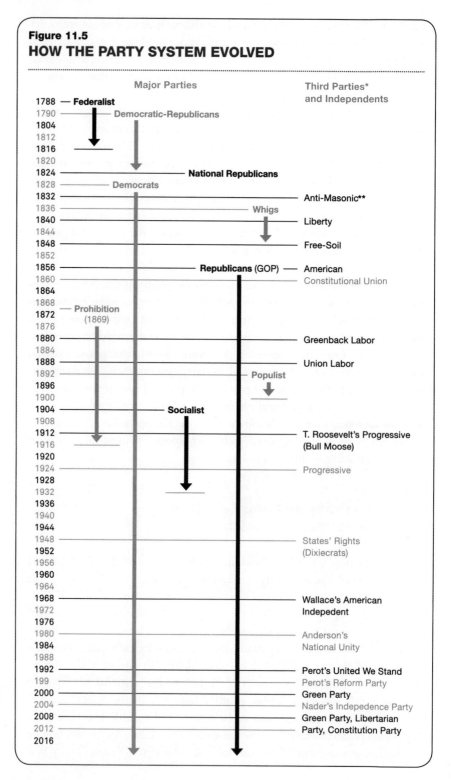

Figure 11.5
HOW THE PARTY SYSTEM EVOLVED

Major Parties

Third Parties*
and Independents

1788	Federalist
1790	Democratic-Republicans
1804	
1812	
1816	
1820	
1824	National Republicans
1828	Democrats
1832	Anti-Masonic**
1836	Whigs
1840	Liberty
1844	
1848	Free-Soil
1852	
1856	Republicans (GOP) — American
1860	Constitutional Union
1864	
1868	
1872	Prohibition (1869)
1876	
1880	Greenback Labor
1884	
1888	Union Labor
1892	Populist
1896	
1900	
1904	Socialist
1908	
1912	T. Roosevelt's Progressive (Bull Moose)
1916	
1920	
1924	Progressive
1928	
1932	
1936	
1940	
1944	
1948	States' Rights (Dixiecrats)
1952	
1956	
1960	
1964	
1968	Wallace's American Indepedent
1972	
1976	
1980	Anderson's National Unity
1984	
1988	
1992	Perot's United We Stand
199	Perot's Reform Party
2000	Green Party
2004	Nader's Indepedence Party
2008	Green Party, Libertarian
2012	Party, Constitution Party
2016	

*In some cases, there was even a fourth party. Most of the parties listed here existed for only one term.

**The Anti-Masonics not only had the distinction of being the first third party but also were the first party to hold a national nominating convention and the first to announce a party platform.

debts, the creation of a national bank, and resumption of commercial ties with England. The Democratic-Republicans opposed these policies, favoring instead free trade, the promotion of agrarian over commercial interests, and friendship with France.

The rationale behind the formation of both parties was primarily that they would create stable voting blocs within Congress around cohesive policy agendas. Although the Federalists and the Democratic-Republicans competed in elections, their ties to the electorate were loose. In 1800, the American electorate was small, and voters generally followed the lead of local political, religious, and social leaders. Nominations were informal, without rules or regulations. Local party leaders would simply gather and agree on the person, usually one of them, who would be the candidate. Meetings where candidates were nominated were called caucuses. In this era, before the secret ballot, many voters were reluctant to defy influential members of their community by publicly voting against them. In this context, the Democratic-Republicans and the Federalists organized political clubs and developed newspapers and newsletters to mobilize elite opinion and draw in more followers. In the election of 1800, Jefferson defeated the incumbent Federalist president, John Adams, and led his party to power. The Federalists continued to weaken and finally disappeared after the pro-British sympathies of some Federalist leaders during the War of 1812 led to charges that the party was guilty of treason.

The Second Party System: Democrats and Whigs

From the collapse of the Federalists until the 1830s, America had only one political party, the Democratic-Republicans. This period of one-party politics is sometimes known as the Era of Good Feeling, to indicate the absence of party competition. Throughout this period, however, there was intense factional conflict within the Democratic-Republican Party, particularly between supporters and opponents of General Andrew Jackson, America's great military hero of the War of 1812. Jackson, one of five significant candidates for president in 1824, won the most popular and electoral votes but a majority of neither, throwing the election into the House of Representatives. His opponents united to deny him the presidency, but he won in 1828 and again in 1832.

Jackson was greatly admired by millions of ordinary Americans living on farms and in villages, and the Jacksonians made the most of the general's appeal to the common people. To bring growing numbers of voters to the polls, the Jacksonians built political clubs and held mass rallies and parades, laying the groundwork for a new and more popular politics. Jackson's vice president and eventual successor, Martin Van Buren, was the organizational genius behind the Jacksonian movement, establishing a central party committee, state party organizations, and party newspapers. In response to complaints about cliques of party leaders dominating the nominations at caucuses, the Jacksonians also established state and national party conventions as the forums for nominating presidential candidates. The conventions gave control of the presidential nominating process to the new state party organizations that the Jacksonians had created and expected to control.

The Jacksonians, whose party became known as the Democratic Party, were not without opponents, however, especially in New England. During the 1830s, groups opposing Jackson for reasons of personality and politics united to form the Whig Party, thus giving rise to the second American party system. During the 1830s and 1840s, the Democrats and the Whigs built party organizations throughout the nation and sought to enlarge their support by eliminating property restrictions and other barriers to voting—although voting was still limited to white men. Support for the Whigs was strongest in the Northeast and among mercantile groups; hence to some extent they were the successors of the Federalists. Many Whigs favored a national bank, a protective tariff, and federally sponsored internal improvements. The Jacksonians opposed all three policies. In 1840, the Whigs won their first presidential election under the leadership of General William Henry Harrison, a military hero. The election marked the first time in American history that two parties competed for the presidency in every state in the Union.

In the late 1840s and early 1850s, conflicts over slavery produced sharp divisions within both parties, despite party leaders' efforts to develop compromises that would bridge the widening gulf between North and South. By 1856, the Whig Party had all but disintegrated under the strain. The Kansas-Nebraska Act of 1854 gave each western territory the right to decide whether to permit slavery. Opposition to this policy led to the formation of a number of antislavery parties, with the Republicans emerging as the strongest.[14] In 1856, the party's first presidential candidate won one-third of the popular vote and carried 11 states.

The early Republican platforms appealed to commercial as well as antislavery interests. The Republicans favored homesteading, internal improvements, construction of a transcontinental railroad, and protective tariffs, as well as containment of slavery. In 1858, the party won control of the House of Representatives; in 1860, the Republican presidential candidate, Abraham Lincoln, was victorious. Lincoln's victory strengthened southern calls for secession from the Union and soon led to civil war.

The Third Party System: Republicans and Democrats, 1860–96

During the war, President Lincoln depended heavily on Republican governors and state legislatures to raise troops, provide funding, and maintain popular support for a long and bloody conflict. The South's secession had stripped the Democratic Party of many of its leaders and supporters, but it nevertheless remained politically competitive and nearly won the 1864 presidential election due to war weariness on the part of the northern public. With the defeat of the Confederacy in 1865, some congressional Republicans sought to convert the South into a Republican bastion through Reconstruction, a program that enfranchised newly freed slaves and provided federal funds for economic recovery and infrastructure rebuilding while disenfranchising many white Democratic voters and disqualifying many white Democratic politicians from seeking office. Reconstruction collapsed in the 1870s as a result of divisions within Republicans in Congress and violent resistance by southern whites.

With the end of Reconstruction, the former Confederate states regained full membership in the Union and full control of their internal affairs. Throughout the South, African Americans were deprived of political rights, including the right to vote, despite post–Civil War constitutional guarantees to the contrary. The postwar South was solidly Democratic, enabling the national Democratic Party to confront the Republicans on a more or less equal basis. From the end of the Civil War to the 1890s, the Republican Party remained the party of the North, with strong business and middle-class support, while the Democratic Party was the party of the South, with support from working-class and immigrant groups in the North.

The Fourth Party System, 1896–1932

During the 1890s, profound social and economic changes led to the emergence of a variety of protest parties, including the Populist Party, which won the support of hundreds of thousands of voters in the South and West. The Populists appealed mainly to small farmers but also attracted western miners and urban workers. In 1892, the party carried four states in the presidential election and elected governors in eight states. In 1896, the Democrats in effect adopted the Populist platform and nominated William Jennings Bryan, a Democratic senator with Populist sympathies, for the presidency. The Republicans nominated the conservative senator William McKinley. In the ensuing campaign, northern and midwestern business interests made an all-out effort to defeat what they saw as a radical threat from the Populist-Democratic alliance. When the dust settled, the Republicans had won a resounding victory. In large urban areas, especially in the Northeast and upper Midwest, workers became convinced that Populist-Democratic policies would threaten the industries that provided their jobs, while immigrants feared the nativist rhetoric of some Populist orators and writers. The Republicans carried the northeastern and midwestern states and confined the Democrats to their bastions in the South and the Far West. For the next

36 years, the Republicans were the nation's majority party, very much the party of business, advocating low taxes, high tariffs, and minimal government regulation. The Democrats were too weak to offer much opposition. Southern Democrats, moreover, were more concerned with maintaining the region's autonomy on issues of race than with challenging the Republicans on other fronts.

The Fifth Party System: The New Deal Coalition, 1932–68

Soon after the Republican candidate Herbert Hoover won the 1928 presidential election, the nation's economy collapsed. The Great Depression produced economic hardship on a scale never seen before in the United States, and millions of Americans blamed the Republican Party for not doing enough to promote recovery. In 1932, voters elected Franklin Delano Roosevelt and a solidly Democratic Congress. Roosevelt's program for economic recovery, the New Deal, led to substantial increases in the size and reach of the national government, which took responsibility for economic management and social welfare to an extent unprecedented in American history. Roosevelt designed many of his programs specifically to expand the Democratic Party's political base. He rebuilt the party around a nucleus of unionized workers, upper-middle-class intellectuals and professionals, southern farmers, Jews, Catholics, and northern African Americans (few blacks in the South could vote), making the Democrats the nation's majority party for 36 years. Republicans groped for a response to the New Deal but often wound up supporting its popular programs, such as Social Security, in what was sometimes derided as "me-too" Republicanism.

The New Deal coalition was severely strained during the 1960s by conflicts over President Lyndon Johnson's Great Society initiative, the African-American civil rights movement, and the Vietnam War. A number of Great Society programs, targeting poverty and racial discrimination, involved the empowerment of local groups that were often at odds with city and county governments. These programs touched off battles between local Democratic political machines and the Johnson administration that split the Democratic coalition. For its part, the struggle over civil rights initially divided northern Democrats, who supported the movement, from white southern Democrats, who defended racial segregation. Subsequently, as the movement launched a northern campaign seeking access to jobs and education and an end to racial discrimination in such realms as housing, northern Democrats also split, with blue-collar workers increasingly tending to vote Republican. The Vietnam War divided the Democrats still further, with liberals opposing Johnson's decision to send U.S. forces to Southeast Asia. These schisms within the Democratic Party provided an opportunity for the Republicans to return to power, which they did in 1968 under Richard Nixon.

The Sixth Party System, 1968–Present

By the 1960s, conservative Republicans, arguing that "me-tooism" was a recipe for continual failure, set out to reposition the party as a genuine alternative to the Democrats. In 1964, Republican presidential candidate Barry Goldwater, author of a book titled *The Conscience of a Conservative*, called for much lower levels of taxation and spending, less government regulation of the economy, and the elimination of many federal social programs. Although Goldwater lost to Johnson, the ideas he espoused continue to be major themes of the Republican Party.

It took Richard Nixon's "southern strategy" to end Democratic dominance of the political process. Beginning with his successful 1968 presidential campaign, Nixon appealed to disaffected white southerners, promising to reduce federal support for school integration and voting rights. With the help of the independent candidacy of former Alabama governor George Wallace, Nixon sparked the voter shift that eventually gave the once-hated "party of Lincoln" a strong position in all the states of the former Confederacy. In the 1980s, under President Ronald Reagan, Republicans added another important group to their coalition: religious conservatives offended by Democratic support of abortion rights as well as alleged Democratic disdain for traditional cultural and religious values.

While Republicans built a political base with economic and social conservatives and white southerners, the Democratic Party maintained support among unionized workers and upper-middle-class intellectuals and professionals. Democrats also appealed strongly to racial minorities. The 1965 Voting Rights Act had greatly increased the participation of black voters in the South and helped the Democratic Party retain some congressional and Senate seats there. And while the Republicans appealed to social conservatives, the Democrats appealed to voters favoring abortion rights, LGBTQ rights, feminism, environmentalism, and other progressive social causes. The results have been something of a draw. Democrats have won the presidency 5 out of 13 elections since the passage of the Voting Rights Act and held at least one chamber of Congress for most of that time. That apparent stalemate masked dramatic changes in the parties' regional bases. Republicans surged in the South but lost ground in the Northeast. New England, once the bedrock of the Republican Party, had only one Republican U.S. House member (of 22 seats) after the 2016 election.

The electoral realignment that began in 1968 laid the foundations for the political polarization that has come to characterize contemporary politics.

The most recent party system was initiated by the shift of Southern Democrats to the Republican Party. The 1968 campaigns of Republican Richard Nixon and Independent Alabama governor George Wallace (right) appealed to disaffected white southerners, cementing this shift.

As southern Democrats and northeastern Republicans faded, the two parties lost their moderate wings. Southern White Democrats had tended to come from rural areas; they were socially conservative but strongly aligned with the New Deal. As the rural population in the South declined, and the suburbs grew beginning in the 1970s, these Southern Democrats were replaced by suburban Republicans whose constituents are much more economically conservative than their predecessors. The opposite dynamic was at work in the North. Republicans in places like New York and New England tended to be socially moderate and fiscally conservative. Social and political shifts in the northeastern states marginalized the Republican Party and led to the emergence of a strong liberal faction within the Democratic Party. As a result, the moderate wings of both parties were substantially reduced, leaving Congress with a void among its moderate ranks and with a more polarized political alignment.

As each political party became ideologically more homogeneous after the 1980s—today there are few liberal Republicans or conservative Democrats—party loyalty in Congress, which had been weak between the 1950s and the 1970s, witnessed a dramatic resurgence. A simple measure of party coherence developed by Professor Stuart Rice in the 1920s and tracked by *Congressional Quarterly* since the 1950s is the party unity score: the percentage of bills on which a majority of one party votes against a majority of the other party. Between the 1950s and the 1970s, unity hovered around 70 percent. Since the 1980s it has regularly exceeded 90 percent.[15]

American Third Parties

Although the United States is said to possess a two-party system, we have always had more than two parties. Typically, third parties in this country have represented social and economic protests that were not given voice by the two major parties.[16] Such parties have significantly influenced ideas and elections. The Populists, centered in rural areas of the West and the Midwest during the late nineteenth century, and the Progressives, representing the urban middle classes in the late nineteenth and early twentieth centuries,

Table 11.1

PARTIES AND CANDIDATES, 2016*

CANDIDATE	PARTY	VOTE TOTAL	PERCENT OF VOTE
Donald Trump	Republican	62,679,259	46.16
Hillary Clinton	Democrat	65,224,847	48.03
Gary Johnson	Libertarian	4,460,030	3.28
Jill Stein	Green	1,432,077	1.05
Evan McMullin	Independent	620,384	0.46
Darrell Castle	Constitution	197,431	0.15
Gloria LaRiva	Socialism and Liberation	72,385	0.05
Rocky de la Fuente	American Delta	33,103	0.02
Others		138,477	0.10

*As of December 2, 2016.
SOURCE: "2016 Presidential General Election Results," U.S. Election Atlas, www.uselectionatlas.org/RESULTS/national.php?year=2016&minper=0&f=0&off=0&elect=0 (accessed 12/2/16).

are important examples. More recently, Ross Perot, who ran for president in 1992 and 1996 as an Independent fiscal conservative, garnered almost 19 percent of the votes in 1992.

The timeplot on pp. 392–5 shows that while in the past, third parties have won entire states, the Democratic and Republican Parties have dominated the electoral map in recent decades. Table 11.1 lists all the parties that offered candidates in one or more states in the presidential election of 2016. The third-party and independent candidates together polled about 6.95 million votes, but they gained no electoral votes for president. Third-party candidacies also arise at the state and local levels. In New York, the Conservative party has been on the ballot for decades, though it generally endorses the Republican candidates. Vermont senator Bernie Sanders is an Independent who caucuses with the Democratic party in the Senate. In 2016, Sanders campaigned for the Democratic presidential nomination.

Although it is difficult for third parties to survive, it is worth noting that the two major parties today themselves started as third parties. As we

Parties' Share of Electoral Votes, 1789–2016

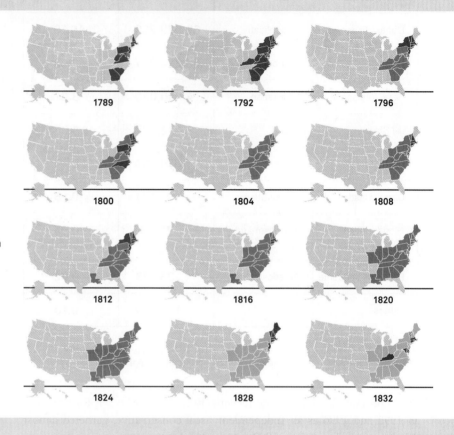

- ■ Federalist
- ▨ Anti-Federalist*
- ■ Democratic-Republican
- ■ Democratic
- ■ National Republican
- ▨ Anti-Masonic
- ■ Independent
- ▨ Whig
- ■ Republican
- ■ American
- ▨ Constitutional Union
- ▨ People's
- ▨ Democrat-Populist

1789 1792 1796

1800 1804 1808

1812 1816 1820

1824 1828 1832

have seen, the Democrats emerged as an alternative to the Federalists and their opponents, loosely, the Antifederalists. The Federalist Party itself gave way to the Whig Party, which was replaced by the Republicans. In some sense, then, the two major parties today started as alternatives to existing parties, and they have reinvented themselves ideologically to change with the times and to co-opt supporters of emerging parties. The Democratic Party, for example, became more liberal when it adopted most of the Progressive program early in the twentieth century. In the 1930s, many socialists felt that Roosevelt's New Deal had adopted most of their party's program, including old-age pensions, unemployment compensation, an agricultural marketing program, and laws guaranteeing workers the right to organize into unions.

(continued on next page)

The major parties' ability to evolve largely explains the short lives of third parties, whose causes are usually eliminated as the major parties absorb their programs and draw their supporters into the mainstream. An additional reason for the short duration of most third parties is the typical limitation of their electoral support to one or two regions. Populist support, for example, was primarily western and midwestern; the 1948 Progressive Party drew nearly half its votes from New York State; the 1968 American Independent Party, which won the most electoral votes ever polled by a third-party candidate (George Wallace), primarily represented the Deep South. Moreover, voters usually assume that only the candidates nominated by the two major parties have any chance of winning and thus that a vote cast for a third-party or an independent candidate is wasted. For instance, in the 2000

Parties' Share of Electoral Votes, 1789–2016

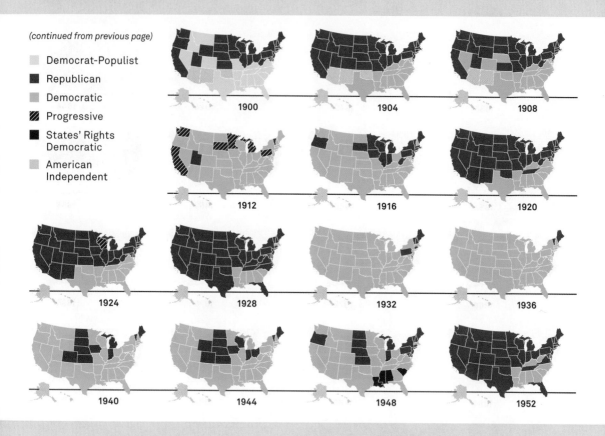

(continued from previous page)

Democrat-Populist
Republican
Democratic
Progressive
States' Rights Democratic
American Independent

1900 1904 1908

1912 1916 1920

1924 1928 1932 1936

1940 1944 1948 1952

race between Al Gore, the Democrat, and George W. Bush, the Republican, the third-party candidate Ralph Nader did better in states where either Bush or Gore was nearly certain of winning and worse in more closely contested states. Third-party candidates must struggle—usually without success—to overcome the perception that they cannot win.

Third-party prospects are also hampered by the United States' single-member-district plurality election system. In many other nations, several individuals are elected to represent each legislative district. With this system of multiple-member districts, weaker parties' candidates have a better chance of winning at least some seats. For their part, voters are less concerned about wasting ballots and usually more willing than Americans to support minor-party candidates.

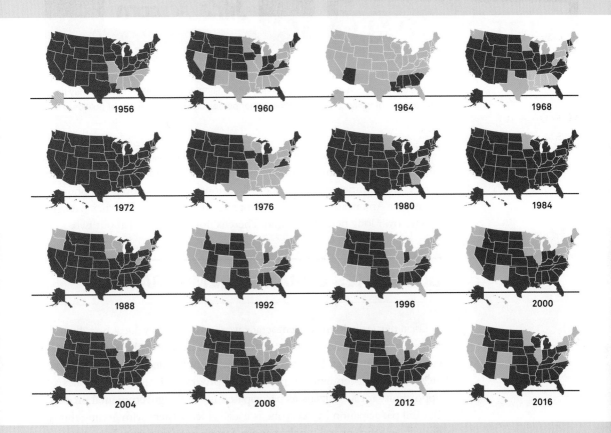

Reinforcing the effects of the single-member district (as noted in Chapter 10), plurality-voting rules generally have the effect of setting a high threshold for victory. To win a plurality race, candidates usually must secure many more votes than they would need under most European systems of proportional representation. For example, to win an American plurality election in a single-member district with only two candidates, a politician must win more than 50 percent of the votes cast. To win a seat in a European multimember district under proportional-representation rules, a candidate may need only 15 or 20 percent of the votes. This high threshold in American elections encourages political factions that might otherwise form minor parties to minimize their differences and remain within the major-party coalitions.[17]

In 2016, candidates from numerous third parties ran for president, including the Libertarian Party's Gary Johnson (left) and the Green Party's Jill Stein (right). Although they may have little chance of winning national office, minor parties can influence national politics.

It would nevertheless be incorrect to assert (as some scholars have) that America's single-member plurality election system guarantees that only two parties will compete for power in all regions of the country. All one can say is that American election law depresses the number of parties likely to survive over long periods of time. There is nothing magical about two.

DO PARTIES ENHANCE DEMOCRACY?

Political parties help make democracy work. Americans value a broadly participatory democracy and an effective government, but these are often at odds with each other. Effective government implies decisive action and the creation of well-thought-out policies and programs. Democracy implies an opportunity for all citizens to participate fully in the governmental process. But full participation by everyone is usually inconsistent with getting things done in an efficient and timely manner. Strong political parties help America balance the ideals of democracy and efficiency in government They can both encourage popular involvement and convert participation into effective government. However, as we have seen, the parties' struggle for political advantage can also lead to the type of intense partisanship that cripples the government's ability to operate efficiently and in the nation's best interest.

Parties also simplify the electoral process. They set the electoral agenda through party platforms, recruit candidates, accumulate and distribute campaign resources, and register and mobilize people to vote. Party control of the nominating process and the pressures toward two-party politics in the United States mean that most voters must decide between just two choices in any election. Parties thus facilitate voters' decision making. Voters can reasonably expect what sorts of policies a candidate with a party's endorsement will pursue if elected. Even before a candidate has been nominated, most voters have already determined themselves to be Democratic or Republican and know for whom they will vote. This binary simplification of politics reduces our society's many complex interests to just two competing teams, whose platforms must accommodate the many subtle differences or ideological nuances among groups inside the party. It further reduces politics into warring factions that have little hope of finding common ground. However, the two-party system does give meaning to the vote. It empowers the voter to say "I want to stay the course with the party in power" or "I want to go in a new direction."

For Further Reading

Aldrich, John H. *Why Parties? A Second Look.* Chicago: University of Chicago Press, 2011.

Campbell, Angus, Philip E. Converse, Warren E. Miller, and Donald E. Stokes. *The American Voter.* Chicago: University of Chicago Press, 1980.

Chambers, William N., and Walter Dean Burnham, eds. *The American Party Systems: Stages of Political Development.* 2nd ed. New York: Oxford University Press, 1975.

Cox, Gary W., and Mathew D. McCubbins. *Legislative Leviathan: Party Government in the House.* Berkeley: University of California Press, 1993.

Cox, Gary W., and Mathew D. McCubbins. *Setting the Agenda: Responsible Party Government in the U.S. House of Representatives.* New York: Cambridge University Press, 2005.

Hershey, Marjorie R. *Party Politics in America.* 15th ed. New York: Pearson, 2013.

Hofstadter, Richard. *The Idea of a Party System: The Rise of Legitimate Opposition in the United States, 1780–1840.* Berkeley: University of California Press, 1969.

Levendusky, Matthew. *The Partisan Sort.* Chicago: University of Chicago Press, 2009.

Mayhew, David. *Electoral Realignments: A Critique of an American Genre.* New Haven, CT: Yale University Press, 2007.

Miller, Gary, and Norman Schofield. "The Transformation of the Republican and Democratic Party Coalitions in the U.S." *Perspectives on Politics* (September 2008): 433–50.

12

Groups and Interests

Democratic politics in the United States does not end with elections. Federal, state, and local governments provide many additional avenues through which individuals and organizations can express their preferences. People may, for example, contact elected officials, their staffs, and bureaucrats directly about a particular decision or problem. They may participate in public meetings about legislation or administrative rulings; some private citizens are even selected to serve on special government commissions because of their expertise or particular concerns. They may file lawsuits to request that a government agency take a particular action or to prevent it from doing so. They may express their opinions through the Internet, in newspapers, on television, or through other venues, and hold public protests. Individuals, organizations, and even governments make frequent use of these many points of access. Many of such encounters are temporary one-time events, as when someone contacts an agency to solve a particular problem. But much political activity in the United States occurs through enduring, organized efforts that bring many individuals into collective action to seek a common goal.

Americans often worry about the power of so-called special interests. Many believe that organized groups following self-seeking agendas dominate government and policy-making; the late Senator Edward Kennedy once said that Americans feel they have the "best Congress money can buy." Certainly a good deal of what Americans see and read about their nation's politics seems to confirm this pessimistic view. For example, after spending millions in campaign contributions and payments to lobbyists, corporations succeeded in having Congress enact legislation that allowed them to sharply cut their required contributions to their employees' pension funds. The savings to major corporations amounted to nearly $160 billion between 2006 and 2009.[1] Similarly, the health care reform program enacted in 2010 contains many provisions to benefit insurance and pharmaceutical companies that lobbied relentlessly for their inclusion.

Most of the time, elected officials have every incentive to pay a good deal of attention to the organized interests that fund their campaigns and far less attention to mere voters. Politicians follow the political golden rule: those who have the gold make the rules.[2] Often enough, voters are not aware that their elected officials are giving them the short end of the stick. How many voters understand the intricacies of the laws governing taxation of profits earned abroad or energy tax credits or Medicare reimbursement rates? In such matters, politicians can serve corporate interests without even considering ordinary citizens, most of whom can safely be assumed to have no views on these topics. But even on matters that many citizens do care about, such as taxes, jobs, and energy costs, politicians will often still follow the golden rule.

The framers of the Constitution foresaw the power that organized interests could wield and feared that the public good would be "disregarded in the conflict of rival [factions]."[3] Yet they recognized that interest groups thrived because of the freedom that all Americans enjoyed to organize and express their views. To the framers, this problem presented a dilemma: If

CORE OF THE ANALYSIS

➡ Interest groups are organized to influence government decisions.

➡ Most interest groups are organized by those segments of society with more education or economic resources and those most directly affected by government actions, especially corporations.

➡ Interest groups use various strategies to promote their goals, including lobbying, using the courts, shaping public opinion, and influencing electoral politics.

the government had the power to regulate or forbid efforts by organized interests to interfere in the political process, it would in effect have the power to suppress freedom. James Madison suggested a solution to this dilemma:

> . . . Take in a greater variety of parties and interest [and] you make it less probable that a majority of the whole will have a common motive to invade the rights of other citizens. . . . [Hence the advantage] enjoyed by a large over a small republic.[4]

According to Madison's theory, a good constitution encourages multitudes of interests so that no single interest can ever tyrannize the others. The assumption is that competition will produce balance and compromise, with all the interests regulating one another.[5] Today, this principle of regulation is called pluralism.

There are tens of thousands of organized groups in the United States competing to influence government, but not all interests are fully and equally represented in the American political process. The political deck is heavily stacked in favor of those able to wield substantial economic, social, and institutional resources on behalf of their cause. Thus, within the universe of interest group politics, it is political power—not some abstract conception of the public good—that is likely to prevail. Moreover, interest group politics, as a whole, works to the advantage of some types of interests more than others. In general, a politics in which interest groups predominate is a politics with a distinctly upper-class bias.

In this chapter, we examine interest group politics in the United States. We analyze the group basis of politics, the challenges groups face in getting individuals to act collectively, and some solutions to these problems. We discuss the character and balance of the interests promoted through the pluralistic American political system and the tremendous growth of interest groups in number, resources, and activity in recent decades. Finally, we examine the strategies that groups use to influence politics and whether their influence has become excessive.

pluralism

The theory that all interests are and should be free to compete for influence in the government. The outcome of this competition is compromise and moderation.

THE CHARACTERISTICS OF INTEREST GROUPS

interest group

An organized group of people that makes policy-related appeals to government

An interest group is an organized group of people that attempts to shape public policies. Individuals form groups to increase the chance that their views will be heard and their interests treated favorably by government. Interest groups are sometimes referred to as lobbies.

Interest groups are sometimes confused with political action committees (see Chapter 10). The difference is that PACs focus on electing officials, whereas interest groups focus on influencing officials. Interest groups also differ from political parties: interest groups concern themselves more with the policies of government, whereas parties concern themselves more with the personnel of government.

Enhancing Democracy

There are an enormous number of interest groups in the United States, and millions of Americans are members of one or more, at least to the extent of paying dues or attending an occasional meeting. By representing the interests of such large numbers of people and encouraging political participation, organized groups enhance American democracy. They educate their members about issues that affect them, lobby members of Congress and the executive branch, mobilize their own members for elections and grassroots lobbying, engage in litigation, and generally represent their members' interests in the political arena. Interest groups also monitor government programs to ensure that they do not adversely affect members. In all these ways, organized interests can be said to promote democratic politics. But because not all interests are represented equally, interest group politics works to the advantage of some and the disadvantage of others.

lobbying

An attempt by a group to influence the policy process through persuasion of government officials

What Interests Are Represented

When most people think about interest groups, they immediately think of groups with a direct economic interest in governmental actions (Table 12.1). These groups are generally supported by producers or manufacturers in a particular economic sector, such as the American Fuel & Petrochemical Manufacturers, the American Farm Bureau Federation, and the National Federation of Independent Business, which represents small business owners. At the same time that broadly representative groups such as these are active in Washington, specific companies—such as Disney, Shell Oil, IBM, and Microsoft—may be active on issues of particular concern to themselves.

Labor organizations, although fewer in number and more limited in financial resources, are extremely active lobbyists. The AFL-CIO, the United Mine Workers, and the Teamsters' union are all groups that lobby on behalf of organized labor. More recently, lobbies have arisen to further the interests of public employees, the most significant being the American Federation of State, County, and Municipal Employees (AFSCME).

Table 12.1

WHO IS REPRESENTED BY ORGANIZED INTERESTS?

WORKFORCE STATUS OF THE INDIVIDUAL	U.S. ADULTS (%)	ORGS. (%)	TYPE OF ORG. IN WASHINGTON	RATIO: % OF ORGS. TO % OF ADULTS
Executives	8.5	70.3	Business association	8.27
Professionals	13	23.7	Professional association	1.82
White collar workers	14	1.1	White collar union	0.08
Blue collar workers	22.2	.4	Blue collar union	0.02
Farm workers	.9	1.6	Agricultural workers' organization	1.78
Unemployed	6.2	1.7	Unemployment organization	0.27
Not in workforce	35.3	1.2	Senior citizens organization, organization for the handicapped, educational organization	.03

SOURCE: Kay Lehman Schlozman, Sidney Verba and Henry E. Brady. *The Unheavenly Chorus: Unequal Voice and the Broken Promise of American Democracy.* (Princeton, NJ: Princeton University Press, 2012), 329. Updated data supplied by Schlozman, Verba, and Brady.

Professional lobbies such as the American Bar Association and the American Medical Association have been particularly successful in furthering their own interests in state and federal legislatures. The "gun lobby," comprising firearms manufacturers and dealers as well as gun owners, is represented by the National Rifle Association (NRA). The NRA mobilized furiously to thwart gun control efforts introduced in Congress in the wake of several mass shootings including a 2016 shooting at a nightclub in Orlando, Florida, that left 50 people dead. Financial institutions, represented by organizations such as the American Bankers Association and the National Savings & Loan League, are also important in shaping legislative policy.

Recent decades have witnessed the growth of a powerful "public interest" lobby purporting to represent concerns not addressed by traditional lobbies. These groups have been most visible in consumer protection and environmental policy, although public interest groups cover a broad range of issues, from nuclear disarmament to civil rights to abortion. Examples include the National Resources Defense Council, the Union of Concerned Scientists, the National Association for the Advancement of Colored People, the Christian Coalition of America, and Common Cause.

The perceived need for representation on Capitol Hill has also generated a public-sector lobby, including the National League of Cities and a "research" lobby. The latter group comprises universities and other institutions, such as the Brookings Institution and the American Enterprise Institute, that seek government funds for research and support. Indeed, many universities have expanded their lobbying efforts even as they have reduced faculty positions and course offerings and increased tuition.[6] Even with the large increase in interest groups, most organizations involved in politics in Washington, D.C., and in the state capitals still represent economic interests. The Policy Principle section on p. 404 gives an example of how the National Association of Realtors and other groups have successfully opposed any changes to the mortgage interest tax deduction, a policy that is in their own economic interests even though it is not in the interest of most homeowners.

The "Free Rider" Problem

Whether organizations need individuals to volunteer or merely to send money, all must recruit and retain members. Yet many groups find this task difficult, even with regard to those who agree strongly with the group's goals. The reason, as the economist Mancur Olson explains, is that the benefits of a group's success are often broadly available and cannot be denied to nonmembers.[7] Such benefits are called collective goods. This term is usually associated with certain government benefits, but it can also be applied to beneficial outcomes of interest group activity.

To follow Olson's theory, suppose a number of private property owners live near a mosquito-infested swamp. Each owner wants the swamp cleared. But if one or a few of the owners were to clear the swamp alone, their actions would benefit all the other owners as well, without any effort on the part of those other owners. Each of the inactive owners would be

The Mortgage Interest Tax Deduction

A home for sale in Durham, North Carolina.

When individuals and groups form coalitions to engage in political action, players may not have equal access to information. Interest groups, for example, are generally better informed than individuals and are thus better able to benefit from collective action in the political arena. Individuals who are poorly informed may find themselves acting in a manner inconsistent with their interests. Take the case of the mortgage tax credit.

Under current U.S. tax law, individuals who file itemized personal income tax returns may deduct the interest on as much as $1 million in mortgage indebtedness plus the interest on another $100,000 in home equity loans. Though the average deduction is only about $1,680 for homeowners who itemize, this law can result in thousands of dollars in savings for an upper-bracket taxpayer with a large mortgage. A family with a $1 million mortgage, for example, currently realizes an average annual tax savings of about $21,000 per year.

Proponents of the mortgage interest tax deduction argue that its chief purpose is to encourage home ownership, which they believe gives people a stake in the community and the nation, making them better neighbors and citizens. However, nearly 80 percent of the benefits provided by the mortgage-interest deduction and other housing tax credits accrue to the wealthiest 20 percent of Americans. Less than 5 percent of these tax benefits are received by the bottom 40 percent of Americans. About half of all families with residential mortgages receive no tax benefit at all.[1]

The mortgage interest deduction is politically almost untouchable. Organized groups representing the housing and lending industries vehemently oppose changing this policy. They have access to information and analyses that show that the deduction drives up home sales and prices. The availability of a tax deduction encourages wealthier Americans to purchase second homes, to purchase more expensive homes, and to borrow against the value of their homes. From the perspective of the housing and lending industries, cuts in the mortgage-interest deduction would shrink these lucrative markets.

The housing industry, though, is not alone in its opposition to eliminating the deduction. Most Americans, even those who are not currently eligible for the mortgage-interest deduction, seem to think that they can benefit from its provisions—if not now, then at some future time.

Though many Americans think the mortgage-interest deduction results in a savings for them, the deduction also hurts them. It drives up home prices by allowing purchasers to assume larger mortgages. If the subsidy had not existed, most Americans would probably have been able to purchase the same house they currently own at a lower price. Americans overwhelmingly support a program they think benefits them, when in fact their taxes pay for a program to reward a wealthy industry. Thus well-organized industry groups with greater access to information than individuals can better engage in collective action to translate their preferences into policy outcomes.

[1] Christian A. L. Hilber and Tracy M. Turner, "The Mortgage Interest Deduction and Its Impact on Homeownership Decisions," *The Review of Economics and Statistics* vol. 96 (October, 2014), pages 618–637, www.mitpressjournals.org/doi/abs/10.1162/REST_a_00427#. V9bT0vkrLIV (accessed 9/12/16).

free riding on the efforts of the ones who cleared the swamp. Thus, there is a disincentive for any of the owners to undertake the job alone.

free riding
Enjoying the benefits of some good or action while letting others bear the costs

Since the number of concerned owners is small in this particular case, they might eventually be able to organize themselves to share the costs as well as enjoy the benefits of clearing the swamp. But suppose the common concern is not the neighborhood swamp but polluted air or groundwater involving thousands of residents in a region, or millions of residents in a whole nation. National defense is the most obvious collective good whose benefits are shared by every resident, regardless of the taxes they pay or the support they provide. As the size of the benefited group increases, the free-rider phenomenon becomes more of a problem. Individuals do not have much incentive to become active members and supporters of a group that is already working more or less on their behalf. The group would no doubt be more influential if all concerned individuals were active members—if there were no free riders. But groups will not reduce their efforts just because free riders get the same benefits as dues-paying activists. In fact, groups may work even harder in the hope that the free riders will be encouraged to join in.

Organizational Components

Most interest groups share certain key organizational components. First, they must attract and keep members. Usually, groups appeal to members not only by promoting certain political goals but also by offering direct economic or social benefits. Thus, for example, AARP (formerly the American Association for Retired Persons), which promotes senior citizens' interests, also offers members insurance benefits and commercial discounts. Similarly, many groups with primarily economic or political goals also seek to attract members through opportunities for social interaction and networking. Thus, the local chapters of many national groups provide a congenial social environment while collecting dues that finance the national office's political efforts.

Another kind of benefit involves the appeal of an interest group's purpose. The best examples of such benefits are those of religious groups. The Christian right is made up of various interest groups that offer virtually no material benefits to members, their appeal depending almost entirely on the members' religious identifications and affirmations. Many religion-based interest groups have arisen throughout American history, such as those that drove the abolition of slavery and Prohibition.

In addition to promoting shared political goals, interest groups may offer their members material benefits. The AARP offers its members insurance benefits and commercial discounts.

The second component shared by interest groups is that each must build a financial structure capable of sustaining an organization and funding its activities. Most interest groups rely on annual dues and voluntary contributions. Many also sell ancillary services, such as insurance and vacation tours.

Third, every group must have a leadership and decision-making structure. For some groups, this structure is very simple. For others, it can be quite elaborate and involve hundreds of local chapters melded into a national apparatus.

Last, most groups include an agency that actually carries out the group's tasks. This may be a research organization, a public-relations office, or a lobbying office in Washington or a state capital.

The Characteristics of Members

Membership in interest groups is not randomly distributed in the population. People with higher incomes, higher levels of education, and managerial or professional occupations are much more likely to join than those on lower rungs of the socioeconomic ladder.[8] Well-educated, upper-income professionals are more likely to have the time, money, and skills needed to play a role in a group. Moreover, for business and professional people, group membership may provide personal contacts and access to information that can help advance their careers. At the same time, corporate entities—businesses and the like—usually have ample resources to form or participate in groups that seek to advance their causes.

The result is that interest group politics in the United States has a pronounced upper-class bias. Although many groups do have a working-class or lower-class membership—labor organizations or welfare-rights organizations, for example—the great majority of interest group members are middle and upper-middle class. In general, interest groups serve the interests of society's "haves." When interest groups take opposing positions on issues and policies, the conflicting positions they espouse usually reflect divisions among upper-income strata rather than conflicts between the upper and lower classes. Even groups associated with a progressive political agenda and support for the rights of the poor tend, in their own membership, to reflect the interests of the middle and upper-middle classes. Consider the National Association for the Advancement of Colored People (NAACP) and the National Organization for Women (NOW). Both groups advocate for the rights of the poor, but both have a middle-class membership and focus on issues relevant to that membership.

The NAACP is concerned with minority access to universities and the professions, a topic primarily of concern to its middle-class supporters. NOW seeks gender equality in education and access to positions in business and the professions—again, matters mainly of interest to its largely middle- and upper-middle-class membership.

In general, to obtain adequate political representation, forces low on the socioeconomic ladder must be organized on the massive scale associated with political parties. Indeed, parties can mobilize the collective energies of large numbers of people who, as individuals, may have very limited resources. Interest groups, in contrast, generally organize smaller numbers of the better-to-do. Thus, the relative importance of political parties and interest groups has far-ranging implications for the distribution of political power in the United States.

Response to Changes in the Political Environment

As long as there is government, as long as government makes policies that provide benefits or impose costs, and as long as there is liberty to organize, interest groups will abound. And if government expands, so will interest groups. For example, a spurt of growth in the national government occurred during the 1880s and 1890s, arising largely from early government efforts to fight monopolies and regulate some aspects of interstate commerce. In the latter decade, a parallel growth spurt occurred in national interest groups, including the imposing National Association of Manufacturers and other trade associations. Many groups organized around agricultural commodities as well, and this period also saw trade unions begin to expand as interest groups. In the 1930s, interest groups with headquarters and representation in Washington began to grow significantly, concurrent with that decade's expansion of the national government.

Recent decades have seen an enormous increase both in the number of interest groups seeking a role in the political process and in the extent of their opportunity to influence that process. Today there are tens of thousands of groups at the national, state, and local levels. One indication of the proliferation of their activity is the enormous number of political action committees (PACs), a vehicle by which interest group money is spent to influence elections. Nearly three times as many PACs operated in 2016 as in the 1970s, increasing from fewer than 500 to more than 7,000.[9] A *New York Times* report, for example, noted that during the 1970s, expanded federal regulation of the automobile, oil, gas, education, and health care industries impelled each of these interests to substantially

political action committee (PAC)

A private group that raises and distributes funds for use in election campaigns

increase its efforts to influence the government's behavior. These efforts, in turn, spurred the organization of other groups to augment or counter the activities of the first.[10] The rise of PACs exhibits one of the most common features of business political activity: businesses are reactive. They are usually drawn into politics in response to regulations, rather than to create a new program.

Similarly, federal social programs have occasionally sparked (1) political organization and action by clientele groups seeking to influence the distribution of benefits and, in turn, (2) the organization of groups opposed to the programs or their cost. AARP, perhaps the nation's largest membership organization, owes its emergence to the creation and expansion of Social Security and Medicare. Once older Americans had guaranteed retirement income and health insurance, they had a clear stake in protecting and expanding these benefits. AARP developed in response to attempts to pare back the program.[11]

Participants in the so-called new politics of the 1960s, which emphasized environmental, consumer and civil rights, civil rights concerns, constructed or strengthened public interest groups such as Common Cause, the Sierra Club, the Environmental Defense Fund, Physicians for Social Responsibility, the National Organization for Women, and the various organizations formed by consumer activist Ralph Nader. These groups were able to influence the media, Congress, and even the judiciary, and enjoyed remarkable success during the late 1960s and early 1970s in securing the enactment of policies they favored. Activist groups also played a major role in securing the enactment of environmental, consumer, and occupational health and safety legislation. More recent social movements include the anti-tax Tea Party movement and Black Lives Matter, protesting racial discrimination in policing and the criminal justice system.

Among the factors contributing to the rise and success of public interest groups was technology. Computerized direct-mail campaigns in the 1980s were perhaps the first innovation that allowed organizations to reach out to potential members. Today, Facebook, Twitter, and other electronic media enable public interest groups to reach hundreds of thousands of potential sympathizers and contributors. Relatively small groups can efficiently identify and mobilize adherents nationwide. Individuals whose perspectives make them a small anonymous minority everywhere can connect and mobilize for national political action through social networking tools unheard of even 30 years ago.

Of course, many individuals who share a common interest do not form interest groups. For example, although college students share an interest in the cost and quality of education, they have seldom organized to demand lower tuition, better facilities, or a more effective faculty. Students could be called a "latent group," of which there are many in American society. Often the failure of a latent group to organize reflects individuals' ability to achieve their goals without joining an organized effort. Individual students, for example, are free to choose among colleges that, in turn, must compete for patronage. Where the market or other mechanisms allow individuals to achieve their goals without joining groups, they are less likely to do so.

STRATEGIES FOR INFLUENCING POLICY

Interest groups work to improve the probability that all branches and levels of government will hear their policy concerns and treat them favorably. The quest for political influence and power takes many forms, which we can roughly divide into "insider strategies" and "outsider strategies."

Insider strategies include gaining access to key decision makers and using the courts. Of course, influencing policy through traditional political institutions requires understanding how those institutions work. A lobbyist who wishes to address a problem with legislation will seek a sympathetic member of Congress, preferably on a committee with jurisdiction over the problem, and will work directly with the member's staff. Likewise, an organization that decides to file a suit will do so in a jurisdiction where it has a good chance of getting a sympathetic judge or appellate court. Gaining access is not easy: legislators and bureaucrats have many requests to juggle. Courts, too, have full dockets. Interest groups themselves have limited budgets and staff. They must choose their battles well and map out the insider strategy most likely to succeed.

Outsider strategies include going public and using electoral tactics. Just as politicians can gain an electoral edge by informing voters, so can groups. A well-planned public-information campaign or targeted campaign activities and contributions can have as much influence as working the corridors of Congress.

Many groups employ a mix of insider and outsider strategies. For example, environmental groups such as the Sierra Club lobby members of Congress and key congressional staff, participate in bureaucratic rule making by offering suggestions to agencies on new environmental rules, and bring suits under various environmental laws, such as the Endangered Species Act. At the same time, the Sierra Club attempts to influence public opinion through media campaigns and to influence electoral politics by supporting candidates who share its environmental views and opposing candidates who do not.

Direct Lobbying

The term "lobbying" refers to efforts by individuals or groups to influence the actions of government officials. Traditionally, lobbying was viewed as an effort to influence members of Congress, but lobbying can also include attempts to influence officials of the executive branch. The First

Amendment to the Constitution provides for the right to "petition the Government for a redress of grievances." But as early as the 1870s, *lobbying* became the common term for petitioning.

The 1946 Federal Regulation of Lobbying Act defines a lobbyist as "any person who shall engage himself for pay or any consideration for the purpose of attempting to influence the passage or defeat of any legislation to the Congress of the United States." According to the 1995 Federal Lobbying Disclosure Act, any person who makes at least one lobbying contact with either the legislative or the executive branch in a year, any individual who spends 20 percent of his or her time in support of such activities, or any firm that devotes 10 percent of its budget to such activities must register as a lobbyist. They must report what topics they discussed with the government, though not which individuals or offices they contacted. The Analyzing the Evidence unit in this chapter looks at the major types of interest groups and their influence on government.

Lobbying involves much activity on the part of someone speaking for an interest. Lobbyists pepper legislators, administrators, and committee staff members with facts and claims about pertinent issues and facts or claims about public support of them.[12] Indeed, lobbyists serve a useful purpose in the legislative and administrative process by providing this kind of information. However, within each industry, the many individuals and organizations involved in government advocacy usually do not speak with a common voice. Rather each advocates for its own interests, often in conflict with other firms in the same industry. What the leading organization or peak association of an industry advocates may be undercut by the activities of individual firms. For example, the Entertainment Software Association likely wants a different set of regulations than Microsoft or Google.

Lobbying Members of Congress. Interest groups have substantial influence in setting the legislative agenda and helping craft the language of legislation (see Figure 12.1). Today sophisticated lobbyists win influence by providing information about policies to busy members of Congress, who actually may refuse to see them unless they have useful information to offer. But this is only one of the many services lobbyists perform. They may also testify on their clients' behalf at congressional committee and agency hearings; help clients identify potential allies with whom to construct coalitions; draft proposed legislation or regulations to be introduced by friendly lawmakers; and talk to reporters and organize media campaigns. Lobbyists are also important in politicians' fund-raising, directing clients' contributions to congressional and presidential candidates. Seeing an opportunity to harness the enthusiasm of political amateurs, they now organize comprehensive efforts that combine simulated grassroots activity with information and election campaign funding for members of Congress.[13]

Interest Group Influence

Contributed by
Beth L. Leech
Rutgers University

Which interest groups have the most influence over political outcomes? It is generally accepted among those who study interest groups that business and economic interests predominate. Economic interests are more likely to form organized groups, are more likely to be active, and on average spend more money and more time on political issues than are noneconomic interests like citizen groups or "public interest" groups. When we look at interest groups' involvement in the policy-making process, however, the sheer number of groups or dollars may not directly equal the amount of influence that those groups have. While numbers and dollars are important indicators of which interests are represented, it would be preferable to try to measure which groups actually were influential in politics. To address this question, the political scientist Frank Baumgartner and his colleagues interviewed 315 lobbyists and government officials about 98 randomly selected policy issues. Citizen groups were more likely to be mentioned as being important in the debates than any other type of group, despite the fact that they spent less and they made up a smaller part of the overall group population.

Why were citizen groups seen as so influential despite their relative lack of resources? It may be that those groups have important ties to constituents, granting them greater legitimacy in the eyes of members of Congress, or it could be that some members of Congress already supported the policies that the citizen groups were advocating. Whatever the reason, it is clear that citizen groups have greater voice in Washington than the dollar counts might suggest.

Groups with Washington Lobbying Offices

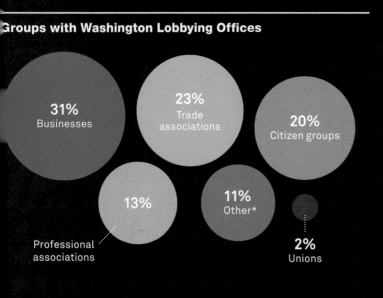

31% Businesses

23% Trade associations

20% Citizen groups

13% Professional associations

11% Other*

2% Unions

These data from the National Survey of Governmental Relations and Lobbyists.Info show the dominance of business organizations in Washington. Businesses make up 31 percent of those with dedicated national lobbying offices. Trade associations, which represent groups of businesses, make up another 23 percent. Citizen groups, professional associations, and unions together have less than half of all lobbying offices, and it is especially striking to note that unions are only 2 percent of the total.

*Includes governmental groups, think tanks, universities, and hospitals

Average Spending on Lobbying and Campaign Contributions

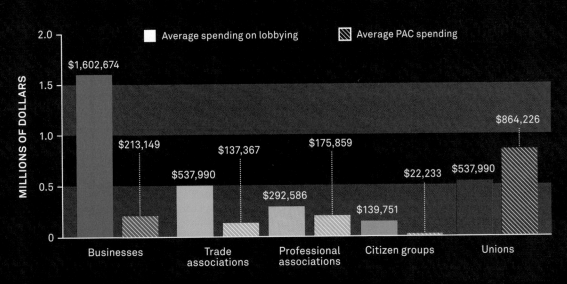

- ■ Average spending on lobbying
- ▨ Average PAC spending

MILLIONS OF DOLLARS

Businesses: $1,602,674 / $213,149
Trade associations: $537,990 / $137,367
Professional associations: $292,586 / $175,859
Citizen groups: $139,751 / $22,233
Unions: $537,990 / $864,226

The graph shows the average amounts spent on lobbying or campaign contributions by interest groups. Citizen groups on average spent much less on lobbying and campaign contributions than other types of groups. Unions on average spent more on campaign contributions than any other type of group, but that spending is tempered by the fact that there are fewer unions. (Note: Lobbying figures represent total reported spending in 2012; PAC campaign contributions are for the two-year election period ending with the 2012 election.)

Who Is Seen as Important in Policy Making?

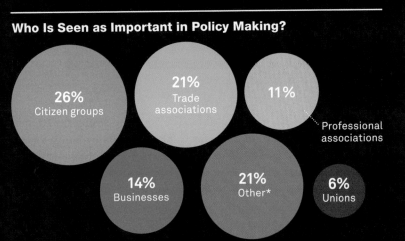

- 26% Citizen groups
- 21% Trade associations
- 11% Professional associations
- 14% Businesses
- 21% Other*
- 6% Unions

*Includes coalitions, governmental associations, and think tanks.

SOURCES:

Frank B. Baumgartner, Jeffrey M. Berry, Marie Hojnacki, David C. Kimball, and Beth L. Leech, *Lobbying and Policy Change: Who Wins, Who Loses, and Why* (Chicago: University of Chicago Press, 2009).

Center for Responsive Politics, www.opensecrets.org/pacs (accessed 12/2/15).

Leech, Beth L., National Survey of Governmental Relations, 2012.

Lobbyists.Info, www.lobbyists.info, (accessed 12/2/15).

Although the overall population of interest groups has fewer citizen groups than business groups, as seen in the figure on the facing page, not all groups are equally influential. Baumgartner and his colleagues interviewed 315 lobbyists and government officials about 98 randomly selected policy issues. Citizen groups were more likely to be mentioned as being important in the debate than any other type of group. More than a quarter of the interest groups seen as being influential were citizen groups.

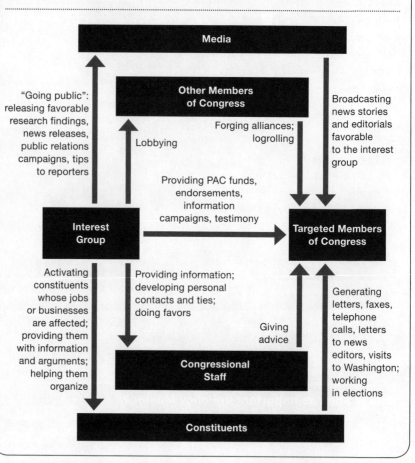

Figure 12.1

HOW INTEREST GROUPS INFLUENCE CONGRESS

ANALYZING THE EVIDENCE

Interest groups can influence members of Congress in a variety of ways. They may seek to mobilize popular support in the form of grassroots campaigns; they may try to generate publicity favorable to their cause; they may work through congressional staffers; or they may seek to lobby members of Congress directly. How might these various strategies work together? What pitfalls might an interest group encounter in trying to influence members of Congress?

Some interest groups go still further. They develop strong ties to individual politicians or policy communities within Congress by hiring former staffers, former members of Congress, or even relatives of sitting members. The frequent rotation of those in positions of power into lobbying jobs, a practice known as revolving-door politics, is driven by the continual turnover of staff, lobbyists, and even the political parties in Washington. Because lobbying firms must stay current and connected to Congress to offer the best service to their clients, most large lobbying firms in Washington have strong ties to both the Democrats and the Republicans on Capitol Hill. This revolving door has been cause for concern among some policy makers.

Lobbying the President. So many individuals and groups clamor for the president's attention that only the most skilled and well-connected can hope

The most powerful interests can sometimes influence presidential decisions. In 2015, President Obama met with members of the business community to discuss efforts to combat climate change.

to influence presidential decisions. When running for president, Barack Obama made a bold promise to "free the executive branch from special interest influence." No political appointee, the Obama campaign promised, "will be permitted to work on regulations or contracts directly and substantially related to their prior employer for two years." That promise proved exceedingly difficult to keep, as many on the Obama transition team had close ties to lobbyists or had worked for lobbying firms.[14] One of President Obama's first executive orders created an ethics standard and pledge for all executive branch appointments, and the administration imposed further restrictions on those receiving funds from the Emergency Economic Stabilization Act and the American Recovery and Reinvestment Act. Anyone wishing to receive funds from those huge economic stimulus bills had to show that they did not have conflicting interests and were not involved in lobbying the government.[15]

Lobbying the Executive Branch. Even when an interest group succeeds in getting its bill passed by Congress and signed by the president, full and faithful implementation of that law is not guaranteed. Often, the group and its allies continue their efforts after the president turns the law over to the appropriate agency. On average, 40 percent of lobbyists regularly contact both legislative and executive branch officials, and 16 percent contact only the executive branch.[16]

In some respects, federal law actually promotes interest group access to the executive branch. The Administrative Procedure Act, enacted in 1946 and frequently amended, requires most federal agencies to provide notice and an opportunity for comment before implementing proposed new rules and regulations. So-called notice and comment rule making gives interests an opportunity to publicize their views and participate in implementing legislation that affects them. Since 1990, the Negotiated Rulemaking Act has encouraged administrative agencies to engage in direct and open negotiations with affected interests when developing new regulations. These two laws have played an important role in opening the bureaucratic process to interest group influence. Today, few federal agencies would consider implementing a new rule without consulting affected interests.[17]

Regulation of Lobbying. Concerns that lobbyists have too much influence have led to the adoption of legal guidelines regulating their activities. For example, since 1993, businesses may no longer deduct the cost of lobbying from their taxes. Trade associations must report to members the proportion of their dues that goes to lobbying, and that proportion may not be claimed as a business expense for tax purposes. Most important, the 1995 Lobbying Disclosure Act significantly broadened the definition of individuals and organizations that must register as lobbyists. According to the filings under this act, almost 10,498 lobbyists were working the halls of Congress in 2016.

Congress also restricted interest group influence by adopting rules that prohibited members from accepting gifts from registered lobbyists. Congressional rules also prohibit members from accepting a gift worth more than $50 from any single source, with a total limit of $100 from any single source during a calendar year. It also banned the practice of paying honoraria, which special interests had used to supplement congressional salaries. Interest groups can still pay for the travel of representatives, senators, or their spouses or staff members as long as a trip is related to legislative business and is disclosed on congressional reports within 30 days. The cost of meals and entertainment on these trips does not count toward the gift limit.

In 2007, congressional Democrats adopted ethics rules prohibiting lobbyists from paying for most meals, trips, parties, and gifts for members of Congress. Lobbyists were also required to disclose the amounts and sources of small campaign contributions they "bundled" into large contributions. And interest groups were required to disclose the funds they used to rally voters for or against legislative proposals. As soon as the rules were enacted, however, lobbyists and politicians found ways to circumvent them, and they have had little impact. In the executive branch, in contrast, policies imposed by President Obama in 2009 have made it much more difficult for lobbying firms to influence decision making, either directly through lobbying or indirectly by hiring people with direct access to decision makers.

Using the Courts

Interest groups sometimes turn to the courts to augment other avenues of access. They can use the courts to affect public policy in at least three ways: (1) by bringing suit directly on behalf of a group; (2) by financing suits brought by individuals; or (3) by filing a companion brief as *amicus curiae* (literally "a friend of the court") to an existing court case.

Significant modern uses of the courts for political influence include those involving the "sexual revolution" and the movement for women's rights. Beginning in the mid-1960s, a series of cases was brought into the federal courts in an effort to force definition of a right to privacy in sexual matters. The effort began in *Griswold v. Connecticut* with a challenge to state restrictions on obtaining contraceptives for nonmedical purposes; here the Supreme Court held that states could neither prohibit the dissemination of information about nor prohibit the use of contraceptives by married couples. In a subsequent case, the Court held that the states could not prohibit the use of contraceptives by single persons A year later, the Court held, in the 1973 case of *Roe v. Wade*, that states could not impose an absolute ban on voluntary abortions. Each of these cases, as well as others, was part of the Court's enunciation of a constitutional doctrine of privacy.[18]

Roe v. Wade sparked a controversy that led conservative groups to make extensive use of the courts to whittle away the scope of the privacy doctrine. They obtained rulings, for example, that prohibit the use of federal funds to pay for voluntary abortions. And in 1989, right-to-life groups used a strategy of litigation to significantly undermine the *Roe v. Wade* decision in the case of *Webster v. Reproductive Health Services*, which allowed states to place some restrictions on abortion.[19]

Another significant use of the courts as a strategy for political influence is found in the history of the NAACP. The most important of these cases was *Brown v. Board of Education of Topeka* (1954), in which the Supreme Court held that legal segregation of public schools was unconstitutional.[20]

Business groups are also frequent users of the courts because so many government programs apply to them, notably in such areas as taxation, antitrust cases, interstate transportation, patents, and product quality and standardization. Major corporations and their trade associations pay tremendous fees each year to prestigious Washington law firms. Some of this money is expended in gaining access, but much of it serves to keep the most experienced lawyers prepared to represent the corporations in court or before administrative agencies.

The new political movements made significant use of the courts to advance their goals during the 1970s and 1980s. Facilitated by changes in the legal rules governing access to the courts (discussed in Chapter 8), the

Political movements often make use of the courts to advance policy preferences. In the thirty years from 1986 to 2016, pro- and antiabortion groups frequently sued state and local governments to challenge the rules surrounding protest outside abortion clinics.

new politics agenda was visible in decisions handed down in several key policy areas. For example, new politics groups forced federal agencies to pay attention to environmental issues, even when the agencies' activities were not directly related to environmental quality. By the 2000s, the courts often were the battleground on which the new political movements waged their fights. Perhaps most dramatic were a string of lawsuits spanning 30 years (1986–2016) in which pro- and antiabortion organizations, such as Pro-Life Action Network, Operation Rescue, and the National Organization for Women, repeatedly sued state and local governments, and sometimes each other, to establish the rules governing protests near abortion clinics. Ultimately, the Supreme Court sided with the antiabortion groups, but not before deciding three separate cases on the matter, at extremely high cost to both sides.[21]

Mobilizing Public Opinion

going public

The effort to influence public opinion for or against some proposed action by the government

Organizations also try to pressure politicians by mobilizing public opinion, a strategy known as going public. When groups go public, they use their resources to try to persuade large numbers of people to pay attention to their concerns in the hope that greater visibility and public support will make those in power see those concerns as important. Increased use of this strategy is traced to the rise of modern advertising at the beginning of the twentieth century. As early as the 1930s, political analysts distinguished between the "old lobby" of group representatives attempting to influence Congress directly and the "new lobby" of public-relations professionals addressing the public in order to reach Congress indirectly.[22]

A casual scan of major newspapers, magazines, and websites will reveal numerous expensive, well-designed ads by major companies and industry associations, such as those from the oil and gas, automobile, and health and pharmaceutical industries. Such ads often highlight what the firms or industries do for the country, not merely the products or services they offer. Their purpose is to create and maintain a positive association between the advertiser and the community at large in the hope that the community's favorable feelings can be drawn on in political controversies later.

Sometimes groups advertise expressly to shift public opinion on a question. One of the most famous such campaigns was run by the Health Insurance Association of America in 1993 and 1994 in opposition to President Bill Clinton's proposed national health insurance plan. These ads featured a couple, Harry and Louise, sitting at their kitchen table disparaging the bureaucratic problems they would face under Clinton's plan. These ads are widely credited with turning public opinion against Clinton's plan, which never got off the ground in Congress. A decade later, when President Barack Obama proposed an extensive overhaul of the health insurance industry, a trade group representing drug makers remade the Harry and Louise spot using the same actors, but this time to support the administration's plan. Louise concludes the new ad by saying, "A little more cooperation, a little less politics, and we can get the job done this time."[23]

A second strategy for going public, grassroots lobbying, entails many of the same organizing methods one sees in political campaigns—developing lists of supporters and having them voice their concern about an issue and recruit others to do so as well. It is common practice today to send "direct mail" that includes a draft letter for recipients to adapt and then send to their representatives in Congress or to send e-mails urging people to contact their members of Congress regarding a particular bill or controversy. A grassroots campaign can cost anywhere from $40,000 to try to sway the votes of one or two crucial members of a committee or subcommittee to millions of dollars to mount a national effort aimed at Congress as a whole. Such grassroots campaigns are often organized around controversial, prominent legislation or appointments, such as Supreme Court nominees.

Grassroots lobbying has become more prevalent in recent decades because congressional rules limiting gifts to members have made traditional lobbying more difficult. But has it reached an intolerable extreme? One case in particular illustrates the extremes of what has come to be known as "Astroturf" lobbying (a play on the brand name of an artificial grass used on many sports fields). Beginning in 1992, 10 giant companies in the financial services, manufacturing, and high-tech industries began a grassroots campaign and spent millions of dollars over three years to influence a decision in Congress to limit investors' ability to sue for fraud. Retaining an expensive consulting firm, these corporations paid for the use of

grassroots lobbying

A lobbying campaign in which a group mobilizes its membership to contact government officials in support of the group's position

One way organized groups attempt to influence popular opinion is by holding protests that generate media attention. Here, teachers, students, and other citizens attend a teachers' union march to protest school closings in Chicago.

specialized computer software to persuade Congress that there was "an outpouring of popular support for the proposal." Thousands of letters about the issue flooded Capitol Hill. Many came from people who sincerely believed that investor lawsuits are often frivolous and should be curtailed, but much of the mail was artificial, generated by the consultants, and came from people who had no strong feelings or even no opinion at all about the issue. Astroturf campaigns have increased in frequency as members of Congress grow more skeptical of Washington lobbyists and far more concerned about demonstrations of support for a particular issue by their constituents. Interestingly, after the firms in the sue-for-fraud campaign spent millions of dollars and generated thousands of letters, they came to the somber conclusion that "it's more effective to have 100 letters from your district where constituents took the time to write and understand the issue," because "Congress is sophisticated enough to know the difference."[24]

Protests are the oldest means of going public. Those who lack money, contacts, and expertise can always resort to protest to bring attention to an issue or pressure on the government. Indeed, the right to assembly is protected in the First Amendment to the Constitution. Protests may have many different consequences, depending on how they are managed. One basic consequence of a successful protest is that it attracts attention. Organized protests also create a sense of community among those involved and raise the consciousness of people outside the protest about the issue involved. In addition, protests often attempt to impose costs on others by disrupting traffic or commerce, thereby forcing people to bargain with the protesters. In 2016, for example, Black Lives Matter protesters disrupted traffic in major cities to call attention to the claim that police forces were too quick to use lethal forces against African Americans.

Using Electoral Politics

In addition to attempting to influence members of Congress and other officials, interest groups also use the electoral process to try to elect the "right" legislators in the first place and to ensure that those elected will owe them a debt of gratitude for their support. To put matters into perspective, groups invest far more resources in lobbying than in electoral politics. Nevertheless, financial support and campaign activism can be important tools for organized interests.

Political Action Committees. By far the most common electoral strategy that interest groups employ is that of giving financial support to political parties or candidates. But such support can easily cross the threshold into outright bribery. Therefore, Congress has occasionally tried to regulate this strategy. For example, the Federal Election Campaign Act of 1971 (FECA; amended in 1974) limits campaign contributions and requires that each candidate or campaign committee provide comprehensive information about each donor who contributes more than $100. These provisions have been effective up to a point, considering the large number of embarrassments, indictments, resignations, and criminal convictions in the aftermath of the Watergate scandal of the early 1970s.

This scandal was triggered by Republican workers breaking into the office of the Democratic National Committee in Washington. But an investigation revealed numerous violations of campaign finance laws, involving millions of dollars passed from corporate executives to President Nixon's re-election committee.

Reaction to Watergate produced further legislation on campaign finance, but the effect has been to restrict individual rather than interest group campaign activity. Individuals may now contribute no more than $2,700 to any candidate for federal office in any primary or general election. A PAC, however, can contribute $5,000, provided it contributes to at least five different federal candidates each year. Beyond this, the laws permit corporations, unions, and other interest groups to form PACs and to pay the costs of soliciting funds for them from individuals.

Electoral spending by interest groups has increased steadily despite these reforms: total PAC contributions increased from nearly $260 million in the 2000 election cycle to $470 million in the 2014 cycle.

Interest groups focus their direct contributions on Congress, especially the House. Because of the enormous cost of running modern political campaigns (see Chapter 10), most politicians are eager to receive PAC contributions. A typical U.S. House incumbent receives half of his or her campaign funds from interest groups. There is little evidence that donations actually buy roll-call votes or other favors from members of Congress, but they do help to keep those sympathetic to groups' interests in office.[25]

The potential influence of interest group campaign donations has prompted frequent calls to abolish PACs or limit their activities. The challenge is how to regulate groups' participation without violating their members' rights to free speech and free association. In 1976, the Supreme Court weighed in on this matter in terms of the constitutionality of the 1974 Federal Elections Campaign Act.[26] In its decision to let the act stand, the majority on the Court ruled that donors' rights of expression were at stake but that these had to be weighed against the government's interest in limiting corruption, or the perception of it. The Court has repeatedly upheld the key tenets of this decision: (1) that money is a form of speech; but (2) that speech rights must be weighed against concerns about corruption.

As we saw in Chapter 10, Congress in 2002 imposed significant limits on independent campaign expenditures in the Bipartisan Campaign Reform Act (BCRA). BCRA restricted donations to nonfederal (for example, state party) accounts to limit corruption, and it imposed limits on the types of campaign commercials groups could air within 60 days of an election. It also raised the limits on direct campaign contributions to compensate for the effect of inflation.

In 2010, the Supreme Court struck down the restrictions on independent advertising.[27] The case involved a political movie critical of then-senator and presidential candidate Hillary Clinton created by an organization called Citizens United. The movie aired on cable television inside the blackout date for independent political advertising stipulated by BCRA. A 5–4 majority on the Court ruled that such imposed blackout dates restricted the rights to free speech of corporations and other associations. This decision firmly established the right of corporations and labor unions to engage in political advocacy and opened the gates to the flood of money in the political arena. This flood was evident during the 2016 national elections, in which independent expenditures amounted to some $1.7 billion (Figure 12.2), and in the 2014 midterms, when the total was $785 million.

Campaign Activism. Financial support is not the only way in which organized groups seek influence through the electoral process. Sometimes activism can be even more important. Perhaps the most notable instance of such

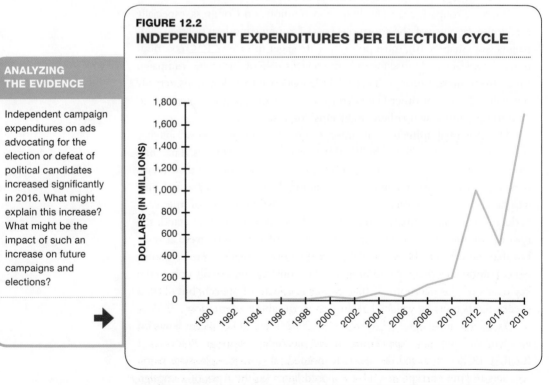

ANALYZING THE EVIDENCE

Independent campaign expenditures on ads advocating for the election or defeat of political candidates increased significantly in 2016. What might explain this increase? What might be the impact of such an increase on future campaigns and elections?

FIGURE 12.2
INDEPENDENT EXPENDITURES PER ELECTION CYCLE

NOTE: The years 1992, 1996, 2000, 2004, 2008, 2012, and 2016 were presidential election years.
SOURCE: Center for Responsive Politics, www.opensecrets.org/outsidespending/fes_summ.php (accessed 11/12/16).

Lobbying

Influencing the passage or defeat of legislation

Access

Developing close ties to decision makers on Capitol Hill and bureaucratic agencies

---

Litigation

Taking action through the courts, usually in one of three ways:

- Filing suit against a specific government agency or program

- Financing suits brought by individuals against the government

- Filing companion briefs as *amicus curiae* (friend of the court) to existing court cases

---

Going Public

Especially by advertising and grassroots lobbying; also by organizing boycotts, strikes, rallies, marches, and sit-ins; generating positive news coverage

---

Electoral Politics

Giving financial support to a party or candidate

Congress passed the Federal Election Campaign Act of 1971 to try to regulate this practice by limiting the amount interest groups can contribute to campaigns.

activism occurs on behalf of Democratic Party candidates through labor unions, which regularly launch massive get-out-the-vote drives. The largest such activities are those of the Service Employees International Union (SEIU), which represents workers ranging from hotel and restaurant workers to clerical staff, and the United Auto Workers (UAW). Other sorts of groups routinely line up behind the Democratic or Republican campaigns. The National Rifle Association, for example, routinely seeks to mobilize its millions of members on behalf of candidates who pledge to support Second Amendment rights.

The cumulative effect of such independent campaign activism is difficult to judge, but an important research initiative within political science seeks to measure the marginal effectiveness of direct campaign contact. In field experiments where campaigns agree to conduct direct activity randomly in some neighborhoods but not others, Alan Gerber and Donald Green have been able to measure the marginal effect of each additional piece of mail, each additional direct canvasser, or each additional phone call. In a typical election context, it costs about $40 to get an additional voter to the polls. Professors Gerber and Green further find that campaign activism can have an initially large impact on persuading voters to go to the polls. The effectiveness of each additional contact after the first tends to diminish, and after a voter has been contacted unsuccessfully six times, additional contacts have no effect and campaign workers may as well give up. This research has given campaigns and reformers some sense of the effectiveness of campaign activism in stimulating turnout and possibly influencing elections. Especially in low-turnout elections, such as those for city councils or state legislatures, interest groups' get-out-the-vote activities can significantly affect the outcome. But as other money enters the scene, especially candidates' own campaign expenditures, the effects of such activities become muted.[28]

The Initiative. Another political tactic that interest groups sometimes use is sponsoring ballot initiatives at the state level. The initiative allows laws proposed by citizens to be submitted directly to the state's voters for approval or rejection, bypassing the state legislature and governor. Perhaps the most famous initiative was Proposition 13 in California in 1978, which limited property tax increases and forever changed the way that state finances education. The initiative was originally promoted by late-nineteenth-century Populists, who saw it as an antidote to interest group influence in the legislative process.

Ironically, most initiative campaigns today are actually sponsored by interest groups seeking to circumvent legislative opposition to their goals. In recent years, for example, the insurance industry, trial lawyers' associations, and tobacco companies have often sponsored them.[29] The role of interest groups in initiative campaigns is no surprise, because such campaigns can cost millions of dollars.

initiative

A process by which citizens may petition to place a policy proposal on the ballot for public vote

ARE INTEREST GROUPS EFFECTIVE?

Do interest groups have an effect on government and policy? A clean answer is difficult to find among the mountains of research on this question. A survey of dozens of studies of campaign contributions and legislative decision making found that in only about 1 in 10 cases was there evidence of a correlation between contributors' interests and legislators' roll-call voting.[30]

Earmarks are a good case in point. Earmarks are expenditures on particular projects in specific districts or states, and they are usually included in a bill late in the legislative process to help secure enough votes for passage. Millions of dollars in earmarks are written into law every year. In a study of lobbyists' effectiveness in obtaining earmarks for college and university clients, lobbying was found to have a limited impact. [31] The more money schools spent on lobbying activities, the more earmarked funds they received; however, the magnitude of the effect depended greatly on institutional factors. A few cases showed exceedingly high returns. Schools in states with a senator on the Senate Appropriations Committee received $18 to $29 in earmarks for every $1 spent on lobbying. Schools in congressional districts whose representative served on the House Appropriations Committee received between $49 and $55 for every $1 spent on lobbying. Having a legislator on the relevant committee, then, explains most of the observed influence. [32]

These results suggest that institutions and politics are profoundly related. Schools without access to influential members of Congress cannot gain much from lobbying. Schools with such access still need to lobby to maximize the potential that representation on congressional appropriations committees can give them. But if they do so, the potential return is substantial.

Do Interest Groups Foster or Impede Democracy?

The institutions of American government embrace an open and democratic process to ensure that government is responsive to the public's preferences and needs. The Bill of Rights provides for free speech, freedom of the press, and freedom of assembly. The nation's laws have further cemented this commitment, requiring open meetings of many governmental bodies, citizen advisory commissions, lobbying, direct contact between legislators and constituents, financial contributions to candidates and causes, trials open to the public, protests, and many other routes through which individuals and groups may advocate for their interests. Through these many points of access, representatives and other government officials learn how their decisions affect the public. Politics is the arena in which many interests compete for the attention and support of government. Indeed, tens of thousands of organizations compete in the political sphere in the United States, and countless other movements and coordinated efforts of citizens rise and fall as issues come into the public arena. This is Pluralism at work, and it aligns closely with the sort of politics the Founders envisioned.

But this system of government is hardly perfect. The policies and laws the U. S. government enacts are often thought to favor those who are organized. The American interest group system creates opportunities for *those who can* use their resources to represent their interests before the government. Individuals and organizations that can muster the most money or manpower can best make their case before the legislature, before executive branch agencies, before the courts, and even before the electorate. Problems of collective action and free riding prevent many latent interests from developing permanent political organizations capable of bringing concerted pressure on the government. Businesses, unions, and professional and industry associations—groups that exist for some other reason than just to gain political influence—usually have less trouble providing the financial resources and overcoming the obstacles to organization and group maintenance that volunteer associations face. Consequently, interest group politics in Washington, D.C., and state governments tends to reflect the interests of and conflicts among those engaged in economic activity.

Even economically based groups do not necessarily succeed in the political arena. Unlike economic activity, politics involves power derived from the ability to vote on measures, introduce legislation or rules, or block actions from happening. Interest groups are outsiders that can do none of these things directly. Nonetheless, these organizations can seek support in the appropriate institutions, such as a court with a sympathetic judge or a congressional subcommittee with a sympathetic chair. Often, groups succeed not by bringing pressure but by providing expertise to the government and by learning from those in office about the impact of new rules and regulations.

Interest group politics today does not neatly fit stereotypical notions of political power and influence. There are as many lobbyists as ever, but the backroom dealings of the "old lobby" are an anachronism. Interest group politics spans all branches of government and involves myriad interests vying for attention in an increasingly crowded field. Moreover, competing interests may very well cancel out a given organization's efforts. And the activities of all groups constitute just one facet of legislators', judges', and executives' deliberations. Those who must ultimately make political decisions and be held accountable weigh other voices as well, especially those of their constituents. Perhaps a better contemporary characterization is that the organized and disorganized interests participating in politics today are really contributing to a much broader sphere of political debate. That debate takes place inside the institutions of government—Congress, courts, executives, and elections.

For Further Reading

Abramoff, Jack. *Capitol Punishment: The Hard Truth about Washington Corruption from America's Most Notorious Lobbyist.* New York: WND Books, 2011.

Ainsworth, Scott. *Analyzing Interest Groups.* New York: Norton, 2002.

Alexander, Robert, ed. *The Classics of Interest Group Behavior*. New York: Wadsworth, 2005.

Ansolabehere, Stephen, John M. de Figueiredo, and James M. Snyder, Jr. "Why Is There So Little Money in U.S. Politics?" *Journal of Economic Perspectives* 17, no. 1 (2003): 105–30.

Birnbaum, Jeffrey H. *The Money Men*. New York: Crown, 2000.

Cigler, Allan J., and Burdett A. Loomis, eds. *Interest Group Politics*. 8th ed. Washington, DC: CQ Press, 2011.

Esterling, Kevin. *The Political Economy of Expertise*. Ann Arbor: University of Michigan Press, 2004.

Gilens, Martin. *Affluence and Influence: Economic Inequality and Political Power in America*. New York and Princeton, NJ: Russell Sage Foundation and Princeton University Press, 2012.

Herrnson, Paul, Christopher Deering, and Clyde Wilcox. *Interest Groups Unleashed*. Washington, DC: CQ Press, 2012.

Nownes, Anthony. *Total Lobbying: What Lobbyists Want and How They Try to Get It*. New York: Cambridge University Press, 2006.

Olson, Mancur, Jr. *The Logic of Collective Action: Public Goods and the Theory of Groups*. Reprinted with new preface and appendix. Cambridge, MA: Harvard University Press, 1965.

Rosenthal, Alan. *The Third House: Lobbyists and Lobbying in the States*. Washington, DC: CQ Press, 2001.

Verba, Sidney, Kay Schlozman, and Henry E. Brady, *The Unheavenly Chorus*. Princeton, NJ: Princeton University Press, 2013.

13 Introduction to Public Policy

public policy

A law, rule, statute, or edict that expresses the government's goals and provides for rewards or punishments to promote their attainment

Public policy is an officially expressed intention backed by a sanction, which can be either a reward or a punishment. Thus public policy may be a law, a rule, a statute, an edict, a regulation, or an order. Its purpose is to provide incentives, whether carrot-like rewards or sticklike punishments, to induce people to change what they are currently doing and do something else or to do more or less of what they are currently doing.

Many policy analysts assert that government action is often required to correct what they call "market failure." This concept refers to inequities, inefficiencies, or other harmful effects produced by the operations of private markets. The presumption underlying the idea of government responsibility for correcting such effects is that government agencies and officials are motivated mainly by a concern for the public's welfare and will intervene in the private sector in ways likely to promote broad public interests.

But does government policy always serve the general interest? In reality, political processes are hardly guaranteed to produce fair and equitable results. Policy makers are often driven by self-interest, partisan predispositions, institutional concerns, and the demands of powerful constituency groups. Often, too, public programs are developed or administered by bureaucracies, courts, private contractors, and other entities whose decision-making processes lack transparency and are open to only a narrow range of participants.[1] Although every governmental program is touted by its proponents as serving the public interest, the unfortunate truth is that many, albeit not all, such programs serve particularistic rather than general interests.

One way in which public programs may benefit narrow groups at the expense of the broader public is through *mobilization bias*. Well-organized groups with substantial resources and a high stake in a particular policy are more likely than ordinary individuals to make successful efforts to pressure officials to enact the policies they favor.[2] Generally, mobilization bias is most likely to succeed when the costs of an interest group's favored program are distributed so widely that no set of potential opponents have much incentive to work against it. Such programs include subsidies to farmers for growing or not growing certain crops and tax benefits for businesses that, for example, produce products within the United States or invest in low-income housing. In other cases, an interest group may design a self-serving program so cleverly that those who pay for it actually believe themselves to be beneficiaries. For example, the guaranteed student loan program is usually supported by students and their parents but is actually a subsidy to colleges and universities, allowing them to charge higher rates for tuition.

A second type of bias, *stealth benefits*, is less obvious. An important example is the mortgage-interest tax deduction, discussed in the Policy Principle case study in Chapter 12, whose nominal purpose is to encourage home ownership. However, nearly 80 percent of the benefits provided by this deduction

CORE OF THE ANALYSIS

➡️ Public policies create incentives for people to alter their behavior.

➡️ In economic policy, government can play an important role in establishing the rules and institutions that allow a market economy to function.

➡️ Government has numerous tools with which to affect the economy, but there is considerable political conflict over which tools to use, how to use them, and when to use them.

➡️ After the Great Depression and the New Deal, the national government assumed greater responsibility for social policies related to broadening opportunity and addressing poverty.

go to the wealthiest 20 percent of Americans and less than 5 percent of these benefits go to the bottom 40 percent.[3] In other words, those families most able to own homes without government help receive most of the government's largesse, while families that struggle to afford their homes receive little or no assistance.

This is one example of public policy not correcting, and possibly even exacerbating, a market failure, though in other instances government policy does ensure effective and efficient markets. In this chapter, we examine several prerequisites for a market economy that are especially important. We then turn to some of the ways government uses social policies to address poverty and broaden opportunity.

HOW DOES GOVERNMENT MAKE A MARKET ECONOMY POSSIBLE?

A market economy is a complex set of arrangements fostered by political provisions that both nourish and protect it. In myriad ways, governments at all levels in our federal system undergird, manage, protect, and sometimes undermine markets.

Conditions Required for a Market Economy

In this section, we explore the conditions required for a functioning market economy and the role of government in providing them.

Establishing Law and Order. The first condition necessary for a market economy is inherent in the very idea of government. There must be a minimal degree of predictability about the basic rules of social interaction—that is, a system of law and order. Participants must be able to assume not only that they can get to the market safely—that they won't be robbed on the way—but also that the people with whom they deal will behave predictably and will be bound by dependable laws.

Defining Rules of Property and Its Exchange. The second condition that encourages people to participate in the market involves defining and dealing with property. If the market involves exchanges of ownership, there must be clear laws about what constitutes property. Property may be many things— your labor or your ideas or the bed you sleep in—but the very concept of property is inconceivable without laws that define what you can call your own.

Property ownership means that we can exercise dominion over something that we have declared our own. Ownership is defined by laws that enable us to exercise that dominion. Something is not our own unless we can be reasonably certain that someone else cannot walk away with or lay claim to it. Trespass laws, for example, confer a legal right to keep others away from certain kinds of property. Before we can enter a market and participate in an exchange, we must be able to expect not only that we can lay claim to something but also that those around us will respect that claim. In this sense, private property has a public component. The probability of enjoying property would be remote without laws that were widely enforced and accepted.

A market exists only when exchanges occur, and there must be rules governing exchange itself. Laws of exchanges structure how, when, and under what conditions you can sell or rent your property. You might think that once the laws of property have defined what you own, you ought to be able to transfer it, but other rules govern the transfer itself. Certain kinds of exchanges are deemed off-limits altogether. For example, you own your own body, but under what conditions can you "transfer" it? Laws about organ donation, prostitution, and slavery prohibit or regulate the selling or renting of one's body.

Enforcing Contracts. A third prerequisite for a market economy is rules governing the enforcement of contracts. Some societies do not have a recognizable concept of contract, but our economy is highly dependent on such notions.

Contracts facilitate exchanges of property, broadly construed. A contract is a voluntary agreement between two or more private persons that governs future conduct. Although the agreement is private, it has a public component: a contract must be enforceable, or it is meaningless. If contracts were meaningless, the economy would grind to a halt. Businesses would not sell goods to one another if each could not count on the other's promise to provide the agreed-upon good, service, or payment. Lenders would not offer loans to home buyers without a legally binding promise to repay. What makes these contracts enforceable is the courts' role arbitrating disputes between parties to a contract. If a homeowner fails to repay her home loan, for instance, the lending institution can follow a legal procedure to demand payment or take possession of the house.

Setting Market Standards. The fourth condition necessary for the modern free market is related to defining property and the conditions for its exchange. When people engage in exchanges that are not face-to-face—where they can't point and say, "I want that tomato"—both parties must have some way of understanding exactly what goods they are bargaining over. To do that, terminology must be standardized, and one of government's essential acts is to establish standard weights and measures.

A lighthouse is a classic example of a public good: its benefits can be enjoyed by everyone and cannot be denied to anyone. By providing public goods, the government helps make a market economy possible.

Providing Public Goods and Ameliorating Externalities.

A fifth condition necessary to the operation of a market economy involves providing public goods, facilities, or services that the government may provide because no single participant can afford or is willing to provide them. The provision of public goods may include (1) providing the physical marketplace itself—like the common in New England towns or the suk in North Africa and the Middle East, (2) building and maintaining transportation infrastructure to facilitate the distribution of goods and people, and (3) providing law and order (as noted above). Public goods are essential to market operation, and how the government provides them affects the market's character. Consider the system of lighthouses established by the U.S. government in the nineteenth century. Before modern electronics, lighthouses were essential for the safety of seagoing vessels, including the transport of goods and people. No individual shipping company, however, would be willing to pay on its own to build a system of lighthouses because its rivals would be able to take advantage of the system free of charge.

A closely related prerequisite to providing public goods is that of allocating responsibility when the social cost of some behavior far exceeds the private cost. For instance, the social cost of driving a gas-guzzling car is more than the total of the owner's monthly payments, insurance, and gasoline, because it also includes the widely distributed impact of smog and carbon monoxide emissions. Broad social effects, such as pollution, that result from market activities are called externalities. When private behavior by individuals or firms leads to such consequences, these externalities provide government with an additional rationale for regulating the economy.

Creating a Labor Force.

A sixth condition necessary for a market economy is the creation of a labor force. Every society has provisions that enable and encourage, or sometimes force, people to work. Consider universal compulsory education: in the United States, parents are required to provide for the education of their children so that all citizens have the opportunity to learn the skills necessary to function in the market. Long before compulsory education, we had poorhouses, vagrancy laws, and other more police-oriented means of forcing people to work; these meant that people might

public good ➡

A benefit that, first, may be enjoyed by anyone if it is provided and, second, may not be denied to anyone once it has been provided

externality ➡

Side effects of an activity, affecting other parties who did not agree to the activity in question

starve or be punished if they failed to earn their keep. Under our welfare system today, the support given is periodically adjusted to remain uncomfortable enough that people will prefer work to welfare.

Promoting Competition. Once markets emerge, they must be maintained. Thus, it should be reasonably easy for a producer to enter and freely compete in the market. If this is not the case, as when one company has a monopoly, the market's efficiency and the equitable distribution of its benefits are threatened. Limited competition provides government with another reason for getting involved in the economy: to function as a watchdog over potential monopoly control and to move against it when it emerges.

◀ monopoly
The existence in a market of a single firm that provides all the goods or services of a particular type for that market; the absence of competition

GOALS OF ECONOMIC POLICY

The previous section surveyed some prerequisites for a market economy. They are means to an end, so to speak—but to what end? Government intervenes in the economy not only to provide the conditions for a well-functioning market but also to achieve other concrete goals, including promoting economic stability, stimulating economic growth, and promoting business development.

Promoting Stable Markets

One of the central reasons for government involvement in the economy is to protect the welfare and property of individuals and businesses. Because such threats change as the economy grows and new technologies emerge, government actions are constantly being updated and adapted. Generally, governments seek to maintain a measure of stability and predictability in the marketplace so that investors, lenders, and consumers will feel confident engaging in economic activity.

One way in which government promotes the viability of the market economy is by regulating competition. Beginning in the nineteenth century, as many sectors of the national economy flourished, certain companies began to exert monopolistic control over them. Decreased competition threatened the market's efficiency and the equitable distribution of its benefits. As a result, the national government stepped in to "level the playing field" by breaking up trusts and conglomerates and by restricting unfair practices such as discriminatory pricing by monopoly railroad lines. In other industries, the government used federal antiracketeering laws to end criminal efforts to control businesses through such means as extortion and kickbacks.

Another major reason that Congress began to adopt national business regulatory policies was that the regulated companies themselves felt burdened by regulatory inconsistencies among the states. These companies often preferred a single national regulatory authority, however burdensome, because it ensured consistency throughout the nation, which could then be treated as a single market.[4] It also enabled companies to lobby a single legislature (Congress) or regulatory agency rather than dozens of them.

Political shifts and advances in technology make the regulation of competition a moving target. In 1913, when telephone service was becoming widely available, the federal government sanctioned AT&T's status as a publicly regulated monopoly. It believed that a single company—publicly regulated—could provide the best service in this industry. By the 1980s, however, views about the necessity and effectiveness of such monopoly control had changed, and the government moved to break up AT&T and open the field to new competitors. Creating competition in the telephone industry, the government hoped, would reduce prices and make the industry more responsive to consumers. And indeed, prices dropped dramatically as competitors arose. In the late 1990s, amid concern about emerging monopolies in high technology, a federal lawsuit charged that Microsoft Corporation's monopoly position would stifle future innovation in software. Subsequently, the public has enjoyed massive innovation of new technologies by both existing competitors like Apple and new market entrants such as Google, Facebook, and Twitter.

Promoting Economic Prosperity

Although the idea that government should stimulate economic growth can be traced back to Alexander Hamilton, it was not until the twentieth century that the federal government assumed a central role in doing so. Americans had long been suspicious of centralized political power, and this suspicion favored state and local governments in engaging with the private economy. By the late nineteenth century, circumstances began to change, as states found themselves unable to deal with the massive growth in interstate economic activity.

Since the 1930s, the federal government has carefully tracked national economic growth in several different ways. The two most important measures are the gross national product (GNP), which is the market value of all goods and services produced in the economy, and the gross domestic product (GDP), which does not include income from foreign investments. In the late 1990s, the GDP grew at a rate of over 4 percent a year, a high rate by modern standards. Growth fell to 0.5 percent during the recession in 2001 and remained modest in the first decade of the 2000s, dipping below

gross domestic product (GDP)

The total value of goods and services produced within a country

zero during the economic crisis years of 2008 and 2009. From 2010 to 2013, annual growth hovered between 1.5–2.5 percent; in 2013–14, the rate increased to the 3–3.5 percent range. In 2016, growth slowed to approximately 1.7 percent, raising concern that the economy might be heading toward another recession.

An important factor in economic growth is strong investment, which government encourages by promoting business, investor, and consumer confidence. When businesses fear political instability, unpredictable government action, or widespread disregard of the law, they are unlikely to invest. When consumers are insecure about the future, they are unlikely to spend. Government officials monitor surveys of business and consumer confidence as they devise economic policy. After the terrorist attacks of 2001, the federal government moved quickly to reassure the financial markets, businesses, and consumers. The Federal Reserve responded with interest-rate cuts aimed at promoting spending and investment. In 2008, the federal government enacted a $700 billion rescue plan to restore investor confidence after several large banks failed. This was followed in 2009 with a $787 billion stimulus package and financial support to Chrysler and General Motors to allow them breathing room to reorganize as profitable enterprises.

Promoting Business Development

Since the beginning of the Republic, the national government has promoted markets. National roads and canals were built to tie states and regions together. National tariff policies promoted domestic markets by restricting imported goods (a tariff is a tax on an import that raises its price, thus weakening its ability to compete with similar domestic products and discouraging its entry into the domestic market). The national government also heavily subsidized the railroad system. Subsidies promote business by making it cheaper for firms to produce their goods. Between 1850 and 1872, Congress granted over 100 million acres of public domain land to railroad interests, and state and local governments contributed roughly $280 million in cash and credit. Before 1900, the United States had 35,000 miles of track—almost half the world's total at the time. Many agricultural sectors received federal subsidies as well.

Agriculture remains highly subsidized: in the first two decades of the twenty-first century, about 40 percent of farms in the United States received subsidies. The total over this period ranged between 10 and 30 billion dollars per year. One of the many criticisms of the farm-subsidy program is that it disproportionately supports large-scale farmers rather than family farmers. The list of farm-subsidy recipients includes many large corporations, and the two postal zip codes receiving the largest agricultural subsidies are Manhattan in New York City and Beverly Hills, California—homes to wealthy, nonresident owners of agricultural land.

The national government also promotes business development indirectly by offering categorical grants-in-aid (see Chapter 3) to states on the condition that the state (or local) government undertakes a particular activity. Thus, to improve national markets by facilitating motor transportation, a 900,000-mile national highway system was built during the 1930s; the national government paid 50 percent of the construction costs as long as the states provided the other 50 percent. Then, beginning in the late 1950s, the federal government constructed over 45,000 miles of interstate highways, paying 90 percent of the costs on the condition that each state provide for 10 percent of the costs of any portion of a highway built within its boundaries.[5] More recently, the federal government has been involved in the subsidization of urban mass transit, airport construction and modernization, and port improvements—a combination of promotional and security concerns at work.

TOOLS OF ECONOMIC POLICY

As it works to meet the multiple goals of economic policy outlined above, the federal government relies on a broad set of tools that has evolved over time. These tools include monetary policy; fiscal policy; and subsidies, tax expenditures, and contracting.

Monetary Policy

monetary policy
Regulation of the economy through manipulation of the supply of money, the price of money (interest rates), and the availability of credit

Monetary policy entails regulation of the economy through manipulation of the supply of money, the price of money (interest rates), and the availability of credit. America's most powerful institution in the area of monetary policy is the Federal Reserve Board.

Early in its history, the national government sought to develop a capacity to employ monetary policy. The Federalist majority in Congress, led by Alexander Hamilton, established a Bank of the United States in 1791. Federalists hoped that a national bank would help the nation create a sound currency and stabilize the new nation's credit. The bank, however, was vigorously opposed by the nation's agrarian interests, led by Thomas Jefferson, who feared that the interests of urban, industrial capitalism would dominate such a bank. The twenty-year charter of the Bank of the United States was not renewed in 1811. The Second Bank of the United States was created in 1816 to deal with the financial chaos following the War of 1812. But like its predecessor, it was terminated after twenty years, during Andrew Jackson's administration. The fear of a central bank lingered eight decades later, when Congress in 1913 established an institution—the Federal Reserve System—to manage the supply of money and credit in the economy.

The core of the Federal Reserve System comprises 12 Federal Reserve banks, each located in a major commercial city. These are not ordinary banks but bankers' banks: they make loans to other banks, clear checks, supply the economy with currency and coins, and seek to prevent both inflation and deflation. The Federal Reserve also regulates the activities of the commercial banks that are members of the Federal Reserve System, each of which must follow national banking rules and must purchase stock in the system (a requirement that helps make it self-financing). State-chartered banks and savings and loan associations may also join if they accept the national rules. At the top of the system is the Federal Reserve Board (the Fed), made up of 7 members appointed by the president (with Senate confirmation) for 14-year terms. Its chairman is selected by the president from among the board members for a 4-year term. In all other respects, the Fed is an independent agency; the president's executive power does not extend to it or its policies. Member banks can borrow money from the Fed, enabling them to expand their own loan operations.

If the Fed significantly decreases the discount rate—the interest it charges member banks for borrowing—that can give a shot in the arm to a sagging economy, because the lower rate pushes down the interest rates charged by leading private banks for loans to their customers. On the other hand, if the economy is expanding too rapidly, threatening inflation, the Fed can put a brake on it by raising the discount rate. Manipulating interest rates is the Fed's most powerful monetary policy tool. During 2001, the Fed cut the discount rate 11 times to combat the combined effects of recession and the terrorist attacks. After the economy began to sag in late 2007, the Fed cut the rate 6 times between September 2007 and March 2008. By 2009, the discount rate had dropped nearly to zero in an effort to stimulate recovery from the deepest recession since the Great Depression of the 1930s; it has remained there for years.

Another monetary policy tool available to the Fed is the ability to increase or decrease the reserve requirement, the amount of cash and negotiable securities every member bank must keep available to cover withdrawals and checks written by its depositors. A third important technique is open-market operations—the buying and selling of Treasury securities to fund government activities and to increase or decrease the supply of money in the economy. Finally, a fourth power is derived from one of the important services rendered by the Federal Reserve System: the opportunity for member banks

Federal Reserve System

A system of 12 Federal Reserve banks that facilitates exchanges of cash, checks, and credit; regulates member banks; and uses monetary policy to fight inflation and deflation

reserve requirement

The amount of liquid assets and ready cash that the Federal Reserve requires banks to hold to meet depositors' demands for their money

open-market operations

The process whereby the Open Market Committee of the Federal Reserve buys and sells government securities to help finance government operations and to reduce or increase the total amount of money circulating in the economy

The Federal Reserve System shapes U.S. monetary policy. At her confirmation hearing in 2013, Fed chair Janet Yellen discussed the role of the Fed in reducing unemployment.

to borrow from each other. This exchange is called the federal funds market, and the interest rate charged by one bank to another, the federal funds rate, can be manipulated just like the discount rate, to expand or contract credit.

The federal government also provides insurance to foster credit and encourage private capital investment. The Federal Deposit Insurance Corporation (FDIC) protects bank deposits up to $250,000. Another important promoter of investment is the federal insurance of home mortgages provided by the Department of Housing and Urban Development (HUD). The arrangements for financing home purchases began to unravel early in the 2000s, however, with the growth of the subprime market for lending. This market made home loans available at variable interest rates to people who could not otherwise afford to buy a home. But it created new instabilities in the market as mortgage payments, low at first, grew more costly with rising interest rates. Indeed, a wave of foreclosures and repossessions began in 2007 when many homeowners could not pay back their loans. The foreclosure crisis sent shock waves through the financial system, as investment banks found themselves holding worthless loans. A massive federal bailout package was required to save the banking system.

federal funds rate

The interest rate on loans between member banks of the Federal Reserve, which the Fed influences by reducing or increasing the supply of money available in the economy

Fiscal Policy

fiscal policy

Regulation of the economy through taxing and spending powers

Fiscal policies include the government's taxing and spending powers.

Taxation. On the tax side, personal and corporate income taxes raise most federal government revenues (Table 13.1). Although the direct purpose of a tax is to raise revenue, each kind of tax has a different impact on the economy, and the government can plan for that impact.

After passing major tax cuts in 2001, President Bush proposed and Congress passed a sweeping new round of cuts in 2003. Bush's plan was intended to promote investment by reducing taxes on most stock dividends, to spur business activity by offering tax breaks to small businesses, and to stimulate the economy by reducing the income tax rates for all taxpayers. In 2006, Congress extended the rate reductions on dividends and capital gains. The Bush tax cuts were criticized on several grounds. Many Democrats argued that they were simply a giveaway to the wealthy and corporations and did nothing to promote growth. There has been concern that the tax cuts are partly responsible for large federal deficits: the federal budget moved from

Table 13.1

FEDERAL REVENUES BY TYPE OF TAX AS PERCENTAGE OF TOTAL RECEIPTS, 1960–2016

FISCAL YEAR	INDIVIDUAL INCOME TAXES	CORPORATION INCOME TAXES	SOCIAL INSURANCE/ RETIREMENT RECEIPTS	EXCISE TAXES	OTHER
1960	44.0	23.2	15.9	12.6	4.2
1970	46.9	17.0	23.0	8.1	4.9
1980	47.2	12.5	30.5	4.7	5.1
1990	45.2	9.1	36.8	3.4	5.4
2000	49.6	10.2	32.2	3.4	4.5
2001	49.9	7.6	34.9	3.3	4.3
2002	46.3	8.0	37.8	3.6	4.3
2003	44.5	7.4	40.0	3.8	4.3
2004	43.0	10.1	39.0	3.7	4.2
2005	43.1	12.9	36.9	3.4	3.8
2006	43.4	14.7	34.8	3.1	4.0
2007	45.3	14.4	33.9	2.5	3.9
2008	45.4	12.1	35.7	2.7	4.2
2009	43.5	6.6	45.3	3.0	4.7
2010	41.5	8.9	40.0	3.1	6.5
2011	47.4	7.9	35.5	3.1	6.1
2012	46.2	9.9	34.5	3.2	6.2
2013	47.4	9.9	34.2	3.0	5.5
2014	46.2	10.6	33.9	3.1	6.3
2015	47.4	10.6	32.8	3.0	6.2
2016*	48.8	8.8	33.0	2.9	6.5

*Estimated

SOURCE: Office of Management and Budget, "Historical Tables" table 2.2, www.whitehouse.gov/omb/budget/historicals (accessed 9/13/16).

ANALYZING THE EVIDENCE

The federal government collects revenue from a variety of different taxes. Most important is the individual income tax. Since 1960, revenues from the corporation income tax have fallen significantly. At the same time, taxes for social insurance and retirement programs have grown substantially. Does the federal government draw more of its revenue from progressive taxes or from regressive taxes?

running surpluses in 2000 to steep deficits throughout the Bush administration. The deficits continued during the Obama years, in part due to spending on recovery from the Great Recession of 2008–10 and on the continuing war in Afghanistan.

A tax is progressive if the proportion of income paid as tax goes up as income goes up. The decision to make the income tax progressive was one of the most important policy choices Congress made. A tax is regressive if people in lower income brackets pay a higher proportion of their income toward the tax than people in higher income brackets. For example, a sales tax is regressive because lower income individuals spend a larger share of their income on consumption covered by a sales tax than higher income individuals do; thus a higher share of their income goes to pay tax on this consumption than the share paid by richer people (even though the sales tax rate is the same for everybody).

Spending and Budgeting. The federal government's power to spend is one of the most important tools of economic policy. Decisions about how much to spend affect the overall health of the economy as well as aspects of American life, ranging from the distribution of income to the availability of different modes of transportation to the level of education. Thus, the fight for control over spending is one of the most contentious in Washington, as interest groups and politicians strive to determine priorities and appropriate levels. Decisions about spending are made as part of the annual budget process. During the 1990s, when the federal budget deficit first became a major political issue, the two political parties were at odds on spending priorities. Partisan divisions have continued to plague the budget process even as federal deficits themselves have diminished (Figure 13.1).

The president and Congress have each created institutions to assert control over the budget process. The Office of Management and Budget (OMB), in the Executive Office of the President, is responsible for preparing the president's budget, which contains the president's spending priorities and the estimated costs of the president's policy proposals. It is viewed as the starting point for the annual debate over the budget. When different parties control the presidency and Congress, the president's budget may have little influence on the budget that is ultimately adopted; indeed, it is often said to be "dead on arrival" on Capitol Hill. Members of the president's own party may also have different priorities.

Congress has its own budget institutions. It created the Congressional Budget Office in 1974 so that it could have reliable information about the costs and economic impact of the policies it considers. At the same time, Congress set up a budget process to establish spending priorities and consider individual expenditures in light of the entire budget. A key element of the process is the annual budget resolution, which designates broad targets for spending. By estimating the costs of policy proposals, Congress hoped to control spending

---

progressive taxation ⇒

A tax is progressive if the proportion of income paid as tax goes up as income goes up

regressive taxation ⇒

A tax is regressive if people in lower income brackets pay a higher proportion of their income toward the tax than people in higher income brackets

budget deficit ⇒

The amount by which government spending exceeds government revenue in a fiscal year

---

Chapter 13: Introduction to Public Policy

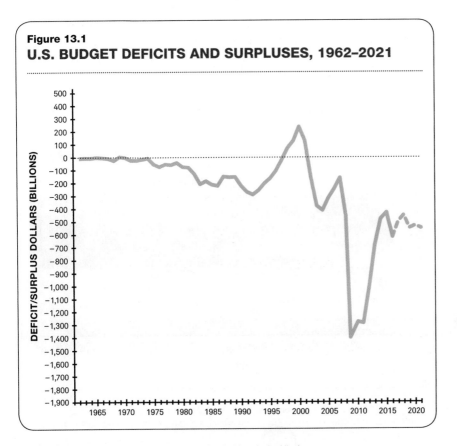

Figure 13.1
U.S. BUDGET DEFICITS AND SURPLUSES, 1962–2021

NOTE: 2015–2020 deficits are estimates (indicated with a dashed line).
SOURCE: Office of Management and Budget, Table 1.1, www.whitehouse.gov/omb/historicals (accessed 9/13/16).

and reduce deficits. When the congressional budget process proved unable to hold down deficits in the 1980s, Congress instituted stricter measures, including spending caps on some types of programs. But even these stricter restrictions have proven ineffective. For one thing, when spending bills that violate the caps arrive on the legislative floor, appropriators seek—and often are granted—waivers of the restriction, permitting the out-of-compliance measure to be taken up. Clearly, small tweaks to the spending process are inadequate. Whether legislators will entertain more drastic reform is an open question.

A very large and growing proportion of the annual federal budget is mandatory spending—expenditures that are, in the words of the OMB, "relatively uncontrollable." Interest payments on the national debt, for example, are determined by the size of the national debt and the cost of borrowed funds. Legislation has mandated payment rates for such programs as retirement under Social Security, retirement for federal employees, unemployment assistance, Medicare, and farm price supports (Figure 13.2). These payments

mandatory spending

Federal spending that is made up of "uncontrollables," budget items that cannot be controlled through the regular budget process. Some uncontrollables, such as the interest on the debt, are beyond the power of Congress because the terms of payments are set in contracts.

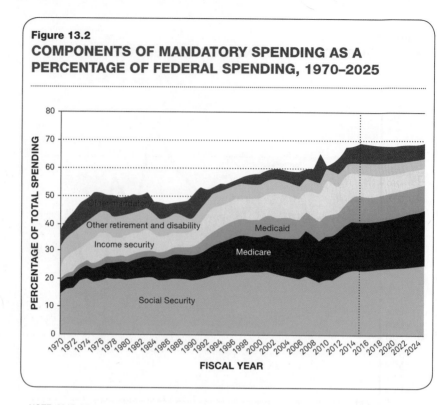

Figure 13.2

COMPONENTS OF MANDATORY SPENDING AS A PERCENTAGE OF FEDERAL SPENDING, 1970–2025

NOTE: 2015–25 percentages are projections (to the right of the dotted line).
SOURCE: Mindy R. Levit, D. Andrew Austin, and Jeffrey M. Stupak, www.senate.gov/CRSReports/crs-publish.cfm?pid=%270E%2C*P%3C%5B%3C%23P%20%20%0A (accessed 6/2/15).

increase with the cost of living as the average age of the population goes up, and as national and world agricultural surpluses go up. In 1970, 38.6 percent of the total federal budget was made up of these uncontrollables; in 1975, it was 52.5 percent; and by 2015, close to 70 percent. Thus the national government now has very little discretionary spending with which to counteract fluctuations in the business cycle.

Government spending as a fiscal policy works fairly well when deliberate deficit spending serves to stop a recession and speed up the recovery, as during the financial crisis of 2008–10. But it does not work well in fighting either inflation or deficits, because elected politicians are politically unable to make the drastic spending cuts necessary to balance the budget, much less to produce a surplus (see the Policy Principle section on p. 443).

discretionary spending

Federal spending on programs that are controlled through the regular budget process

Subsidies, Tax Expenditures, and Contracting

Subsidies, tax expenditures, and contracting are the carrots of economic policy. They encourage people to either do something they might not

Raising the Debt Ceiling

One of the most significant and politically challenging tasks of the federal government is the management of the nation's fiscal affairs. When spending exceeds revenue, the difference (a deficit) must be covered ordinarily either by raising taxes or by borrowing. The first option is naturally unpopular with voters, and so usually—and especially during wars or severe economic downturns, when increased public spending aids in recovery—Congress turns to borrowing, thus accumulating debt. Part of future public spending must then involve paying down the debt, or at the very least paying the interest on the borrowed funds.

For its first 150 years, the national government accumulated only a modest amount of debt. Early in the twentieth century, however, the debt began to grow. The fiscal policy process had grown dysfunctional in Congress: efforts to coordinate appropriations (spending) and taxation (revenue raising) became increasingly ineffective, particularly in the wake of the sizable debt accumulated from World War I, the Great Depression, and attempts at recovery through the New Deal. A large and growing debt became a fixture of the government's finances.

By 1939, Congress had delegated management of the debt (mainly involving maturity of bonds) to the Treasury Department bureaucracy, retaining only the authority to impose a ceiling on total debt. Whenever the debt approaches the limit set by Congress, the Treasury is required to ask Congress to raise it.

Until relatively recently, raising the debt ceiling was an uncontroversial matter routinely handled whenever necessary. Today it has become intensely political for two reasons. First, spending for many of the largest government programs, such as Social Security and Medicare, has, in recent years, gone on automatic pilot and does not require annual appropriations. Spending on these programs, together with interest

A "debt clock" showing the national debt as of July 2016.

payments on the debt, constitute more than three-fourths of all federal outlays. Second, for Congress to direct additional money to such programs and to appropriate resources for new initiatives, it must either raise taxes or borrow, both of which have faced increasing opposition in recent years.

Congressional failure to approve a debt ceiling increase requested by the Treasury results in shutting down some government activities in order to stall spending and thus prevent the existing limit from being exceeded. In highly partisan Washington, members of Congress are often willing to support an increase in the debt ceiling only as part of a bipartisan legislative bargain, with government shutdown the default threat if the bargain is not reached. The policy combination of (1) ensuring funding for existing programs through permanent appropriations, (2) nevertheless seeking funds for new or expanded programs, and (3) resisting increases in taxes has allowed the debt ceiling to become hostage to political extortion. The result is frequent fiscal crises in Washington as conflicting policy goals and the institutional structure of Congress take us right to the edge of the fiscal cliff.

otherwise do or else do more of what they are already doing. Sometimes subsidies merely compensate people for something done in the past.

Subsidies.

Subsidies are government grants of cash or other valuable commodities, such as land. Although subsidies are often denounced as "giveaways," they have played a fundamental role in the history of government in the United States. As the dominant form of public policy of the national government and the state and local governments throughout the nineteenth century, they remain important at all levels of government. The first planning document ever written for the national government, Alexander Hamilton's *Report on Manufactures*, was based almost entirely on Hamilton's assumption that American industry could be encouraged by federal subsidies and that these were not only desirable but constitutional.

Under later policy makers, subsidies in the form of land grants were given to farmers and to railroad companies to encourage western settlement. Substantial cash subsidies have traditionally been given to shipbuilders to develop the commercial fleet and to guarantee the use of their ships as military personnel carriers in wartime. Policies using the subsidy technique have continued into the twenty-first century. Direct crop subsidies for farmers, for example, from the federal government, amounted to approximately $20 billion in 2015. These dollars were distributed to more than 700,000 farmers by the U.S. Department of Agriculture with the bulk going to large corporate farming operations, rather than small family farmers. An additional $5 billion comes as an indirect subsidy in the form of federally sponsored agricultural research and collection of production data.

Politicians have always favored subsidies because they can serve as benefits to be spread widely in response to many demands that might otherwise produce profound political conflict. Subsidies can, in other words, be used to buy off the opposition.

Tax Expenditures.

Tax expenditures are a species of subsidy. Instead of giving cash or something else of direct benefit to encourage a particular activity, government policy releases a citizen or company from a tax obligation. They are especially popular for politicians because they do not show up in the budget as a category of spending. The two largest categories of tax expenditure are on contributions paid by employers for medical insurance premiums and mortgage interest expenses on owner-occupied residences. In the fiscal year beginning in October 2015, the medical insurance shelter amounted to $206 billion of lost tax revenue, while the sheltering of home-mortgage interest cost the Treasury $69 billion.

Contracting.

Like any corporation, a government agency often purchases goods and services by contract. The law requires open bidding for many of these contracts because they are extremely valuable to businesses and the opportunities for abuse are great. But contracting is more than a method of buying goods and services. It is also an important technique of policy because government agencies are often authorized to use their contracting power as a means of helping to build up whole sectors of the economy and of encouraging certain desirable goals or behaviors, such as equal employment opportunity. For example, the infant airline industry of the 1930s was nurtured by the national government's lucrative contracts to carry airmail. A more recent example is the use of government contracting to encourage industries, universities, and other organizations to engage in research and development on issues in basic and applied science.

contracting power
The power of government to set conditions on companies seeking to sell goods or services to government agencies

Military contracting has long been a major element in government spending. So tight was the connection between defense contractors and the federal government during the Cold War that as he was leaving office, President Eisenhower warned the nation to beware of the powerful "military-industrial complex." After the Cold War, as military spending and production declined in the 1990s, major defense contractors sought alternative activities to supplement the reduced demand for weapons. For example, Lockheed Martin, the nation's largest defense contractor, bid on contracts related to welfare reform. After the terrorist attacks of 2001, however, the military budget was awash in new funds: President George W. Bush increased the Pentagon budget by more than 7 percent a year, requesting so many weapons systems that one observer called the budget a "weapons smorgasbord."[6] Military contractors shifted to produce not only weapons for foreign warfare but also surveillance systems to enhance domestic security.

During the financial crisis of 2008–09 the Obama administration, as part of its stimulus package, invited businesses, state and local governments, universities, and laboratories to submit "shovel-ready" and "beaker-ready" project proposals. These were funded on an expedited basis, and tens of billions of dollars were pumped into the economy in the form of contracts to repair roads and bridges, National Institutes of Health grants for research projects, Army Corps of Engineers and Reclamation Bureau activities, and so on.

The government's growing use of contractors can sometimes illustrate the dark side of the relationship between citizens as principals and our governmental institutions as agents. Inherent in all principal-agent relationships is the possibility that the agent will not act in the interest of the principal. Legislative institutions, for example, may enact laws desired by lobbyists rather than by public opinion.

The principal-agent problem is compounded in the case of government contracting. Here, our agent, the U.S. Congress, has delegated power to a secondary agent, a government bureaucracy, which has, in turn, delegated power to a tertiary agent—a private contractor. Thus, the agent of the agent of our agent undertakes actions on behalf of the nation's citizens. We often discover that these tertiary agents are hardly controlled by the bureaucracies that employ them, much less by Congress or the citizenry. Military contractors, for example, were responsible for violent acts against Iraqi civilians that helped to turn Arab opinion against the United States. Although President Obama declared that the government would rely less on contractors and more on civil servants to carry out its responsibilities, its dependence on contractors is so great that it seems unlikely that the role of these tertiary agents will truly be diminished.

THE WELFARE SYSTEM AS FISCAL AND SOCIAL POLICY

Government involvement in relieving poverty and economic insecurity was insignificant until the twentieth century because of Americans' antipathy toward government and their confidence that private efforts alone could care for all those who deserved help. This traditional approach crumbled in 1930s in the wake of the Great Depression, when financial misfortune befell nearly everyone. Americans finally confronted the fact that poverty and dependency could result from imperfections of their economic system itself, rather than individual irresponsibility. Though still distinguishing

The Great Depression helped establish the ideas that unemployment and poverty reflected problems with America's economic system, not just individual irresponsibility, and that the government should take an active role in shaping fiscal and social policy.

Chapter 13: Introduction to Public Policy

between the deserving and undeserving poor, they significantly altered the standards of who was deserving and who was not. And once the idea of an imperfect system was established, a large-scale public approach became practical not only to alleviate poverty but also to redistribute wealth and to manipulate economic activity through fiscal policy.

The architects of the original Social Security system in the 1930s were well aware that a large social welfare system can be good *fiscal* policy. When the economy is declining and more people are losing their jobs or are retiring early, welfare payments go up automatically, thus maintaining consumer demand and making the "downside" of the business cycle shorter and shallower. Conversely, during periods of full employment or high levels of government spending, when inflationary pressures can mount, the taxes that support the system take an extra bite out of consumer dollars, tending to restrain inflation and flatten the "upside" of the cycle.

However, the authors of Social Security were more aware of the *social* policy significance of the welfare system. They recognized that a large proportion of the misery of the 1930s was due to the imperfections of a large industrial economy and not to any fault of the victims of these imperfections. They also recognized that opportunities to achieve financial security, let alone prosperity, were unevenly distributed in our society.

Social Security

The 1935 Social Security Act provided for two separate categories of programs—*contributory* and *noncontributory*. Contributory programs are those financed at least in part by taxation or other mandatory contributions by individuals who are currently receiving benefits or will receive them in the future. Social Security, financed by a payroll tax, is the most important contributory program. In the 1930s, when the original system for old-age insurance was enacted, employers were required to deduct 1 percent of the first $3,000 of wages from the paycheck of each employee and to match this amount with an equal contribution of their own. These figures have increased over the years; in 2016, the total employee contribution was 6.2 percent on the first $118,500 of income for the Social Security program and an additional 1.45 percent on all earnings for Medicare, the national health insurance program for the elderly and disabled (discussed in detail below). Individuals must pay an additional 0.9 percent on earnings over $200,000 for Medicare. Employers pay another 6.2 percent for Social Security and 1.45 percent for Medicare.

Retirees enrolled in the Social Security system receive benefits based on the number of years they have worked, the amount they have contributed, and the age at which they retire. They begin to be eligible for benefits at age 62, but the monthly amount they receive increases substantially the longer they

contributory program

A social welfare program financed in whole or in part by taxation or other mandatory contributions by its present or future recipients. The most important example is Social Security, which is financed by a payroll tax

Social Security

A contributory welfare program into which working Americans contribute a percentage of their wages and from which they receive cash benefits after retirement

wait to begin collecting payments (until age 70 and one-half, when they are required to begin). Spouses and children of deceased enrollees are also often entitled to benefits, as are—under the Social Security Disability Program (SSDI)—workers who become disabled before retirement.

Social Security has some characteristics of an insurance program, but it operates somewhat differently from private insurance. Workers' contributions do not accumulate in a personal account as, say, a private annuity does. Consequently, contributors do not receive benefits in proportion to their contributions, and thus Social Security redistributes wealth: mildly from higher- to lower-income people, and significantly from younger workers to older retirees.

Since 1972, Social Security benefits and costs have been adjusted through indexing. Benefits are automatically increased annually by cost-of-living adjustments (COLAs) based on changes in the Consumer Price Index. To pay for these adjustments, Social Security taxes (contributions) also increase. These changes made Social Security, in the words of one observer, "a politically ideal program. It bridged partisan conflict by providing liberal benefits under conservative financial auspices."[7] In other words, conservatives could more readily yield to the demands of the well-organized and expanding constituency of elderly voters if benefit increases were guaranteed and automatic, and liberals could cement conservative support by agreeing to finance the expanded benefits through increases in the regressive Social Security tax rather than through general revenues from the more progressive income tax.

indexing

The process of periodically adjusting social benefits to account for increases in the cost of living

The Politics of Reforming Social Security. In 2015, some 60 million Americans received around $870 billion in Social Security benefits. For more than half of all American workers, Social Security is their only pension plan. And without it, half of all senior citizens would be living below the poverty line.

Clearly, the Social Security program makes a real difference to many people's lives. However, it faces demographic pressure as the ratio between contributing workers and benefiting retirees has declined, from a comfortable 16 contributors to 1 retiree in the 1950s downward toward 3 contributors to 1 retiree today. With the retirement of the huge baby boom generation under way, the ratio will drop even further, stoking concern that the contributions of today will not pay for the retirements of tomorrow. Until recently, the system has run a surplus. But the low ratio of contributors to retirees coupled with projected higher life expectancies could stress the system—that is, without reform (see the Analyzing the Evidence unit on pp. 450–1). Figure 13.3 shows the actual and projected cost of Social Security and Medicare as a percent of U.S. gross domestic product.

All contributions to the system are deposited in a Social Security Trust Fund, which officially earns interest at the average level for U.S. government

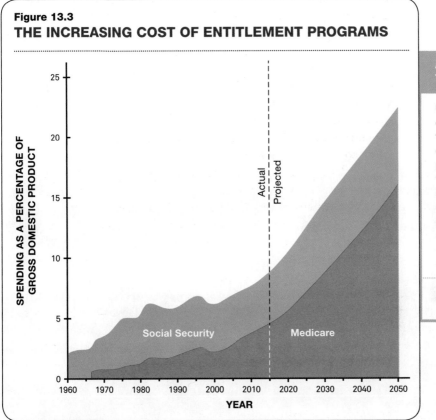

Figure 13.3

THE INCREASING COST OF ENTITLEMENT PROGRAMS

Y-axis: SPENDING AS A PERCENTAGE OF GROSS DOMESTIC PRODUCT (0, 5, 10, 15, 20, 25)

X-axis: YEAR (1960, 1970, 1980, 1990, 2000, 2010, 2020, 2030, 2040, 2050)

Actual | Projected

Social Security

Medicare

SOURCE: Congressional Budget Office, Budget and Economic Outlook (2015).

ANALYZING THE EVIDENCE

Under current eligibility requirements, federal spending on entitlement programs, particularly Medicare, will grow enormously in the future. What accounts for this growth? What are the arguments for and against the welfare state?

securities. But that is a myth. The U.S. Treasury regularly borrows money from the trust fund and leaves IOUs to hide—or soften the impression of—the nation's true national debt. Reforms to safeguard the trust fund have been proposed but tossed aside. One idea from the 1940s was to have the Treasury invest the contributions in private securities, earning interest and at the same time keeping the reserve safely away from politics and government. A more recent proposal was simply to keep the trust fund in interest-bearing government securities but in a "locked box," unavailable for other uses.

Most experts believe that Social Security taxes must be increased and the retirement age raised to maintain the program's solvency. When Social Security was introduced, it seemed fiscally sound to assume a retirement age of 60, the average life expectancy for American workers at that time. Today, however, Americans expect longer and healthier lives than their forebears. Rather than viewing an increase in the national retirement age as a national failure, we should see it as a sign of our success.

Fixing Social Security?

Every month, millions of elderly and disabled Americans receive a check from the U.S. government. These funds are designed to provide a safety net—income for retirement and assistance to those with disabilities. When the Social Security Act passed both houses of Congress and was signed into law by President Franklin D. Roosevelt in 1935, 50 percent of elderly Americans were living in poverty. By the 1950s, that number had fallen to 35 percent. Today, only 10 percent of elderly Americans live in poverty.

However, the number of retired Americans is rising because of an increase in life expectancy and because of a growing population of elderly Americans. In 2010, 54 million people received Social Security. In 2035, a projected 91 million people will receive Social Security. In 1960, the number of workers per beneficiary was five. That number is projected to decline to two by 2035. Thus Social Security faces the challenge of remaining solvent for future generations. Left unchanged, full benefits are possible only through 2033, according to a 2012 report from the Trustees of the Social Security Trust Fund. The figure below, from 2010, shows the projected divergence of program cost and tax revenue over time. More recent analyses have reached similar conclusions.

Social Security Cost vs. Expected Tax Revenue*

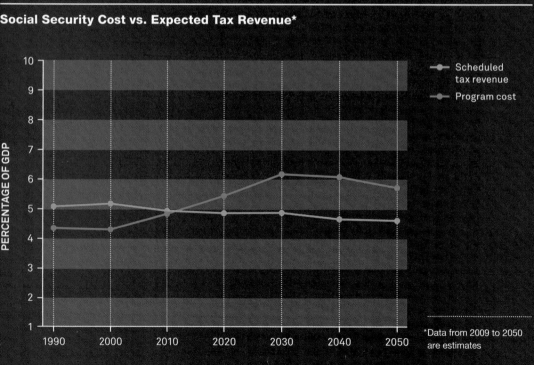

*Data from 2009 to 2050 are estimates

Policy solutions aimed at preserving Social Security fall into three broad categories: raising payroll taxes, reducing benefits to future retirees, or changing eligibility requirements. Currently, 6.2 percent of a person's paycheck is deducted for Social Security, but only on wages and salaries up to $118,500 per year. That means that any income someone earns above $118,500 per year is not deducted. As earnings inequality has increased, the share of earnings that is taxed for Social Security has declined. This is because, according to the Congressional Budget Office, "a greater share of income is above the taxable maximum."[1] Policy makers could lift the ceiling on which payroll taxes are paid, or the tax rate of 6.2 percent could be increased. Finally, the retirement age could be raised from 65 or overall benefits could be cut.

As the figures below show, a 2015 Economist/YouGov poll found that 55 percent of Americans support taxing income above $118,500, while only 23 percent oppose it. A 2012 Pew Research Study found that 66 percent of Americans favored raising payroll taxes on high income earners. At the same time, a majority of Americans has reliably opposed increasing the age of eligibility or reducing benefits.

Percentage of Americans Who:

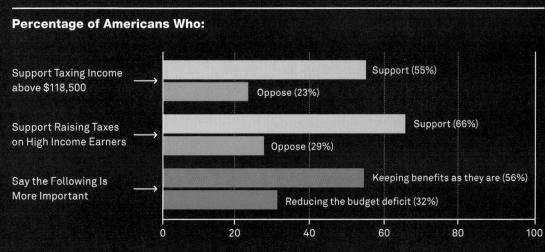

Support Taxing Income above $118,500 → Support (55%) / Oppose (23%)

Support Raising Taxes on High Income Earners → Support (66%) / Oppose (29%)

Say the Following Is More Important → Keeping benefits as they are (56%) / Reducing the budget deficit (32%)

Social Security is a broadly popular program. Since 1984 National Opinion Research Center at the University of Chicago has asked Americans whether they think too much, too little, or just the right amount of money is being spent on Social Security. In every survey, 90 percent or more of the public said too little or just the right amount.[2] Americans support Social Security and also demonstrate support for policy changes that would preserve it and its goals.

1 Noah Meyerson and Sheila Dacey, "How Does Social Security Work?" Congressional Budget Office, September 19, 2013, www.cbo.gov/publication/44590 (accessed 2/25/2016).

2 Fay Lomax Cook and Rachel L. Moskowitz, "What Americans Think About the Future of Social Security," Scholars Strategy Network, 2012, www.scholarsstrategynetwork.org/brief/what-americans-think-about-future-social-security (accessed 2/25/2016).

SOURCES: Steven C. Goss, www.ssa.gov/policy/docs/ssb/v70n3/v70n3p111.html (accessed 4/15/2016); Economist/YouGov Poll, https://d25d2506sfb94s.cloudfront.net/cumulus_uploads/document/5bfxk1yh2f/econTabReport.pdf (accessed 2/25/2016); and Kim Parker, www.pewsocialtrends.org/2012/12/20/the-big-generation-gap-at-the-polls-is-echoed-in-attitudes-on-budget-tradeoffs (accessed 2/25/2016).

Medicare

Medicare ➡
National health insurance for the elderly and for the disabled

The biggest single expansion in contributory programs since 1935 was the establishment in 1965 of Medicare, which provides substantial medical insurance for elderly persons who are already eligible to receive old-age, survivors', and disability insurance under the original Social Security system. Like Social Security, Medicare is not means tested (a procedure that requires applicants to show a financial need for assistance); rather, benefits are provided without regard to recipients' wealth or income. Medicare provides hospital insurance and allows beneficiaries to choose whether to participate in a government-assisted insurance program to cover doctors' fees. A major role is guaranteed to the private health care industry by essentially limiting Medicare to a financing system. Program recipients purchase all their health services in the free market, and then they or their doctors and hospitals are reimbursed by Medicare according to a published fee schedule. As a result, there is little government control over the quality of services and the charges by providers.

As of 2015, more than 55 million senior citizens were covered by Medicare. However, the spectacular increase in the program's cost is only partly attributable to the growing number of participants; much of it is due to the rising cost of health care and to the 2003 prescription drug benefit championed by the George W. Bush administration.

"Obamacare"

In 2010, the Obama administration sponsored a major expansion of federal health care policy. The Patient Protection and Affordable Care Act, popularly known as "Obamacare," was designed to ensure that tens of millions of Americans who could not afford health insurance would have access to at least basic coverage. Among other things, the act required individuals to maintain health insurance and compelled states to establish insurance exchanges or use federal exchanges through which individuals and small employers could obtain low-cost and in some cases federally subsidized health insurance policies. The act also expanded Medicaid, the federally financed, state-operated program providing medical services to low-income people (though states could opt not to expand it); children's health insurance programs; and imposed regulations on providers aimed at cutting costs. Indeed, the administration claimed that the law would ultimately lower health care costs by imposing greater efficiencies on providers and reducing fraud.

The act passed despite vehement and unanimous opposition by Republicans in Congress, who charged that Obamacare would be enormously expensive and would represent a huge expansion of federal government power over Americans' lives. Republicans also feared that an enormous new entitlement program might substantially expand the Democratic Party's base of support as Social Security had in the 1930s.

Opponents of Obamacare challenged the new law in the federal courts. In 2012, the Supreme Court upheld major provisions of the act, but Republicans have vowed to abolish or amend it. In 2013, the Obama administration, citing various problems, delayed implementation of a key provision of the act—the requirement that employers provide health insurance—to 2015. Republicans cited this delay as further proof that the act was unworkable, and they continued their efforts to dismantle Obamacare by attempting to strip it of government funding. The act survived another challenge in 2015 when the Court upheld the Department of Health and Human Services' interpretation of an ambiguously worded provision of the act.[8] During the 2016 campaign, Donald Trump promised to repeal the act.

Public Assistance Programs

Programs to which beneficiaries do not have to contribute—noncontributory programs—are also known as public assistance programs or, derisively, as welfare. Until 1996, the most important noncontributory program was Aid to Families with Dependent Children (AFDC), founded in 1935 (as Aid to Dependent Children, or ADC) by the original Social Security Act. In 1996, Congress replaced AFDC with the Temporary Assistance to Needy Families (TANF) block grant. Eligibility for public assistance is determined by means testing. Between 1935 and 1965, the government also created programs to provide housing assistance, school lunches, and food stamps to other needy Americans. While many of these programs, especially Medicaid, have grown, cash assistance for poor families under TANF has shrunk to about 4 million recipients. TANF grants have not been indexed for inflation and have not increased since 1996. One reason that cash assistance has shrunk relative to other forms of benefits is that the latter generally have provider constituencies (the housing and food industries) who lobby for them. Cash benefits serve only the poor, who have little political power.

Like contributory programs, the noncontributory public assistance programs made their most significant advances in the 1960s and 1970s. The year 1965 saw the establishment of Medicaid, a program that provides extensive medical services to all low-income persons who have established eligibility through means testing. Another major transformation, in the level of benefits provided, occurred in the 1970s. Besides being means tested, noncontributory programs are federal rather than national; grants-in-aid are provided by the national government to the states as incentives to establish

noncontributory program
A social program that assists people based on need they demonstrate rather than contributions they have made. Also known as a public assistance program

Temporary Assistance to Needy Families (TANF)
Federal funds for children in families that fall below state standards of need

means testing
A procedure that determines eligibility for government public-assistance programs. A potential beneficiary must show a need and an inability to provide for that need

Medicaid
A federally financed, state-operated program providing medical services to low-income people

The Supplemental Nutrition Assistance Program (SNAP), formerly known as food stamps, helps people in need buy food. Today recipients use a government-provided debit card.

Supplemental Security Income (SSI)

A program providing a minimum monthly income to people who pass a means test and who are 65 years old or older, blind, or disabled. Financed from general revenues that are not Social Security contributions

Supplemental Nutrition Assistance Program (SNAP)

After Medicaid, the largest in-kind benefits program, administered by the Department of Agriculture for individuals and families who satisfy a means test. SNAP debit cards can be used to buy food at most retail stores

the programs (see Chapter 3). Thus, from the beginning there were considerable disparities in benefits from state to state. In 1974, the national government sought to rectify some of these by creating Supplemental Security Income (SSI) to augment benefits for the aged, the blind, and the disabled. SSI provides uniform minimum benefits nationwide and includes mandatory COLAs. States may be more generous, but no state is permitted to provide benefits below the minimum level set by the national government.

TANF benefit levels, by contrast, still vary widely from state to state. For example, in 2015, monthly TANF benefits for a family varied from $170 in Mississippi to $923 in Alaska. Even the most generous states' TANF payments fall well below the federal poverty line, which in 2016 for a family of three was $20,160 or $1,680 a month.[9]

The number of people receiving AFDC benefits expanded in the 1970s, in part because of the establishment in the mid-1960s of Medicaid and the Supplemental Nutrition Assistance Program (SNAP), originally called the Food Stamp Program, which now provides debit cards that recipients use to buy food at most retail stores. These programs provide in-kind benefits—noncash goods and services that the beneficiary would otherwise have to pay for in cash. The possibility of Medicaid benefits motivated many poor Americans to establish their eligibility for AFDC, which also established their eligibility for Medicaid. At the same time, the government expanded publicity efforts to encourage the unemployed to establish their eligibility for all federal assistance programs.

Welfare Reform

The most dramatic reform of means-tested welfare policy was the 1996 Personal Responsibility and Work Opportunity Act (PRA), which replaced the 61-year-old program of AFDC and its education–work training program, known as JOBS, with block grants to the states for TANF. The act imposed a five-year lifetime limit on TANF benefits to an individual and required work after two consecutive years of benefits. It also required community service after two months of benefits, unless the state administrators agreed to an exemption from the rule. Many additional requirements for eligibility were spelled out in the law, and the states were under severe obligation to impose all these requirements lest they lose their TANF federal grants.

The Welfare State as Fiscal and Social Policy

✓ **Fiscal Policy**

When the economy is declining and more and more people have less money to spend, welfare payments increase, which helps maintain consumer spending, thus shortening the "downside" of the business cycle. On the other hand, if inflation is threatening, then welfare taxes absorb some consumer dollars, having a (desired) damping effect on an economy that is growing too quickly.

✓ **Social Policy**

Contributory programs were established in recognition of the fact that not all people have the means to establish financial security, that is, to save for the future. These programs are financed by taxation of or other mandatory contributions by current or future recipients of benefits. Noncontributory programs provide assistance to those who cannot provide for themselves.

Since this new welfare law was enacted, the number of families receiving assistance has dropped by 61 percent.[10] Some observers take this as a sign that welfare reform is working; indeed, former welfare recipients have been more successful at finding and keeping jobs than many critics of the new law predicted. The law has been less successful in other respects: researchers have found no evidence that it has helped reduce out-of-wedlock births. And critics point out that most former welfare recipients are not paid enough to pull their families out of poverty. Moreover, many families eligible for food stamps and Medicaid stopped receiving these benefits when they left the welfare rolls. The law has helped reduce welfare caseloads, but it has done little to reduce poverty because the low-wage jobs that former welfare recipients typically find offer few employee benefits. Further, the minimum wage that these jobs offer is not a living wage in most parts of the United States.[11]

The importance of the United States's welfare system was underscored during the 2008 economic crisis when millions of Americans lost their jobs. In this period, the federal government provided $5 billion in stimulus funds to the states to help meet welfare needs and extended unemployment benefits.

◀ **in-kind benefits**
Goods and services provided to needy individuals and families by the federal government, as contrasted with cash benefits. The largest in-kind federal welfare programs are Medicaid and SNAP.

WHAT IS THE ROLE OF PUBLIC POLICY IN DEMOCRACY?

Many Americans are deeply suspicious of government. However, without government to provide for the nation's defense, Americans would be vulnerable to foreign foes. Without government to maintain law and order, to define rules of property, to enforce contracts, and to provide public goods, no market economy could function. Without government to provide a safety net for the elderly, poor, and sick, ours would become a brutal society in which we would all be diminished.

Yet, too much or poorly fashioned government intervention—in the form of burdensome regulations, badly designed monetary and fiscal policies, and public policies serving private interests at the public's expense—can stifle a market economy. Poorly conceived national security policies can leave us constantly at war without protecting our safety. Inappropriate social policies can bankrupt the treasury and wreck communities without promoting the public welfare.

What is the proper balance between government intervention and free enterprise, between defense and militarism, between social spending and wasteful extravagance? There is no one answer to these questions. In the United States, as in other liberal democracies, we have a political process designed to allow every citizen to weigh in on it. If this process sometimes seems stalemated, perhaps it is because Americans have not reached any consensus and hope they can have both strong government and maximum individual freedom.

For Further Reading

Bartels, Larry. *Unequal Democracy: The Political Economy of the New Gilded Age.* Princeton, NJ: Princeton University Press, 2008.

Brill, Steven. *America's Bitter Pill: Money, Politics, Backroom Deals, and the Fight to Fix Our Broken Healthcare System.* New York: Random House, 2015.

Campbell, Andrea Louise. *Trapped in America's Safety Net: One Family's Struggle.* Chicago: University of Chicago Press, 2014.

Edin, Kathryn and Luke Shaefer. *$2.00 a Day: Living on Almost Nothing in America.* New York: Houghton Mifflin, 2015.

Gilbert, Neil. *Transformation of the Welfare State*. New York: Oxford University Press, 2004.

Levitsky, Sandra R. *Caring for Our Own: Why There Is No Political Demand for New American Social Welfare Rights*. New York: Oxford University Press, 2014.

McCarty, Nolan, Keith Poole, and Howard Rosenthal. *Polarized America: The Dance of Ideology and Unequal Riches*. Cambridge, MA: MIT Press, 2006.

McCarty, Nolan, Keith T. Poole, Thomas Romer, and Howard Rosenthal, "Political Fortunes: On Finance and Its Regulation," *Daedalus* 139 (Fall 2010): 61–73.

Mettler, Suzanne. *The Submerged State: How Invisible Government Policies Undermine American Democracy*. Chicago: University of Chicago Press, 2011.

Murray, Charles. *In Our Hands: A Plan to Replace the Welfare State*. Washington, DC: American Enterprise Institute Press, 2006.

Putnam, Robert. *Our Kids: The American Dream in Crisis*. New York: Simon and Schuster, 2015.

Schick, Allen. *The Federal Budget*. 3rd ed. Washington, DC: Brookings Institution, 2007.

Wells, Donald. *The Federal Reserve System*. Jefferson, NC: McFarland, 2004.

14 Foreign Policy

The term *foreign policy* refers to the programs and policies that determine the United States' relations with other nations and foreign entities. Foreign policy includes diplomacy, military and security policy, international human rights policy, and various forms of economic policy, such as trade policy and international energy policy. Of course, foreign policy and domestic policy are closely intertwined. Consider security policy. Defending the nation requires the design and manufacture of tens of billions of dollars' worth of military hardware. The manufacture and procurement of this equipment involves numerous economic policies, and paying for it shapes America's fiscal policies.

Much recent debate has centered on the effectiveness of current U.S. foreign policy and whether government actually can—and should attempt to—end violence elsewhere in the world. Some Americans believe that our government is itself too quick to make use of armed violence and should seek peaceful means of solving international differences. Such individuals adhere to two main schools of thought, the Hobbesian and the Kantian. For the seventeenth-century English political philosopher Thomas Hobbes, the solution to the problem of violence was the creation of a powerful sovereign authority that would put an end to violent conflict. For Kant, the solution was an increase in the number of republican governments, a type of regime that in his view was extremely reluctant to engage in armed aggression. Thus, modern-day neo-Hobbesians favor the construction of supranational organizations and the dilution of national sovereignty, while modern-day neo-Kantians count on the spread of liberal democracy to bring about a "democratic peace."

The main problem faced by the neo-Hobbesians is that the establishment and maintenance of a sovereign powerful enough to suppress violence is most likely to be accepted by states or other actors that already have few or relatively manageable antagonisms toward one another and see submission to a single authority as a means of advancing their mutual interests. The thirteen American states in 1789 or the economically advanced western European states today are examples. The imposition of some sort of sovereign authority over mutually antagonistic states and political forces, on the other hand, is likely to require considerable violence and continuing coercion. In other words, it would entail an imperial project that seems more a recipe than a cure for violence.

As for the neo-Kantians, who take their inspiration from the eighteenth-century German philosopher Immaneul Kant, the statistical evidence concerning the peaceful proclivities of liberal democracies is mixed. It is interesting to note that the United States, the world's premier liberal democracy, is also among the most bellicose nations on earth. Since the Civil War, American forces have been deployed abroad on hundreds of occasions for major conflicts as well as minor skirmishes. Writing in 1989, historian Geoffrey Perret commented that no other nation "has had as much experience

CORE OF THE ANALYSIS

➡ The goals of American foreign policy include security, economic prosperity, and—to a lesser extent—humanitarian objectives.

➡ Foreign policy is shaped by domestic actors—such as the president, the bureaucracy, Congress, and interest groups—and through strategic interactions with other foreign actors.

➡ The instruments that the government uses to implement foreign policy may include economic, diplomatic, institutional, or military means. These instruments are deployed strategically to serve the interests of the United States.

of war as the United States."[1] The United States has not become less warlike in the years since: American forces have fought two wars in the Persian Gulf and a war in Afghanistan, while engaging in lesser military actions in Panama, Kosovo, Somalia, and elsewhere. The United States currently spends more than $600 billion per year on its military, more than one-third of the world's total military expenditure and nearly six times the amount spent by China, the nation that currently ranks second. Nonetheless, the United States has justified many of its wars, including the 2002 Iraq War, by the claim that its goal was to transform its adversary into a peaceful liberal democracy.

Often, citizens and politicians denounce the use of force by some groups or nations while casting a tolerant eye at its use by others. Politically progressive groups typically denounce military actions by the United States, but tend to be more accepting of the use of violence by those they regard as oppressed groups. Politically conservative groups generally take the opposite view. The moral implications of American foreign policy are further complicated by important concerns about national security and interests and by the difficult reality that not intervening abroad with violent force may mean effectively condemning some peoples to live under tyranny.

How should our government respond to international violence? Are there peaceful means of solving problems? We also need to remember that many current international threats—climate change, emergent diseases, energy shortages—do not seem solvable by military means. In this chapter, we will consider the goals and tools of American foreign policy, as well as the various makers and shapers of foreign policy decisions. Finally, we will turn to the question of America's role in the world today.

THE GOALS OF FOREIGN POLICY

Although U.S. foreign policy has a number of purposes, three main goals stand out: security, prosperity, and the creation of a better world. These goals are closely intertwined and can never be pursued fully in isolation from one another.

Security

To many Americans, the chief purpose of the nation's foreign policy is protection of America's security in an often hostile world. Traditionally, the United States has been concerned about threats that might emanate from other nations, such as Nazi Germany during the 1940s, and then the

Soviet Union until its collapse in the late 1980s. Today, American security policy addresses not only the actions of other nations but also those of terrorist groups and other hostile non-state actors.[2] To protect against foreign threats, the United States has built an enormous military apparatus and a complex array of intelligence-gathering institutions, such as the Central Intelligence Agency (CIA), charged with evaluating and anticipating challenges from abroad.[3] While all nations are concerned with security, American power and global commitments give U.S. foreign policy a unique focus on security issues.

Security is a broad term. Policy makers must be concerned with Americans' physical security. The September 11 terrorist attacks killed and injured thousands of Americans; the government constantly fears that new attacks could be even more catastrophic. Policy makers must also weigh such matters as the security of food supplies, transportation infrastructure, and energy supplies. Many of our foreign policy efforts in the Middle East, for example, have been aimed at protecting American access to vital oil fields. In recent years, cyberspace has become a new security concern, as the government must be alert to efforts by hostile governments, groups, or even individual "hackers" to damage computer networks.

Isolationism. During the eighteenth and nineteenth centuries, the nation's security was based on its geographic isolation. Separated by two oceans from European and Asian powers, many Americans thought that our security would be best preserved by remaining aloof from international power struggles. This policy was known as isolationism. In his 1796 farewell address, President George Washington warned against permanent alliances with foreign powers, and in 1823, President James Monroe warned foreign powers not to meddle in the Western Hemisphere. Washington's warning and what came to be called the Monroe Doctrine were the cornerstones of U.S. isolationism until the late nineteenth century. The United States saw itself as the dominant power in the Western Hemisphere and believed that its "manifest destiny" was to expand from sea to sea. The rest of the world, however, should remain at arm's length.

In the twentieth century, technology made oceans less of a barrier to foreign threats, and the world's growing economic interdependence meant that the nation could no longer ignore events abroad. Early in the twentieth century, the United States entered World War I on the side of Great Britain and France when the Wilson administration concluded that a German victory would adversely affect America's economic and security interests. In 1941, America was drawn into World War II when Japan attacked the U.S. Pacific fleet anchored at Pearl Harbor, Hawaii. Even before the attack, President Franklin Delano Roosevelt's administration had concluded that the United States must act to prevent a victory by the German-Japanese-Italian

non-state actor

A group other than a nation-state that attempts to play a role in the international system. Terrorist groups are one type of non-state actor.

isolationism

The desire to avoid involvement in the affairs of other nations

Axis alliance. Until Pearl Harbor, however, he had been unable to overcome arguments that our security was best served by leaving foreigners to their own devices. The Japanese attack proved that the Pacific Ocean could not protect the United States from foreign foes and effectively discredited isolationism as a security policy.

Containment and Deterrence.

After World War II, the United States developed a new security policy known as containment to check the Soviet Union's growing power. This policy stressed the need for the United States to contain the Soviets by patiently applying counterpressure wherever the Soviets sought to expand their geopolitical sphere of influence.

By the late 1940s, the Soviets had built a huge empire and enormous military forces. Most threatening, they had built nuclear weapons and intercontinental bombers capable of attacking the United States. The United States was committed to maintaining its own military might as a means of deterrence, to discourage the Soviets from attacking America or its allies. Containment and deterrence remained the cornerstone of American policy toward the Soviet Union throughout the Cold War. Some Americans argued that we should attack the Soviets before it was too late, a policy known as preventive war. Others said that we should show our peaceful intentions and attempt to placate the Soviets, a policy called appeasement.

The policies that the United States actually adopted, deterrence and containment, stand midway between preventive war and appeasement. A nation pursuing deterrence, on the one hand, signals peaceful intentions, but on the other hand indicates willingness and ability to fight if attacked. Thus, during the era of confrontation with the Soviets, known as the Cold War, the United States frequently asserted that it had no intention of attacking the Soviet Union. At the same time, however, the United States built a huge military force, including nuclear weapons and intercontinental missiles, and frequently asserted that should the Soviets attack, we had the ability to respond with overwhelming force. The Soviet Union announced that its nuclear weapons were also intended for deterrent purposes. Eventually the two sides possessed such enormous arsenals that each potentially had the ability to destroy the other. This heavily armed standoff was called a posture of mutually assured destruction.

During the 1962 Cuban missile crisis, the United States and the USSR came to the brink of war when President Kennedy threatened to use force if the Soviets refused to remove their nuclear missiles from Cuba. After several extremely tense weeks, the crisis was defused by a compromise in which the Soviets agreed to remove the missiles in exchange for a U.S. guarantee not to invade Cuba. The two superpowers had come so close to nuclear war that

containment

A policy designed to curtail the political and military expansion of a hostile power

deterrence

The development and maintenance of military strength as a means of discouraging attack

preventive war

The policy of striking first when a nation fears that a foreign foe is contemplating hostile action

appeasement

The effort to forestall war by giving in to the demands of a hostile power

Cold War

The period of struggle between the United States and the Soviet Union, occurring from the late 1940s to about 1990 the leaders of both nations sought ways of reducing tensions. This effort eventually led to a period of détente in which a number of arms control agreements were signed and the threat of war was reduced.

The Soviet Union finally collapsed in 1991, partly because its huge military expenditures undermined its inefficient centrally planned economy. The new post-Soviet nation of Russia, though still a formidable power, seemed to pose less of a threat to the United States. Americans celebrated the end of the Cold War and believed that the enormous expense of the United States' own military forces might be reduced. Within a few years, however, new security threats emerged, requiring new policy responses.

New Security Threats. The September 11 terrorist attacks demonstrated a new type of threat: that non-state actors and so-called rogue states—nations with unstable, ideologically or religiously driven leaders—might acquire significant military capabilities, including nuclear weapons, and not be affected by America's deterrent capabilities. To counter this possibility, the George W. Bush administration shifted from a policy of deterrence to one of preemption, another name for preventive war or a willingness to strike first in order to prevent an enemy attack. The United States declared that if necessary it would disable terrorist groups and rogue states before they could do us harm. The Bush administration's "global war on terror" is an expression of this notion of preemption, as was the U.S. invasion of Iraq. The United States has also refused to rule out the possibility that it would attack North Korea or Iran if it deemed those nations' nuclear programs an imminent threat to American security interests. Accompanying this shift in military doctrines has been an enormous increase in U.S. military spending (see the Analyzing the Evidence unit on pp. 464–5).

preemption
The willingness to strike first in order to prevent an enemy attack

The Obama administration took a different tone, declaring that it would endeavor to establish constructive dialogues with North Korea, Iran, and other hostile states. However, Obama did not renounce the Bush Doctrine for those states that declined to become constructively engaged. Furthermore, he did not immediately withdraw American troops from Iraq and Afghanistan, as many Democrats had expected. Instead, he initially stepped up the United States' military effort in Afghanistan and kept U.S. forces in Iraq. This policy was finally reversed, and the United States began to withdraw from both countries. However, both regions remain unstable and have required U.S. attention. In 2014, for example, the military success of the terrorist group the Islamic State of Iraq and Syria (ISIS) led Obama to send troops back to Iraq to help defend its government, and in 2015 he announced that some American forces would remain in Afghanistan until 2017. Throughout 2015 and 2016, American air power was deployed against ISIS in Syria, special forces teams struck at ISIS in Iraq, and the U.S. armed groups such as Kurdish forces to battle ISIS throughout the region.

Cutting Defense Spending?

Contributed by
Kenneth Mayer
University of Wisconsin

What will happen to the defense budget in the next decade? With the end of large-scale military activity in Iraq and Afghanistan, defense spending has been slowly declining from a peak in 2011 of $705 billion, which was twice what the defense budget was in 2001.

The drawdown of U.S. forces in Afghanistan and Iraq is not complete, as ongoing security problems continue in both countries. In February 2016, there were just under 10,000 military personnel deployed in Afghanistan to assist the government there in its fight with the Taliban. A planned reduction to 5,500 by the end of 2016 was delayed because of ongoing concerns about security. In Iraq, there were 4,000 to 5,000 military personnel deployed at the beginning of 2016, a number that is expected to increase as additional troops are deployed to help fight ISIS forces that control parts of the country.

In his fiscal year 2017 budget, President Obama proposed overall defense outlays of $608 billion, with the total annual spending projected to decline to $606 billion by 2020, with a small increase to $612 billion in 2021. Such projections, however, are notoriously flexible, and the amount actually budgeted in future years will depend crucially on international events. In particular, the future cost of fighting ISIS is so uncertain that the Department of Defense does not predict future spending for Overseas Contingency Operations—the account that funds military combat operations abroad.

U.S. Budget, 2017* (in billions of dollars)   *Estimated

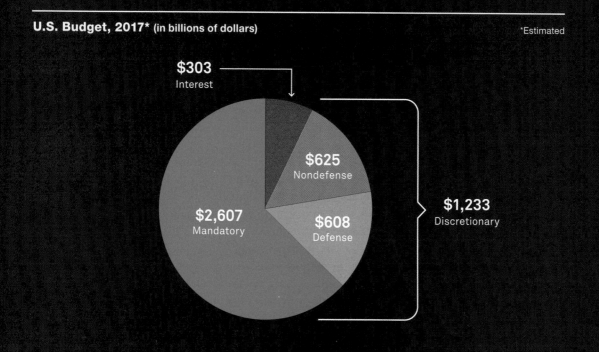

$303
Interest

$625
Nondefense

$2,607
Mandatory

$608
Defense

$1,233
Discretionary

Although the amount spent on defense increased after 2000 (see the first graph below), another way of thinking about the defense budget is not by the dollar amount but as a percentage of overall federal spending. The second graph below shows that defense spending takes up less and less of the federal budget as other types of spending, especially Social Security and Medicare, continue to grow. In 2000, defense spending was 16.5 percent of the budget. Defense spending for 2017 is projected to account for 14.9 percent. However, long-range defense planning is inherently uncertain because it is difficult to forecast concrete threats and predict the likelihood of U.S. intervention.

U.S. Defense Spending (in billions of dollars)

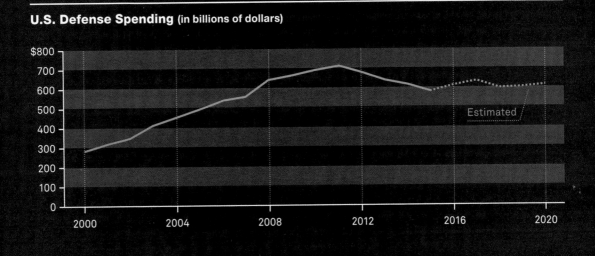

Spending on Defense and Social Security as a Percentage of Total Outlays

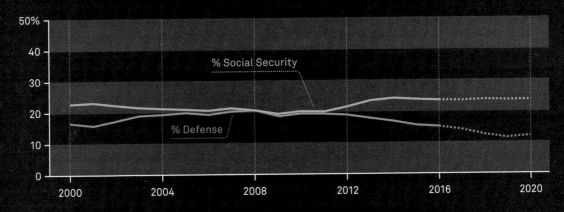

SOURCES: Office of Management and Budget, Table 8.1, www.whitehouse.gov/omb/budget/Historicals (accessed 5/31/16)

Reflecting Obama's promise to establish dialogues with hostile states, his administration brokered a nuclear deal with Iran in 2015. Secretary of State John Kerry met with Iranian Foreign Minister Javad Zarif on numerous occasions to negotiate the deal.

U.S. foreign policy makers also continue to express concern over Iran and North Korea. In 2013, when the North Korean regime began to test missiles that might soon be able to reach U.S. shores, the Obama administration positioned additional antimissile batteries to protect America's west coast. In 2015, the North Koreans pledged to use all means necessary to repel what they called America's aggressive designs and continued testing ever-more-sophisticated missiles. For its part, as Iran continued to work toward the development of nuclear weapons, the West responded with economic sanctions. In 2015, the United States and Iran reached an agreement designed to halt the Iranian nuclear program in exchange for the lifting of U.S. economic sanctions. Critics, however, feared that the Iranians would not truly end their efforts to build nuclear bombs, and during his 2016 campaign Donald Trump promised to abrogate the agreement.

Economic Prosperity

A second major goal of U.S. foreign policy is promoting American prosperity. U.S. international economic policies seek to expand employment domestically, maintain access to foreign energy supplies at a reasonable cost, promote foreign investment in the United States, and lower the prices Americans pay for goods and services.

Among the key elements of U.S. international economic policy is trade policy, which seeks to promote American goods and services abroad.

This effort involves a complex arrangement of treaties, tariffs, and other mechanisms of policy formation. For example, the United States has a long-standing policy of granting most favored nation status to certain countries—that is, we offer to another country the same tariff rate we already give to our most favored trading partners, in return for trade (and sometimes other) concessions. In 1998, to avoid any suggestion that "most favored nation" implied some special relationship with an undemocratic country (China, for example), President Bill Clinton changed the official term from "most favored nation" to "normal trade relations."[4] This continues to be the normal usage.

The most important international organization for promoting free trade is the World Trade Organization (WTO), established in 1995. The WTO grew out of the General Agreement on Tariffs and Trade (GATT) which, after World War II, brought together a wide range of nations for regular negotiations designed to reduce barriers to trade. Such barriers, many believed, contributed to the breakdown of the world economy in the 1930s and helped to cause World War II. The WTO has 161 members worldwide, including the United States. Similar policy goals are pursued in regional arrangements, such as the North American Free Trade Agreement (NAFTA) among the United States, Canada, and Mexico.

For over a half century, the United States has led the world in supporting free trade as the best route to growth and prosperity. Yet the American government, too, has sought to protect domestic industry when politically necessary. Subsidies have long boosted American agriculture, artificially lowering the price of American products on world markets.

In 2015, the Obama administration proposed a free trade agreement between the United States and eleven Pacific Rim nations. The Trans-Pacific Partnership (TPP) would lower tarriffs and other trade barriers throughout the Pacific region. Republicans generally represent industries with an international focus and favor free trade, while Democrats speak for organized labor and other interests threatened by foreign competition and generally favor a more protectionist posture. Even though the TPP was the brainchild of a Democratic president, many Democrats announced qualms about the proposal while many Republicans gave the proposal their support. During the 2016 presidential campaign, however, Donald Trump, positioning himself as a populist, charged that American trade policies had led to a loss of American jobs and called for placing limits on free trade. Trump specifically condemned the TPP, which he said would send even more American jobs to Asia, and promised to withdraw from it. Trump's position produced a strange mix of political alliances in Washington.

most favored nation status

An agreement to offer a trading partner the lowest tariff rate offered to other trading partners

World Trade Organization (WTO)

The international trade agency promoting free trade that grew out of the General Agreement on Tariffs and Trade

General Agreement on Tariffs and Trade (GATT)

The international trade organization, in existence from 1947 to 1995, that set many of the rules governing international trade

North American Free Trade Agreement (NAFTA)

An agreement between the United States, Canada, and Mexico to lower and eliminate tariffs among the three countries

International Humanitarian Policies

A third goal of American policy is to make the world a better place for all its inhabitants, an aim addressed mainly by international environmental policy, international human rights policy, and international peacekeeping. America's wealth often makes the United States the major source of funding for such endeavors. The nation also contributes to international organizations, such as the World Health Organization, that work for global health and against hunger. These policies are often subordinated to the other goals of American foreign policy—security and prosperity—especially if they interfere with achieving those aims. Moreover, although the United States spends billions annually on security policy and hundreds of millions on trade policy, it spends relatively little on environmental, human rights, and peacekeeping efforts. Some critics charge that the United States has the wrong priorities, spending far more to make war than to protect human rights and the global environment. Nevertheless, many American foreign policy efforts do seek, at least in part, to make the world a better place.

U.S.-backed international efforts to protect the environment include the United Nations Framework Convention on Climate Change, an agreement to study and ameliorate harmful changes in the global environment, and the Montreal Protocol, an agreement by more than 150 countries to limit production of substances potentially harmful to the earth's ozone layer. Other nations have criticized the United States for withdrawing from the 1997 Kyoto Protocol, an agreement setting limits on industrial countries' emissions of greenhouse gases, on the grounds that it would harm American economic interests. The Kyoto Protocol expired in 2012, but 37 of its signatories signed the so-called Doha Amendment, which agreed to renew their commitment to reduce greenhouse gas emissions. The United States continued objecting to the mandatory emission reduction targets and refrained from signing this new agreement as well. In 2016, however, the United States did agree to the so-called Paris accords to reduce greenhouse gas emissions. Each signatory country agreed to reduce dangerous emissions but would set its own contribution to the effort. Many Republicans, including Donald Trump, opposed the agreement.

The same national priorities seem apparent in human rights policy. The United States has a long-standing commitment to human rights and is a signatory to many major international agreements about them, including the International Covenant on Civil and Political Rights, the International Convention against Torture, the Convention on the Elimination of All Forms of Racial Discrimination, and various agreements to protect children. The State Department's Bureau of Democracy, Human Rights, and Labor works cooperatively with international organizations to investigate and focus attention on human rights abuses. In 1998, the United States approved the International Religious Freedom Act, which calls on all governments

One way the United States promotes humanitarian goals is by providing assistance to nations facing crises and emergencies. In 2014, the United States sent supplies to Iraqis displaced by Islamist militants who had overrun much of the country.

to respect religious freedom and lists sanctions that signatories may use to punish nations that violate it. The United States has also signed a number of UN resolutions promoting women's and LGBTQ rights.

Backing up such commitments, however, receives a lower priority in American foreign policy than safeguarding security and economic interests. Thus, the United States usually overlooks human rights violations by its major trading partners, such as China, and allies, such as Saudi Arabia. Nevertheless, it does take concrete actions to defend human rights concerns. For example, beginning in 2007, the United States has made available several million dollars annually in small grants to pay medical and legal expenses incurred by victims of retaliation in their own countries for working against their governments' repressive practices.

U.S. foreign policy also often includes support for international peacekeeping and other humanitarian efforts. At any time, border wars, civil wars, and guerrilla conflicts flare somewhere in the world—usually in its poorer regions—and generate humanitarian crises in the form of casualties, disease, and refugees. In cooperation with international agencies and other nations, the United States funds efforts to keep the peace in volatile regions and address conflict-related health and refugee problems. In 2015, for example, the United States provided nearly $2 billion in humanitarian assistance to refugees displaced by the civil war in Syria. By the end of 2016, the United States had donated nearly $5.6 million to the cause. European nations who responded to the Syrian refugee crisis by admitting more than a million refugees to their countries charged that the U.S., which admitted fewer than ten thousand refugees, was not doing enough to deal with the crisis. The United States also assists nations facing nonmilitary crises—for example, sending medical aid, food relief, and rescue teams to Haiti after a devastating earthquake in 2010. Despite the United States' inconsistent application of its professed principles, without its efforts and funding, many international humanitarian programs would be far less successful than they are today.

WHO MAKES AND SHAPES FOREIGN POLICY?

Just as domestic policies are made by governmental institutions but influenced by interest groups, political movements, and even the mass media, the same is true of foreign policy.

The President

The president exercises substantial control over the nation's diplomatic and military institutions, and thus is the most important voice determining with whom, when, and how the United States will engage in the international arena. Since World War II, for example, American military forces have fought numerous engagements throughout the world—Korea, Indo-China, the Middle East, Kosovo, Panama, and others. In every instance, the decision to commit troops to battle was made by the president, often with little or no consultation with Congress. When, following the September 11 terrorist attacks, President George W. Bush ordered American troops into Iraq and Afghanistan, Congress voiced approval, but the president made clear that he did not believe he needed Congress's permission. In 2011, when President Obama ordered American warplanes into action against Libyan rebels, he did not consult with Congress. And when Obama ordered special operations soldiers to attack Osama bin Laden's compound in Pakistan, Congress learned of the operation and bin Laden's death from news broadcasts—just like other Americans. Similarly,

The president's power in the realm of foreign policy has increased since World War II, especially in recent administrations. For example, the 2011 attack on Osama bin Laden's compound in Pakistan was initiated by President Obama without broad congressional consultation.

Chapter 14: Foreign Policy

in 2015, Obama ordered air strikes to combat ISIS in Syria and Iraq without seeking congressional approval. Furthermore, presidents have often made use of private military contractors to pursue their own policy preferences without having to defer to Congress (see the Policy Principle section on p. 472).

The president's foreign policy powers, particularly in the military realm, are far greater than the Constitution's framers had thought wise. The framers gave the power to declare war to Congress and made the president the nation's top military commander if and when Congress chose to go to war.[5] Today, presidents command the troops and decide when to go to war.

The Bureaucracy

The major foreign policy players in the bureaucracy are the secretaries of the departments of State, Defense, and the Treasury; the Joint Chiefs of Staff (JCOS), especially the chair of the JCOS; and the director of the Central Intelligence Agency (CIA). A separate unit in the bureaucracy comprising these people and a few others is the National Security Council (NSC). It comprises the president, the vice president, the secretary of defense, and the secretary of state plus others each president has the authority to add. Since the profound shake-up of September 11, two additional players have been added. The first was the secretary of the new Department of Homeland Security (DHS), made up of 22 agencies relocated from the executive branch on the theory that their expertise could be better coordinated, more rational, and more efficient in a single organization designed to fight international terrorism and domestic natural disasters. The second was imposed during the war in Iraq: a director of national intelligence, to coordinate intelligence from multiple sources and to report a synthesis of it to the president on a daily basis.

To this group another has been added: the Department of Homeland Security. The department has four main divisions: Border and Transportation Security; Emergency Preparedness and Response; Chemical, Biological, Radiological, and Nuclear Countermeasures; and Information Analysis and Infrastructure Protection.

Coordinating the diverse missions of a single agency is a challenge; coordinating those of multiple agencies is especially problematic. The NSC and now the Department of Homeland Security attempt to keep the various players—each with its own authority, interests, and priorities—on the same page.

In addition to top cabinet-level officials, key lower-level staff members have policy-making influence as strong as—and sometimes even stronger than—that of the cabinet secretaries. These include the two or three specialized national security advisers in the White House, the staff of the NSC (headed by the national security adviser), and a few other career bureaucrats in the departments of State and Defense.

The Use of Private Military Contractors

An American private military contractor in Afghanistan.

Since the earliest years of the Republic, Congress and the president have vied for control of American foreign and military policy. The Constitution gives Congress the power to declare war but makes the president commander-in-chief of American military forces. In the realm of foreign and military policy, presidents have worked to develop institutions and procedures that will help implement their own preferences rather than those of Congress. One such institutional procedure is the use of private military contractors—rather than regular military forces—to implement presidential decisions.

George W. Bush relied heavily on private contractors in Iraq in 2003–04 and in Afghanistan during the next several years to provide security and other services for U.S. operations. The use of these private soldiers was brought to the attention of the American public in 2004 when four employees of Blackwater, USA, a North Carolina security firm, were ambushed and killed in the Iraqi town of Fallujah and their bodies dragged through the streets. The horrific event gave rise to questions about the regulation and accountability of private companies. Critics worried that private soldiers showed a lack of discipline and

a lack of commitment to the interests of the states that employ them. To take one example, in 2014, several Blackwater soldiers were found guilty of having murdered 14 innocent Iraqi civilians, including women and children, in 2007.

These concerns have not seemed to deter presidents from employing private military contractors. The ability of private firms to deploy heavily armed professional soldiers has given presidents access to military capabilities outside the scope of public or congressional scrutiny. Indeed, several recent presidents have employed private military contractors to engage in activities that Congress has expressly forbidden U.S. military forces to undertake. For example, when authorizing assistance to Colombia in the War on Drugs in the 1990s, Congress prohibited U.S. forces from engaging in counterinsurgency efforts and providing assistance to Colombian military units with poor human rights records. The Clinton administration, however, believed that drug gangs and antigovernment insurgents were difficult to distinguish and that it would be hard to identify Colombian military units with unblemished human rights records. Accordingly, the administration employed private military contractors to circumvent what it saw as burdensome congressional restrictions. Military Professional Resources Inc. was given a contract to develop the Colombian government's overall military plan and another contractor, Northrop Services, was engaged to provide technical specialists for such tasks as staffing radar sites. Two additional firms provided what amounted to fully equipped combat troops. The use of private contractors allowed the administration to claim it was following the letter of the law regarding the role of U.S. soldiers and, at the same time, provided "deniability" and political cover if military plans went awry. In this and other instances, military contractors have provided presidents with the means to pursue their own policy goals without having to defer to congressional views and priorities.

Congress

For most of American history, the Senate was the only important congressional foreign policy player because of its constitutional role in reviewing and approving treaties. The treaty power is still the primary entrée of the Senate into foreign policy making. However, in recent decades, presidents have chosen to avoid the use of treaties and turned instead to executive agreements as the basic instruments of American foreign policy. This practice has reduced congressional influence. Executive agreements have the force of treaties but do not require prior approval by the Senate. Although the president has become the dominant actor in foreign policy, Congress as a whole has remained influential because most foreign policies require financing, which requires approval from both the House of Representatives and the Senate.

executive agreement
An agreement between the president and another country that has the force of a treaty but does not require the Senate's "advice and consent"

There are two types of executive agreements. The first, a sole executive agreement, entails only presidential action and does not require congressional approval. While they provide presidents with maximum flexibility, sole executive agreements have limited usefulness because they cannot supersede existing law and Congress is not obligated to provide any funding that might be needed to implement the agreement. The second form of executive agreement is called an executive-congressional agreement. Such an agreement is negotiated by the president and then submitted to Congress for approval. Approval consists of a majority vote of both houses rather than a supermajority in the Senate. This generally represents a lower hurdle than the constitutional two-thirds vote in the Senate. In some instances, the president and Congress will agree on a particular procedure for congressional approval of an agreement. In the case of the 2015 Iran nuclear deal, for example, Congress had agreed that it would vote on whether or not to accept the agreement. However, such a vote was subject to a presidential veto. In this way, the constitutional treaty power was turned on its head. Under the Constitution, the president needed two-thirds support in the Senate to carry out his plans. The Iran agreement, however, could have been blocked only if a veto-proof two-thirds of both houses of Congress was prepared to vote against the president's policy.

Other congressional players are the foreign policy, military policy, and intelligence committees: in the Senate these are the Foreign Relations Committee, the Armed Services Committee, and Homeland Security; in the House, they are the Foreign Affairs Committee, the Armed Services Committee, and the Homeland Security and Governmental Affairs Committee. Usually, a few members of these committees with extensive experience in foreign affairs become influential makers of foreign policy. In fact, several members of Congress have left to become key foreign-affairs cabinet members, including the secretary of state during Obama's second term, John Kerry.[6]

Interest Groups

The most important category of nonofficial foreign policy players is the interest group—that is, the interest groups to whom one or more foreign policy issues are of vital relevance. Economic interest groups have a reputation for wielding the most influence, yet myths about their influence far outweigh the realities. The actual influence of organized economic interest groups in foreign policy varies enormously from issue to issue and year to year. Most are *single-issue* groups, most active when their particular issue is on the agenda. On many broader and more sustained issues, such as NAFTA, TPP, or the general question of American involvement in international trade, the larger interest groups have difficulty getting their many members to speak with a single voice. For example, some business groups represent industries dependent on exports and others are those threatened by imports; hence "business" has more than one view on trade policy. Most successful in influencing foreign policy are the single-issue groups such as the tobacco industry, which has prevented heavy restrictions on international trade in and advertising of tobacco products, and the computer hardware and software industries, which have hardened the American attitude toward Chinese piracy of intellectual property rights.

Another type of interest group with significant influence on foreign policy consists of people who strongly identify with their country of origin. For example, wielding great influence are Jewish Americans with family in and emotional ties to Israel. In 2015 many, though not all, Jewish groups lobbied heavily but ultimately unsuccessfully against the Obama administration's agreement with Iran, which they argued posed a threat to both America and Israel. Similarly, some Americans of Irish heritage, despite having lived in the United States for generations, still maintain vigilance about American policies toward Ireland and Northern Ireland. Many other ethnic and national interest groups also exert influence over American foreign policy.

Interest groups comprising citizens with strong attachments to their country of origin or heritage may influence foreign policy. Here, 2016 Democratic candidate Hillary Clinton speaks to the American Israel Public Affairs Committee, which has been prominent in helping shape American foreign policy toward Israel.

IN BRIEF

Makers and Shapers of Foreign Policy

✔ **Makers**

- The president

- The bureaucracy (secretaries of State, Defense, and the Treasury; the Joint Chiefs of Staff; the director of the Central Intelligence Agency; the president's National Security Adviser; the head of the National Security Agency; and the director of Homeland Security.)

- Congress (Senate approves treaties; both chambers vote on financing; foreign policy and military policy committees in each chamber)

✔ **Shapers**

- Interest groups (economic groups, cultural/ethnic groups, human rights groups, environmental groups)

- The media

A third type of interest group, increasingly prominent in recent decades, focuses on human rights. Instead of having self-serving economic or ethnic interests in foreign policy, such groups are concerned about the welfare of people worldwide—particularly those who suffer under harsh political regimes. An example is Amnesty International, whose exposés of human rights abuses have altered the practices of many regimes.

A related type of group with a fast-growing influence is the ecological or environmental group, sometimes called the "greens." Groups of this nature often depend more on demonstrations than on lobbying and electoral politics. Demonstrations in strategically located areas can have significant influence on American foreign policy. In recent years, environmental activists staged major protests at the 2009 London and 2010 Toronto international economic summits, and at the 2015 Paris environmental summit that led to the signing of the 2015 accords discussed earlier.

Putting It Together

Who really makes American foreign policy? First, except for the president, who influences virtually every area of foreign policy, the key players vary from case to case. Second, because the one constant is the president's centrality, it is useful to evaluate other actors and factors as they interact with the president.[7] Third, influence varies from case to case because each case involves not only different conditions but also different time constraints: for issues that arise and are resolved quickly, the opportunity for influence is limited. Fourth, foreign policy experts will often disagree about the level of influence any player or type of player has on policy making.

But we can make some tentative generalizations. When an important foreign policy decision must be made under conditions of crisis, the influence of the presidency is strongest. Within those time constraints, access to the decision-making process is limited almost exclusively to the officially and constitutionally designated participants of the "foreign policy establishment," the collection of institutions and leaders who normally direct American foreign policy. In other words, in a crisis, the foreign policy establishment works as it is supposed to.[8] As time becomes less restricted, the arena of participation expands to include more government players and more nonofficial, informal players—the most concerned interest groups and the most important journalists. In other words, the arena becomes more pluralistic and therefore less distinguishable from the politics of domestic policy making.

THE INSTRUMENTS OF MODERN AMERICAN FOREIGN POLICY

Any government uses certain instruments, or tools, in implementing its foreign policy. While there have been many instruments of American foreign policy, here we discuss those we deem most important in the era since World War II: diplomacy, the United Nations, the international monetary structure, economic aid and sanctions, collective security, military force, and dispute arbitration.

Diplomacy

diplomacy

The representation of a government to other foreign governments

Diplomacy is the instrument to which all others should be subordinated, although they seldom are. Diplomacy is the representation of a government to other, foreign governments. Its purpose is to promote national values or interests by peaceful means.

The first effort to create a modern diplomatic service in the United States was the Rogers Act of 1924, which established the initial framework for a professional foreign service staff. But it took World War II and the Foreign Service Act of 1946 to forge the foreign service into a fully professional diplomatic corps.

Although diplomacy is a powerful tool of foreign policy, by its very nature it is overshadowed by spectacular international events and dramatic initiatives. The traditional American distrust of diplomacy continues today, albeit in weaker form. Impatience with or downright distrust of diplomacy has been built into not only all the other instruments of foreign policy but also the modern presidential system itself.[9] So much personal responsibility has been heaped on the presidency that it is difficult for presidents to entrust any of their authority or responsibility in foreign policy to professional diplomats in the State Department and other bureaucracies.

In 2008, both parties' presidential candidates criticized the Bush administration for having failed to use diplomacy to secure greater international support for the Iraq War. Both promised to revitalize American diplomacy. President Obama appointed Hillary Clinton as his secretary of state in part to underline the importance he attached to diplomacy by appointing such a prominent figure as America's chief diplomat. In 2013, Obama appointed former senators John Kerry as secretary of state and Chuck Hagel as secretary of defense. Both promised continuity with their predecessors' policies. Obama also promised to work to develop a better relationship with China. Though China is among the United States' chief trading partners, the two nations are deeply suspicious of each other. The United States views China as a growing threat, while China believes that the United States wants to undermine its military and economic influence.

Two of the Obama administration's biggest diplomatic achievements took place in 2015. The United States and Iran signed a nuclear deal, discussed earlier, and the United States and Cuba reestablished diplomatic relations that had been severed in 1961. Though the immediate impact was small, over time Cuba was expected to benefit greatly from economic relations with the United States.

In 2016, Democratic candidate Hillary Clinton praised President Obama's foreign policies. Donald Trump, however, declared that Obama had granted too many concessions to the Castro regime when reopening relations with Cuba, and Trump initially promised to dismantle the Iran deal. Trump also seemed to favor a tougher stance toward China and a better relationship with Russia.

The United Nations

United Nations (UN)
An organization of nations founded in 1945 to be a channel for negotiation and a means of settling international disputes peaceably. The UN has had frequent successes in providing a forum for negotiation and on some occasions a means of preventing international conflicts from spreading. On a number of occasions, the UN has been a convenient cover for U.S. foreign policy goals.

The utility of the United Nations (UN) to the United States as an instrument of foreign policy can be underestimated, because the UN is a large, unwieldy institution with few powers and no armed forces to implement its rules and resolutions. Its supreme body is the UN General Assembly, comprising one representative of each of the 192 member states; each representative has one vote, regardless of the size of the country. Important decisions require a two-thirds majority vote of the General Assembly, and its annual session runs only from September to December. It has little organization that can promote effective decision making, with only six standing committees, few tight rules of procedure, and no political parties to provide priorities and discipline. Its defenders assert that although it lacks armed forces, it relies on the power of world opinion, and that should not be taken lightly.

The UN's powers reside mainly in its Security Council, which alone has the real authority to make decisions that member states are obligated by the UN Charter to implement. The Security Council may be called into session at any time, and each member's representative (or a designated alternate) must be present at UN Headquarters in New York at all times. It comprises 15 members: 5 are permanent (the victors of World War II), and 10 are elected by the General Assembly for two-year, nonrepeatable terms. The five permanent members are China, France, Russia, the United Kingdom, and the United States. Each of the 15 members has one vote, and a 9-vote majority is required on all substantive matters. But each of the five permanent members also has a veto power, and one veto is sufficient to reject any substantive proposal.

The UN can be a useful forum for international discussions and an instrument for multilateral action. Most peacekeeping efforts to which the United States contributes, for example, are undertaken under UN auspices.

The International Monetary Structure

Fear of a repeat of the economic devastation that followed World War I brought the United States together with its allies (except the USSR) to Bretton Woods, New Hampshire, in 1944 to create a new international economic structure for the postwar world. The result was two institutions: the International Bank for Reconstruction and Development (commonly called the World Bank) and the International Monetary Fund.

The World Bank was set up to finance long-term capital projects, chiefly development aid to poor countries. Wealthier nations took on the obligation of contributing funds to enable the World Bank to make loans; the U.S. quota has been about one-third of the total.

International Monetary Fund (IMF)

An institution established in 1944 that provides loans and facilitates international monetary exchange

The International Monetary Fund (IMF) was set up to provide for the short-term flow of money. After World War II, the U.S. dollar replaced gold as the chief means by which the currency of one country is "changed into" that of another for purposes of international transactions. The IMF lends dollars or other appropriate currencies to help needy member countries overcome temporary trade deficits and thereby enables them to make purchases and investments. For many years after World War II, the IMF, along with U.S. foreign aid, constituted the only international medium of exchange. During the

1990s, the IMF took on enhanced importance through its efforts to reform the finances of some of the largest debtor nations and formerly communist countries so as to bring them more fully into the global capitalist economy.

Although the IMF, with tens of billions of dollars contributed by its members, has more money to lend poor countries than its leading shareholders—the United States, Europe, western European states, and Japan—do individually, it makes policy decisions in ways generally consonant with those shareholders' interests.[10] For example, two weeks after September 11, 2001, the IMF approved a $135 million loan to economically troubled Pakistan, a key player in the war against the Taliban government of Afghanistan because of its strategic location. Turkey was likewise put back in the IMF pipeline.[11] In 2010 and again in 2015, the IMF organized multibillion-dollar loan packages to save the Greek government from defaulting on its debt, which the United States and major European governments feared might spark a worldwide economic crisis. The future of the IMF, the World Bank, and all other private sources of international investment will depend in part on extension of more credit to developing countries, because credit means investment and productivity. But the future may depend even more on reducing the debt that is already there from previous extensions of credit.

Economic Aid and Sanctions

Every year, the United States provides nearly $30 billion in economic assistance to other nations. Some aid has a humanitarian purpose, such as helping to provide health care, shelter for refugees, or famine relief. Much of it, however, seeks to promote American security or economic concerns or both. For example, the United States provides military assistance to various allies in the form of advanced weapons or loans to purchase such weapons. Generally, loan recipients must purchase the weapons from American firms. In this way, the United States hopes to bolster its security and economic interests with one grant. For years, the two largest recipients of such military assistance have been Israel and Egypt, American allies that fought two wars against each other. The United States believes that its military assistance allows both to feel sufficiently secure to remain at peace with each other.

Aid is an economic carrot. Sanctions are an economic stick. Economic sanctions that the United States employs against other nations include trade embargoes, bans on investment, and efforts to prevent the World Bank or other international institutions from extending credit to nations against which the United States has a grievance. Sanctions are most often used when the United States seeks to weaken a hostile regime or to compel particular action by another regime. Thus, for example, in order to weaken Fidel Castro's communist government in Cuba, the United States long prohibited American firms from doing business there. The United States has maintained economic sanctions against North Korea to try to prevent that nation from pursuing nuclear weapons programs, and in 2014 it imposed them against Russia in response to the Russian annexation of Crimea, which the United States regards as part of Ukraine.

Unilateral sanctions by the United States usually have little effect, since the target can usually trade elsewhere, sometimes even with foreign affiliates of U.S. firms. If allies can be convinced to cooperate, sanctions have a better chance of success. International sanctions applied to Iran, for example, influenced that regime's decision to begin negotiations with the United States that culminated in the nuclear weapons deal of 2015.

Collective Security

In 1947, most Americans hoped that the United States could meet its world obligations through the UN and economic structures alone. But when drafting the UN Charter, most foreign policy makers anticipated future military entanglements by insisting on language that recognized the right of all nations to provide for their mutual defense independent of the UN. And almost immediately after enactment of the Marshall Plan, designed to promote European economic recovery, the White House and a parade of State and Defense Department officials followed up with an urgent request to the Senate to ratify, and to both houses of Congress to finance, treaties providing for mutual-defense alliances.

Initially reluctant, the Senate ultimately agreed with the executive branch. The first collective security agreement was the Rio Treaty (in 1947), which created the Organization of American States (OAS). It anticipated all succeeding collective security treaties by providing that an armed attack against any OAS member "shall be considered as an attack against all the American States," including the United States. A more significant break with U.S. tradition against peacetime entanglements came with the North Atlantic Treaty (signed in April 1949), which created the North Atlantic Treaty Organization (NATO). ANZUS, a treaty tying Australia and New Zealand to the United States, was signed in September 1951. Three years later, the Southeast Asia Treaty created the Southeast Asia Treaty Organization (SEATO). In addition to these multilateral treaties, the United States entered into a number of bilateral treaties—treaties between two countries.

As one author has observed, the United States has been a *producer* of security, whereas most of its allies have been *consumers* of security.[12] This pattern has continued in the post–Cold War era. Its best illustration is the Persian Gulf War, where the United States provided the initiative, the leadership, and most of the armed forces, even though its allies were obliged to reimburse over 90 percent of the cost.

North Atlantic Treaty Organization (NATO)

A treaty organization comprising the United States, Canada, and most of Western Europe, formed in 1949 to counter the perceived threat from the Soviet Union

bilateral treaty

A treaty made between two nations

Chapter 14: Foreign Policy

It is difficult to evaluate collective security or particular treaties as instruments of foreign policy, because their purpose is prevention, and success must be measured in terms of what did *not* happen. Critics have argued that U.S. collective security treaties posed a threat of encirclement to the Soviet Union, forcing it to ensure its own collective security, particularly the Warsaw Pact.[13] Nevertheless, no one can deny the counterargument that more than 60 years have passed without a world war.

In 1998, the expansion of NATO took its first steps toward former Warsaw Pact members, extending membership to Poland, Hungary, and the Czech Republic. Most of Washington embraced this expansion as the true end of the Cold War, and the U.S. Senate with a resounding 80–19 vote inducted the three former Soviet satellites into NATO. After the collapse of the Soviet Union, the importance of NATO as a military alliance seemed to wane. However, beginning in 2014, the resurgence of Russian military aggression forced NATO members to once again look to one another for support. That year, Russia seized the Crimean Peninsula from Ukraine, and it appeared to pose a threat to the Baltic states (Estonia, Latvia, and Lithuania) and other portions of the old Soviet empire as well. Russia also sent military forces to support the regime of President Bashar al-Assad in Syria's civil war.

The September 11 attack on the United States was the first time in NATO's history that Article 5 of the North Atlantic Treaty had to be invoked; it provides that an attack on one member country is an attack on all of them. In fighting the war on terror, the George W. Bush administration recognized that no matter how preponderant American power was, some aspects of its foreign policy could not be achieved without multilateral cooperation. Yet the United States did not want to be constrained by its alliances. The global coalition initially forged after September 11 numbered over 170 countries. Not all joined the war effort in Afghanistan, but most provided some form of support for some aspect of the war on terrorism, such as economic sanctions and intelligence. The war in Iraq, however, put the "coalition of the willing" to a test. The Bush administration was determined not to make its decision to go into Iraq subject to the UN or NATO or any other international organization; the breadth of the U.S. coalition was deemed secondary to this consideration. As a result, no major power except Britain supported the Iraq war.

Military Force

The most visible instrument of foreign policy is military force. The United States has the world's most imposing military—with army, navy, marine, and air force units stationed across the globe—and spends nearly as much on military might as the rest of the world combined (Figure 14.1). The famous Prussian military strategist Carl von Clausewitz called war "politics by other

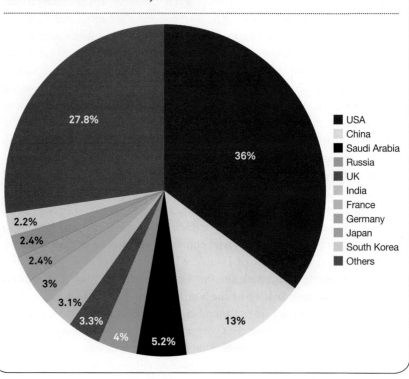

Figure 14.1

SHARES OF WORLD MILITARY EXPENDITURES BY TEN LARGEST SPENDERS, 2015

- USA
- China
- Saudi Arabia
- Russia
- UK
- India
- France
- Germany
- Japan
- South Korea
- Others

27.8%
36%
2.2%
2.4%
2.4%
3%
3.1%
3.3%
4%
5.2%
13%

NOTE: Total world military spending in 2015: $1.67 trillion. Percentages do not sum to 100 because of rounding.
SOURCE: Sam Perlo-Freeman, Aude Fleurant, Pieter D. Wezeman and Siemon T. Wezemand, "Trends in World Military Expenditure, 2015," Stockholm International Peace Research Institute, April 2016.

means." He meant that nations use force not simply to demonstrate their capacity for violence; rather, force or the threat of it sometimes serves to achieve foreign policy goals. Military force may be needed to protect a nation's security interests and economic concerns. Ironically, it may also be needed to achieve humanitarian goals. For example, in 2014 and 2015, international military force was required to protect tens of thousands of Yazidi refugees threatened by ISIS forces in Iraq. Without it, humanitarian assistance to the Yazidis would have been irrelevant.

Military force is generally seen as a last resort and avoided if possible because of problems associated with its use. First, of course, it is extremely costly in both human and financial terms. In the past 50 years, tens of thousands of Americans have been killed and hundreds of billions of dollars spent in America's military operations. Before using military force to achieve national goals, policy makers must be certain that achieving these goals is essential and that other means are unlikely to succeed.

Second, the use of military force is inherently fraught with risk. However carefully policy makers and generals plan for military operations, results can seldom be fully anticipated. Variables ranging from the weather to unexpected weapons and tactics deployed by opponents may turn carefully calculated operations into costly disasters, or maneuvers expected to be quick and decisive into long, drawn-out struggles. For example, American policy makers expected to defeat the Iraqi army quickly and easily in 2003—and they did. They did not anticipate, however, that American forces would still be struggling years later to defeat the insurgency that arose in the war's aftermath.

Finally, in a democracy, any government that addresses policy problems through military means is almost certain to encounter political difficulties. Generally speaking, the American public will support relatively short and decisive military engagements. If, however, a conflict drags on, producing casualties and expenses with no clear outcome, the public loses patience, and opposition politicians decry the government's lies and ineptitude. Korea, Vietnam, and Iraq are all examples of protracted conflicts whose domestic repercussions included dissipating public support.

Thus, military force remains a major foreign policy tool, and the United States currently possesses more powerful and effective military capabilities than any other nation. Nevertheless, the use of military force is fraught with risk and is not to be undertaken lightly.

Arbitration

Dispute arbitration involves referring an international disagreement to a neutral third party for resolution. Arbitration is sometimes seen as a form of "soft power" as distinguished from military force, economic sanctions, and other coercive foreign policy instruments. The United States occasionally turns to international tribunals to resolve disputes with other countries. For example, in 2008, the U.S. government asked the International Court of Justice to resolve a long-standing dispute with Italy over American property confiscated by the Italian government more than 40 years earlier.

More importantly, the United States relies heavily on arbitral panels to maintain the flow of international trade on which the nation's economy depends. American firms would hesitate to do business abroad if they could not be certain that their property and contractual rights would be honored by other nations. Arbitration helps produce that certainty. Almost every international contract contains an arbitration clause requiring that disputes between the parties be resolved by impartial arbitral panels accepted by both sides. By the terms of the New York Convention of 1959, virtually every

International Court of Justice

The UN's chief judicial agency, located in The Hague, Netherlands. The ICJ settles legal disputes submitted by UN member states.

nation in the world has agreed to accept and enforce arbitral verdicts. The United States has incorporated the terms of the New York Convention into federal law, and U.S. courts vigorously enforce arbitral judgments. The United States may not be happy with the outcome of every proceeding, but the arbitral system is essential to America's economic interests.

WHAT IS AMERICA'S ROLE IN THE WORLD?

The nineteenth-century British statesman Lord Palmerston famously said, "Nations have no permanent friends or allies; they only have permanent interests." Palmerston's comment illustrates the "realist" view of foreign policy, which holds that foreign policies should be guided by the national interest—mainly security and economic interest—and that policy makers should be prepared to make decisions that might seem cold and ruthless, as long as those decisions serve the nation's interests. Although many public officials have denounced such views—especially while running for office— many have become realists once in power. Every one of the United States' post–World War II presidents, liberals and conservatives, Democrats and Republicans alike, have been willing to order young Americans into battle and to visit death and destruction on the citizens of foreign states if they believed the national interest required it. As we saw in this chapter's introduction, the long and continuous history of these battles may belie their very justification: ensuring peace.

The harsh reality of foreign policy often clashes with America's history and ideals. Our democratic and liberal traditions lead us to hope for a world in which ideals rather than naked interests govern foreign policy. The ideals that Americans have historically espoused (though not always lived by) assert that our foreign policies should have a higher purpose than the pursuit of interest and that America should use force only as a last resort. Since the realities of our foreign policy often clash with these ideals, our policy makers struggle to explain their actions and avoid admitting to motivations that don't embody those ideals.

"I have previously stated and I repeat now that the United States plans no military intervention in Cuba," said President Kennedy in 1961 as he planned military action in Cuba. "As president, it is my duty to the American people to report that renewed hostile actions against United States ships on the high seas in the Gulf of Tonkin have today required me to order the military forces of the United States to take action in reply," said President Lyndon Johnson in 1964, referring to a fabricated incident used to justify expansion of American involvement in Vietnam. "We did not, I repeat, did

What should the United States' role be in world politics? American foreign policy is often controversial both within the United States and around the world. These Palestinian protesters objected to American policy toward Israel and the Palestinian territories.

not trade weapons or anything else [to Iran] for hostages, nor will we," said President Ronald Reagan in 1986, four months before admitting that U.S. arms had been traded to Iran in exchange for American hostages there. "Simply stated, there is no doubt that Saddam Hussein now has weapons of mass destruction," said Vice President Cheney in 2002. When it turned out that these weapons did not exist, the assistant defense secretary explained, "For bureaucratic reasons, we settled on one issue, weapons of mass destruction [as justification for invading Iraq], because it was the one reason everyone could agree on."[14] These false statements may hide discrepancies between our historic ideals and actual actions in what policy makers deem to be in the national interest.

Such conflicts continue. As a candidate for the presidency in 2008, Barack Obama was praised for denouncing the George W. Bush administration's treatment of enemy combatants. Obama was especially critical of the detention facility at Guantánamo Bay, Cuba, and the creation of military tribunals, outside the regular court system, to hear the cases of alleged combatants incarcerated there. Once in office, however, Obama did not rush to close the Guantánamo facility—though he continued to plan for its closure as he left office. As for the tribunals, the administration indicated in 2010 that it might employ them in some cases after all, not wishing to bring the most important enemy combatant cases to the regular courts. Ideals seemed to have given way to interests again. In 2015, the United States watched as Taliban and ISIS forces routed Afghan government forces and retook control of key regions that American soldiers had captured in bloody battles. As a candidate, President Obama had declared his opposition to endless

American troop commitments abroad and pledged to bring all U.S. troops home from Afghanistan by the end of 2015. The president was, however, forced to acknowledge the reality that absent American troops Afghanistan was likely to be overrun by radical forces and might again become a staging ground for attacks against the United States. The United States' interests again prevailed over its desire for noninvolvement.

Choices made yesterday affect our options today, and the choices we make today will affect our options tomorrow. In response to the 9/11 terrorist attacks, the United States invaded Iraq and Afghanistan, overthrew established governments, and helped replace them with new regimes. In retrospect, many think these actions may have been mistakes. But even if we should never have invaded Iraq and Afghanistan, our having done so produced new political realities that made American disengagement from these countries problematic. As American forces withdrew, new radical forces seized the territory abandoned by the Americans, brutalized local populations, and threatened increases in worldwide terrorism. Hence Americans today see their own options constrained by the choices the United States made 15 years ago. And, of course, the choices we make today may haunt us 15 years from now.

Must America always choose between its ideals and its interests? The Founders believed that America would be different from other nations—that its ideals would be its source of power, allowing it to inspire and lead others as a "shining beacon." If, in the interest of national power and security, our political leaders always choose narrow interests over transcendent ideals, might they be robbing America of its true source of international power and global security?

For Further Reading

Bacevich, Andrew. *The Limits of Power: The End of American Exceptionalism.* New York: Metropolitan Books, 2008.

Berman, Paul. *Terror and Liberalism.* New York: Norton, 2004.

Herring, George. *From Colony to Superpower.* New York: Oxford University Press, 2011.

Jentleson, Bruce. *American Foreign Policy—The Dynamics of Choice in the 21st Century.* 5th ed. New York: Norton, 2013.

Kagan, Robert. *Dangerous Nation.* New York: Knopf, 2006.

Maddow, Rachel. *Drift: The Unmooring of American Military Power*. New York: Crown, 2012.

Mandelbaum, Michael. *The Case for Goliath: How America Acts as the World's Government in the Twenty-First Century*. Washington, DC: Public Affairs Press, 2005.

Mayer, Jane. *The Dark Side: The Inside Story of How the War on Terror Turned into a War on American Ideals*. New York: Doubleday, 2008.

Milner, Helen and Dustin Tingley. *Sailing the Water's Edge: The Domestic Politics of American Foreign Policy*. Princeton: Princeton University Press, 2015.

Nasr, Vali. *The Dispensable Nation: American Foreign Policy in Retreat*. New York: Anchor, 2013.

Nye, Joseph. *Is the American Century Over?* New York: Polity, 2015.

Stent, Angela. *The Limits of Partnership: U.S.-Russian Relations in the Twenty-First Century*. Princeton: Princeton University Press, 2015.

Appendix

The Declaration of Independence

In Congress, July 4, 1776

When in the course of human events, it becomes necessary for one people to dissolve the political bands which have connected them with another, and to assume among the Powers of the earth, the separate and equal station to which the Laws of Nature and of Nature's God entitle them, a decent respect to the opinions of mankind requires that they should declare the causes which impel them to the separation.

We hold these truths to be self-evident, that all men are created equal, that they are endowed by their Creator with certain unalienable rights, that among these are Life, Liberty, and the pursuit of Happiness. That to secure these rights, Governments are instituted among Men, deriving their just powers from the consent of the governed. That whenever any Form of Government becomes destructive of these ends, it is the Right of the People to alter or to abolish it, and to institute new Government, laying its foundation on such principles and organizing its powers in such form, as to them shall seem most likely to effect their Safety and Happiness. Prudence, indeed, will dictate that Governments long established should not be changed for light and transient causes; and accordingly all experience hath shown, that mankind are more disposed to suffer, while evils are sufferable, than to right themselves by abolishing the forms to which they are accustomed. But when a long train of abuses and usurpations, pursuing invariably the same Object evinces a design to reduce them under absolute Despotism, it is their right, it is their duty, to throw off such Government, and to provide new Guards for their future security.—Such has been the patient sufferance of these Colonies; and such is now the necessity which constrains them to alter their former Systems of Government. The history of the present King of Great Britain is a history of repeated injuries and usurpations, all having in direct object the establishment of an absolute Tyranny over these States. To prove this, let Facts be submitted to a candid world.

He has refused his Assent to Laws, the most wholesome and necessary for the public good.

He has forbidden his Governors to pass Laws of immediate and pressing importance, unless suspended in their operation till his Assent should be obtained; and when so suspended, he has utterly neglected to attend to them.

He has refused to pass other Laws for the accommodation of large districts of people, unless those people would relinquish the right of Representation in the Legislature, a right inestimable to them and formidable to tyrants only.

He has called together legislative bodies at places unusual, uncomfortable, and distant from the depository of their public Records, for the sole purpose of fatiguing them into compliance with his measures.

He has dissolved Representative Houses repeatedly, for opposing with manly firmness his invasions on the rights of the people.

He has refused for a long time, after such dissolutions, to cause others to be elected; whereby the Legislative powers, incapable of Annihilation, have returned to the People at large for their exercise; the State remaining in the mean time exposed to all dangers of invasion from without, and convulsions within.

He has endeavored to prevent the population of these States; for that purpose obstructing the Laws of Naturalization of Foreigners; refusing to pass others to encourage their migrations hither, and raising the conditions of new Appropriations of Lands.

He has obstructed the Administration of Justice, by refusing his Assent to Laws for establishing Judiciary powers.

He has made Judges dependent on his Will alone, for the tenure of their offices, and the amount and payment of their salaries.

He has erected a multitude of New Offices, and sent hither swarms of Officers to harass our People, and eat out their substance.

He has kept among us, in times of peace, Standing Armies without the Consent of our legislature.

He has affected to render the Military independent of and superior to the Civil Power.

He has combined with others to subject us to a jurisdiction foreign to our constitution, and unacknowledged by our laws; giving his Assent to their Acts of pretended Legislation:

For quartering large bodies of armed troops among us:

For protecting them, by a mock Trial, from Punishment for any Murders which they should commit on the Inhabitants of these States:

For cutting off our Trade with all parts of the world:

For imposing taxes on us without our Consent:

For depriving us in many cases, of the benefits of Trial by jury:

For transporting us beyond Seas to be tried for pretended offences:

For abolishing the free System of English Laws in a neighboring Province, establishing therein an Arbitrary government, and enlarging its Boundaries so as to render it at once an example and fit instrument for introducing the same absolute rule into these Colonies:

For taking away our Charters, abolishing our most valuable Laws, and altering fundamentally the Forms of our Governments:

For suspending our own Legislatures, and declaring themselves invested with Power to legislate for us in all cases whatsoever.

He has abdicated Government here, by declaring us out of his Protection and waging War against us.

He has plundered our seas, ravaged our Coasts, burnt our towns, and destroyed the lives of our people.

He is at this time transporting large armies of foreign mercenaries to compleat the works of death, desolation, and tyranny, already begun with circumstances of Cruelty & perfidy scarcely paralleled in the most barbarous ages, and totally unworthy the Head of a civilized nation.

He has constrained our fellow Citizens taken Captive on the high Seas to bear Arms against their Country, to become the executioners of their friends and Brethren, or to fall themselves by their Hands.

He has excited domestic insurrections amongst us, and has endeavored to bring on the inhabitants of our frontiers, the merciless Indian Savages, whose known rule of warfare, is an undistinguished destruction of all ages, sexes, and conditions.

In every stage of these Oppressions We have Petitioned for Redress in the most humble terms: Our repeated Petitions have been answered only by repeated injury. A Prince, whose character is thus marked by every act which may define a Tyrant, is unfit to be the ruler of a free people.

Nor have We been wanting in attention to our British brethren. We have warned them from time to time of attempts by their legislature to extend an unwarrantable jurisdiction over us. We have reminded them of the circumstances of our emigration and settlement here. We have appealed to their native justice and magnanimity, and we have conjured them by the ties of our common kindred to disavow these usurpations, which, would inevitably interrupt our connections and correspondence. They too must have been deaf to the voice of justice and of consanguinity. We must, therefore, acquiesce in the necessity, which denounces our Separation, and hold them, as we hold the rest of mankind, Enemies in War, in Peace Friends.

WE, THEREFORE, the Representatives of the UNITED STATES OF AMERICA, in General Congress, Assembled, appealing to the Supreme Judge of the world for the rectitude of our intentions, do, in the Name, and by Authority of the good People of these Colonies, solemnly publish and declare, That these United Colonies are, and of Right ought to be FREE AND INDEPENDENT STATES; that they are Absolved from all Allegiance to the British Crown, and that all political connection between them and the State of Great Britain, is and ought to be totally dissolved; and that as Free and Independent States, they have full Power to levy War, conclude Peace, contract Alliances, establish Commerce, and to do all other Acts and Things which Independent States may of right do. And for the support of this Declaration, with a firm reliance on the Protection of Divine Providence, we mutually pledge to each other our Lives, our Fortunes, and our sacred Honor.

The foregoing Declaration was, by order of Congress, engrossed, and signed by the following members:

John Hancock

NEW HAMPSHIRE	MASSACHUSETTS BAY	RHODE ISLAND
Josiah Bartlett	Samuel Adams	Stephen Hopkins
William Whipple	John Adams	William Ellery
Matthew Thornton	Robert Treat Paine	
	Elbridge Gerry	

CONNECTICUT
Roger Sherman
Samuel Huntington
William Williams
Oliver Wolcott

NEW YORK
William Floyd
Philip Livingston
Francis Lewis
Lewis Morris

NEW JERSEY
Richard Stockton
John Witherspoon
Francis Hopkinson
John Hart
Abraham Clark

PENNSYLVANIA
Robert Morris
Benjamin Rush
Benjamin Franklin
John Morton
George Clymer
James Smith
George Taylor
James Wilson
George Ross

DELAWARE
Caesar Rodney
George Read
Thomas M'Kean

MARYLAND
Samuel Chase
William Paca
Thomas Stone
Charles Carroll,
of Carrollton

VIRGINIA
George Wythe
Richard Henry Lee
Thomas Jefferson
Benjamin Harrison
Thomas Nelson, Jr.
Francis Lightfoot Lee
Carter Braxton

NORTH CAROLINA
William Hooper
Joseph Hewes
John Penn

SOUTH CAROLINA
Edward Rutledge
Thomas Heyward, Jr.
Thomas Lynch, Jr.
Arthur Middleton

GEORGIA
Button Gwinnett
Lyman Hall
George Walton

Resolved, That copies of the Declaration be sent to the several assemblies, conventions, and committees, or councils of safety, and to the several commanding officers of the continental troops; that it be proclaimed in each of the United States, at the head of the army.

The Articles of Confederation

Agreed to by Congress November 15, 1777;
ratified and in force March 1, 1781

To all whom these Presents shall come, we the undersigned Delegates of the States affixed to our Names send greeting. Whereas the Delegates of the United States of America in Congress assembled did on the fifteenth day of November in the Year of our Lord One Thousand Seven Hundred and Seventy seven, and in the Second Year of the Independence of America agree to certain articles of Confederation and perpetual Union between the States of Newhampshire, Massachusetts-bay, Rhodeisland and Providence Plantations, Connecticut, New-York, New-Jersey, Pennsylvania, Delaware, Maryland, Virginia, North-Carolina, South-Carolina and Georgia in the Words following, viz. "Articles of Confederation and perpetual Union between the states of Newhampshire, Massachusetts-bay, Rhodeisland and Providence Plantations, Connecticut, New-York, New-Jersey, Pennsylvania, Delaware, Maryland, Virginia, North-Carolina, South-Carolina and Georgia.

Art. I. The Stile of this confederacy shall be "The United States of America."

Art. II. Each state retains its sovereignty, freedom and independence, and every Power, Jurisdiction and right, which is not by this confederation expressly delegated to the United States, in Congress assembled.

Art. III. The said states hereby severally enter into a firm league of friendship with each other, for their common defence, the security of their Liberties, and their mutual and general welfare, binding themselves to assist each other, against all force offered to, or attacks made upon them, or any of them, on account of religion, sovereignty, trade, or any other pretence whatever.

Art. IV. The better to secure and perpetuate mutual friendship and intercourse among the people of the different states in this union, the free inhabitants of each of these states, paupers, vagabonds and fugitives from Justice excepted, shall be entitled to all privileges and immunities of free citizens in the several states; and the people of each state shall have free ingress and regress to and from any other state, and shall enjoy therein all the privileges of trade and commerce, subject to the same duties, impositions and restrictions as the inhabitants thereof respectively, provided that such restriction shall not extend so far as to prevent the removal of property imported into any state, to any other state of which the Owner is an inhabitant; provided also that no imposition, duties or restriction shall be laid by any state, on the property of the united states, or either of them.

If any Person guilty of, or charged with treason, felony, or other high misdemeanor in any state, shall flee from Justice, and be found in any of the united states, he shall upon demand of the Governor or executive power, of the state from which he fled, be delivered up and removed to the state having jurisdiction of his offence.

Full faith and credit shall be given in each of these states to the records, acts and judicial proceedings of the courts and magistrates of every other state.

Art. V. For the more convenient management of the general interests of the united states, delegates shall be annually appointed in such manner as the legislature of each state shall direct, to meet in Congress on the first Monday in November, in every year, with a power reserved to each state, to recall its delegates, or any of them, at any time within the year, and to send others in their stead, for the remainder of the Year.

No state shall be represented in Congress by less than two, nor by more than seven Members; and no person shall be capable of being a delegate for more than three years in any term of six years; nor shall any person, being a delegate, be capable of holding any office under the united states, for which he, or another for his benefit receives any salary, fees or emolument of any kind.

Each state shall maintain its own delegates in a meeting of the states, and while they act as members of the committee of the states.

In determining questions in the united states, in Congress assembled, each state shall have one vote.

Freedom of speech and debate in Congress shall not be impeached or questioned in any Court, or place out of Congress, and the members of congress shall be protected in their persons from arrests and imprisonments, during the time of their going to and from, and attendance on congress, except for treason, felony, or breach of the peace.

Art. VI. No state without the Consent of the united states in congress assembled, shall send any embassy to, or receive any embassy from, or enter into any conference, agreement, or alliance or treaty with any King, prince or state; nor shall any person holding any office or profit or trust under the united states, or any of them, accept of any present, emolument, office or title of any kind whatever from any king, prince or foreign state; nor shall the united states in congress assembled, or any of them, grant any title of nobility.

No two or more states shall enter into any treaty, confederation or alliance whatever between them, without the consent of the united states in congress assembled, specifying accurately the purposes for which the same is to be entered into, and how long it shall continue.

No state shall lay any imposts or duties, which may interfere with any stipulations in treaties, entered into by the united states in congress assembled, with any king, prince or state, in pursuance of any treaties already proposed by congress, to the courts of France and Spain.

No vessels of war shall be kept up in time of peace by any state, except such number only, as shall be deemed necessary by the united states in congress assembled, for the defence of such state, or its trade; nor shall any body of forces be kept up by any state, in time of peace, except such number only, as in the judgment of the united states, in congress assembled, shall be deemed requisite to garrison the forts necessary for the defence of such state; but every state shall always keep up a well regulated and disciplined militia, sufficiently armed and accoutred, and shall provide and constantly have ready for use, in public stores, a due number of field pieces and tents, and a proper quantity of arms, ammunition and camp equipage.

No state shall engage in any war without the consent of the united states in congress assembled, unless such state be actually invaded by enemies, or shall have received certain advice of a resolution being formed by some nation of Indians to invade such state, and the danger is so imminent as not to admit of a delay, till the united states in congress asssembled can be consulted; nor shall any state grant commissions to any ships or vessels of war, nor letters of marque or reprisal, except it be after a declaration of war by the united states in congress assembled, and then only against the kingdom or state and the subjects thereof, against which war has been so declared, and under such regulations as shall be established by the united states in congress assembled, unless such state be infested by pirates; in which case vessels of war may be fitted out for that occasion, and kept so long as the danger shall continue, or until the united states in congress assembled shall determine otherwise.

Art. VII. When land-forces are raised by any state for the common defence, all officers of or under the rank of colonel, shall be appointed by the legislature of each state respectively by whom such forces shall be raised, or in such manner as such state shall direct, and all vacancies shall be filled up by the state which first made the appointment.

Art. VIII. All charges of war, and all other expences that shall be incurred for the common defence or general welfare, and allowed by the united states in congress assembled, shall be defrayed out of a common treasury, which shall be supplied by the several states, in proportion to the value of all land within each state, granted to or surveyed for any Person, as such land and the buildings and improvements thereon shall be estimated according to such mode as the united states in congress assembled, shall from time to time direct and appoint. The taxes for paying that proportion shall be laid and levied by the authority and direction of the legislatures of the several states within the time agreed upon by the united states in congress assembled.

Art. IX. The united states in congress assembled, shall have the sole and exclusive right and power of determining on peace and war, except in the cases mentioned in the sixth article—of sending and receiving ambassadors—entering into treaties and alliances, provided that no treaty of commerce shall be made whereby the legislative power of the respective states shall be restrained from imposing such imposts and duties on foreigners, as their own people are subjected to, or from prohibiting the exportation of any species of goods or commodities whatsoever—of establishing rules for deciding in all cases, what captures on land or water shall be legal, and in what manner prizes taken by land or naval forces in the service of the united states shall be divided or appropriated—of granting letters of marque and reprisal in times of peace—appointing courts for the trial of piracies and felonies committed on the high seas and establishing courts for receiving and determining finally appeals in all cases of captures, provided that no member of congress shall be appointed a judge of any of the said courts.

The united states in congress assembled shall also be the last resort on appeal in all disputes and differences now subsisting or that hereafter may arise between two or more states concerning boundary, jurisdiction or any other cause whatever; which authority shall always be exercised in the manner following. Whenever the legislative or executive authority or lawful agent of any state in controversy with another shall present a petition to congress stating the matter in question and praying for a hearing, notice thereof shall be given by order of congress to the legislative or executive authority of the other state in controversy, and a day assigned for the appearance of the parties by their lawful agents, who shall then be directed to appoint by joint consent, commissioners or judges to constitute a court for hearing and determining the matter in question: but if they cannot agree, congress shall name three persons out of each of the united states, and from the list of such persons each party shall alternately strike out one, the petitioners beginning, until the number shall be reduced to thirteen; and from that number not less than seven, nor more than nine names as congress shall direct, shall in the presence of congress be drawn out by lot, and the persons whose names shall be so drawn or any five of them, shall be commissioners or judges, to hear and finally determine the controversy, so always as a major part of the judges who shall hear the cause shall agree in the determination: and if either party shall neglect to attend at the day appointed, without shewing reasons, which congress shall judge sufficient, or being present shall refuse to strike, the congress shall proceed to nominate three persons out of each state, and the secretary of congress shall strike in behalf of such party absent or refusing; and the judgment and sentence of the court to be appointed, in the manner before prescribed, shall be final and conclusive; and if any of the parties shall refuse to submit to the authority of such court, or to appear to defend their claim or cause, the court shall nevertheless proceed to pronounce sentence, or judgment, which shall in like manner be final and decisive, the judgment or sentence and other proceedings being in either case transmitted to congress, and lodged among the acts of congress for the security of the parties concerned: provided that every commissioner, before he sits in judgment, shall take an oath to be administered by one of the judges of the supreme or superior court of the state, where the cause shall be tried, "well and truly to hear and determine the matter in question, according to the best of his judgment, without favour, affection or hope of reward:" provided also that no state shall be deprived of territory for the benefit of the united states.

All controversies concerning the private right of soil claimed under different grants of two or more states, whose jurisdictions as they may respect such lands, and the states which passed such grants are adjusted, the said grants or either of them being at the same time claimed to have originated antecedent to such settlement of jurisdiction, shall on the petition of either party to the congress of the united states, be finally determined as near as may be in the same manner as is before prescribed for deciding disputes respecting territorial jurisdiction between different states.

The united states in congress assembled shall also have the sole and exclusive right and power of regulating the alloy and value of coin struck by their own authority, or by that of the respective states—fixing the standard of weights and measures throughout the united states—regulating the trade and managing all affairs with the Indians, not members of any of the states, provided that the legislative right of any state within its own limits be not infringed or violated—establishing and regulating post-offices from one state to another, throughout all the united states, and exacting such postage on the papers passing thro' the same as may be requisite to defray the expences of the said office—appointing all officers of the land forces, in the service of the united states, except regimental officers—appointing all the officers of the united states—making rules for the government and regulation of the said land and naval forces, and directing their operations.

The united states in congress assembled shall have the authority to appoint a committee, to sit in the recess of congress, to be denominated "A Committee of the States," and to consist of one delegate from each state; and to appoint such other committees and civil officers as may be necessary for managing the general affairs of the united states under their direction—to appoint one of their number to preside, provided that no person be allowed to serve in the office of president more than one year in any term of three years; to ascertain the necessary sums of Money to be raised for the service of the united states, and to appropriate and apply the same for defraying the public expences—to borrow money, or emit bills on the credit of the united states, transmitting every half year to the respective states an account of the sums of money so borrowed or emitted,—to build and equip a navy—to agree upon the number of land forces, and to make requisitions from each state for its quota, in proportion to the number of white inhabitants in such state; which requisition shall be binding, and thereupon the legislature of each state shall appoint the regimental officers, raise the men and cloath, arm and equip them in a soldier like manner, at the expence of the united states, and the officers and men so cloathed, armed and equipped shall march to the place appointed, and within the time agreed on by the united states in congress assembled: But if the united states in congress assembled shall, on consideration of circumstances judge proper that any state should not raise men, or should raise a smaller number than its quota, and that any other state should raise a greater number of men than the quota thereof, such extra number shall be raised, officered, cloathed, armed and equipped in the same manner as the quota of such state, unless the legislature of such state shall judge that such extra number cannot be safely spared out of the same, in which case they shall raise, officer, cloath, arm and equip as many of such extra number as they judge can be safely spared. And the officers and men so cloathed, armed and equipped, shall march to the place appointed, and within the time agreed on by the united states in congress assembled.

The united states in congress assembled shall never engage in a war, nor grant letters of marque and reprisal in time of peace, nor enter into any treaties or alliances, nor coin money, nor regulate the value thereof, nor ascertain the sums and expences necessary for the defence and welfare of the united states, or any of them, nor emit bills, nor borrow money on the credit of the united states, nor appropriate money, nor agree upon the number of vessels of war, to be built or purchased, or the number of land or sea forces to be raised, nor appoint a commander in chief of the army or navy, unless nine states assent to the same: nor shall a question on any other point, except for adjourning from day to day be determined, unless by the votes of a majority of the united states in congress assembled.

The congress of the united states shall have power to adjourn to any time within the year, and to any place within the united states, so that no period of adjournment be for a longer duration than the space of six Months, and shall publish the Journal of their proceedings monthly, except such parts thereof relating to treaties, alliances or military operations as in their judgment require secresy; and the yeas and nays of the delegates of each state on any question shall be entered on the Journal, when it is desired by any delegate; and the delegates of a state, or any of them, at his or their request shall be furnished with a transcript of the said Journal, except such parts as are above excepted to lay before the legislatures of the several states.

Art. X. The committee of the states, or any nine of them, shall be authorised to execute, in the recess of congress, such of the powers of congress as the united states in congress assembled, by the consent of nine states, shall from time to time think expedient to vest them with; provided that no power be delegated to the said committee, for the exercise of which, by the articles of confederation, the voice of nine states in the congress of the united states assembled is requisite.

Art. XI. Canada acceding to this confederation, and joining in the measures of the united states, shall be admitted into, and entitled to all the advantages of this union: but no other colony shall be admitted into the same, unless such admission be agreed to by nine states.

Art. XII. All bills of credit emitted, monies borrowed and debts contracted by, or under the authority of congress, before the assembling of the united states, in pursuance of the present confederation, shall be deemed and considered as a charge against the united states, for payment and satisfaction whereof the said united states and the public faith are hereby solemnly pledged.

Art. XIII. Every state shall abide by the determinations of the united states in congress assembled, on all questions which by this confederation are submitted to them. And the Articles of this confederation shall be inviolably observed by every state, and the union shall be perpetual; nor shall any alteration at any time hereafter be made in any of them; unless such alteration be agreed to in a congress of the united states, and be afterwards confirmed by the legislatures of every state.

AND WHEREAS it hath pleased the Great Governor of the World to incline the hearts of the legislatures we respectively represent in congress, to approve of, and to authorize us to ratify the said articles of confederation and perpetual union. KNOW YE that we the undersigned delegates, by virtue of the power and authority to us given for that purpose, do by these presents, in the name and in behalf of our respective constituents, fully and entirely ratify and confirm each and every of the said articles of confederation and perpetual union, and all and singular the matters and things therein contained: And we do further solemnly plight and engage the faith of our respective constituents, that they shall abide by the determination of the united states in congress assembled, on all questions, which by the said confederation are submitted to them. And that the articles thereof shall be inviolably observed by the states we respectively represent, and that the union shall be perpetual. In Witness whereof we have hereunto set our hands in Congress. Done at Philadelphia in the state of Pennsylvania the ninth Day of July in the Year of our Lord one Thousand seven Hundred and Seventy-eight and in the third year of the independence of America.

The Constitution of the United States of America

Annotated with references to *The Federalist Papers*

Federalist Paper
Number (Author)

[PREAMBLE]

We the People of the United States, in Order to form a more perfect Union, establish Justice, insure domestic Tranquility, provide for the common defence, promote the general Welfare, and secure the Blessings of Liberty to ourselves and our Posterity, do ordain and establish this Constitution for the United States of America.

84 (Hamilton)

ARTICLE I

Section 1
[LEGISLATIVE POWERS]

All legislative Powers herein granted shall be vested in a Congress of the United States, which shall consist of a Senate and House of Representatives.

10, 45 (Madison)

Section 2
[HOUSE OF REPRESENTATIVES, HOW CONSTITUTED, POWER OF IMPEACHMENT]

The House of Representatives shall be composed of Members chosen every second Year by the People of the several States, and the Electors in each State shall have the Qualifications requisite for Electors of the most numerous Branch of the State Legislature.

39, 45, 52–53, 57
(Madison)

No Person shall be a Representative who shall not have attained to the Age of twenty-five Years, and been seven Years a Citizen of the United States, and who shall not, when elected, be an inhabitant of that State in which he shall be chosen.

52 (Madison)

60 (Hamilton)
54, 58 (Madison)

Representatives and *direct Taxes*[1] shall be apportioned among the several States which may be included within this Union, according to their respective Numbers, *which shall be determined by adding to the whole Number of free Persons, including those bound to Service for a Term of Years,* and excluding Indians not taxed, *three-fifths of all other Persons.*[2] The actual Enumeration shall be made within three Years after the first Meeting of the Congress of the United States, and within every subsequent Term of ten Years, in such Manner as they shall by Law direct. The Number of Representatives shall not exceed one for every thirty Thousand, but each State shall have at Least one Representative; *and until such enumeration shall be made, the State of New*

55–56 (Madison)

---

1   Modified by Sixteenth Amendment.

2   Modified by Fourteenth Amendment.

Hampshire shall be entitled to chuse three, Massachusetts eight, Rhode-Island and Providence Plantations one, Connecticut five, New-York six, New Jersey four, Pennsylvania eight, Delaware one, Maryland six, Virginia ten, North Carolina five, South Carolina five, and Georgia three.[3]

When vacancies happen in the Representation from any State, the Executive Authority thereof shall issue Writs of Election to fill such Vacancies.

79 (Hamilton)

The House of Representatives shall chuse their Speaker and other Officers; and shall have the sole Power of Impeachment.

Section 3
[THE SENATE, HOW CONSTITUTED, IMPEACHMENT TRIALS]

39, 45 (Madison)
60 (Hamilton)

The Senate of the United States shall be composed of two Senators from each State, *chosen by the Legislature thereof,*[4] for six Years; and each Senator shall have one Vote.

62–63 (Madison)
59, 68 (Hamilton)

Immediately after they shall be assembled in Consequence of the first Election, they shall be divided as equally as may be into three Classes. The Seats of the Senators of the first Class shall be vacated at the Expiration of the second Year, of the second Class at the Expiration of the fourth Year, and of the third Class at the Expiration of the sixth Year, so that one third may be chosen every second Year: *and if vacancies happen by Resignation, or otherwise, during the Recess of the Legislature of any State, the Executive thereof may make temporary Appointments until the next Meeting of the Legislature, which shall then fill such Vacancies.*[5]

62 (Madison)
64 (Jay)

No person shall be a Senator who shall not have attained to the Age of thirty Years, and been nine Years a Citizen of the United States, and who shall not, when elected, be an Inhabitant of that State for which he shall be chosen.

The Vice-President of the United States shall be President of the Senate, but shall have no Vote, unless they be equally divided.

The Senate shall chuse their other Officers, and also a President pro tempore, in the Absence of the Vice-President, or when he shall exercise the Office of President of the United States.

39 (Madison)
65–67, 79 (Hamilton)

The Senate shall have the sole Power to try all Impeachments. When sitting for that Purpose, they shall be on Oath or Affirmation. When the President of the United States is tried, the Chief Justice shall preside: And no Person shall be convicted without the Concurrence of two-thirds of the Members present.

84 (Hamilton)

Judgment in Cases of Impeachment shall not extend further than to removal from Office, and disqualification to hold and enjoy any Office of honor, Trust or Profit under the United States: but the Party convicted shall nevertheless be liable and subject to Indictment, Trial, Judgment and Punishment, according to Law.

Section 4
[ELECTION OF SENATORS AND REPRESENTATIVES]

59–61 (Hamilton)

The Times, Places and Manner of holding Elections for Senators and Representatives, shall be prescribed in each State by the Legislature thereof; but the

---

3 Temporary provision.

4 Modified by Seventeenth Amendment.

5 Modified by Seventeenth Amendment.

Congress may at any time by Law make or alter such Regulations, except as to the Places of chusing Senators.

The Congress shall assemble at least once in every Year, and such Meeting shall be on the first Monday in December, unless they shall by Law appoint a different Day.[6]

Section 5
[QUORUM, JOURNALS, MEETINGS, ADJOURNMENTS]

Each House shall be the Judge of the Elections, Returns and Qualifications of its own Members, and a Majority of each shall constitute a Quorum to do Business; but a smaller Number may adjourn from day to day, and may be authorized to compel the Attendance of absent Members, in such Manner, and under the Penalties as each House may provide.

Each House may determine the Rules of its Proceedings, punish its Members for disorderly Behavior, and, with the Concurrence of two-thirds, expel a Member.

Each House shall keep a Journal of its Proceedings, and from time to time publish the same, excepting such Parts as may in their Judgment require Secrecy; and the Yeas and Nays of the Members of either House on any questions shall, at the Desire of one-fifth of the present, be entered on the Journal.

Neither House, during the Session of Congress, shall, without the Consent of the other, adjourn for more than three days, nor to any other Place than that in which the two Houses shall be sitting.

Section 6
[COMPENSATION, PRIVILEGES, DISABILITIES]

The Senators and Representatives shall receive a Compensation for their Services, to be ascertained by Law, and paid out of the Treasury of the United States. They shall in all Cases, except Treason, Felony and Breach of the Peace, be privileged from Arrest during their Attendance at the Session of their respective Houses, and in going to and returning from the same; and for any Speech or Debate in either House, they shall not be questioned in any other Place.

No Senator or Representative shall, during the time for which he was elected, be appointed to any civil Office under the authority of the United States, which shall have been created, or the Emoluments whereof shall have been encreased during such time; and no Person holding any Office under the United States, shall be a Member of either House during his Continuance in Office.

55 (Madison)
76 (Hamilton)

Section 7
[PROCEDURE IN PASSING BILLS AND RESOLUTIONS]

All Bills for raising Revenue shall originate in the House of Representatives; but the Senate may propose or concur with Amendments as on other Bills.

66 (Hamilton)

Every Bill which shall have passed the House of Representatives and the Senate, shall, before it become a Law, be presented to the President of the United States; if he approve he shall sign it, but if not he shall return it, with his Objections to that House in which it shall have originated, who shall enter the Objections at large on their Journal, and proceed to reconsider it. If after such Reconsideration

69, 73 (Hamilton)

---

6   Modified by Twentieth Amendment.

two-thirds of that House shall agree to pass the Bill, it shall be sent, together with the Objections, to the other House, by which it shall likewise be reconsidered, and if approved by two-thirds of that House it shall become a Law. But in all such Cases the Votes of both Houses shall be determined by Yeas and Nays, and the Names of the Persons voting for and against the Bill shall be entered on the Journal of each House respectively. If any Bill shall not be returned by the President within ten Days (Sundays excepted) after it shall have been presented to him, the Same shall be a Law, in like Manner as if he had signed it, unless the Congress by their Adjournment prevent its Return, in which Case it shall not be a Law.

69, 73 (Hamilton)

Every Order, Resolution, or Vote to which the Concurrence of the Senate and House of Representatives may be necessary (except on a question of Adjournment) shall be presented to the President of the United States; and before the Same shall take Effect, shall be approved by him, or being disapproved by him, shall be repassed by two-thirds of the Senate and House of Representatives, according to the Rules and Limitations prescribed in the Case of a Bill.

Section 8
[POWERS OF CONGRESS]

The Congress shall have Power

30–36 (Hamilton)
41 (Madison)

To lay and collect Taxes, Duties, Imposts and Excises, to pay the Debts and provide for the common Defence and general Welfare of the United States; but all Duties, Imposts and excises shall be uniform throughout the United States;

56 (Madison)

To borrow Money on the Credit of the United States;

42, 45, 56 (Madison)

To regulate Commerce with foreign Nations, and among the several States, and with the Indian Tribes;

32 (Hamilton)

To establish an uniform Rule of Naturalization, and uniform Laws on the subject of Bankruptcies throughout the United States;

42 (Madison)

To coin Money, regulate the Value thereof, and of foreign Coin, and fix the Standard of Weights and Measures;

42 (Madison)

To provide for the Punishment of counterfeiting the Securities and current Coin of the United States;

42 (Madison)

To establish Post Offices and post Roads;

42, 43 (Madison)

To promote the Progress of Science and useful Arts, by securing for limited Times to Authors and Inventors the exclusive Right to their respective Writings and Discoveries;

81 (Hamilton)
42 (Madison)

To constitute Tribunals inferior to the supreme Court;

To define and Punish Piracies and Felonies committed on the high Seas, and Offences against the Law of Nations;

41 (Madison)

To declare War, grant Letters of Marque and Reprisal, and make Rules concerning Captures on Land and Water;

23, 24, 26 (Hamilton)

To raise and support Armies, but no Appropriation of Money to that Use shall be for a longer Term than two Years;

41 (Madison)

To provide and maintain a Navy;

To make Rules for the Government and Regulation of the land and naval forces;

29 (Hamilton)

To provide for calling for the Militia to execute the Laws of the Union, suppress Insurrections and repel Invasions;

To provide for organizing, arming, and disciplining, the Militia, and for governing such Part of them as may be employed in the Service of the United States, reserving to the States respectively, the Appointment of the Officers, and the Authority of training the Militia according to the discipline prescribed by Congress;

29 (Hamilton)
56 (Madison)

To exercise exclusive Legislation in all Cases whatsoever, over such District (not exceeding ten Miles square) as may, by Cession of particular States, and the Acceptance of Congress, become the Seat of the Government of the United States, and to exercise like Authority over all Places purchased by the Consent of the Legislature of the State in which the Same shall be, for the Erection of Forts, Magazines, Arsenals, dock-Yards, and other needful Buildings;—And

32 (Hamilton)
43 (Madison)

To make all Laws which shall be necessary and proper for carrying into Execution the foregoing Powers, and all other Powers vested by this Constitution in the Government of the United States, or in any Department or Officer thereof.

29, 33 (Hamilton)
44 (Madison)

Section 9
[SOME RESTRICTIONS ON FEDERAL POWER]

The Migration or Importation of such Persons as any of the States now existing shall think proper to admit, shall not be prohibited by the Congress prior to the Year one thousand eight hundred and eight, but a Tax or Duty may be imposed on such Importation, not exceeding ten dollars for each Person.[7]

42 (Madison)

The privilege of the Writ of *Habeas Corpus* shall not be suspended, unless when in Cases of Rebellion or Invasion the public Safety may require it.

83, 84 (Hamilton)

No Bill of Attainder or ex post facto Law shall be passed.

84 (Hamilton)

No Capitation, or other direct, Tax shall be laid, unless in Proportion to the Census or Enumeration herein before directed to be taken.[8]

No Tax or Duty shall be laid on Articles exported from any State.

No Preference shall be given by any Regulation of Commerce or Revenue to the Ports of one State over those of another; nor shall vessels bound to, or from, one State, be obliged to enter, clear, or pay Duties in another.

32 (Hamilton)

No Money shall be drawn from the Treasury, but in Consequence of Appropriations made by Law; and a regular Statement and Account of the Receipts and Expenditures of all public Money shall be published from time to time.

No Title of Nobility shall be granted by the United States: And no Person holding any Office of Profit or Trust under them, shall, without the Consent of the Congress, accept of any present, Emolument, Office or Title, of any kind whatever, from any King, Prince, or foreign State.

39 (Madison)
84 (Hamilton)

Section 10
[RESTRICTIONS UPON POWERS OF STATES]

No State shall enter into any Treaty, Alliance, or Confederation; grant Letters of Marque and Reprisal; coin Money; emit Bills of Credit; make any Thing but gold and silver Coin a Tender in Payment of Debts; pass any Bill of Attainder, ex post facto Law, or Law impairing the Obligation of Contracts, or grant any Title of Nobility.

33 (Hamilton)
44 (Madison)

---

7   Temporary provision.

8   Modified by Sixteenth Amendment.

No State shall, without the Consent of the Congress, lay any Imposts or Duties on Imports or Exports, except what may be absolutely necessary for executing its inspection Laws: and the net Produce of all Duties and Imposts, laid by any State on Imports or Exports, shall be for the Use of the Treasury of the United States; and all such Laws shall be subject to the Revision and Control of the Congress.

No State shall, without the Consent of Congress, lay any Duty of Tonnage, keep Troops, or Ships of War in time of Peace, enter into any Agreement or Compact with another State, or with a foreign Power, or engage in War, unless actually invaded, or in such imminent Danger as will not admit of Delay.

ARTICLE II

Section 1
[EXECUTIVE POWER, ELECTION, QUALIFICATIONS OF THE PRESIDENT]

The executive Power shall be vested in a President of the United States of America. *He shall hold his Office during the Term of four years and, together with the Vice-President, chosen for the same Term, be elected, as follows:*[9]

Each State shall appoint, in such Manner as the Legislature thereof may direct, a Number of Electors, equal to the whole Number of Senators and Representatives to which the State may be entitled in the Congress: but no Senator or Representative, or Person holding an Office of Trust or Profit under the United States, shall be appointed an Elector.

The electors shall meet in their respective States, and vote by ballot for two Persons, of whom one at least shall not be an Inhabitant of the same State with themselves. And they shall make a List of all the Persons voted for, and of the Number of Votes for each; which List they shall sign and certify, and transmit sealed to the Seat of the Government of the United States, directed to the President of the Senate. The President of the Senate shall, in the Presence of the Senate and House of Representatives, open all the Certificates, and the Votes shall then be counted. The Person having the greatest Number of Votes shall be the President, if such Number be a Majority of the whole Number of Electors appointed; and if there be more than one who have such Majority and have an equal Number of Votes, then the House of Representatives shall immediately chuse by Ballot one of them for President; and if no person have a Majority, then from the five highest on the List the said House shall in like Manner chuse the President. But in chusing the President, the Votes shall be taken by States, the Representation from each State having one Vote; A quorum for this Purpose shall consist of a Member or Members from two-thirds of the States, and a Majority of all the States shall be necessary to a Choice. In every Case, after the Choice of the President, the person having the greatest Number of Votes of the Electors shall be the Vice-President. But if there should remain two or more who have equal vote, the Senate shall chuse from them by Ballot the Vice-President.[10]

The Congress may determine the Time of chusing the Electors, and the Day on which they shall give their Votes; which Day shall be the same throughout the United States.

---

9 Number of terms limited to two by Twenty-Second Amendment.

10 Modified by Twelfth and Twentieth Amendments.

The Constitution of the United States of America

No Person except a natural born Citizen, or a Citizen of the United States, at the time of the Adoption of this Constitution, shall be eligible to the Office of President; neither shall any Person be eligible to that Office who shall not have attained to the Age of thirty-five Years, and been fourteen Years a Resident within the United States.

64 (Jay)

In Case of the Removal of the President from Office, or his Death, Resignation, or Inability to discharge the Powers and Duties of the said Office, the same shall devolve on the Vice-President, and the Congress may by Law provide for the Case of Removal, Death, Resignation, or Inability, both of the President and Vice-President, declaring what Officer shall then act as President, and such Officer shall act accordingly, until the Disability be removed, or a President shall be elected.

The President shall, at stated Times, receive for his Services, a Compensation, which shall neither be encreased nor diminished during the Period for which he shall have been elected, and he shall not receive within that Period any other Emolument from the United States, or any of them.

73, 79 (Hamilton)

Before he enter on the Execution of his Office, he shall take the following Oath or Affirmation:—"I do solemnly swear (or affirm) that I will faithfully execute the Office of President of the United States, and will to the best of my Ability, preserve, protect and defend the Constitution of the United States."

Section 2
[POWERS OF THE PRESIDENT]

The President shall be Commander in Chief of the Army and Navy of the United States, and of the Militia of the several States, when called into the actual Service of the United States; he may require the Opinion, in writing, of the principal Officer in each of the executive Departments, upon any Subject relating to the Duties of their respective Offices, and he shall have Power to grant Reprieves and Pardons for Offences against the United States, except in Cases of Impeachment.

69, 74 (Hamilton)

He shall have Power, by and with the Advice and Consent of the Senate, to make Treaties, provided two-thirds of the Senators present concur; and he shall nominate, and by and with the Advice and Consent of the Senate, shall appoint Ambassadors, other public Ministers and Consuls, Judges of the Supreme Court, and all other Officers of the United States, whose Appointments are not herein otherwise provided for, and which shall be established by Law: but the Congress may by Law vest the Appointment of such inferior Officers, as they think proper, in the President alone, in the Courts of Law, or in the Heads of Departments.

42 (Madison)
64 (Jay)
66, 69, 76, 77
(Hamilton)

The President shall have Power to fill up all Vacancies that may happen during the Recess of the Senate, by granting Commissions which shall expire at the End of their next Session.

67, 76
(Hamilton)

Section 3
[POWERS AND DUTIES OF THE PRESIDENT]

He shall from time to time give to the Congress Information of the State of the Union, and recommend to their Consideration such Measures as he shall judge necessary and expedient; he may, on extraordinary Occasions, convene both Houses, or either of them, and in Case of Disagreement between them, with Respect to the Time of Adjournment, he may adjourn them to such Time

69, 77, 78
(Hamilton)
42 (Madison)

as he shall think proper; he shall receive Ambassadors and other public Ministers; he shall take Care that the Laws be faithfully executed, and shall Commission all the Officers of the United States.

Section 4
[IMPEACHMENT]

39 (Madison)
69 (Hamilton)

The President, Vice-President and all civil Officers of the United States shall be removed from Office on Impeachment for, and Conviction of, Treason, Bribery, or other high Crimes and Misdemeanors.

ARTICLE III

Section 1
[JUDICIAL POWER, TENURE OF OFFICE]

65, 78, 79, 81, 82
(Hamilton)

The judicial Power of the United States, shall be vested in one supreme Court, and in such inferior Courts as the Congress may from time to time ordain and establish. The Judges, both of the supreme and inferior Courts, shall hold their Offices during good Behavior, and shall, at stated Times, receive for their Services, a Compensation, which shall not be diminished during their Continuance in Office.

Section 2
[JURISDICTION]

80 (Hamilton)

The judicial Power shall extend to all Cases, in Law and Equity, arising under this Constitution, the Laws of the United States, and Treaties made, or which shall be made, under their Authority;—to all Cases affecting Ambassadors, other public Ministers and Consuls;—to all Cases of admiralty and maritime Jurisdiction;—to Controversies to which the United States shall be a party;—to Controversies between two or more States;—*between a State and Citizens of another State;*—between Citizens of different States,—between Citizens of the same State claiming Lands under Grants of different States, *and between a State,* or the Citizens thereof, *and foreign States, Citizens or Subjects.*[11]

81 (Hamilton)

In all Cases affecting Ambassadors, other public Ministers and Consuls, and those in which a State shall be Party, the supreme Court shall have original Jurisdiction. In all the other Cases before mentioned, the supreme Court shall have appellate Jurisdiction, both as to Law and Fact, with such Exceptions, and under such Regulations as Congress shall make.

83, 84 (Hamilton)

The Trial of all Crimes, except in Cases of Impeachment, shall be by Jury; and such Trial shall be held in the State where the said Crimes shall have been committed; but when not committed within any State, the Trial shall be at such Place or Places as the Congress may by Law have directed.

---

11 Modified by Eleventh Amendment.

Section 3
[TREASON, PROOF, AND PUNISHMENT]

Treason against the United States, shall consist only in levying War against them, or in adhering to their Enemies, giving them Aid and Comfort. No Person shall be convicted of Treason unless on the Testimony of two Witnesses to the same overt Act, or on Confession in open Court.

43 (Madison)
84 (Hamilton)

The Congress shall have Power to declare the Punishment of Treason, but no Attainder of Treason shall work Corruption of Blood, or Forfeiture except during the Life of the Person attained.

43 (Madison)
84 (Hamilton)

ARTICLE IV

Section 1
[FAITH AND CREDIT AMONG STATES]

Full Faith and Credit shall be given in each State to the public Acts, Records, and judicial Proceedings of every other State. And the Congress may by general Laws prescribe the Manner in which such Acts, Records and Proceedings shall be proved, and the Effect thereof.

42 (Madison)

Section 2
[PRIVILEGES AND IMMUNITIES, FUGITIVES]

The Citizens of each State shall be entitled to all Privileges and Immunities of Citizens in the several States.

80 (Hamilton)

A person charged in any State with Treason, Felony or other Crime, who shall flee from Justice, and be found in another State, shall on Demand of the executive Authority of the State from which he fled, be delivered up to be removed to the State having Jurisdiction of the Crime.

No person held to Service or Labour in one State, under the Laws thereof, escaping into another, shall, in Consequence of any Law or Regulation therein, be discharged from such Service or Labour, but shall be delivered up on Claim of the Party to whom such Service or Labour may be due.[12]

Section 3
[ADMISSION OF NEW STATES]

New States may be admitted by the Congress into this Union; but no new State shall be formed or erected within the Jurisdiction of any other State; nor any State be formed by the Junction of two or more States, or Parts of States, without the Consent of the Legislatures of the States concerned as well as of the Congress.

43 (Madison)

The Congress shall have Power to dispose of and make all needful Rules and Regulations respecting the Territory or other Property belonging to the United States; and nothing in this Constitution shall be so construed as to Prejudice any Claims of the United States, or of any particular State.

43 (Madison)

---

12 Repealed by Thirteenth Amendment.

Section 4

[GUARANTEE OF REPUBLICAN GOVERNMENT]

39, 43
(Madison)

The United States shall guarantee to every State in this Union a Republican Form of Government, and shall protect each of them against Invasion; and on Application of the Legislature, or of the Executive (when the Legislature cannot be convened) against domestic Violence.

ARTICLE V

[AMENDMENT OF THE CONSTITUTION]

39, 43 (Madison)
85 (Hamilton)

The Congress, whenever two-thirds of both Houses shall deem it necessary, shall propose Amendments to this Constitution, or, on the Application of the Legislatures of two-thirds of the several States, shall call a Convention for proposing Amendments, which, in either Case, shall be valid to all Intents and Purposes, as Part of this Constitution, when ratified by the Legislatures of three-fourths of the several States, or by Conventions in three-fourths thereof, as the one or the other Mode of Ratification may be proposed by the Congress; *Provided that no Amendment which may be made prior to the Year One thousand eight hundred and eight shall in any Manner affect the first and fourth Clauses in the Ninth Section of the first Article;*[13] and that no State, without its Consent, shall be deprived of its equal Suffrage in the Senate.

ARTICLE VI

[DEBTS, SUPREMACY, OATH]

43 (Madison)

All Debts contracted and Engagements entered into, before the Adoption of this Constitution, shall be as valid against the United States under this Constitution, as under the Confederation.

27, 33 (Hamilton)
39, 44 (Madison)

This Constitution, and the Laws of the United States which shall be made in Pursuance thereof; and all Treaties made, or which shall be made, under the Authority of the United States, shall be the supreme Law of the Land; and the Judges in every State shall be bound thereby, any Thing in the Constitution or Laws of any State to the Contrary notwithstanding.

27 (Hamilton)
44 (Madison)

The Senators and Representatives before mentioned, and the Members of the several State Legislatures, and all executive and judicial Officers, both of the United States and of the several States, shall be bound by Oath or Affirmation, to support this Constitution; but no religious Test shall be required as a Qualification to any Office or public Trust under the United States.

ARTICLE VII

[RATIFICATION AND ESTABLISHMENT]

39, 40, 43
(Madison)

The Ratification of the Conventions of nine States, shall be sufficient for the Establishment of this Constitution between the States so ratifying the Same.[14]

---

13 Temporary provision.

14 The Constitution was submitted on September 17, 1787, by the Constitutional Convention, was ratified by the conventions of several states at various dates up to May 29, 1790, and became effective on March 4, 1789.

Done in Convention by the Unanimous Consent of the States present the Seventeenth Day of September in the Year of our Lord one thousand seven hundred and Eighty seven and of the Independence of the United States of America the Twelfth. *In Witness* whereof We have hereunto subscribed our Names,

G:^{0} WASHINGTON—
Presidt, and Deputy
from Virginia

NEW HAMPSHIRE
John Langdon
Nicholas Gilman

MASSACHUSETTS
Nathaniel Gorham
Rufus King

CONNECTICUT
Wm Saml Johnson
Roger Sherman

NEW YORK
Alexander Hamilton

NEW JERSEY
Wil: Livingston
David Brearley
Wm Paterson
Jona: Dayton

PENNSYLVANIA
B Franklin
Thomas Mifflin
Robt Morris
Geo. Clymer
Thos. FitzSimons
Jared Ingersoll
James Wilson
Gouv Morris

DELAWARE
Geo Read
Gunning Bedfor Jun
John Dickinson
Richard Bassett
Jaco: Broom

MARYLAND
James McHenry
Dan of St Thos Jenifer
Danl Carroll

VIRGINIA
John Blair—
James Madison Jr.

NORTH CAROLINA
Wm Blount
Richd Dobbs Spaight
Hu Williamson

SOUTH CAROLINA
J. Rutledge
Charles Cotesworth Pinckney
Charles Pinckney
Pierce Butler

GEORGIA
William Few
Abr Baldwin

Amendments to the Constitution

Amendments I–X, known as the Bill of Rights, were proposed by Congress on September 25, 1789, and ratified on December 15, 1791. *The Federalist Papers* comments, mainly in opposition to a Bill of Rights, can be found in number 84 (Hamilton).

AMENDMENT I
[FREEDOM OF RELIGION, OF SPEECH, AND OF THE PRESS]

Congress shall make no law respecting an establishment of religion, or prohibiting the free exercise thereof; or abridging the freedom of speech, or of the press; or the right of the people peaceably to assemble, and to petition the Government for a redress of grievances.

AMENDMENT II
[RIGHT TO KEEP AND BEAR ARMS]

A well regulated Militia, being necessary to the security of a free State, the right of the people to keep and bear Arms, shall not be infringed.

AMENDMENT III
[QUARTERING OF SOLDIERS]

No Soldier shall, in time of peace be quartered in any house, without the consent of the Owner, nor in time of war, but in a manner to be prescribed by law.

AMENDMENT IV
[SECURITY FROM UNWARRANTABLE SEARCH AND SEIZURE]

The right of the people to be secure in their persons, houses, papers, and effects, against unreasonable searches and seizures, shall not be violated, and no Warrants shall issue, but upon probable cause, supported by Oath or affirmation, and particularly describing the place to be searched, and the persons or things to be seized.

AMENDMENT V
[RIGHTS OF ACCUSED PERSONS IN CRIMINAL PROCEEDINGS]

No person shall be held to answer for a capital, or otherwise infamous crime, unless on a presentment or indictment of a Grand Jury, except in cases arising in the land or naval forces, or in the Militia, when in actual service in time of

War or in public danger; nor shall any person be subject for the same offence to be twice put in jeopardy of life or limb; nor shall be compelled in any Criminal Case to be a witness against himself, nor be deprived of life, liberty, or property, without due process of law; nor shall private property be taken for public use, without just compensation.

AMENDMENT VI
[RIGHT TO SPEEDY TRIAL, WITNESSES, ETC.]

In all criminal prosecutions, the accused shall enjoy the right to a speedy and public trial, by an impartial jury of the State and district wherein the crime shall have been committed, which district shall have been previously ascertained by law, and to be informed of the nature and cause of the accusation; to be confronted with the witnesses against him; to have compulsory process for obtaining Witnesses in his favor, and to have the Assistance of Counsel for his defence.

AMENDMENT VII
[TRIAL BY JURY IN CIVIL CASES]

In suits at common law, where the value in controversy shall exceed twenty dollars, the right of trial by jury shall be preserved, and no fact tried by a jury shall be otherwise re-examined in any Court of the United States, than according to the rules of the common law.

AMENDMENT VIII
[BAILS, FINES, PUNISHMENTS]

Excessive bail shall not be required, nor excessive fines imposed, nor cruel and unusual punishments inflicted.

AMENDMENT IX
[RESERVATION OF RIGHTS OF PEOPLE]

The enumeration in the Constitution, of certain rights, shall not be construed to deny or disparage others retained by the people.

AMENDMENT X
[POWERS RESERVED TO STATES OR PEOPLE]

The powers not delegated to the United States by the Constitution, nor prohibited by it to the States, are reserved to the States respectively, or to the people.

AMENDMENT XI
[Proposed by Congress on March 4, 1794; declared ratified on January 8, 1798]
[RESTRICTION OF JUDICIAL POWER]

The Judicial power of the United States shall not be construed to extend to any suit in law or equity, commenced or prosecuted against one of the United States by Citizens of another State, or by Citizens or Subjects of any Foreign State.

AMENDMENT XII

[Proposed by Congress on December 9, 1803; declared ratified on September 25, 1804.]

[ELECTION OF PRESIDENT AND VICE-PRESIDENT]

The Electors shall meet in their respective states, and vote by ballot for President and Vice-President, one of whom, at least, shall not be an inhabitant of the same state with themselves; they shall name in their ballots the person voted for as President, and in distinct ballots the person voted for as Vice-President, and they shall make distinct lists of all persons voted for as President, and of all persons voted for as Vice-President, and of the number of votes for each, which lists they shall sign and certify, and transmit sealed to the seat of the government of the United States, directed to the President of the Senate;—The President of the Senate shall, in presence of the Senate and House of Representatives, open all the certificates and the votes shall then be counted;—The person having the greatest number of votes for President, shall be the President, if such number be a majority of the whole number of Electors appointed; and if no person have such majority, then from the persons having the highest numbers not exceeding three on the list of those voted for as President, the House of Representatives shall choose immediately, by ballot, the President. But in choosing the President, the votes shall be taken by states, the representation from each state having one vote; a quorum for this purpose shall consist of a member or members from two-thirds of the states, and a majority of all states shall be necessary to a choice. And if the House of Representatives shall not choose a President whenever the right of choice shall devolve upon them, before the fourth day of March next following, then the Vice-President, shall act as President, as in the case of the death or other constitutional disability of the President. The person having the greatest number of votes as Vice-President, shall be the Vice-President, if such a number be a majority of the whole number of Electors appointed, and if no person have a majority, then from the two highest numbers on the list, the Senate shall choose the Vice-President; a quorum for the purpose shall consist of two-thirds of the whole number of Senators, and a majority of the whole number shall be necessary to a choice. But no person constitutionally ineligible to the office of President shall be eligible to that of Vice-President of the United States.

AMENDMENT XIII

[Proposed by Congress on January 31, 1865; declared ratified on December 18, 1865]

Section 1

[ABOLITION OF SLAVERY]

Neither slavery nor involuntary servitude, except as a punishment for crime whereof the party shall have been duly convicted, shall exist within the United States, or any place subject to their jurisdiction.

Section 2

[POWER TO ENFORCE THIS ARTICLE]

Congress shall have power to enforce this article by appropriate legislation.

AMENDMENT XIV

[Proposed by Congress on June 13, 1866; declared ratified on July 28, 1868]

Section 1

[CITIZENSHIP RIGHTS NOT TO BE ABRIDGED BY STATES]

All persons born or naturalized in the United States, and subject to the jurisdiction thereof, are citizens of the United States and of the State wherein they reside. No state shall make or enforce any law which shall abridge the privileges or immunities of citizens of the United States; nor shall any State deprive any person of life, liberty, or property, without due process of law; nor deny to any person within its jurisdiction the equal protection of the laws.

Section 2

[APPORTIONMENT OF REPRESENTATIVES IN CONGRESS]

Representatives shall be apportioned among the several States according to their respective numbers, counting the whole number of persons in each State, excluding Indians not taxed. But when the right to vote at any election for the choice of electors for President and Vice-President of the United States, Representatives in Congress, the Executive and Judicial officers of a State, or the members of the Legislature thereof, is denied to any of the male inhabitants of such State, being twenty-one years of age, and citizens of the United States, or in any way abridged, except for participation in rebellion, or other crime, the basis of representation therein shall be reduced in the proportion which the number of such male citizens shall bear to the whole number of male citizens twenty-one years of age in such State.

Section 3

[PERSONS DISQUALIFIED FROM HOLDING OFFICE]

No person shall be a Senator or Representative in Congress, or elector of President and Vice-President, or hold any office, civil or military, under the United States, or under any State, who, having previously taken an oath, as a member of Congress, or as an officer of the United States, or as a member of any State legislature, or as an executive or judicial officer of any State, to support the Constitution of the United States, shall have engaged in insurrection or rebellion against the same, or given aid or comfort to the enemies thereof. But Congress may by a vote of two-thirds of each House, remove such disability.

Section 4

[WHAT PUBLIC DEBTS ARE VALID]

The validity of the public debt of the United States, authorized by law, including debts incurred for payment of pensions and bounties for services in suppressing insurrection or rebellion, shall not be questioned. But neither the United States nor any State shall assume or pay any debt or obligation incurred in aid of insurrection or rebellion against the United States, or any claim for the loss or emancipation of any slave; but all such debts, obligations and claims shall be held illegal and void.

Section 5
[POWER TO ENFORCE THIS ARTICLE]

The Congress shall have power to enforce, by appropriate legislation, the provisions of this article.

AMENDMENT XV
[Proposed by Congress on February 26, 1869; declared ratified on March 30, 1870]

Section 1
[NEGRO SUFFRAGE]

The right of citizens of the United States to vote shall not be denied or abridged by the United States or by any State on account of race, color, or previous condition of servitude.

Section 2
[POWER TO ENFORCE THIS ARTICLE]

The Congress shall have power to enforce this article by appropriate legislation.

AMENDMENT XVI
[Proposed by Congress on July 12, 1909; declared ratified on February 25, 1913]
[AUTHORIZING INCOME TAXES]

The Congress shall have power to lay and collect taxes on incomes, from whatever source derived, without apportionment among the several States, and without regard to any census or enumeration.

AMENDMENT XVII
[Proposed by Congress on May 13, 1912; declared ratified on May 31, 1913]
[POPULAR ELECTION OF SENATORS]

The Senate of the United States shall be composed of two Senators from each State, elected by the people thereof, for six years; and each Senator shall have one vote. The electors in each State shall have the qualifications requisite for electors of the most numerous branch of the State Legislature.

When vacancies happen in the representation of any State in the Senate, the executive authority of such State shall issue writs of election to fill such vacancies: Provided, That the Legislature of any State may empower the executive thereof to make temporary appointment until the people fill the vacancies by election as the Legislature may direct.

This amendment shall not be so construed as to affect the election or term of any Senator chosen before it becomes valid as part of the Constitution.

AMENDMENT XVIII

[Proposed by Congress December 18, 1917; declared ratified on January 29, 1919]

Section 1

[NATIONAL LIQUOR PROHIBITION]

After one year from the ratification of this article the manufacture, sale, or transportation of intoxicating liquors within, the importation thereof into, or the exportation thereof from the United States and all territory subject to the jurisdiction thereof for beverage purposes is hereby prohibited.

Section 2

[POWER TO ENFORCE THIS ARTICLE]

The Congress and the several states shall have concurrent power to enforce this article by appropriate legislation.

Section 3

[RATIFICATION WITHIN SEVEN YEARS]

This article shall be inoperative unless it shall have been ratified as an amendment to the Constitution by the legislatures of the several states, as provided in the Constitution, within seven years from the date of the submission hereof to the states by the Congress.[15]

AMENDMENT XIX

[Proposed by Congress on June 4, 1919; declared ratified on August 26, 1920]
[WOMAN SUFFRAGE]

The right of the citizens of the United States to vote shall not be denied or abridged by the United States or by any state on account of sex.

Congress shall have power to enforce this article by appropriate legislation.

AMENDMENT XX

[Proposed by Congress on March 2, 1932; declared ratified on February 6, 1933]

Section 1

[TERMS OF OFFICE]

The terms of the President and Vice-President shall end at noon on the 20th day of January, and the terms of the Senators and Representatives at noon on the 3rd day of January, of the years in which such terms would have ended if this article had not been ratified; and the terms of their successors shall then begin.

Section 2

[TIME OF CONVENING CONGRESS]

The Congress shall assemble at least once in every year, and such meeting shall begin at noon on the 3rd day of January, unless they shall by law appoint a different day.

---

15 Repealed by Twenty-First Amendment.

Section 3
[DEATH OF PRESIDENT-ELECT]

If, at the time fixed for the beginning of the term of the President, the President-elect shall have died, the Vice-President-elect shall become President. If a President shall not have been chosen before the time fixed for the beginning of his term, or if the President-elect shall have failed to qualify, then the Vice-President-elect shall act as President until a President shall have qualified; and the Congress may by law provide for the case wherein neither a President-elect nor a Vice-President-elect shall have qualified, declaring who shall then act as President, or the manner in which one who is to act shall be selected, and such person shall act accordingly until a President or Vice President shall have qualified.

Section 4
[ELECTION OF THE PRESIDENT]

The Congress may by law provide for the case of the death of any of the persons from whom the House of Representatives may choose a President whenever the right of choice shall have devolved upon them, and for the case of the death of any of the persons from whom the Senate may choose a Vice-President whenever the right of choice shall have devolved upon them.

Section 5
[AMENDMENT TAKES EFFECT]

Sections 1 and 2 shall take effect on the 15th day of October following ratification of this article.

Section 6
[RATIFICATION WITHIN SEVEN YEARS]

This article shall be inoperative unless it shall have been ratified as an amendment to the Constitution by the legislatures of three-fourths of the several States within seven years from the date of its submission.

AMENDMENT XXI
[Proposed by Congress on February 20, 1933; declared ratified on December 5, 1933]

Section 1
[NATIONAL LIQUOR PROHIBITION REPEALED]

The eighteenth article of amendment to the Constitution of the United States is hereby repealed.

Section 2
[TRANSPORTATION OF LIQUOR INTO "DRY" STATES]

The transportation or importation into any State, Territory, or Possession of the United States for delivery or use therein of intoxicating liquors, in violation of the laws thereof, is hereby prohibited.

Section 3
[RATIFICATION WITHIN SEVEN YEARS]

This article shall be inoperative unless it shall have been ratified as an amendment to the Constitution by conventions in the several States, as provided in the Constitution, within seven years from the date of the submission hereof to the States by the Congress.

AMENDMENT XXII
[Proposed by Congress on March 21, 1947; declared ratified on February 26, 1951]

Section 1
[TENURE OF PRESIDENT LIMITED]

No person shall be elected to the office of President more than twice, and no person who has held the office of President or acted as President for more than two years of a term to which some other person was elected President shall be elected to the Office of the President more than once. But this Article shall not apply to any person holding the office of President when this Article was proposed by the Congress, and shall not prevent any person who may be holding the office of President, or acting as President, during the term within which this Article becomes operative from holding the office of President or acting as President during the remainder of such term.

Section 2
[RATIFICATION WITHIN SEVEN YEARS]

This Article shall be inoperative unless it shall have been ratified as an amendment to the Constitution by the legislatures of three-fourths of the several states within seven years from the date of its submission to the States by the Congress.

AMENDMENT XXIII
[Proposed by Congress on June 21, 1960; declared ratified on March 29, 1961]

Section 1
[ELECTORAL COLLEGE VOTES FOR THE DISTRICT OF COLUMBIA]

The District constituting the seat of Government of the United States shall appoint in such manner as the Congress may direct:

A number of electors of President and Vice-President equal to the whole number of Senators and Representatives in Congress to which the District would be entitled if it were a State, but in no event more than the least populous State; they shall be in addition to those appointed by the States, but they shall be considered, for the purposes of the election of President and Vice-President, to be electors appointed by a State; and they shall meet in the District and perform such duties as provided by the twelfth article of amendment.

Section 2
[POWER TO ENFORCE THIS ARTICLE]

The Congress shall have power to enforce this article by appropriate legislation.

AMENDMENT XXIV

[Proposed by Congress on August 27, 1963; declared ratified on January 23, 1964]

Section 1

[ANTI-POLL TAX]

The right of citizens of the United States to vote in any primary or other election for President or Vice-President, for electors for President or Vice-President, or for Senator or Representative of Congress, shall not be denied or abridged by the United States or any State by reasons of failure to pay any poll tax or other tax.

Section 2

[POWER TO ENFORCE THIS ARTICLE]

The Congress shall have power to enforce this article by appropriate legislation.

AMENDMENT XXV

[Proposed by Congress on July 7, 1965; declared ratified on February 10, 1967]

Section 1

[VICE-PRESIDENT TO BECOME PRESIDENT]

In case of the removal of the President from office or his death or resignation, the Vice-President shall become President.

Section 2

[CHOICE OF A NEW VICE-PRESIDENT]

Whenever there is a vacancy in the office of the Vice-President, the President shall nominate a Vice-President who shall take the office upon confirmation by a majority vote of both houses of Congress.

Section 3

[PRESIDENT MAY DECLARE OWN DISABILITY]

Whenever the President transmits to the President pro tempore of the Senate and the Speaker of the House of Representatives his written declaration that he is unable to discharge the powers and duties of his office, and until he transmits to them a written declaration to the contrary, such powers and duties shall be discharged by the Vice-President as Acting President.

Section 4

[ALTERNATE PROCEDURES TO DECLARE AND TO END PRESIDENTIAL DISABILITY]

Whenever the Vice-President and a majority of either the principal officers of the executive departments, or of such other body as Congress may by law provide, transmit to the President pro tempore of the Senate and the Speaker of the House of Representatives their written declaration that the President is unable to discharge the powers and duties of his office, the Vice-President shall immediately assume the powers and duties of the office as Acting President.

Thereafter, when the President transmits to the President pro tempore of the Senate and the Speaker of the House of Representatives his written declaration that no inability exists, he shall resume the powers and duties of his office unless the Vice-President and a majority of either the principal officers of the executive departments, or of such other body as Congress may by law provide, transmit within four days to the President pro tempore of the Senate and the Speaker of the House of Representatives their written declaration that the President is unable to discharge the powers and duties of his office. Thereupon Congress shall decide the issue, assembling within 48 hours for that purpose if not in session. If the Congress, within 21 days after receipt of the latter written declaration, or, if Congress is not in session, within 21 days after Congress is required to assemble, determines by two-thirds vote of both houses that the President is unable to discharge the powers and duties of his office, the Vice-President shall continue to discharge the same as Acting President; otherwise, the President shall resume the powers and duties of his office.

AMENDMENT XXVI

[Proposed by Congress on March 23, 1971; declared ratified on June 30, 1971]

Section 1

[EIGHTEEN-YEAR-OLD VOTE]

The right of citizens of the United States, who are eighteen years of age or older, to vote shall not be denied or abridged by the United States or by any State on account of age.

Section 2

[POWER TO ENFORCE THIS ARTICLE]

The Congress shall have power to enforce this article by appropriate legislation.

AMENDMENT XXVII

[Proposed by Congress on September 25, 1789; ratified on May 7, 1992]

No law varying the compensation for the services of the Senators and Representatives shall take effect until an election of Representatives shall have intervened.

NO. 10: MADISON

Among the numerous advantages promised by a well-constructed Union, none deserves to be more accurately developed than its tendency to break and control the violence of faction. The friend of popular governments never finds himself so much alarmed for their character and fate as when he contemplates their propensity to this dangerous vice. He will not fail, therefore, to set a due value on any plan which, without violating the principles to which he is attached, provides a proper cure for it. The instability, injustice, and confusion introduced into the public councils have, in truth, been the mortal diseases under which popular governments have everywhere perished, as they continue to be the favorite and fruitful topics from which the adversaries to liberty derive their most specious declamations. The valuable improvements made by the American constitutions on the popular models, both ancient and modern, cannot certainly be too much admired; but it would be an unwarrantable partiality to contend that they have as effectually obviated the danger on this side, as was wished and expected. Complaints are everywhere heard from our most considerate and virtuous citizens, equally the friends of public and private faith and of public and personal liberty, that our governments are too unstable, that the public good is disregarded in the conflicts of rival parties, and that measures are too often decided, not according to the rules of justice and the rights of the minor party, but by the superior force of an interested and overbearing majority. However anxiously we may wish that these complaints had no foundation, the evidence of known facts will not permit us to deny that they are in some degree true. It will be found, indeed, on a candid review of our situation, that some of the distresses under which we labor have been erroneously charged on the operation of our governments; but it will be found, at the same time, that other causes will not alone account for many of our heaviest misfortunes; and, particularly, for that prevailing and increasing distrust of public engagements and alarm for private rights which are echoed from one end of the continent to the other. These must be chiefly, if not wholly, effects of the unsteadiness and injustice with which a factious spirit has tainted our public administration.

By a faction I understand a number of citizens, whether amounting to a majority or minority of the whole, who are united and actuated by some common impulse of passion, or of interest, adverse to the rights of other citizens, or to the permanent and aggregate interests of the community.

There are two methods of curing the mischiefs of faction: the one, by removing its causes; the other, by controlling its effects.

There are again two methods of removing the causes of faction: the one, by destroying the liberty which is essential to its existence; the other, by giving to every citizen the same opinions, the same passions, and the same interests.

It could never be more truly said than of the first remedy that it was worse than the disease. Liberty is to faction what air is to fire, an aliment without which it instantly expires. But it could not be a less folly to abolish liberty, which is essential to political life, because it nourishes faction than it would be to wish the annihilation of air, which is essential to animal life, because it imparts to fire its destructive agency.

The second expedient is as impracticable as the first would be unwise. As long as the reason of man continues fallible, and he is at liberty to exercise it, different opinions will be formed. As long as the connection subsists between his reason and his self-love, his opinions and his passions will have a reciprocal influence on each other; and the former will be objects to which the latter will attach themselves. The diversity in the faculties of men, from which the rights of property originate, is not less an insuperable obstacle to a uniformity of interests. The protection of these faculties is the first object of government. From the protection of different and unequal faculties of acquiring property, the possession of different degrees and kinds of property immediately results; and from the influence of these on the sentiments and views of the respective proprietors ensues a division of the society into different interests and parties.

The latent causes of faction are thus sown in the nature of man; and we see them everywhere brought into different degrees of activity, according to the different circumstances of civil society. A zeal for different opinions concerning religion, concerning government, and many other points, as well of speculation as of practice; an attachment to different leaders ambitiously contending for pre-eminence and power; or to persons of other descriptions whose fortunes have been interesting to the human passions, have, in turn, divided mankind into parties, inflamed them with mutual animosity, and rendered them much more disposed to vex and oppress each other than to co-operate for their common good. So strong is this propensity of mankind to fall into mutual animosities that where no substantial occasion presents itself the most frivolous and fanciful distinctions have been sufficient to kindle their unfriendly passions and excite their most violent conflicts. But the most common and durable source of factions has been the various and unequal distribution of property. Those who hold and those who are without property have ever formed distinct interests in society. Those who are creditors, and those who are debtors, fall under a like discrimination. A landed interest, a manufacturing interest, a mercantile interest, a moneyed interest, with many lesser interests, grow up of necessity in civilized nations, and divide them into different classes, actuated by different sentiments and views. The regulation of these various and interfering interests forms the principal task of modern legislation and involves the spirit of party and faction in the necessary and ordinary operations of government.

No man is allowed to be judge in his own cause, because his interest would certainly bias his judgment and, not improbably, corrupt his integrity. With equal, nay with greater reason, a body of men are unfit to be both judges and parties at the same time; yet what are many of the most important acts of legislation but so many judicial determinations, not indeed concerning the rights of single persons, but concerning the rights of large bodies of citizens? And what are the different classes of legislators but advocates and parties to the causes which they determine? Is a law proposed concerning private debts? It is a question to which the creditors are parties on one side and the debtors on the other. Justice ought to hold the balance between them. Yet the parties are, and must be, themselves the judges; and the most numerous party, or in other words, the most powerful faction must be expected to prevail. Shall domestic manufacturers be encouraged, and in what degree, by restrictions on foreign manufacturers? are questions which would be differently decided by the landed and the manufacturing classes, and probably by neither with a sole regard to justice and the public good. The apportionment of taxes on the various descriptions of property is an act which seems to require the most exact impartiality; yet there is, perhaps, no legislative act in which greater opportunity and temptation are given to a predominant party to trample on the rules of justice. Every shilling with which they overburden the inferior number is a shilling saved to their own pockets.

It is in vain to say that enlightened statesmen will be able to adjust these clashing interests and render them all subservient to the public good. Enlightened statesmen will not always be at the helm. Nor, in many cases, can such an adjustment be made at all without taking into view indirect and remote considerations, which will rarely prevail over the immediate interest which one party may find in disregarding the rights of another or the good of the whole.

The inference to which we are brought is that the *causes* of faction cannot be removed and that relief is only to be sought in the means of controlling its *effects*.

If a faction consists of less than a majority, relief is supplied by the republican principle, which enables the majority to defeat its sinister views by regular vote. It may clog the administration, it may convulse the society; but it will be unable to execute and mask its violence under the forms of the Constitution. When a majority is included in a faction, the form of popular government, on the other hand, enables it to sacrifice to its ruling passion or interest both the public good and the rights of other citizens. To secure the public good and private rights against the danger of such a faction, and at the same time to preserve the spirit and the form of popular government, is then the great object to which our inquiries are directed. Let me add that it is the great desideratum by which alone this form of government can be rescued from the opprobrium under which it has so long labored and be recommended to the esteem and adoption of mankind.

By what means is this object attainable? Evidently by one of two only. Either the existence of the same passion or interest in a majority at the same time must be prevented, or the majority, having such coexistent passion or interest, must be rendered, by their number and local situation, unable to concert and carry into effect schemes of oppression. If the impulse and the opportunity be suffered to coincide, we well know that neither moral nor religious motives can be relied on as an adequate control. They are not found to be such on the injustice and violence of individuals, and lose their efficacy in proportion to the number combined together, that is, in proportion as their efficacy becomes needful.

From this view of the subject it may be concluded that a pure democracy, by which I mean a society consisting of a small number of citizens, who assemble and administer the government in person, can admit of no cure for the mischiefs of faction. A common passion or interest will, in almost every case, be felt by a majority of the whole; a communication and concert results from the form of government itself; and there is nothing to check the inducements to sacrifice the weaker party or an obnoxious individual. Hence it is that such democracies have ever been spectacles of turbulence and contention; have ever been found incompatible with personal security or the rights of property; and have in general been as short in their lives as they have been violent in their deaths. Theoretic politicians, who have patronized this species of government, have erroneously supposed that by reducing mankind to a perfect equality in their political rights, they would at the same time be perfectly equalized and assimilated in their possessions, their opinions, and their passions.

A republic, by which I mean a government in which the scheme of representation takes place, opens a different prospect and promises the cure for which we are seeking. Let us examine the points in which it varies from pure democracy, and we shall comprehend both the nature of the cure and the efficacy which it must derive from the Union.

The two great points of difference between a democracy and a republic are: first, the delegation of the government, in the latter, to a small number of citizens elected by the rest; secondly, the greater number of citizens and greater sphere of country over which the latter may be extended.

The effect of the first difference is, on the one hand, to refine and enlarge the public views by passing them through the medium of a chosen body of citizens, whose wisdom may best discern the true interest of their country and whose patriotism and love of justice will be least likely to sacrifice it to temporary or partial considerations. Under such a regulation it may well happen that the public voice, pronounced by the representatives of the people, will be more consonant to the public good than if pronounced by the people themselves, convened for the purpose. On the other hand, the effect may be inverted. Men of factious tempers, of local prejudices, or of sinister designs, may, by intrigue, by corruption, or by other means, first obtain the suffrages, and then betray the interests of the people. The question resulting is, whether small or extensive republics are most favorable to the election of proper guardians of the public weal; and it is clearly decided in favor of the latter by two obvious considerations.

In the first place it is to be remarked that however small the republic may be the representatives must be raised to a certain number in order to guard against the cabals of a few; and that however large it may be they must be limited to a certain number in order to guard against the confusion of a multitude. Hence, the number of representatives in the two cases not being in proportion to that of the constituents, and being proportionally greatest in the small republic, it follows that if the proportion of fit characters be not less in the large than in the small republic, the former will present a greater option, and consequently a greater probability of a fit choice.

In the next place, as each representative will be chosen by a greater number of citizens in the large than in the small republic, it will be more difficult for unworthy candidates to practise with success the vicious arts by which elections are too often carried; and the suffrages of the people being more free, will be more likely to center on men who possess the most attractive merit and the most diffusive and established characters.

It must be confessed that in this, as in most other cases, there is a mean, on both sides of which inconveniencies will be found to lie. By enlarging too much the number of electors, you render the representative too little acquainted with all their local circumstances and lesser interests; as by reducing it too much, you render him unduly attached to these, and too little fit to comprehend and pursue great and national objects. The federal Constitution forms a happy combination in this respect; the great and aggregate interests being referred to the national, the local and particular to the State legislatures.

The other point of difference is the greater number of citizens and extent of territory which may be brought within the compass of republican than of democratic government; and it is this circumstance principally which renders factious combinations less to be dreaded in the former than in the latter. The smaller the society, the fewer probably will be the distinct parties and interests composing it; the fewer the distinct parties and interests, the more frequently will a majority be found of the same party; and the smaller the number of individuals composing a majority, and the smaller the compass within which they are placed, the more easily will they concert and execute their plans of oppression. Extend the sphere and you take in a greater variety of parties and interests; you make it less probable that a majority of the whole will have a common motive to invade the rights of other citizens; or if such a common motive exists, it will be more difficult for all who feel it to discover their own strength and to act in unison with each other. Besides other impediments, it may be remarked that, where there is a consciousness of unjust or dishonorable purposes, communication is always checked by distrust in proportion to the number whose concurrence is necessary.

Hence, it clearly appears that the same advantage which a republic has over a democracy in controlling the effects of faction is enjoyed by a large over a small republic—is enjoyed by the Union over the States composing it. Does this advantage consist in the substitution of representatives whose enlightened views and virtuous sentiments render them superior to local prejudices and to schemes of injustice? It will not be denied that the representation of the Union will be most likely to possess these requisite endowments. Does it consist in the greater security afforded by a greater variety of parties, against the event of any one party being able to outnumber and oppress the rest? In an equal degree does the increased variety of parties comprised within the Union increase this security? Does it, in fine, consist in the greater obstacles opposed to the concert and accomplishment of the secret wishes of an unjust and interested majority? Here again the extent of the Union gives it the most palpable advantage.

The influence of factious leaders may kindle a flame within their particular States but will be unable to spread a general conflagration through the other

States. A religious sect may degenerate into a political faction in a part of the Confederacy; but the variety of sects dispersed over the entire face of it must secure the national councils against any danger from that source. A rage for paper money, for an abolition of debts, for an equal division of property, or for any other improper or wicked project, will be less apt to pervade the whole body of the Union than a particular member of it, in the same proportion as such a malady is more likely to taint a particular county or district than an entire State.

In the extent and proper structure of the Union, therefore, we behold a republican remedy for the diseases most incident to republican government. And according to the degree of pleasure and pride we feel in being republicans ought to be our zeal in cherishing the spirit and supporting the character of federalist.

PUBLIUS

NO. 51: MADISON

To what expedient, then, shall we finally resort, for maintaining in practice the necessary partition of power among the several departments as laid down in the Constitution? The only answer that can be given is that as all these exterior provisions are found to be inadequate the defect must be supplied, by so contriving the interior structure of the government as that its several constituent parts may, by their mutual relations, be the means of keeping each other in their proper places. Without presuming to undertake a full development of this important idea I will hazard a few general observations which may perhaps place it in a clearer light, and enable us to form a more correct judgment of the principles and structure of the government planned by the convention.

In order to lay a due foundation for that separate and distinct exercise of the different powers of government, which to a certain extent is admitted on all hands to be essential to the preservation of liberty, it is evident that each department should have a will of its own; and consequently should be so constituted that the members of each should have as little agency as possible in the appointment of the members of the others. Were this principle rigorously adhered to, it would require that all the appointments for the supreme executive, legislative, and judiciary magistracies should be drawn from the same fountain of authority, the people, through channels having no communication whatever with one another. Perhaps such a plan of constructing the several departments would be less difficult in practice than it may in contemplation appear. Some difficulties, however, and some additional expense would attend the execution of it. Some deviations, therefore, from the principle must be admitted. In the constitution of the judiciary department in particular, it might be inexpedient to insist rigorously on the principle: first, because peculiar qualifications being essential in the members, the primary consideration ought to be to select that mode of choice which best secures these qualifications; second, because the permanent tenure by which the appointments are held in that department must soon destroy all sense of dependence on the authority conferring them.

It is equally evident that the members of each department should be as little dependent as possible on those of the others for the emoluments annexed to their offices. Were the executive magistrate, or the judges, not independent of the legislature in this particular, their independence in every other would be merely nominal.

But the great security against a gradual concentration of the several powers in the same department consists in giving to those who administer each department the necessary constitutional means and personal motives to resist encroachments of the others. The provision for defense must in this, as in all other cases, be made commensurate to the danger of attack. Ambition must be made to counteract ambition. The interest of the man must be connected with the constitutional rights of the place. It may be a reflection on human nature that such devices should be necessary to control the abuses of government. But what is government itself but the greatest of all reflections on human nature? If men were angels, no government would be necessary. If angels were to govern men, neither external nor internal controls on government would be necessary. In framing a government which is to be administered by men over men, the great difficulty lies in this: you must first enable the government to control the governed; and in the next place oblige it to control itself. A dependence on the people is, no doubt, the primary control on the government; but experience has taught mankind the necessity of auxiliary precautions.

This policy of supplying, by opposite and rival interests, the defect of better motives, might be traced through the whole system of human affairs, private as well as public. We see it particularly displayed in all the subordinate distributions of power, where the constant aim is to divide and arrange the several offices in such a manner as that each may be a check on the other—that the private interest of every individual may be a sentinel over the public rights. These inventions of prudence cannot be less requisite in the distribution of the supreme powers of the State.

But it is not possible to give to each department an equal power of self-defense. In republican government, the legislative authority necessarily predominates. The remedy for this inconveniency is to divide the legislature into different branches; and to render them, by different modes of election and different principles of action, as little connected with each other as the nature of their common functions and their common dependence on the society will admit. It may even be necessary to guard against dangerous encroachments by still further precautions. As the weight of the legislative authority requires that it should be thus divided, the weakness of the executive may require, on the other hand, that it should be fortified. An absolute negative on the legislature appears, at first view, to be the natural defense with which the executive magistrate should be armed. But perhaps it would be neither altogether safe nor alone sufficient. On ordinary occasions it might not be exerted with the requisite firmness, and on extraordinary occasions it might be perfidiously abused. May not this defect of an absolute negative be supplied by some qualified connection between this weaker branch of the stronger department, by which the latter may be led to support the constitutional rights of the former, without being too much detached from the rights of its own department?

If the principles on which these observations are founded be just, as I persuade myself they are, and they be applied as a criterion to the several State constitutions, and to the federal Constitution, it will be found that if the latter does not perfectly correspond with them, the former are infinitely less able to bear such a test.

There are, moreover, two considerations particularly applicable to the federal system of America, which place that system in a very interesting point of view.

First. In a single republic, all the power surrendered by the people is submitted to the administration of a single government; and the usurpations are guarded against by a division of the government into distinct and separate departments. In the compound republic of America, the power surrendered by the people is first divided between two distinct governments, and then the portion allotted to each subdivided among distinct and separate departments. Hence a double security arises to the rights of the people. The different governments will control each other, at the same time that each will be controlled by itself.

Second. It is of great importance in a republic not only to guard the society against the oppression of its rulers, but to guard one part of the society against the injustice of the other part. Different interests necessarily exist in different classes of citizens. If a majority be united by a common interest, the rights of the minority will be insecure. There are but two methods of providing against this evil: the one by creating a will in the community independent of the majority—that is, of the society itself; the other, by comprehending in the society so many separate descriptions of citizens as will render an unjust combination of a majority of the whole very improbable, if not impracticable. The first method prevails in all governments possessing an hereditary or self-appointed authority. This, at best, is but a precarious security; because a power independent of the society may as well espouse the unjust views of the major as the rightful interests of the minor party, and may possibly be turned against both parties. The second method will be exemplified in the federal republic of the United States. Whilst all authority in it will be derived from and dependent on the society, the society itself will be broken into so many parts, interests and classes of citizens, that the rights of individuals, or of the minority, will be in little danger from interested combinations of the majority. In a free government the security for civil rights must be the same as that for religious rights. It consists in the one case in the multiplicity of interests, and in the other in the multiplicity of sects. The degree of security in both cases will depend on the number of interests and sects; and this may be presumed to depend on the extent of country and number of people comprehended under the same government. This view of the subject must particularly recommend a proper federal system to all the sincere and considerate friends of republican government, since it shows that in exact proportion as the territory of the Union may be formed into more circumscribed Confederacies, or States, oppressive combinations of a majority will be facilitated; the best security, under the republican forms, for the rights of every class of citizen, will be diminished; and consequently the stability and independence of some member of the government, the only other security, must be proportionally increased. Justice is the end of government. It is the end of civil society. It ever has been and ever will be pursued until it be obtained, or until liberty be lost in the pursuit. In a society under the forms of which the stronger faction can readily unite and oppress the weaker, anarchy may as truly be said to reign as in a state of nature, where the weaker individual is not secured against the violence of the stronger; and as, in the latter state, even the stronger individuals are prompted, by the uncertainty of their condition, to submit to a government which may protect the weak as well as themselves; so, in the former state, will the more powerful factions or parties be gradually induced, by a like motive, to wish for a government which will protect all parties, the weaker as well as the more powerful. It can be little doubted that if the State of Rhode Island was separated from the Confederacy and left to itself, the insecurity of rights under the popular form of government within such narrow limits would be displayed by such reiterated oppressions of factious majorities that some power altogether independent of the people would soon be called for by the voice of the very factions whose misrule had proved the necessity of it. In the extended republic of the United States, and among the great variety of interests, parties, and sects which it embraces, a coalition of a majority of the whole society could seldom take place on any other principles than those of justice and the general good; whilst there being thus less danger to a minor from the will of a major party, there must be less pretext, also, to provide for the security of the former, by introducing into the government a will not dependent on the latter, or, in other words, a will independent of the society itself. It is no less certain than it is important, notwithstanding the contrary opinions which have been entertained, that the larger the society, provided it lie within a practicable sphere, the more duly capable it will be of self-government. And happily for the *republican cause,* the practicable sphere may be carried to a very great extent by a judicious modification and mixture of the *federal principle.*

PUBLIUS

Endnotes

CHAPTER 1

1   Thomas Hobbes, *Leviathan, or The Matter, Forme, and Power of a Common Wealth, Ecclesiasticall and Civil* (1651; repr., New York: Macmillan, 1947), p. 82.

2   The most instructive treatment of the phenomenon of public goods and the free rider is Mancur Olson, Jr., *The Logic of Collective Action: Public Goods and the Theory of Groups* (1965; repr., Cambridge, MA: Harvard University Press, 1971), pp. 33–43, esp. n. 53.

3   Harold Lasswell, *Politics: Who Gets What, When, How* (New York: Meridian Books, 1958).

4   Quoted in John Cannon, *Parliamentary Reform, 1640–1832* (Cambridge: Cambridge University Press, 1973), p. 216.

5   For a review and analysis of the detrimental consequences of the "opening up" of American democracy since the 1960s, see Morris P. Fiorina, "Parties, Participation, and Representation in America: Old Theories Face New Realities," in *Political Science: State of the Discipline*, Ira Katznelson and Helen V. Milner, eds. (New York: Norton, 2002). For a more general and provocative analysis of the detrimental effects of too much democracy, see Fareed Zakaria, *The Future of Freedom: Illiberal Democracy at Home and Abroad* (New York: Norton, 2003).

CHAPTER 2

1   James Madison, *The Federalist*, no. 62 in *The Federalist Papers*, Clinton Rossiter, ed., (New York: New American Library, 1961), p. 381.

2   Alexei Anishchuk, "Medvedev Says Poor Rule of Law Holds Russia Back," *Reuters*, May 20, 2011, www.reuters.com (accessed 8/16/11).

3   Randall Peerenboom, *China's Long March toward Rule of Law* (Cambridge, UK: Cambridge University Press, 2002).

4   The social makeup of colonial America and some of the social conflicts that divided colonial society are discussed in Jackson Turner Main, *The Social Structure of Revolutionary America* (Princeton, NJ: Princeton University Press, 1965).

5   See Carl Becker, *The Declaration of Independence* (New York: Vintage, 1942).

6   See Merrill Jensen, *The Articles of Confederation* (Madison: University of Wisconsin Press, 1963).

7   There is no verbatim record of the debates, but James Madison's notes are included in Max Farrand, ed., *The Records of the Federal Convention of 1787*, rev. ed., 4 vols. (New Haven, CT: Yale University Press, 1966).

8   Alexander Hamilton, *The Federalist*, no. 70, p. 424.

9   Max Farrand, *The Framing of the Constitution of the United States* (New Haven, CT: Yale University Press, 1962), p. 49.

10   Richard E. Neustadt, *Presidential Power* (New York: Wiley, 1960), p. 33.

11   An excellent analysis of the ratification campaigns is William H. Riker, *The Strategy of Rhetoric: Campaigning for the American Constitution* (New Haven, CT: Yale University Press, 1996).

12   *The Federalist*, esp. nos. 10 and 51.

13   The Fourteenth Amendment is included in this table as well as in Tables 2.3 and 2.4 because it seeks not only to define citizenship but seems to intend also that this definition of citizenship included, along with the right to vote, all the rights of the Bill of Rights, regardless of the state in which the citizen resided. A great deal more is said about this in Chapter 4.

14 See Farrand, *Records of the Federal Convention*, vol. 1, p. 132.

15 *The Federalist*, no. 10.

CHAPTER 3

1 The notion that federalism requires separate spheres of jurisdictions in which lower and higher levels of government are uniquely decisive is developed fully in William H. Riker, *Federalism: Origin, Operation, Significance* (Boston: Little, Brown, 1964). This American version of federalism is applied to the emerging federal arrangements in the People's Republic of China during the 1990s in a paper by Barry R. Weingast, "The Economic Role of Political Institutions: Market-Preserving Federalism and Economic Development," *Journal of Law, Economics, and Organization* 11 (1995): 1–32.

2 For a good treatment of these conflicts of interests between states, see Forrest McDonald, *E Pluribus Unum—The Formation of the American Republic, 1776–1790* (Boston: Houghton Mifflin, 1965), chap. 7, especially pp. 319–38.

3 See David O'Brien, *Constitutional Law and Politics* (New York: Norton, 1997), vol. 1, pp. 602–3.

4 *Obergefell v. Hodges*, 576 U.S. ___ (2015).

5 *Hicklin v. Orbeck*, 437 U.S. 518 (1978).

6 *Sweeny v. Woodall*, 344 U.S. 86 (1953).

7 Marlise Simons, "France Won't Extradite American Convicted of Murder," *New York Times*, December 5, 1997, p. A9.

8 Patricia S. Florestano, "Past and Present Utilization of Interstate Compacts in the United States," *Publius* 24 (Fall 1994): 13–26.

9 A good discussion of the constitutional position of local governments is in York Y. Willbern, *The Withering Away of the City* (Bloomington: Indiana University Press, 1971). For more on the structure and theory of federalism, see Thomas R. Dye, *American Federalism: Competition among Governments* (Lexington, MA: Lexington Books, 1990), chap. 1; and Martha Derthick, "Up-to-Date in Kansas City: Reflections on American Federalism," *PS: Political Science & Politics* 25 (December 1992): 671–5.

10 *McCulloch v. Maryland*, 4 Wheaton 316 (1819).

11 *Gibbons v. Ogden*, 9 Wheaton 1 (1824).

12 In *Wabash, St. Louis, and Pacific Railway Company v. Illinois*, 118 U.S. 557 (1886), the Supreme Court struck down a state law prohibiting rate discrimination by a railroad. In response, Congress passed the Interstate Commerce Act of 1887, creating the Interstate Commerce Commission (ICC), the first federal regulatory agency.

13 *Hammer v. Dagenhart*, 247 U.S. 251 (1918).

14 *National Labor Relations Board v. Jones & Loughlin Steel Company*, 301 U.S. 1 (1937).

15 *Wickard v. Filburn*, 317 U.S. 111 (1942).

16 Kenneth T. Palmer, "The Evolution of Grant Policies," in *The Changing Politics of Federal Grants*, by Lawrence D. Brown, James W. Fossett, and Kenneth T. Palmer (Washington, DC: Brookings Institution, 1984), p. 15.

17 Palmer, "The Evolution of Grant Policies," p. 6.

18 Morton Grodzins, "The Federal System," in *Goals for Americans: The President's Commission on National Goals* (Englewood Cliffs, NJ: Prentice Hall, 1960), p. 265.

19 The concept and the best discussion of this modern phenomenon will be found in Donald F. Kettl, *The Regulation of American Federalism* (Baltimore: Johns Hopkins University Press, 1983 and 1987), especially pp. 33–41.

20 See John DiIulio, Jr., and Donald F. Kettl, *Fine Print: The Contract with America, Devolution, and the Administrative Realities of American Federalism* (Washington, DC: Brookings Institution, 1995), p. 41.

21 Paul Posner, "Unfunded Mandate Reform: How Is It Working?" *Rockefeller Institute Bulletin* (Albany, NY: Nelson A. Rockefeller Institute of Government, 1998), p. 35.

22 Posner, "Unfunded Mandate Reform," p. 36.

23 *King v. Burwell*, 576 U.S. ___ (2015).

24 *United States v. Lopez*, 514 U.S. 549 (1995).

25 *Seminole Indian Tribe v. Florida*, 517 U.S. 44 (1996).

26 *Printz and Mack*, 521 U.S. 898, 117 S. Ct. 2365 (1997).

27 *Gonzales v. Oregon*, 546 U.S. 243 (2006).

28 *Arizona v. United States*, 567 U.S. (2012).

29 *Arizona et al. v. Inter Tribal Council of Arizona, Inc.*, 570 U.S. (2013).

30 *Alabama Legislative Black Caucus v. Alabama* No. 13–1138 (2015) and *Arizona State Legislature v. Arizona Independent Redistricting Commission* No. 13–1314 (2015).

31 Alexander Hamilton, James Madison, and John Jay, *The Federalist Papers*, Clinton L. Rossiter, ed. (New York: New American Library, 1961), no. 47, p. 302.

32 *The Federalist Papers*, no. 48, p. 308.

33 Richard E. Neustadt, *Presidential Power* (New York: Wiley, 1960), p. 33.

34 *Marbury v. Madison*, 1 Cranch 137 (1803).

35 C. Herman Pritchett, *The American Constitution* (New York: McGraw-Hill, 1959), pp. 180–6.

36 *Immigration and Naturalization Service v. Chadha,* 462 U.S. 919 (1983). (See Chapter 7.)

37 Cass R. Sunstein, "Taking Over the Courts," *New York Times,* November 9, 2002, p. A19.

38 Sunstein, "Taking Over the Courts."

39 *Youngstown Sheet & Tube Co. v. Sawyer,* 343 U.S. 579 (1952).

40 *United States v. Nixon,* 418 U.S. 683 (1974).

41 *Clinton v. City of New York,* 524 U.S. 417 (1998).

42 *Hamdi v. Rumsfeld,* 542 U.S. 507 (2004); *Rasul v. Bush,* 542 U.S. 466 (2004).

43 For a good evaluation of divided government, see David Mayhew, *Divided We Govern: Party Control, Law Making and Investigations, 1946–1990* (New Haven, CT: Yale University Press, 1991). See also Charles O. Jones, *Separate but Equal Branches— Congress and the Presidency* (Chatham, NJ: Chatham House, 1995).

CHAPTER 4

1 *Dred Scott v. Sandford,* 60 U.S. 393 (1857).

2 For a spirited and enlightening essay on the extent to which the entire Bill of Rights was about equality, see Martha Minow, "Equality and the Bill of Rights," in Meyer and Parent, eds., *The Constitution of Rights,* pp. 118–28.

3 *Barron v. Mayor and City of Baltimore,* 32 U.S. 243 (1833).

4 The Fourteenth Amendment also seems designed to introduce civil rights. The final clause of the all-important Section 1 provides that no state can "deny to any person within its jurisdiction the equal protection of the laws." It is not unreasonable to conclude that the purpose of this provision was to obligate the state governments as well as the national government to take *positive* actions to protect citizens from arbitrary and discriminatory actions, at least those based on race. This will be explored in the second half of the chapter.

5 The Slaughter-House Cases, 16 Wallace 36 (1873); the Civil Rights Cases, 109 U.S. 3 (1883).

6 *Chicago, Burlington and Quincy Railroad Company v. Chicago,* 166 U.S. 266 (1897).

7 *Gitlow v. New York,* 268 U.S. 652 (1925).

8 *Near v. Minnesota,* 283 U.S. 697 (1931); *Hague v. C.I.O.,* 307 U.S. 496 (1939).

9 All of these were implicitly identified in *Palko v. Connecticut,* 302 U.S. 319 (1937), as "not incorporated" into the Fourteenth Amendment as limitations on the powers of the states.

10 *Brown v. Board of Education of Topeka, Kansas,* 347 U.S. 483 (1954).

11 The one exception was the right to public trial (Sixth Amendment), but a 1948 case (*In re Oliver,* 33 U.S. 257) did not actually mention the right to public trial as such; this right was cited in a 1968 case (*Duncan v. Louisiana,* 391 U.S. 145) as a precedent establishing the right to public trial as part of the Fourteenth Amendment.

12 *Gideon v. Wainwright,* 372 U.S. 335 (1963); Anthony Lewis, *Gideon's Trumpet* (New York: Random House, 1964).

13 *Mapp v. Ohio,* 367 U.S. 643 (1961).

14 *Miranda v. Arizona,* 384 U.S. 436 (1966).

15 *Benton v. Maryland,* 395 U.S. 784 (1969).

16 *NAACP v. Alabama ex rel. Patterson,* 357 U.S. 449 (1958).

17 This section is taken from Benjamin Ginsberg, Theodore J. Lowi, Margaret Weir, and Caroline J. Tolbert, *We the People: An Introduction to American Politics,* 9th ed. (New York: Norton, 2013).

18 For a lively and readable treatment of the possibilities of restricting provisions of the Bill of Rights without actually reversing prior decisions, see David G. Savage, *Turning Right: The Making of the Rehnquist Supreme Court* (New York: Wiley, 1992).

19 *Abington School District v. Schempp,* 374 U.S. 203 (1963).

20 *Engel v. Vitale,* 370 U.S. 421 (1962).

21 *Wallace v. Jaffree,* 472 U.S. 38 (1985).

22 *Lynch v. Donnelly,* 465 U.S. 668 (1984).

23 *Lemon v. Kurtzman,* 403 U.S. 602 (1971).

24 *Elk Grove Unified School District v. Newdow,* 542 U.S. 1 (2004).

25 *Van Orden v. Perry,* 545 U.S. 677 (2005).

26 *McCreary v. ACLU,* 545 U.S. 844 (2005).

27 *Holt v. Hobbs* (574 U.S. ___, 2015) and *E.E.O.C. v. Abercrombie and Fitch Stores* (575 U.S. ___, 2015).

28 *United States v. Carolene Products Company,* 304 U.S. 144 (1938), 384. This footnote is one of the Court's most important doctrines. See Alfred H. Kelly, Winfred A. Harbison, and Herman Belz, *The American Constitution: Its Origins and Development,* 7th ed. (New York: Norton, 1991), vol. 2, pp. 519–23.

29 *Snyder v. Phelps,* 09–751 (2011).

30 *Buckley v. Valeo,* 424 U.S. 1 (1976).

31 *McConnell v. Federal Election Commission,* 540 U.S. 93 (2003).

32 *Federal Election Commission v. Wisconsin Right to Life,* 551 U.S. 449 (2007).

33 *Citizens United v. Federal Election Commission,* 558 U.S. 310 (2010).

34 *United States v. O'Brien,* 391 U.S. 367 (1968).

35 *Texas v. Johnson,* 491 U.S. 397 (1989).

36 *Virginia v. Black,* 538 U.S. 343 (2003).

37 *Near v. Minnesota ex rel. Olson,* 283 U.S. 697 (1931).

38 *Reno v. ACLU,* 521 U.S. 844 (1997).

39 *United States v. American Library Association,* 539 U.S. 194 (2003).

40 *United States v. Williams,* 553 U.S. 285 (2008).

41 *Chaplinsky v. State of New Hampshire,* 315 U.S. 568 (1942).

42 *R.A.V. v. City of St. Paul,* 506 U.S. 377 (1992).

43 *Capital Broadcasting Company v. Acting Attorney General,* 405 U.S. 1000 (1972).

44 Louis Fisher, *American Constitutional Law,* 7th ed. (Durham, NC: Academic Press, 2007), vol. 2, p. 546.

45 *Lorillard Tobacco v. Reilly,* 533 U.S. 525 (2001).

46 *District of Columbia v. Heller,* 554 U.S. 570 (2008).

47 *McDonald v. Chicago,* 561 U.S. 3025 (2010).

48 *Horton v. California,* 496 U.S. 128 (1990).

49 For a good discussion of the issue, see Fisher, *American Constitutional Law,* pp. 884–9.

50 E. S. Corwin and Jack Peltason, *Understanding the Constitution,* 13th ed. (Fort Worth, TX: Harcourt Brace, 1994), p. 286.

51 For a full account of the story of the trial and release of Clarence Earl Gideon, see Lewis, *Gideon's Trumpet.*

52 *Escobedo v. Illinois,* 378 U.S. 478 (1964).

53 *Wiggins v. Smith,* 539 U.S. 510 (2003).

54 *Furman v. Georgia,* 408 U.S. 238 (1972).

55 *Roe v. Wade,* 410 U.S. 113 (1973).

56 *Bowers v. Hardwick,* 478 U.S. 186 (1986). The dissenters were quoting an earlier case, *Olmstead v. United States,* 277 U.S. 438 (1928), to emphasize the nature of their disagreement with the majority in the *Bowers* case.

57 *Lawrence and Garner v. Texas,* 539 U.S. 558 (2003).

58 *Gonzales v. Oregon,* 546 U.S. 243 (2006).

59 Woman Suffrage, *Collier's New Encylopedia,* 1921 edition, http://en.Wikisource.org/wiki/Collier%27s_New_Encyclopedia_%281921%29/Woman_suffrage.

60 V.O. Key, *Southern Politics in State and Nation* (New York: Alfred A. Knopf, 1949).

61 Bernard Taper, *Gomillion v. Lighfoot: The Tuskegee Gerrymander Case* (New York: McGraw-Hill, 1962).

62 *Smith v. Allwright,* 321 U.S. 649 (1944).

63 *Gomillion v. Lightfoot,* 364 U.S. 339 (1960).

64 *Shelby County v. Holder,* 570 U.S. (2013).

65 *Plessy v. Ferguson,* 163 U.S. 537 (1896).

66 *Missouri ex rel. Gaines v. Canada,* 305 U.S. 337 (1938).

67 *Sweatt v. Painter,* 339 U.S. 629 (1950).

68 *Smith v. Allwright* (1944).

69 *Shelley v. Kraemer,* 334 U.S. 1 (1948).

70 The District of Columbia case came up too, but since the District of Columbia is not a state, it did not directly involve the Fourteenth Amendment and its equal protection clause. It confronted the Court on the same grounds, however—that segregation is inherently unequal. Its victory in effect was "incorporation in reverse," with equal protection moving from the Fourteenth Amendment to become part of the Bill of Rights. See *Bolling v. Sharpe,* 347 U.S. 497 (1954).

71 *Brown v. Board of Education* (1954).

72 *Griffin v. Prince Edward County School Board,* 337 U.S. 218 (1964), which forced all the schools of that Virginia county to reopen after five years of being closed to avoid desegregation.

73 *Swann v. Charlotte-Mecklenberg Board of Education,* 402 U.S. 1 (1971).

74 For a good evaluation, see Gary Orfield, *Must We Bus? Segregated Schools and National Policy* (Washington, DC: Brookings Institution, 1978), pp. 144–6. See also Bob Woodward and Scott Armstrong, *The Brethren: Inside the Supreme Court* (New York: Simon & Schuster, 1979), pp. 426–7; and J. Anthony Lukas, *Common Ground* (New York: Random House, 1986).

75 *Parents Involved in Community Schools v. Seattle School District No. 1,* 551 U.S. 701 (2007).

76 *Franklin v. Gwinnett County Public Schools,* 503 U.S. 60 (1992).

77 Jennifer Halperin, "Women Step Up to Bat," *Illinois Issue 21* (September 1995): 11–14.

78 *United States v. Virginia,* 518 U.S. 515 (1996).

79 See especially *Katzenbach v. McClung,* 379 U.S. 294 (1964).

80 *Griggs v. Duke Power Company,* 401 U.S. 24 (1971).

81 *Ledbetter v. Goodyear Tire and Rubber Co.,* 550 U.S. 618 (2007).

82 This and the next five sections are drawn in part from Ginsberg et al., *We the People,* 9th ed.

83 See Jane J. Mansbridge, *Why We Lost the ERA* (Chicago: University of Chicago Press, 1986); and Gilbert Steiner, *Constitutional Inequality* (Washington, DC: Brookings Institution, 1985).

84 See *Frontiero v. Richardson*, 411 U.S. 677 (1973).

85 See *Craig v. Boren*, 423 U.S. 1047 (1976).

86 *Meritor Savings Bank v. Vinson*, 477 U.S. 57 (1986).

87 *Harris v. Forklift Systems*, 510 U.S. 17 (1993).

88 *Burlington Industries v. Ellerth*, 524 U.S. 742 (1998); and *Faragher v. City of Boca Raton*, 524 U.S. 775 (1998).

89 Claire Zillman, "Barnes & Noble is Latest Retailer to Face Transgender Discrimination Lawsuit," *Fortune*, May 7, 2015. http://fortune.com/2015/05/07/barnes-noble-transgender-lawsuit/

90 New Mexico had a different history because not many Anglos settled there initially. (*Anglo* is the term for a non-Hispanic white of European background.) Mexican Americans had considerable power in territorial legislatures between 1865 and 1912. See Lawrence H. Fuchs, *The American Kaleidoscope* (Hanover, NH: University Press of New England, 1990), pp. 239–40.

91 *Mendez v. Westminster*, 161 F2d 744 (Ninth Cir., 1947).

92 On the La Raza Unida Party, see Carlos Muñoz, Jr., and Mario Barrera, "La Raza Unida Party and the Chicano Student Movement in California," in *Latinos and the Political System*, F. Chris Garcia, ed. (Notre Dame, IN: University of Notre Dame Press, 1988), pp. 213–35.

93 *United States v. Wong Kim Ark*, 169 U.S. 649 (1898).

94 *Lau v. Nichols*, 414 U.S. 563 (1974).

95 Dick Kirschten, "Not Black and White," *National Journal*, March 2, 1991, p. 497.

96 See the discussion in Robert A. Katzmann, *Institutional Disability: The Saga of Transportation Policy for the Disabled* (Washington, DC: Brookings Institution, 1986).

97 For example, after pressure from the Justice Department, one of the nation's largest rental car companies agreed to make special hand controls available to any customer requesting them. See "Avis Agrees to Equip Cars for Disabled," *Los Angeles Times*, September 2, 1994, p. D1.

98 *Romer v. Evans*, 517 U.S. 620 (1996).

99 *United States v. Windsor*, 570 U.S. (2013). That same day the Court also cleared the way for the legalization of same-sex marriage in California in the case *Hollingsworth v. Perry*, 570 U.S. (2013).

100 *Regents of the University of California v. Bakke*, 438 U.S. 265 (1978).

101 *United Steelworkers of America v. Weber*, 443 U.S. 193 (1979); and *Fullilove v. Klutznick*, 448 U.S. 448 (1980).

102 *Martin v. Wilks*, 490 U.S. 755 (1989).

103 *Adarand Constructors v. Pena*, 515 U.S. 200 (1995).

104 *Hopwood v. State of Texas*, 78 F3d 932 (Fifth Cir., 1996).

105 *Gratz v. Bollinger*, 539 U.S. 244 (2003).

106 *Grutter v. Bollinger*, 539 U.S. 306 (2003).

107 *Fisher v. University of Texas*, 570 U.S. ___ (2013).

108 *Fisher v. University of Texas*, No. 14-981 (2016).

CHAPTER 5

1 Alexander Hamilton, James Madison, and John Jay, *The Federalist Papers*, Clinton L. Rossiter, ed. (New York: New American Library, 1961), no. 47, p. 378.

2 See Richard F. Fenno, Jr., *Home Style: House Members in Their Districts* (Boston: Little, Brown, 1978). Essays elaborating on Fenno's classic are found in Morris P. Fiorina and David W. Rhode, eds., *Home Style and Washington Work* (Ann Arbor: University of Michigan Press, 1989).

3 For more on political careers generally, see John R. Hibbing, "Legislative Careers: Why and How We Should Study Them," *Legislative Studies Quarterly* 24 (1999): 149–71. See also Cherie D. Maestas, Sarah Fulton, L. Sandy Maisel, and Walter J. Stone, "When to Risk It? Institutions, Ambitions, and the Decision to Run for the U.S. House," *American Political Science Review* 100, no. 2 (May 2006): 195–208.

4 Constituents are not a legislative agent's only principals. He or she may also be beholden to party leaders and special interests, as well as to members and committees in the chamber. See Forrest Maltzman, *Competing Principles* (Ann Arbor: University of Michigan Press, 1997).

5 See Linda L. Fowler and Robert D. McClure, *Political Ambition: Who Decides to Run for Congress* (New Haven, CT: Yale University Press, 1989); and Alan Ehrenhalt, *The United States of Ambition: Politicians, Power, and the Pursuit of Office* (New York: Times Books, 1991).

6 On the thesis of "strategic candidacy," see Gary C. Jacobson, *The Politics of Congressional Elections*, 7th ed. (New York: Pearson Longman, 2008).

7 See James D. Savage, *Funding Science in America: Congress, Universities, and the Politics of the Academic Pork Barrel* (New York: Cambridge University Press, 1999); and Diana Evans, *Greasing the Wheels: Using Pork-Barrel Projects to Build Majority Coalitions in Congress* (New York: Cambridge University Press, 2004).

8 Norman J. Ornstein, Thomas E. Mann, and Michael J. Malbin, *Vital Statistics on Congress, 1995–1996* (Washington, DC: CQ Press, 1996), pp. 60–61

(see also subsequent editions); Robert S. Erickson and Gerald C. Wright, "Voters, Candidates, and Issues in Congressional Elections," in *Congress Reconsidered*, 5th ed., Lawrence C. Dodd and Bruce I. Oppenheimer, eds. (Washington, DC: CQ Press, 1993), p. 99; John R. Alford and David W. Brady, "Personal and Partisan Advantage in U.S. Congressional Elections, 1846–1990," in *Congress Reconsidered*, 5th ed., pp. 141–57.

9 Stephen Ansolabehere and James Snyder, "Campaign War Chests and Congressional Elections," *Business and Politics*, no. 2 (2000): 9–34.

10 Gary W. Cox and Eric Magar, "How Much Is Majority Status in the U.S. Congress Worth?" *American Political Science Review* 93, no. 2 (June 1999): 299–309.

11 Kenneth Bickers and Robert Stein, "The Electoral Dynamics of the Federal Pork Barrel," *American Journal of Political Science* 40 (1996): 1300–26.

12 See Barbara C. Burrell, *A Woman's Place Is in the House: Campaigning for Congress in the Feminist Era* (Ann Arbor: University of Michigan Press, 1994), Chap. 6; and David Broder, "Key to Women's Political Parity: Running," *Washington Post*, September 8, 1994, p. A17.

13 See John H. Aldrich, *Why Parties? The Origin and Transformation of Political Parties in America* (Chicago: University of Chicago Press, 1995); and Gary W. Cox and Mathew D. McCubbins, *Legislative Leviathan: Party Government in the House* (Berkeley: University of California Press, 1993).

14 Richard Fenno, Jr., *Home Style: House Members in Their Districts* (Boston: Little, Brown, 1978).

15 John Gilmour, *Strategic Disagreement* (Pittsburgh: University of Pittsburgh Press, 1995).

16 See Kenneth W. Kollman, *Outside Lobbying: Public Opinion and Interest Group Strategies* (Princeton, NJ: Princeton University Press, 1998).

17 See Janet M. Grenke, "PACs and the Congressional Supermarket: The Currency Is Complex," *American Journal of Political Science* 33, no. 1 (February 1989): 1–24. More generally, see Jacobson, *The Politics of Congressional Elections*. See also Stephen Ansolabehere, John de Figueiredo, and James Snyder, "Why Is There So Little Money in U.S. Politics?" *Journal of Economic Perspectives* 17 (2003): 105–30.

18 See Sven E. Feldmann and Morten Bennedsen, "Informational Lobbying and Political Contributions," *Journal of Public Economics* 90 (2006): 631–56.

19 A recent analysis of how floor time is allocated is found in Gary W. Cox and Mathew D. McCubbins, *Setting the Agenda: Responsible Party Government in the U.S. House of Representatives* (New York: Cambridge University Press, 2005).

20 David Broder, "At 6 Months, House GOP Juggernaut Still Cohesive," *Washington Post*, July 17, 1995, p. A1.

21 Carl Hulse, "Even Some in G.O.P. Call for More Oversight of Bush," *New York Times*, May 31, 2004, p. A13.

22 *U.S. v. Pink*, 315 U.S. 203 (1942). For a good discussion of the problem, see James W. Davis, *The American Presidency* (New York: Harper & Row, 1987), chap. 8.

CHAPTER 6

1 Quoted from the dissenting opinion of Justice Robert Jackson in *Korematsu v. United States*, 323 U.S. 214 (1944).

2 *Authorization for Use of Military Force*, Public Law 107-40, *U.S. Statutes at Large* 115 (2001): 224.

3 Alexander Hamilton, James Madison, and John Jay, *The Federalist Papers*, Clinton L. Rossiter, ed. (New York: New American Library, 1961), no. 39, p. 309.

4 David Fahrenthold, "Senator Obama vs. President Obama," *Washington Post*, June 26, 2011, p. A3.

5 *In re Neagle*, 135 U.S. 1 (1890).

6 James G. Randall, *Constitutional Problems under Lincoln* (New York: Appleton, 1926), chap. 1.

7 Edward S. Corwin, *The President: Office and Powers*, 4th rev. ed. (New York: New York University Press, 1957), p. 229.

8 These statutes are contained mainly in Title 10 of the U.S. Code, Sections 331, 332, and 333.

9 In *United States v. Pink*, 315 U.S. 203 (1942), the Supreme Court confirmed that an executive agreement is the legal equivalent of a treaty, despite the absence of Senate approval.

10 *United States v. Nixon*, 418 U.S. 683 (1974).

11 *Clinton v. City of New York*, 524 U.S. 417 (1998).

12 For the complete list of presidential vetoes, see www.senate.gov/reference/Legislation/Vetoes/BushGW.htm (accessed 9/20/11).

13 Charles M. Cameron, *Veto Bargaining: Presidents and the Politics of Negative Power* (New York: Cambridge University Press, 2000). See also David W. Rohde and Dennis Simon, "Presidential Vetoes and Congressional Response: A Study of Institutional Conflict," *American Journal of Political Science* 29 (1985): 397–427.

14 Theodore J. Lowi, *The Personal President: Power Invested, Promise Unfulfilled* (Ithaca, NY: Cornell University Press, 1985).

15 Timothy Groseclose and Nolan McCarty, "The Politics of Blame: Bargaining before an Audience," *American Journal of Political Science* 45 (2001): 100–19.

16 This point is developed in both Kenneth R. Mayer, *With the Stroke of a Pen: Executive Orders and Presidential Power* (Princeton, NJ: Princeton University Press, 2001); and William G. Howell, *Power without Persuasion: The Politics of Direct Presidential Action* (Princeton, NJ: Princeton University Press, 2003).

17 Richard Neustadt, *Presidential Power: The Politics of Leadership* (New York: Wiley, 1960).

18 For related appraisals, see Jeffrey Tulis, *The Rhetorical Presidency* (Princeton, NJ: Princeton University Press, 1988); Stephen Skowronek, *The Politics Presidents Make: Presidential Leadership from John Adams to George Bush* (Cambridge, MA: Harvard University Press, 1993); and Robert Spitzer, *President and Congress: Executive Hegemony at the Crossroads of American Government* (New York: McGraw-Hill, 1993).

19 See George Krause, "The Secular Decline in Presidential Domestic Policymaking: An Organizational Perspective," *Presidential Studies Quarterly* 34 (2004): 779–92. On the general issue, see James P. Pfiffner, ed., *The Managerial Presidency*, 2nd ed. (College Station: Texas A&M University Press, 1999).

20 Article I, Section 3, provides that the vice president "shall be President of the Senate, but shall have no Vote, unless they be equally divided."

21 Samuel Kernell, *Going Public: New Strategies of Presidential Leadership*, 3rd ed. (Washington, DC: CQ Press, 1997); also Jeffrey Tulis, *The Rhetorical Presidency* (Princeton, NJ: Princeton University Press, 1987).

22 Quoted in Sidney M. Milkis, *The President and the Parties* (New York: Oxford University Press, 1993), p. 97.

23 Kernell, *Going Public*, p. 79.

24 Theodore J. Lowi, *The Personal President: Power Invested, Promise Unfulfilled* (Ithaca, NY: Cornell University Press, 1985).

25 The classic critique of this process is Theodore J. Lowi, *The End of Liberalism* (New York: Norton, 1979).

26 Kenneth Culp Davis, *Administrative Law Treatise* (St. Paul, MN: West Publishing, 1958), p. 9.

27 Elena Kagan, "Presidential Administration," *Harvard Law Review* 2245 (2001): 2265.

28 For example, Douglas W. Kmiec, "Expanding Power," in *The Rule of Law in the Wake of Clinton*, Roger Pilon, ed. (Washington, DC: Cato Institute Press, 2000), pp. 47–68.

29 A complete inventory is provided in Harold C. Relyea, "Presidential Directives: Background and Review," The Library of Congress, *Congressional Research Service Report 98–611*, November 9, 2001.

30 *Youngstown Sheet & Tube Co. v. Sawyer*, 346 U.S. 579 (1952).

31 Mark Killenbeck, "A Matter of Mere Approval: The Role of the President in the Creation of Legislative History," *University of Arkansas Law Review* 48 (1995): 239.

32 Philip J. Cooper, *By Order of the President: The Use and Abuse of Executive Direct Action* (Lawrence: University Press of Kansas, 1998), p. 201.

33 Cooper, *By Order of the President*, p. 201.

34 *Ameron, Inc. v. U.S. Army Corps of Engineers*, 610 F.Supp. 750 (D.N.J. 1985).

35 *Lear Siegler, Inc. v. Lehman*, 842 F.2nd 1102 (1988).

36 Kristy Carroll, "Whose Statute Is It Anyway? Why and How Courts Should Use Presidential Signing Statements When Interpreting Federal Statutes," 16 *Catholic University Law Review* 46 (1997): 475.

CHAPTER 7

1 William A. Niskanen, *Bureaucracy and Representative Government* (Chicago: Aldine, 1971).

2 Stephen Peter Rosen, *Winning the Next War* (Ithaca, NY: Cornell University Press, 1991).

3 Harold Seidman, *Politics, Position, and Power: The Dynamics of Federal Organization*, 5th ed. (New York: Oxford University Press, 1998), chap. 8.

4 James Q. Wilson, *Bureaucracy: What Government Agencies Do and Why They Do It* (New York: Basic Books, 1989), p. 91.

5 When bureaucrats engage in interpretation, the result is what political scientists call bureaucratic drift. Bureaucratic drift occurs because, as we've suggested, the "bosses" (in Congress) and the "agents" (within the bureaucracy) don't always share the same purposes.

6 See Mathew D. McCubbins and Thomas Schwartz, "Congressional Oversight Overlooked: Police Patrols versus Fire Alarms," *American Journal of Political Science* 28 (1984): 165–79.

7 32 Stat. 825; 15 USC 1501.

8 For a detailed account of the creation of the Department of Commerce and Labor and its split into two separate departments, see Theodore J. Lowi, *The End of Liberalism* (New York: Norton, 1979), pp. 78–84.

9 Until 1979, the departments of Education and of Health and Human Services were joined in a single department, the Department of Health, Education, and Welfare (HEW), which had been established by Congress in 1953.

10 Alexander Hamilton, James Madison, and John Jay, *The Federalist Papers*, Clinton L. Rossiter, ed. (New York: New American Library, 1961), no. 51.

11 Niskanen, *Bureaucracy and Representative Government*.

12 John Brehm and Scott Gates, *Working, Shirking, and Sabotage: Bureaucratic Response to a Democratic Public* (Ann Arbor: University of Michigan Press, 1997). For detailed insight about the motivations for government service combining the personal and the patriotic, consider the case of Henry Paulson, who became George W. Bush's Treasury secretary. Paulson's story is described well in Andrew Ross Sorkin, *Too Big to Fail* (New York: Viking, 2009), chap. 2.

13 For an expanded view of bureaucratic autonomy and insulation with historical application to the U.S. Department of Agriculture and the Post Office Department, see Daniel P. Carpenter, *The Forging of Bureaucratic Autonomy: Reputations, Networks, and Policy Innovation in Executive Agencies, 1862–1928* (Princeton, NJ: Princeton University Press, 2001).

14 See John Micklethwait, "Managing to Look Attractive," *New Statesman*, November 8, 1996, p. 24.

15 See Aaron Wildavsky, *The New Politics of the Budgetary Process*, 2nd ed. (New York: HarperCollins, 1992), pp. 15–6.

16 Morris S. Ogul, *Congress Oversees the Bureaucracy: Studies in Legislative Supervision* (Pittsburgh, PA: University of Pittsburgh Press, 1976); and Peter Woll, *American Bureaucracy*, 2nd ed. (New York: Norton, 1977).

17 See McCubbins and Schwartz, "Congressional Oversight Overlooked."

18 This is just under 99 percent of all national government employees. About 2 percent work for the legislative branch and for the federal judiciary. U.S. Bureau of the Census, *Statistical Abstract of the U.S. 2011*, www.census.gov/prod/2011pubs/11statab/pop.pdf (accessed 6/15/16)

19 U.S. Bureau of the Census, *Statistical Abstract of the U.S. 2011*, www.census.gov/prod/2011pubs/11statab/pop.pdf (accessed 6/15/16)

20 Public Law 101-510, Title XXIX, Sections 2,901 and 2,902 of Part A (Defense Base Closure and Realignment Commission).

CHAPTER 8

1 Justices in many state and local courts are elected.

2 *United States v. Nixon*, 418 U.S. 683 (1974).

3 Edward Corwin, *The President: Office and Powers*, 4th rev. ed. (New York: New York University Press, 1957), p. 16.

4 Terry M. Moe and William G. Howell, "The Presidential Power of Unilateral Action," *The Journal of Law, Economics and Organization*, 15 (1) (1999): 151–2.

5 Thomas E. Cronin and Michael A. Genovese, *The Paradoxes of the American Presidency* (New York: Oxford University Press, 1998), p. 271.

6 C. Herman Pritchett, *The American Constitution* (New York: McGraw-Hill, 1959), p. 138.

7 *Marbury v. Madison*, 1 Cranch 137 (1803).

8 For an analysis of the Court's use of judicial review to nullify acts of Congress, see Ryan Emenaker, "Constitutional Interpretation and Congressional Overrides: Changing Trends in Court–Congress Relations," presented at the annual meeting of the Western Political Science Association, Hollywood, CA, March 28–30, 2013.

9 *Shelby County v. Holder*, 570 U.S. ___ (2013)

10 This review power was affirmed by the Supreme Court in *Martin v. Hunter's Lessees*, 1 Wheaton 304 (1816).

11 *Brown v. Board of Education*, 347 U.S. 483 (1954).

12 *Loving v. Virginia*, 388 U.S. 1 (1967).

13 *Obergefell v. Hodges* 576 U.S. ___ (2015).

14 56 Stat. 23 (January 30, 1942).

15 *Chevron v. Natural Resources Defense Council*, 467 U.S. 837 (1984).

16 *Hamdi v. Rumsfeld*, 542 U.S. 507 (2004).

17 *Hamdan v. Rumsfeld*, 548 U.S. (2006).

18 *United States v. Texas*, No. 15-674.

19 Walter F. Murphy, "The Supreme Court of the United States," in *Encyclopedia of the American Judicial System*, Robert J. Janosik, ed. (New York: Scribner's, 1987).

20 Gregory A. Caldeira and John R. Wright, "Organized Interests and Agenda Setting in the U.S. Supreme Court," *American Political Science Review* 82 (1988): 1109–27.

21 *Adarand Constructors, Inc. v. Peña*, 515 U.S. 200 (1995); *Missouri v. Jenkins*, 515 U.S. 70 (1995); *Miller v. Johnson*, 515 U.S. 900 (1995).

22 Mark Joseph Stern, "The Supreme Court Looks Poised to Block Obama's Immigration Actions Indefinitely," Slate, www.slate.com/blogs/the_slatest/2016/04/18/texas_v_united_states_supreme_court_could_block_obama_s_immigration_executive.html (accessed 6/30/16).

23 *Smith v. Allwright*, 321 U.S. 649 (1944).

24 Adam Liptak, "Supreme Court Upholds Health Care Law, 5–4, in Victory for Obama," *New York Times*, June 28, 2012, www.nytimes.com/2012/

06/29/us/supreme-court-lets-health-law-largely-stand.html (accessed 7/15/13).

25 *King v. Burwell,* 576 US ___ (2015).

26 C. Herman Pritchett, *The Roosevelt Court* (New York: Macmillan, 1948).

27 William N. Eskridge, Jr., "Overriding Supreme Court Statutory Interpretation Decisions," *Yale Law Journal* 101 (1991): 331–55.

28 A full strategic analysis of the maneuvering among the legislative, executive, and judicial branches in the separation-of-powers arrangement choreographed by the U.S. Constitution may be found in William Eskridge and John Ferejohn, "The Article 1, Section 7 Game," *Georgetown Law Review* 80 (1992): 523–65.

29 See "Developments in the Law—Class Actions," *Harvard Law Review* 89 (1976): 1318.

30 See Donald Horowitz, *The Courts and Social Policy* (Washington, DC: Brookings Institution, 1977).

31 David Van Drehle, "Court That Liberals Savage Proves to Be Less of a Target," *Washington Post,* June 29, 2003, p. A18.

CHAPTER 9

1 Alan Monroe, "Consistency between Public Preferences and National Policy Decisions," *American Politics Quarterly* 7 (1979): 3–18. See also Alan D. Monroe, "Public Opinion and Public Policy, 1980–1993," *Public Opinion Quarterly* 62, no. 1 (1998): 6–18.

2 Carol Glynn, Susan Herbst, Garret O'Keefe, Robert Shapiro, and Mark Lindeman, *Public Opinion,* 2nd ed. (Boulder, CO: Westview, 2004), p. 293.

3 Lawrence R. Jacobs and Robert Y. Shapiro, *Politicians Don't Pander* (Chicago: University of Chicago Press, 2000), p. xv.

4 Dick Morris, *Behind the Oval Office* (Los Angeles: Renaissance, 1999). Quoted in Jacobs and Shapiro, *Politicians Don't Pander,* p. xv.

5 Michael Graetz and Ian Shapiro, *Death by a Thousand Cuts: The Fight over Taxing Inherited Wealth* (Princeton, NJ: Princeton University Press, 2005).

6 Jacob S. Hacker and Paul Pierson, *Off Center: The Republican Revolution and the Erosion of American Democracy* (New Haven, CT: Yale, 2005), chap. 2.

7 See Louis Hartz, *The Liberal Tradition in America: An Interpretation of American Political Thought since the Revolution* (New York: Harcourt, Brace, 1955).

8 For a discussion of political beliefs of Americans, see Everett Carl Ladd, *The American Ideology* (Storrs, CT: Roper Center, 1994).

9 Jordy Yeager, "House Limits Constituent E-mail to Prevent Crash," *The Hill,* September 30, 2008, http://thehill.com/leading-the-news/house-limits-constituent-e-mails-to-prevent-crash-2008-09-30.html (accessed 3/24/09).

10 The American Values Survey is available at www.people-press.org/values-questions.

11 Rawi Abdelal, Yoshiko M. Herrera, Alastair Iain Johnston, and Rose McDermott, "Identity as a Variable," *Perspectives on Politics* 4, no. 4 (2006): 695–711.

12 Angus Campbell, Philip Converse, Warren Miller, and Donald Stokes, *The American Voter.* John Wiley: New York, 1960.

13 Pew Research Center for the People and the Press, "The Black and White of Public Opinion," October 31, 2005, http://people-press.org/commentary/?anaysisid=121 (accessed 3/24/09).

14 Pew Research Center, September 2014, "Wide Partisan Differences Over the Issues That Matter in 2014," www.people-press.org/files/2014/09/09-12-14-Midterms-Release1.pdf (accessed 12/16/14).

15 Gabriel R. Sanchez, "The Role of Group Consciousness in Latino Public Opinion," *Political Research Quarterly* 59, no. 3 (2006): 435–446. Pamela Johnston Conover, "The Influence of Group Identifications on Political Perception and Evaluation," *Journal of Politics* 46, no. 3 (1984): 760–85.

16 Taeku Lee, "Race, Immigration, and the Identity-to-Politics Link," *Annual Review of Political Science* 11 (2008): 457–78.

17 For data, see Center for American Women and Politics, Eagleton Institute of Politics, Rutgers, State University of New Jersey, www.cawp.rutgers.edu/fast_facts/voters/turnout.php (accessed 4/30/09).

18 Pew Research Center for the People and the Press, "Pragmatic Americans Liberal and Conservative on Social Issues: Most Want Middle Ground on Abortion," August 3, 2006, http://people-press.org/report/283/pragmatic-americans-liberal-and-conservative-on-social-issues (accessed 3/24/09).

19 See Ebonya Washington, "Female Socialization: How Daughters Affect Their Legislator Fathers' Voting on Women's Issues," *American Economic Review* 98 (2008): 311–32.

20 Angus Campbell, Philip E. Converse, Warren E. Miller, and Donald E. Stokes, *The American Voter* (Chicago: The University of Chicago Press, 1960).

21 Rene R. Rocha, and Rodolfo Espino, "Racial Threat, Residential Segregation, and the Policy Attitudes of Anglos," *Political Research Quarterly* 62, no. 2 (2009): 415–26.

22 Being a numerical majority is not necessary. For over a century, blacks in South Africa were

oppressed by Afrikkaners, even though the white population accounted for only about 10 percent of all people in the country.

23 Michael C. Dawson, *Behind the Mule: Race and Class in African-American Politics* (Princeton: Princeton University Press, 1995).

24 Philip E. Converse, "The Nature of Belief Systems in Mass Publics," in *Ideology and Discontent*, David E. Apter, ed. (New York: Free Press, 1964).

25 Anthony Downs, An *Economic Theory of Democracy* (New York: Harper & Row, 1957).

26 For a discussion of the role of information in democratic politics, see Arthur Lupia and Mathew D. McCubbins, *The Democratic Dilemma: Can Citizens Learn What They Need to Know?* (New York: Cambridge University Press, 1998).

27 One of the most detailed analyses of the distribution of the tax burden in advanced industrial democracies in the past half-century is Thomas Piketty and Emmanuel Saez, "How Progressive Is the U.S. Federal Tax System? Historical and International Perspectives," working paper 12404, National Bureau of Economic Research, 2006. www.nber.org/papers/w12404 (accessed 3/25/09).

28 Jacob Hacker and Paul Pierson, *Winner-Take-All Politics* (New York: Simon & Shuster, 2010).

29 Larry M. Bartels, "Homer Gets a Tax Cut: Inequality and Public Policy in the American Mind," *Perspectives on Politics* 3 (2005): 15–31.

30 "Changing Attitudes on Gay Marriage," Pew Research Center, May 12, 2016, www.pewforum. org/2016/05/12/changing-attitudes-on-gay-marriage/ (accessed 10/24/16).

31 Joshua Green, "The Other War Room," *Washington Monthly,* April 2002.

32 Michael Calderone, "White House News Strategy Causes Concerns about Access," February 15, 2011, http://news.yahoo.com/s/yblog_thecutline/20110215/bs_yblog_thecutline/white -house-media-strategy-causes-concerns-about -access (accessed 8/22/11).

33 Cynthia Gorney, "Gambling with Abortion," *Harper's Magazine,* November 2004, pp. 33–46.

34 See David Vogel, "The Power of Business in America: A Reappraisal," *British Journal of Political Science* 13 (January 1983): 19–44.

35 See David Vogel, "The Public Interest Movement and the American Reform Tradition," *Political Science Quarterly* 96 (Winter 1980): 607–27.

36 See Stephen Ansolabehere, Roy Behr, and Shanto Iyengar, *The Media Game* (New York: Macmillan, 1993).

37 Andrew Perrin and Maeve Duggan, "Americans' Internet Access: 2000-2015," Pew Research Center, June 26, 2015, www.pewinternet.org/2015/06/26/americans-internet-access-2000-2015/ (accessed 7/1/16).

38 Michael Barthel, "State of the News Media 2015," Pew Research Center, April 29, 2015, www. journalism.org/2015/04/29/newspapers-fact-sheet/ (accessed 7/1/16).

39 "The 10 Most Endangered Newspapers in America," *Time*, March 9, 2009, www.time.com/time/business/article/0,8599,1883785,00.html (accessed 6/8/09).

40 Jeffrey Gottfried and Elisa Shearer, "News Use Across Social Media Platforms 2016," Pew Research Center, May 26, 2016, www.journalism. org/2016/05/26/news-use-across-social-media-platforms-2016/ (accessed 7/1/16).

41 *Near v. Minnesota ex rel.*, 283 U.S. 697 (1931).

42 See Matthew Baum, *Soft News Goes to War* (Princeton, NJ: Princeton University Press, 2006).

43 The seminal work on priming and framing in public policy and politics is Shanto Iyengar and Donald Kinder, *News That Matters* (Chicago: University of Chicago Press, 1987).

44 Page and Shapiro, "Effects of Public Opinion on Policy."

45 Robert A. Erikson, Gerald Wright, and John McIver, *Statehouse Democracy: Public Opinion and Democracy in the American States* (New York: Cambridge University Press, 1994).

46 The results of separate studies by the political scientists Lawrence Jacobs, Robert Shapiro, and Alan Monroe were reported by Richard Morin in "Which Comes First, the Politician or the Poll?" *Washington Post National Weekly Edition*, February 10, 1997, p. 35.

CHAPTER 10

1 Alexander Hamilton, James Madison, and John Jay, *The Federalist Papers*, Clinton Rossiter, ed. (New York: New American Library, 1961), no. 57.

2 Walter Lippman, *The Essential Lippman,* Clinton Rossiter and James Lare, eds. (New York: Random House, Vintage Books, 1965), p. 12.

3 Senate Committee on the Judiciary, *Hearings before the Subcommittee on Constitutional Amendments on S.J. Res. 8, S.J. Res. 14 and S.J. Res. 78, Relating to Lowering the Voting Age to 18*. 90th Cong., 2nd sess., 1968 (Washington, DC: U.S. Government Printing Office, 1968), p. 12.

4 Senate Committee, *Hearings*, p. 3.

5 Benjamin Ginsberg and Robert Weissberg, "Elections as Legitimizing Institutions," *American Journal of Political Science* 22, no. 1 (February 1978): 31–55.

6 In addition there is the restriction that those currently serving sentences for felonies cannot vote; some states prohibit ex-felons from voting.

7 There are further restrictions in some states that prohibit ex-felons from voting and impose residency requirements.

8 Sidney Verba, Kay Schlozman, and Henry Brady, *Voice and Equality: Civic Volunteerism in America* (Cambridge, MA: Harvard University Press, 1995).

9 See Walter Dean Burnham, "The Changing Shape of the American Political Universe," *American Political Science Review* 59, no. 1 (March 1965): 7–28. It should be noted that other democracies, such as India and Switzerland, have even lower turnout rates, as do some of the new democracies in eastern Europe.

10 See statistics of the U.S. Bureau of the Census and the Federal Election Commission. For voting statistics for 1960 to 2004, see "National Voter Turnout in Federal Elections: 1960–2004," at www.infoplease.com/ipa/A0781453.html (accessed 3/26/09).

11 Not all states report such figures in their certified tally of the vote. In fact, 11 states do not report the number of ballots cast, and researchers must substitute the total votes for all candidates for the presidency or another office on the top of the ballot. Since nearly all voters who turn out do vote on the races at the top of the ticket, counting those totals is a reasonably accurate substitute for official turnout records.

12 These figures exclude undocumented, illegal immigrants, of which there are estimated to be another 12 million persons.

13 Helen Dewar, "'Motor Voter' Agreement Is Reached," *Washington Post*, April 28, 1993, p. A6.

14 Stephen Ansolabehere and Eitan Hersh, "Validation: What Big Data Tell Us about the Actual Electorate," *Political Analysis* (2012).

15 Stephen Ansolabehere and Nathaniel Persily, "Vote Fraud in the Eye of the Beholder," *Harvard Law Review* 121 (2008): 1737; Stephen Ansolabehere, "Effects of Identification Requirements on Voting: Evidence from the Experiences of Voters on Election Day," *PS* (January 2009): 127–130.

16 Jerold G. Rusk, "The Effect of the Australian Ballot Reform on Split Ticket Voting, 1876–1908," *American Political Science Review* 64, no. 4 (December 1970): 1220–38.

17 For definitions of these units, see Bureau of the Census, Geographic Area Reference Manual, www.census.gov/geo/www/garm.html (accessed 6/17/09).

18 For an excellent analysis of voting systems and a complete classification, see Gary Cox, *Making Votes Count* (New York: Cambridge University Press, 1997).

19 *Hollingsworth et. al. v. Perry et. al., 570 U.S.* (2013).

20 This point is developed in Mordon Bennedsen and Sven Fledmann, "Lobbying Legislatures," *Journal of Political Economy* 110 (2002).

21 The most reliable source of information about the demographics of voting is the Current Population Survey, conducted by the Census Bureau. For these and other statistics, see U.S. Census Bureau, "Voting and Registration in the Election of November 2012," www.census.gov/hhes/www/socdemo/voting/publications/p20/2012 /tables.html (accessed 7/17/13).

22 Hawaii has passed an election day registration law, but it will not be implemented until 2018.

23 The classic study in this area is Raymond Wolfinger and Steven Rosenstone, *Who Votes?* (New Haven, CT: Yale University Press, 1978). See also Steven Rosenstone and John Mark Hansen, *Participation, Mobilization and American Democracy* (New York: Macmillan, 1993).

24 This is the wording used by the Gallup Poll. Others ask "In politics today . . ." or offer "or another party" instead of "or what."

25 For an excellent treatment of the meanings of party identification and analysis of the implications of different theories, see Donald Green, Bradley Palmquist, and Eric Schickler, *Partisan Hearts and Minds* (New Haven, CT: Yale University Press, 2003).

26 For a detailed assessment of the political use of information-economizing devices such as party labels, see Arthur Lupia and Mathew D. McCubbins, *The Democratic Dilemma: Can Citizens Learn What They Need to Know?* (New York: Cambridge University Press, 1998).

27 The partitioning of the incumbency effect into officeholder advantages and challenger qualities begins with the important work of Gary C. Jacobson; see, for example, his excellent text *Congressional Elections.* Estimating exactly what fraction of the incumbency effect is due to officeholder benefits is tricky. See Stephen Ansolabehere, James M. Snyder, Jr., and Charles H. Stewart III, "Old Voters, New Voters, and the Personal Vote," *American Journal of Political Science* 44 (2000).

28 See Stephen Ansolabehere, Jonathan Rodden, and James M. Snyder, Jr., "Issue Voting," *American Political Science Review* (May 2008).

29 The classic study showing this is Philip Converse, "The Nature of Belief Systems in Mass Publics," in *Ideology and Discontent*, David Apter, ed. (New York: Free Press, 1964).

30 The FEC's website is an excellent resource for those interested in U.S. campaign finance, www.fec.gov.

31 *Buckley v. Valeo*, 424 U.S. 1 (1976).

32 *Citizens United v. Federal Election Commission,* 558 U.S. 310 (2010).

33 *McConnell v. Federal Election Commission,* 540 U.S. 93 (2003).

34 See Stephen Ansolabehere and James M. Snyder, Jr., "The Incumbency Advantage in U.S. Elections: An

Analysis of State and Federal Offices, 1942–2000," *Election Law Journal* 1 (2002): 315–38.

35 http://www.opensecrets.org/news/ 2014/10/overall-spending-inches-up-in-2014-megadonors-equip-outside-groups-to-capture-a-bigger-share-of-the-pie/)

36 Aaron Blake, "More young people voted for Bernie Sanders than Trump and Clinton combined—by a lot," *Washington Post*, June 20, 2016, www.washingtonpost.com/news/the-fix/wp/2016/06/20/more-young-people-voted-for-bernie-sanders-than-trump-and-clinton-combined-by-a-lot/ (accessed 11/28/16).

37 Michael O'Connell, "TV Ratings: Hillary Clinton's DNC Speech Falls Just Shy of Trump's with 33 Million Viewers," *The Hollywood Reporter*, July 29, 2016, www.hollywoodreporter.com/live-feed/tv-ratings-hillary-clintons-dnc-915706 (accessed 11/22/16).

38 Alan Rappeport, "Who Won the Debate? Hillary Clinton, the 'Nasty Woman,'" *New York Times*, October 20, 2016, www.nytimes.com/2016/10/21/us/politics/who-won-the-third-debate.html (accessed 11/22/16).

39 Exit Polls, CNN Politics, www.cnn.com/election/results/exit-polls (accessed 11/21/16).

40 David Wasserman, The Cook Political Report, November 16, 2016, www.cookpolitical.com/story/10174 (accessed 12/7/16).

41 Michael Lewis-Beck and Charles Tien, "The Political Economy Model: 2016 US Election Forecasts," PS: Political Science & Politics, volume 49, October 2016, pages 661–663, www.cambridge.org/core/journals/ps-political-science-and-politics/article/the-political-economy-model-2016-us-election-forecasts/B4907EFC1CC6D8CC781E575B824F15CE/core-reader (accessed 11/22/16).

CHAPTER 11

1 This distinction is from John H. Aldrich, *Why Parties? The Origin and Transformation of Party Politics in America* (Chicago: University of Chicago Press, 1995).

2 For an excellent analysis of the parties' role in recruitment, see Paul Herrnson, *Congressional Elections: Campaigning at Home and in Washington* (Washington, DC: CQ Press, 1995).

3 For a discussion of some of the effects of primary elections, see Peter F. Galderisi and Benjamin Ginsberg, "Primary Elections and the Evanescence of Third Party Activity in the United States," in *Do Elections Matter?* Benjamin Ginsberg and Alan Stone, eds. (Armonk, NY: M. E. Sharpe, 1986), pp. 115–30.

4 If a group coordinates its activities with a political party, it is subject to additional reporting requirements and contribution limits, and political action can violate the conditions for tax-exempt status of nonprofits.

5 Maurice Duverger, *Political Parties* (New York: John Wiley and Son, 1951).

6 Don Gonyea, "Obama's Winning Streak on Hill Unprecedented," NPR, January 11, 2010, www.npr.org/templates/story/story.php?storyId=122436116 (accessed 10/28/11).

7 Shawn Zeller, "Running on Empty," *CQ Weekly*, March 15, 2015, pp. 26–36, library.cqpress.com/cqweekly/file.php?path=/files/wr20150316-2014_Presidential.pdf (accessed 8/26/16).

8 For what is perhaps still the best discussion of the bases of party identification, see Arthur S. Goldberg, "Social Determinism and Rationality as Bases of Party Identification," *American Political Science Review* 63, no. 1 (March 1969): 5–25. For a more recent article weighing in on economic versus social determinants of party attachments, see Larry M. Bartels, "What's the Matter with *What's the Matter with Kansas?*" *Quarterly Journal of Political Science* 1 (2006): 201–26.

9 "Election 2016: Exit Polls," *New York Times*, November 8, 2016, www.nytimes.com/interactive/2016/11/08/us/politics/election-exit-polls.html (accessed 11/14/16).

10 A recent formulation of the Pluralist model of parties is Kathleen Bawn, Martin Cohen, David Karol, Seth Masket, Hans Noel, and John Zaller, "A Theory of Political Parties: Groups, Policy Demands, and Nominations in American Politics," *Perspectives on Politics* 10 (2012): 571–97.

11 For a useful discussion, see John Bibby and Thomas Holbrook, "Parties and Elections," in *Politics in the American States: A Comparative Analysis*, 6th ed., Virginia Gray and Herbert Jacob, eds. (Washington, DC: CQ Press, 1996), pp. 78–121.

12 See Aldrich, *Why Parties?* chap. 8.

13 See Paul S. Herrnson, *Party Campaigning in the 1980s* (Cambridge, MA: Harvard University Press, 1988).

14 See William E. Gienapp, *The Origins of the Republican Party, 1852–1856* (New York: Oxford University Press, 1994).

15 See David W. Rohde, *Parties and Leaders in the Post-Reform House* (Chicago: University of Chicago Press, 1991). An elaboration of this argument is presented in Gary W. Cox and Mathew D. McCubbins, *Setting the Agenda: Responsible Party Government in the U.S. House of Representatives* (New York: Cambridge University Press, 2005). See also Nolan McCarty, Keith Poole, and Howard Rosenthal, *Polarized America: The Dance of Inequality and Unequal Riches* (Cambridge, MA: MIT Press, 2006).

16 For a discussion of third parties in the United States, see Daniel A. Mazmanian, *Third Parties in Presidential Elections* (Washington, DC: Brookings Institution, 1974).

17 See Maurice Duverger, *Political Parties: Their Organization and Activity in the Modern State*, trans. Barbara North and Robert North (New York: Wiley, 1954).

CHAPTER 12

1 Mary Williams Walsh, "Major Changes Raise Concerns on Pension Bill," *New York Times*, March 10, 2006, p. A1.

2 Thomas Ferguson, *Golden Rule: The Investment Theory of Party Competition and the Logic of Money-Driven Political Systems* (Chicago: University of Chicago Press, 1995).

3 Alexander Hamilton, James Madison, and John Jay, *The Federalist Papers*, Clinton Rossiter, ed. (New York: New American Library, 1961), no. 10, p. 78.

4 *The Federalist*, no. 10, p. 83.

5 *The Federalist*, no. 10.

6 Benjamin Ginsberg, "The Administrators Ate My Tuition," *Washington Monthly* (September/October 2011). http://www.washingtonmonthly.com/magazine/septemberoctober_2011/features/administrators_ate_my_tuition031641.php?page=all (accessed 10/25/16).

7 Mancur Olson, *The Logic of Collective Action* (Cambridge, MA: Harvard University Press, 1971).

8 Sidney Verba, Kay Schlozman, and Henry Brady, *The Unheavenly Chorus*. Princeton University Press, 2013. Gilens, Martin. *Affluence and Influence: Economic Inequality and Political Power in America*. New York and Princeton, NJ: Russell Sage Foundation and Princeton University Press, 2012.

9 "Number of Federal PACs Increases," Federal Election Commission, www.fec.gov/press/press2009/20090309PACcount.shtml (accessed 9/6/16).

10 John Herbers, "Special Interests Gaining Power as Voter Disillusionment Grows," *New York Times*, November 14, 1978.

11 Andrea Campbell, *How Policies Make Citizens: Senior Citizen Activism and the American Welfare State* (Princeton, NJ: Princeton University Press, 2003).

12 For discussions of lobbying, see John Wright, *Interest Groups and Congress* (New York: Longman, 2009).

13 An excellent example is the mobilization of corporate executives in the tax reform efforts in the mid-1980s. See Jeff Birnbaum, *Showdown at Gucci Gulch: Lawmakers, Lobbyists, and the Unlikely Triumph of Tax Reform* (New York: Random House, 1987).

14 David Kirkpatrick, "In Daschle's Tax Woes, a Peek into Washington," *New York Times*, February 2, 2009, p. A1.

15 Jacob Straus, *Lobbying the Executive Branch: Current Practices and Options for Change* (Congressional Research Service, December 6, 2010), Report 7-5700, pp. 3–4.

16 John P. Heinz et al., *The Hollow Core: Private Interests in National Policy Making* (Cambridge, MA: Harvard University Press, 1993).

17 For an excellent discussion of the political origins of the Administrative Procedure Act, see Martin Shapiro, "APA: Past, Present, Future," 72 *Virginia Law Review*, 377 (March 1986): 447–92.

18 *Griswold v. Connecticut*, 381 U.S. 479 (1965); *Eisenstadt v. Baird*, 405 U.S. 438 (1972); *Roe v. Wade*, 410 U.S. 133 (1973).

19 *Webster v. Reproductive Health Services*, 492 U.S. 490 (1989).

20 *Brown v. Board of Education of Topeka*, 347 U.S. 483 (1954).

21 *Scheidler v. National Organization for Women et al.*, 547 U.S. 9 (2006).

22 Pendleton Herring, *Group Representation before Congress* (1928; repr.: New York: Russell & Russell, 1967). See also Kenneth W. Kollman, *Outside Lobbying: Public Opinion and Interest Group Strategies* (Princeton, NJ: Princeton University Press, 1998).

23 Natasha Singer, "Harry and Louise Return, with a New Message," *New York Times*, July 16, 2009, http://www.nytimes.com/2009/07/17/business/media/17adco.html (accessed 11/7/11).

24 Jane Fritsch, "The Grass Roots, Just a Free Phone Call Away," *New York Times*, June 23, 1995, pp. A1, A22.

25 See Stephen Ansolabehere, John M. de Figueiredo, and James M. Snyder, Jr., "Why Is There So Little Money in U.S. Politics?" *Journal of Economic Perspectives* 17, no. 1 (2003): 105–30.

26 *Buckley v. Valeo*, 424 U.S. 1 (1976).

27 *Citizens United v. Federal Election Commission*, 558 U.S. 310 (2010).

28 Donald Green and Alan Gerber, *Get Out the Vote: How to Increase Voter Turnout*, 2nd ed. (Washington, DC: Brookings Institution Press, 2008).

29 Elisabeth R. Gerber, *The Populist Paradox* (Princeton, NJ: Princeton University Press, 1999).

30 Ansolabehere, de Figueiredo, and Snyder, "Why Is There So Little Money in U.S. Politics?"

31 John M. de Figueiredo and Brian S. Silverman, "Academic Earmarks and the Returns to Lobbying" working paper 9064, National Bureau of Economic Research, 2002; substantially rev., 2003, http://web.mit.edu/jdefig/www/papers/academic_earmarks.pdf (accessed 4/7/09).

32 John M. de Figueiredo and Brian S. Silverman, "Academic Earmarks and the Returns to Lobbying," *Journal of Law and Economics* 42 (October 2006): 597–626.

CHAPTER 13

1 Matthew A. Crenson and Benjamin Ginsberg, *Downsizing Democracy: How America Sidelined Its Citizens and Privatized Its Public* (Baltimore: Johns Hopkins University Press, 2002), chaps. 7 and 9.

2 Lester M. Salamon, "Economic Regulation," in *The Tools of Government: A Guide to the New Governance*, Lester M. Salamon, ed. (New York: Oxford University Press, 2002), p. 146.

3 Adam Carasso, Eugene Steuerle, and Elizabeth Bell, "Making Tax Incentives for Home Owners More Equitable and Efficient," Tax Policy Center Discussion Paper No. 21, The Urban Institute, Washington, DC, 2005.

4 Compare with Gabriel Kolko, *The Triumph of Conservatism* (New York: Free Press, 1963), chap. 6.

5 A congressional act of 1956 officially designated the interstate highways the National System of Interstate and Defense Highways. It was indirectly a major part of President Eisenhower's defense program. But it was just as obviously a pork-barrel policy as any rivers and harbors legislation.

6 James Dao, "The Nation: Big Bucks Trip Up the Lean New Army," *New York Times,* February 10, 2002, sec. 4, p. 5.

7 Edward J. Harpham, "Fiscal Crisis and the Politics of Social Security Reform," in *The Attack on the Welfare State*, Anthony Champagne and Edward J. Harpham, eds. (Prospect Heights, IL: Waveland Press, 1984), p. 13.

8 *King v. Burwell* 576 US ___ (2015).

9 2016 Poverty Scorecard, Shriver Center, www.povertyscorecard.org (accessed 9/9/16).

10 *1998 Green Book*, Overview of Entitlement Programs, http://aspe.hhs.gov/98gb/intro.htm (accessed 7/15/09).

11 See the discussion of the law and the data presented in U.S. House of Representatives, Ways and Means Committee, *2000 Greenbook,* www.gpoaccess.gov/wmprints/green/2000.html (accessed 4/16/09).

CHAPTER 14

1 Geoffrey Perret, *A Country Made by War* (New York: Random House, 1989), p. 558.

2 Rupert Smith, *The Utility of Force: The Art of War in the Modern World* (New York: Vintage, 2008).

3 D. Robert Worley, *Shaping U.S. Military Forces: Revolution or Relevance in a Post–Cold War World* (Westport, CT: Praeger Security International, 2006).

4 This was done quietly in an amendment to the Internal Revenue Service Reform Act (PL 105–206), June 22, 1998. But it was not accomplished easily. See Bob Gravely, "Normal Trade with China Wins Approval," *Congressional Quarterly Weekly Report*, July 25, 1998; and Richard Dunham, "MFN by Any Other Name Is . . . NTR?," *Business Week* online news flash, June 19, 1997.

5 Alexander Hamilton and James Madison, *Letters of Pacificus and Helvidius* (New York: Scholars Facsimiles and Reprints, 1999).

6 For example, under President Clinton, Senator Lloyd Bentsen and Representative Les Aspin left Congress to become the secretaries of the Treasury and Defense, respectively.

7 A very good brief outline of the centrality of the president in foreign policy will be found in Paul E. Peterson, "The President's Dominance in Foreign Policy Making," *Political Science Quarterly* 109, no. 2 (Summer 1994): 215, 234.

8 One confirmation of this will be found in Theodore Lowi, *The End of Liberalism,* 2nd ed. (New York: Norton, 1979), pp. 127–30; another will be found in Stephen Krasner, "Are Bureaucracies Important?" *Foreign Policy* 7 (Summer 1972): 159–79. However, it should be added that Krasner was writing his article in disagreement with Graham T. Allison, "Conceptual Models and the Cuban Missile Crisis," *American Political Science Review* 63, no. 3 (September 1969): 689–718.

9 See Theodore Lowi, *The Personal President: Power Invested, Promise Unfulfilled* (Ithaca, NY: Cornell University Press, 1985), pp. 167–9.

10 James Dao and Patrick E. Tyler, "U.S. Says Military Strikes Are Just a Part of Big Plan," *The Alliance*, September 27, 2001; and Joseph Kahn, "A Nation Challenged: Global Dollars," *New York Times*, September 20, 2001, p. B1.

11 "Official Says Turkey Is Advancing in Drive for I.M.F. Financing," *New York Times*, October 6, 2001, p. A7.

12 George Quester, *The Continuing Problem of International Politics* (Hinsdale, IL: Dryden Press, 1974), p. 229.

13 The Warsaw Pact was signed in 1955 by the Soviet Union, the German Democratic Republic (East Germany), Poland, Hungary, Czechoslovakia, Romania, Bulgaria, and Albania. Albania later dropped out. The Warsaw Pact was terminated in 1991.

14 Benjamin Ginsberg, *The American Lie* (Boulder, CO: Paradigm, 2007), p. 3.

Glossary

administrative legislation Rules made by regulatory agencies which have the force of legislation

affirmative action A policy or program designed to redress historical injustices committed against specific groups by making special efforts to provide members of these groups with access to educational and employment opportunities

agency representation The type of representation in which representatives are held accountable to their constituents if they fail to represent them properly. That is, constituents have the power to hire and fire their representatives.

agenda-setting effect The power of the media to focus public attention on particular issues and problems

amicus curiae "Friend of the court," an individual or group that is not a party to a lawsuit but has an interest in influencing the outcome

amnesty A pardon extended to a group of persons

Antifederalists Those who favored strong state governments and a weak national government and who were opponents of the constitution proposed at the American Constitutional Convention of 1787

appeasement The effort to forestall war by giving in to the demands of a hostile power

Articles of Confederation and Perpetual Union America's first written constitution. Adopted by the Continental Congress in 1777, the Articles of Confederation and Perpetual Union were the formal basis for America's national government until 1789, when they were superseded by the Constitution

Australian ballot An electoral format that presents the names of all the candidates for any given office on the same ballot. Introduced at the end of the nineteenth century, the Australian ballot replaced the partisan ballot and facilitated split-ticket voting.

authoritarian government A system of rule in which the government recognizes no formal limits but may nevertheless be restrained by the power of other social institutions

autocracy A form of government in which a single individual rules

bicameral legislature A legislative assembly composed of two chambers, or houses

bicameralism The division of a legislative body into two chambers, or houses

bilateral treaty A treaty made between two nations

Bill of Rights The first 10 amendments to the U.S. Constitution, adopted in 1791. The Bill of Rights ensures certain rights and liberties to the people

block grants Federal funds given to state governments for goods, services, or programs, with relatively few restrictions on how the funds may be spent

brief A written document in which an attorney explains—using case precedents—why a court should rule in favor of his or her client

budget deficit The amount by which government spending exceeds government revenue in a fiscal year

bureaucracy The complex structure of offices, tasks, rules, and principles of organization that all large institutions use to coordinate the work of their personnel

bureaucratic drift The oft-observed phenomenon of bureaucratic implementation that produces policy more to the liking of the bureaucracy than faithful to the original intention of the legislation that created it, but without triggering a political reaction from elected officials

Cabinet The secretaries, or chief administrators, of the major departments of the federal government. Cabinet secretaries are appointed by the president with the consent of the Senate.

casework An effort by members of Congress to gain the trust and support of constituents by providing personal services. One important type of casework is helping constituents obtain favorable treatment from the federal bureaucracy.

categorical grants-in-aid Funds given to states and localities by Congress that are earmarked by law for specific policy categories, such as education or crime prevention

caucus (political) A normally closed meeting of a political or legislative group to select candidates, plan strategy, or make decisions regarding legislative matters

checks and balances The mechanisms through which each branch of government is able to participate in and influence the activities of the other branches

chief justice The justice on the Supreme Court who presides over the Court's public sessions

civil law The branch of law that deals with disputes that do not involve criminal penalties

civil liberties The protections of citizens from improper governmental action

civil rights The legal or moral claims that citizens are entitled to make on the government

class-action suit A lawsuit in which a large number of persons with common interests join together under a representative party to bring or defend a lawsuit, as when hundreds of workers join together to sue a company

clientele agency A department or bureau of government whose mission is to promote, serve, or represent a particular interest

closed primary A primary election in which only those voters who registered with the party a specified period before the primary election day can participate

closed rule The provision by the House Rules Committee that restricts the introduction of amendments during debate

cloture A procedure by which a super-majority of the members of a legislative body can set a time limit on debate over a given bill.

Cold War The period of struggle between the United States and the Soviet Union, occurring from the late 1940s to about 1990

comity clause Article IV, Section 2, of the Constitution, which prohibits states from enacting laws that treat the citizens of other states in a discriminatory manner

commander in chief The power of the president as commander of the national military and the state national guard units (when called into service)

commerce clause The clause found in Article I, Section 8, of the Constitution, which delegates to Congress the power "to regulate Commerce with foreign Nations, and among the several States and with the Indian Tribes." This clause was interpreted by the Supreme Court to favor national power over the economy

concurrence An opinion agreeing with the decision of the majority in a Supreme Court case but not with the rationale provided in the majority opinion

concurrent powers Authority possessed by both state and national governments, such as the power to levy taxes

conference committee A joint committee created to work out a compromise between House and Senate versions of a bill

conservative A person who generally supports the social and economic status quo and believes that a large and powerful government poses a threat to citizens' freedom

constituency The district making up the area from which an official is elected

constitutional government A system of rule—a constitution—specifying formal and effective limits on the powers of the government

containment A policy designed to curtail the political and military expansion of a hostile power

contracting power The power of government to set conditions on companies seeking to sell goods or services to government agencies

contributory program A social welfare program financed in whole or in part by taxation or other mandatory contributions by its present or future recipients. The most important example is Social Security, which is financed by a payroll tax

cooperative federalism A type of federalism existing since the New Deal era in which grants-in-aid have been used strategically to encourage states and localities to pursue nationally defined goals. Also known as intergovernmental cooperation

court of appeals (or appellate court) A court that hears the appeals of trial-court decisions

criminal law The branch of law that regulates the conduct of individuals, defines crime, and specifies punishment for criminal acts

de facto segregation Racial segregation that is not a direct result of law or government policy but a reflection of residential patterns, income distributions, or other social factors

de jure segregation Racial segregation that is a direct result of law or official policy

delegate A legislator who votes according to the preferences of his or her constituency

delegated powers Constitutional powers assigned to one branch of the government but exercised by another branch with the express permission of the first

democracy A system of rule that permits citizens to play a significant part in the governmental process, usually through the selection of key public officials

deregulation The policy of reducing the number of rules promulgated by federal regulatory agencies

deterrence The development and maintenance of military strength as a means of discouraging attack

devolution The policy of delegating a program or passing it down from one level of government to a lower level, such as from the national government to state and local governments

diplomacy The representation of a government to other foreign governments

discretionary spending Federal spending on programs that are controlled through the regular budget process

dissenting opinion A decision written by a justice who voted with the minority opinion in a particular case, in which the justice fully explains the reasoning behind his or her opinion

distributive tendency The tendency of Congress to spread the benefits of a policy over a wide range of members' districts

divided government The condition in American government in which the presidency is controlled by one party, while the opposing party controls one or both houses of Congress

dual federalism The system of government that prevailed in the United States from 1789 to 1937, in which most fundamental governmental powers were shared between the federal and state governments, with the states exercising the most important powers

due process Proceeding according to law and with adequate protection for individual rights

Electoral College An institution established by the Constitution for the election of the president and vice president of the United States. Every four years, voters elect electors who, in turn, cast votes for the president and vice president. The candidate receiving a majority of the electoral vote for president or vice president is elected.

eminent domain The right of the government to take private property for public use, with reasonable compensation awarded

equal protection clause The provision of the Fourteenth Amendment guaranteeing citizens "the equal protection of the laws." This clause has served as the basis for the civil rights of African Americans, women, and other groups.

equal time rule An FCC requirement that broadcasters provide candidates for the same political office an equal opportunity to communicate their messages to the public

establishment clause The First Amendment clause that says, "Congress shall make no law respecting an establishment of religion." This law means that a wall of separation exists between church and state.

exclusionary rule The requirement that courts exclude evidence obtained in violation of the Fourth Amendment

executive agreement An agreement between the president and another country that has the force of a treaty but does not require the Senate's "advice and consent"

executive order A rule or regulation issued by the president that has the effect of legislation

executive privilege The claim that confidential communications between a president and the president's close advisors should not be revealed without the consent of the president

expressed powers The powers that the Constitution explicitly grants to the federal government

externality Side effects of an activity, affecting other parties who did not agree to the activity in question

fairness doctrine An FCC requirement that broadcasters who air programs on controversial issues provide time for opposing views

federal funds rate The interest rate on loans between member banks of the Federal Reserve, which the Fed influences by reducing or increasing the supply of money available in the economy

Federal Reserve System A system of 12 Federal Reserve banks that facilitates exchanges of cash, checks, and credit; regulates member banks; and uses monetary policy to fight inflation and deflation

federalism The system of government in which a constitution divides power between a central government and regional governments

Federalists Those who favored a strong national government and supported the constitution proposed at the American Constitutional Convention of 1787

fighting words Speech that directly incites damaging conduct

filibuster A tactic in which members of the Senate prevent action on legislation they oppose by continuously holding the floor and speaking until the majority abandons the legislation. Once given the floor, senators have unlimited time to speak, and it requires a cloture vote of three-fifths of the Senate to end a filibuster.

fiscal policy Regulation of the economy through taxing and spending powers

formula grants Grants-in-aid for which a formula is used to determine the amount of

federal funds a state or local government will receive

framing The influence of the media over how events and issues are interpreted

free exercise clause The First Amendment clause that protects a citizen's right to believe and practice whatever religion he or she chooses

free riding Enjoying the benefits of some good or action while letting others bear the costs

full faith and credit clause The provision in Article IV, Section 1, of the Constitution, requiring that each state normally honor the government actions and judicial decisions that take place in another state

gender gap A distinctive pattern of voting reflecting the differences in views between women and men

General Agreement on Tariffs and Trade (GATT) The international trade organization, in existence from 1947 to 1995, that set many of the rules governing international trade

gerrymandering The apportionment of voters in districts in such a way as to give an advantage to one political party

going public The effort to influence public opinion for or against some proposed action by the government

government The institutions and procedures through which a land and its people are ruled

grand jury A jury that determines whether sufficient evidence is available to justify a trial. Grand juries do not rule on the accused's guilt or innocence.

grants-in-aid A general term for funds given by Congress to state and local governments

grassroots lobbying A lobbying campaign in which a group mobilizes its membership to contact government officials in support of the group's position

Great Compromise An agreement reached at the Constitutional Convention of 1787 that gave each state an equal number of senators regardless of its population but linked representation in the House of Representatives to population

gross domestic product (GDP) The total value of goods and services produced within a country

home rule The power delegated by a state to a local unit of government to manage its own affairs

impeachment The charging of a governmental official (president or other) with "Treason, Bribery, or other high Crimes and Misdemeanors" and bringing him or her before Congress to determine guilt

implementation The efforts of departments and agencies to the development of rules, regulations and bureaucratic procedures to translate laws into action

implied powers Powers derived from the necessary and proper clause (Article I, Section 8) of the Constitution. Such powers are not specifically expressed but are implied through the expansive interpretation of delegated powers

incumbency Holding the political office for which one is running

indexing The process of periodically adjusting social benefits to account for increases in the cost of living

inherent powers Powers claimed by a president that are not expressed in the Constitution but are said to stem from "the rights, duties and obligations of the presidency," claimed mostly during war and national emergencies

initiative A process by which citizens may petition to place a policy proposal on the ballot for public vote

in-kind benefits Goods and services provided to needy individuals and families by the federal government, as contrasted with cash benefits. The largest in-kind federal welfare programs are Medicaid and SNAP.

institutions The rules and procedures that provide incentives for political behavior, thereby shaping politics

interest group An organized group of people that makes policy-related appeals to government

intermediate scrutiny The test used by the Supreme Court in gender discrimination cases. Intermediate scrutiny places the burden of proof partially on the government to show that the law in question is constitutional and partially on the challengers to show it is unconstitutional.

International Court of Justice The UN's chief judicial agency, located in The Hague, Netherlands. The ICJ settles legal disputes submitted by UN member states.

International Monetary Fund (IMF) An institution established in 1944 that provides loans and facilitates international monetary exchange

isolationism The desire to avoid involvement in the affairs of other nations

issue voting An individual's propensity to select candidates or parties based on the extent to which the individual agrees with one candidate more than others on specific issues

judicial activism The judicial philosophy that the Court should see beyond the text of the Constitution or a statute to consider the broader societal implications of its decisions

judicial restraint The judicial philosophy whose adherents refuse to go beyond the text of the Constitution in interpreting its meaning

judicial review The power of the courts to determine whether the actions of the president, the Congress, and the state legislatures are or are not consistent with the Constitution. The Supreme Court asserted the power to review federal statutes in *Marbury v. Madison* (1803).

jurisdiction The types of cases over which a court has authority.

legislative initiative The president's inherent power to bring a legislative agenda before Congress

legislative supremacy The preeminent position within the national government that the Constitution assigns to Congress

Lemon test Rule articulated in *Lemon v. Kurtzman* according to which governmental action in respect to religion is permissible if it is secular in purpose, does not lead to "excessive entanglement" of government with religion, and neither promotes nor inhibits the practice of religion. The Lemon test is generally used in relation to government aid to religious schools.

libel A written statement made in "reckless disregard of the truth" and considered damaging to a victim because it is "malicious, scandalous, and defamatory"

liberal A person who generally supports political and social reform; governmental intervention in the economy; the expansion of federal social services; more vigorous efforts on behalf of the poor, minorities, and women; and greater concern for consumers and the environment

line-item veto The power of the executive to veto specific provisions (lines) of a bill passed by the legislature

lobbying An attempt by a group to influence the policy process through persuasion of government officials

logrolling Reciprocal agreements between legislators, usually in voting for or against a bill. In contrast to bargaining, logrolling unites legislators who have nothing in common but their desire to exchange support.

majority leader The elected leader of the party holding a majority of the seats in the House of Representatives or in the Senate. In the House the majority leader is subordinate in the party hierarchy to the Speaker.

majority party The party that holds the majority of legislative seats in either the House or the Senate

majority rule A type of electoral system in which, to win an office, a candidate must receive a majority (50 percent plus one) of all the votes cast in the relevant district

mandatory spending Federal spending that is made up of "uncontrollables," budget items that cannot be controlled through the regular budget process. Some uncontrollables, such as the interest on the debt, are beyond the power of Congress because the terms of payments are set in contracts.

means testing A procedure that determines eligibility for government public-assistance programs. A potential beneficiary must show a need and an inability to provide for that need

Medicaid A federally financed, state-operated program providing medical services to low-income people

Medicare National health insurance for the elderly and for the disabled

minority leader The elected leader of the party holding less than a majority of the seats in the House or Senate

Miranda rule The requirement derived from the Supreme Court's 1966 ruling in *Miranda v. Arizona* that persons under arrest must be informed of their legal rights, including the right to counsel, before undergoing police interrogation

monetary policy Regulation of the economy through manipulation of the supply of money, the price of money (interest rates), and the availability of credit

money bill A bill concerned solely with taxation or government spending

monopoly The existence in a market of a single firm that provides all the goods or services of a particular type for that market; the absence of competition

mootness A criterion used by courts to avoid hearing cases that no longer require resolution

most favored nation status An agreement to offer a trading partner the lowest tariff rate offered to other trading partners

National Security Council (NSC) A presidential foreign-policy advisory council comprising the president, the vice president, the secretaries of state, defense, and the treasury, the attorney general, and other officials invited by the president

necessary and proper clause Article I, Section 8 of the Constitution, which enumerates the powers of Congress and provides Congress with the authority to make all laws "necessary and proper" to carry them out; also referred to as the elastic clause

nomination The process by which political parties select their candidate for election to public office

noncontributory program A social program that assists people based on need they demonstrate rather than contributions they have made. Also known as a public assistance program

non-state actor A group other than a nation-state that attempts to play a role in the international system. Terrorist groups are one type of non-state actor.

North American Free Trade Agreement (NAFTA) An agreement between the United States, Canada, and Mexico to lower and eliminate tariffs among the three countries

North Atlantic Treaty Organization (NATO) A treaty organization comprising the United States, Canada, and most of Western Europe, formed in 1949 to counter the perceived threat from the Soviet Union

oligarchy A form of government in which a small group of landowners, military officers, or wealthy merchants control most of the governing decisions

open-market operations The process whereby the Open Market Committee of the Federal Reserve buys and sells government securities to help finance government operations and to reduce or increase the total amount of money circulating in the economy

open primary A primary election in which voters can choose on the primary election day which party's primary to vote in

open rule The provision by the House Rules Committee that permits floor debate and the addition of amendments to a bill

opinion The written explanation of the Supreme Court's decision in a particular case

oral argument The stage in Supreme Court proceedings in which attorneys for both sides appear before the Court to present their positions and answer questions posed by the justices

oversight The effort by Congress, through hearings, investigations, and other techniques, to exercise control over the activities of executive agencies

pardon Forgiveness of a crime and cancellation of relevant penalty

party activist A partisan who contributes time and energy beyond voting to support a party and its candidates

party caucus, or party conference A nominally closed meeting of a political or legislative group to select candidates or leaders, plan strategy, or make decisions regarding legislative matters

party identification An individual's attachment to a particular political party, which may be based on issues, ideology, past experience, upbringing, or a mixture of these elements

party vote A roll-call vote in the House or Senate in which at least 50 percent of the members of one party take a particular position and are opposed by at least 50 percent of the members of the other party. Party votes are less common today than they were in the nineteenth century.

patronage The opportunities available to legislators to provide direct services and benefits to their constituents, especially making partisan appointments to offices and conferring grants, licenses, or special favors to supporters

pluralism The theory that all interests are and should be free to compete for influence in the government. The outcome of this competition is compromise and moderation.

plurality rule A type of electoral system in which victory in an election goes to the individual who gets the most votes, but not necessarily a majority of the votes cast

pocket veto A veto that occurs when Congress adjourns during the 10 days a president has to approve a bill and the president has taken no action on it

political action committee (PAC) A private group that raises and distributes funds for use in election campaigns

political party An organized group that attempts to influence the government by electing its members to important government offices

politics Conflict, struggle, cooperation, and collaboration over the leadership, structure, and policies of government

pork-barrel legislation Legislative appropriations that legislators use to provide government funds for projects benefiting their home district or state

precedents Prior cases whose principles are used by judges as the bases for their decisions in present cases

preemption The willingness to strike first in order to prevent an enemy attack

preventive war The policy of striking first when a nation fears that a foreign foe is contemplating hostile action

priming The use of media coverage to make the public take a particular view of an event or a public figure

principal-agent relationship The relationship between a principal and his or her agent. This relationship may be affected by the fact that each is motivated by self-interest, yet their interests may not be well aligned

prior restraint An effort by a government agency to block the publication of material it deems libelous or harmful in some other way; censorship. In the United States, the courts forbid prior restraint except under extraordinary circumstances.

privatization The act of moving all or part of a program from the public sector to the private sector

progressive taxation A tax is *progressive* if the proportion of income paid as tax goes up as income goes up

project grants Grants-in-aid for which state and local governments submit proposals to federal agencies, who provide funding for them on a competitive basis

proportional representation A multiple-member district system that awards seats to political parties in proportion to the percentage of the vote each party won

prospective voting Voting based on the imagined future performance of a candidate

public good A good that, first, may be enjoyed by anyone if it is provided and, second, may not be denied to anyone once it has been provided

public law Cases involving the powers of government or rights of citizens

public opinion Citizens' attitudes about political issues, personalities, institutions, and events

public policy A law, rule, statute, or edict that expresses the government's goals and provides for rewards or punishments to promote their attainment

recall The removal of a public official by popular vote

referendum A measure that is decided by the vote of the electorate for approval or rejection

regressive taxation A tax is *regressive* if people in lower income brackets pay a higher proportion of their income toward the tax than people in higher income brackets

regulated federalism A form of federalism in which Congress imposes legislation on state and local governments that requires them to meet national standards

regulatory agencies A department, bureau, or independent agency whose primary mission is to ensure that individuals and organizations comply with the statutes under its jurisdiction

regulatory review The Office of Management and Budget function of reviewing all agency regulations and other rule making before they become official policy

reprieve Cancellation or postponement of a punishment

reserve requirement The amount of liquid assets and ready cash that the Federal Reserve requires banks to hold to meet depositors' demands for their money

reserved powers Powers that are not specifically delegated to the national government or denied to the states by the Constitution; under the Tenth Amendment, these powers are reserved to the states

retrospective voting Voting based on the past performance of a candidate or party

right of rebuttal An FCC requirement that broadcasters give individuals the opportunity to respond to the airing of personal attacks on them

right to privacy The right to be left alone, which has been interpreted by the Supreme Court to entail individual access to birth control and abortions

ripeness A criterion used by courts to avoid hearing cases that depend on hypothetical future events

roll-call vote Voting in which each legislator's yes or no vote is recorded

senatorial courtesy The practice whereby the president, before formally nominating a person for a federal district judgeship, finds out whether the senators from the candidate's state support the nomination

seniority The priority or status ranking given to an individual on the basis of length of continuous service on a congressional committee

"separate but equal" rule The doctrine that public accommodations could be segregated by race but still be equal

separation of powers The division of governmental power among several institutions that must cooperate in decision making

signing statement An announcement made by the president when signing a bill into law

single-member district An electoral district that elects only one representative—the typical method of representation in the United States

slander An oral statement made in "reckless disregard of the truth" and considered damaging to a victim because it is "malicious, scandalous, and defamatory"

Social Security A contributory welfare program into which working Americans contribute a percentage of their wages and from which they receive cash benefits after retirement

socialization A process through which individuals assimilate community preferences and norms through social interactions

sovereignty Independent political authority. A sovereign possesses such authority.

Speaker of the House The chief presiding officer of the House of Representatives. The Speaker is elected at the beginning of every Congress on a straight party vote. He or she is the most important party and House leader.

speech plus Speech accompanied by activities such as sit-ins, picketing, and demonstrations. Protection of this form of speech under the First Amendment is conditional, and restrictions imposed by state or local authorities are acceptable if properly balanced by considerations of public order.

standing committee A permanent legislative committee that considers legislation within

its designated subject area; the basic unit of deliberation in the House and the Senate

standing The right to initiate a court case, requiring that one show a substantial stake in the outcome

state sovereign immunity A legal doctrine, based on the Eleventh Amendment to the Constitution, holding that states cannot be sued for violating an act of Congress

states' rights The principle that states should oppose the increasing authority of the national government. This view was most popular before the Civil War

strict scrutiny The most stringent standard of judicial review of a government's actions in which the government must show that the law serves a "compelling state interest"

subsidy A government grant of cash or other valuable commodities, such as land, to an individual or organization; used to promote activities desired by the government, to reward political support, or to buy off political opposition

Supplemental Nutrition Assistance Program (SNAP) After Medicaid, the largest in-kind benefits program, administered by the Department of Agriculture for individuals and families who satisfy a means test. SNAP debit cards can be used to buy food at most retail stores

Supplemental Security Income (SSI) A program providing a minimum monthly income to people who pass a means test and who are 65 years old or older, blind, or disabled. Financed from general revenues that are not Social Security contributions

supremacy clause A clause of Article VI of the Constitution that states that all laws and treaties approved by the national government are the supreme laws of the United States and superior to all laws adopted by any state or other subdivision

supreme court The highest court in a particular state or in the United States. This court primarily serves an appellate function.

tax expenditure A subsidy to an individual or organization in the form of relief from taxes that would otherwise be owed to the government

Temporary Assistance to Needy Families (TANF) Federal funds for children in families that fall below state standards of need

Three-Fifths Compromise An agreement reached at the Constitutional Convention of 1787 stipulating that for the purposes of the apportionment of congressional seats, only three-fifths of slaves would be counted

totalitarian government A system of rule in which the government recognizes no formal limits on its power and seeks to absorb or eliminate other social institutions that might challenge it

trial court The first court to hear a criminal or civil case

trustee A legislator who votes based on what he or she thinks is best for his or her constituency

turnout rate The number of people who vote in a given election divided by the number of people who are allowed to vote

unfunded mandates National standards or programs imposed on state and local governments by the federal government without accompanying funding or reimbursement

United Nations (UN) An organization of nations founded in 1945 to be a channel for negotiation and a means of settling international disputes peaceably. The UN has had frequent successes in providing a forum for negotiation and on some occasions a means of preventing international conflicts from spreading. On a number of occasions, the UN has been a convenient cover for U.S. foreign-policy goals.

veto The president's constitutional power to reject acts of Congress within 10 days of their passage while Congress is in session. A presidential veto may be overridden by a two-thirds vote of each house of Congress.

veto power The president's constitutional power to turn down acts of Congress within 10 days of their passage while Congress is in session; a presidential veto may be overridden by a two-thirds vote of each house of Congress.

War Powers Resolution A 1973 resolution of Congress declaring that the president can send troops into action abroad only by authorization of Congress or if U.S. troops are already under attack or seriously threatened. For the most part, presidents have ignored the resolution.

whip system A party communications network in each house of Congress. Whips poll their party's members to learn their intentions on specific bills and also convey the leadership's views and plans to members.

World Trade Organization (WTO) The international trade agency promoting free trade that grew out of the General Agreement on Tariffs and Trade

writ of *certiorari* A formal request to have the Supreme Court review a decision of a lower court. *Certiorari* is from a Latin word meaning "to make more certain."

writ of *habeas* corpus A court order demanding that an individual in custody be brought into court and shown the cause for detention. *Habeas corpus* is guaranteed by the Constitution and can be suspended only in cases of rebellion or invasion.

Credits

Index

American Bar Association, 402, 408

American Enterprise Institute, 298, 403

American Farm Bureau Federation, 401, 408

American Federation of State, County, and Municipal Employees (AFSCME), 401

American Independent Party, *384,* 393

American Israel Public Affairs Committee (AIPAC), *474*

American Medical Association, 402, 408

American National Election Studies (ANES), 209, 336

American Recovery and Reinvestment Act, 415

American Revolution, 25–27, 29, 383

Americans with Disabilities Act (ADA), 124–25

American Values Survey, 285

American Voter, The, 286

America's Party, *384, 391*

amicus curiae, 264–65

amnesties, Presidential, 176–77

Amnesty International, 475

Amtrak, 215

anarchy, 8

Anderson, Rocky, *391*

ANES (American National Election Studies), 209, 336

Animal and Plant Health and Inspection Service (APHIS), 219

Annapolis Convention, 61

Antifederalists, 44–45, 54, 63, 392

Anti-Masonics, *384*

Antitrust Division of Department of Justice, 218

ANZUS, 480

APHIS (Animal and Plant Health and Inspection Service), 219

appeasement, 462

appellate courts, 246, 248–49, 250, 259

Apple Corporation, 104

appointments, 164–65, 197, 223

appropriations bill, 136

arbitration, 483–84

Arizona, 3–4, 76

Arizona, Miranda v., 90, 92

Arkansas, 95, 116, 175

Armed Services Committee, 473

Army Corps of Engineers, 445

Articles of Confederation, 33, 34, 61, 173, 328

adoption of, 27–28

Constitution *vs.,* 51, 53

flaws of, 28–29, 33

Asian Americans, 123, 373–74

Asian Law Caucus, 124

assembly, freedom of, *90,* 91, 99

assisted-suicide law, 76

Associated Press, 303

Astroturf lobbying, 419–20

atheist

voting for, 97

AT&T, 434

Australia

ANZUS and, 480

voting in, 319

Australian ballot, 326–27

authoritarian governments, 6, 7

autocracy, 6

Baker, Richard, 256

Baker v. Nelson, 256

Bakke, Allan, 127

Bakke case, 127–28

balanced budget, 156

ballot measures, 311

ballots, 326–27

Baltic states, 481

Baltimore, Barron v., 87–89, 91

bank bailout, 435

Bank of the United States, 66, 436

Barr, Roseanne, *391*

Barron v. Baltimore, 87–89, 91

bathroom ban laws, 122

Bayh, Birch, 316

BCRA (Bipartisan Campaign Reform Act), 99, 347–48, 421

"beaker-ready" project proposals, 445

benefit seekers, 362. *see also* interest groups

Benghazi 2012 attack, 163

Benton v. Maryland, 90, 92

Bezos, Jeffrey, 302

bias, organizational, 207–9

bicameralism, 33, 131, 136–37

Biden, Joe, 132, 191–92

bilateral treaties, 480

Bill of Rights, 33, 42, 44, 46, 61, 84–129, 425. *see also specific amendments*

Antifederalist demand for, 44

nationalization of, 87–93, *90*

purpose of, 47, *48*

recent court rulings on, 93–107

state v. national, 87–89, *90*

bin Laden, Osama, 470, *470*

Bipartisan Campaign Reform Act (BCRA), 99, 347–48, 421

Black Americans. *see* African Americans

Black Lives Matter, 409, 420

protests, 115–16

Blackmun, Harry, 269, *271*

Blacks. *See* African Americans

Blackwater, USA, 472

block grants, 72

Board of Education of Topeka, Brown v., 92, 112–13, *114,* 119, 121, 255, 417

Bollinger, Grutter v., 128

"born or naturalized" persons provision, 91

Bosnia, 184

Boston, 25–26

Boston Gazette, 330

Boston Marathon 2013 bombing, 247, 306

Boston Tea Party, 25–26

bourgeoisie, 10–11

Bowers v. Hardwick, 107, 125

BP oil spill, 175

Brady Bill, 73

Brandenburg, Charles, 98

Brandenburg v. Ohio, 98

branding in political parties, 366

Brennan, William J., *271*

Breyer, Stephen G., 94, 252, *253,* 268, *270, 271*

unalienable rights, 26
unfunded mandates, 71
Unfunded Mandates Reform Act
    (UMRA), 71–72
UN General Assembly, 477
Uniform Code of Military
    Justice, 258
uninsured, health insurance, *75*
Union Labor Party, *384*
Union of Concerned Scientists,
    403, 408
unions, 365, 422
    labor, 425
United Auto Workers (UAW),
    423
United Kingdom
    party systems in, 369
    United Nations and, 477
United Mine Workers, 401, 408
United Nations, 284, 468, 477,
    480, 481
United Nations Framework
    Convention on Climate
    Change, 468
United States, Mack v., 73
United States, Printz v., 73
United States' diplomatic
    relations with Cuba, 477
United States v. Lopez, 73
United States v. Nixon, 178, 242,
    257
United States v. O'Brien, 99
United States v. Williams, 101
United States v. Windsor, 256
United We Stand Party, *384*
University of California, 127
University of Michigan, 128
Univision, 300
UN Security Council, 477
U.S. Parole Commission, 216
U.S. Virgin Islands, 247
USA FREEDOM ACT, 150,
    176
USA PATRIOT Act, 60, 150,
    175

Valeo, Buckley v., 99, 347–48
values, 279, 281, 282
Van Buren, Martin, 385
Van Orden v. Perry, 94
Vermont, 126

veto, 36, 80, 151, 178–83, *179,
    180–81,* 184
    impacting Presidential approval
        rating, 181–83
    legislative chambers, 38
    Presidential, 38
veto gates, 38–39
    of countries, 39
vice presidency, 191–92
Vietnam War, 184, 230, 375, 388,
    483
    amnesty for draft evaders, 177
    drafts during, 7
    Johnson and, 484
    media and, 296
    protests against, 99
Virginia
    Constitutional Convention
        and, 34
    gun ownership, 103
    impact of Three-Fifths
        Compromise, 34
    ratification of Constitution, 45
    slavery in, 32
    Virginia Plan and, 30
Virginia, Loving v., 255
Virginia Military Institute, 118
Virginia Plan, 30, 34
voter ID laws, 318
voter registration, 323–26, 365
voter turnout, 204, 319–20,
    325–26, 335–36
    measuring, 321–23
    in presidential elections, 320,
        320, 322
voting, 85, 319–21, 335
    African Americans and, 330–31
    ballots and, 326–27
    compulsory, 319–20
    decisions in, 335–36, *337, 342–43*
    economy's influence on
        presidential elections, 340,
        342–43
    facilitating electoral choice in,
        365–66
    identification and, 318, 325,
        371–73, *372*
    issues and policy preferences
        in, 339–402
    Latino Americans and, 121,
        287, 367

nonvoters and, 335–36
partisanship and, 286, 335,
    336–39, *337,* 341
prospective, 340
religion of candidate, 97
requirements for, 315, 319–20,
    323–26
retrospective, 340
secret ballots and, 326–27
split-ticket, 326–27
voting rights, 108
    African Americans and, 110–111
    property qualifications, 109
    religion, 109
    struggle for, 108–111
    women and, 109–10, *110*
Voting Rights Act, 110, 111, *115,*
    119, 123, 141, 286, 295,
    330, 389

Wade, Roe v. see Roe v. Wade
Wagner Act. *see* National Labor
    Relations Act
Wainwright, Gideon v., 90, 92, 105
Wallace, George, 389, *390,* 393
wall of separation, 94
Wall Street Journal, 303
war. *see also specific wars*
    in Constitution, 23, 61
    declaration of, 61, 175, 184–85
    gender and public opinion on,
        290
War Department, 219
War of 1812, 385
War on Poverty, *115*
war on terrorism, 82, 150, 172,
    175–76, 184, 258, 463,
    481. *see also* Afghanistan
    war; Iraq war
War Powers Resolution, 184
Warren, Earl, 249
Warsaw Pact, 481
Washington, George, 36
    on alliances with foreign
        powers, 461
    Constitution and, 22
    Genêt received by, 177
    House request refused by, 178
    partisan politics and, 360–61,
        383
Washington Post, 302